AN EXEGETICAL SUMMARY OF
JOHN 10–21

AN EXEGETICAL SUMMARY OF
JOHN 10–21

Ronald L. Trail

SIL International®
Dallas, Texas

©2018 by SIL International®

ISBN: 978-1-55671-431-3
Library of Congress Control Number: 2018941111
Printed in the United States of America

All Rights Reserved
No part of this publication may be reproduced, stored in a retrieval system, or transmitted in any form or by any means—electronic, mechanical, photocopy, recording, or otherwise—without the express permission of SIL International®, with the exception of brief excerpts in journal articles or reviews.

Copies of this and other publications of SIL International® may be obtained through distributors such as Amazon, Barnes & Noble, other worldwide distributors and, for select volumes, www.sil.org/resources/publications:

SIL International Publications
7500 West Camp Wisdom Road
Dallas, TX 75236-5629, USA

General inquiry: publications_intl@sil.org
Pending order inquiry: sales_intl@sil.org
www.sil.org/resources/publications

PREFACE

Exegesis is concerned with the interpretation of a text. Exegesis of the New Testament involves determining the meaning of the Greek text. Translators must be especially careful and thorough in their exegesis of the New Testament in order to accurately communicate its message in the vocabulary, grammar, and literary devices of another language. Questions occurring to translators as they study the Greek text are answered by summarizing how scholars have interpreted the text. This is information that should be considered by translators as they make their own exegetical decisions regarding the message they will communicate in their translations.

The Semi-Literal Translation

As a basis for discussion, a semi-literal translation of the Greek text is given so that the reasons for different interpretations can best be seen. When one Greek word is translated into English by several words, these words are joined by hyphens. There are a few times when clarity requires that a string of words joined by hyphens have a separate word, such as "not" (μή), inserted in their midst. In this case, the separate word is surrounded by spaces between the hyphens. When alternate translations of a Greek word are given, these are separated by slashes.

The Text

Variations in the Greek text are noted under the heading TEXT. The base text for the summary is the text of the fourth revised edition of *The Greek New Testament,* published by the United Bible Societies, which has the same text as the twenty-sixth edition of the *Novum Testamentum Graece* (Nestle-Aland). Dr. J. Harold Greenlee researched the variants and has written the notes for this part of the summary. The versions that follow different variations are listed without evaluating their choices.

The Lexicon

The meaning of a key word in context is the first question to be answered. Words marked with a raised letter in the semi-literal translation are treated separately under the heading LEXICON. First, the lexicon form of the Greek word is given. Within the parentheses following the Greek word is the location number where, in the author's judgment, this word is defined in the *Greek-English Lexicon of the New Testament Based on Semantic Domains* (Louw and Nida 1988). When a semantic domain includes a translation of the particular verse being treated, **LN** in bold type indicates that specific translation. If the specific reference for the verse is listed in *A Greek-English Lexicon of the New Testament and Other Early Christian Literature* (Bauer, Arndt, Gingrich, and Danker 1979), the outline location and page number is given. Then English equivalents of the Greek word are given to show how it is translated by those commentaries that have translations of the whole Greek text and, after a semicolon, by twelve major versions. "All versions" refers only to those versions used in the lexicon. "All translations" refers to both the versions and the commentaries used in the lexicon. Sometimes further comments are made about the meaning of the word or the significance of a verb's tense, voice, or mood.

The Questions

Under the heading QUESTION, a question is asked that comes from examining the Greek text under consideration. Typical questions concern the identity of an implied actor or object of an event word, the antecedent of a pronominal reference, the connection indicated by a relational word, the meaning of a genitive construction, the meaning of figurative language, the function of a rhetorical question, the identification of an ambiguity, and the presence of implied information that is needed to understand the passage correctly. Background information is also considered for proper understanding of a passage. Although not all implied information and background information is made explicit in a translation, it is important to consider it so that the translation will not be stated in such a way that prevents a reader from arriving at the proper interpretation. The question is answered with a summary of what commentators have said. If there are contrasting differences of opinion, the different interpretations are numbered and the commentaries that support each are listed. Differences that are not treated by many of the commentaries often are not numbered, but are introduced with a contrastive 'Or' at the beginning of the sentence. No attempt has been made to select which interpretation is best.

In listing support for various statements of interpretation, the author is often faced with the difficult task of matching the different terminologies used in commentaries with the terminology he has adopted. Sometimes he can only infer the position of a commentary from incidental remarks. This book, then, includes the author's interpretation of the views taken in the various commentaries. General statements are followed by specific statements, which indicate the author's understanding of the pertinent relationships, actors, events, and objects implied by that interpretation.

The Use of This Book

This book does not replace the commentaries that it summarizes. Commentaries contain much more information about the meaning of words and passages. They often contain arguments for the interpretations that are taken and they may have important discussions about the discourse features of the text. In addition, they have information about the historical, geographical, and cultural setting. Translators will want to refer to at least four commentaries as they exegete a passage. However, since no one commentary contains all the answers translators need, this book will be a valuable supplement. It makes a greater number of exegetical help sources available to many translators who otherwise would not have had that access. Even if they had all the books available, few would have the time to search through all of them for the answers.

When many commentaries are studied, it soon becomes apparent that they frequently disagree in their interpretations. That is the reason why so many answers in this book are divided into two or more interpretations. The reader's initial reaction may be that all of these different interpretations complicate exegesis rather than help it. However, before translating a passage, a translator needs to know exactly where there is a problem of interpretation and what the exegetical options are.

Acknowledgments

Several people have been involved in the production of this exegetical summary. Richard Blight edited over two thirds of the chapters of this volume for their content and presentation as well as the entire contents of the former volume, John 1–9. Dr. Harold Greenlee prepared all the textual notes found throughout both volumes of the summary. My wife, Gail, did the proofreading of several final chapters of this volume before we sent all the files off to Dennis Felkner for a final checking, formatting, and preparation for printing. Finally, Barbara Shannon and Jim Kakumasu did superb checks of the final copy, highlighting many places needing correction. I would like to express my sincere heartfelt appreciation to each one of these who have participated to make this summary a reality!

ABBREVIATIONS

COMMENTARIES AND REFERENCE BOOKS

AB	Brown, Raymond E. *The Gospel According to John*, (i-xii). The Anchor Bible. Garden City, New York: Doubleday & Company, Inc., 1966.
BAGD	Bauer, Walter. *A Greek-English Lexicon of the New Testament and Other Early Christian Literature*. Translated and adapted from the 5th ed., 1958 by William F. Arndt and F. Wilbur Gingrich. 2nd English ed. revised and augmented by F. Wilbur Gingrich and Frederick W. Danker. Chicago: University of Chicago Press, 1979.
Bar	Barrett, C. K. *The Gospel According to John*. Philadelphia: The Westminster Press, 1978.
BECNT	Köstenberger, Andreas J. *John*. Grand Rapids: Baker Academic, 2004.
Car	Carson, D. A. *The Gospel According to John*. Grand Rapids: Eerdmans, 1991.
CH	Comfort, Phillip W. and Wendall C. Hawley. *Opening the Gospel of John*. Wheaton: Tyndale House Publishers, Inc., 1994.
EGT	Dods, Marcus. *The Gospel of John. The Expositor's Greek Testament*. Grand Rapids: Eerdmans, 1967.
Gdt	Godet, Frederick Louis. *Commentary on the Gospel of John*. Grand Rapids: Zondervan, 1970.
HTC	Schnackenburg, Rudolf. *The Gospel According to St John*, Vol. 1. Montreal: Palm Publishers, 1968.
	Schnackenburg, Rudolf. *The Gospel According to St John*, Vol. 2. New York: The Seabury Press, 1980.
	Schnackenburg, Rudolf. *The Gospel According to St John*, Vol. 3. New York: Crossroad Publishing, 1990.
ICC	Bernhard, J. H. *A Critical and Exegetical Commentary on the Gospel According to St. John*. The International Critical Commentary. Edinburgh: T. & T. Clark, 1928.
IVP	Whitacre, Rodney A. *John*. Downers Grove: Intervarsity Press, 1999.
Kn	Keener, Craig S. *The Gospel of John, a Commentary*, Vol. 1. Peabody, Massachusetts: Hendrikson Publishers, 2003.
LN	Louw, Johannes P., and Eugene A. Nida. *Greek-English Lexicon of the New Testament Based on Semantic Domains*. New York: United Bible Societies, 1988.
Lns	Lenski, R. C. H. *The Interpretation of St. John's Gospel*. Minneapolis: Augsburg Publishing House, 1943.
My	Meyer, Heinrich August Wilhelm. *Critical and Exegetical Hand-book to the Gospel of John*. New York: Funk & Wagnalls Company, 1985.
NICNT1	Morris, Leon. *The Gospel According to John*. The New International Commentary on the New Testament. Grand Rapids: Eerdmans, 1995.
NICNT2	Michaels, J. Ramsey. *The Gospel of John*. The New International Commentary on the New Testament. Grand Rapids: Eerdmans, 2010.
NTC	Hendriksen, William. *The Gospel of John*. London: The Banner of Truth Trust, 1954.
Rd	Ridderbos, Herman. *The Gospel According to John, A Theological Commentary*. Grand Rapids: Eerdmans, 1991.
TH	Newman, Barclay M. and Eugene A. Nida. *A Translator's Handbook on the Gospel of John*. New York: United Bible Societies, 1980.
TRT	Carlton, Matthew E. *The Translator's Reference Translation of the Gospel of John*. Dallas: SIL International, 2003.

WBC Beasley-Murray. *John*. Word Biblical Commentary. Nashville: Thomas Nelson Publishers, 1999.

GREEK TEXT AND TRANSLATIONS

GNT The Greek New Testament. Edited by B. Aland, K. Aland, J. Karavidopoulos, C. Martini, and B. Metzger. 4th ed. London, New York: United Bible Societies, 2001.
CEV The Holy Bible, Contemporary English Version. New York: American Bible Society, 1995.
KJV The Holy Bible. Authorized (or King James) Version. 1611.
NASB The New American Standard Bible. La Habra, California: Lockman Foundation, 1995.
NCV New Century Bible. Dallas: Word Publishing, 1991.
NET The NET Bible, New English Translation. Version 6r,715, Biblical Studies Press, 2006.
NIV The Holy Bible, New International Version. Grand Rapids: Zondervan, 1984.
NJB The New Jerusalem Bible. New York: Doubleday, 1985.
NLT The Holy Bible, New Living Translation. Second edition. Carol Stream, Illinois: Tyndale House, 2006.
NRSV The Holy Bible: New Revised Standard Version. New York: Oxford University Press, 1989.
Ph Phillips, J.B. The New Testament in Modern English. Rev. ed. New York: Harper Collins Publishers, 1960.
REB The Revised English Bible. Oxford: Oxford University Press and Cambridge University Press, 1989.
TEV Good News Bible, Today's English Version. Second ed. New York: American Bible Society, 1992.

GRAMMATICAL TERMS

act.	active	mid.	middle
fut.	future	opt.	optative
impera.	imperative	pass.	passive
imperf.	imperfect	perf.	perfect
indic.	indicative	pres.	present
infin.	infinitive	subj.	subjunctive

MISCELLANEOUS

LXX Septuagint
NT New Testament
OT Old Testament
TR Textus Receptus

EXEGETICAL SUMMARY OF JOHN 10–21

DISCOURSE UNIT—10:1–42 [BECNT, CH, NICNT1, WBC; REB]. The topic is Jesus the Shepherd and Son of God [WBC], Jesus the shepherd [BECNT, CH, NICNT1], victory over death [REB].

DISCOURSE UNIT—10:1–21 [AB, Bar, BECNT, Car, EGT, IVP, Lns, Rd, WBC; CEV, NASB, NET, NIV, NLT, NRSV]. The topic is the good shepherd [Car, IVP, Rd; NASB, NET, NRSV], shepherd and the flock [BECNT, Lns, WBC; NIV, NLT], the good shepherd and the hirelings [EGT], Jesus as sheepgate and shepherd [AB], a story about sheep [CEV].

DISCOURSE UNIT—10:1–18 [Ph]. The topic is Jesus the true shepherd.

DISCOURSE UNIT—10:1–6 [HTC, IVP, NICNT1, Rd, WBC; NCV, TEV]. The topic is the shepherd and his sheep [HTC, WBC], the parable of the shepherd [NICNT1; TEV], misunderstood comparison [Rd], the good shepherd versus robbers [IVP].

DISCOURSE UNIT—10:1–5 [Car]. The topic is the figure of speech.

10:1 Truly[a] truly I-say to-you, "The (one) not entering the sheepfold[b] of-the sheep through the gate[c] but climbing-in[d] some-other-way[e] that (one) is (a) thief[f] and (a) robber.[g]

LEXICON—a. ἀμήν (LN 72.6): 'truly' [LN], 'indeed, it is true that' [LN]. The clause ἀμὴν ἀμὴν λέγω ὑμῖν 'Truly truly I say to you' [HTC; NASB] is also translated 'Verily, verily, I say to you' [Gdt; KJV], 'Amen, amen, I say to/tell you' [NICNT2, WBC], 'Very truly I tell you' [NRSV], 'Believe me when I tell you' [Ph], 'In very truth I tell you' [REB], 'I tell/am telling you the truth' [NCV, NIV, NLT, TEV], 'I tell you the solemn truth' [NET], 'In all truth I tell you' [NJB], 'I tell you for certain' [CEV], 'Truly I assure you' [AB], 'I most solemnly assure you' [NTC]. This particle indicates strong affirmation of what is declared [LN].

b. αὐλή (LN 7.56) (BAGD 1. p. 121): 'sheepfold' [AB, Gdt, HTC, LN, NTC, WBC; KJV, NCV, NET, NJB, NLT, NRSV, Ph, REB], 'fold of the sheep' [NASB], 'sheep pen' [CEV, NIV, TEV], 'courtyard of the sheep' [NICNT2], 'courtyard' [BAGD, LN]. This noun denotes a walled enclosure either to enclose human activity or to protect livestock [LN]. It literally denotes an enclosed space, open to the sky, near a house, or surrounded by buildings, but it is also used to indicate a fold for sheep [BAGD].

c. θύρα (LN 7.39) (BAGD 1.a. p. 365): 'gate' [AB; CEV, NIV, NJB, NLT, NRSV, TEV], 'door' [BAGD, HTC, NICNT2, NTC, WBC; KJV, NASB, NCV, NET, Ph, REB], 'entrance, entranceway, portal' [LN]. This noun denotes the entranceway into a building or structure [LN]. The door was solid and heavily barred to resist attack [EGT].

d. pres. act. participle of ἀναβαίνω (LN 15.101) (BAGD 1.a.α. p. 50): 'to climb in' [AB, HTC, WBC; NCV, NET, NIV, NJB, NRSV, Ph, REB, TEV], 'to climb up' [Gdt; KJV, NASB], 'to climb over' [NTC; CEV], 'to sneak over' [NLT], 'to go up' [BAGD, LN, NICNT2], 'to come up, to ascend' [LN]. This verb means to move up [LN].

e. ἀλλαχόθεν (LN **84.8**) (BAGD p. 39): '(by) some other way' [AB, WBC; Gdt, KJV, NASB, NCV, NET, NIV, NJB, Ph, REB, TEV], 'by/from another way' [HTC, NTC; NRSV], 'from elsewhere' [LN, NICNT2], 'from some other way' [**LN**], 'from another place, at some other place' [BAGD]. The clause 'but climbing in another way' is translated '(thieves and robbers) climb over the fence instead of going in through the gate' [CEV], 'who sneaks over the wall...rather than going through the gate' [NLT]. This adverb describes a thing as being from a source that is different from some other source [LN].

f. κλέπτης (LN 57.233) (BAGD p. 434): 'thief' [BAGD, LN; all translations]. This noun is derived from the verb κλέπτω 'to steal' (57.232) and denotes a person who steals [LN].

g. λῃστής (LN 57.240) (BAGD 1. p. 473): 'robber' [BAGD, LN; all translations except AB; NJB, NRSV, Ph], 'rogue' [Ph], 'bandit' [AB, BAGD; NJB, NRSV], 'highwayman' [BAGD, LN]. This noun is derived from the verb λῃστεύω (not occurring in the NT) 'to practice robbery, piracy' and denotes one who robs by force and violence [LN].

QUESTION—What is the relationship of this chapter to the previous one?

The double Ἀμὴν ἀμὴν 'truly, truly' is never used to start a new discourse in this Gospel. This may indicate that chapter 10 is a continuation of chapter 9 [AB, BECNT, NICNT1]. This teaching arises out of the healing of the blind man [CH, EGT]. Jesus is explaining to the excommunicated man, who it is that has power to allow entrance to the true fold and to exclude from it [EGT]. This picture of thieves and robbers illustrates the work of the Pharisees as they have been 'shepherding' the people of God [Car, Gdt, IVP, Kn, NICNT1]. This chapter is a comment on chapter 9 in which the Pharisees are characterized as hireling shepherds who have thrown out the blind man instead of caring for him [Bar]. The religious leaders who were hostile to Jesus were the thieves and robbers who were trying illegally to gain control over the sheep, the people of Israel [NTC].The reference to the opening the eyes of a blind man in verse 10:21, shows that there is a close connection between this chapter and chapter 9 [My, NICNT1]. Jesus continues to speak to the blind man, his disciples, the Pharisees and other Jews [Lns].

QUESTION—What is the nature of this following teaching?

It is a parable or a figure of speech as seen in verse 6 which describes verses 1–5 as a παροιμίαν 'parable' [ICC, NICNT2, Rd].

QUESTION—What is a sheepfold?

It was a roofless enclosure surrounded by a stone wall with a gate or entranceway [EGT, Gdt, NICNT1, NTC]. It was located either in an open field [NTC] or adjoining a house [AB, Bar, BECNT, HTC, ICC, NICNT1, NICNT2, TH]. At times, the sheepfold was a square marked off on a hillside by stone walls. Here it seems to be a yard in front of a house, surrounded by a stone wall that was probably topped by briars [AB]. Its purpose was to keep sheep safe at night from wild animals [TRT]. The sheepfold or the sheep signify the people of Israel [CH, Gdt, My, NTC].

QUESTION—What is the point of similarity in the figure of the gate?

The gate points to a legitimate entrance into an enclosure [Gdt, HTC, NICNT2]. This in turn points to a divinely instituted office, the Messianic office prophesied and prefigured in the OT [Gdt]. The door is the messiahship [CH].

QUESTION—What is the difference between a thief and a robber?

Both of these steal except that the thief does so by stealth or secrecy while the robber does so by force or violence [BECNT, EGT, HTC, NICNT1, TH]. A robber is characterized more by rudeness and violence than a thief [Gdt]. Although these are different, they point to a single person as shown by the singular ἐκεῖνος 'that one' that precedes it, '*that one* is a thief and a robber' [WBC].

10:2 **But the (one) entering through the gate is (the) shepherd^a of the sheep.**

LEXICON—a. ποιμήν (LN 44.4) (BAGD 1. p. 684): 'shepherd' [BAGD, LN; all translations], 'sheep-herder' [BAGD]. This noun is derived from the verb ποιμαίνω 'to take care of sheep or goats' (44.3) and denotes one who takes care of sheep or goats [LN]. It is used here as a symbol of Christ in an extended allegory [BAGD].

QUESTION—How are the two nouns related in the genitive construction ποιμήν τῶν προβάτων 'shepherd of the sheep'?

The shepherd takes care of the sheep [LN, TH: REB]: 'the shepherd in charge of the sheep' [REB]. He takes care of the sheep either by seeing that they have what they need or taking them out to pasture [TH].

QUESTION—How should the phrase ποιμήν τῶν προβάτων 'shepherd of the sheep' (without a definite article) be translated?

1. The phrase should be translated as 'the shepherd of the sheep' [BECNT, NICNT1, NICNT2, Rd, WBC; CEV, KJV, NCV, NET, NIV, NJB, NLT, NRSV, Ph, REB, TEV]. E. C. Colwell's rule that in the NT definite nouns that precede the verb typically lack the article, justify the translation 'the shepherd' [NICNT1, NICNT2]. The lack of article brings out the strong bond that exists between the shepherd and the sheep, the sheep belong to him (see verse 12) [Rd].
2. The phrase should be translated 'a shepherd' or 'shepherd of the sheep' [AB, Gdt, HTC, Lns, My, NTC; NASB]: 'The one who enters through the gate is shepherd of the sheep' [AB]. In Greek the word shepherd has no definite article and therefore it acts as an adjective, focusing on the quality of a shepherd meaning to enter 'as a shepherd would', rather than to enter

'as a robber' [Gdt, Lns, My]. The lack of article indicates that this shepherd is one among several possible shepherds [HTC].

10:3 To-him the gatekeeper[a] opens, and the sheep hear[b] his voice and he-calls[c] his-own[d] sheep by name and leads- them -out.[e]

LEXICON—a. θυρωρός (LN 46.8) (BAGD 1. p. 366): 'gatekeeper' [HTC; CEV, NJB, NLT, NRSV, TEV], 'doorkeeper' [BAGD, LN, NICNT2, NTC, WBC; NASB, Ph, REB], 'keeper' [AB], 'porter' [Gdt; KJV], 'watchman' [NIV]. This noun is also translated as a clause: 'the one who guards the door' [NCV]. This noun denotes one who guards the door giving access to a house or building [LN].

b. pres. act. indic. of ἀκούω (LN 24.52): 'to hear' [AB; LN, KJV, NASB, NJB, NRSV, REB, TEV], 'to listen to' [NTC, WBC; NCV, NIV], 'to recognize' [NLT, Ph]. The clause 'the sheep hear his voice' is translated 'the sheep know their shepherd's voice' [CEV], 'the sheep recognize his voice and come to him' [NLT].

c. pres. act. indic. of φωνέω (LN 33.307) (BAGD 2.b. p. 870): 'to call' [LN; all translations except Gdt, NICNT2], 'to summon' [BAGD, Gdt, NICNT2], 'to call (someone or something) to oneself' [BAGD]. This verb means to communicate directly or indirectly to someone who is presumably at a distance, in order to tell such a person to come [LN].

d. ἴδιος (LN 57.4) (BAGD 1.b. p. 369): 'one's own' [BAGD, LN], one's property' [LN]. The clause 'he calls his own sheep' [all translations except AB, NICNT2; CEV] is also translated 'he summons his own sheep' [NICNT2], 'he calls (by name) those that belong to him' [AB], 'he calls each of them by name' [CEV]. This adjective describes something or someone as being the exclusive property of someone [LN]. It describes a thing as 'belonging to an individual' or as being 'peculiar to an individual' [BAGD].

e. pres. act. indic. of ἐξάγω (LN **15.174**) (BAGD 1. p. 271): 'to lead out' [BAGD, **LN**; all translations], 'to bring out' [BAGD, LN], 'to lead out, to bring forth' [LN]. This verb means to lead or bring out of a structure or area [LN].

QUESTION—What word is emphasized in this verse?

The word τούτῳ 'to him' (literally, 'to this one') is emphatic in the Greek structure [TH; Ph]: '*It is to him* the doorkeeper opens the door' [Ph].

QUESTION—What is implied by the clause 'the sheep hear his voice'?

The idiom 'to hear someone's voice' means both to hear the voice and to obey the speaker [HTC, ICC, NICNT1, NTC, TRT; NLT]. When the verb ἀκούω 'to hear' is used with a genitive object (as it does here) it means to listen and obey [HTC]. They both hear the voice and recognize who the speaker is [BECNT, Gdt, ICC, Lns, My, NICNT1, NTC, Rd,; CEV, NLT, Ph].

QUESTION—How many flocks are in a fold?
There were probably several flocks in one fold [Bar, BECNT, ICC, Lns, My, NICNT1, TH, WBC]. The existence of a gatekeeper or watchman suggests that the pen held several flocks [BECNT, NICNT1]. The repetition of the phrase τὰ ἴδια 'his own' in verses 3 and 4 suggest that there were more than one flock in the fold [Bar, WBC]. All the sheep in the sheep pen hear the shepherd's voice, but it is only 'his own' flock that responds to his call [HTC]. It is more probable that only the flock of the shepherd was in the fold. The phrase 'his own' simply stresses that the sheep belong to him as objects of his love and care [NICNT2].

QUESTION—What is implied by the phrase 'he calls his own sheep by name'?
It implies that he has a name for each one of his sheep to which they respond [BECNT, Car, HTC, Lns, My, TH].

10:4 When he-brings-out[a] all his own, he-goes before them, and the sheep follow him, because they-know[b] his voice.

LEXICON—a. aorist act. subj. of ἐκβάλλω (LN **15.174**) (BAGD 2. p. 237): 'to bring out' [AB, BAGD, HTC, NICNT2, NTC; NCV, NET, NIV, NJB, NRSV, REB, TEV], 'to lead out' [LN, CEV], 'to put forth' [Gdt; KJV, NRSV], 'to put out' [NTC], 'to gather' [NLT], 'to drive outside' [Ph], 'to bring forth' [LN]. This verb means to lead or bring out of a structure or area [LN].

b. perf. act. indic. of οἶδα (LN 28.1): 'to know' [LN; all translations except AB; NET], 'to recognize' [AB; NET], 'to know about, to have knowledge of, to be acquainted with' [LN]. This verb means to possess information about [LN].

QUESTION—Does the verb ἐκβάλλω 'to bring out' include the sense of force?
1. The verb includes the sense of force or constraint [AB, Gdt, HTC, ICC, Lns, My, NICNT1, NTC; Ph]: 'and when he has driven all his own flock outside' [Ph], 'When he has pushed all his own out' [Lns]. There may be a hint of the helplessness of the sheep, some of which need to be pushed through a gate [AB, BECNT, HTC]. The shepherd energetically and almost roughly helps the hesitant sheep to break away from the others [Gdt]. The shepherd compels the sheep to leave the fold, but for their good. He uses force if necessary but it is in their best interest [NICNT1]. A sheep that delays to come at his call may need a certain amount of constraint [ICC]. The shepherd takes hold of the sheep and brings them out to the gate [My].
2. The verb does not imply force or constraint [BAGD, Car, NICNT2]. While this verb is used to mean 'drive out' in 6:37, here it has a weakened sense much like the verb ἐξάγω 'to lead out' of verse 3 [NICNT2]. The shepherd does not drive the sheep but leads them [Car]. It means 'to bring out' without the connotation of force [BAGD].

10:5 But they-will- never[a] -follow (a) stranger,[b] but will-flee from him because they-do- not -know[c] the voice of-strangers.

LEXICON—a. οὐ μή (LN 69.5) (BAGD D.2. p. 517): 'never' [NICNT2, WBC; NCV, NET, NIV, NJB, Ph], 'in no way' [Lns, NTC], 'by no means, certainly not' [LN], 'not' [AB, Gdt, HTC; CEV, KJV, NLT, NRSV, REB, TEV]. The clause 'they will never follow a stranger' is translated 'a stranger they simply will not follow' [NRSV]. This negative phrase indicates emphatic negation [BAGD, HTC, LN, NICNT2, NTC]. It is the most decisive way of negating something in the future [BAGD, Lns].

b. ἀλλότριος (LN **11.74**) (BAGD 1.b.β. p. 40): 'stranger' [BAGD, LN; all translations except TEV], 'someone else' [TEV], 'foreigner' [LN]. This noun denotes a person from another geographical or cultural region and/or one not known to members of the socio-political group in question. Here the most satisfactory rendering of 'stranger' is often 'someone who is not known,' in other words, 'they will not follow *someone whom they do not know*' or '*recognize*' [**LN**].

c. perf. act. indic. of οἶδα (LN 28.1): 'to know' [Gdt, HTC, LN, NICNT2, NTC, WBC; KJV, NRSV, NRSV, NLT, NRSV], 'to recognize' [AB; CEV, NET, NIV, NJB, Ph, REB], 'to know about, to have knowledge of, to be acquainted with' [LN]. This verb means to possess information about [LN].

QUESTION—What word is emphasized in this verse?

The word 'stranger' comes first in this verse to increase its prominence [TH, TRT].

QUESTION—Which particular 'strangers' are referred to?

They are probably the thieves and robbers mentioned in verses 1, 8, and 10 [Bar, BECNT, Car, Gdt, HTC, ICC, NICNT2]. They are false leaders or seducers whom the sheep refuse to follow [HTC]. It is not merely the ones who climb in another way that are referred to, but everyone in general who is not their shepherd [My].

QUESTION—What relationship is indicated by the conjunction ἀλλά 'but'?

It indicates a sharp contrast between the emphatic negative 'they will *never follow* a stranger' and the words 'they will *flee* from him' [NICNT2].

DISCOURSE UNIT—10:6 [Car]. The topic is misunderstanding.

10:6 Jesus told them this parable[a] but they did- not understand[b] what he-was telling them.

LEXICON—a. παροιμία (LN 33.15) (BAGD 2. p. 629): 'parable' [LN, NICNT2, TH, WBC; KJV, NET, NJB, REB, TEV], 'figure of speech' [NASB, NIV, NRSV], 'figure' [BAGD, LN, HTC], 'illustration' [NLT, Ph], 'allegory' [LN, My, NTC], 'proverb' [CH, EGT, Rd], 'story' [CEV, NCV], 'picture' [AB], 'similitude' [Gdt], 'dark saying' [BAGD], 'enigmatic saying' [CH]. This noun denotes a relatively short narrative with symbolic meaning [LN]. It denotes a figure of speech in which especially lofty ideas are concealed [BAGD].

b. aorist act. indic. of γινώσκω (LN 32.16) (BAGD 3.d. p. 161): 'to understand' [BAGD; all translations except Ph], 'to come to understand, to perceive, to comprehend' [LN]. The statement 'they did not understand what he was telling them' is translated 'they did not understand what it meant that he was telling him' [NTC], 'they did not understand what that meant which he spoke to them' [Gdt], 'they did not understand what it meant' [NCV], 'Those who heard…didn't understand what he meant' [NLT], 'they did not understand what he meant (by it)' [REB, TEV], 'they did not grasp the point of what he was saying to them' [Ph]. This verb means to come to an understanding as the result of the ability to experience and learn [LN].

QUESTION—To whom does the pronoun αὐτοῖς 'to them' refer?

It probably refers back to the Pharisees mentioned in 9:40 [CH, NICNT2, TH]. Jesus had aimed this parable at the Pharisees who had asked him if they were blind too [NICNT2]. It refers to the unbelieving Jews [HTC]. It refers to the Jewish leaders [BECNT, Rd]. It refers to the Jews who were the enemies of Jesus [Bar, Car].

QUESTION—What is a παροιμία 'parable'?

It is a form of speech in which the meaning is not obvious [EGT, ICC, NICNT1] but which, if understood, conveys deep important spiritual truth [NICNT1]. It is an example or illustration used to teach something important. Its meaning is often not understood without thought or explanation [TRT]. It can have several names like, comparison, proverb, cryptic saying, and riddle [Rd]. The writers of the Septuagint used παροιμία to translate the Hebrew word *mashal*, a term that refers to almost all kinds of figurative speech [AB, TH]. The other Gospels use the word παραβολή 'parable' while John uses only this word here and in 16:25, and 29. The Septuagint translation uses both terms to translate the Hebrew word *mashal*. There seems to be no perceptible difference in meaning between the two terms [Bar, BECNT, ICC, TH] so it is probably best to translate them both in the same way [TH]. All three words παροιμία, παραβολή and *mashal* can refer to a wide variety of figures like proverbs, parables, maxims, similes, allegories, fables, riddles, narratives embodying truths, taunts, and others. All have one feature in common, they have something cryptic or enigmatic about them [Car].

QUESTION—Why did they not understand what he was telling them?

They did not understand because it was morally impossible for them to conceive of the Pharisees as being the thieves and robbers [Gdt].

DISCOURSE UNIT—10:7–21 [NCV, TEV]. The topic is Jesus is the good shepherd.

DISCOURSE UNIT—10:7–18 [Car, NICNT1, WBC]. The topic is the application to Christ [NICNT1], meditation on the parable [WBC], expansion [Car].

DISCOURSE UNIT—10:7–10 [HTC, IVP, Rd]. The topic is words about the door.

10:7 **So Jesus again said, "Truly truly I-say to-you(pl) I am the gate of-the sheep.**

QUESTION—What word is emphasized in this verse?

The pronoun ἐγώ 'I' is emphatic [EGT, My, NICNT1, NTC]: 'I alone am the door of the sheep' [NTC]. While the phrase 'truly, truly' marks Jesus' words as being solemn, true and important, his use of 'I am' continues that emphasis [NICNT1].

QUESTION—How are the two nouns related in the genitive construction ἡ θύρα τῶν προβάτων 'the gate of the sheep'?

1. The gate was *for* the sheep to enter and exit the sheepfold [CH, EGT, Gdt, IVP, My, TH, WBC; CEV, NCV, NET, NIV, NLT, NRSV, Ph, TEV]: 'I am the gate for the sheep' [CEV]. The gate was for the sheep to use going in and coming out of the sheepfold [Gdt, TH]. The shepherd would lie down and sleep across the entrance to the sheepfold so that the sheep entered the sheepfold through him [IVP]. Jesus is the door to the sheep in the sense that the true spiritual leaders of God's people receive through him their qualification and appointment as leaders [My].
2. The gate was for access of others *to* the sheep [Bar, BAGD (2.d. p. 366), HTC, ICC, Lns, My, NICNT1, NICNT2]. The primary idea in this verse is that the door provides an entrance for the shepherd to enter the fold, while in verse 9 it is the entrance by which the sheep enter [ICC, NICNT1].
3. The gate was both for the sheep and to them [NTC, Rd]. The following context shows that Jesus is both the door *to* the sheep in verse 8, but the door *for* the sheep to enter and exit in verse 9. For the shepherd he is the door to the sheep but for the sheep he is the door to all the benefits of salvation [NTC]. Verses 1, 2, and 8a show that Jesus is the door that gives access by which others gain entrance to the sheep. On the other hand, verse 9 shows that Jesus is the door through which the sheep gain access to the sheep fold [Rd].

10:8 **All as-many-as[a] came before me are thieves and robbers, but the sheep did not listen-to[b] them.**

TEXT—Instead of ὅσοι ἦλθον πρὸ ἐμοῦ 'who came before me', some manuscripts read ὅσοι πρὸ ἐμοῦ ἦλθον 'who before me came', others read ὅσοι ἦλθον 'who came', and one manuscript omits this phrase. GNT reads 'who came before me' with a C decision indicating difficulty in deciding which variant to place in the text.

LEXICON—a. ὅσος (LN 59.7) (BAGD 2. p. 586): 'as many as' [BAGD, LN], 'who' [BAGD; all translations except WBC; KJV], 'whoever' [WBC], 'that' [KJV]. This pronoun denotes a comparative quantity of objects or events [LN].

b. aorist act. indic. of ἀκούω (LN) (BAGD 4. p. 32): 'to listen to' [BAGD, Gdt, LN, NTC, WBC; CEV, NCV, NET, NIV, NLT, NRSV, Ph, TEV], 'to take notice of' [NJB], 'to heed' [AB, HTC, LN], 'to pay heed to' [REB], 'to follow' [BAGD], 'to hear' [NICNT2; KJV, NASB], 'to accept, to listen and respond, to pay attention and respond' [LN]. This verb means to believe something and to respond to it on the basis of having heard [LN].

QUESTION—Of whom is 'thieves and robbers' a figure?

Jesus is probably referring to the Jewish religious leaders [AB, CH, EGT, Gdt, HTC, IVP, Lns, My, NICNT1, NICNT2, NTC, Rd, TH, TRT, WBC]. He is referring to the Pharisees, the religious leaders of the people [AB, BECNT, Gdt, HTC, Lns, My, NTC, WBC], including the Sadducees (see 9:40 and 10:19) [AB, BECNT, Lns, NICNT1, NTC, TH]. He is referring to the spiritual leaders of the people and to false messiahs [CH, HTC, TH, WBC]. He probably is referring to those who came pretending to be the Messiah [Bar, Car, ICC]. He includes all past leaders, including prophets, priests, and kings who had taken advantage of the people who were placed in their care [TH]. He is not referring to people like Abraham, Moses, God's prophets [Bar, Car, EGT, Gdt, HTC, ICC, IVP, Lns, My, NICNT1, NTC, TH, TRT], or to John the Baptist [Bar, HTC, IVP, NTC, TRT], but to those leaders who led the people astray [TRT]. The word 'all' would include the degraded spiritual leadership of Israel in the past [Rd].

QUESTION—Who are the sheep?

The sheep are the true Israelites [ICC]. They are the true children of God [EGT, Lns, My, Rd]. They are Christ's true disciples [NTC]. They are the people who are truly born again and recognize the truth when they hear it and error when they hear it [CH]. They are those who are given to Jesus by the Father [NICNT1]. They are the ones who have been predestined and who belong to Christ as his own [Bar].

10:9 I am the gate. If anyone enters through[a] me he-will-be-saved[b] and will-go-in and will-go-out and will-find pasture.[c]

LEXICON—a. διά (LN 90.4) (BAGD A.I.1. p. 179): 'through' [AB, BAGD, LN, NICNT2, WBC; CEV, NASB, NCV, NET, NIV, NJB, NLT, Ph, REB], 'by' [Gdt, HTC, LN, NTC; KJV, NRSV, TEV]. This preposition indicates the intermediate agent, with implicit or explicit causative agent [LN].

b. fut. pass. indic. of σῴζω (LN 21.27) (BAGD 2.b. p. 798): 'to be saved' [BAGD, LN; all translations except NJB, Ph, REB], 'to be safe' [NJB, REB], 'to be safe and sound' [Ph], 'to attain salvation' [BAGD]. The active voice of this verb means to cause someone to experience divine salvation [LN]. It means to be saved or preserved from eternal death, from judgment, and from all that might lead to such death, for example, sin. Positively it means to bring Messianic salvation to someone [BAGD].

c. νομή (LN **1.98**) (BAGD 1. p. 541): 'pasture' [BAGD, **LN**; all translations except NLT, Ph], 'good pasture' [NLT], 'food' [Ph], 'fodder' [BAGD]. This noun denotes pastureland in contrast with cultivated fields [LN]. It denotes pasture in the sense of a pasturing-place [BAGD].

QUESTION—Are the words of Jesus, Ἐγώ εἰμι 'I am' significant in John?

It is one of seven emphatic statements in John such as '(I am) the bread of life' (6:35, 48), 'the light of the world' (8:12), 'the gate' (10:7, 9), 'the good shepherd' (10:11, 14), 'the resurrection and the life' (11:25), 'the way, and the truth, and the life' (14:6), and 'the vine' (15:5) [NICNT1].

QUESTION—What was the purpose of the gate?

1. The gate was the entry way *for* the sheep to enter and exit the sheepfold [AB, BAGD (2.d. p. 366), Bar, BECNT, Car, CH, EGT, HTC, ICC, Kn, NICNT1, NICNT2, NTC, Rd, TH]. In verse 7 the meaning seems to be, 'I am the door to the sheep', that is, the means by which a shepherd may enter. But here it is rather, 'I am the door by means of which the sheep may enter into the fold' [Bar, ICC]. This cannot be the door for the shepherd since the one who goes through it will be saved [HTC].
2. The gate was the entry way for the shepherd into the sheepfold [Lns, My]. The gender of τις '(if) anyone (enters)' is masculine while the gender of πρόβατον 'sheep' is neuter. This therefore refers to the shepherd who goes into the sheepfold and goes out to find pasture for the sheep [Lns, My]. The picture in verses 1 and 2 is of the shepherd entering through the door and this reference does not change in this verse [My].

QUESTION—What is indicated by the gate?

It indicates the sole means by which the sheep may enter the safety of the fold or the abundant forage of the pasture [Car]. The shepherd lies across the entrance to the sheepfold and no sheep goes out or wolf comes in without crossing over the shepherd's body. The sheep are perfectly secure in the fold [NICNT1]. The gate also implies a certain exclusivity. With one door, people must enter through it or stay outside [NICNT1, TH].

QUESTION—What words are emphasized in this verse?

The pronoun ἐγώ 'I' is emphatic. Jesus is contrasting himself with all the false shepherds who came before him [TRT]: *I myself* am the door. The phrase δι' ἐμοῦ 'through me' is in the emphatic position [BECNT, ICC, IVP, Lns, My, NICNT1, NTC, TH, TRT], stressing the exclusiveness of the entrance [My, NTC]. The statement 'I am the door' is emphasized by its repetition [EGT].

QUESTION—What does entering the sheepfold signify?

It signifies the act of entering into fellowship with Jesus and coming under his protection [Rd]. It signifies entry into the Messianic community [Bar], into the heavenly world of life (3:5) [HTC], of the gaining of eternal life by believing in Jesus [NICNT2]. The sheepfold is a picture of the Kingdom of God [TH]. It is a picture of salvation [AB, CH, Gdt, NICNT1].

QUESTION—What is indicated by the phrase 'he will go in and go out'?
This action is an OT expression describing the normal activity of daily life (Jeremiah 37:4; Psalm 121:8; Deuteronomy 28:6) [CH, EGT, IVP, Rd]. It is a phrase used in Scripture to indicate the free use of a house. A person goes in and out freely because he belongs to the family [Gdt]. It indicates free and safe movement [Kn, NICNT1, TH], the feeling of being at home [ICC], or that the person will experience perfect freedom from all real harm and danger [NTC].

QUESTION—What does the phrase 'he will be saved' indicate?
It indicates he will gain a place of safety [ICC, NICNT1, NICNT2, Rd, TH] from harm either from thieves and robbers or from natural predators [NICNT2]. It indicates the person will be given eternal life (see verse 10) [NTC]. It means the same as gaining eternal life. The only way for someone to become one of God's people is to believe in Jesus as the sacrifice for their sins [TRT]. It indicates spiritual salvation and spiritual security [CH], or the whole process of being delivered from sin's concequences and being brought into God's blessing [NICNT1]. The shepherd will be made free from all dangers by the protecting door to the sheepfold [My].

QUESTION—What does pasture indicate?
It indicates: the free satisfaction of the sheep's need for nourishment [Gdt], God's provision [BECNT], life and abundance as the following verse shows [NTC], the life-sustaining power that Jesus gives to the believer [TH], or God's blessing into which the sheep is brought [NICNT1].

10:10 The thief does- not -come except[a] so-that[b] he-may-steal and kill[c] and destroy.[d] I came so-that they-may-have life and may-have (it) abundantly.[e]

LEXICON—a. εἰ μή (LN 89.131): 'except' [LN], 'except that, but, however, instead, but only' [LN]. The clause 'The thief does not come except so that he may steal' is translated 'The thief does not come except that he might steal' [NICNT2], 'The thief comes not, but to/for-to steal' [Gdt; KJV], 'The/a thief comes only to steal' [AB, HTC, WBC; NASB, NET, NIV, NJB, NRSV, REB], 'The thief comes only in order to steal' [HTC; TEV], 'A thief comes only to rob' [CEV], 'A thief comes to steal' [NCV], 'The thief's purpose is to steal' [NLT], 'The thief comes with the sole intention of stealing' [Ph]. This conjunction indicates contrast by designating an exception [LN].

b. ἵνα (LN 89.59): 'so that' [LN], 'that' [NICNT2], 'to' [all translations except NICNT2, NTC; KJV; TEV], 'in order to' [LN, NTC; TEV], 'for to' [KJV], 'for the purpose of' [LN]. The clause 'The thief does not come except so that he may steal' is translated 'The thief comes with the sole intention of stealing' [Ph]. This conjunction indicates purpose for events and states (sometimes occurring in highly elliptical contexts) [LN].

c. aorist. act. subj. of θύω (LN **20.72**) (BAGD 3. p. 367): 'to kill' [BAGD, LN; all translations except AB, NICNT2, WBC], 'to slaughter' [AB, Bar, **LN**, NICNT2, TH, WBC]. This verb means to slaughter, either animals or persons. In contexts referring to persons, the implication is of violence and mercilessness [LN]. It refers specifically to the killing of animals and literally means 'to slaughter' [Bar, NICNT2, TH].

d. aorist. act. subj. of ἀπόλλυμι (LN **20.31**) (BAGD 1.a.β. p. 95): 'to destroy' [BAGD, LN; all translations], 'to ruin' [BAGD, LN]. This verb means to destroy or to cause the destruction of persons, objects, or institutions [LN].

e. περισσός (LN **59.51**) (BAGD 2.a. p. 651): 'abundantly' [BAGD, **LN**], 'abundant, profuse, going beyond what is necessary, (have) in abundance' [BAGD], 'that which is more than (something else), more than enough, beyond the norm, superfluous' [LN]. The clause 'they may/might have it abundantly' [Gdt, HTC; KJV, NASB, NET, NRSV] is also translated 'have it in abundance' [BAGD; NICNT2], 'have it in (all) its fullness' [WBC; REB], '(I came to give/I have come in order that you might have) life—life in all its fullness' [NCV, TEV], 'have it in its fullest' [CEV], 'have it to the full' [AB; NIV, NJB], '(My purpose is to give them) a rich and satisfying life' [NLT], '(I came to bring them life) and far more life than before' [Ph], '(in order that people may have life) and may have abundance' [NTC]. This adjective describes quantity so abundant as to be considerably more than what one would expect or anticipate [LN].

QUESTION—To which thief does the phrase '*the* thief' refer?

The definite article is not a reference to any specific thief but is a stylistic reference to a generic thief [AB, TH, TRT; CEV, NCV, REB]: 'A thief comes only to rob' [CEV]. This phrase could also be translated using the plural 'thieves' [TH, TRT].

QUESTION—What word is emphasized in this verse?

The pronoun ἐγώ 'I' is emphatic and contrasts Jesus with the thief [Lns, My, NICNT1]: *I, for my part,* came that they may have life.

QUESTION—What is meant by 'having life in abundance'?

It means that the spiritual pasture will contain more nourishment than the sheep can consume [Gdt]. It means that Jesus always supplies an overflowing measure, a surplus [EGT, NTC]. It means that Jesus gives not merely enough, but more than plenty [BECNT]. It means life in its highest degree, eternal life [CH, HTC, Kn, NICNT2, WBC] that survives bodily death and is indestructible [HTC]. This eternal life refers to a new kind of life, a qualitatively different relationship to God [NICNT2]. It is not life that must somehow be spent, but life at its scarcely imagined best [Car].

DISCOURSE UNIT—10:11–21 [Rd]. The topic is Jesus the Good Shepherd.

DISCOURSE UNIT—10:11–18 [IVP]. The topic is the Good Shepherd lays down his life.

DISCOURSE UNIT—10:11–15 [HTC]. The topic is Jesus the Good Shepherd [HTC].

10:11 I am the good[a] shepherd. The good shepherd lays-down[b] his life[c] for[d] the sheep.

TEXT—Instead of τίθησιν 'lays down', some manuscripts read δίδωσιν 'gives'. GNT reads 'lays down' with a B rating, indicating that the text is almost certain. Gdt; KJV, NCV, Ph seem to read 'gives'.

LEXICON—a. καλός (LN **88.4**) (BAGD 2.c.α. p. 400): 'good' [BAGD, **LN**; all translations except AB], 'model' [AB], 'fine, praiseworthy' [LN], 'blameless, excellent' [BAGD]. This adjective describes a positive moral quality, with the implication of being favorably valued [LN].

b. τὴν ψυχὴν τίθημι (LN 23.113, **88.4**) (BAGD I.1.b.δ. p. 816): 'to lay down one's life' [BAGD, LN (23.113)], 'to give up one's life' [BAGD], 'to die voluntarily, to die willingly' [LN (23.113)]. The clause 'The good shepherd lays down his life for the/his sheep' [HTC, NICNT2, NTC, WBC; NASB, NET, NIV, NJB, NRSV, REB] is also translated 'the model shepherd lays down his life for the sheep' [AB], 'the good shepherd gives his life for the sheep' [Gdt; KJV, NCV], 'The good shepherd will give his life for the sake of his sheep' [Ph], 'the good shepherd gives up his life for his sheep' [CEV], 'the good shepherd…is willing to die for the sheep' [**LN** (88.4); TEV], 'The good shepherd sacrifices his life for the sheep' [NLT]. This phrase literally means 'to lay down one's life' and is an idiom meaning to die with the implication of voluntary or willing action. Though in English the phrases 'to lay down one's life' or 'to give one's life' do suggest a voluntary dying, a literal rendering of such expressions in other languages would not necessarily imply the same. It may therefore be necessary to use such expressions as 'to die willingly' or 'to die without resisting'. In some languages 'willingly' is expressed primarily as a negation of objecting, for example, 'I will not object to dying' [LN (23.113)].

c. ψυχή (LN 23.88) (BAGD 1.a.β. p. 893): 'life' [BAGD, LN; all translations except TEV], 'earthly life, soul' [BAGD]. The clause 'The good shepherd lays down his life for the sheep' is translated 'I am the good shepherd, who is willing to die for the sheep' [TEV]. This noun denotes one's life on earth in its external physical aspects [BAGD, NICNT2]. It connotes the whole person, the self [NTC].

d. ὑπέρ (LN 90.36) (BAGD 1.a.ε. p. 838): 'for' [BAGD, LN; all translations except Ph], 'for the sake of' [BAGD, LN; Ph], 'on/in behalf of' [BAGD, LN, Lns]. This preposition indicates a participant who is benefited by an event or on whose behalf an event takes place [LN]. It suggests sacrifice for the sheep. Everywhere in John that this preposition is used (6:51; 10:11, 15; 11:50–52; 13:37–38; 15:13; 17:19; 18:14), with two exceptions (1:30 and 11:4), it is used to indicate death in behalf of someone else [Bar, Car, IVP]. The shepherd does not die for the sheep as an example, but the sheep are in mortal danger and he loses his life to save them [Car].

QUESTION—What word is emphasized in this verse?

The pronoun ἐγώ 'I' is emphasized [My]: *I myself* am the good shepherd. The adjective 'good' is also emphasized by its occurrence after the noun and with its own article (the shepherd, the good) [Lns, My, NTC].

QUESTION—What is meant by καλός 'good' here?

It means good in the sense of a person who excels at his work [EGT, ICC, Lns, My, NTC]. The good shepherd is the very model or prototype of what a good shepherd should be [My, NICNT2, NTC]. Perhaps 'noble' is a more exact translation of καλός here, while 'model' is a better translation in verse 14 [AB]. It suggests nobility or worth. In contrast to the self-interest of the hired man Jesus is the noble shepherd [Car]. The following context defines the word 'good' as 'devoted' or 'dedicated' that is, 'the shepherd who is devoted to his sheep' or 'the shepherd who gives himself for his sheep' [TH]. Jesus is using 'good' in the sense of 'true' or 'genuine' [NICNT2, WBC]. This shepherd is faithful and trustworthy. A shepherd who deliberately dies for his sheep breaks out of the usual image in which a shepherd may by chance lose his life protecting his sheep [Kn]. Whenever a Palestinian shepherd died protecting the sheep it was an accident and death meant disaster for the sheep. With Jesus, dying for his sheep was his set purpose and his death meant life for them [NICNT1]. All good shepherds will risk their lives for their sheep but only he who is uniquely the Good Shepherd lays down his life for them [ICC].

QUESTION—When does the good shepherd lay down his life for his sheep?

The good shepherd puts himself in danger in order to ensure the safety of the sheep [NICNT2]. The fact that 'the shepherd puts his life at risk' does not mean that he must give up his life. It rather means that he will 'hazard' or 'risk' his life [Rd]. It may be better to translate that the good shepherd *is willing* to lay down his life for his sheep in order to avoid the danger of implying suicide [TRT].

10:12 The hired-man[a] also not being (the) shepherd, whose own the sheep are not, sees the wolf[b] coming and abandons[c] the sheep and flees—and the wolf attacks[d] them and scatters[e] (them)—**10:13** because he-is (a) hired-man and it-does- not -matter[f] to-him about the sheep.

LEXICON—a. μισθωτός (LN **57.174**) (BAGD p. 523): 'hired man' [BAGD, LN; NJB, Ph, REB, TEV], 'hired hand' [AB, WBC; NASB, NET, NIV, NLT, NRSV], 'hireling' [Gdt, HTC, NICNT2, NTC; KJV], 'hired worker' [LN; CEV], 'worker who is paid to keep the sheep' [NCV], 'hired person' [LN]. This noun denotes a person who has been hired to perform a particular service or work [LN]. It denotes a man whose interest is mainly in what he is paid for doing his job, rather than in the job itself [CH, EGT, HTC, ICC, Kn, NICNT1, NTC]. The characteristics of the hired man that are in focus are that the sheep do not belong to him and that he lacks the desire and courage to stay with the sheep in time of danger [Rd]. He is

more committed to his own well-being than to the well-being of the sheep [Car, EGT].
b. λύκος (LN **4.11**) (BAGD 1. p. 481): 'wolf' [BAGD, **LN**; all translations]. In languages that have no word for 'wolf', a similar animal like 'leopard' or a generic term with a modifier such as 'fierce dog' could be used [TH].
c. pres. act. indic. of ἀφίημι (LN 85.45) (BAGD 3.a. p. 126): 'to abandon' [BAGD, Gdt; NET, NIV, NJB, NLT, REB], 'to desert' [NTC; Ph], 'to leave' [AB, BAGD, HTC, LN, NICNT2, WBC; CEV, KJV, NASB, NRSV, TEV], 'to leave alone' [NCV], 'to leave behind' [LN]. This verb means to let something be put behind in a place [LN].
d. pres. act. indic. of ἁρπάζω (LN **39.49**) (BAGD 1. p. 109): 'to attack' [**LN**; CEV, NCV, NET, NIV, NJB, NLT, Ph], 'to snatch' [AB, BAGD, Gdt, HTC, NTC; NASB, NRSV, TEV], 'to seize' [BAGD, LN, NICNT2], 'to harry' [REB], 'to ravage' [WBC], 'to catch' [KJV]. This verb means to attack, with the implication of seizing [LN]. It means to take suddenly and vehemently or take away in the sense of 'to steal, to carry off, to drag away' [BAGD].
e. pres. act. indic. of σκορπίζω (LN **15.135**) (BAGD 1. p. 757): 'to scatter' [BAGD, **LN**; all translations except Ph], 'to send flying' [Ph], 'to disperse' [BAGD], 'to cause to disperse' [LN]. This verb means to cause a group or a gathering to disperse or scatter [LN]. A wolf chases the sheep in all directions [BAGD].
f. pres. act. indic. of μέλει (LN 25.223) (BAGD 2. p. 500): 'to matter' [NICNT2, WBC], 'to be of concern, to be anxious about' [LN]. The clause 'it does not matter to him about the sheep' [NICNT2] is also translated 'the sheep do not matter to him' [WBC], 'they don't care about the sheep' [CEV], 'he…does not care for/about the sheep' [Gdt; TEV], 'he…cares not/nothing for the sheep' [HTC; KJV, NIV, REB], 'a hired hand does not care for the sheep' [NRSV], 'he…does not really care about the sheep' [NCV, NLT], 'he…is not concerned about the sheep' [NTC; NASB, NET], 'he…has no concern for the sheep' [AB; NJB], 'he…has no interest in the sheep' [Ph]. This verb is only used impersonally in the NT and means to be particularly concerned about something, with the implication of some apprehension [LN]. It means 'it is a care or concern to someone'. Here it means the hired man does not 'care for the sheep' [BAGD].

QUESTION—What word is emphasized in this verse?
In the clause, καὶ οὐκ ὢν ποιμήν 'also not being (the) shepherd', the negative phrase καὶ οὐκ 'also not' is unusual since the negative μή (rather than οὐκ) is more frequently used to negate participles (such as ὢν 'being'). As such, the phrase functions to emphasize the factuality of the clause. He is *certainly not* the shepherd [BAGD (3.b. p. 390), NICNT1, similarly ICC, Lns]. The negative particle οὐ(κ) is the correct negative for a statement of downright fact [Bar].

26   JOHN 10:12–13

QUESTION—What is meant by the phrase 'attacks them and scatters them'?
  If the meaning of 'snatch' or 'seize' is chosen for the first verb, it may be difficult for some languages to make sense of the two actions together. In this case it would be better to translate something like, 'he pounces on one of the sheep and scatters the rest' [TH]. It may mean that he seizes some of the sheep and the rest run away in all directions [NICNT1, Rd].
QUESTION—What information is implied between verses 12 and 13?
  Verse 13 refers back to the hired man's fleeing and not to the wolf attacking and scattering the sheep. It may therefore be necessary to begin verse 13 with something like '*He flees* because…' [Gdt, HTC, NTC, TH, TRT, WBC; CEV, KJV, NASB, NIV, NJB, NLT, NRSV, Ph, REB]: '*The hired man runs away* because he is only a hired man' [TEV].

10:14 I am the good shepherd and I-know^a mine^b and mine know me, 10:15 just-as^c the Father knows me and-I know the Father, and I-lay-down^d my life for the sheep.

TEXT—Instead of τίθησιν 'lay down' some manuscripts read δίδωσιν 'give'. GNT reads 'lay down' with a B rating, indicating that the text is almost certain. Gdt; NCV, Ph seem to read 'give'.
LEXICON—a. pres. act. indic. of γινώσκω (LN 27.18) (BAGD 6.a.β. p. 161): 'to know' [BAGD, LN; all translations], 'to come to know someone' [BAGD], 'to become acquainted with, to be familiar with' [LN]. This verb means to learn to know a person through direct personal experience, implying a continuity of relationship [LN]. This knowing is not rational or theoretical knowing, but rather knowing in the OT Semitic sense, indicating a personal intimate relationship with [HTC]. This knowledge is a knowledge of experience [Car, NTC, WBC] and loving fellowship [NTC]. To know in this sense is to enter into an intimate relationship with God [WBC]. It indicates a loving intimacy [IVP, NICNT1]. This kind of knowing indicates a covenant relationship like marital intimacy [Kn]. It is a knowledge that grows out of the most intimate fellowship of love and life [My]. It is a personal knowledge [TH, TRT] based on intimate acquaintance and familiarity with someone [TH].
  b. ἐμός (LN 92.2): 'mine' [LN], 'my' [LN]. The clause γινώσκω τα ἐμά 'I know mine' [NICNT2, WBC] is also translated 'I know my own' [HTC, NTC; NASB, NET, NJB, NRSV, REB], 'I know those that are mine' [Ph] 'I know my sheep' [AB, Gdt; CEV, NCV, NIV, TEV], 'I…know my [sheep]' [KJV], 'I know my own sheep' [NLT].
  c. καθώς (LN 64.14): 'just as' [AB, LN, NICNT2, NTC; NET, NIV, NJB, NLT, NRSV, Ph], 'as' [Gdt, HTC, WBC; KJV, NCV, REB, TEV], 'even as' [NASB], 'in comparison to' [LN]. This conjunction indicates a similarity in events and states, with the possible implication of something being in accordance with something else [LN].
  d. pres. act. indic. of τίθημι (LN 23.113) (BAGD I.1.b.δ. p. 816): 'to lay, to put, to place' [BAGD]. The clause 'I lay down my life for the sheep'

[HTC, NICNT2, NTC, WBC; KJV, NASB, NET, NIV, NJB, NRSV, REB] is also translated 'for these sheep I lay down my life' [AB], 'I give my life for the sheep' [Gdt; NCV], 'I am giving my life for the sake of the sheep' [Ph], 'I give up my life for my sheep' [CEV], 'I sacrifice my life for the sheep' [NLT], 'I am willing to die for them' [TEV]. The idiom τὴν ψυχὴν τίθημι (literally, 'to lay down one's life') means to die, with the implication of voluntary or willing action 'to die voluntarily, to die willingly' [LN]. It means 'to lay down one's life' or 'to give up one's life' [BAGD]. The present tense points to the fact that Jesus' life is presently at risk since the Jews are trying to find a way to kill him, but it also points to the future when Jesus will give up his life on the cross [NICNT2].

QUESTION—What words are emphasized in this verse?

The pronoun Ἐγώ 'I' is emphasized [Gdt, Lns]: '*As for me, I* am the good shepherd' [Gdt]. The statement 'I am the good shepherd' is emphatically repeated from verse 11 [Car, NTC].

QUESTION—What is indicated by the conjunction καθώς 'just as'?

It goes beyond the sense of comparison [Gdt, HTC, Rd] and defines the knowledge that Jesus has of his sheep as being of the same nature as the knowledge that unites him to God [Gdt]. It indicates that the reciprocal knowledge of Jesus and his sheep is patterned after the knowledge of the Father and Jesus [BECNT, NTC]. It indicates that Jesus' knowledge of his sheep is grounded on the mutual knowledge of the Father and the Son [Kn, Rd]. It has both a comparative and a causal sense [Car, HTC, IVP, Rd] because the relationship between the Father and Jesus is both the model and the reason for Jesus' relationship with his own [Car, HTC, IVP].

DISCOURSE UNIT—10:16–21 [HTC]. The topic is Jesus the shepherd and his sheep.

10:16 And I-have[a] other sheep that are not of[b] this fold; it-is-necessary (for) me to-bring[c] them-also and they-will-hear[d] my voice and they-will-become one flock[e] (and) one shepherd.

TEXT—Instead of γενήσονται 'they will become', some manuscripts read γενήσεται 'there will become'. GNT reads 'they will become' with a C rating, indicating difficulty in deciding which variant to place in the text. AB, Bar, Gdt, HTC, Lns; CEV, KJV, NCV, NET, NIV, NJB, NLT, NRSV, Ph, and REB seem to support the reading 'there will become'.

LEXICON—a. pres. act. indic. of ἔχω (LN 57.1) (BAGD p. I.2.a. p. 332): 'to have' [LN; all translations except WBC; REB, TEV], 'to have as one's own' [BAGD], 'to possess' [BAGD, LN], 'to own, to belong to' [LN]. The clause 'other sheep I have' is translated 'There are other sheep which belong to me' [TEV], 'there are other sheep of mine' [WBC; REB]. This verb means to have or possess objects or property [LN].

b. ἐκ (LN 89.3): 'of' [Gdt, HTC; KJV, NASB, NIV, NJB], 'from' [LN, NICNT2]. The phrase 'of this fold' is translated 'in this sheep pen/sheepfold' [CEV, NLT, TEV], 'in this flock' [NCV], 'come from this

sheepfold' [NET], 'belong/belonging to this fold' [AB, NTC, WBC; NRSV, Ph, REB]. This preposition indicates the source from which someone or something is physically or psychologically derived [LN].
c. aorist act. infin. of ἄγω (LN 15.165) (BAGD 1.a. p. 14): 'to bring' [BAGD, LN; all translations except AB, NTC; CEV, NJB, Ph, REB], 'to bring together' [CEV], 'to lead' [AB, BAGD, LN, NTC; NJB, Ph, REB]. This verb means to direct or guide the movement of an object, without special regard to point of departure or goal [LN].
d. fut. act. indic. of ἀκούω (LN 36.14): 'to hear' [BAGD, Gdt, NICNT2; CEV, KJV, NASB, Ph], 'to listen to' [AB, NTC, TRT, WBC; NCV, NET, NIV, NJB, NLT, NRSV, REB, TEV], 'to heed' [HTC], 'to pay attention to and obey' [LN]. This verb means to listen or pay attention to a person, with resulting conformity to what is advised or commanded [LN]. When ἀκούω occurs with a genitive object as it does here it indicates hearing with understanding and obedience [ICC].
e. ποίμνη (LN **11.31**, 4.28) (BAGD p. 684): 'flock' [BAGD, **LN**; all translations except AB; CEV, KJV], 'flock of sheep' [CEV], 'fold' [KJV], 'sheep herd' [AB], 'people who are like a flock' [LN]. This noun is a collective word for a group of sheep and/or goats [LN (4.28)]. Here it is a figurative extension of the meaning of ποίμνη 'flock' referring to the followers of Christ constituting a well-defined membership group [LN]. It refers to the church and to Jesus as its head [BAGD].

QUESTION—To whom does the phrase 'this fold' refer?
It refers to the group in Israel who already believe in Jesus [AB, EGT, HTC] or just to Judaism itself [Bar, NICNT1].

QUESTION—Who are the 'other sheep'?
They are probably the Gentiles who have not yet believed in Jesus [BECNT, Car, CH, EGT, Gdt, ICC, IVP, Lns, my, NICNT1, NICNT2, Rd, TRT]. They are all those heathen who have been chosen by God and who are destined to belong to Jesus' believing community [HTC]. They are future believers who have not seen the historical Jesus personally [Kn].

QUESTION—In what sense does Jesus 'have' these other sheep?
He has them in the sense that the Father has given them to him (6:37, 39; 17:6, 24) [CH, EGT, NTC, WBC].

QUESTION—What is the significance of the sheep becoming one flock and not one fold?
Jesus does not lead the sheep into the fold of Israel. Rather he gathers together the sheep of Israel and the sheep of heathendom into one flock [NTC]. There can be several sheep folds in one flock [ICC].

QUESTION—To whom does the pronoun 'they' refer in the phrase 'they will become'?
It is important to make sure that 'they' refers to both groups of sheep [TRT]: they will all become one flock.

10:17 For-this-reason[a] the Father loves me because I lay-down my life, so-that[b] I-may-take[c] it again.[d]

LEXICON—a. διά τοῦτο (BAGD B.II.2. p. 181): This phrase is translated 'for this reason' [BAGD, HTC, NTC, WBC; NASB, NRSV], 'this is the reason why' [Ph], 'this/that is why' [AB, NICNT2; NET], 'therefore' [Gdt; KJV], 'the reason…is' [NIV], not explicit [CEV, NCV, NJB, NLT, REB, TEV].

   b. ἵνα (LN 89.59): 'so that' [CEV, NASB, NCV, NET], 'in order to' [AB, LN, WBC; NJB, NRSV], 'in order that' [NTC; TEV], 'so' [NLT], 'that' [Gdt, HTC, NICNT2, KJV], 'to' [NIV, Ph, REB], 'for the purpose of, so that' [LN]. This conjunction indicates purpose for events and states [LN].

   c. aorist act. subj. of λαμβάνω (LN 57.55): 'to take' [Gdt, LN, NTC, WBC; KJV, NASB, NCV, NET], 'to take up' [AB, HTC; NIV, NJB, NLT, NRSV, Ph], 'to receive' [NICNT2; CEV, REB, TEV], 'to acquire, to obtain' [LN]. This verb means to acquire possession of something [LN].

   d. πάλιν (LN 67.55) (BAGD 1.a. p. 606): 'again' [AB, Gdt, HTC, LN, NTC, WBC; KJV, NASB, NIV, NJB, NLT, NRSV, Ph], 'back again' [NICNT2; NCV, NET, REB, TEV], 'back' [BAGD; CEV]. The clause 'I may/might take it again' [Gdt, NTC; KJV, NASB] is also translated 'I can/may take it back again' [NCV, NET, NLT], 'I may take it up again' [HTC], 'I may/might receive it back again' [NICNT2; CEV, TEV], 'to take it again' [WBC], 'to take it up again' [AB; NIV, NJB, NRSV, Ph], 'to receive it back again' [REB]. This adverb indicates a subsequent point of time involving repetition [LN].

QUESTION—Does the phrase 'because of this' refer back or forward to something?

1. Although in John this phrase typically refers back to a previous idea, here it refers forward to the ὅτι 'because' and its clause [EGT, Gdt, ICC, Lns, NTC]: *for this reason* the Father loves me *because* I lay down my life for the sheep.
2. The phrase refers back to the preceding context and states the reason the Father loves him, namely, because of his role as Shepherd that he has been describing, while the ὅτι 'because' introduces a more precise explanation of the διά τοῦτο phrase, 'because I lay down my life for the sheep'. This is the main characteristic of the good shepherd [My].

QUESTION—What is meant by the conjunction ὅτι 'because' in the clause 'because I lay down my life'?

This does not indicate that the Father's love for him is dependent on his sacrificing his life for his sheep [Bar, BECNT, Car, IVP, NICNT2, Rd]. Rather, the Father's love for the Son is eternally linked with the Son's unqualified obedience and utter dependence on the Father [Bar, BECNT, Car, IVP, Rd]. It means that his love for his sheep and willingness to die for them is bound up in his very nature as God's Son and for this reason he is the object of the Father's love [NICNT2]. Jesus' laying down his life for the sheep is the supreme manifestation and enactment of the Father's love

[WBC]. Jesus' death fulfilled the Father's will for him and since he is in perfect harmony with the Father's will, he lays down his life. In this way the Father's love is a recognition of their perfect agreement in this matter [NICNT1]. The Father's love is evoked by the self-sacrifice of his Son in the same way that love evokes love [ICC].

QUESTION—What word is emphasized in this verse?

The pronoun ἐγώ 'I' is emphasized [My, Lns, TRT]: '*I, I myself*' [Lns].

QUESTION—What is meant by the conjunction ἵνα 'so that (I may take it again)'?

In this context it indicates the purpose of Jesus' laying down his life [AB, Bar, BECNT, Car, Gdt, ICC, Kn, Lns, NTC, TH]: I lay down my life *with the purpose of* taking it again. This indicates that the resurrection is not a circumstance following Jesus' death, but is the essential completion of his death. Jesus death, resurrection and exaltation are viewed as a unity in this Gospel [AB, Kn]. Jesus' death was endured with his resurrection in view. He died in order to rise again and be glorified and pour out the Spirit so that others may live [Car]. The resurrection was the intention behind Jesus' suffering so that the power of the resurrection might be revealed and released [Bar]. Jesus' death was so that he might continue his life now enriched with life-giving power as never before [ICC]. Jesus lays down his life with the purpose of taking it again so that he may continue his pastoral role until the final goal is reached and all mankind are brought together into one flock [My].

10:18 No-one takes-away[a] it from me, but I lay- it -down of[b] myself. I-have authority[c] to-lay- it -down and I-have authority to-take it again. This command[d] I-received from my Father."

TEXT—Instead of the present tense αἴρει 'takes away', some manuscripts read the aorist tense ἦρεν 'took away'. GNT reads the present tense 'takes' with a B rating, indicating that the text is almost certain. Those preferring the past tense as the correct reading are AB, Bar, NICNT1, NICNT2, NTC; NASB.

LEXICON—a. pres. act. indic. of αἴρω (LN 90.96) (BAGD 4. p. 24): 'to take away' [AB, BAGD, Gdt, LN, NICNT2, NTC, WBC; NCV, NET, REB, TEV], 'to take' [BAGD, HTC; CEV, KJV, NASB, NJB, NLT, NRSV, Ph], 'to remove' [BAGD]. The idiom αἴρω ἀπό (literally 'to take from') means to cause someone to no longer experience something 'to take away from, to remove from' [LN]. It can carry the sense of taking away by force to the extent of killing [BAGD].

b. ἀπό (LN 90.19) (BAGD V.5. p. 88): 'of' [BAGD, LN], 'by' [LN]. The clause 'I lay it down of myself' [KJV] is also translated 'I give it of myself' [Gdt], 'I lay it down on my own' [NICNT2], 'I lay it down/give it up of my own free will' [NET, NJB, Ph, REB, TEV], 'I lay it down of my own accord' [AB, HTC, NTC, WBC; NIV, NRSV], 'I lay it down on my own initiative' [NASB], 'I give it up willingly' [CEV], 'I give my own

life freely' [NCV], 'I sacrifice it voluntarily' [NLT]. This preposition indicates the one who is responsible for an event or state [LN].
c. ἐξουσιά (BAGD 1. p. 277): 'authority' [NICNT2, WBC; NASB, NET, NIV, NLT], 'power' [AB, Gdt, HTC; CEV, KJV, NJB, NRSV, Ph], 'right' [BAGD, NTC; NCV, REB, TEV]. This noun denotes 'freedom of choice', the 'right' to act, decide, or dispose of one's property as one wishes [BAGD]. The clause 'I have authority' is equivalent to saying 'I can' [AB, Bar].
d. ἐντολή (LN 33.330) (BAGD 2. c. p. 269): 'command' [AB, NICNT2, WBC; BAGD; NIV, NJB, NRSV], 'commandment' [BAGD, Gdt, LN; KJV, NASB, NET], 'charge' [HTC, NTC; REB], 'order' [BAGD; Ph]. The clause 'This command I received from my father' is translated 'This is what my Father commanded me to do' [NCV, similarly CEV, NLT, TEV]. This noun denotes that which is authoritatively commanded [LN].

QUESTION—If the aorist tense (took away) of αἴρω 'to take away' is taken as the correct reading, how should it be understood?

It simply means 'No one took it away from me'. Jesus is probably looking back at the times when his enemies tried to arrest or stone him (7:30, 32; 8:20, 59) [NICNT2], or (5:18, 7:25, and 8:59) [AB]. Jesus may be viewing his sacrifice from the perspective of having already accomplished it [NTC]. It may be from John's own perspective as he looked back to the crucifixion as an event in the past [Bar]. To him it is so certain that he considered it already accomplished [ICC, NICNT1, TRT]. Even if taken as a present tense, there is a danger that it may be understood that Jesus was in the process of dying at that very time. If so, it may be necessary to translate 'No one will take my life from me' [TH].

QUESTION—What words are emphasized in this verse?

The pronoun ἐγώ 'I' is emphasized [Lns]: '*I myself* lay it down of myself' [Lns]. Jesus contrasts himself with the οὐδείς 'no one'. He gives his life of his own accord, no one takes it from him [HTC]. The words 'I have authority' are repeated twice for emphasis [Gdt, NICNT1].

QUESTION—What is implied by the statement of Jesus 'I have authority to take it again'?

A dead person needs a living God to bring him back to life. So Jesus is saying that he is God because he takes back his own life after he has died [CH].

DISCOURSE UNIT—10:19–42 [Ph]. The topic is Jesus claims his true identity.

DISCOURSE UNIT—10:19–21 [Car, IVP, NICNT1, WBC]. The topic is the reaction of the Jews.

10:19 Again there-occurred (a) division[a] among the Jews because-of these words. **10:20** And many of them were-saying, "He has (a) demon[b] and he-is-mad.[c] Why do-you(pl)-listen to-him?" **10:21** Others said, "These words are not (those) of-one-being-demon-possessed.[d] Surely-not[e] (a) demon is-able to-open (the) eyes of-(a)-blind-one?"

TEXT—Instead of πάλιν ἐγένετο 'again there occurred', some manuscripts read οὖν πάλιν ἐγένετο 'therefore again there occurred', others read οὖν ἐγένετο πάλιν 'therefore there occurred again', others read οὖν ἐγένετο 'therefore there occurred', and one version manuscript reads ἐγένετο 'there occurred'. GNT reads 'again there occurred' with a B rating, indicating that the text is almost certain.

LEXICON—a. σχίσμα (LN 39.13) (BAGD 2. p. 797): 'division' [BAGD, Gdt, HTC, LN, NTC, WBC; KJV, NASB, NJB, REB, TEV], 'sharp division' [NET], 'split' [NICNT2], 'discord' [LN], 'dissension, schism' [BAGD]. The clause 'There occurred a division among the Jews' is translated 'the Jews were again (sharply) divided' [AB; NIV, NRSV], 'the people were again divided in their opinions (about him)' [NLT], 'the Jews were in two minds (about him)' [Ph], 'the Jews did not agree with each other' [NCV], 'The people took sides' [CEV]. This noun denotes a division into opposing groups, generally two [LN].

b. δαιμόνιον (LN 12.37) (BAGD 2. p. 169): 'demon' [BAGD, LN], 'devil' [AB], 'evil spirit' [BAGD, LN]. The clause 'He has a demon (in him)' [HTC, NICNT2, NTC, WBC; CEV, NASB, NRSV, TEV] is also translated 'He has a devil' [KJV], 'He's possessed of/by a demon' [Gdt; NET], 'He is demon-possessed' [NIV, NLT], 'He is possessed by a devil' [AB], 'He's possessed' [NJB, REB], 'A demon has come into him' [NCV], 'The devil's in him' [Ph]. This noun denotes an evil supernatural being or spirit [LN]. It denotes independent beings who occupy a position somewhere between the human and the divine [BAGD]

c. pres. mid. (deponent = act.) indicative of μαίνομαι (LN 30.24) (BAGD p. p. 486): 'to be mad' [BAGD, LN], 'to be insane' [LN], 'to be out of one's mind' [BAGD, LN], 'to not be in one's right mind' [LN]. The clause 'He is mad' [Gdt, HTC, NICNT2; KJV] is also translated 'He is...raving mad' [NIV], 'He is crazy' [CEV, TEV], '(A demon)...has made him crazy' [NCV], 'He is...insane' [NASB, Ph], 'he is raving' [WBC; NJB], 'He...raves' [NTC], 'He's...out of his mind' [AB; NLT, NRSV, REB], 'He...has lost his mind' [NET]. This verb means to think or reason in a completely irrational manner [LN]. The result of this condition is 'to have no control over oneself' [BAGD].

d. pres. mid. (deponent = act.) participle of δαιμονίζομαι (LN 12.41) (BAGD p. 169): 'to be demon possessed' [LN], 'to be possessed by a demon' [BAGD]. The clause 'These are not the words of one being demon possessed' [NICNT2; similarly NRSV, NET, NIV, NJB] is also translated 'These are not the remarks of a demon-possessed (person)' [NTC], 'These words are not from a demon-possessed man' [WBC], 'This

doesn't sound like a man possessed by a demon' [NLT], 'These are not the discoursings of one possessed' [Gdt], 'No one possessed by a demon could speak like this' [REB], 'This is not the sort of thing a devil-possessed man would say' [Ph], 'These are not the words of a demented person' [AB], 'These are not the sayings of one who has a demon' [HTC; similarly KJV, NRSV], 'A man with a demon could not talk like this' [TEV], 'A man who is crazy with a demon does not say things like this' [NCV], 'How could anyone with a demon in him say these things?' [CEV]. This verb means to be possessed by a demon [LN].
- e. μή (LN 69.3, 69.15): 'surely not' [AB], 'not' [LN (69.3)]. The question 'Surely not a demon is able to open the eyes of a blind one?' is translated 'Surely a devil cannot open the eyes of the blind!' [AB], 'Can/could a devil/demon open the eyes of the blind?' [Gdt, HTC, NICNT2; KJV, NCV, NIV, NJB, NLT, NRSV], 'Can a devil make a blind man see?' [Ph], 'A demon cannot open the eyes of the-blind/blind people, can he?' [NTC; NASB], 'How could a demon give sight to blind people?' [TEV]. 'No one like that could give sight to a blind person' [CEV]. This negative particle indicates that a negative response is expected to a question [LN (69.15)].

QUESTION—To what event does the word πάλιν 'again' refer?

There were two other divisions among the people before, one at 7:43 and the other at 9:16, hence now a third [Lns, NICNT2, TRT]. It is probably to the latter (9:16) that this refers where the Pharisees were divided about him after he healed the blind man [BECNT, ICC, IVP, NICNT2, Rd]. Other times there were differences of opinion among Jesus' listeners (6:52; 7:43; and 9:16) [NTC].

QUESTION—To whom does the phrase 'the Jews' refer?

This probably refers to the Pharisees [ICC, My, NICNT2]. It probably refers to the people at large including their leaders [BECNT, Car, NICNT1].

QUESTION—To what does the phrase 'these words' refer?

The Jews react to the explanation of Jesus' parable in 10:7–18 about being the Good Shepherd [AB, Bar].

QUESTION—What word is emphasized in this verse?

The word δαιμόνιον 'demon' is placed forward and so emphasized, '*A demon* he has' [NICNT1].

QUESTION—What is the relationship between the clauses 'He has a demon' and 'he is mad'?

In ancient times being demon-possessed was frequently linked together with being insane [BECNT]. Insanity was thought to be the result of demon possession [AB, Bar, Car, CH, IVP, My, TH, TRT; NCV]: 'A demon has come into him and made him crazy' [NCV], 'He is possessed by a devil—out of his mind' [AB].

QUESTION—What is implied by the rhetorical question 'Why do you listen to him?'

The question implies either that there was no reason to listen to Jesus or that they should not do so [TRT].

QUESTION—What response is implied to the question 'Surely not a demon is able to open the eyes of a blind one'?
A negative response is expected to the question [AB, Car, EGT, LN, Lns, My, NICNT1, NTC, TH, TRT, WBC; CEV, NASB]: 'A demon cannot open the eyes of the blind, can he?' [NASB]. The question implies the answer 'Certainly not!' [Lns, NTC].

DISCOURSE UNIT—10:22–42 [Bar, BECNT, IVP, Lns, NICNT1, NICNT2, WBC; CEV, NCV, NET, NIV, NLT, NRSV, TEV]. The topic is titles and works [NICNT2], Jesus at the Feast of Dedication [Lns, WBC; NET], the rejection of the Jews [BECNT, NICNT1; CEV, NCV, NIV, NRSV, TEV], Jesus claims to be the Messiah [IVP], who is Jesus? [Bar], Jesus asserts his deity [NASB, NLT].

DISCOURSE UNIT—10:22–39 [AB, Car, EGT, Rd]. The topic is Jesus as Messiah and Son of God [AB], final dialogues with the Jews [Rd], Jesus at the Feast of Dedication [Car, EGT].

DISCOURSE UNIT—10:22–30 [Car, HTC, NICNT1, WBC]. The topic is the unity of Father and Son [NICNT1], at the Feast of Dedication [HTC], Jesus the Messiah [Car, WBC].

10:22 Then[a] the Festival-of-dedication-of-the-Temple[b] occurred[c] in Jerusalem. It was winter.[d]

TEXT—Instead of τότε 'then', some manuscripts read δέ 'and/but', others read δὲ τότε 'and/but then', still others omit this word. GNT reads τότε 'then' with a B rating, indicating that the text is almost certain.

LEXICON—a. τότε (LN 67.47): 'then' [LN, NICNT2, NTC, WBC; NET, NIV, Ph], 'at that time' [NASB, NRSV], 'the time (came)' [NCV], 'it (was) the time' [NJB], 'it (was winter)' [AB; REB, TEV], 'it (was) now (winter)' [NLT], 'that (winter)' [CEV], 'it (was the feast)' [HTC], not explicit [Gdt; KJV]. This adverb describes a point of time subsequent to another point of time [LN]. It looks forward to what follows and sets the time frame for the Festival as is evident from the verb 'occurred' or 'came about' [NICNT2].

b. ἐγκαίνια (LN **51.9**) (BAGD I.3.a. p. 159): 'the festival of dedication of the Temple' [LN]. The clause 'Then the Festival of Dedication of the Temple in Jerusalem occurred' is translated 'the time came to celebrate the dedication of the Temple in Jerusalem' [**LN**], 'the Festival of the Dedication of the Temple was being celebrated in Jerusalem' [TEV], 'Then came the feast of (the) Dedication in/at Jerusalem' [NTC; NET, NIV], 'Then came the dedication festival at Jerusalem' [Ph], 'Then came the Rededication in Jerusalem' [NICNT2], 'It was the feast of the Dedication at Jerusalem' [HTC], 'At that time the Feast/festival of Dedication took place at Jerusalem' [NASB, NRSV], 'The time came for the Feast of Dedication at Jerusalem' [AB; NCV], 'It was the time of the feast of Dedication in Jerusalem' [NJB], 'And it was at Jerusalem the feast of dedication' [KJV], 'Now they were celebrating the feast of the Dedication at Jerusalem' [Gdt], 'the festival of Dedication was being held

in Jerusalem' [REB], 'The festival of the Dedication then took place in Jerusalem' [WBC], 'Jesus was in Jerusalem for the Temple Festival' [CEV], 'Jesus was in Jerusalem at the time of Hanukkah, the Festival of Dedication' [NLT]. This noun denotes a Jewish festival commemorating the rededication of the Temple in the time of Judas Maccabaeus in 165 B.C. It may be possible to speak of this Festival of Dedication as 'the festival to celebrate the time when the Temple was again made pure and ready for worship' [LN].
   c. aorist mid. (deponent = act.) indic. of γίνομαι (LN 13.107): 'to occur' [LN], 'to happen' [BAGD, LN], 'to come to be' [LN], 'to come, to take place, to be held' [BAGD]. This verb means to happen, with the implication that what happens is different from a previous state [LN]. See the previous lexical item for version rendering.
   d. χειμών (LN 67.165) (BAGD 2. p. 879): 'winter' [BAGD, LN; all translations except Ph], 'winter time' [Ph]. This noun denotes the coldest season of the year. In a number of languages it may be important to translate χειμών as simply 'the time of the cold rains'. Such rains may actually occur during the growing season or as a part of the rainy season [LN]. It denotes the season of bad weather [BAGD] or the rainy season [NTC]. Rather than try to translate 'winter' in terms of a particular season of the year, it may be better to translate it as 'a cold time' or 'a cold season'. If the term 'winter' is translated, it might be necessary, especially for people from the tropics or the southern hemisphere, to explain in a footnote that at that time of year the weather was cold [TH].
QUESTION—What was the Festival of Dedication?
   This Festival was also known also as Hanukkah, or 'Tabernacles of the month of Kisl'ev' (2 Maccabees 1:9). It was roughly equivalent to December. The festival celebrated the rededication of the Temple in 164 B.C., after the Syrians had profaned it for three years (Maccabees 4:54). It lasted for eight days, and was a time of great happiness for the Jews [TH]. It might be good to add a footnote to the effect: In 167 B.C. the Syrians, led by Antiochus Epiphanes, took over Jerusalem and profaned the temple by sacrificing pigs in it to Zeus, their chief god. Three years later the Jews, led by Judas Maccabaeus, recaptured Jerusalem and rededicated the temple and altar to God. The Jews celebrated this event during the Festival of the Temple Dedication, that took place every December, about two months after the Festival of Tabernacles. It lasted eight days. During this very joyful celebration, people were especially hopeful that the Messiah would come [TRT]. The festival is also called the Festival of Lights because people lit so many lamps in their homes to celebrate [Bar, Car, ICC, My, NICNT2, NTC, TRT, WBC]. Hannukah is the Hebrew word for 'dedication' [AB].
QUESTION—What is the significance of the temporal note, 'It was winter'?
   The note helps explain why Jesus was in a covered part of the temple, Solomon's Porch [BECNT, Bar, Car, CH, EGT, Gdt, Kn, Lns, My, NTC, WBC]. The porch gave shelter from the cold winds [WBC].

10:23 And Jesus was-walking[a] in the temple[b] on the Porch[c] of Solomon.[d]

LEXICON—a. imperf. act. indic. of περιπατέω (LN 15.227) (BAGD 1.a. p. 649): 'to walk' [all translations except Gdt; NJB, NLT, Ph], 'to walk up and down' [NJB], 'to walk through' [NLT], 'to walk about' [Gdt; Ph], 'to go about' [BAGD], 'to walk along' [LN], 'to walk around' [BAGD, LN], 'to go' [LN]. This verb means to walk along or around [LN]. Jesus was walking there to teach and invite discussion (see Mark 11:27), not simply to escape the cold weather [NICNT2].

b. ἱερόν (LN **7.16**) (BAGD 2. p. 372): 'Temple' [**LN**; NCV, NJB, NLT, Ph, TEV], 'temple' [BAGD, Gdt, HTC, NICNT2, NTC; CEV, KJV, NASB, NRSV], 'temple area' [WBC; NET, NIV], 'temple precincts' [AB, TH; REB]. This noun denotes a temple or sanctuary and the surrounding consecrated area [LN]. It denotes the temple at Jerusalem, including the whole temple precinct with its buildings, courts, etc. [BAGD].

c. στοά (LN 7.40) (BAGD p. 768): 'porch' [LN], 'collonade' [BAGD], 'portico' [BAGD, LN], 'cloister' [BAGD]. The phrase 'Porch of Solomon' is translated 'Solomon's Porch/porch' [Gdt; CEV, KJV, NCV, TEV], 'Solomon's Portico' [AB, similarly HTC, NICNT2, NTC; NASB, NET, NJB, NRSV, REB], 'Solomon's Collonade/Collonade of Solomon' [NIV, WBC], 'the section known as Solomon's Collonade' [NLT], 'Solomon's cloisters' [Ph]. This noun denotes a covered colonnade, open normally on one side, where people could stand, sit, or walk, protected from the weather and the heat of the sun. In many parts of the world the closest equivalent to a στοά 'porch' would be a veranda, an extensive type of porch. Such a porch may be described as 'a long outside room' or 'an open room made with pillars' [LN]. The word 'colonnade' denotes a roofed structure supported on pillars [NICNT1]. It was a covered porch open on the inside facing the temple but closed on the outside [TH]. The temple area was surrounded by a huge, stone wall. The inner sides of the wall were lined with porches that were open toward the temple. Each porch had a roof that was held up by two or more rows of stone pillars that were around 40 feet (12 meters) high. Solomon's Porch ran along the length of the east side of the temple's outer court. It was the only part of Solomon's temple that was not destroyed by King Nebuchadnezzar in 586 B.C. Christians later met regularly at Solomon's Porch (see Acts 3:11, 5:12) [TRT]. In the cold weather it gave protection from the raw east wind [BECNT, HTC].

d. Σολομών (LN 93.344) (BAGD p. 759): 'Solomon' [BAGD, LN; all translations]. This name denotes the son and successor of King David [BAGD, LN].

QUESTION—How are the nouns related in the genitive construction στοᾷ τοῦ Σολομῶνος 'Porch of Solomon'?

If translated literally, it may suggest a porch belonging to Solomon [TH, TRT]. In fact, it was a porch associated with Solomon's name and so it may be best to translate, 'a porch called Solomon's Porch' [TH, TRT; NLT]. It was called 'Solomon's portico' because it was said to have been the only remnant of the original temple built by him [Kn, Lns, NTC].

10:24 So^a the Jews gathered-around^b him and were-saying to-him, "Until when do-you-lift-up^c our soul? If you(sg) are the Christ,^d tell us plainly.^e"

LEXICON—a. οὖν (LN 89.50, 91.7): 'so' [HTC, NICNT2, NTC; NRSV, Ph], 'therefore' [Gdt, Lns, WBC], 'then' [KJV], 'and' [CEV], not explicit [NASB, NCV, NET, NIV, NJB, NLT, REB, TEV]. This conjunction indicates that the Jews see their opportunity and take it [Lns].

b. aorist act. indic. of κυκλόω (LN **15.147**) (BAGD p. 456): 'to gather around/round' [AB, HTC, NTC; CEV, NASB, NCV, NIV, NJB, NRSV, REB, TEV], 'to surround' [BAGD, Gdt, **LN**, NICNT2, WBC; NET, NLT], 'to close in on' [Ph], 'to come round about' [KJV], 'to encircle' [BAGD], 'to be around' [LN]. This verb means to move in such a way as to encircle an object [LN]. It can mean simply 'to surround someone' or it may carry the sense of surrounding or encircling someone with a hostile intent [BAGD].

c. pres. act. indic. of αἴρω (LN 15.203, **30.36**) (BAGD 1.b. p. 24): 'to lift up' [BAGD, LN (15.203)], 'to take up, to pick up' [BAGD], 'to keep in suspense, to keep someone from being able to form a conclusion about something' [LN (30.36)]. The clause 'Until when do you lift up our soul?' is translated 'How long will you take away our life?' [NICNT2], 'how long will you keep us in suspense?' [HTC, **LN** (30.36); NASB, NET, NIV, NRSV, similarly AB, NJB, NTC; NLT, Ph, REB, TEV], 'How long will you hold our minds in suspense?' [Gdt], 'How long are you going to keep us guessing?' [CEV], 'How long do you make us doubt?' [KJV], 'How long will you make us wonder about you?' [NCV], 'How long are you going provoke us?' [WBC]. Primarily the verb means 'to lift up and carry (away), to carry off, to remove, to take (away)' [LN (15.203)]. The idiom αἴρω τὴν ψυχήν τινος 'to lift up the soul of someone' means to keep someone in suspense [BAGD, LN (30.36)] so that one cannot come to a conclusion in one's thinking [LN (30.36)].

d. Χριστός (LN 53.82) (BAGD 1. p. 887): 'Christ' [BAGD, Gdt, HTC, LN, NICNT2, NTC, WBC; KJV, NASB, NCV, NET, NIV, NJB, Ph], 'Messiah' [AB, BAGD, LN; CEV, NLT, NRSV, REB, TEV], 'the Anointed One' [BAGD]. This noun literally denotes 'one who has been anointed'. In the NT it is used as a title for Jesus as the Messiah [LN]. The phrase 'the Christ' is a technical term referring to the Jewish Messiah [TH; CEV, NLT, NRSV, REB, TEV].

e. παρρησίᾳ (LN 28.29) (BAGD 1. p. 630): 'plainly' [BAGD, Gdt, HTC, NICNT2, NTC, WBC; CEV, KJV, NASB, NCV, NET, NIV, NLT, NRSV, REB], 'openly' [BAGD; NJB], 'publicly, in an evident manner' [LN]. The clause 'tell us plainly' is translated 'tell us so straight out' [Ph], 'Tell us the plain truth' [TEV], 'tell us so in plain words' [AB]. This noun denotes, in an evident or publicly known manner [LN]. It does not just mean 'publicly' but 'in so many words' rather than in metaphors [NICNT2].

QUESTION—What is indicated by the imperfect tense of the verb ἔλεγον 'they were saying'?

The imperfect tense probably indicates that the action was repeated [IVP, NICNT1, TRT]: they kept asking. The tense suggests persistence. They pressed their question [NICNT1].

QUESTION—Who are the Jews who gather around him?

They are those Jews who did not believe in Jesus as the Messiah [Bar, CH, HTC, Lns, My, WBC]. They are probably a mixture of Jewish leaders and the common people [TH, TRT].

QUESTION—Is the intent of the Jews friendly or hostile?

Their intent may have been hostile [BAGD, CH, EGT, Lns, My, NICNT2, WBC]. Their request was not a search for truth but a trap to catch him in some act of blasphemy. This is shown by their actions a few moments later when they take stones to stone him [CH]. If the idiom, 'to lift up our soul', is taken as 'annoy/provoke us' the Jews would be clearly antagonistic [Bar, Car, NICNT1]. The Jewish leaders wish to discredit Jesus rather than become his disciples [WBC]. Otherwise they may not be hostile but simply those who want the matter cleared up as to what Jesus' real status is [Bar, Car, NICNT1].

QUESTION—What is meant by 'lift up one's soul'?

Although the meaning 'to keep one in suspense' makes excellent sense in the context, this meaning is nowhere attested in biblical, classical, or Hellenistic Greek. It may rather be that the idea of 'killing' or 'taking away life' is used figuratively here. It would be the sense of someone else 'taking away their soul' or 'life'. This then would yield the idea of a prolonged death as an expression of their frustration. The English expression 'the suspense is killing me' would capture the idea [NICNT2]. The meaning of 'keeping a person in suspense' is the sense that is intended as seen by the next sentence, 'Tell us plainly', that is, do not keep us on tenterhooks [NTC].

QUESTION—What is the function of the rhetorical question, 'Until when do you lift up our soul?'

They brusquely *demand* an answer [EGT]. The question is an *accusation* and coupled with their command acts like a *challenge*. Their question *charges* Jesus with keeping them on tenterhooks and not coming out squarely and answering the main question as to his Messiahship [Lns]. Their question implies that Jesus has not been fair with them, he has kept them in suspense [NICNT1, TRT].

QUESTION—What word is emphatic in this verse?

The pronoun σύ 'you' in the question, 'If you are the Christ, tell us plainly', is emphatic [ICC, NICNT1]: If *you yourself* are the Christ. This may indicate that in their opinion Jesus is far from being the glorious being that Christ should be [NICNT1].

10:25 Jesus answered them, "I-told you(pl) and[a] you(pl)-do- not -believe. The works[b] that I do in the name[c] of my Father testify[d] about me. **10:26** But you(pl) do- not -believe, because you(pl)-are-not of[e] my sheep.

TEXT—Following ἐμῶν 'my (sheep)', some manuscripts add καθὼς εἶπον ὑμῖν 'just as I said to you'. GNT rejects this addition with a B rating, indicating that the omission is almost certain.

LEXICON—a. καί (LN 89.93): 'and' [Gdt, HTC, LN, NICNT2, WBC; CEV, KJV, NASB, NET, NLT, NRSV, Ph, REB], 'but' [AB, NTC; NCV, NIV, NJB, TEV]. Here καί is used for καίτοι 'and yet' [ICC]. It is used to indicate an adversative relationship 'but' [HTC].

b. ἔργον (LN 42.11) (BAGD 1.c.α. p. 308): 'work' [AB, BAGD, Gdt, HTC, NICNT2, NTC, WBC; KJV, NASB, NJB, NLT, NRSV], 'deed' [BAGD, LN; NET, REB, TEV], 'miracle' [BAGD; NCV, NIV], 'act' [LN], 'accomplishment' [BAGD]. The clause 'the works that I do' is translated 'the things I do' [CEV], 'what I have done' [Ph]. This noun denotes that which is done, with possible focus on the energy or effort involved [LN]. Jesus' works include his miracles although they are not limited to them [BECNT, Car, NICNT1]. They may include all his works of kindness [NICNT1].

c. ὄνομα (LN 33.126) (BAGD I.4.c.γ. p. 572–573): 'name' [BAGD, LN]. The clause 'in the name of my Father' is translated 'in my Father's name' [all translations except CEV, TEV], 'by my Father's authority' [CEV, TEV]. This noun denotes the proper name of a person or object [LN]. The formula 'in the name of' means, 'with the mention of the name, while naming/calling on the name' [BAGD].

d. pres. act. indic. of μαρτυρέω (LN 33.262) (BAGD 1.a. p. 492): 'to testify' [BAGD], 'to witness' [LN]. The phrase '(The works)…testify about me' [NICNT2; NET] is also translated 'testify of/to me' [NASB, NRSV], 'give testimony for me' [AB], 'bear witness of/to/concerning/about me' [Gdt, HTC, NTC, WBC; KJV], 'are my witness' [NJB], 'are my credentials' [REB], 'speak for me' [NIV], 'speak on my behalf' [TEV], 'show who I am' [CEV, NCV], 'the proof is the work I do' [NLT], '(What I have done)…is sufficient to prove my claim' [Ph]. This verb means to provide information about a person or an event concerning which the speaker has direct knowledge [LN].

e. ἐκ (LN 63.20) (BAGD 4.a.δ. p. 236): The clause 'you are not *of* my sheep' [Gdt, NTC; KJV, NASB] is also translated 'you are no sheep of mine' [NJB], 'you are not sheep of my flock' [REB], 'you are not my sheep' [AB, WBC; CEV, NCV, NET, NIV, NLT, Ph, TEV], 'you do not belong to my sheep' [HTC, NICNT2; NRSV]. This preposition indicates a part of a whole, whether consisting of countable nouns or of mass nouns, 'one of, one among, a part of' [LN]. It is used here with the verb 'to be' to mean 'to belong to someone' [BAGD].

QUESTION—What is significant about Jesus' reply?

His reply was in essence an affirmation that he was the Messiah [Lns]. He could not reply 'Yes!' because their conception of the Messiah was different from his own. Nor could he answer 'No!' because he really was the Messiah, the one promised by God and so in truth the one that they were expecting [Gdt]. Although Jesus had not told them in so many words that he was the Messiah, he had done so to the Samaritan woman (4:26) and to the man born blind (9:35–37). He may have meant that his teaching was so clear that had they come to him with the right attitude they would have believed. Or he may have meant that his statement 'before Abraham was born, I am' was the answer [NICNT1]. Although he does not reply directly, his reply may mean that his teaching made the matter clear enough for those with eyes to see and ears to hear [WBC]. Both Jesus words and works together had already told them plainly enough. If Jesus had spoken plainly to them about his suffering they would have dismissed him as a fool [Car]. Jesus replies by calling attention to his works. Chief among them would be the healing of the man born blind which the Jews themselves brought up in verse 21. He had replied in a similar way to the disciples John had sent to him by calling their attention to his works for the blind and lame etc. (Matthew 11:2–6) [AB].

QUESTION—Where had Jesus told them before about his Messiahship?

He had already spoken about this in John 5:17–47; 6:29, 35, 51–65; 7:37–39; 8:12–20, 28–29, 42, 56–58; and 10:7–18 [HTC]. Other examples are 6:27–59; 7:14–30; 8:12–29, and 42–59 [TRT]. The time when the Jews first resolved to kill him for making himself equal with God is one case where they had realized what he was claiming (5:17) [Lns].

QUESTION—What did it mean 'to do things in the name of the Father'?

It meant to do the works by his direction, in cooperation with him, and with the purpose of revealing his character and power to the people [HTC]. It meant that the work was done representing the Father [EGT, TH] and his authority [TH, TRT; CEV, TEV]. It could be translated as 'just as my Father told me to do' [TH]. It meant that his works were all the works of the Father since they were done while naming his Father's name [Gdt]. His works agreed with all that the Father stood for or they fit in with the Father's revealed character [NICNT1].

QUESTION—In what way do Jesus' works testify about him?

They testify about him in the sense of proving who he is [TRT]. Others translate the phrase 'testify about me' as: 'show who I am' [CEV, NCV], 'are my credentials' [REB], 'the proof is the work I do' [NLT], '(What I have done)…is sufficient to prove my claim' [Ph].

QUESTION—What words are emphasized in these verses?

The pronoun ἐγώ 'I' is emphatic [NICNT2]: The works that *I myself* do. The pronoun ὑμεῖς 'you(pl)' is emphatic [EGT, Lns, NICNT2, TH, TRT]: 'But as for *you, you* do not believe' [NICNT2]. A sharp contrast is drawn between the 'I' of verse 25 and the 'you' of verse 26 [My, TH].

10:27 **My sheep hear^a my voice, and-I know^b them and they-follow^c me,**
LEXICON—a. pres. act. indic. of ἀκούω (LN 36.14) (BAGD p. 31): 'to hear' [AB, BAGD, Gdt, HTC, NICNT2; KJV, NASB], 'listen to' [NTC, WBC; NCV, NET, NIV, NJB, NLT, NRSV, REB, TEV], 'to recognize' [Ph], 'to know' [CEV], 'to pay attention to and obey' [LN]. This verb means to listen or pay attention to a person, with resulting conformity to what is advised or commanded [LN]. It means to hear with obedient attention [ICC]. The present tenses of the verbs 'to hear, to know' and 'to follow' all indicate a timeless aspect, 'they always hear, I always know' and 'they always follow' [Lns].
  b. pres. act. indic. of γινώσκω (LN 27.18) (BAGD 6.a.β. p. 161): 'to know' [BAGD, LN; all translations except Ph], 'to have come to know' [BAGD], 'to become acquainted with, to be familiar with' [LN]. The clause 'I know them' is translated 'I know who they are' [Ph]. This verb means to learn to know a person through direct personal experience, implying a continuity of relationship [LN]. It means to be on familiar terms with and united with [HTC], to acknowledge as one's own [NTC], to know personally [TRT].
  c. pres. act. indic. of ἀκολουθέω (LN 36.31): 'to follow' [LN; all translations], 'to be a disciple of' [LN]. This verb means to be a follower or a disciple of someone, in the sense of adhering to the teachings or instructions of a leader and in promoting the cause of such a leader [LN]. The present tense indicates habitual following [NICNT1].
QUESTION—What words are emphasized in these verses?
  The phrases κἀγώ 'and I' in the clauses 'I know them' and 'I give them' (next verse) are emphatic [EGT, Lns]: '*I myself* know…*I myself give*' [Lns].

10:28 **and-I give them eternal-life^a and they-will- never^b -perish^c forever^d and no one will-snatch^e them from my hand.^f**
LEXICON—a. ζωὴ αἰώνιος (LN 67.96): 'eternal life' [LN]. The phrase ζωὴν αἰώνιον 'eternal life' [all translations except NTC] is also translated 'everlasting life' [NTC]. This adjective describes a thing as pertaining to an unlimited duration of time. The most frequent use of αἰώνιος in the NT is with ζωή 'life', for example, 'so that everyone who believes in him may have eternal life' John 3:15. In combination with ζωή there is evidently not only a temporal element, but also a qualitative distinction. In such contexts, αἰώνιος evidently carries certain implications associated with αἰώνιος in relationship to divine and supernatural attributes. If one translates 'eternal life' as simply 'never dying', there may be serious misunderstandings, since persons may assume that 'never dying' refers only to physical existence rather than to 'spiritual death'. Accordingly, some translators have rendered 'eternal life' as 'unending real life', so as to introduce a qualitative distinction [LN]. Eternal life is a present possession and it is a quality of life, God's life [CH]. The phrase 'eternal

life' is a significant one in John and occurs 17 times at 3:15, 16, 36; 4:14, 36; 5:24, 39; 6:27, 40, 47, 54, 68; 10:28; 12:25, 50; 17:2, 3.

b. οὐ μή (LN 69.5) (BAGD D.1.a. p. 517): 'never' [BAGD, LN], 'certainly not' [BAGD, LN], 'by no means' [LN]. The clause 'they will never perish forever' is translated 'they shall certainly never perish' [NTC], 'they will never never be lost' [WBC], 'they will/shall never perish' [AB, Gdt, HTC; KJV, NASB, NET, NIV, NLT, NRSV, REB], 'they will/shall never die' [NCV, Ph, TEV], 'they will never be lost' [NICNT2; CEV, NJB]. This negative combination indicates emphatic negation [LN]. In combination with οὐ 'not', μή 'not' has the effect of strengthening the negation [BAGD]. It is the most decisive way of negating something in the future [BAGD, Lns].

c. aorist mid. (deponent = act.) subj. of ἀπόλλυμαι (LN) (BAGD 2.a.α. p. 95): 'to perish' [AB, BAGD, Gdt, HTC, LN, NTC; KJV, NASB, NET, NIV, NLT, NRSV, REB], 'to be lost' [LN, NICNT2, WBC; CEV, NJB], 'to die' [BAGD; NCV, Ph, TEV], 'to be destroyed, to be ruined' [BAGD]. This verb means to be lost, in the religious or spiritual sense [LN]. It means to be separated from God, from life, and from blessedness forever [Lns].

d. εἰς τὸν αἰῶνα (LN 67.95): 'forever' [BAGD, LN], 'always, forever and ever, eternally' [LN]. This phrase indicates unlimited duration of time, with particular focus on the future [LN]. See item b. above for version rendering.

e. fut. act. indic. of ἁρπάζω (LN **37.28**) (BAGD 2.a. p. 109): 'to snatch' [BAGD], 'to seize' [BAGD, **LN**], 'to snatch away' [BAGD, LN], 'to take away' [BAGD], 'to gain control over' [LN]. The clause 'no one will snatch them from my hand' [AB; NET] is also translated 'no one shall/will/can snatch them out of my hand' [Gdt, HTC, NTC, WBC; NASB, NIV, NRSV, Ph], 'no one will snatch them from my care' [REB], 'no one can snatch them away from me' [NLT, TEV], 'no one will seize them from/out-of my hand' [NICNT2, **LN**], 'neither shall any man pluck them out of my hand' [KJV], 'no one can steal them out of my hand' [NCV], 'no one will ever steal them from my hand' [NJB]. This verb means to gain control over someone by force [BECNT, LN, NICNT1, TRT] and can be translated 'no one will be able to take them away from my control' [**LN**]. It means to take suddenly and vehemently [BAGD].

f. χείρ (LN 37.14) (BAGD 2.a.δ. p. 880): 'hand' [BAGD, LN]. This noun figuratively denotes a state of control exercised by a person [LN]. The hand of Christ means his power [BAGD, Lns]. Hand here is more the sense of one's property than of one's power, 'They shall not cease to be *mine*' [Gdt]. See item e. above for version rendering.

QUESTION—What word is emphasized in this verse?

The phrase κἀγώ 'and I' is emphasized [EGT, Lns]: '*I myself* give' [Lns].

QUESTION—To whom does the pronoun 'them' refer in the words 'I give them eternal life'?

While it apparently refers to 'sheep', to translate it literally could imply to some that sheep can have eternal life. Sheep is figurative of disciples [NICNT2, TH]. To avoid this wrong meaning it could be translated 'I give to my followers eternal life' [TH].

QUESTION—What is meant by the addition of the phrase εἰς τὸν αἰῶνα 'forever' to the clause 'they will never perish'?

1. The phrase merely strengthens the word 'never' [Bar, Lns, WBC; probably CEV, KJV, NASB, NCV, NET, NIV, NJB, NLT, NRSV, Ph, REB, TEV]: 'they will *never never* be lost' [WBC]. The phrase simply strengthens the negative οὐ μή 'never'. It does not mean they will not perish eternally, but simply that they will never perish [Bar].
2. The phrase does not simply strengthen the negative 'never'. It here modifies the meaning of 'die'. It is not mere physical death that is indicated but *eternal* death, 'They will not perish *eternally*'. Jesus told Martha the same thing when he told her with identical negative phrasing, 'whoever lives and believes in me *will never die*'(11:26). He meant that although men may die naturally, if they would believe in him, they would never die *eternally* [NICNT1].

10:29 That-which my Father has-given to-me is greater-than[a] all, and no-one is-able to-snatch (them) from the hand of-the Father.

TEXT—Instead of ὁ πατήρ μου ὃ ('that which') δέδωκέν μοι πάντων μεῖζόν ἐστιν 'that which my Father has given to me is greater (*neuter*) than all', some manuscripts read ὁ πατήρ μου ὅς ('who') δέδωκέν μοι μείζων πάντων ἐστίν 'my Father who has given to me is greater (*masculine*) than all', others read ὁ πατήρ μου ὅς ('who') δέδωκέν μοι αὐτὰ μείζων πάντων ἐστίν 'my Father who has given them to me is greater (*masculine*) than all', others read ὁ πατήρ μου ὃ ('that which') δέδωκέν μοι πάντων μείζων ἐστιν 'my Father is greater (*masculine*) than all that which he has given me', and one manuscript reads ὁ πατήρ μου ὅς ('who') δέδωκέν μοι τὴν ἐξουσίαν μείζων πάντων ἐστίν 'my Father who has given to me the authority is greater (*masculine*) than all'. GNT reads 'that which my Father has given me is greater (*neuter*) than all' with a D rating, indicating great difficulty in deciding which text is authentic.

LEXICON—a. μέγας (LN 87.22) (BAGD p.): 'great' [LN; all translations except NTC; NLT], 'powerful' [NLT], 'excellent' [NTC], 'important' [LN]. This adjective describes someone or thing as being great in terms of status [LN]. 'Great' in this context refers especially to God's power [ICC, Lns, TRT; NLT]. The Father's power exceeds that of every being opposing the sheep [Lns].

QUESTION—Which text is correct?

1. The text that reads ὁ πατήρ μου ὃ ('that which') δέδωκέν μοι πάντων μεῖζόν ἐστιν 'That which my Father has given to me is greater

(masculine) than all' is the correct text [GNT, NICNT1, NICNT2, NTC, TH; NRSV, TEV]: 'What my Father has given me is greater than all else/everything' [NRSV, TEV]. The sheep are the antecedent of 'that which' [NICNT1, NICNT2, NTC, TH] in the sense that they consitute 'the Father's gift to the Son' in that he has predestined them. They are of all people the object of God's very special providence [NTC]. The picture is confusing but the best explanation is that this text is the original and other readings are attempts to make better sense of it. The sheep or believers are the gift to the Son that is greater in the Father's eyes than anything else on earth and so he will look after them to the end [NICNT1]. Because the Father is who he is, his gift therefore is greater than all things. No one is able to snatch the sheep from Jesus' hand and similarly no one is able to snatch them from the Father's hand. Believers are a gift of incalculable value to God [NICNT2].

2. The text that reads ὁ πατήρ μου ὅς ('who') δέδωκέν μοι μεῖζων πάντων ἐστίν 'My Father who has given (them) to me, is greater (masculine) than all' [Bar, BECNT, Car, EGT, Gdt, HTC, Lns, ICC, My, Rd, WBC; CEV, KJV, NASB, NCV, NET, NIV, NJB, NLT, Ph, REB]. The Father is greater than all things or all persons so the security of the sheep is assured [Car]. Although the weight of manuscript evidence favors option 1., the resulting meaning, 'As for my Father, that which He has given me is greater than all', is unsuited to the context. Therefore the reading, 'My Father, who gave (them) to me, is greater than all things' is the one we adopt [ICC].

3. Other renderings are 'My Father, as to what He has given me, is greater than all' [AB], 'The Father, for what he has given me, is greater than anyone' [NJB]. Whichever reading is chosen, the alternative may be placed in a footnote [TRT].

QUESTION—What is the implied object of ἁρπάζω 'to snatch'?

The implied object is the sheep [Gdt, HTC, NICNT1, NICNT2, NTC, TH, WBC; CEV, KJV, NASB, NCV, NET, NIV, NLT, NRSV, REB, TEV]. The implied object is either the indefinite pronoun 'anything', or the verb is being purposefully used without an object in order to refer to the general action of snatching [AB; NJB, Ph]: 'no one can steal anything from the Father's hand' [NJB], 'no one can tear anything out of the Father's hand' [Ph], 'from the Father's hand no one can snatch away' [AB].

DISCOURSE UNIT—10:31–39 [Car, HTC, NICNT1, WBC]. The topic is the blasphemy rebutted [NICNT1], dispute about claim to deity [HTC], Jesus the Son of God [Car, WBC].

10:30 I and the Father are one.[a] **10:31** Again the Jews[b] picked-up[c] stones that they-might-stone[d] him.

LEXICON—a. ἕν (LN 63.4) (BAGD 1.b. p. 230): 'one' [BAGD, LN; all translations]. This pronominal adjective describes something as being united as one in contrast with being divided or consisting of separate parts

[LN]. It refers to a unity of parts in contrast to the individual parts of which the whole is made up [BAGD].
b. Ἰουδαῖος (LN 93.172) (BAGD 2.e. p. 379): 'Jew' [BAGD, LN]. The phrase οἱ Ἰουδαῖοι 'the Jews' [AB, Gdt, HTC, NICNT2, NTC, WBC; KJV, NASB, NCV, NIV, NJB, NRSV, Ph, REB] is also translated 'the Jewish leaders' [NET], 'the people' [CEV, NLT, TEV]. This noun is derived from 'Judah' (93.173), and denotes the ethnic name of a person who belongs to the Jewish nation [LN]. In John the Ἰουδαῖοι are the enemies of Jesus [BAGD].
c. aorist act. indic. of βαστάζω (LN 15.201) (BAGD 1. p. 137): 'to pick up' [CEV, NASB, NCV, NET, NIV, NLT, REB, TEV], 'to take up' [BAGD, HTC; KJV, NRSV], 'to lift' [NICNT2], 'to reach for' [Ph], 'to fetch' [WBC; NJB], 'to get' [AB], 'to bring' [Gdt], 'to carry' [NICNT1, NTC], 'to remove, to carry away, to take away' [LN]. This verb means to carry away from a place [ICC, LN], with the probable implication of something that is relatively heavy [LN]. In 8:59 the Jews ἦραν 'took up' stones, here they 'bring' them [Gdt]. They probably did not have them at hand so it was necessary to go some distance to the court to find them [Gdt, Lns, NICNT1, NTC].
d. aorist act. subj. of λιθάζω (LN 20.79) (BAGD p. 474): 'to stone' [BAGD; all translations except [CEV, NCV, NET, NLT, Ph], 'to stone to death' [LN, TRT; NET, Ph], 'to throw (stones) at' [TEV], 'to kill' [CEV, NCV, NLT]. This verb means to kill or attempt to kill by means of hurling stones, normally carried out by angry mobs [LN]. It is a means of capital punishment or punishment for certain crimes such as adultery or blasphemy [BAGD].

QUESTION—What is meant by the words 'I and the Father are one'?
1. It means 'one' in the sense of equality or unity of essence, being, or nature [Bar, Car, Gdt, HTC, IVP, Kn, Lns, NICNT1, NICNT2, NTC]. This unity is one not only of moral but also of essential unity, while the plural subject 'we' (ἐσμεν 'we are') establishes the difference of persons [Gdt, NTC]. Jesus is speaking of his divine nature [HTC, IVP]. By saying this Jesus is making it very clear to the Jews that he is making himself God [NICNT2]. He is affirming his equality with the Father [NTC]. His claim means more than merely that Jesus' will was one with the Father [NICNT1]. In addition to being a unity of essence, it is also a unity of love and obedience [Bar]. The claim means that the Father and Son were equal in power, namely, almighty power [Lns].
2. It does not necessarily denote equality or unity of essence [AB, Car, CH, EGT, ICC, My, Rd, TH, WBC]. They are one in purpose, that of protecting the sheep. But no matter how it is taken, the Jews recognized it as a claim to deity which to them was blasphemy [CH]. In the present context the oneness seems to mean that Christ reflects the Father in all that he says and does [TH]. It is a unity of power and operation [AB], a unity of fellowship, will, and purpose [ICC]. The oneness refers to the

Father and Son's care for the sheep. It is a unity of function or action [Car, WBC]. Jesus refers to the agreement that he has with the Father so that whatever he does will be confirmed by the power of his Father [Rd]. Although an ambassador may say that he and his sovereign are one, he does not mean to claim to be royalty himself. He merely asserts that what he does, his sovereign also does, and that his promises are backed by all the resources of his sovereign. Here Jesus is saying that his claims are backed by the power of the Father [EGT]. The unity consists in the Father being in the Son and acting in the works that the Son performs [My].

QUESTION—Is it possible for a plural subject have a singular predicate ('we are one')?

In some languages it may be impossible to say, 'The Father and I are one' since there must be concord between subject and predicate and two ('the Father and I') do not mathematically equal one). It may then be necessary to translate something like, 'the Father and I are just like one person' or '…are the same as one person' or '…are joined together as one person' [TH]. It is important that the translation of 'I and the Father are one' does not mean that they are one person [TRT].

QUESTION—What is indicated by the *neuter* adjective ἕν 'one'?

If the masculine εἷς 'one' were used, it could have indicated that the Son is the Father and so the distinctiveness of each would have been lost [Car, IVP, Lns]. The neuter means 'one thing' not 'one person' [Car, NICNT1]. It refers to one substance or essence. Jesus and the Father are two persons with one substance [NTC]. It is not identity that is claimed but essential unity [NICNT1]. The neuter points to a unity of purpose [CH].

QUESTION—To what does the adverb πάλιν 'again' refer?

The Jews had tried to stone Jesus to death before in John 8:59 [AB, CH, Gdt, HTC, NICNT1, NICNT2, NTC, Rd, TRT]. Also in 5:18 the Jews had tried to kill Jesus [TRT].

QUESTION—Why do the Jews pick up stones to stone Jesus?

They take his claim as blasphemous [Bar, CH, Gdt, HTC, Kn, My, NICNT1] and the punishment for blasphemy was stoning (Leviticus 24:16). They had asked him to tell them plainly if he was the Christ. But this was more than they had expected [NICNT1]. They intend to stone him because they interpret his words as a claim to equality with God [Car, CH, My]. A claim to equality with God to them was blasphemous [CH].

10:32 Jesus answered them, "I-showed[a] you(pl) many good[b] works from[c] the Father. For[d] which[e] work of-them do-you(pl)-stone[f] me?"

LEXICON—a. aorist act. indic. of δείκνυμι (LN 28.7) (BAGD 1.a. p. 172): 'to show' [BAGD, LN], 'to make known' [BAGD, LN], 'to demonstrate' [LN], 'to point out' [BAGD]. The clause 'I showed/have shown you many good works' [Gdt, similarly HTC, NICNT2, NTC; KJV, NASB, NET, NJB, NRSV, Ph] is also translated 'I have shown you many great miracles' [NIV], 'Many a noble work I have shown you' [AB], 'Many noble works of power I have set before you' [WBC], 'I have shown you many good things' [CEV], 'I have done many good works' [NCV], 'I have done many good deeds in your presence' [TEV], '(At my Father's direction) I have done many good works' [NLT], '(By the Father's power) I have done many good deeds before your eyes' [REB]. This verb means to make known the character or significance of something by visual, auditory, gestural, or linguistic means [LN]. Since Jesus' miracles were signs that pointed the way, the verb δείκνυμι 'to show' is appropriate [NICNT1].

b. καλός (LN 88.4) (BAGD 2.b. p. 400): 'good' [BAGD, LN; all translations except AB, WBC; NIV], 'noble' [AB, BAGD, WBC], 'great' [NIV], 'praiseworthy' [BAGD, LN], 'fine' [LN], 'useful, morally good, contributing to salvation' [BAGD]. This adjective describes something as having positive moral quality, with the implication of being favorably valued [LN]. In this context the word should be translated 'beautiful' [Car, Gdt] in the sense that Jesus' works are morally beautiful [Gdt]. The word suggests powerful and morally excellent works that resulted in health and well-being [Bar].

c. ἐκ (LN 90.16) (BAGD 3.c. p. 235): 'from' [BAGD, LN]. The phrase 'from the/my Father' [all translations except Gdt; NLT, REB, TEV] is also translated 'At my Father's direction [NLT], 'by the power of my Father' [Gdt; similarly REB], 'which the Father gave me to do' [TEV], 'that my Father sent me to do' [CEV]. This preposition indicates the source of an activity or state, with the implication of something proceeding from or out of the source [LN]. It indicates that Jesus does these things by the will and power of the Father [Gdt, TRT; REB] or at his direction [HTC, TRT; NLT].

d. διά (LN 89.26): 'for' [all translations], 'because of' [LN], 'on account of, by reason of' [BAGD]. This preposition indicates cause or reason, with focus on instrumentality, either of objects or events [LN].

e. ποῖος (LN 92.36) (BAGD 2.a.α. p. 284): 'which?' [BAGD, LN], 'which one?, which sort of?' [LN]. This interrogative adjective refers to one among several objects, events, or states [LN]. It indicates the quality of the work ('of what kind?') [Lns, NICNT1, NTC] and points to their divine origin [NICNT1].

f. pres. act. indic. of λιθάζω (LN 20.79): 'to stone' [all translations except NCV], 'to stone to death' [LN], 'to kill' [NCV]. This verb means to kill or attempt to kill by means of hurling stones, normally carried out by angry mobs [LN]. The present tense indicates the intention of the Jews [TH; Ph, TEV], or what they were trying to do [Lns, NTC], or what they were beginning to do [Lns].

QUESTION—How did Jesus 'answer' them?

He did not answer the people, he answered the thought that led them to try to stone him [ICC]. His reply was to their action of picking up stones [Lns].

QUESTION—What was implied by Jesus' question 'For which of them do you stone me?'

Jesus' question implied that if he were a blasphemer he would not have been able to perform these good works [BECNT, HTC]. It implies that all that he has done has been the work of the Father himself, for they were works from the Father [Car]. Jesus actually asks, 'Does any work that I have shown you contradict my assertion that I and the Father are one so that what I have said must be ranked as blasphemy?' [Lns].

10:33 **The Jews answered him, "For[a] (a) good work we-do- not -stone you(sg) but for blasphemy,[b] and because you(sg) being (a) man[c] make[d] yourself God."**

LEXICON—a. περί (LN 89.36) (BAGD 1.b. p. 644): 'for' [BAGD, LN; all translations except NICNT2; CEV, NCV, TEV], 'because of' [BAGD, LN; CEV, NCV, TEV], 'on account of' [BAGD, LN], 'about' [NICNT2], 'concerning' [BAGD]. This preposition indicates cause or reason as an implied content of speaking [LN]. It indicates the object or person to which an action refers or relates [BAGD].

b. βλασφημία (LN 33.401) (BAGD): 'blasphemy' [LN; all translations except AB; CEV, NCV], 'blaspheming' [AB], 'serious insult' [LN]. The phrase 'for blasphemy' is translated 'because you did a terrible thing' [CEV], 'because you speak against God' [NCV]. This noun is derived from the verb βλασφημέω 'to blaspheme' (33.400) or to speak against someone in such a way as to harm or injure his or her reputation (occurring in relation to persons as well as to divine beings) 'to revile, to defame'. One way in which βλασφημία 'blasphemy' and βλασφημέω 'to blaspheme' were used in speaking of 'defaming God' was by claiming some kind of equality with God. Any such statement was regarded by the Jews of biblical times as being harmful and injurious to the nature of God [LN].

c. ἄνθρωπος (LN **9.1**) (BAGD 1.a.β. p. 68): 'man' [BAGD; all translations except NCV, NRSV], 'human being' [BAGD, LN; NRSV], '(a) human' [NCV], 'person, individual' [LN]. The clause 'you being a man make yourself God' is translated 'you are only a human being, but you make yourself God' [**LN**]. This noun denotes a human being (normally an adult) [LN].

d. pres. act. indic. of ποιέω (LN 42.29) (BAGD I.1.b.ι. p. 682): 'to make' [BAGD, LN], 'to fashion' [LN], 'do' [BAGD]. The clause 'you being a man make/are making yourself God' [Gdt, HTC, NICNT2, NTC; KJV] is also translated 'You being a man, make Yourself out to be God' [NRSV], 'you, who are only a man are making yourself out to be God' [Ph], 'You who are only a man make yourself God' [AB], 'You are only a man, but you are trying to make yourself God!' [TEV], 'You are just a man, and here you are claiming to be God!' [CEV], 'you, a man, are claiming to be God' [NET, REB], 'you, a mere man, claim to be God' [NIV, NLT], 'though you are only a man, you claim to be God' [NJB], 'you, though you are but a man, are making yourself God' [WBC], 'you, though only a human being, are making yourself God' [NRSV], 'You are only a human, but you say you are the same as God!' [NCV]. This verb means ' to make someone something'. Specifically it means 'to claim that someone is something' or 'to pretend that someone is something' [BAGD]. The present tense is durative [BECNT, Rd] indicating that this was something that Jesus kept doing and the Jews could no longer tolerate it [Rd].

QUESTION—What is the relationship of the clause, 'and because you being a man make yourself God', to the charge of blasphemy?

The accusation 'you being a man make yourself God' specifies what form of blasphemy the Jews had in mind [EGT, Gdt, Lns, My]. It clarifies the meaning of blasphemy [BECNT]. The phrase 'and because' does not introduce a new charge but explains and amplifies the charge of blasphemy [NICNT1, TRT]. 'And because' could be translated 'even because' [NICNT1], or 'namely that' [Lns].

QUESTION—What is meant by βλασφημέω 'to blaspheme'?

To blaspheme meant to usurp divine status [HTC]. Jesus was trying to make people believe that he was God and this was blasphemy [EGT, ICC, NTC, WBC]. That the Jews understood that Jesus was claiming equality with God is shown from the following verses John 5:17–18; 8:58–59; and 10:30–31, 33 [NTC]. The Jews understood that the statement 'I and the Father are one' (verse 30) meant that 'Jesus was making himself God' and therefore he was guilty of blasphemy [Lns]. To blaspheme was to speak evil against God or to insult him. For Jesus, a mere man, to make himself God, was insulting to God [TH]. Jewish law specified the penalty of death for dishonoring God in this way (Leviticus 24:13–16; 1 Kings 21:13) [TRT].

QUESTION—What words are emphasized in this verse?

The pronoun su 'you(sg)' is emphasized [TH]: *You yourself* being a man. The adverb 'only' in the TEV shows the emphasis of the Greek [TH]: You are only a man' [TEV].

10:34 Jesus answered them, "Is-it not[a] written in your(pl) law,[b] 'I said, you(pl)-are gods?[c]'

LEXICON—a. οὐ (LN 69.11): 'not' [LN]. This negative particle indicates that a positive reply is expected to a question [LN, TH, WBC; NCV, NLT, TEV]. The words 'Is it not written?' [KJV, NET, NIV, NRSV, Ph, REB] is also translated 'Has it not been written?' [NASB], 'It is written…isn't it' [WBC], 'It is written' [NLT, NCV, TEV], 'In your Scriptures doesn't God say' [CEV].

b. νόμος (LN **33.56**) (BAGD 4.b. p. 543): 'law' [BAGD, Gdt, HTC, NICNT2, NTC; KJV, NCV, NET, NRSV, REB], 'Law' [AB, WBC; NASB, NIV, NJB, Ph, TEV], 'Scriptures' [**LN**; CEV, NLT], 'sacred/holy writings' [LN]. This noun denotes the sacred writings of the OT. It is clear from the content of the quotation in John 10:34 that the reference to the law is not restricted to the first five books of the OT, for the passage comes from the Psalms [LN]. It refers to the Holy Scriptures generally on the principle that the most authoritative part gives its name to the whole [BAGD].

    c. θεός (LN 12.22) (BAGD 4.a. p. 358): 'god' [BAGD, LN; all translations], 'God' [BAGD]. This noun denotes any one of many different supernatural beings regarded as having authority or control over some aspect of the universe or human activity [LN]. It refers figuratively to someone who is worthy of reverence or respect [BAGD].

QUESTION—Why does Jesus specify the word 'law' as 'your(pl) law'?

He is not distancing himself from the law itself, but from the Jews' approach to it [BECNT]. He meant 'your law' in the sense of, 'your law, because you make so much of it' [NTC, Rd].

QUESTION—To what does the word νόμος 'law' refer?

The word 'law' refers to the whole OT [AB, BECNT, Car, CH, EGT, ICC, Lns, My, NICNT1, TH, TRT, WBC]. The particular Scripture referred to is Psalm 82:6, 'I say, You are gods, sons of the Most High, all of you' [All commentaries].

QUESTION—To whom does the pronoun 'I' in the words 'I said' refer?

It refers to God [CH, Lns, My, Rd, TH, TRT; CEV, NCV, TEV]: 'It is written in your Law that God said' [TEV].

QUESTION—To whom did God say this?

This question is translated 'It is written in your own Scriptures that God said *to certain leaders of the people*, 'I say, you are gods!' [NLT].

10:35 If he-called them gods to whom the word of God came, and the Scripture[a] cannot be-broken,[b] **10:36** do- you(pl) -say that he-blasphemes whom the Father sanctified[c] and sent into the world, because I-said I-am (the) Son of-God?"

LEXICON—a. γραφή (LN 33.53) (BAGD 2.b.β. p. 166): 'Scripture' [AB, Gdt, LN, NICNT2, WBC; NASB, NCV, NIV], 'Scriptures' [CEV, NLT], 'scripture' [HTC, NTC; KJV, NET, NJB, NRSV, Ph, REB, TEV], 'Scripture passage' [LN]. This noun denotes a particular passage of the OT [LN]. It is used in the NT exclusively with a sacred meaning, of Holy Scripture and refers here to the Scripture as a whole [BAGD].

    b. aorist pass. infin. of λύω (LN 13.100) (BAGD 4. p. 484): 'to be broken' [Gdt, HTC, NTC; KJV, NASB, NET, NIV, Ph], 'to be set aside' [WBC; NJB, Ph], 'to be annulled' [NRSV], 'to be altered' [NLT], 'to be abolished' [BAGD, NICNT2], 'to be destroyed, to be brought to an end, to be done away with' [BAGD], 'to be caused to come to an end, to be caused to become nothing, to be put an end to' [LN]. The clause 'the Scripture cannot be broken' is translated 'You can't argue with the Scriptures' [CEV], 'the Scripture is always true' [NCV], 'what the scripture says is true forever' [TEV], 'the Scripture cannot lose its force' [AB]. This verb means to cause to cease to exist [LN]. The phrase 'cannot be broken' means that the validity of Scripture cannot be dissolved [HTC, My], or the Scripture cannot be kept from fulfillment [AB, IVP], or the Scripture cannot be emptied of its force by being shown to be false [NICNT1].

c. aorist act. indic. of ἁγιάζω (LN 53.44, 88.26) (BAGD 2. p. 8): 'to sanctify' [BAGD, Gdt; KJV, NASB, NRSV], 'to consecrate' [AB, BAGD, HTC, LN (53.44), NICNT2, NTC, WBC; NJB, Ph, REB], 'to set apart' [NET, NLT], 'to dedicate (to God)' [BAGD, LN (53.44)], 'to set apart as one's own' [NIV], 'to choose' [NCV, TEV], 'to make holy' [LN (88.26)]. The clause 'whom the Father (has) sanctified' [Gdt; KJV, NASB, NRSV] is also translated 'it is the Father who prepared me for this work' [CEV]. This verb means to dedicate to the service of deity and to show loyalty to that deity [LN (53.44)] or to cause someone to have the quality of holiness [LN (88.26)]. It means to include in the inner circle of what is holy [BAGD]. It means to appoint a person to fulfill an important task or office [BECNT], or to set someone or thing apart for God's purpose [Bar], or a holy purpose [ICC], or the setting aside of an object for a special religious function [TH].

QUESTION—Does the word εἶπεν mean 'he called' or 'it called'?

If its meaning is personal, 'he called', the speaker will be taken as God [HTC, NICNT2, NTC; CEV, KJV, NASB, NIV, Ph, TEV]. If it is taken as impersonal, 'it called', the subject will be the law (or Scripture) [AB, Gdt, WBC; NCV, NJB]. In either case a very high authority is being referred to [NICNT1].

QUESTION—Is there any implied meaning in the phrase 'to whom the word of God came'?

The phrase amounted to a divine call on a person. Similar instances of it are God's call to Hosea (Hosea 1:1), Jeremiah (Jeremiah 1:2), and John the Baptist (Luke 3:2) [AB]. It is found at the introduction to prophetic books such as Hosea, Joel, Micah, and Zephaniah, as well as Luke 3:2 [BECNT]. This word of God that came to them, is the one that appointed them to their offices as judges [Lns]. In some prophetic books in the OT, this expression was equivalent to saying, 'God spoke his message to…' [TH]. The ones to whom the word of God came can be judges or authorities who have been commissioned to act as God's agents [CH, EGT, ICC, IVP, Lns, My, NICNT1, TRT], or prophets [NICNT2], or Israelites who received the law [Bar, Car, IVP], or people in general [Rd].

QUESTION—What is the force of the argument in these two verses?

Jesus' point is that if this Psalm (82:6) may be true of men, then much more it applies to the one whom the Father sanctified and sent into the world [NICNT1]. It is an argument from the lesser to the greater [EGT, IVP, Kn, Lns, My, NICNT1]. That is, if those to whom God spoke could be called 'gods', then certainly Jesus who was sanctified and sent into the world, could claim to be God's Son. In brief, Jesus is merely showing that even a man could call himself 'Son of God' without blaspheming [EGT]. His argument is in the form of a syllogism. *Major premise*: The Scriptures cannot be broken; *Minor premise*: The Scripture calls men who are ordained by God, 'gods'; *Conclusion*: Jesus, whom God sanctified and sent into the world is rightly called 'God' [Lns]. If Scripture called the people of Israel gods, how could they protest if Jesus called himself the Son of God, a lesser claim' [Kn]. Jesus is not only interested in the term 'gods' but also in the synonymous phrase in the same psalm 'sons of the Most High', because he refers to himself as Son of God in verse 36 [AB]. The force of the argument is that the One who speaks God's words, whom God has sent into the world, stands in an incomparably closer relationship to God than those who had received God's words and are called 'gods'. This one, therefore, may refer to himself as the Son of God without fear of blasphemy [HTC]. The basis of the reasoning is the accepted principle that the Scripture cannot blaspheme [Gdt].

QUESTION—What words are emphasized in this verse?

The pronoun ὑμεῖς 'you(pl)' is emphasized [BECNT, ICC, My, NICNT1, Rd]: Do *you, on your part*, say that he blasphemes? Jesus means, 'You who consider yourselves to be the keepers and teachers of the Law' [NICNT1]. By this, Jesus emphatically pits the Jews against the words of God and the inviolability of Scripture [BECNT, My, Rd]. The pronoun 'whom (the Father sancified)' is emphatic in the Greek sentence structure [TH].

QUESTION—What is the implied response to this rhetorical question?

The question implied that they should not accuse Jesus of blaspheming because he called himself the Son of God [CH, NTC, TRT]. The Jews had no right to say to Jesus, 'You are blaspheming', when he said, 'I am the Son of God' [NTC]. Jesus' purpose was to invalidate the charge of blasphemy for calling himself the Son of God [Rd]. Jesus denies that the Jews are right in their evaluation of the situation [NICNT1].

QUESTION—What is the significance of the lack of the definite article in the statement 'Son of God I am'?

The correct meaning of the phrase is '*the* Son of God' on the principle given by E.C. Colwell that in the New Testament definite nouns that precede the the verb typically lack the article (see also 1:1) [NICNT1].

10:37 If I-do- not -do[a] the works my Father, do- not -believe[b] me. **10:38** But if I-do, even-though[c] you(pl)-do- not believe me, believe the works, so-that you(pl)-may-know[d] and may-continue-to-know[e] that the Father (is) in[f] me and-I (am) in the Father.

TEXT—Instead of γνῶτε καὶ γινώσκητε 'you may know and may continue to know', some manuscripts read γνῶτε καὶ πιστεύσητε 'you may know and believe', and others read γνῶτε 'you may know'. GNT reads 'you may know and may continue to know' with a B rating, indicating that the text is almost certain. The reading 'you may know and believe' is taken by KJV.

LEXICON—a. pres. act. indic. of ποιέω (LN 42.7) (BAGD I.1.b.α. p. 681): 'to do' [BAGD, LN; all translations except AB], 'to perform' [AB, LN], 'to accomplish' [LN, BAGD], 'to make, to manufacture, to produce' [BAGD], 'to act, to carry out' [LN]. This verb is also translated as a noun: '(my) deeds' [REB]. This verb means to do or perform (it is highly generic for almost any type of activity) [LN]. It refers to actions that one undertakes, of events or states of being that one brings about, 'to cause, to bring about, to prepare' [BAGD]. The present tense indicates continuing action [Lns].

b. pres. act. impera. of πιστεύω (LN 31.85) (BAGD 1.b. p. 661): 'to believe' [BAGD, LN; all translations except AB], 'to put faith in' [AB], 'to believe in, to have confidence in, to have faith in, to trust [LN]. This verb means to believe to the extent of complete trust and reliance [LN]. The person to whom one 'gives credence' or whom one 'believes' is in the dative case (as here) [BAGD]. The present tense imperative should mean to stop an activity already occurring, 'stop believing!' But because such a meaning is impossible here it must be taken to mean 'do not have a continual trust' [NICNT1].

c. κἄν (LN 89.73) (BAGD 2. p. 402): 'even though' [AB, BAGD, HTC, LN, NTC; NCV, NIV, NRSV, Ph, TEV], 'even if' [BAGD, LN, WBC; CEV, NET, NJB, NLT, REB], 'though' [Gdt; KJV]. This conjunction is a combination of καί + ἐάν ('and' + 'if') and is an emphatic marker of concession [LN].

d. aorist act. subj. of γινώσκω (LN 28.1): 'to know' [Gdt, HTC, LN, WBC; all versions except NET, Ph, REB], 'to come to know' [AB; NET, Ph], 'to come to realize' [Lns; NTC], 'to recognize' [REB], 'to learn' [NICNT2], 'to know about, to have knowledge of, to be acquainted with' [LN]. The clause 'so that you may know and may continue to know' is translated 'so that/that you may (come to) know and understand' [AB, HTC; NASB, NET, NIV, NRSV], 'to the end that you may know and may understand' [Gdt], 'then you will know and understand' [NCV, NLT], 'then you may come to know and realize' [Ph], 'so that you may recognize and know' [REB], 'in order that you may come to realize and may continue to realize' [NTC], 'that you may know and come to grasp' [WBC], 'so that you might learn and know' [NICNT2], 'then you will know for certain' [CEV, NJB], 'in order that you may know once and for all' [TEV], 'that you may know, and believe' [KJV]. This verb means to possess information about [LN]. The aorist tense indicates 'to come to know' while the present tense of the following occurrence of the same verb means 'and keep on knowing' [NICNT1, NICNT2]. Jesus wants them to have a moment of insight and then to remain permanently in this knowledge [NICNT1]. The aorist indicates 'that you may begin to know' [Bar, CH, HTC, ICC, Lns, NICNT1, NICNT2, Rd, TH].

e. pres. act. subj. of γινώσκω (LN 28.1) 'to know' [LN], 'to know about, to have knowledge of, to be acquainted with' [LN]. This verb means to possess information about [LN]. The present tense indicates to continue to know [Bar, Car, CH, ICC, Lns, NICNT1, NICNT2, Rd, TH]. See previous item for version evidence.

f. ἐν (LN 89.119) (BAGD I.5.d. p. 259): 'in' [LN; all translations except CEV], 'one with' [LN; CEV], 'in union with, joined closely to' [LN]. This preposition indicates a close personal relation with someone [BAGD, LN]. The mutual indwelling of Jesus and the Father point to Jesus' oneness with the Father [Bar, BECNT, CH, HTC, NTC, WBC]. It indicates the closest conceivable fellowship [HTC]. This preposition could be translated 'one with' or 'one united with' or 'in close relationship with' [TRT].

QUESTION—How are the nouns related in the genitive construction τὰ ἔργα τοῦ πατρός μου 'the works of my Father'?

The works of the Father are the works that the Father does [My, NICNT1, TRT; CEV, NCV, NIV, Ph]. Jesus is identifying his works as the works of his Father [Bar, ICC, IVP, Kn, NICNT2, NTC, Rd; REB]. They are the works that the Father has accomplished through Jesus [Gdt]. This phrase is translated 'the things my Father wants me to do' [TEV].

QUESTION—What is the implied object of the clause 'But if I do'?

The object is 'the works of my Father/what my Father is doing' [AB, Gdt, HTC, NICNT2, NTC, Rd, TH, TRT, WBC; CEV, NASB, NCV, NET, NIV, NJB, NLT, NRSV, REB, TEV]: 'But if I do his work, believe in the evidence of the miraculous works I have done' [NLT].

QUESTION—What is meant by the phrase 'believe the works'?

Jesus means that they should consider his works and see that they are the works of the Father, and so come to believe in him [Bar, NTC]. He means to 'take seriously my works' or 'have confidence in what I say because of what I have done' [TH]. Jesus means to invite them to believe in him by means of his works [Kn]. It means to believe as true what the works are showing them [My]. Looking at the works they will be convinced of Jesus' trustworthiness and begin to believe what he says. This in turn will lead them to believe in him [ICC].

10:39 Therefore[a] they-were-trying again to-arrest[b] him, but he-went-out[c] from their hand.

TEXT—Instead of ἐζήτουν οὖν 'therefore they were trying', some manuscripts read ἐζήτουν 'they were trying', others read ἐζήτουν δέ 'but they were trying', still others read καὶ ἐζήτουν 'and they were trying'. GNT reads 'therefore they were trying' with a C decision indicating difficulty in deciding which variant to place in the text.

LEXICON—a. οὖν (LN 89.50): 'therefore' [Gdt, LN, WBC; KJV, NASB], 'so' [LN, NICNT2, NTC], 'then' [AB, LN; NET, NJB, NRSV], 'consequently, accordingly, so then' [LN], not explicit [HTC; CEV, NCV, NIV, NLT, Ph, TEV]. This conjunction is also translated as a phrase: 'this provoked them (to make another attempt to seize him)' [REB]. This conjuction indicates result, often implying the conclusion of a process of reasoning

[LN]. It indicates that as a result of Jesus' defence, the Jews had abandoned their intention to stone him (10:31) [EGT, Gdt, My], or that Jesus' appeal only served to cause their opposition to him to become stronger and led to the attempt to arrest him [Rd].
b. aorist act. infin. of πιάζω (LN 37.110) (BAGD 2.a. p. 657): 'to arrest' [AB, BAGD, HTC, LN, NICNT2, NTC; CEV, NJB, NLT, NRSV, Ph], 'to seize' [BAGD, LN, WBC; NASB, NET, NIV, REB, TEV], 'to take' [Gdt; KJV, NCV], 'to take into custody' [BAGD]. This verb means to take a person into custody for alleged illegal activity [BAGD, LN], with hostile intent [BAGD].
c. aorist act. indic. of ἐξέρχομαι (LN 15.40) (BAGD 1.b.γ. p. 275): 'to go out of' [LN], 'to depart out of, to leave from within' [LN], 'to disappear, to be gone' [BAGD]. The clause 'he went out from their hand' [NICNT2] is also translated 'he went forth out of their hands' [Gdt], 'he escaped out of their hand' [NTC; KJV], 'he escaped from their hands' [HTC; NRSV], 'he slipped out of their hands' [TEV], 'he slipped away out of their hands' [WBC], 'he escaped (from) their clutches' [NET, REB], 'he slipped out of their clutches' [AB], 'he eluded their clutches' [NJB], 'he escaped from them' [NCV], 'he escaped their grasp' [NIV], 'he escaped' [CEV], 'he eluded their grasp' [NASB], 'he got away and left them' [NLT], 'he moved out of their reach' [Ph]. This verb means to move out of an enclosed or well-defined two or three-dimensional area [LN].

QUESTION—To what previous events does the term πάλιν 'again' refer?
The previous times that the Jews tried to arrest Jesus were at 7:30 [AB, Bar, Car, EGT, HTC, ICC, Kn, Lns, My, NICNT2, NTC, Rd, WBC], 7:44 [AB, EGT, ICC, HTC, Lns, My], and 8:20 [AB, Bar, ICC, WBC].
QUESTION—Was Jesus' escape miraculous?
It seems to indicate that his escape was miraculous [Bar, Car, HTC, NTC, TH]. Jesus was protected by the Father's hand [HTC, IVP]. The Jews have no power over him until his hour comes [Bar, Car, TH]. Jesus is able to break the circle formed around him [Gdt]. This was was not necessarily miraculous [Gdt, BECNT, ICC, Lns, My, NICNT1].

DISCOURSE UNIT—10:40–42 [AB, Car, HTC, NICNT1, Rd, WBC]. The topic is conclusion to public ministry [AB], back to the beginning [Rd], strategic retreat [Car], retirement beyond Jordan [HTC, NICNT1, WBC].

10:40 And he-went-away again[a] across[b] the Jordan to the place where John was first[c] baptizing and he-stayed there. 10:41 And many came to him and were-saying, "John on-one-hand did no sign,[d] but-on-the-other-hand all (the) things-whichever John said about this-man were true. 10:42 And many believed in him there.

LEXICON—a. πάλιν (LN 67.55): 'again' [Gdt, HTC, LN, NTC, WBC; KJV, NICNT2, NRSV, Ph, REB], 'back again' [NICNT2; NET, NJB, TEV], 'back' [AB, NICNT1, Rd; NCV, NET, NIV], not explicit [CEV, NLT]. This adverb indicates a subsequent point of time involving repetition

[LN]. Here it should be translated 'back' [NICNT1, Rd]. The emphasis lies on returning to 'where it all began' rather than repeated going to the same place [Rd].

b. πέραν (LN 83.43) (BAGD 2.a. p. 643): 'across' [AB, HTC, NICNT2, NTC, WBC; NCV, NET, NIV, NRSV, Ph, REB, TEV], 'beyond' [Gdt; KJV, NASB, NLT], 'on the other side of' [BAGD, LN], 'to the far side of' [NJB], 'opposite, across from' [LN]. This preposition is also translated as a verb: '(he...) crossed (the Jordan)' [CEV]. It indicates a position opposite another position, with something intervening [LN].

c. πρῶτος (LN 60.46) (BAGD 2.a. p. 726): 'first' [BAGD, LN, WBC; NASB, NCV, NLT, Ph], 'at first' [HTC, NICNT2, NTC; KJV, NJB], 'earlier' [AB, BAGD; CEV, NRSV, REB], 'in the first place, before, to begin with' [BAGD]. This adverb is also translated as a phrase: 'at an earlier time' [NET], 'in the early days' [NIV], 'at the beginning' [Gdt], not explicit [TEV]. This adverb indicates the first in a series involving time, space, or set [LN].

d. σημεῖον (LN 33.477) (BAGD 2.a. p. 748): 'sign' [AB, BAGD, HTC, LN, NICNT2, NTC, WBC; NASB, NJB, NRSV, Ph], 'miracle' [BAGD, Gdt; CEV, KJV, NCV, TEV], 'miraculous sign' [NET, NIV, NLT, REB]. This noun denotes an event which is regarded as having some special meaning [LN]. It is a sign consisting in a 'wonder' or 'miracle', an event that is contrary to the usual course of nature. It is a miracle of divine origin, performed by God himself, by Christ, or by men of God [BAGD]. Σημεῖον as an event with special meaning was inevitably an unusual or even miraculous type of occurrence, and in a number of contexts it may be rendered as 'miracle'. Certainly that is the referent of the term in John 2:23 'many believed in him as they saw the signs he did'. For the Gospel of John, however, a σημεῖον is not simply a miraculous event but something that points to a reality with even greater significance. A strictly literal translation of σημεῖον as 'sign' might mean nothing more than a road sign or a sign on a building, and therefore in some languages σημεῖον in a context such as John 2:23 may be rendered as 'a miracle with great meaning' [LN]. In John this word denotes 'miracle' [NICNT1]. It is a key word in John and occurs at 2:11, 18, 23; 3:2, 4:48, 54; 6:2, 14, 26, 30; 7:31; 9:16; 10:41; 11:47; 12:18, 37; and 20:30.

QUESTION—Where did Jesus go when he went away across the Jordan?

He went to Batanea [BECNT, Car, TRT], in the northeast, in the tetrarchy of Philip [BECNT, Car], or to Perea [Bar, CH, Gdt, ICC, Kn, Lns, My]. He returned to Bethany (1:28) [AB, Gdt, HTC, ICC, NICNT2, NTC, TRT, WBC], which was in the province/district of Perea [ICC, TRT]. Bethany was located just east of the Jordan River, about 13 miles south of the Sea Galilee and about 20 miles southeast of Nazareth [NTC]. He returned to the area of his earliest ministry [ICC, NTC].

QUESTION—Did Jesus stay permanently in this area?
If it is necessary to choose the correct verb, it is best to indicate that his stay there was a temporary one [My, TH, TRT], lasting perhaps for several weeks [TH, TRT]. His stay there lasted about three months [EGT, ICC].

QUESTION—To whom did the people say these words?
They probably said them to each other [TH, TRT; NLT]: 'they remarked to one another' [NLT].

DISCOURSE UNIT—11:1–12:50 [AB, Car, Kn, Lns, Rd]. The topic is Jesus approaches his time of death and resurrection [AB], prelude to Jesus' suffering [Kn, Rd], transition: life and death [Car], final attestation before the people [Lns].

DISCOURSE UNIT—11:1–12:36 [IVP]. The topic is Jesus' raising of Lazarus and his reception as King leads to death.

DISCOURSE UNIT—11:1–12:11 [Kn]. The topic is dying to live.

DISCOURSE UNIT—11:1–57 [BECNT, NICNT1]. The topic is Jesus raises Lazarus.

DISCOURSE UNIT—11:1–54 [AB, HTC, IVP, WBC]. The topic is Jesus gives men life—they condemn him [AB], Jesus raises Lazarus [HTC, IVP], Jesus the resurrection and the life [WBC].

DISCOURSE UNIT—11:1–46 [NASB]. The topic is the death and resurrection of Lazarus.

DISCOURSE UNIT—11:1–44 [AB, Bar, Car, Kn, Lns, Rd; NJB, NLT, Ph]. The topic is Lazarus [Bar], Jesus raises Lazarus [AB, Car, Kn, Lns, Rd; NJB, NLT], Jesus shows his power over death [Ph].

DISCOURSE UNIT—11:1–16 [BECNT, Car, ICC, IVP, NICNT1, NICNT2, NTC, Rd, WBC; CEV, NCV, NET, NIV, NRSV, TEV]. The topic is Lazarus's illness reported [ICC, Rd], Lazarus dies [BECNT, Car, IVP, NICNT1, WBC; CEV, NIV, NET, NRSV, TEV], going to Bethany [NICNT2].

DISCOURSE UNIT—11:1–6 [AB, Kn]. The topic is the setting [AB], the request [Kn].

DISCOURSE UNIT—11:1–5 [HTC]. The topic is setting the scene for the raising of Lazarus.

11:1 Now a-certain-one was-sick,[a] Lazarus from Bethany,[b] of the village of-Mary and her sister Martha. **11:2** Mary was the-one-who anointed[c] the Lord with-perfume[d] and wiped[e] his feet with her hair, whose brother Lazarus was-sick.

LEXICON—a. pres. act. participle of ἀσθενέω (LN 23.144) (BAGD 1.a. p. 115): 'to be sick' [AB, BAGD, Gdt, LN, NICNT2; CEV, KJV, NASB, NCV, NET, NIV, NLT], 'to be ill' [HTC, LN, NTC, WBC; NJB, NRSV],

'to become sick' [TEV], 'to become seriously ill' [Ph], 'to fall ill' [REB], 'to be disabled' [LN]. This verb means to be sick and, as a result, to be in a state of weakness and incapacity [LN].
b. Βηθανία (LN **93.427**) (BAGD 1. p. 139): 'Bethany' [BAGD, **LN**; all translations]. This noun denotes a village on the Mount of Olives [BAGD, Car, LN]. It was 2.775 kilometers or nearly 2 miles from Jerusalem [BAGD, EGT, TRT]. It is about three-quarters of an hour's walk from Jerusalem [My]. It was east of Jerusalem [AB, TH, TRT, WBC], on the eastern slope of the Mount of Olives [BECNT, Car, EGT, Gdt, My]. It is distinct from the Bethany mentioned in 1:28 (the one beyond the Jordan River) [AB, Bar, BECNT, Car, EGT, IVP, Lns, Rd, My, TH, TRT].
c. aorist act. participle of ἀλείφω (LN 47.14) (BAGD 1. p. 35): 'to anoint' [AB, BAGD, Gdt, HTC, LN, NICNT2, NTC, WBC; KJV, NASB, NET, NJB, NRSV, REB], 'to pour (on)' [CEV, NIV, NLT, Ph, TEV], 'to put (on)' [NCV]. This verb means to anoint with a liquid, normally oil or perfume [LN].
d. μύρον (LN 6.205) (BAGD p. 529): 'perfume' [AB, BAGD, HTC, LN, NICNT2; CEV, NCV, NIV, NRSV, Ph, TEV], 'expensive perfume' [NLT], 'perfumed oil' [LN; NET], 'ointment' [BAGD, Gdt, NTC, WBC; KJV, NASB, NJB, REB]. This noun denotes a strongly aromatic and expensive ointment [LN].
e. aorist. act. participle of ἐκμάσσω (LN 79.83) (BAGD p. 243): 'to wipe' [BAGD; all translations except AB; NET], 'to wipe dry' [LN; NET], 'to dry' [AB]. This verb means to cause something to become dry by wiping with a dry substance [LN].

QUESTION—What is the meaning of Lazarus?

Lazarus means 'God helps/he whom God helps/God has helped/God is my help' [AB, Bar, BECNT, EGT, HTC, Lns, NICNT1, NTC, TH, TRT, WBC] and is a shortened form of the name Eleazar [AB, Bar, BECNT, ICC, Lns, NTC, TRT, WBC].

QUESTION—To which event does John refer when he talks about Mary's anointing Jesus with perfume?

He is referring ahead to the account in John 12:1–8 [AB, Bar, BECNT, Car, CH, EGT, HTC, Kn, NICNT2, NTC, Rd, TH, WBC] and presupposes that his readers have already heard about it [Bar, BECNT, Car, IVP, Kn, Rd, WBC].

QUESTION—On which part of his body did Mary anoint Jesus?

She anointed him on his feet [HTC, Kn, TH, TRT; NLT, TEV], or on his head [CEV].

QUESTION—Who was eldest of three siblings, Lazarus, Mary and Martha?

Probably Martha was the oldest [BECNT, Gdt, Lns, NICNT1, NTC, TRT], followed by Mary and then Lazarus as this is the order in which they are listed in verses 5 and 19. Often in Scripture names of siblings are listed according to their ages beginning with the eldest [TRT]. That Martha may have been the oldest may be supported by Luke 10:38 [Gdt, NICNT1, NTC], where she is described as being the hostess [NICNT1].

11:3 So[a] the sisters sent[b] to him saying, "Lord,[c] look[d] the-one-whom you(sg)-love[e] is-sick.

LEXICON—a. οὖν (LN 89.50): 'so' [AB, HTC, LN, NICNT2, NTC; NASB, NCV, NET, NIV, NLT, NRSV, Ph], 'therefore' [LN, Gdt, WBC; KJV], 'consequently, accordingly, then' [LN], not explicit [CEV, NJB, REB, TEV]. This conjunction indicates result, often implying the conclusion of a process of reasoning [LN].

b. aorist act. indic. of ἀποστέλλω (LN 15.67) (BAGD 1.d. p. 99): 'to send' [BAGD], 'to send a message, to send word' [LN]. The clause 'the/his sisters sent to him/Jesus' [Gdt, HTC, NICNT2, NTC, WBC; KJV] is also translated 'the sisters sent word to Him/Jesus' [NASB, NIV, Ph], 'Mary and Martha sent someone to tell Jesus' [NCV], 'the sisters sent a message to the Lord/Jesus/him' [CEV, NET, NRSV, REB, similarly NJB, NLT, TEV], 'the sisters sent to inform Jesus' [AB]. This verb means to send a message, presumably by someone [LN].

c. κύριος (LN 12.9): 'Lord' [LN; all translations except WBC; REB], 'Sir' [REB], 'Master' [WBC], 'Ruler, One who commands' [LN]. This noun denotes one who exercises supernatural authority over mankind. It is a title for God and for Christ [LN]. It should probably be translated 'Sir' here [NICNT1].

d. ἰδού (LN 91.13) (BAGD 2. p. 369): 'look' [LN, NICNT2; NET], 'behold' [Gdt; KJV, NASB], 'listen' [LN, NTC], 'pay attention' [LN], not explicit [AB, HTC; CEV, NCV, NIV, NJB, NLT, NRSV, Ph, TEV]. This particle is also translated as a clause: '(Sir) you should know' [REB], 'we want you to know' [WBC]. This particle functions as a prompter of attention emphasizing the statement that follows [LN]. It serves to introduce something unexpected [BAGD], or to emphasize the urgency of the sisters' appeal [HTC].

e. pres. act. indic. of φιλέω (LN 25.33) (BAGD 1.a. p. 859): 'to love' [AB, BAGD, Gdt, HTC, LN, NICNT2, NTC, WBC; KJV, NASB, NCV, NET, NIV, NJB], 'to have affection for' [BAGD, LN], 'to like' [BAGD]. The phrase ὃν φιλεῖς 'the one/he whom you love' [NRSV] is also translated 'his good friend' [CEV], 'your (dear) friend' [NLT, Ph, REB, TEV]. This verb means to have love or affection for someone or something based on association [LN].

QUESTION—What do the sisters imply by sending this information to Jesus?
It is a subtle request for Jesus to come and help them in this crisis [BECNT, EGT, Gdt, HTC, ICC, IVP, Kn, NICNT1, NICNT2, NTC, Rd, TRT], and to heal their brother Lazarus [HTC, TRT].

QUESTION—Who is the antecedent of the pronoun 'him' in the phrase πρὸς αὐτὸν '(sent) to him'?

The antecedent is Jesus [AB, Gdt, ICC, TH; CEV, NCV, NET, NIV, NJB, NLT, NRSV, Ph, TEV]: 'The sisters sent Jesus a message' [TEV]. It may be necessary to make this explicit since the previous two verses are all about Lazarus [TH].

QUESTION—What other information is there that the clause ὃν φιλεῖς 'the one whom you love' refers to Lazarus?

The only objective indication is that the relative pronoun ὅν 'the one whom' is masculine gender [NICNT2]: 'he whom you love' [Gdt, HTC; KJV, NASB, NRSV], 'the man you love' [NCV].

11:4 **And Jesus having-heard (this) said, "This sickness is not toward**[a] **death but for**[b] **the glory of God, so-that the Son of God may-be-glorified**[c] **through**[d] **it."**

LEXICON—a. πρός (LN 89.44) (BAGD III.3.b. p. 710): 'toward' [NICNT2], 'result in, end in, have as a consequence' [LN]. The clause 'this sickness is not toward death' [NICNT2], is also translated 'this sickness is not unto death' [Gdt, HTC, NTC; KJV], 'this illness is not with a view to death' [WBC], 'this sickness/illness is not to end in death' [NASB, REB], 'his sickness won't end/is not to end in death' [AB; CEV, NCV, NIV, NJB, similarly NLT], 'this illness is not meant to end in death' [Ph], 'this sickness/illness will not/does not lead to death' [NET, NRSV], 'the final result of this sickness will not be the death of Lazarus' [TEV], 'the final outcome of this illness is not death' or 'this illness will not end in death' [**LN**], 'this disease is not of the kind that will lead to death' [BAGD]. The clause 'this sickness is not unto death' means that 'death will not be the final result of this sickness' [Bar, EGT, Gdt, LN, Lns, NICNT1, NTC, TH; TEV]. This preposition indicates result, with focus on the end point [LN]. It indicates that death is not the goal aimed at or striven toward or the result that will follow a set of circumstances [BAGD].

b. ὑπέρ (LN 90.36) (BAGD 1.b. p. 838): 'for' [LN], 'for, on behalf of, for the sake of' [LN]. The phrase 'for the glory of God/God's glory' [AB, Gdt, HTC, NICNT2, NTC; KJV, NASB, NCV, NIV, NJB, NLT] is also translated 'for the sake of the glory of God' [WBC], 'it will bring glory to God' [CEV, similarly Ph], '(this sickness) will lead to God's glory' [NET], 'in order to bring glory to God' [TEV], 'through it God's glory is to be revealed' [REB], 'to reveal the glory of God' [BAGD]. This preposition indicates the participant who is benefited by an event or on whose behalf an event takes place [LN]. The phrase 'for the glory of God' means 'in the interest of the glory of God' [NTC].

c. aorist pass. subj. of δοξάζω (LN 87.24) (BAGD 2. p. 204): 'to be glorified' [BAGD, LN], 'to be made gloriously great' [LN], 'to be clothed in splendor' [BAGD]. The clause 'so that/that/in order that the Son of God/God's Son may be glorified through/by/by means of it' [AB, HTC,

NTC, WBC; NASB, NET, NIV, NRSV, similarly NICNT2; NJB] is also translated 'through it...the son of God is to be glorified' [REB], 'that the Son of God may be glorified thereby' [Gdt; KJV], 'to bring glory to the Son of God' [NCV], 'it will bring glory to...his Son' [CEV], 'so that the Son of God will receive glory from this' [NLT], 'it will show the glory of the Son of God' [Ph], 'it will be the means by which the Son of God will receive glory' [TEV]. This verb means to cause someone to have glorious greatness [LN]. The glorifying of the Son is brought about by the miracles that the Father has him perform [BAGD].
   d. διά (LN 89.76): 'through' [AB, LN, NICNT2, WBC; NET, NIV, NJB, NRSV, REB], 'by means of' [LN, HTC, NTC], 'by' [Gdt, LN; KJV, NASB], 'from' [NLT]. The phrase δι' αὐτῆς 'through it' is translated 'it will bring (glory to God and his Son)' [CEV], '(it is...to bring glory) to the Son of God' [NCV], 'it will show (the glory of the Son of God)' [Ph], 'it will be the means by which (the Son of God will receive glory)' [TEV]. This preposition indicates the means by which one event makes another event possible [LN].

QUESTION—To whom was Jesus speaking?
   He may have been replying to the sisters [Lns, NICNT2], to his disciples [EGT], to the sisters and his disciples [Gdt], or to the messenger and to those present with him [My]. It is likely that Jesus' was speaking to the two sisters as is indicated by Jesus' later reminding Martha 'Did I not tell you that if you believed you will see the glory of God' (verse 40) [NICNT2].

QUESTION—What did Jesus mean when he said, 'This sickness is not unto death'?
   He did not mean that the sickness was not fatal, but simply that it would not *ultimately* end in death [Bar, Car, EGT, Lns, NICNT1].

QUESTION—What does the phrase 'for the glory of God' mean?
   It means 'for revealing the glory of God' [Bar, ICC, NICNT1, TRT]. It does not mean, so that God may be praised or honored, but so that his glory may be revealed because in John's Gospel God's glory is more his self-disclosure than his receiving praise [Car]. As verse 40 shows, it does not mean 'so that God may be glorified'. The glory of God is not his praise but his activity [Bar, NICNT1]. Glory here means God's power to give life to people [TRT]. To bring glory to God may mean 'to reveal how powerful God is' or 'to show people how wonderful God is' [TH], or 'to reveal God's greatness/power to people' [TRT]. 'For the glory of God' means 'for the sake of glorifying God' [EGT].

QUESTION—What is the relationship between the purposes expressed by the two expressions, 'for (ὑπέρ) the glory of God' and 'so that (ἵνα) 'the Son of God may be glorified'?
   The words 'so that the son of God may be glorified' explain the means by which the phrase 'for the glory of God' will be realized [EGT, Gdt, Lns, My, NICNT2]. The revealing of God's glory was that the Son might be honored by God as shown in his granting him the power to raise a man from the dead

[ICC]. The phrase 'for the glory of God' explains the clause 'so that the Son of God may be glorified' making it clear that God intends to reveal himself in a unique way through his son's action [HTC].

QUESTION—What is the antecedent of the pronoun αὐτῆς 'it' in the phrase 'through it'?

The pronoun refers back to the word 'sickness' [AB, EGT, Gdt, ICC, Lns, TH].

11:5 **Now Jesus loved**[a] **Martha and her sister and Lazarus.**

LEXICON—a. imperf. act. indic. of ἀγαπάω (LN 25.43) (BAGD 1.b.α. p. 4): 'to love' [BAGD, LN; all translations except AB, NTC], 'to really love' [AB], 'to hold in loving esteem' [NTC], 'to cherish' [BAGD], 'to regard with affection' [LN]. This verb means to have love for someone or something based on sincere appreciation and high regard [LN]. In translating this verb it is important to not use a word that would imply anything romantic or sexual [TH, TRT].

QUESTION—What is the purpose of supplying this information?

It is intended to assure the reader that Jesus' failure to go to Lazarus immediately does not mean that he was indifferent to his condition [AB]. It may be intended to soften the implications of his not going immediately to him (verse 6) [BECNT, Car] or to explain that it was not a lack of love that kept Jesus from going to them [Bar, CH, Lns, NICNT1, TH]. The verse seems to be parenthetical [AB, CH, Lns; NET].

QUESTION—Is there a difference in meaning between the two words for 'to love', ἀγαπάω here, and φιλέω in verse 3?

1. There is no difference in meaning between the two verbs [AB, Bar, BECNT, Car, EGT, ICC, NICNT1, NICNT2, TH]. There is little distinction in meaning between these two verbs. The use of two words for love seems to be explained by the evangelist's tendency for stylistic variation [BECNT].

2. There is a difference between these two verbs [Gdt, HTC, Lns, My, NTC; probably CEV, NLT, Ph, REB, TEV]: 'your *dear* friend is sick'…(Verse 3) 'Jesus *loved* Martha…(Verse 5)' [TEV]. The verb ἀγαπάω is a verb of dignity or nobleness, while φιλέω expresses tenderness [Gdt]. While ἀγαπάω means 'to hold in loving esteem', φιλέω means 'to have an affection for' someone [NTC]. The verb φιλέω carries a sense of natural affection, while ἀγαπάω, although not excluding affection, places the emphasis on a spiritual relationship [HTC]. While φιλέω expresses affection and personal attachment, ἀγαπάω expresses the love of the spirit and reason, the all-comprehending and purposeful love of God's Son [Lns].

QUESTION—What is indicated by the order in which the three, 'Martha and her sister and Lazarus' are mentioned?

There is a tendency in the NT to mention the oldest first so they were probably listed in that way here with Lazarus being the youngest [Lns, TH].

Martha is mentioned first because she is eldest [My, TH] and the mistress of the house (compare verse 19) [My]. Mary was probably the younger sister [NICNT1, TRT]. The fact that Martha is mentioned first and Mary is not named may suggest that Martha was the eldest [Car].

DISCOURSE UNIT—11:6–16 [HTC]. The topic is the journey to Bethany.

11:6 So[a] when he-heard that he-is-sick, then he-remained two days in (the) place in-which he-was.

LEXICON—a. οὖν (LN 89.50, 89.127) (BAGD 5. p. 593): 'so' [HTC, LN (89.50), NTC; NASB, NET, Ph], 'yet, and so' [AB], 'therefore' [Gdt, WBC; KJV], 'therefore though' [REB], 'accordingly, though' [NRSV], 'then' [LN, NICNT2], 'consequently, accordingly, so then' [LN (89.50], 'but' [LN (89.127); CEV, NCV], yet' [NIV, NJB, TEV], 'although' [NLT]. This conjunction indicates result, often implying the conclusion of a process of reasoning (89.50) or it indicates relatively weak contrast (89.127) [LN].

QUESTION—What is indicated by the conjunction οὖν?

1. It indicates the consequence of Jesus' love for them [BECNT, Car, EGT, Gdt, IVP, NICNT1, NICNT2, NTC, WBC; NRSV, Ph]: therefore. Three factors tell us that Jesus purposely intended to remain where he was for two days: (1) By this time Lazarus was already dead, (2) Jesus' life was determined by the Father's will, not by the will of people, (3) the disciples' faith would be strengthened by the raising of Lazarus from the dead [WBC]. The delay is explained when one considers that Jesus' ultimate motivation was the glory of God, and that God was the one who was sovereignly guiding him [BECNT]. The word 'therefore' refers ahead to verse 7 where Jesus said, '*Let us go* to Judea', rather than pointing to the words 'he remained for two days' of this verse [EGT, Gdt]: 'When therefore he heard of it, he remained, *it is true* (μέν), but afterward he said, Let us go…' [Gdt].
2. It indicates a counter-expectation relationship [AB; CEV, NCV, NIV, NJB, NLT, REB, TEV]: 'Yet Jesus really loved…Lazarus. And so, even when he heard that Lazarus was sick, he stayed on where he was two days longer' [AB], 'So although Jesus loved Martha, Mary, and Lazarus, he stayed where he was for the next two days' [NLT]. It was out of love that Jesus refrained from going immediately knowing that would be of more help to Lazarus when Lazarus was dead [AB].
3. It indicates the resumption of the narrative from verse 4 [ICC, Lns, My]: then. Jesus' knew that this sickness was not to result in death but rather result in glory to God, so he was not in a hurry to go immediately [ICC].

QUESTION—Who is the antecedent of the pronoun 'he' in the clause 'he is sick'?

Since the pronoun 'he' is repeated four times in this verse, it may be advisable to make the one pronoun that refers to Lazarus explicit to avoid ambiguity [TH; NCV, NET, NIV, NRSV, Ph, REB, TEV]: 'when he received news that Lazarus was sick' [TEV].

QUESTION—Why did Jesus remain where he was for two days?

It is likely that he meant to indicate that his actions were determined by God rather than by the desires of people [Bar, Car, IVP, My, NICNT1, NICNT2, TH]. He waited so as to raise Lazarus from the dead rather than merely to heal him so he could add to God's glory [My, NICNT2, NTC]. But he also did so to strengthen the faith of those who believed in him [NICNT2, NTC]. Raising Lazarus was a better way to strengthen the faith of the family and his disciples than merely healing him [Car, NTC]. He remained two days because he felt that he could do more good for Lazarus by raising him from the dead, than healing him [AB].

QUESTION—When did Lazarus die?

Jesus did not delay so as to allow Lazarus to die. He was already dead by the time the messenger reached Jesus [Bar, CH, Kn, NICNT1, TH, WBC]. By the time Jesus arrives in Bethany it has been four days, one for the journey of the messenger, two for the stay where he was, and one more for the journey to Judea [CH, NICNT1, WBC]. If the place where Jesus was staying is Bethany beyond Jordan in the south, it would take the messenger one day to reach Jesus and one for Jesus to reach Lazarus, this plus the two days that Jesus delayed plus the day to travel to Lazarus (five days) indicates that Lazarus must have died the same day that the messenger set out. But if Jesus were in Batanea in the north, a journey of four days away, he would have been only half way to Lazarus by the time he died [IVP].

DISCOURSE UNIT—11:7–16 [AB, Kn]. The topic is going to Judea.

11:7 Then after this he-says to-the disciples, "Let-us-go^a to Judea again."
11:8 The disciples say to-him, "Rabbi, the Jews were- just-now^b -trying to-stone you, and^c you-go there again?"

LEXICON—a. pres. act. subj. of ἄγω (LN **15.34**) (BAGD 5. p. 14): 'to go' [BAGD; all translations], 'to go off' [**LN**], 'to depart for' [**LN**] 'to go away, to leave' [**LN**]. This verb means to move away from a reference point [**LN**].

  b. νῦν (LN **67.39**) (BAGD 1.b. p. 545): 'just now' [AB, BAGD, **LN**, NICNT2, NTC, WBC; NASB, NET, NRSV], 'but now' [Gdt, HTC], 'now' [BAGD], 'of late' [KJV], 'presently' [**LN**], not explicit [CEV]. This adverb is also translated as a phrase: 'only a short time ago' [NCV], 'a short while ago' [NIV], 'just a short time ago' [TEV], 'only a few days ago' [NLT, Ph], and as a clause: 'it is not long since' [NJB, REB]. This adverb indicates a time shortly before or shortly after the time of the discourse [BAGD, **LN**]. Here it has the meaning of 'recently' [Car, ICC].

  c. καί (LN **91.12**) (BAGD): 'and' [AB, Gdt HTC, NICNT2, NTC, WBC; KJV, NASB, NRSV, TEV], 'and yet' [NIV], 'yet, indeed, how is it then, then' [**LN**], 'now' [NCV], not explicit [NET, NJB, NLT, Ph, REB]. This conjunction indicates emphasis, involving surprise and unexpectedness [LN]. It is used here in the sense of καίτοι 'and yet' [NICNT1].

QUESTION—What is indicated by Jesus' referring to Judea, rather than Bethany?

Judea, rather than Bethany was the significant location. It was where crucifixion awaited him [NICNT1]. It indicates that Jesus knew he was going into danger and by this he evokes the fear in his disciples that he wants to overcome before beginning the journey [Gdt]. All the emphasis is put on the place of danger and stress [Bar].

QUESTION—To what incident were the disciples probably referring?

They were probably referring to the incident in 10:31 where after Jesus said that he and the Father were one, the Jews picked up stones to stone him [AB, Bar, Car, TH, TRT, WBC]. They may have been referring to the incident in 10:39 [Bar, Car, HTC, WBC]. The desire of the Jews to kill Jesus is seen at 5:18; 7:1; 8:37, 40, 59; and 10:31 [NICNT2].

QUESTION—What is indicated by the rhetorical question, 'You go there again?'

The question indicates that the disciples protest Jesus' going to Judea [Gdt, NICNT1]. It indicates that the disciples think Jesus should not go back there [Rd, TRT]. The disciples are surprised [EGT, NTC] and puzzled that Jesus would wish to return where there was so much danger [NTC]. They are aghast [Car, WBC] and think it foolish for him to risk his life again [WBC]. They are incredulous at Jesus' suggestion [CH]. The question shows the disciples' concern for the safety of their beloved Master [My].

11:9 Jesus answered, "Are-there not[a] twelve hours of-the day? If anyone walks[b] in the day, he-does- not stumble,[c] because he-sees the light of-this world.

LEXICON—a. οὐχί (LN 69.12) (BAGD 3. p. 598): 'not' [BAGD, LN; all translations except NLT]. The question 'Are there not twelve hours of the day' is translated 'There are twelve hours of daylight every day' [NLT], 'You know that the sun shines for twelve hours a day' [TRT], 'There are twelve hours in the day, are there not?' [NTC, WBC; similarly Ph], 'A day has twelve hours, doesn't it?' [TEV]. Οὐχί is a strengthened form of οὐ [BAGD]. This negative particle indicates that a somewhat more emphatic positive response (than οὐ would indicate) is expected to a question [BAGD, LN]. The question expects the answer 'Yes' [BAGD, LN, TH].

b. pres. act. subj. of περιπατέω (LN 15.227): 'to walk' [LN; all translations except AB; NET], 'to walk around' [LN; NET], 'to go walking' [AB], 'to go' [LN]. This verb means to walk along or around [LN].

c. pres. act. indic. of προσκόπτω (LN 15.228) (BAGD 1.b. p. 716): 'to stumble' [BAGD, **LN**; all translations except NLT]. The clause 'If anyone walks in the day, he does not stumble' is translated 'During the day people can walk safely' [NLT]. This verb means to strike one's foot against something [BAGD, LN] as one walks and in this way to lose one's balance temporarily [LN].

QUESTION—What is meant by this metaphor?

Figuratively it can either mean: (1) While I am with you, no harm can come to us, because God has given us the time that we need to do his will [NTC, TRT]. After that time is over, no one will be able to work. Or (2) Follow Me, the Light of the world, so that you know God's will and are safe, because without Me you will stumble in sin [TRT]. It means, I can go without fear to Bethany where God's will directs me [Gdt, HTC] because the sunshine of God's will shines on my path and I will not stumble [Gdt]. Jesus is assuring his disciples that until his hour arrives, as long as they are with him, they are safe from stumbling and threats of the Jews [BECNT]. The Lord's 'day' was now in its final hour, but Jesus still had work to do before his death [CH]. The primary meaning is directed toward the disciples indicating that as long as Jesus, the light, is with them, his light enables them to see where they are going [IVP, Rd]. The metaphor can either apply to Jesus meaning that as long as he performs God's will he is safe. Though the time is short he must not quit before the twelve hours are complete. Or it can apply to his disciples meaning that as long as they have Jesus the light, they should perform the works assigned to them [Car]. The time of Jesus' ministry is limited so he must use the time he has regardless of the consequences [Bar]. He means that the time assigned to him by the Father for working is not yet finished. Until it does, no one can harm him. When it is finished, he will fall into the power of his enemies [My]. In brief Jesus is simply saying, 'My hour has not yet come' [NICNT2].

QUESTION—To what length of time does the word 'day' refer?

The Jews and the Romans both recognized that a day was made up of the time from sunrise to sunset [Bar, TH] or of twelve one-hour periods [Bar, BECNT, Car]. One day was the time from sunrise to sunset [NICNT2, NTC, Rd, TRT, WBC]. Jesus is reminding his hearers that twelve hours are all the time there is in a day [NICNT1].

QUESTION—To what does the phrase 'the light of this world' refer?

It refers to the sun or sunlight [AB, Car, HTC, My, NICNT1, NICNT2, NTC, TH, TRT, WBC]. It may also refer to Jesus as the spiritual light [AB, TH, TRT]. While it literally applies to the sun, it points to the knowledge of God's will, man's moral light that guides him [EGT].

11:10 **But if anyone walks-around in the night, he stumbles, because the light[a] is not in him.**

LEXICON—a. φῶς (LN 14.36) (BAGD 1.a. p. 871): 'light' [BAGD, LN; all translations except Ph]. The clause 'the light is not in him/them' [Gdt, HTC, NICNT2, NTC, WBC; NASB, NET, NRSV] is also translated 'he has no light in him' [AB], 'there is no light in him' [KJV], 'he has/they have no light' [NIV, NLT, TEV], 'there is no light to help him see' [NCV], 'having no light as a guide' [NJB], 'the light fails him' [REB], 'he cannot see where he is going' [Ph], 'you don't have any light' [CEV]. This noun denotes light, in contrast with darkness usually in relationship to some source of light such as the sun, moon, fire, lamp, etc. [LN].

QUESTION—Does this part of the metaphor apply to Jesus or to people?
1. It applies to Jesus [Gdt, NICNT2]. If Jesus should try to extend his time on earth beyond God's allotted time for him, he could stumble, sin, or perish [Gdt]. The present context indicates that this applies to Jesus. When 'night' comes Jesus is in danger (13:30). Once set free from the context, it applies to the disciples or to anyone who hears his message [NICNT2].
2. It applies to people [Bar, HTC, WBC]. Here the metaphor switches to symbolic language and applies now to people who refuse to walk with Jesus and so have no inner light by which to be led. As such, they stumble, that is they fail to obtain salvation [HTC]. Men can walk safely in the light that Jesus provides. Apart from him they stumble and become emersed in sin [Bar].
3. It can apply to either 1 or 2 [CH]. On one level this shows that Jesus had only a short time left and he must do the work he had to do before his death. On another level the light refers to Jesus' presence among his people. People should utilize his presence as long as he is available. But the believers have Jesus' light with them and so they need not fear stumbling [CH].

QUESTION—What is meant by the clause 'the light is not in him'?
It either means he has no light to help him see, or he has no light in him [TRT]. It means he has no internal light, or the capacity to see in the darkness [TH]. To have no light in oneself means that the person is dead. This applies to Jesus as well as to his followers [Lns]. It means that the sun of God's will no longer directs his way [Gdt]. He does not have the Light of the world, Jesus shining within him [WBC]. The person no longer has the light of the eye through which the body receives light (Matthew 6:2) [Rd]. Men should not follow some supposed inner light, but receive Jesus as the light of the world [Bar]. The Jews conceived of light as residing in the eye (Matthew 6:22–23) [AB, BECNT, HTC, Kn].

11:11 He-said these-things, and after this he says to-them, "Lazarus our friend^a has-fallen-asleep,^b but I-am-going so-that I-may-wake- him -up.^c"
11:12 Therefore the disciples said to-him, "Lord, if he-has-fallen-asleep he-will-be-healed.^d

LEXICON—a. φίλος (LN 34.11) (BAGD 2.a.α. p. 861): 'friend' [BAGD, LN; all translations except AB]. This noun is also translated as an adjective: '(our) beloved (Lazarus) [AB]. It denotes a male person with whom one associates and for whom there is affection or personal regard [LN]. It had become a technical term for 'Christian believer' (Luke 12:4; Acts 27:3; 3 John 15; John 15:13–15) [Bar, TH].
  b. perf. mid. or pass. (deponent = act.) indic. of κοιμάομαι (LN 23.104, 23.66) (BAGD 2.a. p. 437): 'to fall asleep' [BAGD, LN (23.66); all

68   JOHN 11:11–12

translations except Gdt; CEV, KJV, NJB], 'to sleep' [BAGD, Gdt, LN (23.66); KJV], 'to be asleep' [LN (23.66); CEV], 'to be at rest' [NJB], 'to die, to pass away' [BAGD]. This verb means the state of being asleep [LN (23.66)], or to sleep as a euphemistic expression for the state of being dead, 'to be dead, to have died' [LN (23.104)]. It is figurative of the sleep of death [BAGD]. While this verb can be used euphemistically, the disciples understand it literally as referring to natural sleep. Therefore it is important to translate it literally here [TH, TRT].
- c. aorist act. subj. of ἐξυπνίζω (LN **23.77**) (BAGD p. 279): 'to wake (someone) up' [AB, BAGD, LN, NICNT2, NTC; CEV, NIV, NLT, Ph, TEV], 'to awaken (someone)' [Gdt, LN; NASB, NET, NRSV], 'to wake (someone)' [NCV, NJB, REB], 'to awake/wake (someone) out of sleep' [HTC, WBC; KJV], 'to arouse (someone)' [BAGD], 'to cause (someone) to wake up' [LN]. This verb means to cause someone to awaken [LN].
- d. fut. pass. indic. of σῴζω (LN 23.136) (BAGD 1.a. p. 798): 'to be healed, to be cured, to be made well' [LN], 'to be saved' [BAGD]. The phrase 'he will be healed' is translated 'he will be saved' [NJB], 'his life will be saved' [AB], 'he will recover' [Gdt, HTC, NTC; NASB, NET, REB], 'he will get better' [NICNT2; CEV, NIV], 'he will soon get better' [NLT], 'he will get well' [WBC; TEV], 'he shall do well' [KJV], 'he will be all right' [NCV, NRSV, Ph]. This verb means to cause someone to become well again after having been sick [LN]. It means here to be saved from death [BAGD].

QUESTION—What is significant about Jesus' plan to go and awaken Lazarus?
Jesus is revealing his intention to raise Lazarus from the dead, otherwise his reply makes no sense. If Lazarus were sleeping, he would certainly be awake by the time they arrive at Bethany and not need to be awakened [NICNT2]. The disciples should have realized by the length of the journey to Bethany that Jesus was not talking about natural slumber [Lns, NTC]. His reply implies that if he does not go and wake Lazarus up, he will remain asleep. But this the disciples fail to understand [Lns].

QUESTION—Was the misunderstanding of the disciples realistic?
Jesus had told them in verse 4 that, 'This sickness is not unto death', so it was understandable that they would take his words as referring to natural sleep [EGT, Lns, My, NTC].

11:13 **Now Jesus had-spoken about his death, but those (men) thought[a] that he-speaks about the sleep[b] of-sleep.[c]**

LEXICON—aorist act. indic. of δοκέω (LN 31.29) (BAGD 1.d. p. 202): 'to think' [BAGD, LN; all translations except WBC], 'to suppose' [BAGD, LN, WBC], 'to believe' [BAGD, LN], 'to presume, to assume, to imagine' [LN], 'to consider' [BAGD]. This verb means to regard something as presumably true, but without particular certainty [LN].
- b. κοίμησις (LN **23.66**) (BAGD 1. p. 437): 'sleep' [BAGD, LN]. The clause 'he speaks about the sleep of sleep' is translated 'he meant/he had spoken

of taking of rest in sleep' [HTC; KJV], 'he was speaking of the rest of sleep' [Gdt], 'he spoke about the repose of sleep' [NTC], 'he was talking only about sleep' [CEV], 'he was speaking of literal sleep' [NASB], 'he meant Lazarus was really sleeping' [NCV], 'he had been talking about real sleep' [NET], 'he meant/he was speaking of natural sleep' [**LN**, NICNT2; NIV, REB, TEV], 'he was speaking about falling into natural sleep' [Ph], '(they thought that) by "rest" he meant "sleep"' [NJB], 'Jesus meant Lazarus was simply sleeping' [NLT], 'he was referring merely to sleep' [NRSV], 'he was/had been talking about sleep in the sense of slumber' [AB, WBC]. This noun denotes the state of being asleep [LN]. The phrase 'the sleep of sleep' means 'natural sleep' [TH], or 'the sleep of slumber' [BAGD].
- c. ὕπνος (LN **23.66**) (BAGD p. 843): 'sleep' [BAGD, **LN**]. This noun denotes the state of being asleep [LN]. For translations see lexical item b. above.

QUESTION—What is the relationship between the two clauses of this verse?

There is a contrastive relationship between these clauses [BECNT, NICNT1, TH, TRT; all translations except Gdt]. The contrast between what Jesus meant and what the disciples thought he meant should be indicated in some languages by an adversative conjunction, such as 'but', or 'on the other hand' [TH].

QUESTION—What word is emphasized in this verse?

The pronoun ἐκεῖνοι 'those (men)' is emphatic [BECNT, ICC, NICNT1] and contrasts them with Jesus who is mentioned first [BECNT, NICNT1].

11:14 So then[a] Jesus told them plainly,[b] "Lazarus died, 11:15 and I-am-glad for- your(pl) -sakes[c] that you(pl)-may-believe,[d] that I-was not there. But let-us-go to him.

LEXICON—a. τότε (LN 67.47) (BAGD): 'then' [LN; all translations except AB; NJB, NLT, Ph, TEV], 'finally' [AB], not explicit [NJB, NLT, Ph, TEV]. The clause 'So then Jesus told them plainly' is translated 'This made Jesus tell them quite plainly' [Ph]. This adverb indicates a point of time subsequent to another point of time [LN]. It introduces something that follows another in time [BAGD].
- b. παρρησία (BAGD 1. p. 630): 'plainly' [BAGD; all translations except Gdt; Ph], 'quite plainly' [Ph], 'openly' [BAGD, Gdt]. This noun denotes 'outspokenness, frankness, plainness' of speech that conceals nothing and passes over nothing [BAGD]. It indicates speaking in plain terms without figures [EGT, Gdt, My, NICNT2], without the possibility of not understanding [EGT], without obscurity or ambiguity of speech [Bar].
- c. διά (LN 90.38): 'for the sake of' [BAGD; all translations except CEV], 'for, on behalf of, for the benefit of' [LN]. The clause 'I am glad for your sakes that I was not there' is translated 'I am glad that I wasn't there, because now you will have a chance (to put your faith in me)' [CEV].

This preposition with accusative object indicates a participant who is benefited by an event or for whom an event occurs [LN].
   d. aorist act. subj. of πιστεύω (LN 31.102) (BAGD 2.b. p. 661): 'to believe' [BAGD], 'to be a believer, to be a Christian' [LN]. This verb means to believe in the good news about Jesus Christ and to become a follower [LN]. The aorist tense of the verb may mean 'begin to believe' [AB, Lns, NICNT1, TH]. The translation 'come to have faith' is an attempt to render the sense of a single act implicit in the aorist tense [AB].
QUESTION—What is the implied object of the verb 'believe'?
   Jesus is the obvious object intended [TH, TRT; CEV]: 'you will have a chance to put your faith *in me*' [CEV].
QUESTION—Does the phrase 'so that you may believe' indicate that the disciples did not believe before this?
   The disciples were already believers so this indicates that their faith would grow to a new stage [EGT, Gdt, ICC, IVP, Kn, Lns, NICNT1, NTC, TRT] and this would almost make their earlier faith seem like unbelief [Gdt]. Their faith would now receive a new and stronger stimulus [HTC]. The raising of a dead man would be a more effective way of strengthening their faith than merely healing a sick man [NTC].
QUESTION—Should the clause 'I am glad' be construed with 'that you may believe' or with 'that I was not there'?
   Jesus' words, 'I am glad' are directly dependent on the clause 'I was not there'. It is sometimes better for the disciples that Jesus not be there with them (16:7) [Bar, NICNT2, NTC; all translations]: 'I am glad that I wasn't there' [CEV].
QUESTION—What is the relationship between the clauses 'that I was not there' and 'so that you may believe'?
   The purpose clause 'so that you may believe' explains why Jesus was glad that he was not there when Lazarus was still alive [ICC]. Jesus realized that if he had been there, he would not have been willing to allow Lazarus to die [NICNT2]. He therefore chose to allow this so that he might be glorified (verse 4) and so that the disciples might believe [NICNT1, NICNT2].

11:16 So Thomas[a] the (one) called[b] Didymus[c] said to-the fellow-disciples,[d] "Let-us-go also so-that we-may-die with him."

LEXICON—a. Θωμᾶς (LN 93.155) (BAGD p. 367): 'Thomas' [BAGD, LN; all translations]. This noun denotes one of the twelve apostles [BAGD, LN]. The name 'Thomas' is derived from the Hebrew word *Te'oma* and means 'twin' [Bar, BECNT, Car, Gdt, NICNT1, NICNT2, NTC, TH, TRT].
   b. pres. pass. participle of λέγω (LN 33.129) (BAGD II.3. p. 470): 'to be called' [BAGD, LN; all translations except AB; CEV, NJB, NLT, Ph], 'to be nicknamed' [NLT, similarly CEV], 'to be known as' [NJB, Ph], 'to mean' [AB, BAGD], 'to be named' [BAGD, LN]. This verb means to speak of a person or object by means of a proper name [LN].

c. Δίδυμος (LN **93.95**) (BAGD p. 192): 'Didymus' [Gdt, LN; KJV, NASB, NCV, NET, NIV], 'Didymos' [NICNT2], 'Twin' [AB, BAGD, HTC, NTC, WBC; CEV, NJB, NLT, NRSV, REB, TEV], 'twin' [Ph]. The phrase 'called Didymus/Didymos' [Gdt, NICNT2; KJV, NASB, NCV, NET, NIV] is also translated 'called the Twin' [HTC, NTC, WBC; NRSV, REB, TEV], "Didymus" meaning 'Twin'" [**LN**], 'nicknamed the Twin' [NLT, similarly CEV], 'known as the Twin/twin' [NJB, Ph], 'this name means "Twin"' [AB]. This noun denotes the Greek name of the apostle Thomas [BAGD, LN]. The Greek word 'Didymus' means 'Twin' [Bar, BECNT, Car, Gdt, Lns, NICNT1, NTC, TH, TRT].

d. συμμαθητής (LN **36.42**) (BAGD p. 778): 'fellow disciple' [BAGD, **LN**; all translations except NTC; NCV, NIV, NJB], 'other disciples' [NJB], 'the rest of the disciples' [NIV], 'the disciples' [NTC], 'fellow pupil' [BAGD], 'other followers' [NCV]. This noun denotes a person who, along with someone else, is a disciple or follower [LN].

QUESTION—Did the disciples call Thomas, 'Didymus', or 'Twin'?

1. They called him 'Didymus' [Car, Gdt, ICC, Lns, My, NICNT2; KJV, NASB, NCV, NET, NIV]. Didymus was his Greek name and was not a mere translation of the Hebrew name 'Thomas' [Lns]. He undoubtedly was called Didymus in the churches of Asia Minor [Gdt]. If John had meant merely to translate Thomas, he probably would have used the verb ἑρμηνεύω 'to interpret, to translate' instead of λέγω 'to be called' [ICC].

2. They called him 'Twin' [AB, Bar, BAGD, EGT, HTC, NTC, WBC; CEV, NJB, NLT, NRSV, Ph, REB, TEV]: 'this name means "Twin"' [AB]. In all of the lists of the Twelve, he is known as Thomas, never Didymus. John always explains his name (20:24; 21:2) [AB].

QUESTION—Does the conjunction καί 'also', modify 'go' or 'we'?

1. It modifies 'go' [all translations except CEV, Ph which left this word implicit]: 'Let us *also* go' [KJV].

2. It modifies 'we' [Lns]: 'Let us go, that we, *too* may die with him' [Lns]. 'We too' is emphatic in the Greek sentence [Lns].

QUESTION—To whom does the pronoun αὐτοῦ 'him' refer in the phrase μετ' αὐτοῦ 'with him'?

1. It refers to Jesus [Bar, EGT, Gdt, ICC, My, NICNT1, NTC, TH, WBC]. It may be important to make this referent explicit as TEV has done [TH]: 'Let us all go along with the Teacher, so that we may die with him!' [TEV]. Thomas's comment refers back to verse 8 where the disciples remind Jesus that the Jews in Judea were seeking to kill him [Bar].

2. It refers to Lazarus [Lns, NICNT2]. Looking at the pronominal references to the pronoun 'him' in these verses suggests that Lazarus is the referent. In verse 15 Jesus says, 'Let us go to *him* (Lazarus)'. In this verse Thomas says, 'Let us go also so that we may die with *him* (Lazarus)'. Then in verse 17 the words 'Jesus found *him* (Lazarus) having been already four days in the tomb'. This being the case, it is unlikely that the middle pronoun would abruptly refer to Jesus [NICNT2].

DISCOURSE UNIT—11:17–54 [NICNT2]. The topic is the raising of Lazarus and its consequences.

DISCOURSE UNIT—11:17–44 [CEV]. The topic is Jesus brings Lazarus to life [CEV].

DISCOURSE UNIT—11:17–37 [BECNT, NTC; NIV, NET]. The topic is Jesus arrives at Bethany [NTC], Jesus comforts Martha and Mary [BECNT; NIV, NET].

DISCOURSE UNIT—11:17–33 [AB]. The topic is Jesus arrives at Bethany.

DISCOURSE UNIT—11:17–27 [Car, HTC, ICC, IVP, Kn, NICNT1, Rd, WBC; NCV, NRSV, TEV]. The topic is Jesus the resurrection and the life [Car, WBC; NRSV, TEV], Jesus meets with Martha [HTC, ICC, IVP, Kn, NICNT1, Rd], Jesus in Bethany [NCV].

11:17 So Jesus having-come[a] found[b] him having-been already four days in the tomb.[c]

LEXICON—a. aorist act. participle of ἔρχομαι (LN 15.81): 'to come' [LN]. The clause 'Jesus having come' is translated 'when Jesus came' [HTC, NTC; KJV, NASB], 'when Jesus had come' [NICNT2], 'when Jesus arrived' [AB, WBC; NCV, NET, NRSV, Ph, TEV], 'Jesus on his arrival' [Gdt; similarly NJB, NIV, REB], 'when Jesus got-to/arrived-at (Bethany)' [CEV, NLT]. This verb means to move toward or up to the reference point of the viewpoint character or event [LN]. The place to which Jesus came was Bethany [My].

b. aorist act. indic. of εὑρίσκω (LN 27.1): 'to find' [all translations except NCV, NLT], 'to learn' [LN; NCV], 'to be told' [NLT], 'to find out, to discover' [LN]. This verb means to learn something previously not known, frequently involving an element of surprise [LN]. It probably indicates that he had been informed [Gdt, TRT], had learned [EGT, HTC, TH], or had inquired about Lazarus [NTC, TRT].

c. μνημεῖον (LN 7.75) (BAGD 7. p. 524): 'tomb' [BAGD, LN; all translations except KJV, Ph], 'grave' [BAGD, LN; KJV, Ph]. This noun is also translated as a verb: '(Lazarus) had been buried (four days before)' [TEV]. This noun denotes a construction for the burial of the dead [LN]. This would be a kind of cave so it may be important to not translate as though he had been buried in a grave or under the ground [TH, TRT].

QUESTION—What was the significance of the information that Lazarus had been in the tomb for four days?

There was a belief among Jewish rabbis that the soul stayed near the body for three days, but after that there was no hope of resuscitation [AB, BECNT, Rd, TH]. Tradition held that the soul hovers near the body for three days, intending to reenter it, but when it sees that the facial features have become disfigured, it departs [IVP, NICNT2, similarly Car, NICNT1, NTC, WBC]. The fact that Lazarus had been four days in the tomb stresses the magnitude of the miracle [NTC, TRT]. It shows the certainty of his being genuinely dead [AB, BECNT, HTC, WBC].

11:18 **Now Bethany was near Jerusalem about fifteen stadia**[a] **away.**[b] **11:19 And many of the Jews had come to Martha and Mary so-that they-might-comfort**[c] **them about (their) brother.**

LEXICON—a. στάδιος (LN 81.27) (BAGD 1. p. 764): 'stade' [BAGD, LN]. This noun denotes a measure of distance of about 600 feet or 185 meters [BAGD, LN], but is normally translated using familiar measurements of distance [LN]. A 'stade' was a Roman measurement equal to a little more than 600 feet. So 15 stadia would be a little less than two miles [Car, ICC, NICNT1, NICNT2, TH, TRT] or about three kilometers [TH, TRT]. 15 stadia would be about 1.75 miles [AB, BECNT, Car, TRT]. A stadium was equal to one-eighth of a mile [HTC]. It would be a walk of about forty minutes [Gdt]. See next item for version evidence.

b. ἀπό (LN **84.3**) (BAGD III. p. 87): 'away' [BAGD, **LN**], 'away from' [BAGD, LN], 'from' [LN]. The phrase 'about fifteen stadia away' is translated 'about fifteen stadia distant' [WBC], 'some fifteen stadia away' [NICNT2], 'about fifteen furlongs off' [KJV], 'at the distance of about fifteen furlongs' [Gdt], 'some two miles away' [NRSV], 'rather less than two miles away' [Ph], 'about two miles off' [HTC, NTC; NASB], 'about/less-than/just-under two miles from (Jerusalem)' [CEV, NCV, NET, NIV, NJB, REB, TEV], 'not far from (Jerusalem) just under two miles' [AB], 'only a few miles down the road from (Jerusalem)' [NLT]. This genitive preposition indicates extension from or away from a source [LN].

c. aorist mid. (deponent = act.) subj. of παραμυθέομαι (LN 25.153) (BAGD p. 620): 'to comfort' [BAGD, LN, NICNT2; CEV, KJV, NCV, NIV, NJB, TEV], 'to console' [BAGD, Gdt, HTC, LN, NTC, WBC; NASB, NET, NLT, NRSV], 'to condole' [REB], 'to offer sympathy to' [AB; Ph], 'to encourage' [BAGD, LN], 'to cheer up' [BAGD]. This verb means to cause someone to become consoled [BAGD, LN], especially in connection with death or other tragic events [BAGD]. An equivalent expression might be 'to speak helpful words to' [TH].

QUESTION—What is the purpose of including the close distance of Bethany to Jerusalem?

It probably explains the presence of so many Jews who came to express their sympathy to Mary and Martha [Bar, BECNT, EGT, NICNT1, NICNT2, NTC, Rd, TH]. It suggests that these Jews were from Jerusalem [WBC]. John includes the note about so many Jews to emphasize the number who would be the witnesses to the miracle [AB]. It may highlight the risk that Jesus took in coming to Judea [Car, BECNT, Kn]. It heightens the drama. Judea was a place of hostility, the very heart of the opposition to Jesus [IVP].

QUESTION—Are these Jews hostile or friendly to Jesus?
1. They are probably friendly [Bar, BECNT, Car, ICC, Rd]. These Jews are sincere in their sympathy. John uses the term 'Jew' in a historical as well as a theological sense [Bar].
2. They are probably hostile [Lns, My, NICNT1]. Perhaps these Jews, although sympathetic with Mary and Martha, were hostile to Jesus [NICNT1].
3. They are a mixed group, some hostile, some friendly [Gdt, HTC, TH]. They are Jews from the province of Judea some of whom opposed Jesus and some of whom accepted him [TH]. It should not be assumed that because Mary and Martha were disciples, that therefore those who came to express their sympathy were all friendly to the Lord [HTC]. The phrase 'the Jews' maintains an unfavorable sense throughout this Gospel. So these would be mostly hostile to Jesus [Gdt].

QUESTION—What was the custom of mourning among the Jews?
The burial would occur on the day of death because of the warm climate and lack of embalming. Mourning then would follow the burial and continue for 30 days [AB, similarly BECNT]. Judaism required burial on the day of death followed by six days of mourning in which the bereaved family would stay home and friends would come to offer sympathy and food [Kn].

11:20 So when Martha heard that Jesus comes she-went-to-meet^a him. But Mary was-sitting^b in the house.

LEXICON—a. aorist act. indic. of ὑπαντάω (LN 15.78) (BAGD p. 837): 'to go to meet' [AB, BAGD, WBC; NASB, NCV, NJB, NLT, REB], 'to go and meet' [HTC, NTC; KJV, NRSV], 'to go out and meet' [Ph], 'to go out to meet' [Gdt; CEV, NET, NIV, TEV], 'to meet' [LN, NICNT2], 'to come to meet' [BAGD], 'to draw near, to meet up with' [LN]. This verb means to come near to and to meet, either in a friendly or hostile sense [LN].

b. imperf. mid. (deponent = act.) indic. of καθέζομαι (LN 17.12) (BAGD): 'to sit' [BAGD, LN], 'to sit down, to be seated' [LN]. The clause 'Mary was sitting in the house' [NICNT2; NET] is also translated 'Mary continued to sit in the house' [NTC, WBC], 'Mary sat [still] in the house' [KJV], 'Mary (still) sat in the house' [Gdt, HTC], 'Mary remained sitting in the house' [NJB], '(left) Mary sitting at home' [REB], 'Mary sat quietly at home' [AB], 'Mary stayed in/at the house' [CEV, NASB, NLT, Ph, TEV], 'Mary stayed (at) home' [NCV, NIV, NRSV]. This verb means to be in a seated position or to take such a position [LN]. Sitting was the usual position in which a person in mourning received the condolences of friends [BECNT, My, NICNT1, TH, TRT, WBC].

QUESTION—What is the significance of the present tense Ἰησοῦς ἔρχεται 'Jesus comes'?
It probably indicates that this was the exact message that Martha heard, 'Jesus is coming' [ICC, Lns].

QUESTION—Why did Mary stay home?
> She probably had not yet been told that Jesus had come (verse 29) [AB, EGT, ICC, NICNT2, Rd, TH, TRT]. Martha was first to hear of Jesus' arrival and ran to him, not thinking to tell Mary [Gdt]. It may be that a messenger from Jesus came and only told Martha of his coming and she slipped out without informing Mary [Lns].

11:21 Then Martha said to Jesus, "Lord, if you-were here my brother would not have-died. 11:22 But even now I-know that whatever you-should-ask God God will give you."

TEXT—Some manuscripts omit κύριε 'Lord'. GNT includes 'Lord' with an A rating, indicating that the text is certain.

QUESTION—How should a contrary to fact sentence be translated?
> It may be necessary in some languages to translate 'You should have been here Lord, then my brother would not have died'. In others it may be necessary to be more explicit and translate 'If you were here, Lord (but you were not), my brother would not have died (but he did)' [TH].

QUESTION—What do Martha's words to Jesus in verse 21 indicate?
> They express Martha's heartfelt regret that Jesus had not been there [EGT, Gdt, Lns, NICNT1, TH]. They were an expression of poignant grief [Car, EGT, Lns, My, NTC, WBC], or disappointment at Jesus' delay [BECNT, Rd]. In view of verse 22, her words were a tribute to Jesus' love and power to heal [NICNT2]. Her words are an expression of faith that Jesus would have healed her brother, had he been present [BECNT, Bar, Car, Kn, NICNT1, TH].

QUESTION—What is implied in the cryptic words καὶ νῦν 'even now'?
> The meaning is, 'even now that Lazarus is dead and buried...' [EGT, Bar, Lns, My].

QUESTION—Is Martha asking Jesus to raise Lazarus from the dead?
> 1. Martha's words that God would give Jesus whatever he asked, imply that she is requesting him to raise her brother from the dead [Bar, EGT, Kn, Lns, My, NTC, TH]. Although verses 24 and 39 seem to indicate that Martha had abandoned hope in resurrection, still the messenger had returned from Jesus and had reported Jesus' words, 'This sickness is not unto death'. So in her mind, the raising of Lazarus is certainly included in the words 'whatever you ask' [NTC].
> 2. It is unlikely that she is asking this in view of her statement in verse 24 where she interprets Jesus' words that her brother would rise again only in terms of the 'last day', and of verse 39 where she objects to having Lazarus's tomb opened [TRT, similarly HTC, NICNT1, WBC].

QUESTION—What did Mary indicate by her statement, 'I know that whatever you ask God God will give you'?
> It may be important to translate the words 'God *will give you*' as 'God *will do for you*' in order to avoid the impression that Jesus was not asking for an object [TRT; CEV]: 'I know that God will do anything you ask' [CEV].

11:23 Jesus says to-her, "Your brother will-rise-again.ᵃ" **11:24** Martha says to-him, "I-know that he-will-rise-again in the resurrectionᵇ on the last day.ᶜ"

LEXICON—a. fut. mid. indic. of ἀνίσταμαι (LN 23.93) (BAGD 2.a. p. 70): 'to rise again' [AB, Gdt, HTC, NTC; KJV, NASB, NIV, NJB, NLT, NRSV, Ph, REB], 'to rise' [BAGD; NICNT2], 'to rise to life' [WBC; TEV], 'to rise and live again' [NCV], 'to live again' [LN; CEV], 'to come back to life (again)' [LN; NET], 'to be resurrected' [LN], 'to stand up, to get up' [BAGD]. This verb means to come back to life after having once died [LN]. It is used literally to mean to rise from a sitting or lying down position and means 'to rise to speak' and is especially used often of the dead [BAGD].
- b. ἀνάστασις (LN 23.93) (BAGD 2.a. p. 60): 'resurrection' [BAGD, LN; all translations except CEV, NLT, TEV], not explicit [TEV]. This noun is also translated as a clause: 'when all the dead are raised' [CEV], 'when everyone else rises' [NLT]. This noun denotes the state of having come back to life after having once died [LN]. Martha assumes that Jesus is referring to the Jewish belief in the resurrection that was to occur on the last day when all of God's people will rise again [TH].
- c. ἡμέρα (BAGD 3.b.β. p. 347): 'day' [BAGD]. The phrase 'on the last day' is translated 'on/at the last day' [all translations]. It indicates the day of God's final judgment and refers to the last day of this age [BAGD]. Some languages may also require a reference to some event as in 'the last day of the world' or 'of the age' [TH, TRT], or 'of time' [TRT].

11:25 Jesus said to her, "I am the resurrection and the life.ᵃ The (one) believing in me will-live even-if he-should-die. **11:26** And every one living and believing in me will- neverᵇ -die forever.ᶜ Do-you(sg)-believe this?"

TEXT—Some manuscripts omit the words καὶ ἡ ζωή 'and the life'. GNT includes 'and the life' with an A rating, indicating that the text is certain. NJB omits this phrase and AB and WBC place it in parentheses or brackets.
LEXICON—a. ζωή (BAGD 2.a.b. p. 340): 'life' [BAGD; all translations except NICNT2; NJB], 'Life' [NICNT2], not explicit [NJB]. The statement 'I am the resurrection and the life' is translated 'I am the one who raises the dead to life!' [CEV]. This noun denotes the supernatural life belonging to God and Christ, that the believers will receive in the future but which they also enjoy here and now [BAGD].
- b. οὐ μή (LN 69.5) (BAGD D.1.a. p. 517): 'never' [BAGD], 'certainly not' [BAGD, LN], 'by no means' [LN]. This phrase is a marker of emphatic negation [LN]. In combination with οὐ, μή has the effect of strengthening the negation. It is the most decisive way of negating something in the future [BAGD]. See the following item for version renderings.
- c. εἰς τὸν αἰῶνα (LN 67.95): 'forever' [LN], 'always, forever and ever, eternally' [LN]. The phrase 'will never die forever' is translated 'shall/will never die' [Gdt, HTC; KJV, NASB, NCV, NET, NIV, NJB,

NRSV, REB, TEV], 'will/shall never never die' [WBC; NTC], 'will never ever die' [NICNT2; NLT], 'shall/will never die at all' [AB; Ph], 'will never really die' [CEV]. This phrase indicates unlimited duration of time, with particular focus on the future [LN].

QUESTION—What word is emphasized in this verse?

The pronoun Ἐγώ 'I' is emphasized [HTC, My; Ph]: 'I, and no other than I' [My] 'I myself' [Ph]. The double negative is emphatic [BAGD, LN, Lns, NICNT1]: '*in no way* shall he die forever' [Lns].

QUESTION—What is meant by the phrase 'I am the resurrection'?

Jesus meant that he is the one who raises people from the dead [My, TH, TRT; CEV]. Jesus is the resurrection in the sense that whoever believes in *him* will receive eternal life even though he should die [AB]. Jesus was telling Martha that resurrection and life were not merely abstract events, but a person—himself [Car, CH, EGT, ICC, IVP, Lns, My]. Jesus is the source of resurrection for people [Bar, ICC, NTC], and the agent [ICC]. Jesus makes resurrection possible for people [BECNT]. The consolation that Jesus offered Martha was that her brother was alive even now because he had touched the eternal life of God when he believed in Jesus. Thus his true life was never really extinguished. In this sense he had already experienced the resurrection [ICC].

QUESTION—What is meant by the phrase 'I am the life'?

It means that Jesus is the one who gives people life [BECNT, HTC, IVP, Rd, TH, TRT, WBC]. He is the power that makes them live [My]. Jesus gives life by becoming life in the one believing [IVP]. Jesus is the source of eternal life for people [Bar, NTC]. Jesus offers life to men, so that the believer receives eternal life through Jesus and will never die a spiritual death [AB]. This life is eternal life [AB, Car, CH, HTC, My, NICNT1, NTC, TH, WBC].

QUESTION—What kind of death is indicated by the phrase 'even if he should die'?

It refers to physical, not spiritual death [AB, Gdt, HTC, ICC, Lns, My, NICNT1, NTC, Rd, TH, TRT].

QUESTION—Does the phrase 'everyone living' refer to physical or spiritual life?

1. It refers to spiritual life [AB, Car, EGT, ICC, Lns, NTC, TH, TRT, WBC]. Since the sense of 'live' in verse 25 in the words 'the one believing in me will live even if he should die' is spiritual, it is best to take the words 'everyone living' in verse 26 as referring to the same sense of spiritual living [ICC]. The fact that only one article in the Greek governs both participles 'living' and 'believing', indicates that both are on the same level and refer to spiritual life [AB].
2. It refers to physical life [Gdt, HTC, My, Rd]. 'Everyone living' applies to the two sisters and all who are physically alive [Gdt]. A person is alive naturally but through believing comes to have eternal life [HTC]. If the word 'living' is taken to mean the same as the preceding phrase 'will live'

of verse 25 referring to spiritual life, then here in this verse it is redundant to again repeat 'and believing'. Rather here 'lives' refers to being alive physically and then believing [Rd].

QUESTION—What figure of speech is the phrase 'will never die forever'?

It is the figure of *litotes* in which two negatives make a positive. So 'will never die forever' means 'shall most certainly live forever' [NTC].

11:27 She-says to-him, "Yes Lord, I have-believed that you(sg) are the Christ[a] the Son of-God the (one) coming into the world."

LEXICON—a. Χριστός (LN 53.82) (BAGD 1. p. 887): 'Christ' [BAGD, Gdt, HTC, LN, NICNT2, NTC, WBC; CEV, KJV, NASB, NCV, NET, NIV, NJB], 'Messiah' [AB, BAGD, LN; NLT, NRSV, REB, TEV], 'Anointed One' [BAGD]. This noun literally means 'one who has been anointed' and serves as a title for Jesus as the Messiah in the NT. In a number of languages Χριστός (or Μεσσίας) as a reference to the Messiah occurs in a transliterated form based either on Χριστός in Greek or on Messiah in Hebrew. However, in some languages an attempt is made to represent the significance of the terms Χριστός and Μεσσίας by translating 'God's appointed one' or 'God's specially chosen one' or 'the expected one,' in the sense of one to whom everyone was looking for help and deliverance. [LN].

QUESTION—What did Martha mean by her reply, 'Yes Lord'?

She meant that she agreed with what Jesus had just said that he was the resurrection and the life as well as the two propositions that followed it [Bar, EGT, ICC, Lns, My, NICNT1, NTC].

QUESTION—What words are emphasized in this verse?

The pronoun ἐγώ 'I' is emphatic [BECNT, ICC, Lns, NICNT1, NICNT2, NTC]: *I myself* have believed. No matter that others had rejected Jesus, Martha herself had believed [Lns, NICNT1, NTC]. The pronouns ἐγώ 'I' and σύ 'you(sg)' are emphatic [NICNT2]: *I myself* believe that *you yourself* are the Christ.

QUESTION—What is indicated by the perfect tense πεπίστευκα 'I have believed'?

It indicates that she had come to believe and that it was a settled conviction in her thinking [BECNT]. She began to believe and continued to do so [CH, NICNT1, Rd, TH]. It may indicate emphasis 'I do believe' [TH; TEV, Ph].

QUESTION—What sense does the phrase 'Son of God' add to Martha's description?

It lifts the Jewish idea of Messiahship up and surpasses all their expectations [HTC].

QUESTION—What is indicated by the present tense participle ἐρχόμενος, '(the one) coming (into the world)'?

Instead of referring to the present tense, it refers to an action that was anticipated, 'the one who was to come into the world' [AB, Gdt, TH: CEV, NIV, NJB, Ph, REB, TEV]: 'the one we hoped would come into the world'

[CEV]. This may be difficult to translate in some languages so it may be necessary to be more explicit by translating 'whom God promised would come into the world' or 'of whom God said, He will come into the world' [TH].

QUESTION—To whom does the phrase 'the one coming into the world' refer?

This is a reference to the prophet to whom Moses referred when he said in Deuteronomy 18:15 'The Lord your God will raise up for you a prophet like me from among your own brothers. You must listen to him' [AB, Bar, Car, ICC, Lns, NICNT1]. It refers to the words of Moses and the prophets who had prophesied about his coming (see John 1:45) [CH]. This phrase echoes the Messianic claim of Psalm 118:26 'Blessed is he who comes in the name of the LORD' [BECNT, WBC].

DISCOURSE UNIT—11:28–44 [Rd, WBC]. The topic is Jesus' anger in the face of unbelief [WBC], Jesus raises Lazarus [Rd].

DISCOURSE UNIT—11:28–37 [Car, Kn; NCV, NRSV, TEV]. The topic is Jesus outraged and grief-stricken [Car], Jesus cries [NCV, NRSV, TEV], mourning with Mary [Kn].

DISCOURSE UNIT—11:28–32 [AB, HTC, ICC, IVP, NICNT1]. The topic is Jesus arrives at Bethany [AB], Jesus meets with Mary [HTC, ICC, IVP, NICNT1].

11:28 And having-said this she-left and called[a] Mary her sister privately[b] saying, "The Teacher is-here and calls you." **11:29** When she heard (it) she-got-up quickly and was-coming[c] to him.

- LEXICON—a. aorist act. indic. of φωνέω (LN 33.307) (BAGD 2.b. p. 870): 'to call' [BAGD, LN; all translations except Gdt, NICNT2; CEV, NCV], 'to summon' [BAGD, LN, NICNT2], 'to call to oneself' [Gdt], 'to talk to' [NCV], not explicit [CEV]. This verb means to communicate directly or indirectly with someone who is presumably at a distance, in order to tell such a person to come [LN].
- b. λάθρα (LN 28.71) (BAGD 1. p. 462): 'privately' [LN, NICNT2, WBC; CEV, NET, NRSV, TEV], 'secretly' [Gdt, BAGD, LN; KJV, NASB], 'quietly' [HTC, NTC], 'alone' [NCV], 'aside' [NIV, NLT], 'in secret, in private' [LN]. This adverb is also translated as a phrase: 'in a low voice' [NJB], as a participle: 'whispering' [Ph], and as a clause: 'she whispered' [AB], 'taking her aside' [REB]. It describes an event as not being able to be known by the public but known by some in-group or by those immediately involved [LN]. Translated literally 'to call' may imply using a loud voice. This cannot be done privately. It may be better to translate something like 'spoke to her so that others would not hear' [TH].
- c. imperf. mid. (deponent = act.) indic. of ἔρχομαι (LN 15.81): 'to come' [LN, Gdt, NICNT2, NTC; KJV, NASB], 'to go' [HTC; NCV, NET, NIV, NCV, NLT, NRSV, Ph, REB], 'to go out' [CEV]. The clause 'she got up quickly and was coming to him' is translated 'she got up and hurried out

to meet him' [TEV], 'she got up quickly and started out toward him' [AB], 'she got up quickly and made her way to him' [WBC]. This verb means to move toward or up to the reference point of the viewpoint character or event [LN].

QUESTION—Does λάθρα 'secretly' modify the verb 'to call', or the verb 'to say'?

1. It modifies 'to call' [Lns, NTC, Rd; KJV, NIV, NLT, TEV]: 'called her sister Mary aside' [NIV], 'called her sister Mary privately' [TEV]. It is best to construe 'privately' with the main verb 'called' rather than with the incidental participle 'saying' [Lns].
2. It modifies the verb 'to say' [AB, HTC, NICNT2, WBC; CEV, NASB, NET, NJB, NRSV, Ph, REB]: 'saying privately' [NET].
3. The two verbs complement each other so it makes little difference whether the adverb is construed with one verb or the other [NICNT1].

QUESTION—Why did Martha communicate to Mary privately?

Both Jesus and the sisters wanted to maintain a little privacy in the middle of such a public affair [Car]. It was to get her away from the Jews, not merely to avoid attracting attention [HTC, NICNT2]. It was probably to conceal from the Jews there, the fact that Jesus was present [Bar]. She did not want to cause a scene [Rd]. She wanted to protect Jesus from publicity [Kn]. She wanted to avoid having the Jews follow Mary to Jesus [CH, My], and disturb what comfort she already had received [My]. Martha wanted Mary to meet with Jesus alone, without any company [EGT, ICC].

QUESTION—Where was Jesus?

Translating the words 'The Teacher is here' literally may indicate that Jesus was present in the same room. It may be better in some languages to simply say he was nearby [TH].

QUESTION—Does the adverb 'quickly' modify 'get up' or 'was coming'?

1. It modifies how she got up [AB, Gdt, HTC, NICNT2, NTC, TH, TRT, WBC; KJV, NASB, NCV, NET, NIV, NJB, NRSV, Ph]: she got up quickly.
2. It modifies how she was coming [TEV]: 'she got up and hurried out to meet him' [TEV].
3. Both actions were done quickly [CEV, NLT, REB]: 'So Mary immediately went to him' [CEV].

QUESTION—What is indicated by the imperfect tense 'was coming to him'?

It may indicate that the action is inchoative or incipient [AB, NICNT1]: 'she got up quickly and *started out* toward him' [AB]. It maintains the sense of haste and raises the reader's expectation level [NICNT2]. The tense enables the reader to picture the action [NTC]. It indicates that more will yet be said about her going [Lns].

11:30 Now Jesus had- not-yet -come into the village, but was still in the place where Martha met him. **11:31** So the Jews the (ones) being with her in the house and comforting[a] her, having-seen that Mary got-up quickly[b] and went-out, followed her having-supposed[c] that she-is-going to the tomb that she-might-weep[d] there.

TEXT—Instead of δόξαντες 'having supposed', some manuscripts read δοξάζοντες 'glorifying', and others read λέγοντες 'saying'. GNT reads 'having supposed' with a B rating, indicating that the text is almost certain. KJV reads 'saying'.

LEXICON—a. pres. mid. (deponent = act.) participle of παραμυθέομαι (LN 25.153) (BAGD p. 620): 'to comfort' [BAGD, Gdt, **LN**, NICNT2; CEV, KJV, NCV, NIV, NJB, TEV], 'to console' [AB, BAGD, HTC, LN, WBC; NASB, NET, NLT, NRSV, NTC], 'to condole with' [Ph, REB], 'to cheer up' [BAGD], 'to encourage' [BAGD, LN]. This verb means to cause someone to become consoled [LN].

b. ταχέως (LN 67.110) (BAGD 1.a. p. 806): 'quickly' [AB, BAGD, HTC, LN, NICNT2, WBC; CEV, NASB, NCV, NET, NIV, NJB, NRSV, Ph], 'hastily' [KJV, NLT], 'hurriedly' [LN, NTC], 'suddenly' [Gdt], 'swiftly, speedily' [LN], 'at once, without delay' [BAGD]. This adverb is also translated as a verb: '(the Jews...saw her) hurry out' [REB, similarly TEV]. This adverb describes an action as being of a very short extent of time [LN].

c. aorist act. participle of δοκέω (LN 31.29) (BAGD 1.d. p. 202): 'to suppose' [BAGD, Gdt, HTC, LN, NTC, WBC; NASB, NIV], 'to think' [AB, BAGD, LN, NICNT2; CEV, NCV, NET, NJB, NRSV], 'to assume' [LN; NLT, REB], 'to imagine' [LN; Ph], 'to believe' [BAGD, LN], 'to presume' [LN], 'to consider' [BAGD]. This verb means to regard something as presumably true, but without particular certainty [LN].

d. aorist act. subj. of κλαίω (LN 25.138) (BAGD 1. p. 433): 'to weep' [BAGD, LN; all translations except NICNT2; CEV, NCV, NIV], 'to cry' [BAGD, NICNT2; CEV, NCV], 'to mourn' [NIV], 'to wail, to lament' [LN]. This verb means to weep or wail [AB, LN], with emphasis on the noise accompanying the weeping [LN]. It does not indicate quiet weeping, but the unrestrained wailing of Easterners [ICC]. It indicates private mourning, lamentation, and weeping [HTC].

11:32 So when Mary came (to) where Jesus was (and) seeing him she-fell[a] at his feet saying to-him, "Lord if you-were here my brother would not have-died."

LEXICON—a. aorist act. indic. of πίπτω (LN 17.22) (BAGD 1.b.α. p. 659): 'to fall, to fall down' [BAGD], 'to prostrate oneself before, to fall down before' [LN]. The phrase 'she fell (down) at his feet' [AB, HTC, NICNT2, NTC, WBC; KJV, NASB, NCV, NET, NIV, NLT, Ph, REB, TEV] is also translated 'she knelt at his feet' [CEV, NRSV], 'she threw herself at his feet' [NJB]. This verb means to prostrate oneself before someone, implying entreaty [LN]. It means to throw oneself to the ground before high-ranking persons or divine beings as a sign of devotion, especially when one approaches with a petition [BAGD].

QUESTION—What did Mary's falling at Jesus' feet indicate?
It probably showed her respect/reverence for him [HTC, NICNT1, Rd, TRT], and/or her grief about her brother's death [EGT, HTC, TRT].

DISCOURSE UNIT—11:33–44 [IVP, NICNT1]. The topic is Jesus raises Lazarus.

DISCOURSE UNIT—11:33–41a [HTC]. The topic is visit to the tomb.

DISCOURSE UNIT—11:33–38 [ICC]. The topic is Jesus goes to the tomb.

DISCOURSE UNIT—11:34–44 [AB]. The topic is the raising of Lazarus.

11:33 So when Jesus saw her weeping[a] and the Jews (who had) come-with her weeping, he-was-deeply-moved[b] in-the spirit and troubled[c] himself **11:34** and said, "Where have-you-put him?" They-say to-him, "Lord, come and see."

LEXICON—a. pres. act. participle of κλαίω (LN 25.138) (BAGD 1. p. 433): 'to weep' [BAGD, LN; all translations except NICNT2; CEV, NCV, NIV], 'to cry' [BAGD, NICNT2; CEV, NCV], 'to wail, to lament' [LN]. This verb is also translated as a noun: '(At the sight of her) tears' [NJB]. This verb means to weep or wail [AB, LN], with emphasis upon the noise accompanying the weeping [LN]. It indicates loud weeping and wailing [NICNT1]. The repeated verb '(her) weeping…(the Jews…)weeping' serves to emphasize this action [My].

b. aorist mid. (deponent = act.) indic. of ἐμβριμάομαι (LN **25.56**) (BAGD p. 254): 'to be deeply moved' [BAGD], 'to feel strongly, to be indignant' [LN]. The clause 'he was deeply moved in the spirit' [NTC, similarly HTC; NIV] is also translated 'he was intensely moved in spirit' [NET], 'he was greatly disturbed in spirit' [NRSV], 'he shuddered in his spirit' [Gdt], 'he groaned in the spirit' [KJV], 'he was deeply moved' [Ph], 'he was upset' [NCV], 'Jesus was greatly distressed' [NJB], 'his heart was touched' [TEV], '(he was) moved with deepest emotions' [AB], 'he was moved with indignation' [REB], 'a deep anger welled up within him' [NLT], 'he became very angry in spirit' [WBC], 'Jesus…got angry in the spirit' [NICNT2]. The clause 'he was deeply moved in the spirit and troubled himself' is translated 'he was terribly upset' [CEV]. This verb means to have an intense, strong feeling of concern, often with the implication of indignation. It can either mean 'his feeling was intense' or 'he was indignant' [**LN**]. The middle voice might favor an active translation such as 'he bristled' in contrast to a passive one like 'he was deeply moved' [BECNT].

c. aorist act. indic. of ταράσσω (LN **25.244**) (BAGD 2. p. 805): 'to stir up' [BAGD, LN], 'to cause great mental distress' [LN], 'to disturb, to unsettle, to throw into confusion' [BAGD]. The words ἐτάραξεν ἑαυτὸν 'he troubled himself' is translated 'he was troubled' [BAGD, Gdt, HTC; KJV, NIV], 'he was deeply troubled' [NCV, NLT], 'he was agitated'

[BAGD, NTC], 'he was very agitated' [WBC], '(he was) greatly distressed' [**LN**; NET], '(he was) deeply distressed' [REB], '(he was) visibly distressed' [Ph], '(he was) deeply moved' [NRSV, TEV], 'with a profound sigh (he said)' [NJB], 'he shuddered' [AB], '(he) shook himself' [NICNT2]. This verb is used figuratively to mean to cause acute emotional distress or turbulence [LN]. This must refer to Jesus' intense concern and anger at the mourners' attitude and their misunderstanding of the nature of death and the Person of the Son [NICNT1].

QUESTION—What is indicated by the verb κλαίω 'to weep'?

Jesus saw a large group of people weeping and wailing and this aroused his anger. The verb κλαίω is a strong term for weeping and wailing and is typically used for lamentation on the day of burial. (See a similar scene at the bedside of Jairus' daughter Mark 5:38–39). It also contrasts with the word δακρύω 'to weep' in reference to Jesus in verse 35 [HTC].

QUESTION—What is meant by the phrase 'he was deeply moved in spirit'?

1. The verb denotes anger or indignation [AB, BECNT, Bar, Car, CH, Gdt, HTC, IVP, Lns, My, NTC, TH, NICNT2, Rd, WBC; NLT, REB]. Etymologically the verb means 'to snort like a horse' while in the LXX of Daniel 11:30 it means 'to be enraged' or 'to be greatly angry'. Here it cannot mean anything less than to be angry [Bar, HTC, NICNT2, TH]. Basically the verb seems to imply a silent expression of anger [AB]. It indicates a shudder of indignation [Gdt]. Although indignant with sin as the cause of this sorrow, he also sympathized with the grief of those around him [NTC]. When used about people, this verb implies anger, outrage or emotional indignation [Car].
2. The verb rather denotes a general deep emotion [EGT, ICC, NICNT1; probably also NET, NIV, NRSV, Ph, TEV]. John probably means that Jesus was deeply moved [NICNT1]. This verb is found in Matthew 9:30, Mark 1:43, and here. In all three it expresses intense emotion. But in Matthew and Mark where he sternly warned those he had healed not to tell others about their healing, the verb may just suggest the powerful emotion on his voice as he spoke. It is probably best to render it simply 'he groaned in spirit', where the groaning was the physical evidence of tremendous inward spiritual agitation and effort [ICC].

QUESTION—If the meaning of ἐμβριμάομαι is taken to mean 'he was angry', what was the cause of his anger?

It may have been because he found himself face to face with the realm of Satan which, in this instance, was represented by sickness and death [AB, BECNT, Car, CH, Gdt, IVP, Lns, Rd], and what it does to families and friends [CH]. Although the ostensible cause of Jesus anger is the sobbing of Mary and her friends, it goes deeper into the underlying cause of that sobbing, namely the sin and death that is causing such pain to the ones he loves [Lns]. Jesus was angry at sin as being the underlying cause of all suffering, grief, and sorrow but he also sympathized with the sorrow of those present [NTC]. His anger was perhaps owing to the unbelief of the mourners

[Car, CH, HTC, Kn, TH, WBC]. Jesus was the 'Resurrection and the Life' and was right there with them but still they were without hope. It was this that angered him [WBC]. Jesus had been able to speak with Martha privately but the presence of the Jews at this encounter with Mary invaded that privacy and may have caused Jesus' anger [NICNT2]. The Jews here are the hostile party and it is at their hypocritical mourning that Jesus is angry as though they felt the same sorrow that Mary displayed by her weeping [My]. The verb ἐμβριμάομαι is used elsewhere in the NT in Matthew 9:30 and Mark 1:43 where Jesus sternly warns those healed to not tell others what had happened. In both cases, it was the secret of his Messiahship that he was protecting. Similarly here Jesus perceives the grief of the sisters and of the Jews as almost forcing him to perform a miracle. This miracle will be impossible to hide and will precipitate his death and this arouses his anger [Bar].

QUESTION—Does the phrase ἐτάραξεν ἑαυτὸν 'he troubled himself' have an active or passive sense and what does it mean?

1. It has an active sense [AB, BECNT, Bar, ICC, Lns, My, NICNT2, TH; NJB]: 'he shook himself' [Lns, NICNT2], 'he shuddered' [AB, ICC], 'he agitated himself' [My], 'with a profound sigh (he said)' [NJB]. It literally means 'he troubled himself' and implies a deep kind of disturbance. The same verb occurs in 13:21 where Jesus is troubled in spirit over the thought of being betrayed by Judas. It may indicate the same emotion that came over Jesus in Gethsemane—emotional distress brought on by his approaching death and struggle with Satan [AB]. If this phrase is not merely a variation of the previous one, it shows that Jesus is troubled at the approaching climax of his ministry and troubles himself, thus revealing his mastery over himself and his circumstances/emotions [Bar, TH].
2. It has a passsive sense [BECNT, Gdt, HTC, LN, NICNT1, TH; KJV, NCV, NET, NIV, NLT, Ph, REB, TEV]: 'he was (deeply) troubled [Gdt, HTC; KJV, NCV, NIV, NLT], 'he was greatly/deeply/visibly distressed' [NET, Ph, REB], 'he was deeply moved' [NRSV, TEV], 'he became very agitated' WBC]. Although the verb is transitive with an object ('he troubled himself') it may be that it is a kind of substitute passive [TH]. The verb implies inner agitation and turmoil [BECNT]. It indicates a profound emotion. Rieu translates, 'he gave way to such distress of spirit as made his body tremble' [NICNT1].

QUESTION—To whom does Jesus direct the question 'Where have you put him', and who replies to him?

He must be speaking to the two sisters since the Jews with her had no responsibility for the burial [My, NICNT2]. It is the two sisters who reply to him [BECNT, ICC, My, NICNT1, NICNT2]. Several speak at once including the two sisters [Lns].

11:35 Jesus wept.[a] **11:36** So the Jews were-saying, "See[b] how he-loved[c] him.

LEXICON—a. aorist act. indic. of δακρύω (LN 25.137) (BAGD p. 170): 'to weep' [**LN**; all translations except NTC, WBC; CEV, NCV], 'to cry' [LN; CEV, NCV], 'to burst into tears' [BAGD, Bar, NICNT1, NTC, WBC]. This verb means to weep, with the clear implication of shedding tears [LN]. Some took the aorist tense of the verb to indicate ingressive or inchoative aspect 'to begin/start to weep/cry' [AB, Bar, HTC, NICNT1, NTC; CEV, NRSV]. This weeping contrasts with the verb κλαίω 'to weep' of verse 33 [BECNT, Gdt, ICC, IVP, My, NICNT1, NICNT2, NTC. TH]. It means the expression of a calm and gentle grief [Gdt]. Κλαίω denotes loud wailing, this is a more quiet expression of grief [BECNT, My, NICNT1, TH].

b. ἰδού (LN 91.13) (BAGD 1. p. 369): 'see' [AB, BAGD, HTC, NICNT2, NTC; CEV, NASB, NCV, NIV, NJB, NLT, NRSV, TEV], 'look' [LN, WBC; NET, Ph], 'behold' [Gdt, KJV], 'How dearly (he must have loved him!' [REB], 'listen, pay attention' [LN]. This particle functions as a prompter of attention, which serves also to emphasize the following statement [LN]. It points out something to which the speaker wishes to draw attention [BAGD].

c. imperf. act. indic. of φιλέω (LN 25.33) (BAGD 1.a. p. 859): 'to love' [BAGD, LN; all translations], 'to have affection for' [BAGD, LN], 'to like' [BAGD]. This verb means to have love or affection for someone or something based on association [LN].

QUESTION—Why did Jesus weep?
1. His tears were for the grief of the people affected by death [AB, BECNT, EGT, Gdt, HTC, IVP, Lns, Kn, My, NTC, Rd, WBC], not for Lazarus whom he will raise [BECNT, Car, IVP, WBC]. His sorrow is over the grief that both Lazarus and the sisters were facing at the separation they were experiencing [Gdt]. His sympathy arose out of his love for Lazarus and the sisters [NTC]. He is moved by the bleak inevitability of death [BECNT, HTC, WBC], and the chaos and confusion that it causes those who experience it [IVP, Rd, WBC]. Jesus wept with those who wept [Lns, My].
2. He wept because of the wrong attitude of the Jews [NICNT1]. Both when Jesus wept over Jerusalem (19:41) and here, his grief was over the misconception of the Jews, who here regard darkness and death as being in control of the situation [NICNT1].
3. He wept both out of sympathy for those facing death, and also over the unbelief of the Jews. Grief and outrage go together—grief over the sin and death facing humanity and anger over the unbelief of some of the onlookers [Bar, Car].

QUESTION—To whom were the Jews talking?
They were talking among themselves [TH, TRT].

11:37 But[a] some of them said, "Was- not[b] -able this (man) the (one) having-opened the eyes of-the blind (one) to-bring-(it)-about[c] that this (man) also[d] should- not -die?"

LEXICON—a. δέ (LN 89.124): 'but' [LN; all translations except CEV, KJV, Ph], 'though' [Ph], 'on the other hand' [LN], 'and' [KJV], not explicit [CEV]. This conjunction indicates contrast [LN].
- b. οὐκ (LN 69.11) (BAGD 2. p. 590): 'not' [BAGD]. This particle indicates that an affirmative reply is expected to a question [EGT, LN, TRT, WBC].
- c. aorist act. infin. of ποιέω (LN 13.9) (BAGD I.1.b.θ. p. 681): 'to bring (it) about' [BAGD, LN], 'to cause to be, to make to be, to result in, to bring upon' [LN], 'to make' [BAGD, LN]. The clause 'to bring it about that this man also should not die' are translated 'Could not this man/he…have caused that this man also should not have died?' [Gdt], 'Could not he…have caused that even this man should not have died?' [KJV], 'Could not this man…have made it so that this man would not die?' [NICNT2], 'Could not this man/he…have kept (also) this man from dying?' [NTC; NASB], 'Couldn't he also have done something to stop this man from dying?' [AB; similarly NET, REB], 'Could not he…have kept this man/Lazarus from dying?' [HTC; NIV, NLT, NRSV, Ph, TEV], 'Could he not have prevented this man's death?' [NJB], 'why couldn't he have-kept/keep Lazarus from dying?' [CEV, NCV], 'Surely he…was able to do something to prevent this man from dying?' [WBC]. This verb means to cause a state to be [LN]. It indicates actions that one undertakes or of events or states of being that one brings about [BAGD].
- d. καί (LN 89.93): 'also' [AB, Gdt, LN, NTC; NASB], 'even' [LN; KJV], 'and, and also, in addition' [LN], not explicit [NICNT2, NTC, WBC; CEV, NET, NIV, NJB, NLT, NRSV, Ph, REB, TEV]. This conjunction indicates an additive relation which is not coordinate [LN].

QUESTION—Are these Jews hostile or friendly?
1. They are hostile [Car, Gdt, HTC, My, WBC]. John identifies these Jews with those of verse 46 who report the healing of Lazarus to the Pharisees by the identical form of the phrase 'some of them' [Gdt]. The particle δέ 'but' indicates that these form a negative conclusion to the tears of Jesus [HTC]. They are critical of him [HTC, My, WBC]. At least these are a different group than those who remarked about Jesus' love in verse 36 [WBC].
2. They are friendly [Bar, Car, ICC, Lns, NICNT1]. They are not mocking [Car, NICNT1] although their question does express massive unbelief. Their faith is in its infancy and does not rest on who Jesus is, but on his miracles [Car]. There is no reason for doubting their sincerity [NICNT1]. They were thinking much like Martha and Mary [ICC, NICNT1].

QUESTION—What response is expected to this question and what does it express?

The particle οὐκ indicates that an affirmative reply is expected to the question [EGT, HTC, TRT, WBC]: 'Surely he…was able to do something to prevent this man from dying?' [WBC]. The question is rhetorical [TRT, WBC]. They are *puzzled* at the fact that even though Jesus loved Lazarus, yet he failed to be there and to heal him before he died [Car, IVP, Lns, NTC]. Their question expresses *criticism* [HTC, My, NTC, WBC]. Their question expresses *skepticism*, implying that Jesus possibly did not love Lazarus. If he had the power to prevent his death, he must have been unwilling to do so [NICNT2]. In their minds Jesus could have prevented the death of Lazarus but he didn't [HTC, WBC]. They imply that Jesus did not come sooner because he was unable to save Lazarus [My].

DISCOURSE UNIT—11:38–44 [BECNT, Car, Kn; NCV, NIV, NET, NRSV, TEV]. The topic is Jesus raises Lazarus [BECNT, Car; NCV, NIV, NET, NRSV, TEV], the miracle [Kn].

11:38 So[a] **Jesus comes to the tomb being-deeply-moved[b] again[c] in[d] himself. Now it-was (a) cave and (a) stone was-lying across it.**
LEXICON—a. οὖν (LN 89.50): 'so' [NICNT2, NTC; NASB], 'therefore' [Gdt, LN, WBC; KJV], 'with this' [AB], 'then' [HTC; NRSV], 'consequently, accordingly, so then' [LN], not explicit [CEV, NCV, NET, NIV, NJB, NLT, Ph, REB, TEV]. This conjunction indicates result, often implying the conclusion of a process of reasoning [LN].
  b. pres. mid. (deponent = act.) participle of ἐμβριμάομαι (LN 25.56) (BAGD p. 254): 'to be deeply moved' [BAGD]. The phrase 'being deeply again moved in himself' is translated 'again (being) deeply moved within (himself)' [NTC, NASB], 'again deeply moved' [HTC; similarly Ph, REB], 'once more deeply moved' [NIV, similarly TEV], 'again groaning in himself' [KJV], 'still terribly upset' [CEV], 'again feeling very upset' [NCV], 'again greatly disturbed' [NRSV], 'intensely moved again' [NET], '(With this) again arousing his emotions' [AB], 'sighing again' [NJB], 'shuddering in himself again' [Gdt], 'again angry within himself' [NICNT2], 'again in a state of anger within' [WBC], '(Jesus) was still angry' [NLT]. This verb means to have an intense, strong feeling of concern, often with the implication of indignation [LN].
  c. πάλιν (LN 67.55): 'again' [LN; all translations except CEV, NIV, NLT, TEV], 'once more' [NIV, TEV], 'still' [CEV, NLT]. This adverb indicates a subsequent point of time involving repetition [LN]. Here it has a sense more like 'still' given the present tense of the verb 'being deeply moved'. Jesus' anger probably had not subsided even in his grief [NICNT2].
  d. ἐν (LN 90.56) (BAGD I.5.b. p. 259): 'in' [Gdt; KJV], 'within' [NICNT2; NASB, NTC, WBC], 'in relation to, with respect to' [LN], 'to' [BAGD, LN], not explicit [all translations except Gdt, NICNT2, NTC, WBC; KJV, NASB]. This preposition indicates the experiencer of an event [LN]. It indicates a very close connection especially to describe certain mental processes, whereby their inward quality is to be emphasized. Here it means 'to himself', that is, in silence [BAGD]. The expression 'in himself' here and the phrase 'in spirit' in verse 33 mean about the same

thing [Bar, Lns, NICNT2, NTC, TH]. The phrase 'in himself' interprets the phrase 'in spirit' [Bar].

QUESTION—What is meant by the phrase 'he was deeply moved within himself'?

1. It denotes anger or indignation [AB, BECNT, Bar, Car, CH, Gdt, HTC, Lns, My, NICNT2, NTC, Rd, TH, WBC; NLT]. His anger was apparently the result of the remark of the Jews about his inability to have prevented the death of Lazarus [Gdt, HTC, My, NICNT2, WBC]. It is not the remark of the Jews that angers Jesus [Lns], it is the sight of the tomb, the evidence of death that angers him [BECNT, IVP, Lns, Rd]. It is the undeveloped faith of the Jews expressed in the previous verse that causes Jesus' anger [Bar].
2. It denotes rather a general deep emotion [ICC, NICNT1]. The emotion of being deeply moved is explained by his reaction to the cruelty of death which he had to conquer [NICNT1].

QUESTION—What was the form of the tomb?

1. It was a cave with the opening perpendicular to the ground and the stone lying against it [BECNT, Kn, NICNT1, NICNT2, NTC, TH, TRT]. The entrance would be either perpendicular to the ground or slanting back a bit and the actual cave would be hewn from the rock [NTC]. The weight of evidence favors this style of cave [TH]. Verse 44 favors this option where Lazarus comes out from the tomb [NICNT1, TRT].
2. It was probably a vertical shaft with the stone lying over the entrance [AB, HTC]. This would be a hole in the ground leading to an antechamber or outer room with a stone covering the entrance [HTC].

DISCOURSE UNIT—11:39–44 [ICC]. The topic is the raising of Lazarus.

11:39 Jesus says, "Take-away[a] the stone." Martha the sister of-the (one) having-died says to-him, "Lord, already he-smells[b] for it-is (the) fourth[c] (day)."

LEXICON—a. aorist act. imperative of αἴρω (LN 15.203) (BAGD 3. p. 24): 'to take away' [AB, BAGD, Gdt, HTC, LN, NTC; KJV, NET, NIV, NJB, NRSV, Ph, REB, TEV], 'to remove' [BAGD, LN, WBC; NASB], 'to roll away' [CEV], 'to roll aside' [NLT], 'to move away' [NCV], 'to lift' [NICNT2], '(to lift up and) carry away' [BAGD], 'to carry (away), to carry off' [LN]. This verb means to lift up and carry (away) [LN].

b. pres. act. indic. of ὄζω (LN **79.47**) (BAGD p. 555): 'to smell' [BAGD], 'to stink' [**LN**], 'to give off an odor' [BAGD], 'to have a bad smell' [LN]. The clause 'already he smells' is translated 'already it stinks' [NICNT2], 'already there is a stench' [NRSV], 'by now he will smell' [NJB], 'by this time/now he stinks' [Gdt, WBC; KJV], 'by this time the smell must be offensive' [BAGD], 'by now/this time there will/must be stench' [AB; NASB, REB], 'by this time the body will have a bad smell' [NET], 'by this time there is a bad odor' [NIV], 'by this time there will be/is an odor' [HTC, NTC], 'by this time he will be decaying' [Ph], 'there will be a bad

smell' [CEV, NCV, TEV], 'the smell will be terrible' [NLT]. This verb means to cause a foul-smelling odor [LN].
  c. τεταρταῖος (LN **67.181**) (BAGD p. 813): 'fourth' [BAGD, LN]. The clause 'it is the fourth day' [**LN**, WBC] is also translated '(he has been dead) (for) four days' [BAGD, Gdt, HTC, **LN**, NTC; KJV, NASB, NLT, NRSV, Ph], 'Lazarus has been dead four days' [CEV], 'it has been four days since he died' [NCV], 'it has been four days' [NICNT2], 'he has been buried four days' [NET, TEV], 'he has been there four days' [NIV, REB], 'this is the fourth day since he died' [NJB], 'it is four days' [AB]. This pronominal adjective indicates the fourth in a series of days [LN]. It refers to an event happening on the fourth day [BAGD].
QUESTION—What is indicated by the clause 'it is the fourth day'?
The Jews believed that there was no hope for anyone who had been dead for four days. By then the body showed signs of decay and the soul, which was thought to hover over the body for three days, had left [AB, Bar, Car, EGT, ICC, TH, WBC]. The soul/spirit stays close three days hoping perhaps to reenter the body [Car, EGT, ICC, WBC].

11:40 **Jesus says to-her, "Did-I- not**[a] **-tell you(sg) that if you(sg)-believed you(sg)-will-see the glory**[b] **of God?"**
LEXICON—a. οὐκ (LN 69.11): 'not' [all translations]. This negative particle indicates that a positive response is expected to a question [LN].
  b. δόξα (LN 79.18): 'glory' [LN; all translations except Ph], 'splendor' [LN]. The phrase 'the glory of God' is translated 'the wonder of what God can do' [Ph]. This noun denotes the quality of a splendid, remarkable appearance [LN]. The mention of glory here ties this last of Jesus' signs to the first one at Cana (2:11) where glory is also connected to that sign. It also connects with the first mention of glory in 11:4 where Jesus tells his disciples that the death of Lazarus is for the glory of God [AB].
QUESTION—What reply is expected to Jesus' rhetorical question and what is its function?
The question with the negative particle οὐκ indicates that a positive reply is expected to the question [LN, TH, WBC]: 'I told you, didn't I, that if you believed you would see the glory of God?' [WBC]. This verse is a *gentle reprimand* to Martha [EGT, ICC, My] for her lack of understanding [ICC]. It is a *challenge* to her faith [BECNT]. He *reminds* her that she would see God's glory if she believed [Lns, NICNT1, WBC]. In effect, Jesus has just told Martha what he is about to do so they will see the glory of God [NICNT2].
QUESTION—When had Jesus said this to Martha before this?
There is no record of his having said this, but Jesus knew that the messenger had reported it to the sisters on returning from him, 'This sickness is not unto death but for the glory of God' (in verse 4) [Gdt]. Jesus refers indirectly to this statement in verses 25–26 where he spoke of being the resurrection and the life [HTC]. This must be a summary statement of all that was promised

in 23–26. That is, to raise to life a person who has died is an act that reveals God's glory in Christ [Bar, Car].

QUESTION—What is the meaning of τὴν δόξαν τοῦ θεοῦ 'the glory of God'?
It means 'the splendid triumph of the omnipotence of God, in the service of His love, over death and corruption' [Gdt]. In the context it means 'the power of God that rules over death and decay' [HTC]. This clause may be translated 'you will see God reveal how powerful he is' or 'you will see how wonderful God is' [TH], or 'you will see how great God is' [TRT]. The mention of glory in verses 4 and 40 point to the raising of Lazarus as being the greatest sign of the presence of God's saving power in Jesus [HTC]. This miracle is a revelation of Jesus' power and authority [IVP, NICNT1] as the creator of all things [IVP]. The glory is probably the power of God that effected the raising of Lazarus [ICC].

DISCOURSE UNIT—11:41b–44 [HTC]. The topic is Jesus raises Lazarus.

11:41 So they-took-away the stone. And Jesus lifted (his) eyes up and said, "Father, I-thank[a] you(sg) that you-listen-to[b] me. **11:42** And I knew that you- always -listen-to me, but I said (it) because-of the crowd standing-around,[c] so-that they-may-believe that you sent me."

LEXICON—a. pres. act. indic. of εὐχαριστέω (LN 33.349) (BAGD 2. p. 328): 'to thank' [BAGD, LN; all translations], 'to give thanks, to render thanks, to return thanks' [BAGD]. This verb means to express gratitude for benefits or blessings [LN].

b. aorist act. indic. of ἀκούω (LN 31.56) (BAGD 5. p. 32): 'to listen to' [BAGD, LN], 'to listen and respond, to accept, to pay attention and respond, to heed' [LN]. The clause 'that you listen/have listened to me' [NET, TEV] is also translated 'that/because you (have) heard me' [AB, Gdt, HTC, NICNT2, NTC, WBC; KJV, NASB, NCV, NIV, Ph], 'for hearing/having heard me' [NLT, NRSV, REB], 'for hearing my prayer' [NJB], 'for answering my prayer' [CEV]. This verb means to believe something and to respond to it on the basis of having heard [LN].

c. perf. act. participle of περιΐστημι (LN **17.4**) (BAGD 1.b. p. 647): 'to stand around' [BAGD, **LN**], 'to stand by' [BAGD], 'to be around' [LN]. The phrase 'the crowd standing around (here)' [AB, NICNT2; NET] is also translated 'the crowd standing here' [NRSV], 'the crowd that is standing by' [WBC], 'the multitude who surround me' [Gdt], 'the multitude that is standing around' [Gdt], 'these who are standing around me' [NJB], 'the people standing (a)round' [NASB, REB], 'the people standing/which-stand by' [HTC; KJV], 'the people standing here' [NIV], '(all) these people standing here' [NLT, Ph], 'the people here around me' [NCV], 'the people here' [CEV, TEV]. This verb means to stand around someone or to encircle [LN].

JOHN 11:41–42 91

QUESTION—Why did Jesus look up?
> This action was a natural prelude to prayer. Jesus did this before he multiplied the loaves (Mark 6:41) and before the High Priestly Prayer (John 17:1) [AB, ICC].

QUESTION—To whom does the pronoun 'they' in the phrase 'they took away' refer?
> It probably refers to the people with Martha and Mary [NICNT1, NICNT2, TH, TRT], not to the sisters themselves as the stone would have been too heavy for them to lift [NICNT2, TH].

QUESTION—What was the significance of Jesus praying at this time?
> That Jesus prayed before calling Lazarus out of the tomb concentrates all the attention on the miracle as being the working of Jesus and the Father together [Rd]. His prayer showed that he was no miracle worker on his own, and that he had no power apart from the Father [Bar, BECNT, NICNT1]. Jesus had already asked God to raise Lazarus from the dead [Car, NICNT1, TRT]. This prayer had been prayed while Jesus was still in Peraea (where he had received the news of Lazarus' illness) [EGT].

QUESTION—What word is emphasized in this verse?
> The pronoun ἐγώ 'I' is emphatic [Gdt, HTC, Lns, My; NJB]: Yet *on my part, I* know…' [Lns]. He did not pray for his own sake but for the sake of those with him that they would understand that the miracle showed God's backing of his mission [HTC]. The pronoun σύ 'you(sg)' in the phrase 'you sent me' is emphatic [My, TH; NJB]: '*it was you who* sent me' [NJB]. The emphasis shows Jesus was interested not in displaying his power as a miracle worker but to show that through his miracles it was the power *of God* that was active in him [TH].

QUESTION—What relationship is indicated by the conjunction ἵνα 'so that' in the clause 'so that they may believe that you sent me'?
> It signals that Jesus' *purpose* was that the crowd might believe that he had been sent by God [ICC, Lns, NICNT1].

11:43 And having-said these-things he-cried[a] (with) (a) loud voice, "**Lazarus, come-here**[b] **out.**[c]"

LEXICON—a. aorist act. indic. of κραυγάζω (LN 33.83) (BAGD 2.b. p. 449): 'to cry' [BAGD, Gdt, HTC; KJV, NJB, NRSV], 'to cry out' [BAGD; NASB, NCV], 'to shout' [AB, LN, NICNT2, NTC, WBC; CEV, NET, NLT], 'to call' [NIV], 'to call out' [Ph, TEV], 'to utter a (loud) sound' [BAGD], 'to scream' [LN]. The clause 'he cried with a loud voice' is translated 'he raised his voice in a great cry' [REB]. This verb means to shout or cry out, with the possible implication of the unpleasant nature of the sound [LN]. It means 'to cry (loudly)' [BAGD].
  b. aorist act. impera. of δεῦρο (LN **84.24**) (BAGD 1. p. 176): 'come here' [BAGD, LN], 'come' [BAGD], 'here, hither' [LN]. The command δεῦρο ἔξω 'come here out' is translated 'come out here' [**LN**, WBC], 'come out' [AB, BAGD, HTC, NTC; CEV, NCV, NET, NIV, NJB, NLT, NRSV, Ph,

REB, TEV], 'come forth' [Gdt; KJV, NASB], '(Lazarus!) Out!' [NICNT2]. This adverb indicates extension toward a goal at or near the speaker and implies movement [LN]. Δεῦρο is an adverb of place used as an imperative like our 'Here!' [Bar, NICNT1, TH]. It is wonderfully succinct: 'Here! Outside!' [BECNT, NICNT1], or 'Here/hither, out!' [EGT, Lns, My, TH].

c. ἔξω (LN 83.20) (BAGD 1.b. p. 279): 'out' [BAGD], 'outside' [LN]. This adverb indicates a position not contained within a particular area [LN]. See previous item for version renderings.

QUESTION—What is the significance of the description of Jesus' voice?

The verb κραυγάζω by itself means 'to cry loudly'. The addition of 'with a loud voice' reinforces the strength with which it was said. Wizards muttered their spells. Perhaps this loud command was to show the people there that this was no work of magic, but the very power of God [NICNT1]. He used a loud cry in order that everyone in the crowd might know that the dead would respond to his call [NTC].

QUESTION—How does this authenticate another promise of Jesus?

Jesus had said, 'Truly, truly I say to you that an hour is coming and now is when the dead will hear the voice of the Son of God and the ones having heard will live' (John 5:25, 28–29) [Car, WBC].

11:44 The (one) having-died came-out the (his) feet and hands having-been-bound[a] with-graveclothes[b] and his face having-been-wrapped[c] with-(a)-cloth.[d] Jesus says to-them, "Untie[e] him and permit him to-go."

LEXICON—a. perf. pass. participle of δέω (LN 18.13) (BAGD 1.a. p. 177): 'to be bound' [BAGD, all translations except CEV, NCV, NET, NIV, TEV], 'to be wrapped' [CEV, NCV, NIV, TEV], 'to be tied up' [LN; NET], 'to be tied' [BAGD, LN], 'to be tied together [LN]. This verb means to tie objects together [LN].

b. κειρία (LN **6.156**) (BAGD p. 427): 'graveclothes' [BAGD; KJV, NLT, Ph, TEV], 'strip of linen' [AB, WBC; NIV], 'strip of cloth' [**LN**; NET, NRSV], 'strip of burial cloth' [CEV], 'strip of material' [NJB], 'piece of cloth' [NCV], 'grave band' [NTC], 'band of cloth' [LN], 'wrapping' [NASB], 'bandage' [BAGD, Gdt, NICNT2; HTC], 'linen bandage' [REB]. This noun probably refers to strips of linen used to wrap a corpse [TH]. One custom was to lay the corpse on a linen sheet, wide enough to envelop the whole body and twice its length. The end of the sheet was then pulled over the head and back down to the feet. The feet were bound at the ankles and the arms were tied to the body with cloth strips [BECNT, Car, WBC]. Lazarus was apparently prepared in this way [BECNT, Car]. Here one may translate 'the strips of cloth that had been put around the body of Lazarus' [**LN**].

c. pluperfect pass. indic. of περιδέω (LN **18.14**) (BAGD p. 646): 'to be wrapped' [AB, Gdt, HTC, NICNT2; NLT, NRSV, REB], 'to be wrapped around' [BAGD, **LN**; NASB, NET], 'to be wrapped up' [LN], 'to be bound' [BAGD; KJV], 'to be bound about' [NTC], 'to be muffled' [Ph], 'to be covered' [LN, WBC], 'to be tied around' [**LN**]. The phrase 'his face having been wrapped with a face cloth' is translated 'a cloth around/over his face' [NCV, NIV, NJB, TEV], 'a cloth wrapped around his face' (literally, his face tied around with cloth)' [**LN**]. This verb means to tie or wrap an object around something [LN].

    d. σουδάριον (LN **6.159**) (BAGD p. 759): 'cloth' [HTC, NICNT2, WBC; CEV, NASB, NCV, NET, NIV, NJB, NRSV, REB, TEV], 'face cloth' [BAGD, **LN**], 'headcloth' [NLT], 'handkerchief' [AB, BAGD, LN; Ph], 'napkin' [Gdt LN; KJV], 'sweat-band' [NTC], 'towel' [LN]. This noun denotes a small piece of cloth used as a towel, napkin, or face cloth [LN]. It is somewhat similar to our 'handkerchief' [BAGD]. The head cloth probably was about one yard square [Kn].

    e. aorist act. impera. of (LN 18.18) (BAGD 2.a. p. 483): 'to untie' [AB, BAGD, LN, NTC; CEV, TEV], 'to unbind' [BAGD, HTC; NASB, NJB, NRSV, Ph], 'to unwrap' [NET, NLT], 'to loose' [BAGD, Gdt; KJV, REB], 'to loosen' [LN, NICNT2] , 'to take off' [NCV, NIV], 'to release' [WBC], 'to set free' [BAGD]. This verb means to reverse the result of tying by untying [LN]. To avoid the idea that Lazarus was somehow tied up with ropes it may be good to translate something like, 'unwind the cloths from around him' or 'take off the cloths that are wound around him' [TH].

QUESTION—If Lazarus was bound head and foot, how could he have come out of the tomb?

It may be that each leg was wrapped separately [Gdt, NICNT1, TRT] or that the cloths were wrapped loosely enough to allow for movement [BECNT, Gdt, Lns, My, TRT]. He was at least able to shuffle or walk with difficulty to the door of the tomb [Car, IVP, Kn, Lns, NTC, TRT, WBC], or hop [Car, IVP, TRT]. We should assume that Lazarus was able to get up without aid and to have enough movement to get to the door of the tomb [Lns]. It is possible that a second miracle occurred and Lazarus does not walk out of the tomb but is somehow drawn out bound as he was [NICNT1].

DISCOURSE UNIT—11:45–12:11 [Kn]. The topic is responses to the raising.

DISCOURSE UNIT—11:45–57 [BECNT, Lns; CEV, NCV, NIV, NET, NRSV, Ph]. The topic is the plot to kill Jesus [BECNT; NCV, NIV, NRSV], the response to the raising of Lazarus [Lns; NET, Ph].

DISCOURSE UNIT—11:45–54 [AB, Bar, Car, HTC, IVP, Rd, WBC; NJB]. The topic is the Sanhedrin decides Jesus' death sentence [AB, Car, HTC, Rd, WBC; NJB], the plot against Jesus [Bar], some believe in Jesus while others reject him [IVP].

DISCOURSE UNIT—11:45–46 [Kn, ICC]. The topic is faith and betrayal among witnesses [Kn], impression made on bystanders [ICC].

DISCOURSE UNIT—11:45 [NICNT1]. The topic is the reaction of faith.

11:45 Therefore[a] many of the Jews the (ones) having-come to[b] Mary and having-seen the-things he-did believed in him.

LEXICON—a. οὖν (LN 89.50): 'therefore' [Gdt, HTC, LN, NTC, WBC; NASB, NIV, NRSV], 'so then' [LN, NICNT2], 'then' [KJV, NET], 'so, consequently, accordingly, then' [LN], not explicit [CEV, NCV, NJB, NLT, Ph, REB, TEV]. This conjunction is also translated as a clause: 'this caused' [AB]. This conjunction indicates result, often implying the conclusion of a process of reasoning [LN].

b. πρός (LN 84.18) (BAGD): 'to' [LN]. The words 'had come/having come/came to Mary' [Gdt, NICNT2, NTC, WBC; KJV, NASB] are also translated 'come to visit Mary' [CEV, NCV, NIV, NJB, REB, TEV], 'had come with Mary' [HTC; NET, NRSV], 'had accompanied Mary' [Ph], '(who) were with Mary' [NLT]. This preposition indicates extension toward a goal, with the probability of some type of implied interaction or reciprocity [LN].

QUESTION—What is implied by the phrase 'having come to Mary'?

These Jews had come *to visit* Mary [AB, Car, NICNT1, TH, TRT; CEV, NCV, NIV, NJB, REB, TEV].

DISCOURSE UNIT—11:46–57 [NICNT1]. The topic is the reaction of unbelief.

11:46 But some of them went to the Pharisees and told them the-things Jesus did.

QUESTION—Who is the antecedent of the pronoun 'them' in the clause 'some of them went away to the Pharisees'?

1. It refers to some of the ones who believed in Jesus in verse 45 [ICC, Lns, My, NICNT2]. This may imply that those who believed had not actually believed and had other than pure motives for telling the Pharisees what had happened [NICNT2]. Their action was not necessarily malevolent [ICC, Lns, My]. We may assume that they went to convince the Pharisees that they had been wrong in their opinion of Jesus [Lns].
2. It refers to other Jews who witnessed the miracle but had not come to visit Mary [Bar, Gdt, NICNT1, NTC]. There are two classes of witnesses here. Those who believe and those who are hostile and go to convince the Pharisees that some action must be taken. This is supported by what occurs in 47–48 [NTC]. These others certainly must have acted out of a spirit of hostility [NICNT1].

DISCOURSE UNIT—11:47–57 [NASB, NLT, TEV]. The topic is the plot to kill Jesus.

DISCOURSE UNIT—11:47–53 [ICC, Kn]. The topic is the elite plot Jesus' death [Kn], the counsel of the Sanhedrin [ICC].

11:47 So the chief-priests and the Pharisees called-together[a] (the) Sanhedrin[b] and were-saying, "What do-we (do) for this man is-doing many signs?[c] **11:48** If we-let[d] him (do) thus,[e] all-men will-believe in him, and the Romans will-come and take-away[f] both our place[g] and nation?"

LEXICON—a. aorist act. indic. of συνάγω (LN 15.125) (BAGD 2. p. 782): 'to call together' [BAGD, LN; CEV, NET, NLT], 'to call a meeting' [NCV, NIV, NJB, NRSV], 'to call' [NTC], 'to gather' [BAGD, Gdt, HTC, NICNT2, WBC; KJV], 'to gather together' [AB, LN], 'to convene' [NASB, REB], 'to summon' [Ph], 'to bring together' [BAGD]. The words 'called together the Sanhedrin' is translated 'met with the council' [TEV]. This verb means to cause to come together, whether of animate or inanimate objects [LN].

b. συνέδριον (LN **11.80**) (BAGD 2. p. 786): 'Sanhedrin' [AB, BAGD, LN, WBC; NIV], 'meeting of the Sanhedrin' [**LN**], 'Sanhedrin-session' [NTC], 'Jewish council' [NCV], 'Council' [TEV], '(the/a) council' [HTC, NICNT2; CEV, KJV, NASB, NET, NRSV, Ph], 'the council of the Jews' [LN], 'meeting of the council' [BAGD; REB], 'the high council' [BAGD; NET], 'assembly' [Gdt]. This noun denotes the highest Jewish council, exercising jurisdiction in civil and religious matters, but having no power over life and death or over military actions or taxation [LN]. In Roman times this was the highest indigenous governing body in Judaea, composed of high priests, elders, and scholars (scribes), and meeting under the presidency of the ruling high priest. This body was the ultimate authority not only in religious matters, but in legal and governmental affairs as well, in so far as it did not encroach on the authority of the Roman procurator. The latter had to confirm any death sentence passed by the council [BAGD]. The Sanhedrin was a council composed of 71 members with the high priest presiding. The majority were Sadducees and the minority Pharisees [CH]. This can be translated 'the gathering of the leaders' [TH].

c. σημεῖον (LN 33.477) (BAGD 2.a. p. 748): 'sign' [AB, BAGD, HTC, LN, NICNT2, NTC, WBC; NASB, NJB, NRSV, REB], 'remarkable sign' [Ph], 'miracle' [Gdt; CEV, KJV, NCV, TEV], 'miraculous sign' [NET, NIV, NLT]. A σημεῖον as an event with special meaning was inevitably an unusual or even miraculous type of occurrence, and in a number of contexts it may be rendered as 'miracle'. For the Gospel of John, however, a σημεῖον is not simply a miraculous event but something which points to a reality with even greater significance. A strictly literal translation of it as 'sign' might mean nothing more than a road sign or a sign on a building, and therefore in some languages σημεῖον may be rendered as 'a miracle with great meaning' [LN]. This word occurs at 2:11, 18; 3:2; 4:48, 54; 6:2, 14, 26, 30; 7:31; 9:16; 10:41, 47; 12:18, 37; 20:30.

d. aorist act. subj. of ἀφίημι (LN 13.140) (BAGD 4. p. 126): 'to let' [BAGD, LN], 'to allow, to leave it to' [LN], 'to let go, to tolerate'

[BAGD]. The clause 'if we we let him do thus' is translated 'if we let him alone (thus)' [Gdt, NTC; KJV], 'if we let him go on like this/in this way/thus' [AB, BAGD, HTC, NICNT2, WBC; NASB, NIV, NJB, NRSV, REB, TEV], 'if we allow him to go on this way/like this' [NET, NLT], 'if we let him go on doing this sort of thing' [Ph], 'if we let him continue doing these things' [NCV], 'if we don't stop him now' [CEV]. This verb means to leave it to someone to do something, with the implication of distancing oneself from the event [LN].

e. οὕτως (LN 61.9) (BAGD): 'thus' [BAGD, HTC, LN, NTC; KJV], 'like this' [AB, NICNT2; NASB, NIV, NLT, NRSV, REB], '(in) this way' [LN, WBC; NET, NJB, TEV], 'so' [BAGD, LN], 'in this manner' [BAGD]. This adverb refers to that which precedes. 'If we let him do thus' (that is, in accordance with what he had been doing, namely, performing various miracles) [BAGD, LN]. See previous item for more version translations.

f. fut. act. indic. of αἴρω (LN **20.43**) (BAGD 4. p. 24): 'to take away' [AB, BAGD, NICNT2, NTC, WBC; KJV, NASB, NCV, NET, NIV], 'to destroy' [Gdt, HTC, LN; CEV, NLT, NRSV], 'to take action and destroy' [TEV], 'to suppress' [NJB], 'to be the end of' [Ph], 'to sweep away' [REB], 'to do away with' [LN], 'to conquer, to remove, to take over' [BAGD]. The clause 'the Romans will come and take away both our place and nation' is translated 'the Roman authorities will take action and destroy our Temple and our nation' [**LN**], '(we shall have) the Romans coming and that will be the end of our holy place and our very existence as a nation' [Ph]. This verb means to destroy, with the implication of removal and doing away with [LN]. It implies take away by force, even by killing [BAGD].

g. τόπος (LN **80.1**) (BAGD 1.a./1.b. p. 822): 'place' [Gdt, LN, NICNT2, NTC; KJV, NASB, NIV], 'Holy Place' [NJB], 'holy place' [AB, HTC, WBC; NRSV, Ph], 'Temple' [NCV, NLT, TEV], 'temple' [CEV, REB], 'sanctuary' [NET], 'space, room' [LN]. This noun denotes an area of any size, regarded in certain contexts as a point in space [LN]. Here it refers to the Temple [**LN**]. It can refer to either the Temple or Jerusalem [BAGD].

QUESTION—What may be implied by the lack of an article before the word 'Sanhedrin'?

It may indicate that this was not a formal meeting of the whole council [My, NICNT2]. The fact that Caiaphas, the presiding high priest, is called 'one of them' in verse 49 may indicate that this was an informal meeting, but this may be pressing the lack of article before 'Sanhedrin' too far. John does not mention a trial after Jesus' arrest perhaps indicating that this was the trial itself [NICNT1].

QUESTION—What do the Pharisees mean when they say, 'What do we do'?

1. This is a deliberative question or a rhetorical question with the function of deliberation—they are asking each other what must be done [AB, Gdt, HTC, NICNT2, NTC, Rd, WBC; CEV, NCV, NLT, NRSV, Ph, TEV].

The present tense is future in sense meaning [Gdt, HTC]. 'It is absolutely necessary to do something, but what?' [Gdt]. The following clause and the next verse force us to choose this deliberative interpretation of the question. It expresses their dismay and anxiety about what they should do [HTC].
2. This is a rhetorical question with the function of negative evaluation— 'We are doing nothing' [Bar, Car, EGT, ICC, Lns, NICNT1, TRT]: 'Here is this *man* working all these signs, and what action are we taking?' [NJB]. Their question means that they have plans and are wondering how effective their actions have been. In fact they may be implying that they are accomplishing nothing in comparison with Jesus' many miracles [NICNT1]. The question means 'What are we *now* doing?' and implies the response, 'Nothing' [Bar]. They ask, 'Why are we doing nothing?' [EGT, ICC]. The natural mood to indicate deliberation would be the subjunctive. But this is the present indicative asking what is being done about Jesus, and implying, 'Nothing at all' [Lns].

QUESTION—What is indicated by referring to Jesus as οὗτος ὁ ἄνθρωπος 'this man'?

It indicates the contempt or disrespect they had for him [ICC, My, TRT]. It is used derogatorily and shows a reluctance to mention his name [Lns].

QUESTION—What is indicated by the phrase 'our place'?
1. It refers to the Jewish Temple [AB, Bar, BECNT, Car, HTC, ICC, IVP, Kn, LN, NICNT1, Rd, TH, WBC; CEV, NCV, NET, NJB, NLT, REB, TEV]. That it probably refers to the temple is supported by the following references: John 4:20; Matthew 24:15; Acts 6:13(–14); 21:28 [HTC, NICNT2]. The reference in 2 Maccabees 5:19 is clearly to the Temple, 'the Lord did not choose the nation for the place's sake, but the place for the nation's sake' [NICNT1].
2. It refers to Jerusalem [Gdt, My]. 'Our place' refers to their capital as the seat of government. This alternative also fits more naturally with the word 'nation' that follows [Gdt].
3. Other views [EGT, Lns, NTC]. It refers to both Jerusalem and the temple. It may refer more specifically to the latter [Lns, NTC]. The natural rendering for 'our place' is 'our land'. This is also a fitting partner to join with the word 'nation' [EGT]. When the explanations are given they usually vary between the country, the city and the Temple. But in fact, they always refer to the position of authority held by the rulers no matter in which place that rule held sway. The rulers are chiefly concerned with their *position* [Lns].

QUESTION—What words are emphasized in verse 48?

The pronoun ἡμῶν 'our' in the phrase 'both our place and nation' is emphasized [Car, EGT, Gdt, HTC, ICC, IVP, Lns, My, Rd]: both our own place and nation. The possessive pronoun is placed before the two nouns serving to emphasize the concern of the rulers over the possible loss of their power [Gdt]. Since the Sanhedrin had so much at stake in this matter, it is better to take the pronominal genitive 'our' and treat it as a sympathetic dative (from us) modifying the verb: 'will take away from us' [Car, Rd].

11:49 **But (a) certain one of them Caiaphas, being high-priest^a that year, said to them, "You(pl) do- not -know^b anything.**

LEXICON—a. ἀρχιερεύς (LN 53.89) (BAGD 1.b. p. 112): 'high priest' [BAGD, LN; all translations except NICNT2], 'Chief Priest' [NICNT2], 'most important priest' [LN]. This noun denotes the principal member among the chief priests [LN]. He was the president of the Sanhedrin [BAGD, TRT]. The High Priest held office for life [AB, Bar, Car, Gdt, ICC, NICNT1, TH], though in Jesus' time the length of time in office depended on the favor of the Roman government [AB, Car, Gdt, ICC, TH].

   b. pres. act. indic. of οἶδα (LN 32.4): 'to understand, to comprehend' [LN]. The clause 'You do not know anything' [NICNT2, NTC] is also translated 'You know nothing at all' [Gdt, HTC, WBC; KJV, NASB, NET, NIV, NRSV], 'You people know nothing!' [NCV], 'You have no grasp of the situation at all' [REB], 'You do not seem to have grasped the situation at all' [NJB], 'You don't know what you're talking about!' [NLT], 'You plainly don't understand what's involved here' [Ph], 'You have no sense at all' [AB], 'You people don't have any sense at all!' [CEV], 'What fools you are!' [TEV]. This verb means to comprehend the meaning of something, with focus on the resulting knowledge [LN].

QUESTION—What is indicated by the clause 'being high priest that year'?

John's statement that he was high priest that year probably means that this was the memorable year in which Jesus was crucified [AB, Bar, Car, CH, EGT, Gdt, HTC, ICC, IVP, Lns, My, NICNT1, NICNT2, Rd, TH]. The same phrase is repeated in verse 51 and in 18:13 showing that John was using it not to point out that the high priest only served a year, but to emphasize the historic nature of the council's decision and the events following it [NICNT2].

QUESTION—What is implied by the statement, 'You do not know anything'?

It implies that he was being *rude* [BECNT, Gdt, NICNT1, NTC, TRT], or *arrogant* [CH, HTC, WBC], or *ill-mannered* [NTC], or *critical* [TRT]. He was being *discourteous, rough, and insulting* [Lns]. It implies that they knew nothing in view of the fact that they could still ask, 'What do we do?' [My].

QUESTION—What words are emphasized in this verse?

The pronoun ὑμεῖς 'you(pl)' is emphatic [NICNT1, NICNT2]: *You, for your part* do not know anything. The emphasis on 'you' implies that *he himself* understands what they are failing to understand [NICNT2]. The emphatic 'you' is probably contemptuous [EGT, ICC, NICNT1]. He himself sees things clearly and he scornfully dismisses the others because they do not see things his way [NICNT1]. The double negative ('*not* know *nothing*') is also emphatic [AB, Gdt, HTC, WBC; CEV, KJV, NASB, NET, NIV, NRSV, REB]: You know nothing at all! The final word οὐδέν 'anything' is

JOHN 11:49

emphasized [Bar]. The demonstrative adjective ἐκεῖνος 'that' in the phrase 'that year' is emphatic [Gdt, HTC]: *that very* year. John is emphasizing that year as the year in which the Messiah was put to death and the priesthood came to an end [Gdt, HTC].

11:50 **Nor do-you-realize**[a] **that it-is-better**[b] **for-you that one man should-die for**[c] **the people and not all the nation should-perish."**

TEXT—Instead of ὑμῖν 'for you' some manuscripts read ἡμῖν 'for us', while others omit this word. GNT reads 'for you' with a B rating, indicating that the text is almost certain. Gdt, My; KJV, Ph adopt the reading 'for us'.

LEXICON—a. pres. mid. (deponent = act.) indic. of λογίζομαι (LN 30.9) (BAGD 2. p. 476): 'to realize' [AB, NICNT2, WBC; NCV, NET, NIV, NLT, Ph, REB, TEV], 'to consider' [BAGD, Gdt; KJV], 'to take into account' [NTC; NASB], 'to see' [NJB], 'to understand' [HTC; NRSV], 'to know' [CEV], 'to think about, to ponder' [BAGD, LN], 'to reason about' [LN], 'to let one's mind dwell on' [BAGD]. This verb means to think about something in a detailed and logical manner [LN].

b. pres. act. indic. of συμφέρω (LN **65.44**) (BAGD 2.a. p. 780): 'to be better' [BAGD, Gdt; CEV, NCV, NIV, NLT, NRSV, TEV], 'to be expedient' [HTC, NTC; KJV, NASB], 'to be to one's advantage' [AB, **LN**, NICNT2, WBC; NET, NJB], 'to be (a) good (thing)' [BAGD; Ph], 'to be to one's interest' [REB], 'to be advantageous' [BAGD, LN], 'to be better off' [LN], 'to help, to confer a benefit, to be profitable, to be useful' [BAGD]. This verb means to be of an advantage to someone [LN].

c. ὑπέρ (LN **90.36**) (BAGD 1.a.ε. p. 838): 'for' [BAGD, LN; all translations except Ph], 'for the sake of' [BAGD, LN; Ph], 'on behalf of' [BAGD, LN]. This preposition (with the genitive case) indicates a participant who is benefited by an event or on whose behalf it takes place [LN]. It is used after expressions of suffering, dying, or devoting oneself for someone [BAGD].

QUESTION—What is indicated by the pronoun ὑμῖν 'for you'?

It separates Caiaphas from his fellow council members and puts distance between them. It is in keeping with his scolding attitude that he expressed in verse 49 [NICNT2] and may imply contempt for them [ICC, NICNT2].

11:51 **But he-did- not -say this of-himself,**[a] **but being high-priest that year he prophesied**[b] **that Jesus was-about**[c] **to-die on-behalf-of the nation.**

LEXICON—a. ἀφ' ἑαυτοῦ (BAGD 1.a. p. 212): The clause 'he did not say this of himself' [Gdt; similarly KJV] is also translated 'he did not say this on his own (initiative)' [NICNT2; NASB, NET, NIV, NLT, NRSV], 'he did not make this remark on his own initiative' [Ph], 'Caiaphas did not say this on his own' [CEV], 'it was not on his own that he said this' [AB], 'he did not say this of his own accord' [HTC, WBC; REB, TEV], 'this he said not (merely) of his own accord' [NTC], 'he did not speak in his own person' [NJB], 'Caiaphas did not think of this himself' [NCV]. This pronoun denotes a reflexive reference to a person or thing spoken or

written about [LN]. This clause means 'to speak on one's own authority' without orders from a higher authority [BAGD], or to speak at one's own instigation [EGT].
   b. aorist act. indic. of προφητεύω (LN **33.459**) (BAGD 3. p. 723): 'to prophesy' [BAGD, **LN**; all translations except Ph], 'to foretell the future' [BAGD], 'to make inspired utterances' [LN]. The phrase 'he prophesied' is translated 'he was in fact inspired to say' [Ph]. This verb means to speak under the influence of divine inspiration, with or without reference to future events [LN]. He prophesied means that when he spoke God also spoke. Caiaphas meant one thing, but God used his words to mean another thing [Car]. In this verse 'to prophesy' means 'to predict' [TH]. 'He prophesied' means that God controlled his words [Lns].
   c. imperf. act. indic. of μέλλω (LN 67.62) (BAGD 1.c.δ. p. 501): 'to be about to' [LN]. The clause 'Jesus was about to die' [NTC, WBC; NRSV] is also translated 'Jesus was going to die' [NICNT2; NASB, NET, Ph, TEV], 'Jesus would die' [CEV, NCV, NIV, NLT, REB], 'Jesus should die' [Gdt, HTC; KJV], 'Jesus was to die' [AB; NJB]. This verb means to occur at a point of time in the future which is subsequent to another event and closely related to it [LN]. It denotes an action that necessarily follows a divine decree. For example, 'he is destined to suffer' [BAGD, ICC]. It adds a touch of certainty to Jesus' sacrifice [NICNT1].
QUESTION—Who is the speaker of this verse?
   It is John's own editorial remark [BECNT, Gdt, HTC, ICC, IVP, Lns, My, NICNT1, NICNT2, Rd]. Several translations put verses 51–52 in parentheses [AB; NET, Ph].
QUESTION—What relationship is indicated by the clause 'being high priest that year'?
   It has a causal relationship to the verb 'he prophesied' [Gdt, NICNT1, TH, TRT; NET, Ph]: '*because* he was high priest that year, he prophesied' [NET]. The Jews believed that the High Priest possessed a certain degree of prophetic ability [TH]. It was because of his being High Priest that God spoke through him [NICNT1]. It was not merely as High Priest, but as High Priest *that* year that he so spoke [Gdt].

11:52 **And not on-behalf-of the nation only but that he-might- also -gather[a] into one the children[b] of-God the (ones) having-been-scattered.[c]**
LEXICON—a. aorist act. subj. of συνάγω (LN 15.125) (BAGD 2. p. 782): 'to gather' [BAGD], 'to gather together' [AB, LN], 'to call together' [BAGD, LN], 'to bring together' [BAGD]. The phrase 'to gather into one' [HTC, NICNT2, NTC, WBC; NRSV] is also translated 'to gather together into one' [NET, NJB], 'to gather in one body' [Gdt], 'to gather together…and make them one' [AB], 'to bring them (all) together and make them one' [NCV, NIV], 'to bring together into one (body)' [Ph, TEV], 'to bring together and unite' [NLT]. The phrase means 'to unite, bring together'

[BAGD 2.a. p. 231]. This verb means to cause to come together, whether of animate or inanimate objects [LN].
- b. τέκνον (BAGD 2.e. p. 808): 'child' [BAGD]. The phrase 'the children of God' [all translations except CEV, NCV, TEV] is also translated 'God's children' [NCV], 'God's people' [CEV, similarly TEV].
- c. perf. pass. participle of διασκορπίζω (LN 15.136) (BAGD p. 188): 'to be scattered' [BAGD, LN, NICNT2; CEV, NCV, NET, NIV, NJB, REB, TEV], 'to be scattered abroad' [Gdt, HTC, NTC, WBC; KJV, NASB], 'to be scattered around the world' [NLT], 'to be dispersed' [AB, BAGD; NRSV], 'to be caused to disperse' [LN]. This verb means to cause a group or gathering to disperse or scatter, with possible emphasis on the distributive nature of the scattering (that is to say, each going in a different direction) [LN]. To avoid the idea that these people were somehow physically thrown around by someone, it may be better to translate something like, 'all the children of God who were living in different lands' [TH].

QUESTION—To whom does the phrase 'children of God' refer?

It is used figuratively here to denote the believers as those who had been born of God (1:12) [AB, BAGD, Bar, Car, Gdt, HTC, ICC, IVP, Kn, My, NICNT1, NICNT2, NTC]. They are the Gentiles who are destined to believe in Jesus [AB, BECNT, EGT, Gdt, HTC, My. NICNT1, NICNT2, NTC, TH], the ones the Father has given to Jesus (8:42). The OT speaks of gathering the dispersed children of Israel (Isaiah 11:12; Micah 2:12; Jeremiah 23:3; Ezekiel 34:16), so these Gentiles now become part of that community forming the true Israel [AB]. It refers both to Jews and Gentiles who will believe in Jesus [Bar, Car, CH, Kn, Lns, Rd, TRT], and who though not at that time were believers, were considered to be 'children of God' because they were predestined to become his children (see 10:16) [Car, Lns].

11:53 **Therefore from that day they-planned^a that^b they-might-kill him.**

LEXICON—a. aorist mid. indic. of βουλεύομαι (LN 30.56) (BAGD 2. p. 145): 'to plan' [AB, LN; NCV, NRSV, Ph], 'to plan together' [NASB, NET], 'to make plans' [CEV, TEV], 'to plot' [NTC; NIV, NLT, REB], 'to take counsel' [HTC; KJV], 'to take counsel together' [Gdt], 'to be determined' [NJB], 'to resolve' [BAGD, NICNT2], 'to make a resolution' [WBC], 'to purpose, to intend' [LN], 'to decide' [BAGD]. This verb means to think, with the purpose of planning or deciding on a course of action [LN]. The sense of 'to resolve' is intended here [BAGD, Car, NICNT1, NICNT2, WBC], or 'to decide' [BAGD, NICNT1].
- b. ἵνα (LN 90.22) (BAGD II.1.a.α. p. 377): 'that' [LN]. The clause 'that they might kill him' is translated 'that they would kill him' [NICNT2], 'to kill him/Jesus' [AB; NASB, NCV, NET, NJB, Ph, TEV], 'to put him/Jesus to death' [WBC; CEV, NRSV], 'for to put him to death' [KJV], 'how to put him to death' [HTC], 'in order that they might put him to death' [NTC], 'to the end that they might put him to death' [Gdt], 'to take

his life' [NIV], 'to plot Jesus' death' [NLT, similarly REB]. This conjunction indicates the content of a discourse, particularly if and when purpose is implied [LN]. It serves as a substitute for an infinitive that supplements the verb, or as an accusative with infinitive after verbs with the senses of 'wish, desire, strive' [BAGD].

QUESTION—What is implied by the conjunction οὖν 'therefore'?

It implies that the Jewish council accepted the High Priest's proposition [Gdt, ICC, My]: So, accepting his counsel they planned from that day…. All that was now left to decide were the timing and method [Gdt]. This decision was precipitated by Jesus' action in raising Lazarus (11:47) [Bar, Car].

QUESTION—What is irregular about their decision?

They do not plan to arrest him for trial, but to kill him. They have already arrived at a verdict about the matter [BECNT, Car, WBC].

DISCOURSE UNIT—11:54–57 [ICC, Kn]. The topic is danger during Passover season [Kn], Jesus withdraws [ICC].

11:54 Therefore[a] Jesus was- no-longer -walking[b] openly[c] among the Jews, but he-went from-there into the country[d] near the desert,[e] into (a) city called Ephraim, and-there he-stayed with the disciples.

LEXICON—a. οὖν (LN 89.50) (BAGD): 'therefore' [Gdt, HTC, LN; KJV, NASB, NIV], 'so' [LN, NTC; TEV, NCV, NJB, NRSV], 'thus' [NET], 'as a result' [NLT], 'as a consequence' [Ph], 'for this reason' [AB], 'accordingly' [LN, WBC; REB], 'then' [LN, NICNT2], 'consequently, so then' [LN]. This conjunction is also translated as a clause: 'because of this plot against him' [CEV]. This conjunction indicates result, often implying the conclusion of a process of reasoning [LN]. Here οὖν has a more strict meaning indicating that it was because of the hostile plans of the Jews that Jesus left that area [ICC, NICNT1, TH].

b. imperf. act. indic. of περιπατέω (LN 15.227) (BAGD 1.a. p. 649): 'to walk' [LN, NICNT2; KJV, NASB], 'to walk about' [NTC; NRSV], 'to walk around' [BAGD], 'to go about' [BAGD, HTC, WBC; NJB, REB], 'to go around' [CEV, NET], 'to go' [LN], 'to travel' [NCV, TEV], 'to move about' [AB; NIV], 'to abide' [Gdt], 'to appear (among the Jews)' [BAGD]. The clause 'Jesus was no longer walking openly among the Jews' is translated 'Jesus stopped his public ministry among the Jews' [NLT], 'Jesus made no further public appearance among the Jews' [Ph]. This verb means to walk along or around [LN]. The imperfect tense indicates an ongoing action 'continued to walk' [NASB].

c. παρρησία (BAGD 2. p. 630): 'openly' [AB, Gdt, HTC, NICNT2, NTC; KJV, NCV, NJB, NRSV, REB, TEV], 'publicly' [BAGD, WBC; NASB, NET, NIV], 'in public' [BAGD; CEV]. This adverb is also translated as an adjective: '(stopped his) public (ministry)' [NLT]. It indicates 'openness' and sometimes develops into 'openness to the public' before whom one is speaking and actions are taking place [BAGD].

d. χώρα (LN 1.87) (BAGD 1.a. p. 889): 'country' [BAGD, Gdt, HTC, NTC; KJV, NASB, NJB, REB], 'countryside' [LN; Ph], 'region' [AB, BAGD, NICNT2; NET, NIV, NRSV], 'place' [BAGD, NCV, NLT, TEV], 'territory' [WBC], 'land, district' [BAGD], 'rural area' [LN], not explicit [CEV]. This noun denotes a rural area in contrast with a population center. A rural area is often identified by a term or phrase meaning 'an extension of fields' or 'a place of field after field' or 'an area of farms' [LN].

e. ἔρημος (LN 1.86) (BAGD 2. p. 309): 'desert' [AB, BAGD, NICNT2, NTC; CEV. NIV, NJB, Ph, REB, TEV], 'wilderness' [BAGD, Gdt, HTC, LN, WBC; KJV, NASB, NET, NLT, NRSV], 'lonely place' [LN], 'grassland' [BAGD]. This noun denotes a largely uninhabited region, normally with sparse vegetation (in contrast with πόλις 'a population center'). Throughout the NT ἔρημος focuses primarily on the lack of population rather than on sparse vegetation, though the two features are closely related ecologically in the Middle East. In most languages the most satisfactory equivalent of ἔρημος is a word or phrase suggesting a place where few if any people live. Such expressions are generally far better than a word meaning 'a bare place' or 'a place of sand', since in some languages such expressions could mean only a clearing in the forest or a sandy beach along a river bank. In the case of translations being made for people living in jungle areas, it may, however, be necessary to describe in a footnote the nature of an ἔρημος in NT times [LN]. This noun refers to the Judean wilderness, the stony barren eastern slopes of the Judaean mountains toward the Dead Sea and lower Jordan Valley [BAGD].

QUESTION—Where was the town of Ephraim located?

It may have been fifteen miles northeast of Jerusalem in northern Judea [IVP, TRT]. If Ephraim is the same as the village of Ophrah [BECNT, CH, NICNT1, NTC], it was about fourteen miles north northeast of Jerusalem [NICNT1, NTC]. Ephraim is probably the present village of Et-taiyibe [Bar, BECNT, Car, EGT, HTC, ICC], about 12 miles northeast of Jerusalem [BECNT, Car, HTC]. The ancient name of Et-taiyibe was Ophrah [EGT]. According to Eusebius it was eight miles north of Jerusalem. But Jerome places it twenty miles northeast of Jerusalem [Gdt, My].

QUESTION—Who were the Jews mentioned in the phrase 'openly among the Jews?

They were the hostile leaders of the Jews [ICC, NTC]. They were probably the Jews in the province of Judea [Car].

DISCOURSE UNIT—11:55–12:50 [WBC]. The topic is Jesus, victor over death.

DISCOURSE UNIT—11:55–12:36 [Car, HTC]. The topic is Jesus' journey to his final passover in Jerusalem [HTC], victory and impending death [Car].

DISCOURSE UNIT—11:55–12:19 [NICNT2]. The topic is to Jerusalem again.

DISCOURSE UNIT—11:55–12:11 [Bar, IVP]. The topic is Jesus is anointed at Bethany.

DISCOURSE UNIT—11:55–12:8 [Rd]. The topic is Jesus' journey to the Passover Feast and anointing at Bethany.

DISCOURSE UNIT—11:55–57 [AB, Car, HTC; NJB]. The topic is will Jesus come for Passover? [AB], the setting: the Jewish Passover [Car], the final Passover [HTC; NJB].

11:55 Now the Passover[a] of-the Jews was near, and many went-up[b] from the country to Jerusalem before the Passover so-that they-might-purify[c] themselves.

LEXICON—a. πάσχα (LN 51.6) (BAGD 1. p. 633): 'Passover' [AB, BAGD, Gdt, HTC, LN, NICNT2, NTC, WBC; NASB, NIV, NJB, NRSV, Ph, REB], 'passover' [KJV], 'Passover festival' [LN], 'Passover (Festival)' [BAGD]. The phrase 'the Passover of the Jews' is translated 'Passover' [CEV], 'the Passover Festival' [TEV], 'the Jewish feast of Passover' [NET], the Jewish Passover celebration' [NLT], 'the Jewish Passover Feast' [NCV]. This noun denotes the Jewish festival commemorating the deliverance of the Jews from Egypt. In some languages the term πάσχα has been borrowed in one form or another, but frequently it is necessary to have some qualifying statement to identify this festival, for example, 'a festival to celebrate the passing over of the angel' or 'a festival to celebrate deliverance from Egypt' [LN]. It is a Jewish festival, celebrated on the 14th of the month of Nisan, and continuing into the early hours of the 15th. This was followed immediately by the Feast of Unleavened Bread on the 15th to the 21st. Popular usage merged the two festivals and treated them as a unity, as they were for practical purposes [BAGD].

b. aorist act. indic. of ἀναβαίνω (LN 15.101) (BAGD 1.a.α. p. 50): 'to go up' [BAGD, LN; all translations except CEV, KJV, NLT], 'to ascend' [BAGD, LN], 'to go out' [KJV], 'to come to' [CEV], 'to arrive in' [NLT], 'to come up' [LN]. This verb means to move up [LN]. The Jewish pilgrims who traveled from Galilee at 680 feet below sea-level literally 'went up' to Jerusalem which was located at 2500 feet above sea-level. [NTC]. This is the normal verb used to describe a pilgrimage to Jerusalem [TH].

c. aorist act. subj. of ἁγνίζω (LN **53.30**) (BAGD 1.a. p. 11): 'to purify' [AB, BAGD, Gdt, HTC, **LN**, NICNT2, NTC, WBC; KJV, NASB, NJB, NRSV, REB]. The clause 'so that they might purify themselves' is translated 'to make themselves pure' [NCV], 'for their ceremonial cleansing' [NIV], 'to go through a ceremonial cleansing' [Ph], 'so they could go through the purification ceremony' [NLT], 'to get themselves ready for the festival' [CEV], 'to cleanse themselves ritually' [NET]. This verb means to purify and cleanse ritually and thus acquire a state of ritual acceptability [LN]. God required the Jews to purify themselves before taking part in the

Passover celebration [TRT]. Some languages have no way to express spiritual purity and it may be necessary to translate 'to do what was necessary so that God would look upon them as being good' or '...that God would accept them' [TH].

QUESTION—How many may have been meant by the word 'many'?

The number of pilgrims may have varied between 85,000 and 125,000 [AB, TRT]. The Jerusalem population was normally about 25,000. The Passover pilgrims would increase that to more than 100,000 [TH]. According to some estimates, the population of Jerusalem increased from 100,000 to one million during this festival [BECNT].

QUESTION—What is the sense of the noun χώρα 'country'?

It refers to the rest of the country as opposed to Jerusalem itself [Bar, Car, HTC, ICC, Lns, My, NTC]. It may refer specifically to the province of Judea [HTC]. The reference is probably to the 'country near the desert' of the previous verse [NICNT2].

QUESTION—How did the Jews purify themselves?

They needed to perform the Levitical purification ceremony (Numbers 9:6–13; 2 Chronicles 30:15–19) [HTC, NICNT2, NTC]. See also Exodus 19:10–15 [NTC]. It was the purification required for them to participate in the Passover [NICNT2]. For certain purification rituals a period of seven days was required [Car, EGT, HTC, ICC, Kn, NICNT1, TH, TRT, WBC].

11:56 So they-were-looking-for[a] Jesus and standing in the temple they-were-talking with each-other, "What does-(it)-appear[b] to-you(pl)? He-will-certainly-not[c] -come to the Festival?" **11:57** Now/but the chief-priests and the Pharisees had-given commands that if anyone knew where he-is he-should-report[d] (it) so-that they-might-arrest[e] him.

LEXICON—a. imperf. act. indic. of ζητέω (LN 27.41) (BAGD 1.c. p. 339): 'to look for' [BAGD, HTC, NTC; LN; NCV, NET, NIV, NLT, NRSV, Ph, TEV], 'to look around for' [CEV], 'to look out for' [NJB, REB], 'to seek' [BAGD, Gdt, NICNT2; KJV, NASB], 'to try to find, to try to learn where something is' [LN]. This verb means to try to learn the location of something, often by movement from place to place in the process of searching [LN]. The imperfect tense indicates ongoing action [NICNT1].

b. pres. act. indic. of δοκέω (LN 31.30) (BAGD 3.a. p. 202): 'to appear' [LN], 'to think' [BAGD, LN], 'to believe' [BAGD], 'to seem, to assume' [LN]. The question 'What does it appear to you?' is translated 'What do you think?' [all translations except WBC; CEV], 'You don't think he...' [CEV], 'What is your opinion?' [WBC]. This verb means to hold an opinion based upon appearances which may be significantly different from reality [LN].

c. οὐ μή (LN 69.5, 69.13) (BAGD D.1.a. p. 517): 'certainly not' [BAGD, LN (69.5)], 'by no means' [LN (69.5)], 'never' [BAGD]. The question 'He will certainly not come to the Festival?' is translated 'Do you think that he will not come to the feast?' [Gdt], 'Surely he won't come to the festival?' [Ph], '(What do you think) that he will not/won't come to the feast?' [HTC; KJV, NET], '(What do you think) that he will not come to the feast at all?' [KJV, NASB], 'Isn't he coming to the Feast at all?' [NIV], 'Will he come to the festival or not?' [NJB], 'Perhaps he is not coming to the festival' [REB], 'Is there really a chance that he'll come for the feast?' [AB], 'That he surely won't come to the festival?' [NICNT2], 'that he will certainly not come to the feast?' [NTC], 'Is he coming to the feast?' [NCV], 'You don't think he will come here for Passover, do you?' [CEV], 'He won't come for Passover, will he?' [NLT], 'Surely he will not/won't come to the festival, will he?' [WBC; NRSV, TEV]. This negative particle combination indicates that a strongly emphatic positive response is expected to a question [LN (69.13)]. In combination with οὐ, μή has the effect of strengthening the negation [BAGD, LN (69.5)]. It is the most decisive way of negativing something in the future. In a rhetorical question, it indicates that a positive reply is expected [BAGD].

d. aorist act. subj. of μηνύω (LN **33.209**) (BAGD p. 519): 'to report' [AB, NTC, WBC; NASB, NET, NIV, NLT, REB, TEV], 'to make known' [BAGD, NICNT2], 'to inform' [**LN**; NJB], 'to declare' [Gdt], 'to show' [KJV], 'to reveal' [BAGD, LN], 'to give information (to the authorities)' [BAGD]. The clause 'he should report it' is translated 'he must tell them' [NCV, similarly Ph], 'he should let them know' [HTC; similarly NRSV, CEV]. This verb means to provide information concerning something, with emphasis on the fact that such information is secret or known only to a select few [LN].

e. aorist act. subj. of πιάζω (LN 37.110) (BAGD 2.a. p. 657): 'to arrest' [BAGD, LN; all translations except Gdt; KJV, NASB], 'to seize' [BAGD, LN; NASB], 'to take' [Gdt; KJV], 'to take into custody' [BAGD]. This verb means to take a person into custody for alleged illegal activity [LN]. It implies that the action is done with hostile intent [BAGD].

QUESTION—What response is expected to the question 'He will certainly not come to the festival?'

1. The form of the question either expects the answer 'No', or introduces an element of doubt about his coming [Bar, BECNT, ICC, My, NICNT1, NICNT2, NTC, Rd, TRT, WBC; CEV, NLT, NRSV, TEV]: 'Surely he will not come to the festival, will he?' [TEV]. The question expresses doubt and anticipates the answer 'No, he will not come' [TH, TRT]. While a negative reply is expected, still there is a hint of a positive reply as well implying that if he does come it will be a really bold move on his part [NICNT2]. The question implies tense uncertainty but assumes that he will not risk coming [BECNT, Rd]. Their negative evaluation is the result of the edict of arrest given by the chief priests and the Pharisees (verse 57) [ICC, Lns, NTC, My, Rd]. The Jews consider it unlikely that he would be so foolish as to appear at the festival [NICNT1]. It is more likely that the question expresses merely an element of doubt about his coming rather than a strong denial [Bar].

2. A positive response is expected [BAGD, HTC, LN]: He certainly will come, won't he? The combination οὐ μή in a question indicates that a positive reply is expected (See Blass-Debrunner 365,4; 427,2 and John 18:11) [HTC].

QUESTION—What is indicated by the conjunction δέ 'now/but' in verse 57?

It indicates that the chief priests and Pharisees are being contrasted with the common people [HTC]. Rather than contrast, the conjunction indicates that this verse is a parenthetical statement that is necessary to understand the situation. The author explains that prior to the arrival of these pilgrims the authorities had already issued orders demanding that he be reported [Lns, My]. This conjunction is translated 'now' [Gdt, HTC, NICNT2, NTC; KJV, NASB, NET, NRSV, REB], 'but' [WBC; NCV, NIV], 'meanwhile' [NLT], 'it should be understood that' [Ph], not explicit [AB; CEV, NJB, TEV].

DISCOURSE UNIT—12:1–50 [NICNT1]. The topic is the close of Jesus' public ministry.

DISCOURSE UNIT—12:1–11 [BECNT, Car, Gdt, HTC, Lns; NASB, NET, NIV, NLT, Ph]. The topic is the supper at Bethany [Gdt], the anointing at Bethany [BECNT, Car, HTC, Lns; NASB, NET, NIV, NLT], an act of love as the end approaches [Ph].

DISCOURSE UNIT—12:1–8 [AB, Kn, NICNT1, WBC; CEV, NRSV, TEV]. The topic is Mary anoints Jesus for his death [AB, NICNT1, WBC; NRSV, TEV], Mary's lavish devotion [Kn], Bethany [CEV, NCV].

12:1 Then/therefore six days before the Passover[a] Jesus came to Bethany, where Lazarus was, whom Jesus raised from the dead.

TEXT—Following Λάζαρος 'Lazarus' some manuscripts add ὁ τεθνηκώς 'the one having been dead'. GNT rejects this addition with an A rating, indicating that the omission is certain.

LEXICON—a. πάσχα (LN 51.6) (BAGD 1. p. 633): 'Passover' [BAGD, LN; all translations except WBC; KJV, NCV, NLT, REB], 'passover' [WBC; KJV], 'Passover festival' [LN; REB], 'Passover Feast' [NCV], 'Passover celebration' [NLT]. This noun denotes the Jewish festival commemorating the deliverance of Jews from Egypt [LN]. It denotes a Jewish festival, celebrated on the 14th of the month of Nisan, and continuing into the early hours of the 15th. It is followed by the Feast of Unleavened Bread on the 15th to the 21st. Popular usage merged the two festivals and treated them as a unity, as they were for practical purposes [BAGD].

QUESTION—What relationship is indicated by the conjunction οὖν 'then/therefore'?

1. A resumptive or transitional relationship is indicated [HTC, ICC, Lns, My, NICNT2, NTC; KJV, NET]: then.
2. A causal relationship is indicated [EGT, Gdt, NICNT1; NASB]: therefore. This conjunction ties this event to the preceding narrative. The Jews were

looking for a way to have Jesus killed. Although there was no need to rush needlessly into danger, Jesus had come to lay down his life for others. 'Therefore' at the set time he came to the place where this would be accomplished [NICNT1].

QUESTION—On which day did Jesus come to Bethany?
1. Jesus came to Bethany on a Saturday [AB, BECNT, Bar, Car, EGT, ICC, Kn, My, Rd, TH, WBC]. In John's Gospel, the Passover began on the next Friday evening (13:1; 18:28; 19:31,42). So the anointing must have taken place on the preceding Saturday evening [TH]. John seems to take the Passover as beginning Thursday evening. Therefore six days before brings us back to the preceding Saturday [BECNT, Car].
2. Jesus came to Bethany on Friday [Lns, TRT]. Not counting the day being counted from, the 14th of Nisan (Passover) and counting back, according to the Greek system, Jesus arrived in Bethany the Friday morning of the 8th of Nisan [Lns].
3. Jesus came to Bethany on Sunday evening. Counting the day of arrival, Sunday, and the day of Preparation of the Passover, the 14th of Nisan, there are six days. Sunday then is the day on which Jesus arrived at Bethany [Gdt].

QUESTION—What is indicated by the clause 'where Lazarus was'?
It indicates that Bethany was his home village or where he lived [AB, TH, TRT; NCV, NET, NIV, NLT, NRSV, Ph, REB, TEV].

12:2 Then/therefore[a] they-made him (a) dinner[b] there, and Martha was-serving[c] and Lazarus was one of the (ones) reclining[d] with him.

LEXICON—a. οὖν (LN 89.50): 'then' [LN, NICNT2], 'therefore' [Gdt, LN], 'so' [NTC; NASB, NET], 'accordingly' [LN, Lns, WBC], 'consequently, so then' [LN], not explicit [AB, HTC; CEV, KJV, NCV, NIV, NJB, NLT, NRSV, Ph, REB, TEV]. This conjunction indicates result, often implying the conclusion of a process of reasoning [LN]. The word 'accordingly' suggests that this banquet was the result of Jesus' friends taking advantage of the occasion to honor him [Lns]. It indicates that this feast was given in gratitude for Jesus' miracle of bringing Lazarus back to life [Gdt].

b. δεῖπνον (LN 23.25) (BAGD 2. p. 173): 'dinner' [AB, BAGD, NICNT2, WBC; NCV, NET, NIV, NJB, NLT, NRSV, TEV], 'supper' [BAGD, Bar, HTC, LN, Lns, NTC; KJV, NASB, Ph, REB], 'feast' [Gdt], 'meal' [CEV, '(formal) dinner' [BAGD], 'banquet' [BAGD]. This noun denotes the principal meal of the day, usually in the evening [BAGD, LN, Lns].

c. imperf. act. indic. of διακονέω (LN 46.13) (BAGD 1. p. 184): 'to serve' [LN; all translations except NCV, NJB, Ph, TEV], 'to serve the food' [NCV], 'to help serve' [TEV], 'to wait on/upon' [LN; NJB, Ph], 'to wait on someone at table' [BAGD]. This verb means to serve food and drink to those who are eating [LN].

d. pres. mid. (deponent = act.) participle of ἀνάκειμαι (LN 17.23) (BAGD 2. p. 55): 'to recline' [LN, NICNT2, NTC], 'to recline at (the) table' [BAGD, WBC; NASB, NIV], 'to sit at (the) table' [KJV, TEV], 'to be at (the) table' [AB, BAGD, Gdt, HTC, LN; NJB, NRSV], 'to be present at the table' [NET], 'to take one's place at table' [Ph], 'to be among the guests' [REB], 'to eat' [LN; NCV, NLT], 'to dine, to sit down to eat' [LN], not explicit [CEV]. This verb means to be in a reclining position as one eats (with the focus either on the position or the act of eating) [LN]. That they reclined at this meal may indicate that this was a banquet rather than a regular meal [BECNT].

QUESTION—What was the occasion for the dinner?

The dinner may have been given in gratitude to Jesus for raising Lazarus from the dead [NTC]. It was an expression of gratitude by the residents of Bethany to Jesus for his having honored the village by performing so notable a miracle there [Gdt]. It was given to welcome Jesus back from his time away and to celebrate with him the raising of Lazarus [NICNT2].

QUESTION—To whom does the pronoun 'they' in the verb ἐποίησαν 'they made (him a dinner)' refer?

1. The pronoun reference is indefinite and refers to the villagers or friends [Gdt, ICC, Lns, NICNT1, TH]. It is impossible to identify with certainty who the antecedent was. If it is necessary to make the referent explicit a phrase like 'Jesus' friends' could be used. If this is not made explicit, there is the possibility that people may assume that it refers back to the chief priests and Pharisees just mentioned in 11:57 [TH].
2. It refers to Mary and Martha and Lazarus [Bar, My, NICNT2]. 'They' refers to the family of Bethany which is clear from the words 'and Martha was serving' [My].

QUESTION—What is indicated by the mention of Martha serving and Lazarus being among the guests?

The mentioning of the two events indicates that this dinner was at a home different from that of Martha, Mary and Lazarus. Otherwise Martha would not be characterized as serving, or Lazarus as being among the guests [Gdt, Lns]. The note that Lazarus was among the guests is indicative of the meal being held in someone else's home [AB, EGT, Gdt, ICC, NICNT1]. If it were in Lazarus' home, his presence would have been merely assumed and not remarked about [Lns, NICNT1]. Mark and Matthew write that this was at the home of Simon the leper (Matthew 26:6–13; Mark 14:3–6) [CH, EGT, Gdt, IVP, Lns, NTC]. That Martha was serving would be more natural to mention if she were in her own house [ICC].

12:3 Then/therefore[a] Mary having-taken (a) pound[b] of pure[c] expensive[d] nard[e] perfume[f] anointed[g] Jesus' feet and wiped[h] his feet with her hair. The house was filled with fragrance[i] of-the ointment.

LEXICON—a. οὖν (LN 89.50): 'then' [LN, NICNT2; KJV, NASB, NET, NIV, NLT, Ph, REB, TEV], 'therefore' [Gdt, LN, NTC, WBC], 'accordingly' [LN], 'consequently, so then' [LN], not explicit [AB, HTC; CEV, NCV, NJB, NRSV]. This conjunction indicates result, often implying the conclusion of a process of reasoning [LN]. It may have the full meaning of 'therefore' here indicating that since Lazarus had been brought back from death and was now present and completely healthy at table with Jesus, 'therefore' Mary did this noble act on Jesus [NTC]. Failing to translate this word as 'therefore' misses the fact that John is connecting the anointing of Jesus with the preceding events [NICNT1].

b. λίτρα (LN **86.4**) (BAGD p. 475): 'pound' [AB, BAGD, Gdt, HTC, **LN**, NICNT2, NTC, WBC; KJV, NASB, NRSV, REB], 'whole pound' [Ph], 'pint' [LN; NCV], 'whole pint' [TEV], 'about a pint' [NIV], 'three quarters of a pound' [NET], 'twelve-ounce jar' [NLT], 'bottle' [CEV]. This noun denotes a Roman pound, weighing about twelve ounces or about 325 grams [BAGD, LN]. In speaking of perfume in John 12:3 it may be far better to indicate quantity rather than weight, and therefore one may translate 'then Mary took a pint of perfume.' In translating λίτρα in the NT, one need not identify the pound as being 'a Roman pound' [LN]. This much perfume was a very large amount [BECNT, Car, Lns, NICNT1, NTC, TH]. In the metric system this would be 'about half a liter' [TH, TRT].

c. πιστικός (LN **79.97**) (BAGD): 'pure' [Gdt, HTC, **LN**, NTC; NASB, NCV, NET, NIV, NJB, NRSV, REB, TEV], 'geniuine' [NICNT2, WBC], 'real' [AB], not explicit [CEV, KJV, Ph]. This adjective is also translated as a noun: 'essence (of nard)' [NLT]. It describes something as being pure, with the possible implication of a quality that can be trusted [LN].

d. πολύτιμος (LN 65.3) (BAGD p. 690): 'expensive' [AB, LN, NICNT2; NET, NIV, NLT], 'very expensive' [WBC; CEV, NCV, Ph, TEV], 'costly' [HTC; NRSV], 'very costly' [KJV, NASB, NJB, REB], 'very precious' [BAGD, NTC], 'of great price' [Gdt], 'valuable' [BAGD, LN]. This adjective describes something as being of great value or worth, implying in some contexts a monetary scale [LN].

e. νάρδος (LN 6.210) (BAGD 2. p. 534): 'nard' [AB, Gdt, HTC, NICNT2, NTC, WBC; NASB, NCV, NIV, NJB, NLT, NRSV, TEV], 'perfume of nard' [BAGD, LN], 'oil of nard' [BAGD, LN; REB], 'aromatic oil' [NET], 'spikenard' [KJV], 'ointment' [BAGD], not explicit [CEV, Ph]. The phrase '(a) pound of pure expensive nard perfume' is translated 'a very expensive bottle of perfume' [CEV], 'a pound of ointment of spikenard, very costly' [KJV], 'a pound of very costly perfume of pure nard' [NASB], 'a pint of very expensive perfume made from pure nard' [NCV], 'three quarters of a pound of expensive aromatic oil from pure nard' [NET], 'about a pint of pure nard, an expensive perfume' [NIV], 'a pound of very costly ointment, pure nard' [NJB], 'a twelve-ounce jar of expensive perfume made from essence of nard' [NLT], 'a pound of costly perfume made of pure nard' [NRSV], 'a whole pound of very expensive perfume' [Ph], 'a pound of very costly perfume, pure oil of nard' [REB], 'a whole pint of a very expensive perfume made of pure nard' [TEV], 'a pound of expensive perfume made from real nard' [AB], 'a pound of very expensive ointment, made from genuine nard' [WBC], 'a pound of expensive perfume of genuine nard' [NICNT2], 'a pound of ointment of pure nard, which was of great price' [Gdt], 'a pound of costly ointment of pure nard' [HTC], 'a pound of very precious ointment of pure nard' [NTC]. This noun denotes an aromatic oil extracted from a plant called nard [AB, LN]. Translators normally borrow the term 'nard' but employ some type of classifier, for example, 'a perfume called nard' or 'a sweet-smelling substance, nard' [LN]. The fragrant oil was derived from the root and hair stem or spike of the nard plant, hence the name 'spikenard'. The nard plant was grown in the mountains of Northern India [AB, TH].

f. μύρον (LN 6.205) (BAGD p. 529): 'perfume' [AB, NICNT2, BAGD, LN; CEV, NCV, NIV, NLT, NRSV, Ph, REB, TEV], 'ointment' [BAGD, Gdt, HTC, NTC, WBC; KJV, NJB], not explicit [KJV, NASB, NET]. This noun denotes a strongly aromatic and expensive ointment [LN]. It refers to a perfume or ointment made from myrrh. It is either a dry powder or a liquid, secreted from the balsam tree. It was used as incense or perfume in cosmetics, medicines and in burial preparation [AB]. Μύρον is a generic name for all liquid perfumes and νάρδος 'nard' is the most precious kind of perfume [Gdt].

g. aorist act. indic. of ἀλείφω (LN 47.14) (BAGD 1. p. 35): 'to anoint' [BAGD, LN; all translations except CEV, NCV, NIV, TEV], 'to pour on' [CEV, NCV, NIV, TEV]. This verb means to anoint with a liquid, normally oil or perfume [LN]. The perfume is actually poured out on the feet of Jesus [NTC]. It means 'to smear with oil' [Bar]. If it is understood that the perfume is liquid, then a verb such as 'to pour' would be appropriate. If it is understood to be a more solid ointment or cream, then a verb such as 'to rub on' or 'to put on' could be used [TH].

h. aorist act. indic. of ἐκμάσσω (LN 79.83) (BAGD p. 243): 'to wipe' [BAGD; all translations except NET, REB], 'to wipe dry' [LN; NET, REB]. This verb means to cause something to become dry by wiping with a dry substance [LN].

i. ὀσμή (LN 79.45) (BAGD 1.a. p. 586): 'fragrance' [AB, BAGD, HTC, NICNT2, NTC, WBC; NASB, NET, NLT, NRSV, Ph, REB], 'sweet smell' [CEV, TEV], 'odor' [BAGD, Gdt, LN; KJV], 'scent' [LN; NJB], 'smell' [LN]. This noun denotes the scent or odor of a substance, whether agreeable or disagreeable [LN].

QUESTION—How are the nouns related in the genitive construction μύρου νάρδου 'perfume of nard'?

The perfume is made of nard [AB, TH, TRT, WBC; NCV, NLT, NRSV, TEV].

QUESTION—What is indicated by Mary's drying Jesus' feet with her hair?

It was looked on with distinct disfavor for a woman to let her hair down in the presence of men [NTC]. Lightfoot notes that among the Jews it was a disgrace for a woman to let her hair down and appear in public with disheveled hair [Gdt]. Jewish women (especially married women) did not let their hair down in public [BECNT, Kn, NICNT1] as it would have been a sign of loose morals [BECNT, NICNT1]. For a woman to let down her hair before outsiders was considered indecent [Lns]. The action of Mary was an expression of devotion [IVP, Kn] done out of gratitiude for what Jesus had done for her brother [IVP]. It was an act of humility [Kn, Lns] and affection for Jesus as a woman's hair was her glory [Kn]. Mary lays her woman's honor at Jesus feet and uses her honor as a towel to dry his feet [Lns]. The phrase 'his feet' is twice repeated to correlate with the phrase 'with her hair' and to emphasize the greatness of her love [My].

QUESTION—What is indicated by Mary's anointing of Jesus feet in this way?

It was an act of self-humbling devotion and love [Car]. It was an act of absolute humility and great devotion [NICNT1, TRT]. Anointing of the feet is equated with anointing of the whole body (13:9–10). If so, this may be a symbolic anointing of Jesus' body for burial [NICNT1].

12:4 But[a] one of his disciples Judas Iscariot,[b] the-one being-about-to[c] betray[d] him says, **12:5** "Why was this perfume not sold (for) three-hundred denarii[e] and given to-the-poor?[f]"

TEXT—There is a slight textual problem here as EGT, Gdt; KJV, NJB, REB are translating an οὖν 'then/therefore' instead of δέ 'but/and' at the beginning of this verse. GNT has δέ without comment.

LEXICON—a. δέ (LN 89.124, 89.94): 'but' [HTC, LN (89.124), Lns, NICNT2, NTC, WBC; NASB, NET, NIV, NLT, NRSV, Ph], 'on the other hand' [LN (89.124)], 'and' [LN (89.94)], 'then' [Gdt; KJV, NJB], 'at this' [REB], not explicit [AB; CEV, NCV, TEV]. This conjunction indicates a contrastive relation [LN (89.124)]. It can also indicate an additive relation, but with the possible implication of some contrast [LN (89.94)]. There is a striking contrast between the generosity of Mary and the selfishness of Judas [NTC].

b. Ἰσκαριώθ (LN 93.181, 93.496) (BAGD p. 381): 'Iscariot' [BAGD, LN (93.181); all translations except Gdt, NICNT2], 'the Iscariot' [Gdt, NICNT2]. This noun denotes an identifying name (probably based on a place name; see 93.496) of Judas, the betrayer of Jesus. Καρυῶτος, a place in southern Judea 'Carioth' or 'Kerioth' [LN (93.496)].

c. pres. act. participle of μέλλω (LN 67.62) (BAGD 1.c.γ. p. 501): 'to be about to' [LN, NTC, WBC; NRSV], 'to be going to' [AB, NICNT2; CEV, NET, Ph, TEV], 'to intend' [BAGD; NASB], 'to propose, to have in mind' [BAGD]. The clause 'the one being about to betray him' is translated 'which should betray him' [KJV], 'who would later turn against him' [NCV], '(he) who was (later) to betray him' [HTC; NIV, NJB, REB], 'he who was soon to betray him' [Gdt], 'who would soon betray him' [NLT]. This verb means to occur at a point of time in the future which is subsequent to another event and closely related to it [LN].

d. pres. act. infin. of παραδίδωμι (LN 37.111) (BAGD 1.b. p. 614): 'to betray' [Gdt, HTC, LN, NTC, WBC; CEV, KJV, NASB, NET, NIV, NJB, NRSV, Ph, REB, TEV], 'to hand over' [AB, BAGD, LN, NICNT2], 'to turn against' [NCV], 'to turn over' [BAGD, LN], 'to give up a person' [BAGD]. This verb means to deliver a person into the control of someone else, involving either the handing over of a presumably guilty person for punishment by the authorities or the handing over of an individual to an enemy who will presumably take undue advantage of the victim [LN]. It is used as a technical term of the police and courts meaning 'to hand over into the custody of'. Here it refers to the betrayal of Jesus by Judas [BAGD].

e. δηνάριον (LN 6.75) (BAGD p. 179): 'denarius' [BAGD, Gdt, HTC, LN, NICNT2, NTC, WBC; NASB, NJB, NRSV, REB], 'silver coin' [CEV, NET, TEV], 'silver piece' [AB], 'pence' [KJV], not explicit [NCV]. This question is translated 'Why wasn't it sold and the money given to the poor?' [NCV]. The phrase '(for) three hundred denarii' is translated '(worth) a year's wages' [NIV, NLT], '(worth) thirty pounds' [Ph]. This noun denotes a Roman silver coin equivalent to a day's wage of a common laborer [BAGD, LN].

f. πτωχός (LN 57.53) (BAGD 1.a. p. 728): 'poor' [BAGD, LN], 'destitute' [LN]. This pronominal adjective is translated 'to the poor' [all translations except NASB], 'to poor people' [NASB]. It describes someone as being poor and destitute, implying a continuous state [LN]. It is mainly used as a substantive and indicates someone who is dependent on others for support [BAGD].

QUESTION—What is the meaning of ὁ Ἰσκαριώτης 'the Iscariot'?

It probably means that he was a man from Kerioth [BAGD, Car, EGT, ICC, LN, Lns, NICNT1, NTC, TRT]. This was a place (town) in the province of Judah [BAGD, EGT, LN, Lns, NTC]. Kerioth may have been located in Judah or Moab [ICC, NICNT1].

QUESTION—Was Judas asking for information, or was his question rhetorical? If it is rhetorical, what is its function?

His question is essentially rhetorical making a strong statement, 'This perfume should have been sold for three hundred silver coins, and then the money given to the poor' [TH, TRT; NLT]: 'It should have been sold and the money given to the poor' [NLT]. His question voices his *objection* to Mary's noble action [BECNT, Car, HTC, Lns, NICNT2]. Judas is *indignant* at the waste [Gdt]. He *thinks it would have been better* if Mary had sold the perfume and given the proceeds to the poor [NTC]. He *strongly disapproves* of Mary's action [Rd]. He *complains* about the waste [CH]. He is *shocked* seeing such a waste [IVP]. 'Jesus replied to *this outburst*' (12:7) [Ph].

QUESTION—What was to be given to the poor, the perfume or the proceeds from the sale?

Translating literally the question, 'Why wasn't this perfume sold for three hundred denarii and given to the poor?' might imply that the perfume should be given to the poor. To avoid this meaning, it would be better to translate 'Why wasn't this perfume sold for three hundred denarii and *then the money* given to the poor? [AB, Gdt, TH, TRT; CEV, NCV, NET, NIV, NJB, NLT, NRSV, Ph, REB, TEV].

QUESTION—What is the value of three hundred denarii and how is it best to translate it?

A denarius is worth a laborer's daily wage, so three hundred would be three hundred days' wages and allowing for Sabbaths would amount to about a year's wages for a working man [NICNT1]. Considering the rapid change in the purchasing power of money from one time to another, it may be best to translate denarii as 'silver pieces' with a footnote about the value of a silver piece as being the average daily wage of a laborer [TH]. This amount was translated variously: 'three hundred silver coins' [CEV, NET, TEV], 'three hundred silver pieces' [AB], 'a year's wages' [NIV, NLT], 'thirty pounds' [Ph].

12:6 Now he-said this not because it-was-a-concern[a] to-him about the-poor, but because he-was (a) thief and having the money-box[b] he-was-stealing[c] the-things being-put (into it).

LEXICON—a. imperf. act. indic. of μέλει (LN 30.39) (BAGD 2. p. 500): 'to be a concern' [BAGD], 'to be a care' [BAGD], 'to be concerned about, to think about' [LN]. The clause 'not because it was a concern to him about the poor' is translated 'not out of any concern for the poor' [REB], 'not because he was concerned about/for the poor' [AB, NTC, WBC; NASB, NET], 'not because it mattered to him about the poor' [NICNT2], 'Judas did not really care about the poor' [CEV, NCV], 'not that he cared for the poor' [Gdt, HTC; KJV, NLT], 'not because he cared about the poor' [NIV, NJB, NRSV, Ph, TEV]. This verb means to think about something in such a way as to make an appropriate response [LN]. It is also used of the hired hand about whom it was said, 'it does not matter to him about the sheep' (10:13) [NICNT1].

b. γλωσσόκομον (LN 6.143) (BAGD p. 162): 'money box' [AB, BAGD, HTC, LN, NICNT2, NTC; NASB, NCV, NET], 'collecting box' [WBC], 'money bag' [CEV, NIV, TEV], 'bag' [KJV], 'purse' [Gdt, Ph], 'common purse' [NRSV, REB], 'common fund' [NJB], '(the) disciples' money' [NLT], 'case, container' [BAGD]. This noun denotes a box in which money was kept [LN]. It was probably a small portable cash box [Gdt]. It was probably not a bag, but a box made of wood or other rigid material [BECNT, NICNT1]. It was a box or coffer with several compartments [ICC].

c. imperf. act. indic. of βαστάζω (LN 15.201) (BAGD 3.b. p. 137): 'to steal' [BAGD, NICNT2; CEV, NCV, NET, NLT, NRSV], 'to pilfer' [BAGD; NCV, REB], 'to help oneself' [WBC; NIV, NJB, Ph, TEV], 'to take' [Gdt, HTC], 'to take away' [LN, NTC], 'to remove, to carry away' [BAGD, LN], 'to take surreptitiously' [BAGD]. The clause 'he was stealing the things being put into it' is translated 'he was stealing from what was being put in' [NICNT2], 'he...sometimes would steal from it' [CEV], 'he...bare what was put therein' [KJV], 'he used to pilfer/steal what was put into it' [NASB, NET, NRSV], 'he used to pilfer the money kept in it' [REB], 'he often stole from it' [NCV], 'he often stole some for himself' [NLT], 'he took what was put therein' [Gdt], 'he used to take (away) what was put into it' [HTC, NTC], 'he used to help himself to what was put into/in it' [WBC; NIV], 'he used to help himself to/from the contents' [NJB, Ph], 'he would help himself from it' [TEV], 'he could help himself to what was put in' [AB]. This verb means to carry away from a place, with the probable implication of something that is relatively heavy [LN]. The imperfect tense indicates that this was repeated [NICNT1, NTC, TH], habitual action [EGT, TH]. Judas did not take all the money [Gdt, My, NTC, TH], but small amounts off and on [NTC].

QUESTION—What is indicated by the clause 'he was having the money box'?
It indicates that he was the treasurer for Jesus and the disciples [Car, ICC, NICNT1, NTC, Rd, TH, TRT].

QUESTION—What is meant by the words 'the things being put into it'?
These were gifts from friends and followers for the purchase of daily necessities and charitable gifts [My, TH].

12:7 Therefore/then Jesus said, "Let- her -be,[a] so-that she-may-keep[b] it for the day of my burial.[c] **12:8** For the-poor you(pl)- always -have with you, but you(pl)-do- not always -have me."

TEXT—Instead of including these two verses, some manuscripts omit 12:8, one manuscript omits both 7 and 8, and others omit from 12:8 the words μεθ' ἑαυτων, ἐμὲ δὲ οὐ πάντοτε ἔχετε 'with you, but me you do not always have'. GNT includes verses 12:7–8 with an A rating, indicating that the inclusion is certain.

LEXICON—a. aorist act. impera. of ἀφίημι (LN 13.140) (BAGD 4. p. 126): 'to let be' [NICNT2, NTC], 'to let' [BAGD, LN], 'to allow, to leave it to' [LN], 'to let go, to tolerate' [BAGD]. The command Ἄφες αὐτήν, 'Let her be' [NICNT2, NTC] is also translated 'Leave her alone [AB; CEV, NCV, NET, NIV, NJB, NLT, NRSV, Ph, REB, TEV], 'Let her alone' [Gdt, HTC, WBC; KJV, NASB]. This verb means to leave it to someone to do something, with the implication of distancing oneself from the event [LN].

b. aorist act. subj. of τηρέω (LN 13.32) (BAGD 2.a. p. 814): 'to keep' [BAGD, LN; all translations except NCV, NIV, NLT, REB], 'to save' [NCV, NIV, REB], 'to cause to continue, to retain' [LN], 'to hold, to reserve, to preserve someone or something' [BAGD], not explicit [NLT]. The clause 'so that she may keep it for the day of my burial' [NASB], is also translated 'so as to keep it for the day of my burial' [NICNT2], '(it was) in order that she might keep it for the day of my burial' [NTC], 'It was intended that she should save this perfume for the day of my burial'

[NIV], 'The purpose was that she might keep it for the day of my embalming' [AB], 'She has kept this perfume/it for the day of my burial' [Gdt; CEV, NET], 'against the day of my burying has she kept this' [KJV], 'She bought it so that she might keep it for the day of my burial' [NRSV], 'she had to keep it for the day of my burial' [WBC], 'She did this in preparation for my burial' [NLT], 'It was right for her to save this perfume for today, the day for me to be prepared for my burial' [NCV], '(Let her) keep it/this for the day of my burial' [HTC; NJB, Ph, REB], 'Let her keep what she has for the day of my burial' [TEV]. This verb means to cause a state to continue [LN].

c. ἐνταφιασμός (LN 52.6) (BAGD p. 268): 'burial' [BAGD, all translations except AB; KJV, NCV, NLT], 'burying' [KJV], 'embalming' [AB], 'preparation for burial' [BAGD, LN; NLT], 'the day for me to be prepared for burial' [NCV]. This noun denotes the preparation of a body for burial [EGT, Gdt, ICC, LN, NICNT1].

QUESTION—Is there ellipsis before the clause 'so that she may keep it'?

The implied information was probably 'Let her be. (She did not sell it), so that she may keep it for the day of my burial' [BECNT, TRT]. It may be that Jesus' reply is an elliptical rhetorical question meaning, 'Let her alone! Do you suppose she should have kept it (the ointment) until the day of my burial?' [Rd].

QUESTION—Did Mary use all the perfume or only part of it?

1. She used it all to anoint Jesus' body beforehand for burial [AB, EGT, Gdt, HTC, Lns, NICNT1, NICNT2, NTC, Rd]. The idea is that Mary was unknowingly keeping the perfume to embalm Jesus. It was not intended for some future use. This agrees with Mark 14:3 where the woman breaks the jar using it all. This also explains Judas's anger that all the perfume had been used. Also Mary did not keep part of it to prepare Jesus' body for burial later since she had no role in that event [AB]. In reply to Judas' question of 'why?', the purpose of Mary's having kept the perfume was to anoint Jesus before his burial [Gdt]. Perhaps the meaning is that Mary should keep the perfume for the purpose she had in mind rather than selling it as Judas had suggested [NICNT1].

2. Mary used only part of the perfume and kept the rest for Jesus' burial [ICC, My]. Jesus' reply is in response to Judas' complaint and means to let her alone that she may not give the ointment to the poor, but rather preserve the remainder for the day of Jesus' embalming [My]. We should translate 'Let her alone, in order that she may keep it (namely the remainder of the spikenard) against the day of my burying' [ICC].

QUESTION—What relationship is indicated by the conjunction γάρ 'for'?

It indicates that this verse is the reason why anointing Jesus was appropriate in place of giving to the poor [EGT, My]: Let her keep...*because* the poor you always have with you.

QUESTION—What words are emphasized in this verse?
>
> The pronoun 'me' is emphasized [BECNT, NICNT1, TH]. The emphatic pronoun 'me' is in sharp contrast with the phrase 'the poor' [NICNT1]. The phrase 'the poor' and the pronoun 'me' are in emphatic positions in the Greek sentence [TH].

QUESTION—Is the care of the dead more important than giving to the poor?
>
> The Jewish rabbis ranked the care of the dead more important than almsgiving [BECNT, NICNT1, TH].

DISCOURSE UNIT—12:9–19 [AB, Kn, NICNT1, Rd, WBC]. The topic is the entry into Jerusalem [AB, Kn, NICNT1, Rd, WBC], Jerusalem and its king [Kn].

DISCOURSE UNIT—12:9–11 [Kn; CEV, NCV, NRSV, TEV]. The topic is plot to kill Lazarus.

12:9 Now the great crowd of the Jews learned^a that he-is there and they-came not only because-of Jesus, but also so-that they-might-see Lazarus whom he-raised from (the) dead.

TEXT—Instead of ἔγνω οὖν [ὁ] ὄχλος πολὺς ἐκ τῶν Ἰουδαίων 'now the great crowd of the Jews knew', some manuscripts read ἔγνω οὖν ὁ ὄχλος ὁ πολὺς ἐκ τῶν Ἰουδαίων 'now the great crowd of the Jews knew', others read ἔγνω οὖν ὄχλος πολὺς ἐκ τῶν Ἰουδαίων 'now a great crowd of the Jews knew', and still others read ὄχλος δὲ πολὺς ἐκ τῶν Ἰουδαίων ἤκουσαν 'but a great crowd of the Jews heard'. GNT reads ἔγνω οὖν [ὁ] ὄχλος πολὺς ἐκ τῶν Ἰουδαίων 'now the great crowd of the Jews knew' with a C rating, indicating difficulty in deciding which variant to place in the text.

LEXICON—a. aorist act. indic. of γινώσκω (LN 27.2) (BAGD 2.b. p. 161): 'to learn' [BAGD, Gdt, HTC, LN, NTC; NASB, NET, NRSV, REB], 'to find out' [AB, BAGD, LN, NICNT2; NIV], 'to hear' [CEV, NCV, NJB, NLT, TEV], 'to discover' [Ph], 'to ascertain' [BAGD], 'to know' [WBC; KJV]. This verb means to acquire information by whatever means, but often with the implication of personal involvement or experience [LN].

QUESTION—Should the article 'the' be retained in the phrase 'the great crowd' as some manuscripts have it or be omitted as others do. And what is its meaning?

1. The article should be retained [AB, CKB, HTC, Lns, NICNT1, NTC, Rd, WBC; NASB, NRSV, Ph]: *the* great crowd. The reading that includes the article is the most difficult and so probably the correct reading. There seems to be no reason for inserting an article if there were none while omitting one from the text would be an obvious correction [NICNT1]. The crowd referred to was probably the pilgrims who had come up to the festival [Bar, HTC]. The Jews described in 11:55–56 who had come to the festival are the ones referred here to as 'the great crowd of the Jews' [Rd].
2. It should be omitted [EGT, Gdt, ICC, NICNT2; CEV, KJV, NCV, NET, NIV, NJB, NLT, REB, TEV]: *a* great crowd. It is unlikely that the author

would have used the article to refer to a group not previously mentioned. The article may have been added by scribes [NICNT2]. They are the pilgrims who came with Jesus from Jericho and told of his coming. Then those pilgrims (11:55–56) from Judea who heard came to see him and Lazarus [Gdt].

QUESTION—Are τῶν Ἰουδαίων 'the Jews' the common people or the Jewish authorities?

They are the common people who found out he was there [AB, Bar, EGT, Lns, NTC]. In John the expression 'of the Jews' usually refers to Jesus' enemies. But many common people were also included [ICC]. They are the Jewish opposition [Gdt, My, NICNT1].

QUESTION—To which place does the clause ἐκεῖ ἐστιν 'he is there' refer?

It refers to Bethany [Lns, TH, TRT; NCV, TEV]: 'A large number of people heard that Jesus was in Bethany' [TEV].

12:10 But the chief-priests planned^a that they-might- also -kill Lazarus, 12:11 because on-account-of^b him many of the Jews were-going-away^c and were-believing in Jesus.

LEXICON—a. aorist mid. indic. of βουλεύομαι (LN 30.56) (BAGD 2. p. 145): 'to plan' [AB, HTC, LN, NTC, WBC; NASB, NET, NRSV, Ph], 'to make plans' [CEV, NCV, NIV, TEV], 'to decide' [NJB, NLT], 'to consult' [KJV], 'to resolve' [NICNT2; REB], 'to take counsel' [Gdt], 'to purpose, to intend' [LN]. This verb means to think, with the purpose of planning or deciding on a course of action [LN]. The middle voice indicates that the priests consulted with each other [BECNT, Lns].

b. διά (LN 90.44): 'on account of' [AB, HTC, LN, NICNT2, NTC, WBC; NASB, NET, NJB, NIV, NRSV, REB, TEV], 'because of' [LN; NCV, NLT], 'for this reason' [LN], not explicit [Gdt]. The phrease 'on account of him' is translated 'he was the reason' [CEV, Ph], 'by reason of him' [KJV]. This preposition, with an accusative object, indicates that a participant constitutes the cause or reason for an event or state [LN]. If the two causes, 'because' and 'on account of/because of' present difficulty in translation, they could be translated 'The chief priests made plans to kill Lazarus also, *because* the Jews were rejecting them and believing in Jesus. They were doing so *because of* what happened to Lazarus' [TH].

c. imperf. act. indic. of ὑπάγω (LN 15.52) (BAGD 2. p. 836): 'to go away' [Gdt, HTC, LN, NTC; KJV, NASB, NET, Ph], 'to go off' [NICNT2], 'to go' [BAGD], 'to depart' [LN], 'to leave' [LN; NJB], 'to turn from' [CEV], 'to go over to' [AB; NIV, REB], 'to desert' [NLT, NRSV], 'to reject' [TEV]. This verb means to depart from someone's presence, with the implication of a changed relation [BAGD]. The imperfect tense indicates inchoative or inceptive aspect 'began to go away' [ICC, NICNT1], or continuous aspect 'were going away' [NICNT1].

JOHN 12:10–11 119

QUESTION—What may have been a factor in the chief priests' decision to kill Jesus and Lazarus?

The chief priests were Sadducees and did not believe in the resurrection of the dead [BECNT, EGT, NICNT1, NTC]. Lazarus was a living witness to the resurrection and to the power of Jesus over death [EGT].

QUESTION—To whom does the pronoun αὐτὸν 'him' in the phrase 'on account of him' refer?

It refers to Lazarus [TRT; CEV, NCV]: 'Because of Lazarus' [NCV].

QUESTION—Should the verb 'going away' be interpreted metaphorically or literally?

1. It should be interpreted metaphorically meaning to leave one's allegiance to the Jewish leaders or their teaching [AB, Bar, Car, CH, ICC, IVP, NICNT1, TH, WBC; CEV, NCV, NIV, NJB, TEV, CKB, Go, HC, ICC]: 'many of the people were turning *from them* and putting their faith in Jesus [CEV]. While it could mean going over to Bethany, it more likely means to go over to Jesus' side [AB].
2. 'Going away' should be interpreted literally as 'leaving a place' [ICC, My, NTC]. Many of the Jews began to go away, perhaps to Bethany [ICC], or Jerusalem [My].

QUESTION—Is the phrase τῶν Ἰουδαίων 'of the Jews' a partitive genitive to mean 'many *of* the Jews', or is it a genitive of separation to mean 'many were going away *from* the Jews'?

1. The phrase 'of the Jews' is a partitive genetive to mean 'many of the Jews' [AB, Gdt , Lns, HTC, ICC, NICNT2, NTC; all versions except CEV, NCV, NJB, TEV]: 'many of the Jews were going over to Jesus and believing in him' [AB]. The words 'many' and 'of the Jews' are separated in the Greek sentence by several words but should be translated together as 'many of the Jews'. This is a partitive genitive rather than a genitive of separation [AB].
2. The phrase is a genitive of separation meaning 'were going away *from* the Jews' [TH, TRT, WBC; CEV, NCV, NJB, TEV]: 'many Jews were rejecting them and believing in Jesus' [TEV]. The genitive construction is a genitive of separation indicating that many were leaving the Jewish leaders [TH].

DISCOURSE UNIT—12:12–50 [Ph]. The topic is Jesus experiences a temporary triumph.

DISCOURSE UNIT—12:12–19 [Bar, BECNT, Car, Gdt, HTC, IVP, Kn, Lns; CEV, NASB, NET, NIV, NLT, NRSV, TEV]. The topic is Jesus' entry into Jerusalem.

DISCOURSE UNIT—12:12–16 [NCV]. The topic is Jesus enters Jerusalem.

12:12 The next day the large crowd that had-come to the Festival, having heard that Jesus is-coming to Jerusalem, **12:13** took palm-branches[a] of palm-trees[b] and went-out to (a) meeting with-him and were-crying-out, "Hosanna[c] blessed[d] (is) the-one coming in (the) name of (the) Lord, even the King-of-Israel.[e]"

LEXICON—a. βάϊον (LN **3.53**) (BAGD p. 130): 'palm branch' [BAGD, LN]. The phrase 'palm branches of palm trees' is translated 'branches of palm trees' [BAGD, Gdt, HTC, NTC, WBC; KJV, NASB, NCV, NET, NRSV, TEV], 'palm branches' [BAGD, **LN**; CEV, NIV, NLT, Ph, REB], 'branches of palm' [NJB], 'branches of the palms' [NICNT2], 'palm fronds' [AB].

b. φοῖνιξ (LN **3.8**) (BAGD I.1. p. 864): 'palm tree' [BAGD, LN], 'date palm' [BAGD].

c. ὡσαννά (LN 33.364) (BAGD p. 899): 'Hosanna' [BAGD, LN; all translations except CEV, NCV, NLT, TEV, Ph], 'Hooray!' [CEV], 'Praise God!' [NCV, NLT, TEV], 'God save him!' [Ph]. This is an Aramaic expression meaning 'help, I pray' or 'save, I pray', but which had become a strictly liturgical formula of praise. It is a shout of praise or adoration [LN].

c. perf. pass. participle of εὐλογέω (LN 33.470) (BAGD 2.a. p. 322): 'to bless' [BAGD, LN]. The participle εὐλογημένος 'having been blessed' is translated 'blessed (is/be)' [AB, Gdt, HTC, NICNT2, NTC, WBC; KJV, NASB, NET, NJB, NIV, NRSV, REB], 'God bless' [LN; NCV, Ph, TEV], 'blessings (on the one who comes)' [NLT]. This verb means to ask God to bestow his favor on, with the implication that the verbal act itself constitutes a significant benefit [LN]. It means to call down God's gracious power on someone [BAGD]. When God is acting toward people the verb means 'to bless'. When people are acting toward God or his representative it means 'to praise' [TRT].

e. βασιλεὺς τοῦ Ἰσραήλ (BAGD 2.a. p. 136): 'King of Israel' [BAGD; all translations]. This noun phrase refers to the Messianic king [BAGD]. See this phrase also at 1:49.

QUESTION—To what day of the week does the word ἐπαύριον 'next day' refer?

It probably refers to Sunday [AB, BECNT, Car, EGT, ICC, IVP, HTC, Lns, My, NICNT2, TH, TRT].

QUESTION—To which festival does this refer?

It refers to the Passover Festival [Bar, BECNT, Car, IVP, TH; CEV, NCV, NLT, TEV] and it is important to make this explicit here [TH].

QUESTION—Why did the crowd take palm branches?

It is an expression of victory used here of the triumph of Jesus [NICNT1]. The palm branch was a symbol of strength, beauty, joy, and salvation [Gdt], a symbol of life and salvation [Lns]. People used them to wave in Jesus' honor [ICC, TRT]. The waving of the palm branch was to show the joy of victory or military triumph [EGT, IVP, Kn, NTC, Rd]. The people felt that from now on things were going to be better [NTC]. It may indicate an expression of hope that a messianic liberator had arrived in Jesus [BECNT, Car]. It signifies a joyful welcome to a notable person [Bar, My].

QUESTION—Is the word ὡσαννά 'hosanna' an exclamation of praise or a prayer?

1. It is an exclamation of praise rather than a prayer [AB, Bar, BECNT, Car, LN, HTC, IVP, Lns, NICNT1, NICNT2, TH, TRT, WBC; CEV, NCV, NLT, TEV]: 'Praise God!' [NCV, NLT, TEV]. This is an Aramaic expression meaning 'help, I pray' or 'save, I pray,' but which had become a strictly liturgical formula of praise [LN]. Luke's account of the triumphal entry (Luke 19:37) speaks of the crowd praising God. This is the meaning of 'hosanna' here [AB]. Although this word was originally a request meaning 'Please help', it became a greeting and a shout of homage [HTC]. Their greeting was a joyful acclamation, a little like our: 'All hail!' [Lns].

2. It is a request to be saved rather than an exclamation of praise [BAGD, CH, Gdt, Kn, NTC; Ph]: 'God save him!' [Ph]. This is an Aramaic expression meaning 'help I pray' or 'save I pray' [BAGD]. It is a prayer addressed to Jehovah and expresses 'We beseech thee, O Jehovah, save now'. It is a request that God may no longer delay his promised salvation [NTC]. They were probably expecting the Messiah had come to save them from Roman domination [CH]. The word 'hosanna' is a prayer addressed to God by the people on behalf of His Messiah King. It is like the exclamation 'God save the King!' [Gdt].

QUESTION—The clause 'Blessed is the one coming in the name of the Lord' is taken by some to be an acclamation and by others a prayer.

1. It is a statement that God has blessed Jesus [AB, BECNT, HTC, Lns, NICNT1, NICNT2, NTC, WBC; KJV, NASB, NET, NJB, NIV, NRSV, REB]. The people are proclaiming the blessedness of Jesus rather than praying that he might be blessed [NICNT1]. The people are saying that Jesus has been blessed by Jehovah in that he comes to Jerusalem bearing the gifts and treasures. They have in mind the great miracles he has done including the raising of Lazarus. The perfect εὐλογημένος, 'having been blessed', has its usual present force, 'having been and now still blessed' [Lns].

2. It is a request for God to bless Jesus [Bar, Gdt, TH; CEV, NCV, NLT, Ph, TEV]: 'God bless him who comes in the name of the Lord' [TEV]. The blessing here comes from God [TH]. John means to say, 'Blessed be he who comes in the name of the Lord' [Bar].

QUESTION—To whom does the word 'Lord' refer in the phrase 'the name of the Lord'?

It refers to God since Jesus is the one who comes in His name [TH].

QUESTION—What does it mean to 'come in the name of the Lord'?

It means to come representing the Lord or to come as his ambassador [TH]. To come in the Lord's name is to come to the work and with the authority of the Lord [Bar]. Coming in the name of the Lord means coming to reveal the Lord [Lns]. 'The one who comes' functions as a messianic title [Car, Kn,

Lns, NICNT1], especially when it is coupled with 'in the name of the Lord' [Lns].

QUESTION—Who is the King of Israel?
He is the same as the one who comes in the name of the Lord [Bar, BECNT, Car, NICNT2, Rd, TH]: the one who comes in the name of the Lord, that is, the King of Israel. The King of Israel may be better translated 'the one who will rule over Israel' since Jesus was not yet their king [TH]. This title implied that the person referred to is the Messiah [Car, Lns, NICNT1, NICNT2, WBC].

12:14 And Jesus having-found[a] (a) young-donkey[b] he-sat on it, just-as it-is written, **12:15** "Do- not -fear daughter-of-Zion.[c] Look[d] your king comes sitting on (the) colt[e] of-(a)-donkey.[f]"

- LEXICON—a. aorist act. participle of εὑρίσκω (LN 27.27) (BAGD 1.b. p. 325): 'to find' [BAGD, LN; all translations], 'to come upon' [BAGD, LN], 'to learn the whereabouts of something, to discover, to happen to find' [LN]. This verb means to learn the location of something, either by intentional searching or by unexpected discovery [LN]. It means to come upon accidentally, without seeking [BAGD]. It may be necessary to avoid the sense that Jesus accidentally came across a donkey. A better tranlation would be that 'he procured a donkey' [Gdt, TH]. Make sure that the translation does not indicate that the donkey was lost [TRT]. Jesus acquires the donkey. Mark 11:2ff. tells that Jesus sent disciples to get the animal [Rd]. 'Finds' can include the sense of 'finds by the agency of others' as the Synoptic accounts tell us [Bar, Car, NICNT1].
- b. ὀνάριον (LN **4.33**) (BAGD p. 570): 'young donkey' [AB, NICNT2, NTC, WBC; NASB, NET, NJB, NIV, NLT, NRSV], 'young ass' [Gdt, HTC; KJV, Ph], 'donkey' [BAGD, **LN**; CEV, REB, TEV], 'colt' [LN; NCV], 'foal' [LN]. This noun denotes the young of a donkey [LN]. The word means literally 'little donkey' but in many cases the diminutive of ὄνος 'donkey' is diminutive in form only [BAGD].
- c. θυγάτηρ Σιών (LN 11.66) (BAGD 2.a. p. 752; 2.e. p. 365): 'daughter of Zion' [AB, Gdt, HTC, LN, NTC, WBC; NASB, NJB, NIV, NRSV, Ph, REB], 'daughter of Sion' [KJV], 'daughter Zion' [NICNT2], 'city of Zion' [TEV], 'people of Zion' [LN, TRT; NET], 'people of Jerusalem' [LN; CEV, NCV, NLT]. This noun phrase is literally 'daughter of Zion' but this is an idiom meaning the inhabitants of Jerusalem [BECNT, Car, Gdt, LN, Lns, NICNT1, NTC, TH, TRT]. It poetically refers to Jerusalem/the city of Zion and its inhabitants. The noun Σιών itself refers to Mount Zion, a hill within the city of Jerusalem [BAGD]. 'Daughter Zion indicates Jerusalem [NICNT2].
- d. ἰδού (LN 91.13) (BAGD): 'look' [LN, NICNT2, NTC, WBC; NET, NJB, NLT, NRSV], 'behold' [Gdt, HTC; KJV, NASB, Ph], 'see' [AB; NIV, REB], 'listen, pay attention, come now' [LN], not explicit [NCV]. The clause 'Look your king comes' is translated '*Here* comes your king'

[TEV], 'Your king is *now* coming' [CEV]. This particle is a prompter of attention, that serves also to emphasize the following statement [LN].

e. πῶλος (LN **4.33**) (BAGD p. 731): 'colt' [LN; all translations except CEV, NJB, TEV], 'foal' [**LN**; NJB], 'young animal, ass's foal, young donkey' [BAGD], not explicit [CEV]. This noun denotes the young of a donkey [LN].

f. ὄνος (LN **4.31**) (BAGD): 'donkey' [AB, BAGD, **LN**, NICNT2, WBC; NASB, NCV, NET, NJB, NIV, NLT, NRSV, REB], 'ass' [Gdt, HTC, LN, NTC; KJV, Ph]. The phrase 'colt of a donkey' is translated 'donkey' [CEV], 'young donkey' [TEV]. In this context the reference is obviously to a female donkey [LN].

QUESTION—Where was this written?

It was written in Zechariah 9:9, 'Rejoice greatly, people of Jerusalem! Shout for joy, people of Jerusalem! Your king is coming to you. He does what is right, and he saves. He is gentle and riding on a donkey, on the colt of a donkey' [all commentaries]. The first part, 'Do not fear daughter of Zion' probably comes from Zephaniah 3:16 [IVP, TH] or Isaiah 40:9 [Car, TH]. The rest comes from Zechariah 9:9 [Car, IVP]. Since the place where it was written is important it may be necessary to translate 'This happened just as the *Scripture* says' or 'This happening was just as the *Scripture* says' [TH], or 'Just as one of God's prophets wrote in the Scriptures' or 'Just as God's Word says' [TRT].

QUESTION—What is indicated by the present tense of the command 'Do not fear'?

The present tense imperative indicates that the action has been going on [NET; REB]: 'Stop being afraid' [NTC], 'Fear no more, daughter of Zion' [REB]. A king who comes riding on a donkey is no cause for fear [Gdt].

QUESTION—What is indicated by Jesus riding on the colt of a donkey?

The donkey is a symbol of peace/humility contrasted with a horse which would symbolize war and conquest [BECNT, Car, CH, EGT, HTC, IVP, Lns, My, NICNT1, NICNT2, NTC, TH, WBC]. Riding on a donkey symbolized humility and peace. Jesus wanted to show the spiritual nature of his royalty in the most humble way [BECNT, Gdt]. Here Jesus accepts that he is a king, but the kind of a king who comes sitting on a donkey's colt [BECNT, NICNT2]. From such a king the people can expect peace and well-being [Rd]. Riding on a donkey did not indicate humility since the donkey and mule were used by great people. The people understood that Jesus came as the Prince of Peace [ICC].

12:16 His disciples at-first[a] did- not understand[b] these-things, but when Jesus was-glorified[c] then they-remembered that these-things were-written about him and they-did these-things to-him.

LEXICON—a. τὸ πρῶτος (BAGD 2.a. p. 726): 'at first' [BAGD; all translations except Gdt; NASB, NET, NLT, Ph, REB, TEV], 'at the first' [NASB], 'at the time' [NLT, Ph, REB, TEV], 'at the moment' [Gdt], 'when they first happened' [NET]. It is better to translate this phrase 'at the time' since the contrast is between the disciples' understanding when these events took place and their understanding after Jesus was glorified [TH].

b. aorist act. indic. of γινώσκω (LN 32.16) (BAGD 3.a. p. 161): 'to understand' [BAGD; all translations except NLT, Ph], 'to come to understand' [LN], 'to understand…that this was a fulfillment of prophecy' [NLT], 'to realize the significance of' [Ph], 'to comprehend' [BAGD, LN], 'to perceive' [LN]. This verb means to come to an understanding as the result of the ability to experience and learn [LN].

c. aorist pass. indic. of δοξάζω (LN 87.24) (BAGD 2. p. 204): 'to be glorified' [BAGD, LN; all translations except CEV, NCV, NLT, TEV], 'to be given glory' [CEV], 'to be raised to glory' [NCV, TEV], 'to be made gloriously great' [LN], 'to be clothed in splendor' [BAGD]. The clause 'when Jesus was glorified' is translated 'after Jesus entered into his glory' [NLT]. This verb means to cause someone to have glorious greatness [LN]. It describes the glory that comes in the next life [BAGD].

QUESTION—What is indicated by the pronoun ταῦτα 'these things'?

These things include the waving of the palm branches, the spreading of the branches in the way, and the cheering [NTC]. They point to Jesus' riding the donkey and the prophecy relating to it [Rd, TRT]. This is what they did not understand but in which they had played a part [Rd]. The part the disciples did not understand was the fact that this event was prophesied in Scripture [CH]. What the disciples did not understand was the significance of these events. They probably thought of Jesus as a political Messianic king but they did not understand the true nature of his kingship. After his resurrection they understood the true nature of his kingship [NICNT1].

QUESTION—What is indicated by the three-fold repetition of the pronoun ταῦτα 'these things'?

The repetition may be intended to emphasize the way these events fulfilled prophecy [NICNT1]. The pronoun 'these things' is in an emphatic position in the Greek [TH, TRT].

QUESTION—When was Jesus glorified?

Jesus' glorification refers to his resurrection [Rd, TH] or exaltation [TH]. His glorification meant his resurrection and exaltation [Car]. It took place after his resurrection and the sending of the Spirit (7:39). The two events-- are considered his glorification (12:23, 32) [HTC]. Jesus was glorified both in his death on the cross and his resurrection [NTC, WBC].

QUESTION—To whom does the pronoun 'they' in the clause 'they did these things to him' refer?

1. It refers to the disciples [Bar, Gdt, ICC, Lns, My, NICNT1, Rd, TH; KJV, NASB, NASB, NIV, Ph, TEV]. This may be the simplest solution although it is not clear what the disciples had done for Jesus. It may refer to their procuring of a donkey and/or to the larger group of disciples and their part in praising Jesus as he entered Jerusalem [TH]. The subject of

'they did' must be the same as the subject of 'they understood' and 'they remembered'. What they had done is recorded in Luke 19:29–36, they brought the donkey to Jesus [Gdt]. In bringing the donkey to Jesus they had become instruments in the fulfillment of the prophecy [My].
2. It refers to the people [EGT, NICNT2]. It was the acclaim of the crowds welcoming Jesus as the King of Israel that the disciples remembered [EGT].
3. The agents in this case should not be specified (AB, NTC; NET, NJB, NLT, NRSV, REB]. It is perhaps better to take the verb 'did' as being equivalent to a passive 'this was done to him' [AB, NTC].

DISCOURSE UNIT—12:17–19 [NCV]. The topic is people tell about Jesus.

12:17 Now the crowd that was with him when he-called Lazarus from the tomb and raised him from (the) dead were-testifying.[a] **12:18** Because-of this the crowd also met him because they-heard (that) he had-done this sign.

TEXT—Instead of ὅτε 'when' some manuscripts read ὅτι 'that'. GNT reads 'when' with a B rating, indicating that the text is almost certain.

LEXICON—a. imperf. act. indic. of μαρτυρέω (LN 33.262) (BAGD 1.a. p. 492): 'to testify' [BAGD, NTC], 'to bear witness' [BAGD; HTC], 'to witness' [LN], 'to be a witness' [BAGD], 'to bear record' [KJV]. The verb ἐμαρτύρει 'were testifying' is translated 'continued to testify' [NRSV], 'continued to testify about him' [NASB], 'were continuing to testify about it' [NET], 'kept testifying to it' [AB], 'kept testifying that he called Lazarus from the tomb and raised him from the dead' [NICNT2], 'bore testimony to the fact' [WBC], 'bore witness to him' [Gdt], 'kept bearing witness to it' [NJB], 'continued to spread the word' [NIV], 'kept talking about him and this miracle' [CEV], 'were continually talking about him' [Ph], 'they were telling others about what Jesus did' [NCV], 'were telling others about it' [NLT], 'kept telling what they had seen and heard' [REB], 'reported what had happened' [TEV]. This verb means to provide information about a person or an event concerning which the speaker has direct knowledge [LN]. The imperfect tense indicates continuing or repeated action [HTC, NICNT1, TH].

QUESTION—Is there one crowd or two in these two verses,?
1. There are two crowds [AB, Bar, Car, Gdt, HTC, ICC, Lns, NICNT1, NICNT2, NTC, TH, TRT]. One crowd was telling about the raising of Lazarus, the other crowd was the one coming out of Jerusalem because of what it has learned from the first crowd [TH]. One crowd was accompanying Jesus into the city and was telling about the miracle, the other was coming out of the city to meet Jesus. But the crucial point of these verses is that it was the raising of Lazarus that accounted for the excitement of the great crowd that had come to the festival and whose enthusiasm had frustrated the plans of the elders of the Jews [NICNT2].

2. There is only one crowd [BECNT, Rd; CEV, NLT; and perhaps KJV, NASB, NET, NJB, NIV, NRSV]: 'Many in the crowd had seen Jesus call Lazarus from the tomb, raising him from the dead, and they were telling others about it. That was the reason so many went out to meet him—because they had heard about this miraculous sign' [NLT]. The two crowds are identical, that is the same crowd that saw the miracle is now coming to meet Jesus in this triumphal entry [BECNT].

QUESTION—What word is emphasized in these two verses?

The emphasis is on the pronoun τοῦτο 'this' in the phrase 'because of this' [Bar, My. TH]. 'Because of this' stresses the fundamental and decisive importance of the miracle of raising Lazarus [Bar].

12:19 Then/therefore[a] the Pharisees said to themselves, "See you(pl) do-not -accomplish[b] anything. Look[c] the world[d] went after him."

LEXICON—a. οὖν (LN 89.50): 'then' [HTC, LN, NICNT2; NJB, NLT, NRSV, TEV], 'therefore' [LN, WBC; KJV], 'so' [Lns, NTC; NASB, NCV, NIV], 'at that' [AB], 'whereupon' [Gdt], 'thus' [NET], 'but' [CEV], 'consequently, accordingly' [LN], not explicit [REB]. This conjunction indicates result, often implying the conclusion of a process of reasoning [LN].

b. pres. act. indic. of ὠφελέω (LN 68.33) (BAGD 2.a. p. 900): 'to accomplish' [BAGD, LN], 'to do' [LN]. The clause 'you do not accomplish anything' is translated 'you're accomplishing nothing' [NICNT2], 'you are gaining nothing' [NTC], 'you are doing no good at all' [WBC], 'you are not doing any good' [NASB], 'you prevail nothing' [Gdt; KJV], 'you can do nothing' [HTC; NET, NRSV], 'you are making no progress' [NJB], 'we/you are getting nowhere' [AB; REB], 'we are not succeeding at all!' [TEV], 'There's nothing that we can do' [NLT], 'this is getting us nowhere' [NIV], 'nothing is going right for us' [NCV], 'There's nothing that one can do!' [Ph], 'There is nothing that can be done!' [CEV]. This verb means to be successful in accomplishing some goal, with the implication that such might be useful [LN]. The TEV shifts from second person 'you' to 'we' because the Pharisees are speaking to each other [TH].

c. ἴδε (LN 91.13) (BAGD 2. p. 369): 'look' [AB, HTC, LN, NICNT2, NTC, WBC; NASB, NCV, NET, NJB, NIV, NLT, NRSV, TEV], 'behold' [Gdt; KJV], 'see' [BAGD], 'listen, pay attention' [LN], not explicit [CEV, Ph, REB]. This particle acts as a prompter of attention that serves also to emphasize the following statement [LN].

d. κόσμος (LN 9.23) (BAGD 5.a. p. 446): 'the world' [AB, Gdt, HTC, NICNT2, NTC, WBC; KJV, NASB, NET, NRSV], 'the whole world' [NCV, NJB, NIV, Ph, TEV], 'all the world' [BAGD; REB], 'everybody' [BAGD], 'everyone' [NLT], 'everyone in the world' [CEV], 'people of the world' [LN]. This noun denotes 'cosmos, universe' but here is used figuratively to mean people who are associated with a world system and estranged from God [LN]. Here it denotes 'the world' as mankind [BAGD].

QUESTION—What can describe these words of the Pharisees?

They are a cry of dismay [IVP, WBC]. The Pharisees are exasperated [BECNT, CH], desperate [ICC, My, Rd], frustrated [IVP, TRT], pessimistic [NICNT1]. Their words mean, 'We have proved ineffective in stopping Jesus' [Kn].

QUESTION—Among the Pharisees, who is speaking to whom, and what does their complaint mean?

It is probably the more radical Pharisees who wanted to take drastic measures to stop Jesus who are speaking and, talking to the more conservative ones who were holding out for less violent tactics [Lns, NTC]. They are trying to encourage each other to use the extreme measures Caiaphas had advised [Gdt].

QUESTION—Should the phrase 'You see' be taken as a statement, a question, or an imperative?

1. This should be taken as a statement [AB, Bar, Gdt, ICC, Lns, NICNT1, NICNT2, TH; all other versions]: 'You can see that you are accomplishing nothing' [NICNT2]. This verb form can be taken as imperative but it is better to take it as indicative, that is, as a statement [Gdt].
2. It should be taken as an interrogative [EGT; KJV, Ph]: 'Do you see how helpless you are?' [EGT].
3. It should be taken as an imperative [NIV]: 'See, this is getting us nowhere' [NIV].

QUESTION—What figure of speech is the phrase 'the world'?

It is a hyperbole—an exaggerated statement used to emphasize the large number of people who were believing in Jesus [Bar, Car, HTC, IVP, Kn, Lns, NICNT1, NICNT2, Rd, TRT, WBC].

QUESTION—What does it mean that the world went after him?

It means that they were giving him their allegiance or following him as disciples [NICNT2]. It implies that the world was going away from them [My, TRT].

DISCOURSE UNIT—12:20–36 [AB, Bar, BECNT, Car, Gdt, IVP, Kn, Lns, NICNT2, Rd, WBC; NCV, NET, NIV, NLT]. The topic is the coming of the hour [AB], the hour of glorification [IVP, NICNT2], the last scene in the temple [Gdt], the Greeks [Bar; NET], Gentiles and the cross [Car, Kn, Lns, WBC], dawning age of the Gentiles [BECNT], Jesus predicts his death [NCV, NIV, NLT].

DISCOURSE UNIT—12:20–36a [NICNT1]. The topic is the Greeks.

DISCOURSE UNIT—12:20–28 [HTC]. The topic is Jesus and the Greeks, death and glorification.

DISCOURSE UNIT—12:20–26 [NASB, NRSV, TEV]. The topic is Greeks seek Jesus.

DISCOURSE UNIT—12:20–22 [CEV]. The topic is Greeks ask to meet Jesus.

12:20 Now there-were some Greeks[a] among the-ones going-up[b] so-that they-might-worship[c] at the festival.

LEXICON—a. Ἕλλην (LN 11.40): 'Greek' [LN; all translations except NCV, REB], 'Greek people' [NCV], 'Gentile' [LN; REB], 'non-Jew' [LN]. This noun denotes a person who is a Gentile in view of being a Greek [LN, TH]. The term 'Greek' was used as a cover term for Gentiles because the Greek culture and language dominated the Greco-Roman world [BECNT]. It describes a person as being of non-Jewish birth [Bar, TH] but not necessarily of the Greek race [Bar].

b. pres. act. participle of ἀναβαίνω (LN 15.101) (BAGD): 'to go up' [HTC, LN, NICNT2, NTC, WBC; NASB, NET, NJB, NIV, NRSV, Ph, REB], 'to come up' [AB, LN; KJV], 'to ascend' [LN]. The phrase 'the ones going up' is translated 'Some Greeks had gone to Jerusalem' [CEV], 'who came/had come/had gone to Jerusalem' [NCV, NLT, TEV], 'who went up to Jerusalem' [Gdt]. This verb means to move up. The upward movement may be of almost any gradient, for example, in going up a road to Jerusalem [LN]. This verb is commonly used for talking about a journey to Jerusalem [Bar, ICC, NTC, Rd, TH], or going up to celebrate the festivals [NICNT1]. The present tense indicates that they were accustomed to going up [Lns, NTC].

c. aorist act. subj. of προσκυνέω (LN 53.56) (BAGD 2.a. p. 717): 'to worship' [LN; all translations except NLT], 'to prostrate oneself in worship, to bow down and worship' [LN], 'to fall down and worship, to do obeisance to, to prostrate oneself before, to do reverence to, to welcome respectfully' [BAGD]. The clause 'so that they might worship at the festival' is translated '(who had come to Jerusalem) for the Passover celebration' [NLT]. This verb means to express by attitude and possibly by position one's allegiance to and regard for deity [LN]. It is used to designate the custom of prostrating oneself before a person and kissing his feet, the hem of his garment, or the ground [BAGD].

QUESTION—Who were these Greeks?
They were Greeks by birth who adopted Judaism as full or semi-proselytes. They were known as God-fearers who came to the feast but who were not allowed to eat of the Passover lamb [HTC]. They were proselytes [Gdt, IVP]. They were either proselytes or God-fearing Gentiles [Car, CH]. They were proselytes of the gate [ICC, Lns, My, NTC] or God-fearers who had converted to Judaism but were uncircumcised [NTC]. Had they been circumcised they would have become 'proselytes of righteousness' [Lns]. They may or may not have been proselytes, that is, full-converts to Judaism who had been circumcised [TRT]. They were restricted to the Court of the Gentiles [BECNT, NTC]. They were God-fearers [BECNT, Kn] who had not

formally converted to Judaism [BECNT]. They were half-proselytes who accepted Jewish monotheism and observed parts of the Mosaic law but were uncircumcised [Rd]. They were not full proselytes as they were not permitted to eat the Passover [Bar]. They were not Greek-speaking Jews [AB, Gdt, HTC, ICC, IVP, NTC, Rd, TH].

QUESTION—What was the significance of the appearance of these Greeks at this point?

They serve to introduce Jesus to the whole world, Jewish and non-Jewish alike, which is soon to be addressed [NICNT2]. Jesus sees in their arrival a sign that the climax of his work had come [NICNT1].

12:21 Then these-ones approached[a] Philip from Bethsaida[b] of Galilee and were-asking him, "Sir, we-want to-see[c] Jesus. **12:22** Philip comes and tells Andrew, Andrew and Philip come and tell Jesus.

LEXICON—a. aorist act. indic. of προσέρχομαι (LN 15.77) (BAGD 1. p. 713): 'to approach' [AB, BAGD, LN, WBC; NET, NJB, Ph, REB], 'to come to' [BAGD, Gdt, HTC, NICNT2, NTC; KJV, NASB, NIV, NRSV], 'to go to' [BAGD; CEV, NCV, TEV], 'to pay a visit to' [NLT], 'to move toward, to come near to' [LN]. This verb means to move toward a reference point, with a possible implication in certain contexts of a reciprocal relationship between the person approaching and the one who is approached [LN].

b. Βηθσαϊδά (LN 93.432) (BAGD 1. p. 140): 'Bethsaida' [BAGD, LN; all translations]. This noun denotes a place northeast of the Lake of Galilee [BAGD, LN]. It is east of the Jordan River, near where it empties into the lake [BAGD]. It was a town in Galilee [Ph]. Bethsaida was the hometown of Philip and Andrew (see 1:44) [EGT, HTC, NTC, Rd].

c. pres. act. infin. of ὁράω (LN 34.50) (BAGD 6. p. 221): 'to see' [all translations except CEV, NLT], 'to meet' [CEV, NLT], 'to visit' [BAGD, LN], 'to go to see' [LN], 'to come to know, to learn to know' [BAGD]. This verb means to go to see a person on the basis of friendship and with helpful intent [LN]. It may have the sense of 'to visit with' or 'to meet' [AB, BECNT, My, NTC, TH], or 'to have an interview with' [Bar, BECNT, Car, EGT, ICC, Lns, NICNT1, NTC]. In John it may well have the sense of 'believe in' [AB]. The Greeks desired a more intimate relationship with Jesus, to have a private conversation with him [Gdt].

QUESTION—Why may these Greeks have chosen to come to Philip?

It is not clear why they would have gone to Philip rather than one of the other disciples except that he had a Greek name [Bar, BECNT, Car, CH, Gdt, ICC, IVP, My, NICNT1, NICNT2, NTC, TH], or knew Greek [EGT]. These Greeks may have come from the province of Decapolis that had a large Greek population. They may also have known Philip and Andrew who were from nearby Bethsaida [TRT]. Galilee was more Hellenized than most of the rest of Palestine [BECNT]. These Greeks may have been from a region in Galilee like Decapolis where the cities were completely Greek [Gdt].

DISCOURSE UNIT—12:23–36a [CEV]. The topic is the lifting up of the Son of Man.

12:23 **Jesus answers them saying, "The hour[a] has-come that the Son of Man may-be-glorified.[b]**

LEXICON—a. ὥρα (LN 67.1) (BAGD 3. p. 896): 'hour' [BAGD; all translations except CEV, NCV, NET, NLT, Ph], 'time' [BAGD, LN; CEV, NCV, NET, NLT, Ph], 'occasion' [LN]. This noun denotes points of time consisting of occasions for particular events [LN]. It denotes the time when something took place, is taking place, or will take place. It is used especially of Jesus, whose ὥρα John speaks of the time of his death and of the glorification that is inextricably bound up with it [BAGD]. 'Hour' is used in a wider sense to refer to a specific date and appropriate time, here the time for Jesus' death [Lns]. Possible renderings of 'hour' might be 'the time has now come', or 'now is the occasion for', or 'it will soon happen that' [TH].

b. aorist pass. subj. of δοξάζω (LN 87.24) (BAGD 2. p. 204): 'to be glorified' [BAGD, LN; all translations except CEV, NCV, NLT, TEV], 'to receive glory/great glory' [NCV, TEV], 'to be given glory' [CEV], 'to enter into one's glory' [NLT], 'to be made gloriously great' [LN], 'to be clothed in splendor' [BAGD]. This verb means to cause someone to have glorious greatness [LN].

QUESTION—What is indicated by the phrase 'Jesus answered'?

Jesus does not reply as much to the disciples' words as to the situation that their words created [Bar, AB].

QUESTION—Why does Jesus seem to disregard the request of the Greeks to talk about his hour?

The arrival of the Greeks means to Jesus the evangelization of the Gentiles which does not belong to his earthly ministry. The way to accomplish this is through crucifixion and resurrection. It will be the mission of the church that will accomplish this. Jesus' ministry to the Jews must finish before the true spritual conversation with the Greeks may begin [Bar]. In the Greeks Jesus saw his seed. This had been promised to him, 'When his soul shall make *an offering for sin*, he shall see *his seed*' (Isaiah 53:10, A.R.V.). It was only through Jesus' voluntary sacrifice that Jesus could do anything for these Greeks [NTC]. Jesus must first die before he can bring salvation to the Greeks [HTC].

QUESTION—What is meant by the glorification of the Son of Man?

1. Jesus' death, resurrection, ascension, and exaltation were included in his glorification [BAGD, Car, CH, Kn, Lns, NICNT2, My, NTC, Rd, TH, TRT, WBC]. Jesus could not be arrested because his hour had not yet come (7:30; 8:20). Therefore it follows that when his hour does come, he would be arrested and put to death. But how does this 'hour' relate to the prospect of glorification? It must be that the two are the same event. The prospect of resurrection or ascension are joined with death itself. What

was from a human perspective was death, from God's perspective was glorification [NICNT2]. This was the hour when Jesus' intense suffering was followed by his resurrection, ascension and coronation [NTC]. This hour is comprised of Jesus' passing out of the world to the Father. It would begin with his approaching death and be completed in his return to Heaven's glory [Rd]. On the one hand Jesus is exalted to a position of honor but on the other he is lifted up on the cross and crowned 'king of the Jews' [Kn].
2. His glorification was his ascension to the Father's presence [Gdt, HTC]. For Jesus, his glorification was the regaining of the glory he had with the Father before the world began. The time had come when he would be given the fullness of saving power to draw all men to himself. He would now be able to give life to all believers and so fulfill his mission. This was the meaning of his death as seen in the next verse [HTC]. Glorification primarily means the heavenly exaltation of Jesus' person [Gdt].
3. Jesus' death was his glorification [Bar, IVP, ICC, NICNT1]. Jesus' death is the way that he reveals the Father, for God is love and love is the laying down of one's life for his beloved. In Jesus' cross God's heart is revealed most clearly [IVP]. Jesus speaks of his death in terms not of tragedy but of triumph. He will not be dishonored, he will be glorified and by this he meant crucified [NICNT1]. Jesus' hour is his death and death means glorification [Bar]. This is the paradox of Jesus' cross. He was glorified in his suffering [ICC].

QUESTION—Who is the actor of the passive verb 'may be glorified'?

The Father is the actor [Lns, TH, TRT]. If a language requires this information to be made explicit, it could be translated 'for God to show how wonderful the Son of Man is' [TH], or 'for the Son of Man to be glorified by God' or 'for God to reveal to people my greatness as the Son of Man' [TRT]. Both here and in verse 28 where Jesus asks the Father to glorify his name, the focus seems to be on revealing the true nature of the Son of Man and the Father. So a good rendering would then be 'the hour has now come for the true glory of the Son of Man to be revealed' [TH].

12:24 **Truly^a truly I-say to-you(pl), unless the grain^b of wheat^c having-fallen into the ground dies,^d it remains^e alone. But if it-dies, it-bears- much -fruit.^f**

LEXICON—a. ἀμήν (LN 72.6): 'truly' [LN], 'indeed, it is true that' [LN]. The clause 'Truly truly I say to you' [HTC; NASB] is also translated 'Verily, verily, I say to you' [Gdt; KJV], 'Amen, amen, I say to/tell you' [NICNT2, WBC], 'Very truly I tell you' [NRSV], 'I tell you truly' [Ph], 'In very truth I tell you' [REB], 'I tell/am telling you the truth' [NCV, NIV, NLT, TEV], 'I tell you the solemn truth' [NET], 'In all truth I tell you' [NJB], 'I tell you for certain' [CEV], 'I solemnly assure you' [AB], 'Most solemnly I declare to you' [NTC]. This particle indicates strong affirmation of what is declared [LN].

b. κόκκος (LN 3.35) (BAGD 1. p. 440): 'grain' [BAGD, all translations except KJV, NET, NIV, NLT], 'kernel' [NET, NIV, NLT], 'corn' [KJV], 'seed' [BAGD, LN]. This noun denotes the kernel part of fruit [LN].

c. σῖτος (LN **3.31**) (BAGD p. 752): 'wheat' [BAGD, **LN**; all translations], 'grain' [BAGD]. The phrase 'the grain of wheat' is translated 'a wheat grain' [NJB], 'the seed of wheat' [**LN**]. This noun denotes the wheat plant [LN]. Elsewhere in the NT σῖτος, when used alone, refers to wheat as grain, but even in John 12:24 τοῦ σίτου may be interpreted as a so-called 'appositional genitive', that is, 'seed which is wheat' or 'wheat seed' [LN].

d. aorist act. subj of ἀποθνῄσκω (LN 23.99) (BAGD 1.a.β. p. 91): 'to die' [BAGD, LN]. This verb means the process of dying [LN]. When used of grains of wheat placed in the ground it means 'to decay' [BAGD]. In some languages the idea of a seed dying may be strange so it may be necessary to translate 'if it does, as it were, die' or 'if it dies, so to speak' [TH].

e. pres. act. indic. of μένω (LN 85.55) (BAGD 1.b. 504): 'to remain' [BAGD, LN; NASB, NET, NJB, NLT], 'to stay' [BAGD, LN], 'to abide' [Gdt; KJV]. The clause αὐτὸς μόνος μένει 'it remains alone' [HTC, NTC, WBC] is also translated 'it remains alone by itself' [NICNT2], 'it remains only a single seed' [NCV, NIV], 'it remains only/just a single grain' [NJB, NRSV], 'it remains a single grain of wheat' [Ph], 'it remains just a grain of wheat' [AB], 'it remains no more than a single grain' [TEV], '(unless a grain of wheat falls into the ground and dies) it remains that and nothing more' [REB] '(a grain of wheat)…will never be more than one grain' [CEV]. This verb means to remain in the same place over a period of time [LN]. It means for a thing to remain in the state in which it is found [BAGD].

f. καρπὸν φέρω (LN **23.199**) (BAGD 2. p. 855; 1.a. p. 404): 'to bear fruit' [BAGD, LN], 'to produce fruit' [BAGD, LN], 'to yield fruit' [BAGD], to produce seed' [LN]. The clause 'it bears much fruit' [AB, Gdt, HTC, NTC; NASB, NRSV] is also translated 'it yields much fruit' [**LN**], 'it yields a rich harvest' [NJB], 'it produces much/many grain/grains/seeds' [NET, NIV, TEV], 'it produces a great harvest' [WBC], 'it will produce lots of wheat' [CEV], '(its death) will produce many new kernels—a plentiful harvest of new lives' [NLT], 'it brings forth much fruit' [KJV], 'it brings a good harvest' [Ph], 'it bears a rich harvest' [REB], 'it bears a great crop' [NICNT2], '(wheat must…die) to make many seeds' [NCV]. This verb means to produce fruit or seed (of plants) [LN]. The fruit mentioned here are people, the result of evangelism [IVP, Kn, Lns; NLT].

QUESTION—What is implied by this saying?

It illustrates the paradox that life comes through death [ICC]. Jesus is speaking about his own death as a means of bringing life to all men (12:32) [AB, Bar, ICC, Lns, My, NICNT1, TH, TRT]. A seed in the granary remains as it is without the strength to reproduce itself. What is needed is that it be sown in the earth and die so that it may live again and may produce a multitude of beings like itself [Gdt]. Here the 'grain of wheat' does not refer uniquely to Jesus but also to his disciples [Kn, NICNT2]. The 'much fruit' may hint at a coming mission to the Gentiles [NICNT2].

QUESTION—What is indicated by the article in the phrase ὁ κόκκος τοῦ σίτου '*the* grain of wheat'?

In parabolic speech of this kind the definite article is frequently used to introduce the subject (see Luke 8:5, 11: 'the sower…the seed') [AB].

12:25 The-one loving[a] his life[b] loses[c] it, and the-one hating[d] his life in this world[e] will-keep[f] it to eternal-life.[g]

LEXICON—a. pres. act. participle of φιλέω (LN 25.33) (BAGD 1.b. p. 859): 'to love' [BAGD, LN; all translations], 'to have affection for' [BAGD, LN], 'to like' [BAGD]. This verb means to have love or affection for someone or something based on association [LN]. If a language cannot express 'loving life' this clause could be expressed as 'the one living just for himself' or 'the one loving to do only what he wants to do' [TH].

b. ψυχή (LN 23.88) (BAGD 1.d. p. 894): 'life' [BAGD, LN; all translations except REB], 'himself' [REB], 'soul' [BAGD]. This noun denotes life on earth in its external physical aspects. Since the soul is the center of both the earthly and the supernatural life, a man can find himself facing the question in which character he wishes to preserve it for himself [BAGD]. The ψυχή refers to the natural life with all of its appetites, desires, and affections [Gdt, NICNT1]. It is not limited to the physical life but includes one's whole being or self [IVP].

c. pres. act. indic. of ἀπόλλυμι (LN 57.68) (BAGD 1.b. p. 95): 'to lose' [BAGD; all translations except AB; NET, Ph, REB], 'to destroy' [AB, NET, Ph]. The clause 'the one loving his life loses it' is translated 'whoever loves himself is lost' [REB]. This verb means to lose something which one already possesses [LN].

d. pres. act. participle of μισέω (LN 88.198) (BAGD 2. p. 522): 'to hate' [BAGD, LN; all translations except CEV, NLT], 'to detest' [BAGD, LN], 'to abhor' [BAGD]. The clause 'the one hating his life' is translated 'If you give up your life' [CEV], 'Those who care nothing for their life' [NLT]. This verb means to dislike strongly, with the implication of aversion and hostility [LN]. If a language cannot speak of hating life, this could be expressed as 'the one living for others' [TH].

e. κόσμος (LN 1.39) (BAGD 4.b./7. p. 446): 'world' [BAGD, LN; all translations], 'earth' [LN]. This noun denotes the surface of the earth as the dwelling place of mankind, in contrast with the heavens above and the world below [BAGD (4.b), LN]. It denotes everything that belongs to the world, appears as that which is hostile to God, i.e., lost in sin, wholly at odds with anything divine, ruined and depraved [BAGD (7)].

f. fut. act. indic. of φυλάσσω (LN 37.120) (BAGD 1.c. p. 868): 'keep' [HTC, NICNT2, NTC; KJV, NASB, NCV, NJB, NIV, NLT, NRSV,

TEV], 'to preserve' [AB, BAGD, Gdt, WBC; Ph], 'to guard' [BAGD; NET], 'to guard closely' [LN], 'to protect' [BAGD]. The clause '(the one hating his life) will keep it to eternal life' is translated 'you will be given eternal life' [CEV], 'he…will be kept safe for eternal life' [REB]. This verb means to hold someone or something in close custody [LN].

  g. ζωὴ αἰώνιος (LN 67.96): 'eternal life' [LN; all translations except AB, NTC; KJV, NASB, NCV, NLT, NTC, TEV], 'life eternal' [Gdt; KJV, NRSV, TEV], 'everlasting life' [NTC]. The clause 'will keep it to eternal life' is translated 'will keep true life forever' [NCV], 'will keep it for eternity' [NLT], 'will keep it with a view to everlasting life' [NTC], 'preserves it to live eternally' [AB], 'you will be given eternal life' [CEV]. The adjective αἰώνιος describes a thing as pertaining to an unlimited duration of time. The most frequent use of αἰώνιος in the NT is with ζωή 'life', for example, 'so that everyone who believes in him may have eternal life' John 3:15. In combination with ζωή there is evidently not only a temporal element, but also a qualitative distinction. In such contexts, αἰώνιος evidently carries certain implications associated with αἰώνιος in relationship to divine and supernatural attributes. If one translates 'eternal life' as simply 'never dying', there may be serious misunderstandings, since persons may assume that 'never dying' refers only to physical existence rather than to 'spiritual death'. Accordingly, some translators have rendered 'eternal life' as 'unending real life' so as to introduce a qualitative distinction [LN]. Eternal life is a present possession and it is a quality of life, God's life [CH]. The phrase 'eternal life' is a significant one in John and occurs 17 times at 3:15, 16, 36; 4:14, 36; 5:24, 39; 6:27, 40, 47, 54, 68; 10:28; 12:25, 50; 17:2, 3.

QUESTION—What is the underlying meaning of this verse?
  It means that loss of life is the condition for the emergence of new life [BECNT, Rd].

QUESTION—What does it mean to hate one's life?
  It means to regard one's life as having secondary importance and desirability [Bar, TH]. The loving and hating contrast indicate preference rather than actual hatred [BECNT, Car]. To hate has the sense of 'to love less' [BECNT, TH]. Jesus is speaking of choices and attachments rather than absolute hatred. He means that devotion to himself must be so thorough that nothing else is distracting [IVP]. The love-hate contast is a Jewish way of comparing degrees of love and faithfulness [TRT].

QUESTION—What is meant by the clause 'will keep it to eternal life'?
  It means he will keep life forever [AB, NICNT2; NCV], or he will have eternal life [TRT], or he will be given eternal life [CEV].

12:26 **If anyone serves[a] me, let- (him) -follow[b] me, and where I am there also my servant will-be. If anyone serves me the Father will honor[c] him.**

LEXICON—a. pres. act. subj. of διακονέω (LN 35.19) (BAGD 2. p. 184): 'to serve' [BAGD, LN; CEV, KJV, NASB, NCV, NJB, NIV], 'to render service, to help' [LN]. The clause 'if anyone serves me' is translated 'if anyone wants to serve me' [NET], 'whoever wants to serve me' [TEV], 'if a man wants to enter my service' [Ph], 'anyone who wants to be my disciple' [NLT], 'if anyone would serve me' [AB, NICNT2]. This verb means to render assistance or help by performing certain duties, often of a humble or menial nature [LN]. To say 'if anyone would serve me' is about the same as saying 'If anyone wants to serve me' [NICNT2]. Here 'serving' is defined as 'following' [Bar, NICNT2] and serving entails imitating his behavior and being a servant to others [NICNT2], or of dying in his service [Bar]. The present subjunctive indicates a lifetime of continual service [Lns]. To avoid the idea that serving might mean 'to serve meals to', it may be helpful to translate 'If anyone wants me to be their master' [TH].

b. pres. act. impera. of ἀκολουθέω (LN 36.31): 'to follow' [LN; all translations except CEV, Ph], 'to be a disciple of' [LN]. The clause 'let him follow me' is translated 'you must go with me' [CEV], 'he must follow my way' [Ph]. This verb means to be a follower or a disciple of someone [BECNT, LN], in the sense of adhering to the teachings or instructions of a leader and in promoting the cause of such a leader. Though many translators have attempted to employ the metaphorical significance of 'to follow' in the sense of 'to be a disciple of,' there are certain dangers in a number of languages. For example, 'to follow' may often have the connotation of 'to pursue after with evil intent'. In many languages the appropriate equivalent of 'to follow' (in the sense of 'to be a disciple') is literally 'to accompany' or 'to go along with' or 'to be in the group of' [LN]. Following Jesus implies that a person may have to follow him to death [HTC, ICC, TH], or to follow in the pathway of sacrifice [Gdt]. The followers must risk death by denying themselves and taking up their cross [BECNT, IVP, NICNT2, NTC]. Following meant along the pathway of Jesus' life-surrender [My].

c. fut. act. indic. of τιμάω (LN 87.8) (BAGD 2. p. 817): 'to honor' [BAGD, LN; all translations], 'to respect' [LN], 'to revere, to reward' [BAGD]. This verb means to attribute high status to someone [LN]. The Father honors a disciple by letting him participate in the honor and glory of his Son [Gdt, Rd].

QUESTION—What words are emphasized in this verse?

The pronoun ἐγώ 'I/me' [Lns, TH], and the pronoun αὐτόν '(will honor) him' are emphasized in the Greek structure [TH]: 'where I myself am' [Lns]. There is special emphasis on the pronoun 'me' in the clause 'if anyone serves me' but throughout the whole verse the first person is emphasized [NICNT1]. The pronoun 'me' is emphatically contrasted with the phrase 'his life' in verse 25 [Lns]. There is also emphasis on the possessive adjective '*my own* (servant will be)' [Lns].

QUESTION—What does Jesus mean by the words 'where I am'?

He means 'where I am in Heaven' [Gdt, HTC].

JOHN 12:27

12:27 Now[a] my soul[b] is-troubled,[c] and what should-I-say?[d] Father, save me from this hour?[e] But[f] because-of this I-came to this hour.

LEXICON—a. νῦν (LN 67.38) (BAGD 1.a.β. p. 545): 'now' [BAGD, LN; all translations], 'at the present time' [BAGD]. This adverb indicates a point of time simultaneous with the event of the discourse itself [LN]. It designates a point of time as well as its extent. The verbs with which it is used are found in the perfect tense when it has a present meaning [BAGD]. Jesus means now that the hour has come and death is all but here [Bar].

b. ψυχή (LN 26.4) (BAGD 1.b.g. p. 893): 'soul' [BAGD; KJV, NASB, NET, NJB, NLT, NRSV, REB], 'heart' [LN, WBC; NIV, TEV], 'inner self, mind, thoughts, feelings, being' [LN]. The clause 'my soul is troubled' is translated 'I am deeply/very troubled' [CEV, NCV], '(Now comes the hour) of my heart-break' [Ph]. This noun denotes the essence of life in terms of thinking, willing, and feeling [LN]. It refers to the seat and center of the inner life of man in its many and varied aspects, feelings and emotions [BAGD]. We could translate 'I am troubled' [AB, NCV, TH, TRT] but the word 'soul' helps to express the sensory aspects of a person [AB].

c. perf. pass. indic. of ταράσσω (LN 25.244) (BAGD 2. p. 805): 'to be troubled' [AB, HTC, Gdt, NTC; KJV, NJB, NIV, NRSV, TEV], 'to be very troubled' [NCV], 'to be deeply troubled' [CEV, NLT], 'to be greatly distressed' [NET], 'to become troubled' [NASB], 'to be in turmoil' [WBC; REB], 'to be shaken' [NICNT2], 'to be caused great mental distress' [LN], 'to be stirred up, to be disturbed, to be unsettled, to be thrown into confusion' [BAGD]. The statement Νῦν ἡ ψυχή μου τετάρακται 'Now my soul is troubled' is translated 'Now comes my hour of heart-break' [Ph]. This verb is a figurative extension of the meaning of ταράσσω 'to stir up' and means to cause acute emotional distress or turbulence [LN]. The perfect tense indicates a continuous state of being deeply perturbed [NICNT1]. It indicates agitation, horror, convulsion and shock of spirit [WBC].

d. aorist act. subj. of λέγω (LN 33.69) (BAGD 1. 226): 'to say' [BAGD, LN; all translations except NLT], 'to pray' [NLT], 'to talk, to tell, to speak' [LN]. The clause 'What should I say?' is translated 'I don't know what to say' [CEV]. This verb means to speak or talk, with apparent focus on the content of what is said [LN]. It is a deliberative subjunctive [Bar, BECNT, Lns, ICC, NICNT1, NTC] indicating hesitation [Bar], or indecision [ICC].

e. ὥρα (LN 67.1) (BAGD 3. p. 896): 'hour' [BAGD; all translations except CEV, NCV], 'time' [LN; NCV], 'time of suffering' [CEV], 'occasion' [LN]. This noun denotes points of time consisting of occasions for particular events [LN].

f. ἀλλά (LN 89.125): 'but' [Gdt, LN, NTC, WBC; CEV, KJV, NJB, NLT, TEV], 'No' [AB, HTC, NICNT2; NCV, NET, NIV, NRSV, Ph, REB], 'instead, on the contrary' [LN]. This conjunction indicates more emphatic contrast than δέ, 'but' (see 89.124) [LN]. It can be taken to mean 'No!' as in classical Greek after a question to oneself [NICNT1, Rd].

QUESTION—Is the question 'What should I say?' asking for information or is it rhetorical?

It is rhetorical [NICNT2, TRT; CEV]: 'I don't know what to say' [TH, TRT; CEV]. Jesus addresses the question to himself, but it is not a real question for he already knows the answer [NICNT2].

QUESTION—Should the clause 'Father save me from this hour' be taken as a question or as a prayer?

1. It should be taken as a question [AB, BECNT, Bar, EGT, Gdt, HTC, Kn, Lns, NICNT1, NICNT2, Rd; CEV, NASB, NCV, NET, NJB, NIV, NLT, NRSV, Ph, REB, TEV]: 'Shall I say, Father, do not let this hour come upon me?' [TEV]. If we do not take it as a question it is difficult to see why he used the deliberative subjunctive, 'What should I say?' Also the strong adversative 'but' that follows argues that this was intended as a question [BECNT, NICNT1]. The whole structure is a rhetorical question—he refuses to pray such a prayer [NICNT1]. The deliberative question 'What should I say?' suggests that taking this as a question is the better choice, but little difference is made in either case [Bar].

2. This clause should be taken as a prayer [Car, ICC, My, NTC, WBC]. This prayer of Jesus parallels his prayer in Gethsemane as recorded in Matthew 26:39 'My Father, if it is possible, may this cup be taken from me. Yet not as I will, but as you will' (see also Mark 14:36; Luke 22:42) [NTC]. This statement expresses what Jesus really wanted to pray so it is a genuine prayer. He seeks to avoid this fearful experience [WBC].

QUESTION—What did Jesus mean by saying 'Save me from this hour?'

The figurative language 'save me from this hour' is difficult to translate in some languages. It could be translated 'do not make me suffer as I know I will have to' [TH], or 'make it so that I don't have to go through this suffering' [TRT].

QUESTION—What did Jesus mean by 'because of this (I came to this hour)'?

He meant 'because of laying down my life' [Bar, EGT, Gdt, ICC, Lns, Rd, TH, TRT; TEV]: 'that is why I came—so that I might go through this hour of suffering' [TEV].

12:28 Father, glorify[a] your name.[b]" Then (a) voice came from heaven,[c] "I-glorified (it) and I-will-glorify (it) again."

TEXT—Instead of σου τὸ ὄνομα 'your name', one manuscript reads μου τὸ ὄνομα 'my name', other manuscripts read σου τὸν υἱόν 'your Son', another reads σου τὸν υἱόν ἵνα καὶ ὁ υἱός σου δοξάσῃ σέ 'your Son in order that your Son may glorify you', and still others read σου τὸ ὄνομα ἐν τῇ δόξῃ ᾗ εἶχον παρὰ σοὶ πρὸ τοῦ τὸν κόσμον γενέσθαι 'your name in the glory which I had with you before the world came to be'. GNT reads 'your name' with an A rating, indicating that the text is certain.

JOHN 12:28

LEXICON—a. aorist act. impera. of δοξάζω (LN 87.24) (BAGD 2. p. 204): 'to glorify' [BAGD, LN; all translations except CEV, NCV, NLT, Ph, TEV], 'to bring glory to' [CEV, NCV, NLT, TEV], 'to honor' [Ph], 'to clothe in splendor' [BAGD], 'to make gloriously great' [LN]. This verb means to cause someone to have glorious greatness [LN]. The glory given is the glory that comes in the next life [BAGD].
  b. ὄνομα (LN 33.126): 'name' [LN]. The clause 'glorify your name' [AB, Gdt, HTC, NICNT2, NTC, WBC; KJV, NASB, NET, NJB, NIV, NRSV, REB] is also translated 'bring glory to your name' [NCV, NLT, TEV], 'honor your own name' [Ph], 'bring glory to yourself' [CEV]. This clause could be translated 'reveal to people how glorious you are' or 'show people how wonderful you are' [TH], or 'show everyone how great you are' [TRT]. This noun denotes the proper name of a person or object [LN]. The name of the Father is his revelation in Christ [NTC]. To glorify someone's name is to reveal their glory [TH] or to clearly present it to men in all its truth, grace, and power [Lns]. To glorify a person's name is to glorify the person him/herself [IVP, Lns]. In the cross the heart of God is seen more clearly than anywhere else [IVP].
  c. οὐρανός (LN 1.11) (BAGD 2.a. p. 594): 'heaven' [BAGD, LN; all translations except AB, NICNT2], 'sky' [AB, NICNT2]. This noun denotes the supernatural dwelling place of God and other heavenly beings. Οὐρανός also contains a component denoting that which is 'above' or 'in the sky', but the element of 'abode' is evidently more significant than location above the earth [LN]. It refers to the dwelling place or throne of God [BAGD]. The fact that the crowd later confuses the voice with thunder suggests that 'sky' is the correct interpretation here. This also is similar to the voice from the cloud that was heard at Jesus' baptism [NICNT2].

QUESTION—Whose voice came from heaven?
  It was the voice of God himself [BECNT, HTC, Lns, NICNT1, Rd, TH, TRT].

QUESTION—What did Jesus mean by the request 'glorify your name'?
  He was asking God to obtain glory from him by doing through him what God willed [Gdt] or that the Father would reveal himself in the Son so that the beauty of his majestic character traits would be displayed to people [NTC]. The aorist tense of δοξάζω may indicate a single act in which case the cross would be referred to [NICNT1]. He was asking God to fulfill his mission of saving the world through his suffering [ICC, Lns, My]. He wanted God to reveal his holiness and love through him even through the cross [EGT].

QUESTION—In what ways had the Father glorified the Son?
  He had glorified him at his baptism, transfiguration [CH, Lns, NTC], and by the great miracles that he had performed [Bar, Car, ICC, Lns, NTC]. The raising of Lazarus was where God had glorified his name [ICC]. He had glorified him in his complete ministry [BECNT, Car, My, Rd, TRT, WBC]

including his death on the cross. The future tense refers to his resurrection [WBC]. The future glorifying refers to Jesus' crucifixion and related events [Bar, BECNT, Car, EGT, ICC, IVP, Lns, My, NICNT1, TRT].

DISCOURSE UNIT—12:29–36 [HTC]. The topic is the entry into Jerusalem.

12:29 Then the crowd (that) stood (there) and heard (it) were-saying "Thunder happened.ᵃ" Others were-saying, "(An) angelᵇ has-spoken to-him."

LEXICON—a. perf. act. infin. of γίνομαι (LN 13.107) (BAGD I.1.b.α. p. 158): 'to happen' [LN], 'to come to be' [BAGD, LN], 'to occur' [LN], 'to arise, to come about, to become, to originate' [BAGD]. The words βροντὴν γεγονέναι 'thunder happened' is translated 'thunder had come' [NICNT2], 'it (had) thundered' [Gdt, HTC, NTC, WBC; KJV, NASB, NET, NIV, Ph], 'it was thunder' [AB; CEV, NCV, NLT, NRSV, REB, TEV], 'it was a clap of thunder' [NJB]. This verb means to happen, with the implication that what happens is different from a previous state [LN].

b. ἄγγελος (LN 12.28) (BAGD 2.a. p. 7): 'angel' [BAGD, LN; all translations]. This noun denotes a supernatural being that attends or serves as a messenger of a superior supernatural being. In many languages a term for 'angels' is borrowed from another dominant language, but in other instances a somewhat descriptive phrase may be employed. The most common expressions for the angels of God are 'messengers' and 'messengers from heaven'. Sometimes these angels are called 'spirit messengers' and even 'flying messengers' [LN], or 'heavenly messengers', or 'a messenger from heaven', or 'one of God's messengers' [TH].

QUESTION—What had the crowd heard?
They had heard the voice/sound from heaven [TH, TRT, WBC; CEV, NCV, NET, NLT, TEV]. While not all heard the voice, all heard the sound [BECNT, NICNT1]. Some heard a voice while others only heard noise [Bar, Car, EGT].

12:30 Jesus answered and said, "This voice has- not -come for- my -sakeᵃ but for- your(pl) -sakes. **12:31** Now is (the) judgmentᵇ of-this world, now the rulerᶜ of-this world will-be-drivenᵈ out.

LEXICON—a. διά (LN 90.38): 'for the sake of' [AB, Gdt, HTC, LN, NICNT2, NTC, WBC; NASB, NCV, NJB, NRSV, Ph, TEV], 'for the benefit of' [LN; NET, NIV, NLT], 'because of' [KJV], 'for, on behalf of' [LN]. The phrase 'for your sake' is translated 'to help you' [CEV]. This preposition with the accusative indicates a participant who is benefited by an event or for whom an event occurs [LN].

b. κρίσις (LN 56.20) (BAGD 1.a.β. p. 452, 3. p. 453): 'judgment' [BAGD (1.a.β.)], 'judging' [BAGD (1.a.β.)], 'right, justice' [BAGD (3)]. The clause 'Now is the judgment of this world' [AB, Gdt, HTC, NICNT2, NTC, WBC; KJV, NET, NRSV] is also translated 'Now judgment is upon this world' [NASB], 'Now is the time for judgment on this world' [NIV], 'Now is the hour of judgment for this world' [REB], 'Now is the time for the judgment of this world to begin' [Ph], 'Now is the time for the/this world to be judged' [NCV, TEV], 'The time for judging this world has come' [NLT], 'This world's people are now being judged' [CEV], 'Now sentence is being passed on this world' [NJB]. This noun is derived from the verb κρίνω meaning to decide a question of legal right or wrong, and thus determine the innocence or guilt of the accused and to assign appropriate punishment or retribution [LN]. The word often means 'judgment' that goes against a person, 'condemnation', and the 'punishment' that follows [BAGD (1.a.β.)]. The sense of 'right, justice' may also play a role in John 12:31 [BAGD (3)]. If this noun is translated as a verb 'to judge' and an actor is required it is probably best to introduce God as the agent [TH, TRT].

c. ἄρχων (LN 37.56) (BAGD 3. p. 114): 'ruler' [BAGD, HTC, LN, NICNT2; CEV, NASB, NCV, NET, NRSV, TEV], 'Satan, the ruler' [NLT], 'prince' [AB, BAGD, Gdt, NTC, WBC; KJV, NJB, NIV, REB], 'governor' [LN], 'lord' [BAGD]. The phrase 'the ruler of this world' is translated 'the spirit that rules this world' [Ph]. This noun denotes one who rules or governs [LN]. It denotes here a ruler of evil spirits whose hierarchy resembles a human political institution [BAGD].

d. fut. pass. indic. of ἐκβάλλω (LN 15.44) (BAGD 1. p. 237): 'to be driven out' [AB, BAGD, LN, NICNT2; NET, NJB, NIV, NRSV, Ph, REB], 'to be cast out' [Gdt, HTC, NTC; KJV, NASB, NLT], 'to be thrown out' [BAGD, WBC; CEV], 'to be thrown down' [NCV], 'to be overthrown' [TEV], 'to be expelled' [BAGD, LN], 'to be sent away' [LN]. This verb means to cause to go out or leave, often, but not always, involving force [LN]. It literally means 'to be thrown out' more or less forcibly [BAGD].

QUESTION—How did the voice benefit those who heard it?

It was a sign to them that Jesus' prayer had received a response [NICNT2, NTC] and that a decisive moment had come [Car, NICNT2], a turning point in the history of man's salvation [Car]. It was a signal to them that Jesus' entire mission included them and was now coming to completion [Rd]. It was given to cause the people to pay attention to what Jesus was saying [CH]. In saying this Jesus was giving them the chance to see that they were missing something and to enquire about the meaning of his words [IVP]. Hearing the voice was a sign for them to believe [Kn]. Jesus did not mean that the voice was not for his sake as well, to encourage him in his impending suffering. He meant that it was not exclusively for his sake but also for theirs [Car, NTC, Rd]. It was very important that the disciples understand that the transition from the triumphal entry to the cross was not a defeat but the fulfillment of God's purpose [EGT]. The disciples did understand the voice with Jesus and to them it was a clear affirmation that Jesus was God's beloved Son [Lns].

QUESTION—To what does the word 'now' refer in this verse?

It refers to the same event as the 'the hour' in verse 23, 'The hour has come that the Son of Man may be glorified', and 'this hour' of verse 27, 'Father save me from this hour' [Car, HTC, NICNT2]. This whole train of thought about his 'hour' was triggered by the arrival of the Greeks in verse 20 [Car]. The fact that the word 'now' is repeated twice gives it great emphasis [Bar, Lns].

QUESTION—What is the relationship between the two clauses beginning with the word 'now'?

The second clause explains the first: 'Now is the judgment of this world, *that is*, now the ruler of this world will be driven out' [CH, Lns, NICNT2].

QUESTION—What is indicated by the term 'world' and its judgment?

The term world indicates the whole society of evil men who were led by Satan as its ruler [NTC]. The world here is all that is in rebellion against God [Car, IVP]. The judgment of the world would be accomplished by Jesus' death on the cross. The world is self-condemned because it does not believe [CH]. The people of the world will condemn (judge) themselves by how they treat God's Son [NICNT1]. The cross of Jesus poses a judgment on the world in the sense that some are drawn to it, while others are repelled by it [Bar].

QUESTION—To whom does the phrase 'ruler of this world' refer?

It is John's term for Satan [AB, Bar, Car, EGT, My, NICNT1, NICNT2, NTC, Rd, TH]. It refers to the enemy of God and Christ [HTC].

QUESTION—How is the ruler of the world judged?

His crime in causing the crucifixion of the Son of God was detestable and unpardonable and it ends God's long-suffering and therefore it ends his dominion over mankind [Gdt]. The judgment of the world occurs in the crucifixion-exaltation of the Son of Man. Satan is dethroned and the Son of Man is enthroned over the world he died for [Rd, WBC]. Satan is doomed by the death and resurrection of Jesus [Lns].

QUESTION—Who is the implied actor of ἐκβληθήσεται 'will be driven out' and how will the ruler of this world be driven out?

The actor may be God [NICNT2, TH, TRT]. God's part in this action may indicate some of what is involved in glorifying his name [NICNT2]. In the next verse Jesus designates himself the one to drive out the ruler of this world [Gdt, NTC]. Jesus' drawing all men to himself is the casting out of the ruler of this world. In this context the Greeks represent the nations over which Satan had ruled. Jesus' death broke the power of Satan over the nations [NTC]. He is being cast out of his position of opposing Christ, dislodged from his place of authority, and stripped of his power in heaven [Kn]. He will be put out of office and relieved of his authority [Bar]. He will be thrown out of the world over which he has held dominion [ICC, My].

12:32 And-I[a] if[b] I-am-lifted-up[c] from the earth, I-will-draw[d] all (people) to myself.

TEXT—Instead of πάντας ἑλκύσω 'I will draw all (people)', some manuscripts read πάντα ἑλκύσω 'I will draw all (things)'. GNT reads 'I will draw all (people)' with a B rating, indicating that the text is almost certain.

LEXICON—a. κἀγώ (BAGD 1. p. 386): 'and I' [AB, BAGD, Gdt, HTC, NICNT2, NTC, WBC; KJV, NASB, NLT, NRSV, REB], 'but I' [NIV], 'I' [CEV, NCV, NET, NJB, TEV], 'as for me' [Ph]. This word is a contraction formed by joining καί 'and' with ἐγώ 'I' [BAGD].

b. ἐάν (LN **67.32**) (BAGD I.1.d. p. 211): 'if' [NICNT2, WBC; CEV, KJV, NASB, NCV, Ph], 'when' [AB, BAGD, Gdt, HTC, **LN**, NTC; NET, NJB, NIV, NLT, NRSV, REB, TEV], 'when and if' [LN], 'whenever' [BAGD]. This conjunction indicates a point of time which is somewhat conditional and simultaneous with another point of time [LN]. It is used with the subjunctive to denote 'what is expected to occur, under certain circumstances, for a given standpoint in the present either general or specific'. At times the meaning approaches that of 'when' or 'whenever' as here [BAGD].

c. aorist pass. subj. of ὑψόω (LN 81.5) (BAGD 1. p. 850): 'to be lifted up' [BAGD, LN; all translations], 'to be raised up' [LN], 'to be raised high' [BAGD]. This verb means to cause something to become high [LN]. It can mean being lifted up on a cross before the eyes of all. For Jesus this 'lifting up' is not to be separated from the 'exaltation' into heaven, since the heavenly exaltation presupposes the earthly [BAGD].

d. fut. act. indic. of ἕλκω (LN 33.301) (BAGD 1.b. p. 251): 'to draw' [BAGD, LN; all translations except CEV], 'to attract' [LN], 'to drag' [BAGD]. The clause 'I will draw all people to myself' is translated 'I will make everyone want to come to me' [CEV]. This verb means to draw and is figurative of the pull on a man's inner life by God [BAGD]. To avoid the meaning 'to drag' that a literal translation of 'draw' might imply one could translate 'I will cause all people to come to me' [TH, TRT], or 'cause everyone to believe in me' [TRT].

QUESTION—What word is emphasized in this verse?

The pronoun ἐγώ 'I' is emphasized [HTC, Lns, My, NICNT1: Ph]: '*As for me*, if *I* am lifted up from the earth, I will draw all men to myself' [Ph]. Jesus contrasts himself with the ruler of this world [HTC, Lns, My, Rd] and with this world itself [Lns, Rd].

QUESTION—What is implied by the verb phrase ὑψωθῶ 'I am lifted up'?

The words '(lifted up) on the cross' are implied [AB, Bar, BECNT, Car, CH, EGT, Gdt, HTC, ICC, Kn, NICNT1, NTC, Rd, TH, TRT, WBC]. 'Lifting up' was a common idiom meaning to hoist onto a cross [CH]. The cross is also the means of Jesus' being elevated and so exalted to God's throne through his ascension [Bar, Gdt, Kn, My, WBC]. The lifting up includes crucifixion, resurrection, ascension, and coronation [NTC]. Lifting up has a double interpretation of Jesus' physical lifting up on a cross and his exaltation to God's presence [BECNT, Car, CH, EGT, Rd, TH]. Verse 33 shows that Jesus was talking about his death on a cross and verse 34 shows that the people understood this [TRT].

QUESTION—How does Jesus draw all people to himself?
Jesus draws people to himself by the work of his Spirit [My, NTC] and his Word. This action precedes a person's believing in Jesus for salvation [NTC]. He draws people to himself by bringing them under his saving power [Rd]. He leads people to have a relationship with himself [TRT]. The drawing is a pull on a person's inner life [BAGD]. The drawing to himself is only thwarted by a person's unbelief [HTC, Lns, WBC]. Jesus will draw all people to himself when he causes the general resurrection. 'All who are in their graves will hear his voice and come out' (5:28–29) [NICNT2].

12:33 Now he-was-saying this signifying[a] by-what-kind-of death he-was-about[b] to-die.

LEXICON—a. pres. act. participle of σημαίνω (LN 33.153) (BAGD 2. p. 747): 'to signify' [BAGD, Gdt, NICNT2, NTC, WBC; KJV], 'to indicate' [AB; NASB, NJB, NLT, NRSV, REB, TEV], 'to indicate clearly' [LN; NET], 'to show' [HTC; NCV, NIV, Ph], 'to indicate (beforehand), to foretell' [BAGD], 'to make clear' [LN]. This verse is translated 'Jesus was talking about the way he would be put to death' [CEV]. This verb means to cause something to be both specific and clear [LN].

b. imperf. act. indic. of μέλλω (LN 67.62) (BAGD 1.c.δ. p. 501): 'to be about to' [LN, NTC], 'to be destined to' [BAGD]. The clause 'he was about to die' [WBC] is also translated 'he was going to die' [AB, NICNT2; NET, NIV, NLT, Ph], 'he was to die' [HTC; NASB, NRSV, REB], 'he would die' [NCV, NJB], 'he should die' [Gdt; KJV], 'he would be put to death' [CEV], '(the kind of) death he was going to suffer' [TEV]. This verb means to occur at a point of time in the future which is subsequent to another event and closely related to it [LN]. It denotes an action that necessarily follows a divine decree 'is destined, must, will certainly' [BAGD]. It indicates the inevitability of Jesus' death as an event foreordained by God [ICC].

QUESTION—What is the purpose of this verse and what kind of death is being indicated?
Its purpose is to explain verse 32 [Gdt, HTC, ICC, NICNT1, TH] and it points to crucifixion as the meaning of the phrase 'to lift up' [AB, BECNT, Car, EGT, Gdt, HTC, ICC, Kn, Lns, NICNT1, NICNT2, NTC, Rd, TRT, WBC]. The following translations put this verse in parentheses [AB; NET, Ph, TEV].

12:34 Then the crowd answered him, "We heard from the law[a] that the Christ[b] remains[c] forever,[d] and how[e] do- you(sg) -say that it-is-necessary (for) the Son of Man to-be-lifted-up? Who is this Son of-Man?"

LEXICON—a. νόμος (LN 33.56) (BAGD 4.b. p. 543): 'law' [BAGD, Gdt, HTC, NICNT2, NTC; KJV, NCV, NET, NRSV, REB], 'Law' [AB,

WBC; NASB, NJB, NIV, Ph, TEV], '(the) Scriptures' [LN; CEV], 'Scripture' [NLT], 'Holy Scripture' [BAGD], 'holy writings, sacred writings' [LN]. This noun denotes the sacred writings of the OT [LN]. It denotes Holy Scripture in the wider sense generally, on the principle that the most authoritative part gives its name to the whole [BAGD].

b. Χριστός (LN 53.82) (BAGD 1. p. 887): 'Christ' [BAGD, Gdt, HTC, LN, NICNT2, NTC, WBC; KJV, NASB, NCV, NET, NJB, NIV, Ph], 'Messiah' [AB, BAGD, LN; CEV, NLT, NRSV, REB, TEV]. This noun in the NT (literally 'one who has been anointed') functions as a title for Jesus as the Messiah [LN]. It is a title for 'the Anointed One, the Messiah, the Christ' [BAGD].

c. pres. act. indic. of μένω (LN 13.89) (BAGD 1.c.α. p. 504): 'to remain' [AB, BAGD, HTC, LN, NICNT2, NTC, WBC; NASB, NET, NJB, NIV, NRSV, REB], 'to live' [CEV, NCV, NLT, Ph, TEV], 'to continue to live' [BAGD], 'to abide' [Gdt; KJV], 'to continue, to continue to exist, to still be in existence' [LN], 'to last, to persist' [BAGD]. This verb means to continue to exist [LN].

d. εἰς τὸν αἰῶνα (LN 67.95) (BAGD 1.b. p. 27): The phrase εἰς τὸν αἰῶνα 'to the age' is translated 'forever' [AB, BAGD, LN, NICNT2, NTC, WBC; CEV, KJV, NASB, NCV, NET, NIV, NLT, NRSV, TEV], 'for ever' [Gdt, HTC; KJV, NJB, Ph, REB], 'eternally' [BAGD, LN], 'always, forever and ever' [LN], 'to eternity, in perpetuity' [BAGD]. This phrase indicates unlimited duration of time, with particular focus on the future [LN].

e. πῶς (LN 92.16) (BAGD 1.a. p. 732): 'how?' [BAGD, LN], 'by what means?' [LN], 'in what way?' [BAGD]. The question πῶς λέγεις σὺ 'how do you say?' [Gdt; KJV], is also translated 'how can you say?' [HTC, NICNT2; CEV, NASB, NET, NJB, NIV, NLT, NRSV, Ph], 'how can you claim?' [AB], 'how, then, can/do you say?' [NTC; TEV], 'then how is it that you are saying?' [WBC], 'why do you say?' [NCV], 'what do you mean by saying?' [REB]. This interrogative adverb questions the means by which something happens [LN]. It is used to question how something has come to be, how something is happening, or should happen, with the special meaning 'with what right?' or 'in what sense?' [BAGD].

QUESTION—How did the crowd 'hear from the law'?
Probably their priest or rabbi read to them from the law [TRT]. Since it is not possible in some languages to make the law an agent, it is possible to translate 'in our laws we read that' or 'from our laws we learn that' [TH].

QUESTION—To what did the word 'law' refer?
It referred to the Scripture as a whole [BAGD, Bar, Car, CH, EGT, LN, Lns, My, NICNT1, NICNT2, NTC, Rd, TH, WBC; CEV, NLT]. It probably refers to the OT [Bar, LN, Lns, NTC, WBC] or to the entire Jewish Bible [TH]. The word law often refers to more than the Pentateuch [ICC]. That this term does not refer to a legal code or the pentateuch is clear from a similar use in 10:34 where 'law' is used to refer to a verse in the Psalms [NICNT2].

QUESTION—What specific reference may the crowd have had in mind?

They may have been referring to a Targum of Isaiah 9:5 where the child that is born to us is said to live forever [IVP]. There are the various scriptures noted by the commentaries as being those the crowd may have had in mind: Psalms 45:9; 61:6–7; 72:17; 89:3–4, 29, 35–37; 110:2–4; 132:12; Isaiah 9:5–7; Ezekiel 37:25; Daniel 2:44; 7:13–14; 8:13–14; 2 Samuel 7:12–13, 16.

QUESTION—What words are emphasized in this verse?

Both pronouns ἡμεῖς 'we' and σύ 'you(sg)' are emphatic [BECNT, Lns, NICNT1]: *We, on our part* (heard)…(how do) *you on your part* (say)? The pronoun 'you' is being contrasted with the 'we' [BECNT, Gdt, Lns], that is, we who are acquainted with the law and have those among us who can explain it [Gdt].

QUESTION—What is implied by the question 'How do you say that it is necessary for the Son of Man to be lifted up?'

The people are incredulous that Jesus could claim this [HTC]. They take for granted that Jesus is the Son of Man, but as such he does not qualify in their minds as the Christ for they believe that the Messiah will live forever. But Jesus was claiming that he must be lifted up, that is, die by crucifixion [NICNT2]. What they do not understand is Jesus' resurrection [Kn]. The question is rhetorical [TRT] and could be translated 'Isn't it wrong for you to say?' or 'It is wrong for you to say' [TRT].

QUESTION—What is implied by the question 'Who is this Son of Man'?

The question means, 'What kind of person is this anyway, this Son of man who, strange to say, must be lifted up?' [Car, Lns, NTC, WBC]. They are really asking Jesus 'Who are you?' [IVP, NICNT2]. They cannot understand how he can be the Christ if he maintains that he is going to be crucified [NICNT2]. They are not asking for the identity of the Son of Man, but what his function is? Is he distinct from the Messiah whom they understood would live forever [NICNT1]. They were not asking for his identity for they had correctly understood him to be the Messiah. They were asking about his nature—'What kind of Son of Man?' [Rd]. The question can be taken either as asking about the Son of Man's identity or what his relationship to the Messiah is [TH].

12:35 Then Jesus said to-them, "Yet (a) little time the light[a] is among you(pl). Walk[b] while[c] you(pl)-have the light, so-that darkness[d] does- not -overtake[e] you(pl). And the-one walking in the darkness does- not -know where he-is-going.

LEXICON—a. φῶς [BAGD 2. p. 872]: 'light' [BAGD; all translations except NASB, NLT], 'Light' [NICNT2; NASB], 'my light' [NLT]. Light is the element and sphere of the Divine. In the Fourth Gospel it is used of the Divine Redeemer [BAGD].

b. pres. act. impera. of περιπατέω (LN 41.11) (BAGD 1.d. p. 649): 'to walk' [KJV], 'to go about' [BAGD], 'to walk around' [BAGD], 'to go about doing, to live, to behave' [LN]. The clause 'Walk while you have the light/Light' [AB, Gdt, HTC, NICNT2, NTC; KJV, NASB, NCV, NET, NIV, NRSV] is also translated 'Walk in the light while you can' [CEV, NLT], 'Go/continue on your way while you have the light' [NJB, REB, TEV], 'Go on walking while you have the light' [WBC], 'Go on while the light is good' [Ph]. This clause means 'Live and act according to the light that you have' [NICNT1]. This verb means to live or behave in a customary manner, with possible focus on continuity of action [LN]. Here it does not refer to literal walking but is used figuratively [BAGD]. It refers to conduct or behavior [ICC]. The present tense imperative indicates that they should continue an action that is already begun [TH; TEV].

c. ὡς (LN **67.139**) (BAGD IV.1.b. p. 898): 'while' [BAGD, LN; all translations], 'as long as' [BAGD, **LN**], 'when' [BAGD]. This conjunction indicates an extent of time of the same length as another extent or unit of time [LN]. The sense of this conjunction is, 'as' or 'in keeping with the fact that' you have the light. He means 'Because of the fact that you have the light, come to it, believe' [Gdt].

d. σκοτία (LN 88.125) (BAGD 2. p. 757): 'darkness' [all translations except CEV], 'dark' [CEV], 'evil world, realm of evil' [LN]. This noun is used figuratively and denotes the realm of sin and evil [LN]. It is figurative of the mind or spirit, of ignorance in moral and religious matters. Especially in Johannine usage it is used as a category including everything that is at enmity with God, earthly and demonic [BAGD]. It symbolizes the realm of all that is hostile to God, the realm of sin and death, judgment and annhilation [HTC].

e. aorist act. subj. of καταλαμβάνω (LN 37.19) (BAGD 1.b. p. 413): 'to overtake' [BAGD], 'to seize with hostile intent, to come upon' [BAGD], 'to overcome, to gain control of' [LN]. The clause 'so that (the) darkness does/will not overtake you' [NASB, NLT] is also translated 'so that the darkness may not overtake you' [NET, NRSV, REB], 'so that the darkness will not come upon you' [TEV], 'or darkness will overtake you' [NJB], 'or the darkness will come over you' [AB], 'lest (the) darkness overtake you' [Gdt, HTC, NICNT2, NTC, WBC], 'lest darkness come upon you' [KJV], 'before darkness overtakes you' [NIV], 'before the darkness comes down upon you' [Ph], 'Then the darkness will not catch you' [NCV], 'Then you won't be caught walking blindly in the dark' [CEV]. This verb means to gain control over [LN]. When the darkness overtakes a person it gets the better of them [ICC].

QUESTION—Does Jesus directly answer their question?

He does not answer their question directly [AB, BECNT, EGT, Gdt, HTC, Lns, My, NICNT1, NTC]. Jesus does reply to their question. They talked about the Christ remaining forever but he emphasizes the shortness of his time with them as the light of the world and the necessity of their believing while time remained [Rd]. Jesus answers the people's real need which was not to solve the problem of the Son of Man but to realize that there was judgment associated with him [AB, BECNT]. His answer amounts to believe in the light and you will know how the Son of Man must be lifted up [Lns]. While not a direct answer to their question, he replies to the insulting spirit they used to ask it, reminding them of their serious responsibility [NTC]. Jesus is counselling them to leave their prejudice about the Messiah and act on the light or truth that he is giving them [NICNT1]. He bids them to leave questions about Messiahship and to permit the light of truth to enter their lives [EGT]. There is a connection however between Jesus as the light of the world and as the Son of Man. Chapter 9 begins with him as the light of the world (9:5) and ends with him as the Son of Man (9:35–37) [AB].

QUESTION—Who is the topic of the metaphor of φῶς 'light'?

The topic is Jesus [AB, Bar, BECNT, Car, EGT, Gdt, HTC, ICC, IVP, NICNT2, NTC, TH, TRT; NLT]: 'My light will shine for you just a little longer' [NLT]. Jesus spoke of himself as 'the light' (see 1:9; 8:12; 12:46) [Lns].

QUESTION—To what does the 'little time' refer?

The little time refers to the brief time left that Jesus would be on earth with them [NICNT1]. It refers to the brevity of Jesus' remaining ministry and the urgency of deciding one way or another [Bar].

QUESTION—What is implied by the verb περιπατεῖτε 'walk'?

Jesus is referring to the act of believing [Bar, BECNT, Gdt, HTC, Rd] and he is addressing the unbelieving [Gdt]. 'Walking' here refers to getting to know the Son of Man [NICNT1]. To walk in the light is to show by one's behavior that they have accepted the truth that Jesus has proclaimed [NTC]. To walk in the light is to become Jesus' disciples and follow him [IVP].

DISCOURSE UNIT—12:36b–43 [NICNT1; CEV, NRSV, TEV]. The topic is the witness of prophecy to Jesus [NICNT1], unbelief in Jesus [CEV, NRSV, TEV].

12:36 **While you(pl)-have the light, believe in the light, so-that you(pl)-may-become sons-of-light.**[a]**" Jesus spoke these-things and having-gone-away he-was-hidden**[b] **from them.**

LEXICON—a. υἱοὶ φωτός (LN **11.14**) (BAGD 1.c.δ. p. 834): 'sons of (the) light' [AB, HTC, LN, NICNT2, NTC, WBC; NET, NIV, Ph], 'sons of Light' [NASB], 'children of (the) light' [Gdt, LN; CEV, KJV, NCV, NJB, NLT, NRSV, REB], 'people of the light' [TEV], 'people of God' [**LN**]. The clause 'so that you may become sons of light' is translated 'so that you will be God's people' [**LN**]. This phrase is an idiom denoting persons to whom the truth of God has been revealed and who are presumably living according to such truth [LN]. The noun υἱός 'son' with the genitive case of the noun φῶς 'light', denotes one who shares in the light or who is worthy of it, or who stands in some other close relation to it, often made clear by the context [BAGD].

b. aorist pass. indic. of κρύπτω (LN 21.12) (BAGD 1.c. p. 454): 'to be hidden' [BAGD, LN], 'to be kept safe, to be caused to be protected, to be protected' [LN]. The clause '(he) was hidden from them' [NICNT2; NLT] is also translated '(he) hid himself from them' [Gdt, HTC, NTC, WBC; KJV, NASB, NCV, NET, NIV, TEV], '(he) went/went away into hiding' [AB; CEV, REB], '(he) hid from them' [NRSV], '(he) was hidden from their sight' [NJB], 'Jesus…went away, out of their sight' [Ph]. This verb means to cause to be safe or protected by hiding, in some contexts with the intent of not being found [LN]. It means 'to hide' or 'to conceal oneself' [BAGD]. Although the verb is passive, most commentators take it as being middle voice meaning 'he hid himself'. If it is a passive, God is the agent [NICNT1]. (See the question about treating this verb as passive or reflexive also at verse 8:59).

QUESTION—What is indicated by the period 'while you have the light'?

It refers to the time that Jesus is with them [EGT, Gdt, ICC, NICNT1, NICNT2, NTC, Rd]. To believe in the Light means 'to believe in me' NICNT2].

QUESTION—What does it mean to be 'sons of light'?

This is a Semitic expression describing people who have a close relationship to someone or something in terms of sonship [EGT, HTC, ICC]. It means to have the light of Christ in your hearts and minds [NTC], to become a possessor of the nature of light [WBC], to be characterized by light [Bar, BECNT, Car, IVP, NICNT1, TH], to become a follower of light [BECNT, Car, TRT], to become an enlightened person [ICC, My], or to become like the Light [TRT]. John uses the phrase to indicate those who believe in Jesus [AB]. The person believing in Christ becomes so penetrated by light that he himself becomes brilliant [Gdt]. To become 'sons of light' means 'to become people who belong to God' [NICNT2]. The word 'son' implies that the person is derived from the light and the light becomes the very nature of that person [Lns].

DISCOURSE UNIT—12:37–50 [Bar, BECNT, IVP, Lns, NICNT2, WBC; NCV, NIV, NLT]. The topic is the verdict on the world [NICNT1], conclusion of Jesus' public ministry [IVP, WBC], the Messiah's signs rejected [BECNT], theology of unbelief [Car], the unbelief of the people [NCV, NIV, NLT].

DISCOURSE UNIT—12:37–43 [AB, Gdt, HTC, IVP, Kn, Rd; NET]. The topic is an evaluation of Jesus' ministry [AB], the riddle of unbelief [HTC, IVP], Jewish unbelief [Gdt, Kn, Rd], Jesus' public ministry's outcome foretold [NET].

12:37 And although he performed so-many[a] signs[b] before them they-were-not -believing in him.

LEXICON—a. τοσοῦτος (LN 59.6) (BAGD 1.b. p. 823): 'so many' [AB, BAGD, Gdt, HTC, LN, NICNT2, NTC; KJV, NASB, NET, NJB, NRSV, Ph], '(the) many' [NCV, REB], 'a lot of' [CEV], 'all these' [NIV, TEV], 'all the' [NLT], 'such great' [WBC], 'this many' [LN], 'so great, so large, so much, so strong' [BAGD]. This adjective describes a quantity of objects or events considerably beyond normal expectations [LN].

b. σημεῖον (LN 33.477) (BAGD 2.a. p. 748): 'sign' [AB, BAGD, HTC, LN, NICNT2, NTC, WBC; NASB, NJB, NRSV, Ph, REB], 'miracle' [BAGD, Gdt, LN; CEV, KJV, NCV, TEV], 'miraculous sign' [NET, NIV, NLT]. This noun denotes an event which is regarded as having some special meaning. It was inevitably an unusual or even miraculous type of occurrence, and in a number of contexts it may be rendered as 'miracle'. Certainly that is the referent of the term in John 2:23. Since 'sign' combines the concepts of pointing to something and miracle, it may be rendered in some languages as 'a miracle with great meaning' [LN]. It denotes a 'wonder' or 'miracle', an event that is contrary to the usual course of nature and is performed by God himself, by Christ, or by men of God [BAGD]. The word σημεῖον brings to mind God's purpose in giving these signs [Gdt]. This word occurs at 2:11, 18; 3:2; 4:48, 54; 6:2, 14, 26, 30; 7:31; 9:16; 10:41, 47; 12:18, 37; 20:30.

QUESTION—Why do most translations of this verse treat it as a concessive sentence?

The genitive absolute, 'he had done so many signs before them', is concessive [Lns; KJV, NASB, NCV, NET, NIV, NLT, NRSV, Ph, TEV]: 'But though He had performed so many signs before them, *yet* they were not believing in Him' [NASB].

QUESTION—Does τοσοῦτος 'so many/such great' refer here primarily to quantity or to quality?

1. It refers to quality or quality as well as quantity [BECNT, NICNT1, WBC]: 'Although he had performed such great signs before them' [WBC]. Quality is more likely here in view of the fact that John selected only a few of Jesus' most outstanding signs and recorded them in detail [BECNT]. John has in mind not only the great number of signs, but also the kind of signs he had performed [NICNT1].
2. It refers rather only to quantity [Gdt, HTC, ICC, Lns, My, Rd; all other translations]. In the Gospels τοσοῦτος always refers to quantity not quality [Gdt]. Τοσοῦτος can mean either 'so many' or 'so great' but since the evangelist has selected only a few significant signs, the choice for quantity seems to fit better [HTC].

QUESTION—To whom do the pronouns 'them' and 'they' refer?

They refer to the people in general, not to every single one of them [Car, ICC, Rd, TRT].

QUESTION—What is indicated by the imperfect tense of the verb 'they were not believing'?

The imperfect tense indicates that they were continuing in their unbelief [Gdt, NICNT1, WBC]. It is an action that is now in progress [Lns].

12:38 So-that[a] the word of-the prophet Isaiah[b] might-be-fulfilled[c] that said, "Lord, who believed our report?[d] And to-whom was-revealed[e] the arm[f] of-(the)-Lord?

LEXICON—a. ἵνα (LN 89.59) (BAGD II.2. p. 378): 'so that' [LN, NICNT2; NET, Ph, TEV], 'that' [Gdt, WBC; KJV], 'in order that' [NTC], 'in order to, for the purpose of' [LN], 'for' [REB]. The words 'so that...might be fulfilled' are translated 'This happened so that...would come true' [CEV], 'This was to fulfill' [AB, NASB, NJB, NIV, NRSV], 'This was to bring about' [NCV], 'This is...what Isaiah...had predicted' [NLT], 'It was that...might be fulfilled' [HTC]. This conjunction indicates purpose for events and states (sometimes occurring in highly elliptical contexts) [LN]. Very often the sense of purpose is greatly weakened, or disappears altogether. In this case the ἵνα-construction serves as a substitute for the infinitive of result, when the result is considered probable, but not actual. But this distinction is not always strictly observed. In many cases purpose and result cannot be clearly differentiated, and hence ἵνα is used for the result which follows according to the purpose of the subject or of God. As in Jewish and pagan thought, purpose and result are identical in declarations of the divine will. The formula ἵνα πληρωθῇ 'so that...might be fulfilled', is to be understood in this way, since the fulfillment is according to God's plan of salvation [BAGD].

b. Ἡσαΐας (LN 93.147) (BAGD p. 348): 'Isaiah' [BAGD, LN; all translations except KJV], 'Esaias' [KJV]. This noun denotes a major OT prophet, 'Isaiah'[LN].

c. aorist passive subj. of πληρόω (LN 13.106) (BAGD 4.a. p. 671): 'to be fulfilled' [BAGD, Gdt, HTC, LN, NICNT2, NTC, WBC; NET, Ph, REB], 'to cause to happen, to make happen' [LN]. The clause 'the word of the prophet Isaiah might be fulfilled' is translated 'what the prophet Isaiah had said would come true' [CEV], 'what the prophet Isaiah had said might come true' [TEV], 'this is exactly what Isaiah the prophet had predicted' [NLT]. This verb is also translated actively: '(This was) to fulfill' [AB; NASB, NJB, NIV, NRSV], '(This was) to bring about' [NCV]. This verb means to cause to happen, with the implication of fulfilling some purpose [LN]. It means to fulfill divine predictions or promises [BAGD].

d. ἀκοή (LN 24.57) (BAGD 2.b. p. 31): 'report' [BAGD, HTC, NTC, WBC; KJV, NASB, Ph], 'message' [LN, NICNT2; CEV, NET, NIV, NLT, NRSV, TEV], 'preaching' [LN, Gdt], 'account' [BAGD], 'what is heard' [LN]. This noun is also translated as a phrase: 'what we told them' [NCV], 'what we reported' [REB], 'what they have heard from us' [NJB], 'what we have heard' [AB], 'the message we have heard' [NICNT2]. This noun is derived from the verb ἀκούω 'to hear' and denotes that which is heard by someone [LN].

e. aorist pass. indic. of ἀποκαλύπτω (LN 28.38) (BAGD 1. p. 92): 'to be revealed' [AB, BAGD, Gdt, HTC,LN, NICNT2, NTC, WBC; KJV, NASB, NET, NIV, NRSV, Ph, REB], 'to be disclosed' [BAGD, LN], 'to be made fully known' [LN], 'to be uncovered, to be brought to light' [BAGD]. This verb means to cause something to be fully known [LN]. See other version evidence in f. below.

f. βραχίων (LN 76.3) (BAGD p. 147): 'arm' [BAGD, Gdt, HTC, NICNT2, NTC, WBC; KJV, NASB, NET, NIV, NRSV, Ph], 'power' [LN; REB], 'might' [AB]. The question 'to whom was revealed the arm of the Lord?' is translated 'to whom has the Lord revealed his powerful arm?' [NLT], 'to whom did the Lord reveal his power?' [TEV], 'who has seen your mighty strength?' [CEV], 'who saw the Lord's power in this?' [NCV], 'who has seen it in a revelation of the Lord's arm?' [NJB]. This noun is a figurative extension of the meaning of βραχίων 'arm' and indicates power as an expression of the activity of a person or supernatural being. In some languages there is no abstract term for 'power'. The equivalent of doing something by the power of someone is 'someone makes it possible to do' or, in a figurative sense, 'someone gives strength to do' [LN]. This noun is an anthropomorphic symbol of God's power [BAGD].

QUESTION—What relationship is indicated by the conjunction ἵνα 'so that'?

It is a relationship of purpose [AB, Car, EGT, ICC, Lns, My, NICNT1, NICNT2, NTC, TH]. In order to bring out the purpose of this conjunction it may be necessary add the implied introductory clause and translate something like 'All this happened so that what the prophet Isaiah had said might come true' [TH]. It was necessary for the OT prophecies to be fulfilled [AB].

QUESTION—Which particular OT reference is being quoted?

John refers to Isaiah 53:1 [Bar, BECNT, Car, CH, EGT, Gdt, HTC, ICC, IVP, Lns, My, NICNT1, NICNT2, NTC, WBC].

QUESTION—If the question 'Lord, who believed our report?' is taken as a rhetorical question, what does it imply?

It implies that no one believed our report [HTC, NICNT2, TRT]. It might be translated 'It seems like no one believes our report' [TRT]. It implies that hardly anyone has believed [Lns, Rd], or that it is difficult for them to believe [IVP].

QUESTION—How are the nouns related in the genitive construction ἀκοῇ ἡμῶν 'our report'?

1. 'Our report' means 'the report that we gave' [Gdt, Lns, My, TH; all translations except AB, NICNT2].
2. 'Our report' means 'the report that we heard' [AB, NICNT2, Rd]: 'Lord who has believed what we have heard?' [AB].

QUESTION—What was the content of the report or message?

It was the word/teachings of Jesus [Bar, BECNT, Car, EGT, ICC, WBC]. It was the message about the suffering Messiah [Gdt].

QUESTION—What is symbolized by the 'arm of the Lord'?

The arm of the Lord symbolizes his power, strength, or might [AB, BAGD, BECNT, CH, EGT, Gdt, ICC, IVP, LN, Lns, My, NTC, WBC; CEV, NCV, NLT, REB, TEV]: 'To whom did the Lord reveal his power?' [TEV]. Jesus the Messiah is the arm of the Lord [CH, Gdt] as are his acts of divine power [Gdt]. It is the power of God shown in the signs that Jesus performed [Bar, Car, BECNT, EGT, ICC, Lns, My, NTC, WBC]. It is God's great power seen in his acts of deliverance as in the exodus [IVP].

QUESTION—If the question 'To whom was revealed the arm of the Lord?' is taken as being rhetorical, what does it imply?

It implies either that it was revealed to no one [Gdt, HTC, TRT] or to a small number of people [Gdt, NTC]. It could be translated 'No seems to recognize your power that you have revealed to them' [TRT].

QUESTION—How does God reveal his power to someone?

It may not make sense to translate this literally so it could be rendered 'To whom did God reveal how powerful he is?' or 'To whom did God show how much power he has?' or 'To whom did God reveal how he is able to control?' [TH].

QUESTION—Who is the implied actor of ἀπεκαλύφθη 'was revealed'?

God is the actor [TH, TRT; NLT, TEV]: 'To whom did the Lord reveal his power?' [TEV].

12:39 For-this-reason[a] they were- not -able to-believe, because again Isaiah said, **12:40** "He-has-blinded[b] their eyes[c] and hardened[d] their heart,[e] so-that they-may- not -see with-the eyes and understand with-the heart[f] and might-turn,[g] and I-will-heal[h] them."

LEXICON—a. διὰ τοῦτο (BAGD B.II.2. p. 181): 'for this reason' [BAGD, NTC; NASB, NET, NIV], 'therefore' [HTC, NICNT2; KJV], 'on this account' [WBC], 'this is why' [NCV], 'thus' [Ph], 'and so' [NRSV, TEV], 'but' [NLT], '(And) indeed' [Gdt; NJB], not explicit [CEV]. The clause 'For this reason they were not able to believe, because Isaiah said' is translated 'And there is another saying of Isaiah which explains why they could not believe' [REB], 'The reason they could not believe was that, as Isaiah said elsewhere' [AB]. The phrase διὰ τοῦτο indicates the reason for an event, in this case the reason is given in the following clause introduced by ὅτι 'that'—'for this reason, (namely) that' [BAGD].

b. perf. act. indic. of τυφλόω (LN **32.25**) (BAGD p. 381): 'to blind' [BAGD, LN; all translations], 'to deprive of sight' [BAGD], 'to cause to not understand, to make unable to comprehend' [LN]. The clause 'he has blinded their eyes' is translated 'he has made it impossible for them to understand' [LN]. The phrase τυφλόω τοὺς ὀφθαλμούς is an idiom (literally 'to blind the eyes') meaning to cause someone to no longer have the capacity for understanding [LN].

c. ὀφθαλμός (BAGD 2. p. 599): 'eye' [BAGD: all translations]. The literal meaning of this noun is here transferred from physical sense perception to mental and spiritual understanding [BAGD].

d. aorist act. indic. of πωρόω / πηρόω (LN **27.51**, **27.53**) (BAGD p. 732): 'to harden' [BAGD, Gdt, HTC, LN (27.51), NICNT2, NTC; KJV, NASB, NET, NJB, NLT, NRSV, Ph], 'to dull' [REB], 'to numb' [AB], 'to deaden' [NIV], 'to callous' [WBC], 'to petrify' [BAGD], 'to make dull, to make obtuse, to make blind' [BAGD]. The clause '(he has) hardened their heart(s)' [Gdt, NICNT2, NTC; KJV, NASB, NET, NJB, NLT, NRSV, Ph] is also translated 'he has made their hearts unable to learn' [**LN** (27.53)], 'he (has) closed their minds' [**LN** (27.51); NCV, TEV], 'he has made the people stubborn' [CEV], 'he has...dulled their minds' [REB], 'he has...numbed their minds' [AB], 'he has deadened their hearts' [NIV], 'he has calloused their hearts' [WBC]. The phrase πηρόω τὴν καρδίαν, literally 'to maim the heart' is an idiom meaning to cause someone to be unwilling to learn, 'to close someone's mind, to make someone unable to learn' [LN (27.53)]. The verb πωρόω is used figuratively with καρδία 'heart' to mean to cause someone to be completely unwilling to learn and to accept new information, 'to cause to be completely unwilling to learn, to cause the mind to be closed' [LN (27.51)]. It refers to 'numbness' rather than hardness and would be better translated 'He has...darkened their hearts' since it is parallel to the blinding of their eyes [ICC].

e. καρδία (LN **27.53**) (BAGD 1.b.β. p. 403): 'heart' [BAGD, LN; all translations except AB; NCV, REB, TEV], 'mind' [AB, BAGD, LN; NCV, REB, TEV]. The heart is the seat of physical, spiritual and mental life as the center and source of the whole inner life with its thinking, feeling, and volition in the case of the natural man as well as the redeemed man. It denotes the faculty of thought, of the thoughts themselves, of understanding, as the organ of natural and spiritual enlightenment. Here it refers to a lack of understanding [BAGD]. The word 'heart' in Hebrew is the equivalent of 'mind' for the western reader [TH].

f. καρδία (LN 26.3) (BAGD 1.b.β. p. 403): 'heart' [BAGD, LN, Gdt, NICNT2, WBC; KJV, NET, NJB, NIV, NRSV HTC, NTC NASB, NLT, Ph], 'mind' [BAGD, LN; AB, NCV, REB, TEV], 'inner self' [LN]. The phrase 'understand with the/their heart(s)' [Gdt, NICNT2 KJV, NET, NIV, NRSV] is also translated 'understand' [CEV], 'perceive with their heart' [HTC, NTC, WBC; NASB, Ph], 'using their heart to understand' [NJB], 'their hearts cannot understand' [NLT], 'perceive with their minds' [AB; REB], 'understand in their minds' [NCV], 'their minds would not understand' [TEV]. This noun is used figuratively to denote the causative source of a person's psychological life in its various aspects, but with special emphasis on thoughts [LN]. Here 'to understand with the heart' means 'to think' [BAGD].

g. aorist pass. subj. of στρέφω (LN **31.60**) (BAGD 2.b. p. 771): 'to turn' [BAGD, LN, NICNT2, NTC, WBC; NIV, NRSV, Ph], 'to be converted' [AB, Gdt, BAGD; KJV, NASB], 'to change one's ways' [NJB], 'to turn to me' [NET, NLT, REB, TEV], 'to turn to the Lord' [CEV], 'to come back to me' [NCV], 'to turn to, to come to believe, to come to accept' [LN], 'to change (inwardly)' [BAGD]. The clause 'they...might turn and I will heal them' is translated 'they...turn for me to heal them' [HTC]. This verb

means to change one's belief, with focus on that to which one turns [LN]. It means here to turn to God from one's sinful ways of life [TRT].
- h. fut. mid. (deponent = act.) indic. of ἰάομαι (LN 13.66) (BAGD 2. p. 368): 'to heal' [BAGD, LN; all translations except CEV, NCV, NJB], 'to cure' [BAGD], 'to renew' [LN]. The clause 'I will heal them' is translated 'be healed' [CEV, NCV], 'being healed by me' [NJB]. This verb is used figuratively to cause something to change to an earlier, correct, or appropriate state [LN]. It is used figuratively here of deliverance from ills of many kinds [BAGD]. It refers to saving people from their sin [TRT].

QUESTION—Does the phrase 'for this reason' refer to what precedes or to what follows?

1. It refers forward to the ὅτι 'because' which follows [BAGD, NICNT2; REB]: 'And there is another saying of Isaiah which explains why they could not believe' [REB]. The phrase διὰ τοῦτο indicates the reason for an event, in this case the reason is given in the following clause introduced by ὅτι 'that'—'for this reason, (namely) that' [BAGD]. The reason they were not able to believe was because…. The prophecy brought about their unbelief, it was not that unbelief resulted in the fulfillment of prophecy [NICNT2].
2. It refers to what precedes and what follows [EGT, My]. Διὰ τοῦτο 'therefore' always refers to what precedes in John. It means that on account of such a small positive response to the message of salvation and the strength of the Lord (verse 38), they were unable to believe. The ὅτι 'because', which follows, gives a more detailed reason why they could not believe, namely that, 'He has blinded…' [My].

QUESTION—What is the Scripture reference referred to?

The verse quoted is Isaiah 6:9–10 [AB, Bar, BECNT, Car, Gdt, HTC, ICC, Kn, Lns, My, NICNT1, NICNT2, NTC, Rd, TH, TRT, WBC].

QUESTION—Who is the person indicated by the pronoun 'he' in the verb phrases 'he has blinded…and hardened'?

It refers to God [Car, Gdt, HTC, IVP, Lns, My, NICNT1, NICNT2, Rd, TH, TRT; CEV, NLT, TEV]: The Lord has blinded the eyes of the people, and he has made the people stubborn' [CEV].

QUESTION—What does it mean to 'blind the eyes' of a person?

It means to deprive someone of intellectual light [Gdt], or to blind someone's means of perceiving spiritual truth [EGT]. It means to cause someone to no longer have the capacity for understanding [LN].

QUESTION—What does it mean to 'harden the heart' of a person?

It means to deprive someone of moral sensibility. The result of having one's eyes blinded and one's heart hardened is necessarily unbelief [Gdt]. It means to make them incapable of believing and inwardly understanding [HTC]. It means hardening their sensibility to religious and moral impressions so that they are prevented from seeing the significance of Jesus' miracles and understanding his teaching [EGT]. To harden the heart means 'to cause someone to be unable to understand' [TRT].

QUESTION—To how many following verbs does the purpose conjunction ἵνα μὴ 'so that…(they may) not (see…)' apply?

It applies to all four verbs—*so that* they may *not see* with the eyes and *understand* with the heart, and might *turn* and I will *heal* them' [Gdt, HTC, My, NICNT1].

12:41 Isaiah said these-things because he-saw his glory,[a] and he-spoke about him.

TEXT—Instead of ὅτι 'because', some manuscripts read ὅτε 'when', and another reads ἐπεί 'since'. GNT along with all translations except Gdt; KJV read 'because' with a B rating, indicating that the text is almost certain. Gdt; KJV accept the reading 'when'.

LEXICON—a. δόξα (LN 79.18): 'glory' [LN; all translations], 'splendor' [LN]. This noun denotes the quality of splendid, remarkable appearance [LN].

QUESTION—To what does the pronoun ταῦτα 'these things' refer?

It refers to the two quotations from Isaiah in the previous verses [IVP, Lns, NICNT2].

QUESTION—To whom do the pronouns 'his' and 'him' refer?

They refer to Jesus [AB, BECNT, Car, EGT, Gdt, HTC, ICC, Lns, My, NICNT1, NICNT2, Rd, TH, TRT; CEV, NCV, NET, NJB, NIV, NLT, Ph, TEV]: 'he saw the glory of Jesus and spoke about him' [CEV].

QUESTION—On what occasion did Isaiah see Jesus' glory?

1. Isaiah saw Jesus' glory when he saw the Lord, high and exalted in the temple in Isaiah 6:1–4 [Bar, EGT, Gdt, ICC, IVP, Kn, Lns, My, NICNT1, NICNT2, NTC, Rd, TRT, WBC]. The Adonai whom Isaiah saw in his vision in Isaiah 6 was Jesus. In this John and Paul concur as seen in 1 Corinthians 10:4 where Paul refers to the One who guided Israel in the cloud, as Christ [Gdt]. In addition to the scene of glory in the temple (Isaiah 6:1–10), the reference about God's servant being glorified and lifted up (Isaiah 52:13–53:1) is also included [Car, Kn]. What Isaiah saw was the glory of the exalted Son after his return to the Father (12:28) [Lns].

2. He saw Jesus' glory after his resurrection [TH]. Isaiah probably had a prophetic vision of Jesus' glory that he received resulting from his death and resurrection [TH].

3. He saw the glory of the pre-existent Christ [HTC, Rd]. John 17:5 talks about the glory that Jesus had with the Father before the world began. This was the glory that Isaiah saw [HTC]. This same glory was to be shown to the world in the incarnation of Christ (17:4; 1:14, 18) [Rd].

4. He foresaw the glory of a suffering Messiah. Isaiah foresaw that God would be pleased with a suffering Servant who would be raised and highly exalted (Isaiah 52:13) that his glory would be shown through one who was 'pierced for our transgressions' and 'who bore the sins of many' (53:5, 12) [BECNT].

QUESTION—What is indicated by the word δόξα 'glory'?

Christ's glory indicates his supreme greatness and at the same time his death on the cross as a symbol of that greatness. Part of this greatness was his rejection by mankind [NICNT1].

12:42 Nevertheless[a] even of the rulers[b] many believed in him, but because-of the Pharisees they-were- not -confesssing[c] (him) so-that they-should- not -be put-out-of-the-synagogue.[d] **12:43** For they-loved[e] the praise[f] of-men more than the praise of God.

LEXICON—a. ὅμως μέντοι (LN **89.75**) (BAGD p. 569, 2. p. 503): 'nevertheless' [AB, BAGD, HTC, LN, NICNT2, NTC, WBC; KJV, NASB, NET, NRSV, Ph], 'however' [NLT], 'but' [NCV], 'even then' [CEV, TEV], 'and yet' [**LN**; NJB], 'yet' [BAGD; NIV], 'it is true, nevertheless' [Gdt], 'for all that' [REB], 'all the same, despite that' [BAGD]. This phrase is a marker of an implied clause of concession [LN]. The combination of ὅμως and μέντοι forms a strong adversative [HTC, IVP, NICNT1, Rd]. This phrase could be translated 'There were in fact (many...)' or 'Actually there were (many...)' [TH]. This phrase indicates a contrast between the people of verses 37–41 and those of this verse [TRT].

b. ἄρχων (LN 37.56) (BAGD 2.a. p. 114): 'ruler' [BAGD, Gdt, LN, NICNT2, NTC; NASB, NET], 'chief ruler' [KJV], 'leader' [CEV, NCV, NIV], 'Jewish leader' [NLT], 'leading man' [NJB], 'authority' [HTC, WBC; NRSV, Ph], 'Jewish authority' [BAGD; TEV], 'those in authority' [REB], 'Sanhedrin' [AB], 'governor' [LN], 'lord' [BAGD]. This noun is derived from the verb ἄρχω 'to rule' and denotes one who rules or governs [LN]. It refers to Jewish authorities [BAGD].

c. imperf. act. indic. of ὁμολογέω (LN 33.274) (BAGD 4. p. 568): 'to confess' [HTC, LN, NICNT2, NTC, WBC; KJV, NASB, NIV, NRSV], 'to profess' [LN]. The clause 'they were not confessing him' is translated 'they did not tell anyone about it' [CEV], 'they did not talk about it openly' [TEV], 'they did not say they believed in him' [NCV], 'they would not confess Jesus to be the Christ' [NET], 'they did not confess their faith' [Gdt], 'they would not acknowledge him' [REB], 'they did/would not admit it' [NJB, NLT, Ph], 'they refused to admit it' [AB]. This verb means to express openly one's allegiance to a proposition or person [LN]. 'To confess' means to publicly acknowledge their faith [NICNT2]. The imperfect tense points to the continuing failure to confess [BECNT, EGT, NTC].

d. ἀποσυνάγωγος (LN 11.46) (BAGD p. 100): 'put out of the synagogue' [AB, Gdt, HTC, NICNT2, NTC; KJV, NASB, NCV, NET, NIV, NRSV], 'banned from the synagogue' [NJB, REB], 'expelled from a/the synagogue' [BAGD, LN; TEV], 'thrust out of the synagogue' [WBC], 'excommunicated' [BAGD; Ph]. The words 'because of the Pharisees...so that they should not be put out the synagogue' are translated 'The

Pharisees had already given orders for the people not to have anything to do with anyone who had faith in Jesus' [CEV], 'for fear that the Pharisees would expel them from the synagogue' [NLT]. This adjective denotes a state of having been excommunicated from membership in a synagogue. It is important to indicate clearly that this is not a matter of an individual merely being forced outside of a synagogue building, but also being excluded from membership and thus from worship in the synagogue. In some languages this is made explicit by saying 'his name will be erased from the list of those belonging to the synagogue' or 'he will no longer be able to enter a synagogue' or 'he will be rejected as a member of the synagogue' [LN].

e. aorist act. indic. of ἀγαπάω (LN **25.104**) (BAGD 2. p. 5): 'to love' [BAGD, Gdt, HTC, **LN**, NICNT2, NTC, WBC; KJV, NASB, NCV, NET, NIV, NLT, NRSV, TEV], 'to prefer' [AB, Bar, Lns, My], 'to value' [BAGD; REB], 'to like' [LN; CEV], 'to take pleasure in' [Bar, LN]. The words 'they loved the praise of men more than the praise of God' is translated 'they put human glory above God's glory' [NJB], 'they were more concerned to have the approval of men than to have the approval of God' [Ph]. This verb means to like or love something on the basis of a high regard for its value or importance [LN]. It has to do with the love for things, denoting high esteem for or satisfaction with something [BAGD]. The sense of 'love' here is 'to choose' or 'to prefer' [NICNT2].

f. δόξα (LN 33.357) (BAGD 3. p. 204): 'praise' [AB, BAGD, HTC, LN; CEV, KJV, NCV, NET, NIV, NLT], 'glory' [Gdt, NICNT2, NTC; NJB, NRSV], 'approval' [BAGD; NASB, Ph, TEV], 'reputation' [REB], 'honor' [BAGD, WBC], 'fame, renown' [BAGD]. This noun denotes something that is unusually fine and deserving of honor [LN]. It has the sense of 'opinion' or 'approbation' [Gdt].

QUESTION—What contribution does verse 42 add to the narrative?

It serves to counter the idea that the blinding and hardening by God locks men into an inescapable destiny. Men still need to decide for themselves [HTC, WBC].

QUESTION—Who were the rulers?

They were members of the Jewish high council, the Sanhedrin [AB, HTC, ICC, Lns, My, Rd, TH].

QUESTION—To whom does the pronoun 'him' refer in the phrase 'believed in him'?

There is a possibility that Isaiah could be taken as the one referred to. Therefore it is advisable to make Jesus explicit, 'believed in Jesus' [TH, TRT; CEV, NCV, TEV].

QUESTION—The Greek structure allows for two interpretations: either, many rulers believed, or many people believed including some rulers?

1. Many rulers believed in Jesus [Gdt, HTC, NICNT1, NTC, TRT, WBC; CEV, KJV, NASB, NCV, NET, NJB, NIV, NRSV,Ph, REB, TEV].

2. Only some of the rulers believed in Jesus [NICNT2; NLT]: 'many, even some of the rulers, did believe in him' [NICNT2]. The text means that included in the many who believed, some rulers also believed. The genitive phrase ἐκ τῶν ἀρχόντων 'of the rulers' is partitive [NICNT2].

QUESTION—How are the nouns related in the genitive constructions τὴν δόξαν τῶν ἀνθρώπων 'the praise of men' and τὴν δόξαν τοῦ θεοῦ 'the praise of God'?

In each case the men and God are the ones who praise, or give praise to the believers [ICC, Lns, My, TRT].

QUESTION—What is indicated by the conjunction γάρ 'for'?

It indicates that this verse is the explanation of how this refusal to publicly confess their faith in Jesus operated in their hearts [Lns].

DISCOURSE UNIT—12:44–50 [AB, Gdt, HTC, Kn, NICNT1, Rd; CEV, NET, TEV]. The topic is a summary of Jesus' teaching [AB, IVP; NRSV], Jesus' revelatory discourse [HTC, Rd], consequences of faith and unbelief [Gdt], Jesus is God's standard of judgment [Kn; TEV], final challenge to believe [NICNT1], Jesus' purpose to save the world [CEV], Jesus' final public words [NET].

12:44 But[a] Jesus cried-out[b] and said, "The-one believing in me does- not - believe in me but in the-one-who sent me, **12:45** And the-one seeing me sees the-one-who sent me.

LEXICON—a. δέ (LN 89.124, 89.94): 'but' [LN (89.124), NICNT2, TH, WBC; NET, Ph], 'on the other hand' [LN (89.124), My], 'and' [LN (89.94), HTC, NTC; NASB], 'then' [NCV, NIV, NRSV], 'now' [Gdt], not explicit [CEV, KJV, NJB, NLT, REB, TEV]. This conjunction indicates contrast [LN (89.124)], or an additive relation, but with the possible implication of some contrast [LN (89.94)]. It should be taken here as marking contrast with the preceding verses [NICNT1].

b. aorist act. indic. of κράζω (LN 33.83) (BAGD 2.a. p. 447): 'to cry out' [HTC, NICNT2, NTC, WBC; NASB, NCV, NIV], 'to cry aloud' [NRSV, Ph], 'to cry' [BAGD, Gdt; KJV], 'to shout' [LN], 'to shout to the crowd' [NLT], 'to shout out' [NET], 'to scream' [LN], 'to say in a loud voice' [CEV, TEV], 'to declare publicly' [NJB], 'to proclaim' [REB], 'to proclaim aloud' [AB], 'to call, to call out' [BAGD]. This verb means to shout or cry out, with the possible implication of the unpleasant nature of the sound [LN]. The phrase 'cried and said' is a formula that indicates speaking in public [HTC, ICC, Lns; NJB]. That Jesus spoke loudly probably indicates the importance of what he was saying [NICNT1]. This action implies a solemn announcement or formal declaration of some kind [ICC, NICNT2, WBC].

QUESTION—How is faith in Jesus the same as faith in his sender?

As the Father's agent, Jesus does what the Father wants him to do, in fact what he does is what the Father does (see 3:31–36; 5:19ff.; 6:37–40; 7:27–

29; 8:14–17, 28–29, 42–43; 10:34–36). So to believe in Jesus is to believe in his sender, the Father [Car].

QUESTION—What is implied by the 'The one believing in me does not believe in me'?

The word 'alone' or 'only' is implied [ICC, IVP, Lns, NICNT1, NTC, TH, TRT, WBC; CEV, NIV, NLT, TEV]: 'When a man believes in me, he does not believe in me *only*, but in the one who sent me' [NIV]. This could be translated as 'he believes both in me and in him who sent me' or 'he believes in him who sent me as well as believing in me' [TH]. Verses 44 and 45 imply that believing in Jesus is equivalent to believing in his sender and seeing him is seeing his sender [AB]. The one believing in Jesus and seeing Jesus is actually believing in and seeing the one who sent him on the principle of the Jewish theory of representation that the ambassador merely represents the one who sends him [BECNT, HTC, NICNT2].

QUESTION—What is the relationship between believing in Jesus and seeing Jesus?

They are synonomous, to do one is to do the other [HTC, NICNT2, WBC] showing the influence of Jewish parallelism. So here, θεωρέω 'to see' refers to the sight of faith [HTC, WBC]. 'Seeing' means 'seeing with faith' [WBC].

QUESTION—How does 'seeing' Jesus equate with 'seeing' his sender?

When a person looks intently at Jesus and notes how the glory of his sender is reflected in his words and works, then that person is actually looking at his sender [NTC]. When a person sees with faith they are able to see the Father in Jesus [WBC]. Jesus is the image of God (Hebrews 1:3) so to see him is to see the Father (8:19; 14:9; 5:19, 30) [Kn, Lns]. The Son is so closely identified with the Father (1:1, 18) that to see him is to see the Father [Car]. Looking at Jesus is like looking through a clear lens to see God [EGT]. 'Seeing' Jesus here refers to a spiritual seeing. Not everyone who saw Jesus, saw the Father [ICC].

12:46 I have-come (a) light[a] into the world, so-that[b] every one believing in me may- not -remain[c] in the darkness.[d]

LEXICON—a. φῶς (LN 14.36) (BAGD 2. p. 872): 'light' [BAGD, LN; all translations]. The clause 'I have/am come a light into the world' [KJV] is also translated 'I am the light that has come into the world' [CEV], 'I have come as Light/light into the world' [NASB, similarly AB, HTC, NICNT2, WBC; NJB, NRSV, TEV], 'I have come as (a) light into the world' [Gdt, NTC; NCV, NET, similarly NIV, Ph, REB], 'I have come as a light to shine in this dark world' [NLT]. This noun denotes light, in contrast with darkness usually in relationship to some source of light such as the sun, moon, fire, lamp [LN]. It is the element and sphere of the Divine [BAGD]. Light is a figure of truth [Lns].

b. ἵνα (LN 89.59) (BAGD I.1.b. p. 377): 'so that' [AB, LN, NICNT2; NASB, NCV, NET, NIV, NLT, NRSV, Ph, REB, TEV], 'that' [BAGD,

Gdt, HTC; KJV], 'in order that' [BAGD, NTC, WBC], 'in order to, for the purpose of' [LN], not explicit [CEV]. The clause 'so that every one believing in me may not remain in the darkness' is translated 'to prevent anyone who believes in me from staying in the dark any more' [NJB]. This conjunction indicates purpose for events and states (sometimes occurring in highly elliptical contexts) [LN]. It is used to denote purpose, aim, or goal [BAGD].

c. aorist act. subj. of μένω (LN 68.11) (BAGD 1.a.β. p. 504): 'remain' [BAGD, LN; all translations except Gdt; CEV, KJV, NCV, NIV, NJB], 'to stay' [BAGD; CEV, NCV, NIV, NJB], 'to abide' [BAGD, Gdt; KJV], 'to continue' [BAGD, LN], 'to keep on' [LN]. This verb means to continue in an activity or state [LN]. It is used figuratively of someone who does not leave the realm or sphere in which he finds himself [BAGD].

d. σκότος (LN 88.125) (BAGD 2. p. 757): 'darkness' [BAGD, LN; all translations except CEV, NJB, NLT, Ph], 'dark' [CEV, NJB, NLT, Ph], 'evil world, realm of evil' [LN], 'gloom' [BAGD]. This noun is used to symbolize the realm of sin and evil [LN]. It is used figuratively to indicate the darkening of the mind or spirit of ignorance in moral and religious matters. In John it includes all that is at enmity with God, earthly and demonic [BAGD]. The definite article with darkness, 'the darkness', indicates the evil power of falsehood, deception, ignorance, and error [Lns].

QUESTION—What word is emphasized in this verse?

The pronoun ἐγώ 'I' is emphatic [BECNT, HTC, My, NICNT2, Rd]: *I myself* have come a light into the world. The noun 'light' is also emphatic by its fronted position in the Greek sentence [NICNT1]. *Jesus himself* is the one who rescues men from darkness [HTC].

QUESTION—If this is a simile, 'I have come as a light', in what sense is Jesus like light?

This may be translated 'I have come as one who causes light to shine on people' or '…as one who causes light for people' or '…as one who causes people to be in light' [TH], or 'I have come as a light to shine on people/enlighten people/to enable people to know God's truth' [TRT]. Jesus possesses and communicates divine truth and salvation [My].

QUESTION—What does it mean to 'remain in darkness'?

It means to remain as subject to the wrath of God, to be under the sentence of eternal death, as darkness is synonymous with the sphere of death [HTC]. It means to remain in a state of alienation from God [IVP]. To be in darkness is to be in a state of unbelief [My].

12:47 And if anyone hears[a] my words[b] and does- not -keep[c] (them), I do- not -judge[d] him, for I-did- not -come so-that I-may-judge the world,[e] but so-that I-may-save the world.

LEXICON—a. aorist act. subj. of ἀκούω (LN 24.52) (BAGD 1.b.γ. p. 32): 'to hear' [BAGD, LN; all translations except AB; CEV], 'to listen to' [AB], not explicit [CEV]. 'Hearing' here with the genitive case implies to hear with appreciation and understanding of what one means [AB, ICC, NICNT1]. If it were the accusative case it would mean only physical hearing [ICC]. It means to accept inwardly [Gdt, HTC], possess [Gdt], or believe the words [WBC].

  b. ῥῆμα (LN 33.98) (BAGD 1. p. 735): 'word' [AB, BAGD, LN, NICNT2, WBC; KJV, NCV, NET, NIV, NJB, NRSV, REB], 'saying' [BAGD, Gdt, HTC, LN, NTC; NASB, Ph], 'teaching' [CEV], 'message' [LN; TEV], 'statement' [LN], 'that which is said, expression' [BAGD]. The clause 'And if anyone hears my words and does not keep them, I do not judge him' is translated 'I will not judge those who hear me but don't obey me' [CEV]. This noun denotes that which has been stated or said, with primary focus on the content of the communication [LN]. It denotes the words of (Christian) teaching or of divine understanding [BAGD].

  c. aorist act. subj. of φυλάσσω (LN 36.19): 'to keep' [AB, Gdt, HTC, NICNT2, NTC, WBC;NASB, NIV, NRSV, Ph], 'to keep faithfully' [NJB], 'to obey' [LN; CEV, NCV, NET, NLT, TEV], 'to believe' [KJV], 'to keep commandments' [LN]. The phrase 'does not keep them' is translated 'disregards them' [REB]. 'Keep' is used in the sense of 'do' or 'obey' Jesus' words [AB, Bar, IVP, Kn, Rd, TH, TRT, WBC], or believe them [HTC, Lns, My].

  d. pres. act. indic. of κρίνω (LN 56.30) (BAGD 4.b.α. p. 452): 'to judge' [BAGD; all translations except AB; REB], 'to condemn' [AB, BAGD. LN], 'to judge as guilty' [LN], 'to punish' [BAGD]. This verb is also translated as a noun: '(I am not his) judge' [REB]. This verb means to judge a person to be guilty and liable to punishment [LN]. Here it is a technical term meaning 'to judge, decide, hale before a court, condemn, and hand over for judicial punishment. Often the emphasis is unmistakably laid on that which follows the Divine Judge's verdict, on the condemnation or punishment [BAGD]. It is used here in a condemnatory sense [My, TH].

  e. κόσμος (LN 9.23) (BAGD 5.b. p. 446): 'world' [BAGD; all translations except CEV], 'people of the/this world' [LN; CEV]. This noun denotes 'cosmos, universe', but is used figuratively here to denote people associated with a world system and estranged from God [LN]. It denotes 'the world' as all of mankind, but especially of believers, as the object of God's love [BAGD].

QUESTION—What word is emphasized in this verse?

  The pronoun ἐγώ 'I' is emphatic [HTC, Rd, NICNT2, TRT]: '*I, for my part*, do not judge him' [Lns]. The emphasis on Jesus' himself not doing the judging serves to include by implication the fact that people are, nevertheless, going to be judged [Lns, NICNT2].

12:48 **The-one rejecting^a me and not receiving^b my words has one judging him, the word that I-spoke will-judge him on the last day.^c**

LEXICON—a. pres. act. participle of ἀθετέω (LN 31.100) (BAGD 1.b. p. 21): 'to reject' [BAGD, LN; all translations except WBC], 'to set aside' [LN; WBC], 'to not rely on' [LN], 'to not recognize' [BAGD]. This verb means to believe that something or someone cannot be trusted or relied on and hence to reject [LN].

b. pres. act. participle of λαμβάνω (LN **31.50**) (BAGD 1.e.β. p. 464): 'to receive' [BAGD, Gdt, HTC, LN, NICNT2, NTC, WBC; KJV, NASB, NRSV], 'to accept' [AB, LN; NCV, NET, NIV, Ph, REB, TEV], 'to come to believe' [LN], 'to take up' [BAGD], not explicit [CEV]. The phrase 'not receiving my words' is translated 'refuses my words' [NJB], '(all who) reject my message' [NLT]. This verb means to come to believe something and to act in accordance with such a belief [LN].

c. ἡμέρα (BAGD 3.b.β. p. 347): 'day' [BAGD]. The phrase 'the last day' [all translations except NLT] is also translated 'the day of judgment' [NLT]. This 'day' refers to a day appointed for a very special purpose, especially of the day of final judgment [BAGD, ICC], fixed by God. Here it refers to 'the last day' (of this age) [BAGD].

QUESTION—What is the sense of the word 'judge' that is indicated here?

The word 'to judge' is used in the sense of 'to condemn' [AB, IVP, TH], or 'to pass sentence on' [TH].

QUESTION—How can Jesus' word judge a person?

God will use the word that Jesus spoke to judge that person: 'On the last day he will be judged by God on the basis of what I said' [TRT]. What Jesus said is the same as what God said (3:34; 5:47; 17:8) because all that he said was spoken in obedience to the Father. Therefore Jesus' word would be the criterion for judgment on the last day [Kn].

12:49 **Because I did- not -speak of myself,^a but the-one-who sent me (the) Father he has-given (a) command to-me what I-should-say^b and what I-should-speak.^c**

LEXICON—a. ἐμαυτοῦ (LN 92.3) (BAGD 3. p. 254): 'myself' [BAGD, LN], 'me' [LN]. The phrase ἐξ ἐμαυτοῦ 'of/from myself' [Gdt; KJV, NCV] is also translated 'on/from my own authority' [BAGD, HTC, NTC, WBC; NET, NLT, Ph, REB, TEV], 'on my own' [AB, NICNT2; CEV, NRSV], 'of my own accord' [NIV, NJB], 'on my own initiative' [NASB]. This reflexive pronoun denotes the first person singular within the immediate context [LN].

b. aorist act. subj. of λέγω (LN 33.69): 'to say' [LN], 'to talk, to tell, to speak' [LN]. The clauses 'what I should say, and what I should speak/utter' [NICNT2, NTC; KJV, NET], is also translated 'what to say and what to speak' [HTC, WBC; NASB, NJB, NRSV, Ph], 'what to say

and what to teach' [NCV], 'I only say what (the Father who sent me has told me) to say' [CEV], 'what I must say and speak' [TEV], 'what to say and how to say it' [NIV, NLT], 'what to say and how to speak' [AB; REB], 'what I should say and how I should say it' [Gdt]. This verb means to speak or talk, with apparent focus upon the content of what is said [LN].
- c. aorist act. subj. of λαλέω (LN 33.70) (BAGD 2.b. p. 463): 'to speak' [BAGD, LN], 'to say' [BAGD, LN], 'to talk, to tell' [LN], 'to assert, to proclaim' [BAGD]. This verb means to speak or talk, with the possible implication of more informal usage (though this cannot be clearly and consistently shown from NT contexts) [LN]. See previous item for version evidence.

QUESTION—What relationship is indicated by ὅτι 'because'?

This conjunction indicates that this verse is the reason why Jesus' word will be the judge on the last day—it is not only Jesus' word but also the word of the Father [Bar, BECNT, Car, EGT, HTC, IVP, ICC, My, NICNT1; TEV]: 'The words that I have spoken will be their judge on the last day! This is true because I have not spoken on my own authority, but the Father who sent me has commanded me what I must say and speak' [TEV].

QUESTION—What word is emphasized in this verse?

The pronoun αὐτός 'he' is emphasized indicating that it is the Father and no other who commands [AB, Gdt, HTC, Lns, NICNT1, NTC; NASB, NET, NRSV, REB]: *he himself* has given a command.

QUESTION—Do the two clauses 'what I may say' and 'what I may speak' mean the same thing or are they distinct in meaning?
1. The two clauses mean the same thing [Bar, ICC, NICNT1, NICNT2, NTC, TH; CEV, probably all other versions except NIV, NLT, REB]: 'I say only what the Father...has told me to say' [CEV]. The two expressions merely emphasize the same event, that is, '(Has commanded me) just what I must say' [TH]. The two verbs together emphasize the whole of Jesus' message [NICNT1, NTC]. It may be that the first verb deals with the substance of what is said and the second with the form, but it is simpler to treat them as being identical [ICC].
2. The two verbs have distinct meanings [AB, Car, EGT, Gdt, Lns, My; NIV, NLT, REB]: 'what to say and how to say it' [NIV, NLT]. The first verb designates the contents of what is to be said, the second designates the manner in which it is to be said [EGT]. Both the content of what is to be said and the very sounds of how it is to be said are given by God [Lns].

12:50 **And I-know that his command is eternal-life.[a] Therefore the-things I say, I-say as the Father has-told me.**

LEXICON—a. ζωὴ αἰώνιος (LN 67.96): 'eternal life' [LN]. The phrase ζωὴν αἰώνιον 'eternal life' [all translations except NTC] is also translated 'everlasting life' [KJV, NTC]. This adjective describes a thing as pertaining to an unlimited duration of time. The most frequent use of αἰώνιος in the NT is with ζωή 'life', for example, 'so that everyone who believes in him may have eternal life' John 3:15. In combination with ζωή there is evidently not only a temporal element, but also a qualitative distinction. In such contexts, αἰώνιος evidently carries certain implications associated with αἰώνιος in relationship to divine and supernatural attributes. If one translates 'eternal life' as simply 'never dying', there may be serious misunderstandings, since persons may assume that 'never dying' refers only to physical existence rather than to 'spiritual death'. Accordingly, some translators have rendered 'eternal life' as 'unending real life', so as to introduce a qualitative distinction [LN]. Eternal life is a present possession and it is a quality of life, God's life [CH]. The phrase 'eternal life' is a significant one in John and occurs 17 times at 3:15, 16, 36; 4:14, 36; 5:24, 39; 6:27, 40, 47, 54, 68; 10:28; 12:25, 50; 17:2, 3.

QUESTION—What is meant by 'his command is eternal life'?

It means that God's command brings eternal life to those who believe [Gdt, HTC, NICNT2, NTC, TH]. It means that obedience to the Father's command results in life [Kn]. The command indicates a relationship with God, one that shares his life [IVP]. The command of the Father was for Jesus to announce eternal life [EGT]. In Mark 10:18 when the rich young man asked what he must do to inherit eternal life, Jesus referred him to the commandments. This means that God's commandment, when fully realized is eternal life [ICC]. This clause is translated 'his commandment/his command(s)/what he commands mean(s) eternal life' [AB, WBC; NJB, Ph], 'his command(s) will bring/brings eternal life' [CEV, TEV], 'eternal life comes from what the Father commands' NCV], 'his command(s) lead(s) to eternal life' [NIV, NLT]. Since 'his command' means 'what he has commanded' and 'eternal life' means 'people live forever', this could be translated 'what he has commanded causes people to live forever' [TH, TRT].

QUESTION—What word is emphasized in this verse?

The pronoun ἐγώ 'I' is emphasized [Lns]: The things, *I myself* say. This emphasis corresponds to Jesus' counterpart in this verse, the Father [Lns].

QUESTION—What relationship is indicated by οὖν 'therefore (the things I say…)'?

It indicates that the clause 'his command is eternal life' is the reason why Jesus speaks to people just as the Father has spoken to him without making any changes to it [Gdt]. It indicates that since the command of the Father results in such a great benefit, Jesus sees no way that he could speak anything else than what the Father had said to him [My].

DISCOURSE UNIT—13:1–20:31 [BECNT, Car, WBC]. The topic is the passion and resurrection [WBC], book of glory [BECNT], Jesus' self-disclosure [Car].

DISCOURSE UNIT—13:1–17:26 [AB, BECNT, IVP, Kn, NICNT1, NICNT2, WBC]. The topic is Jesus' self-revelation [NICNT2], the last supper [AB], ministry in the upper room [BECNT, IVP, WBC], farewell discourse [Kn, NICNT1].

DISCOURSE UNIT—13:1–38 [Kn; REB]. The topic is a model for love and service [Kn], farewell discourses [REB].

DISCOURSE UNIT—13:1–30 [Bar, BECNT, Car, CH, NICNT1]. The topic is the footwashing and Judas's departure [Bar, BECNT, NICNT1], Jesus, master and servant [CH], the last supper [Car].

DISCOURSE UNIT—13:1–20 [AB, IVP, NICNT2, WBC; CEV, NCV, NJB, NRSV, TEV]. The topic is the footwashing [AB, IVP, WBC; CEV, NCV, NJB, NRSV, TEV], Jesus at supper [NICNT2].

DISCOURSE UNIT—13:1–17 [BECNT, Car; NET, NIV, NLT, Ph]. The topic is the footwashing [BECNT, Car; NET, NIV, NLT], Jesus teaches about humility [Ph].

DISCOURSE UNIT—13:1–11 [NICNT1]. The topic is the footwashing.

DISCOURSE UNIT—13:1–5 [HTC]. The topic is the footwashing.

13:1 Now before the Festival of-the Passover, Jesus having-known that his hour had-come that he-should-depart[a] from this world to the Father, having-loved his own in the world he-loved[b] them to (the) end.[c]

LEXICON—a. aorist act. subj. of μεταβαίνω (LN 15.2) (BAGD 1.a.α. p. 510): 'depart' [HTC, LN, NTC; KJV, NASB, NET, NRSV], 'to leave' [Gdt; CEV, NCV, NIV, NLT, Ph, REB, TEV], 'to pass' [AB, WBC; NJB], 'to be taken out' [NICNT2], 'to pass over, to go (from one place to another)' [BAGD], 'to move from one place to another, to change one's location' [LN]. This verb means to effect a change of location in space, with the implication that the two locations are significantly different [LN].

b. aorist act. participle of ἀγαπάω (LN 25.43) (BAGD 1.c. p. 4): 'to love' [BAGD, LN; all translations except AB, Gdt, WBC; NIV], 'to regard with affection' [LN], 'to cherish' [BAGD]. The clause 'he loved them' [NICNT2, NTC, CEV, KJV, NASB NCV, NET, NJB, NLT, NRSV, Ph, REB, TEV] is also translated 'he showed his love for them' [AB, WBC], 'he now showed them the full extent of his love' [NIV], 'he perfectly testified to them all his love' [Gdt]. This verb means to have love for someone or something, based on sincere appreciation and high regard [LN]. It means to have affection for people [BAGD]. The aorist tense indicates a definite act—he showed them his love [AB, Gdt, ICC]. He did this by washing their feet [ICC].

c. εἰς τέλος (LN **78.47**) (BAGD 3. p. 229; 1.d.γ. p. 812): 'into end' [LN], 'completely' [BAGD (3. p. 229), LN], 'to the uttermost' [BAGD (3. p. 229)], 'totally, entirely, wholly' [LN], 'fully, absolutely' [BAGD (3. p.

229]. This phrase is translated 'to the end' [BAGD, HTC, **LN**, NICNT2; KJV, NASB, NJB, NRSV, Ph, REB], 'to the very end' [AB; CEV, NET, NLT, TEV], 'all the way to the end' [NCV], '(now he showed them) the full extent (of his love)' [NIV], '(now showed his love for them) to the limit' [WBC], '(he perfectly testified to them) all his love' [Gdt], 'to the uttermost' [NTC]. This phrase indicates a degree of completeness, with the possible implication of purpose or result. It can also have a temporal sense meaning 'to the end' [BAGD (3. p. 220), **LN**].

QUESTION—What is indicated by the phrase 'before the festival'?

It indicates that it was the day before the Passover Festival [AB, Bar, EGT, Gdt, ICC, My, Rd, TH; TEV]: 'It was now the day before the Passover Festival' [TEV]. This verse gives us the setting for Jesus' last supper with his disciples [TH].

QUESTION—To whom does the phrase 'his own' refer?

It refers to his followers [Gdt, HTC, NICNT1, TH, TRT, WBC]. Make sure in the translation that it does not refer to his family or to the Jews [TRT]. Also make sure that these are not slaves whom he owned [TH, TRT]. Before this time Jesus ministered to people in general. From now on he focuses on those he loves intimately [NICNT1].

QUESTION—Should the phrase 'before the Festival of the Passover' be construed with the verb 'having known' or with 'he loved'?

1. It should be construed with 'having known' [Lns, NTC, TH; KJV, NET, NLT, NRSV, REB, Ph]: 'Before the festival of the Passover began, Jesus realised' [Ph]. It is most natural to construe the phrase with the nearest verbal form which here is 'having known' [NTC].
2. It should be construed with 'he loved' [Gdt]. The time reference should be construed with the principle verb 'he loved', not with the participles 'having known' or 'having loved'. It was on the evening before the festival when he was about to leave his disciples that he showed all his love for them [Gdt].
3. It should be construed with both verbs. The phrase probably modifies both Jesus knowing and his loving and we should not try be too precise as to which one is specified here [AB].

QUESTION—What is meant by the phrase εἰς τέλος 'to the end'?

1. 'To the end' means 'utterly, completely, to the limit' [EGT, Gdt, HTC, ICC, NTC, WBC; NIV]: 'he...showed his love for them to the limit' [WBC]. To say that Jesus loved them to the end would be useless. Rather Jesus showed his love in an exhaustive way, completely pouring it out [Gdt]. Jesus loved them to the uttermost, that is, in the footwashing, his farewell address, his high priestly prayer, and his crucifixion [NTC]. It is pointless to translate that he loved them to the end. The meaning is that 'He exhibited his love for them to the uttermost' or in a very remarkable manner [ICC]. While this sense is primary the temporal sense should not be abandoned. He loved them to the end, that is the hour of his death [HTC].

2. 'To the end' means means 'to the end of his life' [AB, Bar, Lns, My, NICNT2, TH; CEV, KJV, NASB, NCV, NET, NJB, NLT, NRSV, Ph, REB, TEV]. It means 'to the end of life', meaning 'to the death'. Jesus said in John 15:13 that death for someone else was the supreme expression of love [AB]. Both meanings are possible but in view of the fact that Jesus will soon be taken out of the world suggests that separation is near. This in connection with the statement 'his hour had come' suggests that the temporal meaning is primary [NICNT2]. The senses 'at the end, finally, at last' are in focus meaning that he showed them the last proof of his love before his death [My].
3. Both senses are in focus [Bar, BECNT, CH, IVP, Kn, NICNT1, Rd]. This refers to love in it greatest intensity as well as love to the last breath [Kn, Rd]. The meaning is that Jesus continued to love his disciples to the end and he showed them the full extent of his love [CH]. Since love means the giving up of one's life, to love to the full extent is to love to the end of one's life. This extent of this love is seen in the crucifixion [IVP].

13:2 And supper[a] taking-place, the devil[b] already having-put[c] into the heart (of) Judas (son) of-Simon Iscariot[d] that he-should-betray[e] him, **13:3** (and Jesus) having-known that the Father gave him all-things into (his) hands[f] and that he-came from God and is-going to God,

TEXT—Instead of the present tense γινομένου 'taking place' some manuscripts read the aorist tense γενομένου 'having taken place'. GNT reads the present tense 'taking place' with a B rating, indicating that the text is almost certain. Gdt; KJV read 'having taken place'.

TEXT—Instead of Ἰούδας Σίμωνος Ἰσκαριώτου 'Judas of Simon Iscariot', some manuscripts read Ἰούδας Σίμωνος Ἰσκαριώτης 'Judas of Simon of Iscariot', others read Ἰούδα Σίμωνος ἀπὸ Καρυώτου 'of Judas of Simon from Kerioth', still others read Σίμωνος Ἰσκαριώτου 'of Simon Iscariot'. GNT reads 'Judas of Simon Iscariot' with a C rating, indicating difficulty in deciding which variant to place in the text.

LEXICON—a. δεῖπνον (LN **23.25**) (BAGD 2. p. 173): 'supper' [**LN**], 'evening dinner' [BAGD], 'main meal' [BAGD, LN], 'evening meal' [Bar, BAGD]. The words 'supper taking place' is translated 'supper being ended' [KJV], 'supper having taken place' [Gdt], 'during supper' [AB, HTC; NASB, NRSV, REB], 'during the (evening) meal' [WBC; NCV], 'at supper' [NTC], 'while supper was going on' [NICNT2], 'they were at supper' [NJB, similarly TEV], 'the evening meal was in progress/was being served' [NET, NIV], 'before the evening meal started' [CEV], 'it was time for supper' [NLT], 'by supper-time' [Ph]. This noun denotes the principal meal of the day, usually in the evening [LN]. It denotes a formal dinner or banquet [BAGD].

b. διάβολος (LN 12.34) (BAGD 2. p. 182): 'devil' [BAGD; all translations except WBC; TEV], 'Devil' [LN, WBC; TEV], 'Satan' [LN], 'slanderer' [BAGD]. This noun literally means 'slanderer' and is a title for the Devil the principal supernatural evil being. In a number of languages there is a well-known proper name for the Devil as the chief of all demons. In other instances, however, he is given a descriptive name, for example, 'the ruler of the evil spirits', 'the chief of the demons', 'the truly bad one', 'the left-handed one' (as the one who is opposed to all which is right or correct), 'the no-good one', 'the avaricious one'. In some instances a term for the Devil may be highly idiomatic as, for example, 'the barking one', a reference to the Devil's presumed activity in animal guise [LN].

c. perf. act. participle of βάλλω (LN **30.29**) (BAGD 2.b. p. 131): 'to put' [BAGD], 'to place, to lay' [BAGD]. The phrase βάλλω εἰς τὴν καρδίαν is an idiom, meaning literally 'to throw into the heart' and means to cause someone to think in a particular manner, often as a means of inducing some behavior 'to make think, to fill the heart, to cause to decide'. This idiom is translated 'put (it) into the heart (of Judas)' [Gdt, HTC, **LN**, NTC, WBC; KJV, NASB, NET, NRSV], 'put into the heart (of Judas the thought)' [TEV], 'put it into the heart (so that Judas...might hand him over)' [NICNT2], 'put the thought (of betraying Jesus) into the mind (of Judas)' [Ph], 'put it into the mind (of Judas)' [NJB, REB], '(the devil) had made (Judas) decide' [CEV], '(the devil) had already persuaded (Judas)' [NCV], '(the devil) had already prompted (Judas) [NIV, NLT], '(the devil) had already induced (Judas)' [AB].

d. Ἰσκαριώθ (LN 93.181, 93.496) (BAGD p. 381): 'Iscariot' [BAGD, LN (93.181); all translations]. This noun is an identifying name (probably based on a place name; see 93.496) of Judas, the betrayer of Jesus [LN (93.181)]. Καρυῶτος a place in southern Judea 'Carioth' or 'Kerioth' [LN (93.496)]. It is usually taken to refer to the place of his origin, 'from Kerioth' in southern Judea [BAGD].

e. aorist act. subj. of παραδίδωμι (LN 37.111) (BAGD 1.b. p. 614): 'to betray' [BAGD, LN; all translations except NCV, NICNT2], 'to hand over' [BAGD, LN, NICNT2], 'to turn against' [NCV], 'to turn over (to)' [BAGD, LN], 'to give up' [BAGD]. This verb means to deliver a person into the control of someone else, involving either the handing over of a presumably guilty person for punishment by authorities or the handing over of an individual to an enemy who will presumably take undue advantage of the victim [LN]. It is used especially of the betrayal of Jesus by Judas [BAGD].

f. χείρ (BAGD 2.a.δ. p. 880): 'hand' [BAGD]. The idiom πάντα ἔδωκεν εἰς τὰς χεῖρας 'he gave all things into the hands' is translated 'the Father had given all things into his hands' [Gdt, HTC, NICNT2, NTC, WBC; KJV, NASB, NRSV], 'the Father had put everything into his hands' [NJB, Ph], 'the Father had entrusted everything to him' [REB], 'the Father had handed all things (over) to him' [AB; NET], 'the Father had put all things under his power' [NIV], 'the Father had given him complete power' [CEV, TEV], 'the Father had given him power/authority over everything' [NCV, NLT]. The hand of God means his power [BAGD].

JOHN 13:2–3   169

QUESTION—Which reading is correct, 'Judas, son of Simon Iscariot' or 'Judas Iscariot, son of Simon'?
    1. The reading 'Judas, son of Simon Iscariot' is preferred [AB, GNT, TRT, WBC; CEV, NLT, NRSV, REB, TEV].
    2. The reading 'Judas Iscariot, son of Simon' is preferred [Gdt, HTC, NICNT2, NTC; KJV, NASB, NCV, NET, NIV, NJB, Ph].

QUESTION—Into whose heart did the devil put this idea?
    1. He put it into the heart of Judas [AB, Gdt, HTC, ICC, IVP, Lns, NTC, Rd, WBC; all translations]: 'The Devil had already put into the heart of Judas…the thought of betraying Jesus' [TEV]. Although the reading of nominative case for the name of Judas is the preferable one, still the obvious meaning is that the devil put the thought of betrayal into Judas's heart [Lns].
    2. He put it into his own heart [Bar, CH, My, NICNT1]. The common interpretation that the devil put the idea into Judas's heart can only be accepted if the genitive case of the name of Judas is read (here Judas is in the nominative case) [Bar]. The best text in which the name of Judas is in the nominative case indicates that the devil had made up his own mind that Judas should betray Jesus. The alternative reading that makes the name of Judas genitive (of Judas) tells us that the devil put the thought into Judas's mind, but this seems to contradict verse 27 where only at that point did Satan enter Judas [NICNT1].

QUESTION—Who is the subject of the participle 'having known'?
Jesus is the one who knew these things [HTC, ICC, TH, TRT; all translations except NICNT2].

QUESTION—What relationship is indicated by the perfect participle εἰδώς 'having known'?
    1. The participial clause is causative 'because he knew' [BECNT, EGT, Gdt, ICC; probably CEV, NCV, NET, NIV, NLT, TEV]: '*Because* Jesus knew that the Father had handed all things over to him…he got up from the meal' [NET]. It is because he knew of his greatness that he humbled himself [Gdt]. Jesus, fully conscious of the majestic dignity of his person, even because of it, takes up the humble chore of washing the disciples' feet [ICC].
    2. The participial clause is concessive 'although he knew' [Lns, My]: 'although he knows that the Father did give all things into his hands…he rises from the supper' [Lns]. In spite of the fact that all things were in Jesus' hands, still he used those hands to wash the disciples' feet [Lns].

DISCOURSE UNIT—13:5–20 [NASB]. The topic is Jesus washes the disciples' feet.

13:4 He-rises from supper and take-off[a] the (his) garments[b] and having-taken (a) towel[c] he-girded[d] himself. **13:5** Then[e] he-puts water into the basin[f] and began to-wash[g] the feet of-the disciples and to-wipe (them) with-the towel with-which he-was girded.

LEXICON—a. pres. act. indic. of τίθημι (LN **49.21**) (BAGD I.1.b.δ. p. 816): 'to take off' [AB, BAGD, **LN**; NCV, NIV, NLT, NRSV, Ph, REB, TEV], 'to remove' [BAGD, LN; CEV, NET, NJB], 'to lay aside' [Gdt, HTC, NTC, WBC; KJV, NASB], 'to lay down' [NICNT2]. This verb means to remove or take off clothing [LN].
  b. ἱμάτιον (LN 6.162) (BAGD 3. p. 376): 'garment' [BAGD, Gdt, HTC, NICNT2, NTC; KJV, NASB], 'outer garment' [CEV, NJB, REB, TEV], 'outer clothing' [NCV, NIV], 'outer clothes' [NET, Ph], 'robe' [AB, BAGD, WBC; NLT], 'outer robe' [NRSV], 'cloak' [BAGD], 'clothing, apparel' [LN]. This noun denotes any kind of clothing [LN]. It indicates either a garment or an outer piece of clothing [BAGD]. Jesus was probably wearing a tunic under His robe. A tunic was a short-sleeved shirt much like an extra long T-shirt reaching to the knees. A robe, worn over it, was long-sleeved and reached to the feet. He may have taken off one or both of these [TRT].
  c. λέντιον (LN **6.161**) (BAGD p. 471): 'towel' [BAGD, LN; all translations], 'linen cloth' [BAGD]. This noun denotes a piece of cloth (probably made of linen) used primarily for drying [LN]. Jesus tied a long towel [BECNT, EGT, NTC, TRT] around his waist so that the end would be available for drying the disciples' feet [BECNT, NTC, TRT]. The towel was a linen cloth [BAGD, EGT, HTC, IVP, Kn, LN, Lns, NTC].
  d. aorist act. indic. of διαζώννυμι (LN **49.14**) (BAGD p. 182): 'to gird' [LN], 'to tie around oneself' [BAGD, **LN**], 'to fasten one's belt, to wear a narrow band of cloth around the waist' [LN]. The words 'he girded/girds himself' [Gdt, HTC, NICNT2; KJV, NASB] is also translated 'he wrapped a towel around his waist' [CEV, NIV, NLT, similarly NCV, NJB], 'he...tied it around himself' [AB, NET, similarly WBC; NRSV, REB], 'he...tied a towel around his waist' [TEV, similarly NTC], 'he...fastened it around his waist' [Ph]. This verb means to tuck up or hold a garment firmly in place by wrapping a belt, girdle, or piece of cloth around it [LN].
  e. εἶτα (LN 67.44) (BAGD 1. p. 233): 'then' [BAGD, LN; all translations except KJV, NET], 'after that' [KJV], 'afterwards, later' [LN], 'next' [BAGD], not explicit [NET]. This adverb indicates a point of time following another point [LN].
  f. νιπτήρ (LN **6.122**) (BAGD): 'basin' [BAGD, Gdt, HTC, LN, NICNT2, WBC; KJV, NASB, NIV, NJB, NLT, NRSV, Ph, REB], 'washbasin' [BAGD, LN, NTC; NET, TEV], 'bowl' [NCV], 'large bowl' [CEV], 'pitcher' [AB]. This noun denotes a basin used for washing [LN]. It is more likely that a basin used to catch the water was the utensil referred to here [NICNT1].

g. pres. act. infin. of νίπτω (LN **47.9**) (BAGD 1. p. 540): 'to wash' [BAGD, LN; all translations]. This verb means to wash a part of a body, usually the hands or feet [LN]. Jesus probably poured water from one utensil over the feet and into another utensil [ICC, Kn, NICNT1].

QUESTION—Did Jesus take off a single piece of clothing or several?

1. Ἱμάτια 'garments' should rather be taken as a singular, such as a 'robe, coat' or 'cloak' [AB, BAGD, EGT, Gdt, HTC, ICC, TH, WBC: CEV, NLT, NRSV, REB, TEV]: 'took off his outer garment' [TEV]. He took off his upper garment and was left dressed in just his tunic [EGT, Gdt, ICC], the dress of a slave [Gdt].
2. Ἱμάτια 'garments' is plural and denotes more than one piece of clothing [Lns, NICNT1, NICNT2, NTC; KJV, NASB, NET, NJB, Ph]. Since John is careful to use the singular for a single garment in 19:2, 5 and the plural for several of Jesus' garments in 19:23–24, it is more likely that the plural is indicated here. If so, Jesus took off his outer garments and was left with just his loin cloth, just like a slave [NICNT1, NTC].

QUESTION—What is the significance of the present tense of 'he rises'?

It is as though John sees the very scene reenacted before his eyes and so he writes in the present tense [NICNT1].

QUESTION—What is the significance of the definite article in the phrase '*the* basin'?

This was *the* basin that was there for footwashing [EGT, Gdt, Lns, TRT] and belonged to the furnishings of the dining hall [EGT, Gdt]. It indicates that this was the normal utensil used for a meal. The custom of footwashing was not usually done in a basin of water but rather by pouring water over the feet [AB].

QUESTION—What was unusual about Jesus washing his disciples' feet?

Foot washing was not even considered the work of a Jewish slave. It was relegated to non-Jewish slaves to perform [Bar, BECNT, IVP].

QUESTION—How were Jesus and his disciples dining?

They would probably be lying on couches [AB, ICC, Kn] on their left sides with their left hand supporting their heads. With their right hands they would reach food off the table placed in the center of the couches at their heads. Jesus then could wash their feet that were extended out behind them [AB]. They would be lying on mats around a low table with their feet extending outward from the table. The person would typically lean on the left arm [Car].

DISCOURSE UNIT—13:6–11 [HTC]. The topic is conversation with Peter.

13:6 Then he-comes to Simon Peter. He says to-him, "Lord do-you(sg) wash my feet?" **13:7** Jesus answered and said to-him, "What I do you(sg) do- not know[a] now, but after these-things you(sg)-will-know.[b]"

LEXICON—a. perf. act. indic. of οἶδα (LN 32.4): 'to know' [Gdt, HTC, NTC; KJV, NJB, NRSV], 'to really know' [CEV], 'to realize' [AB, WBC; NASB, NIV, Ph, REB], 'to understand' [LN, NICNT2; NCV, NET, NLT,

TEV], 'to comprehend' [LN]. This verb means to comprehend the meaning of something, with focus on the resulting knowledge [LN].

b. fut. mid. (deponent = act.) indic. of γινώσκω (LN 32.16): 'to understand' [AB, HTC, NICNT2, NTC; CEV, NASB, NCV, NET, NIV, NJB, NLT, NRSV, Ph, REB, TEV], 'to come to know' [WBC], 'to know' [Gdt; KJV], 'to come to understand, to perceive, to comprehend' [LN]. This verb means to come to an understanding as the result of ability to experience and learn [LN].

QUESTION—What words are emphasized in verse six?

The pronouns σύ 'you(sg)' (wash)' and μου 'my (feet)' are emphasized [Bar, Car, ICC, IVP, Kn, Lns, NICNT1, NICNT2, NTC, TH, TRT, WBC]: 'Lord, *you*? Of *me*?' [NICNT2]. The pronoun μου 'my' is emphasized [AB, My]. The two pronouns are in contrast [Bar, EGT, Gdt, NICNT1, NTC]. To Peter it was not fitting that such a holy person of God should do such a lowly service for one so undeserving [NICNT2]. The two pronouns are placed side by side σύ μου 'you my' highlighting the contrast [EGT, Kn, Bar]. Also placing 'Lord' at the beginning and 'feet' at the end of the question puts them in the most emphatic point of a Greek sentence [Kn]. Although the primary emphasis is on 'you' [HTC, My] the secondary emphasis is on the word 'feet' [My].

QUESTION—What is indicated by the rhetorical question of Peter?

Peter was shocked at Jesus' intention [NICNT2, NTC], embarrassed [AB, Car], incredulous [NICNT2], astonished [WBC]. He emphatically rejects Jesus' action [NTC, WBC]. The question could be translated 'Surely you aren't going to wash my feet, are you?' or 'You shouldn't wash my feet!' [TRT].

QUESTION—What is indicated by the present tense of the verb νίπτω 'to wash', 'Do you wash my feet?'

The present tense indicates an action not yet begun and could be translated 'Do you intend to wash my feet?' or 'Is it your plan to wash my feet?' [TH].

QUESTION—What words are emphasized in verse seven?

The pronouns ἐγώ 'I' and σύ are emphasized [EGT, HTC, ICC, Lns, NICNT1, NICNT2, TH] and in emphatic contrast [NICNT1]. Jesus echoes Peter's emphatic pronouns in verse six and perhaps gently mocks his emphasis [NICNT2].

QUESTION—To what time does the phrase 'after these things' refer?

1. It refers to after Jesus' death and resurrection and/or after the coming of the Holy Spirit [Bar, Car, CH, HTC, IVP, Lns, NICNT1, NTC, Rd, TH]. It refers to the time after Jesus' death, burial, resurrection and glorification. But it refers especially to Pentecost which will clarify the meaning of his action [Lns]. It does not refer to the footwashing but to the suffering on the cross to which footwashing points. Only after this and the descent of the Holy Spirit will they understand [Car]. It may refer to Jesus' explanation in the next few verses, but the primary reference is to the time when the Holy Spirit will make all things clear [NICNT1].

2. It refers rather to Jesus' explanation in the following verses [EGT, Gdt, My]. Beginning at verse 12, Jesus explains his action and helps Peter to understand [EGT]. If Jesus had meant in the future after my death and resurrection, he would have used the adverb ὕστερος 'later' as he does in verse 36. Here the phrase 'after these things' refers to after he finishes washing their feet [My].
3. It may refer to either or both interpretations [BECNT, NICNT1, NICNT2, WBC]. Jesus may have meant that Peter would understand after Jesus was taken out of the world to the Father after which the meaning of Jesus' action would come clear to him. Or it may refer to Jesus explanation beginning at verse 12 [NICNT2].

QUESTION—Do the two verbs for knowing have the same meaning or do they refer to different senses?
1. The two words for know should be kept distinct [AB, HTC, ICC, Lns, NTC; NASB, NIV, NJB, NRSV, Ph, REB]. The first verb οἶδα is the common verb for knowing, but the second, γινώσκω, indicates real/full understanding [Lns].
   'to know…understand' [HTC, NTC; NJB, NRSV]
   'to realize…understand' [AB; NASB, NIV, Ph, REB]
   'to realize…come to know' [WBC]
2. They mean essentially the same thing [Bar, NICNT2; KJV, NCV, NET, NLT, TEV].
   'to know…know' [Gdt; KJV]
   'to understand…understand' [NICNT2; NCV, NET, NLT, TEV].

13:8 Peter says to-him, You(sg)-will- certainly-not[a] -wash my feet forever.[b]" Jesus answered him, 'If I-do- not -wash you(sg), you(sg)-do- not have (a) part[c] with me."

LEXICON—a. οὐ μή (LN 69.5) (BAGD D. 1.a. p. 517): 'certainly not' [BAGD, LN], 'by no means' [LN], 'never' [BAGD]. This negative phrase is a marker of emphatic negation [LN]. The combination of two negative particles has the effect of strengthening the negation [BAGD]. It indicates a very strong negation in the Greek [TH]. The combination of this strong negative phrase plus the word 'forever' strengthens the negation to the point of excess [NICNT2]. The effect of Peter's use of the double negative plus 'forever' means 'never, no, not in all eternity' [NTC].
b. εἰς τὸν αἰῶνα (LN 67.95): 'forever' [LN], 'always, forever and ever, eternally' [LN]. The sentence 'You will certainly not wash my feet forever' is translated 'By no means shall you wash my feet ever' [NTC], 'you shall not wash my feet—ever' [AB], 'you will never ever wash my feet' [NICNT2; NLT], 'Never at any time will you wash my feet' [TEV], 'Never, never shall you wash my feet' [WBC], 'You will/shall never wash my feet' [HTC; CEV, KJV, NASB, NET, NIV, NJB, NRSV], 'You must never wash my feet' [Ph], 'No, you will/shall never wash my feet' [Gdt;

NCV], 'I will never let you wash my feet' [REB]. This phrase indicates unlimited duration of time with particular focus on the future [LN].

c. μέρος (BAGD 2. p. 506): 'part' [BAGD], 'share' [BAGD], 'place' [BAGD]. The sentence 'you do not have a part with/in me' [Gdt, HTC, NICNT2, WBC; KJV, NASB, NIV, REB] is also translated 'you (can) have no share with me' [NTC; NET, NJB, NRSV], 'you will have no heritage with me' [AB], 'you don't really belong to me' [CEV], 'you won't belong to me' [NLT], 'you cannot share my lot' [Ph], 'you are not one of my people' [NCV], 'you will no longer be my disciple' [TEV].

QUESTION—What information is implied in the clause 'If I do not wash you'?

Jesus implies Peter's feet as is seen from Peter's reply in the next verse [TH; NCV, TEV]: 'If I don't wash your feet' [NCV].

QUESTION—What is meant by the verb νίπτω 'to wash'?

It has a double meaning in this verse. It means to wash physically and it also means to wash from sin [BECNT, NICNT1].

QUESTION—What is meant by Jesus' words 'You do not have a part with me'?

It means that he will not share in the benefits of Jesus' death and so will not have a place among the people of God [Bar, TH]. The word μέρος 'part' means more than fellowship. This word is used to translate the Hebrew word *heleq* 'God given heritage' in the LXX. So what is in focus is rather eternal life and being part of God's kingdom [AB, BECNT]. It means you will not enter the Kingdom of God [Gdt]. It means that Peter will not be one of Jesus' own [NICNT2]. Jesus is the Son, the true Heir and believers are joint heirs with him (Romans 8:17). But if Jesus does not wash Peter, Peter will not share in this inheritance [NTC]. To lose one's part with Jesus is to reject one's salvation [My, Rd]. It is a loss of eternal fellowship with Jesus [Kn]. To have part with someone meant to share in their work and reward [ICC].

13:9 **Simon Peter says to-him, "Lord, not only my feet but also the (my) hands and the (my) head.** **13:10** **Jesus says to-him, "The-one having-bathed**[a] **does- not -have need to-wash except the (his) feet, but is clean**[b] **all-over.**[c] **And you(pl) are clean,**[d] **but not all.**

TEXT—Instead of οὐκ ἔχει χρείαν εἰ μὴ τοὺς πόδας νίψασθαι 'he does not have need except to wash his feet', some manuscripts read οὐκ ἔχει χρείαν νίψασθαι 'he does not have need to wash', others read οὐ χρείαν ἔχει εἰ μὴ τοὺς πόδας μόνον νίψασθαι 'he does not have need except only to wash his feet', others read οὐ χρείαν ἔχει ἢ τοὺς πόδας νίψασθαι 'he does not have need than to wash his feet', and still others read οὐ χρείαν ἔχει τὴν κεφαλὴν νίψασθαι εἰ μὴ τοὺς πόδας μόνον 'he does not have need to wash his head except his feet only'. GNT reads 'he does not have need except to wash his feet' with a B rating, indicating that the text is almost certain.

LEXICON—a. perf. mid. or pass. participle of λούω (LN 47.12) (BAGD 2.a.β. p. 481): 'to bathe' [AB, BAGD, HTC, LN, NICNT2, WBC; CEV, NASB, NET, NJB, NLT, NRSV, Ph, REB], 'to bathe all over' [NLT], 'to be

bathed' [Gdt, NTC], 'to be washed' [KJV], 'to have a bath' [NCV, NIV], 'to take a bath' [TEV], 'to wash' [BAGD, LN]. This verb means to wash one's body [LN]. It refers to religious washings. Here it contrasts with the person who has his feet washed, and with allusion to the cleansing of the whole body in baptism [BAGD]. It differs from νίπτω 'to wash' in that it tends to mean to wash the whole body whereas νίπτω tends to mean to wash part of the body [AB, HTC, NICNT1, NICNT2]. The perfect tense indicates a permanent state. The person continues in the state of being a 'bathed one' [Lns, NICNT1]. The two verbs meaning 'to wash/bathe' are synonyms [Lns, NICNT2]. The passive mood of this verb is to be understood with Jesus as the one who does the washing [Lns]. (AB, HTC, NICNT2, WBC; CEV, NASB, NET, NIV, NJB, NLT, NRSV, Ph, REB, TEV, take the verb to be active).
   b. καθαρός (LN **79.48**) (BAGD 1. p. 388): 'clean' [BAGD, LN; all translations], 'pure' [BAGD]. This adjective describes a thing as not being dirty [LN]. Here it should be taken in the physical sense [BAGD].
   c. ὅλος (LN **78.44**) (BAGD 2.c. p. 565): 'all over' [AB, BAGD, HTC, NICNT2, WBC; CEV, NJB, Ph, REB], 'completely' [**LN**; NASB, NET, TEV], 'entirely' [NLT, NRSV], 'altogether' [Gdt, NTC], 'every whit' [KJV], 'totally' [LN], 'complete' [BAGD, LN]. The phrase 'is clean all over' is translated 'his whole body is clean' [NCV, NIV]. This adjective describes a degree of totality or completeness [LN].
   d. καθαρός (LN 79.48) (BAGD 3.a. p. 388): 'clean' [BAGD, LN; all translations], 'pure' [BAGD]. Here καθαρός should be taken in the moral and religious sense: 'pure, free from sin' [BAGD, NICNT1]. It changes from the physical to the spiritual sense [EGT, ICC]. The disciples may have thought that their feet were still dusty, but he meant that not all of them were clean because one of them was a sinner [AB].
QUESTION—To what custom may verse 10 refer?
   When invited to a banquet people would typically bathe at home before going but then on arrival at the banquet, having walked over dusty roads, would need their feet washed before dining. Once washed they would be completely clean again [Bar, BECNT, Car, EGT, IVP, NICNT1, NTC, Rd].
QUESTION—Does the word ὅλος 'completely' intensify the word clean or does it mean '(clean) all over'?
   1. It intensifies 'clean' meaning 'completely clean' [TRT; NASB, NET, TEV].
   2. It means that a person is clean all over [AB, BAGD, HTC, NICNT2, WBC; CEV, NCV, NIV, NJB, Ph, REB].
QUESTION—Does the word 'bathed' refer to baptism or to some other form of cleansing?
   1. 'Bathed' refers to baptism and what it symbolizes [AB, BAGD, Bar, Gdt, Lns]. Jesus is thinking here about baptism as the sign of general cleansing [Gdt]. The verb λούω is a common verb in the NT to refer to baptism. Note Acts 22:16 where Ananias says to Paul, 'Get up, be baptized and

wash (ἀπολούω) your sins away, calling on his name' (See also Titus 3:5) [AB].
2. 'Bathed' refers to something other than baptism [BECNT, Car, CH, HTC, IVP, Kn, My, NICNT1, NICNT2, Rd, WBC]. Jesus does not speak of baptism here nor even of bathing, he only says that they are clean [NICNT2]. In 15:3 Jesus tells his disciples, 'You are already clean because of the word I have spoken to you' [BECNT, Car, CH, IVP, Kn, My, NICNT2, Rd, WBC]. John 15:3 is the only other place in the NT where Jesus tells his eleven disciples that they are clean [Car]. Jesus' word must be received and believed for it to be effective in one's life. Judas, however, rejected Jesus' word [WBC]. The disciples received the cleansing salvation by faith. Genuine cleansing is made possible only through Jesus' revealed word and atoning sacrifice [Car]. At the cross the blood and water flowing from Jesus' side is the blood that cleanses from all sin (1 John 1:7) [HTC].

QUESTION—What is implied by the explicit pronoun ὑμεῖς 'you(pl)'?
It is commonly assumed that only men were present [AB, ICC, NICNT2, WBC; CEV, NCV, NET, NLT]: 'you men are clean—but not all of you' [NICNT2], 'you, my disciples are clean, except for one of you' [CEV].

QUESTION—What is implied by the phrase 'but not all'?
The words 'of you' are implied [AB, Kn; all translations except Gdt]: 'And now you men are clean, though not all of you' [AB].

DISCOURSE UNIT—13:12–17 [HTC]. The topic is a model of service for the disciples.

DISCOURSE UNIT—13:12–20 [NICNT1]. The topic is a lowly service.

13:11 For he-knew the-one betraying him. Therefore he-said, "(You(pl)) are not all clean. **13:12** So when he-washed their feet and took his garments and reclined[a] again, he-said to them, "Do-you(pl)-know[b] what I-have-done to-you(pl)?"

LEXICON—a. aorist act. indic. of ἀναπίπτω (LN 17.23) (BAGD 1. p. 59): 'to recline' [BAGD, LN, NICNT2], 'to recline at the table' [WBC; NASB], 'to take one's place at the table' [NET], 'to go to the table' [NJB, NRSV], 'to go to one's place (at the table)' [AB; NIV, TEV], 'to sit down' [CEV, NCV, NLT, Ph, REB], 'to be set down' [KJV], 'to lie down' [BAGD], 'to eat, to be at table, to dine, to sit down to eat' [LN]. The phrase 'reclined again' is translated 'having resumed his seat at table' [Gdt], '(had) resumed his place' [HTC, NTC]. This verb means to be in a reclining position as one eats [BAGD, LN] (with the focus either on the position or the act of eating) [LN].

b. pres. act. indic. of γινώσκω (LN 32.16) (BAGD 3.d. p. 161): 'to know' [Gdt, HTC, NTC, WBC; KJV, NASB, NRSV], 'to understand' [AB, NICNT2; BAGD; CEV, NCV, NET, NIV, NJB, NLT, REB, TEV], 'to realize' [Ph], 'to comprehend' [BAGD, LN], 'to come to understand, to perceive' [LN]. This verb means to come to an understanding as the result of the ability to experience and learn [LN].

QUESTION—Is verse 11 a parenthetical statement?

The following consider this verse parenthetical and place it in parentheses [AB, TH; NET, Ph, TEV].

QUESTION—What relationship is indicated by the conjunction γάρ 'for'?

It indicates that this verse gives the reason why he had said, 'you are clean, but not all' [AB, ICC, NICNT1, NICNT2, NTC, WBC]: 'The reason he said, "Not all of you are clean," was that he knew his betrayer' [AB]. The words 'not all' could indicate more than one, so John explains what Jesus meant [Lns].

QUESTION—What may be indicated by the present participle 'the one betraying'?

It may indicate that the betrayal was already in process [AB, ICC, Lns, NICNT1, NTC; possibly NICNT2; NASB]: 'He knew the one who was betraying him' [NASB]. If the word 'betrayer' is used to translate 'the one betraying him', it could indicate that Jesus was only personally acquainted with him rather than being aware of his activities [TH].

QUESTION—Is Jesus' question rhetorical, and if so, what is its function?

The question is rhetorical [Lns, NICNT1, NICNT2]. Jesus *challenged* them to ponder the significance of his action [NICNT1]. Jesus does not wait for their answer but goes on to explain the meaning of what he had done [NICNT2]. The rhetorical question was at least designed to attract the attention of the disciples so he could make them realize the full import of what they had seen [Lns]. The verb γινώσκετε 'you know' can be interpreted either as interrogative or as imperative, 'Do you know?' or 'Understand!' [ICC, NICNT1, TH, TRT].

13:13 You(pl) call[a] me the Teacher[b] and the Lord,[c] and you(pl) say well,[d] for I-am. **13:14** Therefore if I (being) the Lord and the Teacher washed your feet, you(pl) also ought[e] to wash the feet of-each-other. **13:15** For I-gave you(pl) an example[f] so-that as I did to you(pl) you(pl) also may-do.

LEXICON—a. pres. act. indic. of καλέω (LN 33.131) (BAGD 2.a. p. 870): 'to call' [BAGD, LN; all translations except AB, WBC], 'to address (as)' [AB, WBC], 'to name' [LN]. This verb means to use an attribution in speaking of a person [LN]. It means 'to call' in the sense of 'address as' [BAGD].

b. διδάσκαλος (LN 33.243) (BAGD p. 191): 'Teacher' [all translations except Gdt; CEV, KJV, NJB, Ph], 'teacher' [BAGD, LN; CEV, Ph], 'Master' [Gdt; KJV, NJB], 'master' [BAGD], 'instructor' [LN]. This is derived from the verb διδάσκω 'to teach' and denotes one who provides instruction [LN]. It was the Hebrew equivalent of 'Rabbi', the term commonly used by disciples addressing a religious leader [Car, NICNT1]. This title with the definite article carries the connotation of divinity [Lns].

c. κύριος (LN 12.9) (BAGD 2.c.γ. p. 460): 'Lord' [BAGD, LN; all translations except WBC], 'Master' [BAGD, WBC], 'Ruler, One who commands' [LN]. This noun is a title for God and Christ and denotes one who exercises supernatural authority over mankind [LN]. It expresses very high reverence, possibly carrying the connotations of divinity [NICNT1]. This title does carry the connotation of divinity [Lns].

d. καλῶς (LN 72.12) (BAGD 4.b. p. 401): 'well' [BAGD, Gdt, NICNT2; KJV], 'rightly' [BAGD, WBC], 'correctly' [BAGD, LN], 'accurate, right' [LN]. The clause 'you say well' is translated 'you are right' [HTC; NASB, NCV, NLT, NRSV], 'you are quite right' [Ph], 'you do so correctly' [NET], 'you say (this) correctly' [NTC], 'it is right that you do so' [TEV], 'and rightly' [NJB], 'and rightly so' [ABNIV, REB], 'you should' [CEV]. This adverb describes an action as being accurate and right, with a possible implication of being commendable [LN].

e. pres. act. indic. of ὀφείλω (LN 71.25) (BAGD 2.a.β. p. 599): 'ought' [BAGD, Gdt, HTC, LN, NICNT2, NTC, WBC; KJV, NASB, NET, NLT, NRSV, REB], 'should' [CEV, NCV, NIV, TEV], 'must' [AB, BAGD; NJB], 'must be ready (to)' [Ph], 'to be obligated' [BAGD], 'to be under obligation' [LN]. This verb means to be obligatory in view of some moral or legal requirement [LN]. If followed by an infinitive this verb has the meaning 'ought' or 'must' [BAGD]. The present tense indicates that they should continue doing this [NTC].

f. ὑπόδειγμα (LN **58.59**) (BAGD): 'example' [BAGD, **LN**; all translations], 'model' [BAGD, LN], 'pattern' [BAGD]. The clause 'I gave you an example' is translated 'it was an example that I gave you' [AB], 'I have given you an example to follow' [NLT], 'I have set the example' [CEV], 'I have set you an example' [NIV, NRSV, REB, similarly TEV], 'I did this as an example' [NCV]. This noun denotes a model of behavior as an example to be imitated or to be avoided [LN]. Here it denotes model in a good sense as something that does or should spur one on to imitate it [BAGD].

QUESTION—Are the titles 'Teacher' and 'Lord' vocatives or simply titles?

1. These titles are used as vocatives [Bar, Gdt, ICC, My, NICNT1, NICNT2, NTC; all translations except CEV].
2. These titles are not used as vocatives [Lns; and possibly CEV]: 'You call me your teacher and Lord' [CEV]. Both of these titles have the definite article 'the Teacher' and 'the Lord' and both are in the nominative case, not the vocative. The phrase 'You call me' meant 'you call me when you speak of me' to others, not 'when you adddress me'. In speaking about Jesus to others they would refer to him as 'the Teacher'. This form of expression gives the titles a specific and exalted sense—*the* Teacher, and *the* Lord who ranks above others with similar titles [Lns].

QUESTION—What words are emphasized in this verse?

The pronoun ὑμεῖς 'you(pl)' in verse 13 in the phrase 'you call me Lord' is emphatic [Lns, TRT]: *you yourselves* call me Teacher. The pronoun ἐγώ 'I', in the phrase 'I the Lord and the Teacher' is emphasized [Lns, My, NTC]: *I, on my part*. The pronoun ὑμεῖς 'you(pl)' in the phrase 'you also ought' emphasizes the role of the disciples [Lns, NICNT1, NTC]. The following pronouns in italics in verses 14 and 15 are being emphasized, 'If, therefore, *I* your Lord and Teacher, have washed *your* feet, *you* also ought to wash *each other's* feet, for I have given you an example, in order that just as *I* did to you so also *you* should do' [NTC].

QUESTION—Does the conjunction εἰ 'if' indicate a condition?

It does not indicate a condition, but a fact [NTC, TH] so TEV renders it as a statement 'I, your Lord and Teacher, have just washed your feet...' [TH; TEV]. These others also assume it as a fact: NICNT2; NIV, NLT, TEV.

QUESTION—Did Jesus mean that the disciples should literally wash each other's feet?

Although they might from time to time do so, Jesus' real point is that they should be ready to do even the lowliest form of service for each other [NICNT1]. Central to this example is humility and helpfulness to Christian brothers and sisters rather than observing a literal footwashing sacrament [Car]. The adverb καθώς 'as' means 'in the same manner' not 'the same identical thing' [Lns]. It is the spiritual action symbolized by footwashing not its specific form that Jesus intended his disciples to imitate [My]. Jesus wanted his disciples to be humble and serve each other. He just used foot washing to teach them this principle [TRT].

QUESTION—What is the form of the argument that Jesus uses in verse 14?

The argument style is called *argumentum a majori ad minus* which means in essence that if a greater thing is true, how much more is the lesser true. That is, if a teacher undertakes a given action, how much more is it incumbent on the student to do the same [TH].

DISCOURSE UNIT—13:17–19 [NCV]. The topic is people tell about Jesus.

13:16 Truly[a] truly I-say to-you(pl), (a) slave is not greater-than[b] his master[c] nor (a) messenger[d] greater-than the-one having-sent him. **13:17** If[e] you(pl)-know these-things, happy[f] are-you(pl) if you(pl)-do them.

LEXICON—a. ἀμήν (LN 72.6): 'truly' [LN], 'indeed, it is true that' [LN]. The clause 'Truly truly I say to you' [HTC; NASB] is also translated 'Verily, verily, I say unto you' [Gdt; KJV], 'Very truly, I tell you' [NRSV], 'Amen, amen, I tell you/say to you' [NICNT2, WBC], 'I tell you for certain' [CEV], 'I tell/am telling you the truth' [NCV, NIV, NLT, TEV], 'I tell you the solemn truth' [NET], 'In all/very truth I tell you' [NJB, REB], 'Most solemnly do I assure you' [NTC], 'Let me firmly assure you' [AB], 'Believe me' [Ph]. This particle indicates strong affirmation of what is declared [LN].

b. μέγας (LN 87.22) (BAGD 2.b.α. 498): 'great' [BAGD, LN], 'important' [LN], 'prominent, outstanding' [BAGD]. The comparative form of this adjective μείζων is translated 'greater than' [all translations except AB],

'more important' [AB]. This adjective describes a person as being great in terms of status [LN], rank, and dignity [BAGD].
  c. κύριος (LN **57.12**) (BAGD 1.a.β. p. 459): 'master' [BAGD, **LN**; all translations except Gdt, NICNT2, NTC; KJV], 'lord' [Gdt, LN, NICNT2, NTC; KJV], 'owner' [LN]. This noun denotes one who owns and controls property, including especially servants and slaves, with important supplementary semantic components of high status and respect [LN].
  d. ἀπόστολος (LN **33.194**) (BAGD 1. p. 99): 'messenger' [AB, BAGD, LN, NICNT2; CEV, NCV, NET, NIV, NJB, NLT, NRSV, Ph, REB, TEV], 'envoy, delegate' [BAGD]. This noun is also translated as a clause: 'he that/he who/one who is sent' [Gdt, HTC, NTC; KJV, NASB, similarly WBC]. This noun is derived from ἀποστέλλω 'to send a message' and denotes one who is sent with a message [LN].
  e. εἰ (LN 89.65) (BAGD III p. 219): 'if' [BAGD, Gdt, HTC, LN, NTC, WBC; KJV, NASB, NCV, NET, NRSV, REB]. The clause 'if you know these things' is translated 'Once you have realized these things' [Ph], 'Now that you know these things/this/this truth' [NIV, NJB, NLT, TEV], 'Now that you understand these things' [NICNT2], 'Now, once you understand this' [AB], 'You know these things' [CEV]. This conjunction indicates condition, real or hypothetical, actual or contrary to fact [LN]. It indicates a condition that is true to fact [Lns, NICNT2, TH]. This if-clause implies that they did know them [AB, EGT, Gdt, Lns, My, TH; CEV, NIV, NJB, NLT, TEV].
  f. μακάριος (LN 25.119) (BAGD 1.b. p. 486): 'happy' [LN], 'blessed' [BAGD], 'fortunate' [BAGD]. The words 'happy are you' [AB, Gdt, WBC; KJV, REB] are also translated 'you will be happy' [NCV], 'how happy you will be' [TEV], 'you will find your happiness (in doing them)' [Ph], 'you are blessed' [NJB, NRSV, similarly HTC, NICNT2, NTC; NASB], 'you will be blessed' [NET, NIV], 'God will bless you' [CEV, NLT]. This adjective describes a person as being happy, with the implication of enjoying favorable circumstances [LN]. It has the sense of being a 'privileged recipient of divine favor' [BAGD]. It does not refer to how a person feels, but to the inner spiritual condition of those who are the objects of God's favor [NTC, TRT], although joy would be the result of being in God's favor. One could translate 'will prosper spiritually' [TRT]. It means spiritually contented and fulfilled [CH]. The focus is on the subjective state of happiness experienced by people who have received God's blessings [TH].

QUESTION—What did Jesus mean to imply by saying that a slave was not greater than his master and a messenger was not greater than his sender?
  He implied that no slave or messenger should think of himself as being too important to do something his master or sender had already willingly done [TRT].

QUESTION—To what does the pronoun ταῦτα 'these things' refer?

It refers to the words of Jesus in verses 13–16 [EGT, My, NTC, TH], or to the verses 14–15 [Car]. He probably refers to his teaching about how to be humble and love and serve others [TRT]. He means, if you know that it is a good thing to wash each other's feet, you will be happy if you do it [Bar].

QUESTION—What is indicated by the present tense of the verb in the clause 'if you do them'?

The present tense indicates repeated activity. The disciples are to do repeatedly what Jesus has done for them [AB, BECNT, Lns, NICNT2, NTC, WBC; TEV]: 'how happy you will be if you put it into practice' [TEV].

DISCOURSE UNIT—13:18–38 [Ph]. The topic is Jesus foretells his betrayal.

DISCOURSE UNIT—13:18–30 [BECNT, Car; NCV, NIV, NLT]. The topic is the betrayal.

DISCOURSE UNIT—13:18–20 [HTC]. The topic is the betrayal.

13:18 I-do- not -speak about all of-you(pl). I know whom I-chose.[a] But so-that[b] the Scripture may-be-fulfilled, The-one eating my bread[c] raised[d] his heel against me.

TEXT—Instead of μου 'my' some manuscripts read μετ' ἐμοῦ 'with me', others read μετ' ἐμοῦ 'with me' and add another μου 'my' following ἄρτον 'bread'. GNT reads 'my' with a C rating, indicating difficulty in deciding which variant to place in the text. AB, Gdt; CEV, KJV, REB read 'with me'.

LEXICON—a. aorist. mid. indic. of ἐκλέγομαι (LN 30.92) (BAGD 2.a. p. 242): 'to choose' [BAGD, LN; all translations], 'to select' [BAGD]. This verb means to make a special choice based on significant preference, often implying a strongly favorable attitude toward what is chosen [LN]. It means to choose someone for oneself [BAGD].

b. ἵνα (LN 89.59) (BAGD III.1. p. 378): 'so that' [LN], 'in order to, for the purpose of' [LN]. The clause 'so that/that the Scripture may be fulfilled' [Gdt; KJV] is also translated 'the purpose is to have the Scripture fulfilled' [AB], 'it is that the scripture/Scriptures may be fulfilled' [HTC; NASB], 'this is to bring about what the Scripture said' [NCV], 'this is to fulfill the scripture' [NET, NIV, NRSV], '(this happened) in order that the scripture may be fulfilled' [NTC], 'this fulfills the Scripture' [NLT], 'what the Scriptures say must come true/be fulfilled' [CEV, NJB], 'the scripture/Scripture must come true/be fulfilled (that says)' [NICNT2, WBC; TEV], 'there is a text of scripture to be fulfilled' [REB], 'let this scripture be fulfilled' [Ph]. This conjunction indicates purpose for events and states (sometimes occurring in highly elliptical contexts) [LN]. It is used elliptically here to mean something like 'this has happened that' where the verb to be supplied must be inferred from the context [BAGD].

c. ἄρτος (LN 5.1) (BAGD 2. p. 111): 'bread' [AB, BAGD, Gdt, HTC, NICNT2, NTC, WBC; KJV, NASB, NET, NIV, NRSV, Ph, REB], 'food' [BAGD, LN; NLT, TEV]. The phrase 'the one eating my bread' is translated 'the man who ate with me' [CEV], 'he who shares my table' [NJB], 'the man who ate at my table' [NCV]. This noun denotes any kind of food or nourishment. In the place of a general term or phrase such as 'that which is eaten', some languages generalize the meaning of a particular term. For example, in certain parts of the Orient the term meaning specifically 'rice' also refers to 'food' in general. A similar type of meaning has developed in English with respect to 'bread'. For example, in rendering Luke 4:4 'man shall not live by bread alone', it would be wrong to employ a strictly literal rendering, since this might mean simply that people should not live on a diet consisting solely of bread. The meaning is, of course, 'to live means more than merely eating' [LN]. The idiom 'to eat someone's bread' means 'be the guest of someone' [BAGD], It signifies close fellowship [NICNT1, TRT]. In Semitic cultures when a person ate bread at a superior's table, it was a sign of a pledge of one's loyalty. Therefore betraying a superior with whom one had eaten was a flagrant breach of hospitality [BECNT, ICC].

d. aorist act. indic. of ἐπαίρω (LN **39.3**, 15.105) (BAGD 1. p. 282, p. 727): 'to raise' [BAGD, LN (15.105)], 'to turn against' [**LN** (39.3)], 'to oppose' [LN]. The clause '(he has) raised his heel against me' [AB] is also translated '(has) lifted (up) his heel against me' [Gdt, HTC, NICNT2, NTC, WBC; KJV, NRSV, NIV, NRSV, Ph], '(has) turned against me' [**LN**; CEV, NCV, NET, NLT, REB, TEV], 'takes advantage of me' [NJB]. The phrase ἐπαίρω τὴν πτέρναν 'to lift one's heel against' is an idiom meaning to oppose someone by turning against such a person [LN, TRT], possibly with focus on the initial aspect of becoming opposed to [LN]. It means to 'raise one's heel' to tread on someone [BAGD (p. 282), Lns], or kick them [BAGD (p. 727), My], or refers to the lifting up of a horse's hoof to prepare to kick someone [NICNT1]. It is a sign of contempt [AB, EGT, Kn] to show someone the bottom of one's foot in the Near East [AB]. It is a sign of brutal hatred [Gdt], of treachery [Kn, Rd], of violence [ICC]. The tragedy of the betrayal was that it was done by an intimate friend [Car, NICNT1].

QUESTION—To whom do the words 'I do not speak about all of you' apply and what is that one excluded from?

This is an obvious reference to Judas [Bar, NICNT1, TH]. Judas would exclude himself from the blessing Jesus has just declared, 'If you know these things, happy are you if you do them' [Bar, EGT].

QUESTION—What word is emphasized in this verse?

The pronoun ἐγώ 'I' is emphasized [EGT, Lns, My]: '*I, for my part* know' [Lns].

QUESTION—What words are implied with the verb 'to choose'?

Jesus meant that he chose them *to be his disciples* [NTC, TRT].

QUESTION—Does the text imply that Judas was not chosen with the others?

Judas was chosen with the other apostles. What Jesus meant was that he knew the kind of men he had chosen [AB, Bar, Car, CH, EGT, Gdt, ICC,

IVP, Kn, Lns, My, NICNT1, NTC, Rd, TH, TRT]. In 6:70 Jesus said, 'Have I not chosen you, the Twelve? Yet one of you is a devil!' [AB, Bar, Car, Gdt, Lns, Rd, TH]. Jesus chose Judas, but he was not surprised by his treachery [EGT].

QUESTION—What relationship is indicated by the conjunction ἵνα 'so that'?

It indicates purpose [AB, BECNT, Car, EGT, Gdt, Kn, NICNT1, NTC, Rd]. This occurred in order to fulfill the OT Scriptures [AB]. Judas was chosen because his character would lead him to fill the role of betrayer that was prophesied in Scripture [Kn]. This may also be interpreted as a third person imperative, 'Let the Scripture be fulfilled' [Ph].

QUESTION—What words may be implied with the conjunction 'so that'?

It is natural to understand an ellipsis meaning: 'This has happened/is happening, in order that' [Gdt, NTC, TRT], 'I have nevertheless chosen him in order that' [Car, Gdt, TRT], or 'what is about to happen will happen' [TRT]. It is better to understand this in a general sense 'this is to fulfill Scripture' [BECNT, NICNT1, Rd; NCV, NET, NIV, NRSV]. If Judas is among the chosen there must be a rather large ellipsis, such as '*I know whom I have chosen. Therefore I know that Judas is a traitor but I have chosen him* in order that' [Bar]. Jesus meant, 'I know whom I chose, but *none the less this treachery will come*, that the Scripture might be fulfilled' [ICC]. He meant, 'But I made this choice in obedience to the divine destiny, in accordance with which the Scripture could not but be fulfilled' [My].

QUESTION—What specific Scripture does Jesus refer to here?

He is referring to Psalm 41:9 (40:10, LXX) 'Even my close friend, whom I trusted, he who shared my bread, has lifted up his heel against me' [AB and most other commentaries].

13:19 **From now^a (on) I-tell you(pl) before the occurrence, so-that when it-occurs you-may-believe that I am (he).**

LEXICON—a. ἄρτι (LN 67.38) (BAGD 3. p. 110): 'now' [BAGD, LN], 'at the present time' [BAGD]. The phrase ἀπ' ἄρτι 'from now on/onwards' [BAGD, My, NICNT2, NTC; NASB, Ph] is also translated 'from henceforth' [Gdt], 'now' [AB, HTC; KJV, NCV, NET, NIV, NJB, NRSV, REB, TEV]. The meaning of 'from now' is 'at this time' [AB], or 'now' [Bar, HTC, TH], or 'already' [HTC]. This adverb indicates a point of time simultaneous with the event of the discourse itself [LN].

QUESTION—What does the ability to accurately foretell the future indicate?

In the OT, both God and his prophets were known to be true by their ability to accurately predict the future (Isaiah 48.5) [IVP]. Such an ability was proof of God's omnipotence (Ezekiel 24:24; Isaiah 43:10; 46:10). Here it makes Jesus' power and authority indisputable [Rd]. The fulfillment of a prophet's prediction assures the prophet's bona fides (Deuteronomy 18:22) [Kn].

QUESTION—What had Jesus told his disciples?

1. He had told them about the betrayal of Judas [AB, Bar, Car, CH, HTC, ICC, Kn, Lns, NICNT1, NTC, TRT; CEV, NCV, NET, NJB, NLT,

NRSV, REB, TEV]: 'I am telling you *this* before it all happens' [CEV]. The word 'occurrence' refers to the betrayal of Judas as does the phrase 'when *it* does' [Bar, Lns]. Jesus knows that the treachery of Judas may upset the other disciples and undermine their faith. He wants them to know that this has not taken him by surprise, that it was included in God's plan, and that when it does happen their faith may be strengthened [NICNT1, NTC]. Jesus' purpose is to strengthen the disciples faith [NICNT1].
  2. He would tell them about things before they happened [NICNT2; Ph]: 'From now onwards, I shall tell you about things before they happen' [Ph]. Jesus is warning the disciples of coming events so that when they happen the disciples will believe. It is more likely that the disciples would have understood Jesus' words in a broad sense than they would have understood that he was talking about the betrayal of one of their number just then [NICNT2].

QUESTION—Did Jesus mean that they would come to believe or continue to believe?
  1. There is better evidence for the aorist tense indicating that they would come to full faith than for the present tense that would indicate a continuing belief. He means that Jesus' suffering, death, resurrection, and ascension put altogether would lead the disciples to put their full faith in Jesus [AB].
  2. The present tense is the correct reading [NTC]: 'you may continue to believe that I am (he)' [NTC].

QUESTION—What did Jesus mean by saying 'you may believe that I am'?
  1. He meant to claim that he was God [AB, BECNT, HTC, ICC, IVP, Kn, NICNT1, TH, TRT; TEV]: 'I Am Who I Am' TEV]. This is probably the absolute use of the phrase 'I am' on analogy with other occurrences like 8:58, where Jesus makes a claim to deity [AB]. In the OT, God predicted the future so that people would recognize his identity as Yahweh (Isaiah 43:9–10). So here Jesus' predicts Judas' betrayal so that the disciples might realize that he was the 'I am' [Kn]. Jesus' words almost certainly indicate his divine status [NICNT1]. When the phrase 'I am' is used without a predicate, as here, it identifies the speaker with God. It is used by God in a similar way in Isaiah 43:10. But some languages have no equational verb, that is, they cannot say 'I am'. For them the phrase 'I am good' would be expressed as 'I good'. Therefore in such languages this could be translated as 'I (am) the one who has always existed' [TH]. He meant that he was all that he claimed to be—the One sent by the Father, the One from above, the Son of man, the only-begotten Son of God, equal with God, One who has life in himself, the bread of life, the light of the world, etc. [NTC].
  2. He meant that he was the Messiah [EGT, My, Rd]. 'I am he' means that 'I am the Messiah, the Son of God' (20:31) [Rd].

3. Another view [Lns]. It must mean, I am he, that is, 'the one who tells you this in advance in order that you may believe' [Lns].

13:20 **Truly^a truly I-say to-you, 'Whoever receives^b whom I-send receives me, and the-one receiving me receives the-one-who sent me.'**

LEXICON—a. ἀμήν (LN 72.6): 'truly' [LN], 'indeed, it is true that' [LN]. The clause 'Truly truly I say to you' [HTC; NASB] is also translated 'Verily, verily, I say unto you' [Gdt; KJV], 'Very truly, I tell you' [NRSV], 'Amen, amen, I tell you/say to you' [NICNT2, WBC], 'I tell you for certain' [CEV], 'I tell you plainly' [Ph], 'I tell/am telling you the truth' [NCV, NIV, NLT, TEV], 'I tell you the solemn truth' [NET], 'In all/very truth I tell you' [NJB, REB], 'I most solemnly assure you' [NTC], 'Let me firmly assure you' [AB]. This particle indicates strong affirmation of what is declared [LN].
    b. pres. act. participle of λαμβάνω (BAGD 1.e.α. p. 464]): 'to receive' [BAGD, Gdt, HTC, NICNT2, NTC, WBC; KJV, NASB, NRSV, REB], 'to welcome' [AB; CEV, NJB, NLT], 'to accept' [NCV, NET, NIV, Ph]. This verb means to receive someone in the sense of recognizing his authority [BAGD]. Receives may be understood in the sense of 'welcomes into one's heart' [TH].

QUESTION—What is the function of this verse and its relationship to the preceding context?
    This verse may serve to encourage the disciples to stand firm in view of Judas's approaching defection. To do so Jesus reminds them of their close relationship to him in their mission [BECNT, Rd]. Jesus assures the disciples that although Judas has defected, their own commission remains strong [Lns]. Verses 18–19 are a digression contrasting the fate of Judas and the happiness of the other disciples. Verse 20 now picks up the theme of the happiness of the one, who in receiving Jesus, also receives God himself [Gdt]. In both Jesus' mission and the mission of his followers the world confronts God himself [Bar, IVP].

QUESTION—What word is emphasized in this verse?
    The pronoun ἐμέ 'me' is emphatic by its position before the verb in the Greek text [NICNT1, TRT] and by its form [NICNT1].

DISCOURSE UNIT—13:21–38 [NASB]. The topic is Jesus predicts his betrayal.

DISCOURSE UNIT—13:21–35 [NICNT2; NCV]. The topic is prediction of the departure of Judas [NICNT2], Jesus talks about his death [NCV].

DISCOURSE UNIT—13:21–30 [AB, IVP, NICNT1, WBC; CEV, NJB, NRSV, TEV]. The topic is prediction of the betrayal [AB, IVP, NICNT1; NJB, NRSV, TEV], exposure of the betrayer [WBC], Jesus foretells his testing [CEV].

DISCOURSE UNIT—13:21–26 [HTC]. The topic is the exposure of the traitor.

13:21 Having said these-things Jesus was-troubled[a] in (his) spirit and testified[b] and said, "Truly truly I-say to-you(pl) that one of you(pl) will-betray[c] me."

LEXICON—a. aorist. pass. indic. of ταράσσω (LN 25.244) (BAGD 2. p. 805): 'to be troubled' [BAGD], 'to cause great mental distress' [LN], 'to be agitated, to be frightened, to be terrified' [BAGD]. The phrase 'he was troubled in (the/his) spirit' [Gdt, HTC, NTC; KJV, NIV, NRSV] is also translated 'he became troubled in spirit' [NASB], 'he was greatly distressed in spirit' [NET], 'he became agitated in spirit' [WBC], 'he was shaken in the spirit' [NICNT2], 'he was deeply troubled' [AB; CEV, NJB, NLT, TEV], 'he was very troubled' [NCV], 'he was clearly in anguish of soul' [Ph], '(he exclaimed) in deep distress' [REB]. This verb is a figurative extension of the basic meaning of ταράσσω 'to stir up' indicating to cause acute emotional distress or turbulence [LN]. The phrase 'to be troubled in spirit' means 'to be inwardly moved' [BAGD]. Jesus was in a state of turmoil at the thought of one of his closest followers betraying him [BECNT]. Jesus was profoundly agitated [Rd]. Jesus' love for Judas was what caused him to be in anguish over his loss [IVP].

b. aorist act. indic. of μαρτυρέω (LN 33.262) (BAGD 1.a. p. 493): 'to testify' [NET], 'to witness' [LN], 'to bear witness' [BAGD]. The phrase 'he testified and said' [Gdt, NICNT2, NTC; KJV, NASB] is also translated 'he bore witness and said' [WBC], 'he testified' [HTC; NET, NIV], 'he told his disciples' [CEV], 'he said openly' [NCV], 'he declared' [AB; NJB, NRSV], 'he declared openly' [TEV], 'he exclaimed' [NLT, REB], 'he added (solemnly)' [Ph]. This verb means to provide information about a person or an event concerning which the speaker has direct knowledge [LN]. This verb means that he made an open declaration in an impressive manner [NTC]. It indicates a clear and emphatic statement [WBC]. It marks the following statement as a solemn declaration [Bar, NICNT1, Rd].

c. fut. act. indic. of παραδίδωμι (LN 37.111) (BAGD 1.b. p. 614): 'to betray' [LN; all translations except NICNT2; NCV], 'to turn against' [NCV], 'to hand over' [BAGD, LN, NICNT2], 'to turn over to' [BAGD, LN], 'to give (someone) up' [BAGD]. This verb means to deliver a person into the control of someone else, involving either the handing over of a presumably guilty person for punishment by authorities or the handing over of an individual to an enemy who will presumably take undue advantage of the victim. As is the case in English, a number of languages make a clear distinction between legitimate handing over of a presumably guilty person to a civil authority and the betrayal of a person in the in-group to someone in the out-group [LN]. This verb is a technical term of police and courts meaning 'to hand over into the custody of' [BAGD].

QUESTION—What is the function of the phrase 'Having said these things'?

It signals an end of the previous discourse as if Jesus pauses for breath before announcing this next solemn declaration [NICNT2]. It introduces a transition to a new phase in the story [Rd].

13:22 The disciples were-looking at each-other being-uncertain^a about whom he-speaks.

LEXICON—a. pres. mid. participle of ἀπορέω (LN **32.9**) (BAGD p. 97): 'to be uncertain' [BAGD, LN], 'to be at a loss' [BAGD, **LN**], 'to be in doubt' [BAGD, LN], 'to be anxious' [LN]. The phrase 'being uncertain' is translated 'uncertain' [BAGD, HTC], 'doubting' [KJV], 'worried and perplexed' [NICNT2; NET], 'completely mystified' [Ph], 'puzzled' [AB], 'completely puzzled' [TEV], 'at a loss' [**LN**, NTC, WBC; NASB, NIV], 'confused' [CEV], 'wondering' [NJB, NLT], 'in bewilderment' [REB], 'not able to understand' [Gdt], 'they did not know' [NCV]. This verb means to be in perplexity, with the implication of serious anxiety [LN].

QUESTION—What is indicated by the imperfect tense of the verb 'were looking'?

It indicates that they continued to look at each other [NICNT2, NTC; CEV, NIV, Ph]: 'The disciples kept looking at each other' [NICNT2, NTC], 'they just stared at each other' [CEV]. It indicates an inchoative or inceptive aspect [NASB, NET]: 'The disciples began looking at one another' [NASB].

13:23 One of his disciples whom Jesus loved^a was reclining on Jesus' bosom.^b 13:24 So Simon Peter nods^c to-this-one to-ask who it-may-be about whom he-speaks.

LEXICON—a. imperf. act. indic. of ἀγαπάω (LN 25.43) (BAGD 1.b.α. p. 4): 'to love' [BAGD, LN], 'to regard with affection' [LN], 'to cherish' [BAGD]. The clause 'whom/he-whom/the-one-whom Jesus loved' [Gdt, NTC, WBC, NICNT2, HTC, KJV, NASB, NET, NIV, NRSV, Ph, TEV] is translated 'the follower/disciple Jesus/he loved' [AB; NCV, NJB, NLT, REB], 'Jesus' favorite disciple' [CEV]. This verb means to have love for someone or something, based on sincere appreciation and high regard [LN]. It refers to the love of supernatural beings for humans [BAGD]. The imperfect tense indicates that the action of Jesus was continuous or constant [Lns, NTC]. It is important in translating this clause that people not mistakenly understand that Jesus did not therefore love the other disciples [TRT].

b. κόλπος (LN **17.25**) (BAGD 1. p. 442, 2. p. 55): 'bosom' [BAGD (1. p. 422), LN], 'breast, chest' [BAGD (1. p. 422)]. The clause 'was reclining on Jesus'/his bosom' [Gdt, NASB, similarly NTC] is also translated 'was leaning on Jesus' bosom' [KJV], 'was reclining next to him/Jesus' [NIV, NJB, NRSV, similarly NICNT2; REB], 'was reclining at table close to the breast of Jesus' [WBC], 'was lyng close to the breast of Jesus' [HTC], 'was sitting next to him at the meal' [CEV], '(was) sitting next to Jesus' [NCV, NLT], 'was sitting very close to him' [Ph], 'was at the table close beside Jesus' [AB], 'was dining in the place of honor next to Jesus' [**LN**], 'was at the table to the right of Jesus in a place of honor' [NET]. The phrase ἀνάκειμαι ἐν τῷ κόλπῳ literally 'to recline on the bosom' is an idiom that means 'to take the place of honor at a meal' or 'to dine in the place of honor'. These expressions in John 13:23 and John 13:25 would mean that the so-called 'beloved disciple' would be at the right of Jesus, since guests at a meal would be reclining on their left sides so as to permit freedom for the right hand in dining. It may, of course, be that the same expression could be used of persons sitting at a table rather than reclining on couches [LN]. It means 'to lean on someone's breast' meaning 'to take the place of honor' in case it was the breast of the head of the house [BAGD (2. p. 55)].

c. pres. act. indic. of νεύω (LN **33.485**) (BAGD p. 536): 'to nod' [BAGD, LN, NICNT2, NTC; Ph], 'to motion' [**LN**; CEV, NCV, NIV, NLT, NRSV, TEV], 'to beckon' [Gdt, HTC, LN; KJV], 'to gesture' [LN; NASB, NET], 'to sign' [NJB], 'to make signs' [WBC], 'to signal' [AB; REB]. This verb means to signal to someone by means of part of the body, especially by means of the head or hands [LN].

QUESTION—Who was the disciple whom Jesus loved?

It was probably John, the author of this Gospel [AB, BECNT, Car, CH, EGT, Gdt, ICC, Lns, My, NICNT1, NTC, TRT].

QUESTION—Did Jesus love John more than the other disciples?

Jesus loved all the disciples in the same way. John, however, had greater capacity for receiving his love than the others [Lns].

QUESTION—What was the seating arrangement at the supper?

The usual arrangement was several couches arranged in a U formation around the table. The participants would lie on their left sides with their heads toward the table and their feet stretched out away from it. They would support their head on their left hand and eat from the table with their right. The host reclined between two other guests on the chief table placed at the center of the U between its two arms. The place of honor was to his left and behind him and the second place was to his right or in front of him. The person reclining there, the beloved disciple, would have his head near the breast of the host [NICNT1]. Eating in a reclining position was observed only for special occasions, but was virtually obligatory for the Passover meal [Bar, Car, WBC].

QUESTION—In which position would the beloved disciple have been sitting?

He was probably seated to the right, or in front of Jesus [AB, Car, CH, EGT, ICC, IVP, Kn, LN, Lns, NICNT1, NTC, Rd, TH, WBC], so that when he leaned back, his head would be close to Jesus' breast [AB, Car, Lns, NICNT1, WBC].

QUESTION—In which position may Judas have been sitting?

He may have been sitting in the place of honor to the left of or just behind Jesus [AB, Car, ICC, Kn, NICNT1]. This position would facilitate Jesus' handing of the bread to him as he does in verse 26 [AB, Kn], or would have allowed him to speak to Judas privately [ICC]. Since this was the place of honor, it is possible that Jesus gave this place to Judas as part of a last appeal to him [NICNT1]. His being treasurer may have qualified him to have the place of honor [AB]

QUESTION—There are two possible readings of this verse. The first has Peter signaling the disciple *to ask* Jesus, the second has Peter signaling the disciple *to tell* who it was that Jesus spoke about. Which reading is correct?

1. The reading in which Peter signals John *to ask* Jesus is correct [AB, BECNT, Gdt, ICC, NICNT2, Rd, WBC; CEV, KJV, NCV, NET, NIV, NJB, NLT, NRSV, REB, TEV]: 'Simon Peter motioned to him and said, Ask him whom he is talking about' [TEV]. Against the following interpretation is the observation that they were all puzzled (13:22) and John would not know more than the others [ICC].
2. The reading in which Peter signals John *to tell* who it was that Jesus spoke about is correct [Bar, HTC, Lns, My, NICNT1, NTC; NASB, Ph]: 'Simon Peter nodded to this man and said, Tell us who he means' [Ph]. Peter assumes that because John was the confidant of Jesus, he would know about whom Jesus was speaking [My].

13:25 So that-one having-leaned-back^a thus^b on the chest^c of Jesus says to-him, "Lord, who is-it?" **13:26** Jesus answers, "It-is that-one to-whom I will-dip^d the piece-of-bread^e and give to-him. So having-dipped the piece-of-bread he-takes (it) and gives (it) to-Judas (the son)-of-Simon of-Iscariot.

TEXT—Instead of βάψω τὸ ψωμίον καὶ δώσω αὐτῷ 'I will dip the piece of bread and give to him', some manuscripts read βάψας τὸ ψωμίον ἐπιδώσω 'having dipped the piece of bread I give', others read ἐμβάψας τὸ ψωμίον ἐπιδώσω 'having dipped the piece of bread in I give', another reads βάψας τὸ ψωμίον ἐπιδώσω αὐτῷ 'having dipped the piece of bread I give to him', and one manuscript reads δώσω ἐνβάψας τὸ ψωμίον 'I give having dipped the piece of bread in'. GNT reads 'I dip the piece of bread and give to him' with a C rating, indicating difficulty in deciding which variant to place in the text.

TEXT—Instead of βάψας οὖν τὸ ψωμίον λαμβάνει καὶ δίδωσιν 'so having dipped the piece of bread he takes and gives', some manuscripts read βάψας οὖν τὸ ψωμίον δίδωσιν 'so having dipped the piece of bread he gives', others read καὶ ἐμβάψας τὸ ψωμίον δίδωσιν 'and having dipped the piece of bread in, he gives', and another reads καὶ βάψας τὸ ψωμίον δίδωσιν 'and having dipped the piece of bread he gives'. GNT reads 'so having dipped the piece of bread he takes and gives' with a C decision indicating difficulty in deciding which variant to place in the text.

LEXICON—a. aorist act. participle of ἀναπίπτω (LN **17.25**) (BAGD 2. p. 59): 'to lean back' [BAGD], 'to lean' [BAGD]. The clause 'that one having leaned back thus on the chest of Jesus' is translated 'having leaned on Jesus' breast like this, that one' [NICNT2], 'having leaned back on the breast of Jesus, he' [NTC], 'he, leaning back thus on Jesus' breast/bosom' [Gdt; NASB], 'the one who was dining in the place of honor next to Jesus' [**LN**], 'while reclining next to Jesus, he' [NRSV], 'the disciple leaned toward Jesus' [CEV], 'that disciple leaned over to Jesus' [NLT], 'that follower leaned closer to Jesus' [NCV], 'the/that disciple/he…leaned back against/on Jesus' chest' [AB, WBC; NET], 'that disciple leaned back close to Jesus' [REB], 'leaning back against Jesus, he' [NIV], 'leaning back close to Jesus' chest he' [NJB], 'lying thus, close to the breast of Jesus he' [HTC], 'he then lying on Jesus' breast' [KJV], 'he simply leaned forward on Jesus' shoulder' [Ph], 'that disciple moved closer to Jesus' side' [TEV]. The phrase ἀναπίπτω ἐπὶ τὸ στῆθος, literally 'to recline on the bosom' means to take the place of honor at a meal. It is possible, however, in view of the aorist participle in John 13:25 that the phrase could also be understood in a more literal sense to mean 'to move closer to the side (of Jesus)' [LN]. The aorist tense probably indicates a change of position [NICNT1].
  b. οὕτως (LN 61.9) (BAGD 4. p. 598): 'thus' [HTC, LN; NASB], 'simply' [BAGD; Ph], 'from his position' [AB], 'like this' [NICNT2], 'in this way, so' [LN], 'just, without further ado' [BAGD], not explicit [all translations except AB, HTC, NICNT2; NASB, Ph]. This adverb may refer back to what precedes [LN, BAGD] and means 'accordingly', that is, following Peter's nod [AB, BAGD, Rd].
  c. στῆθος (LN 8.36) (BAGD p. 767): 'chest' [AB, BAGD, LN, WBC; NET, NJB], 'breast' [BAGD, Gdt, HTC, NICNT2, NTC; KJV], 'bosom' [NASB], 'side' [TEV], 'shoulder' [Ph], not explicit [CEV, NCV, NIV, NLT, NRSV, REB]. This noun denotes the trunk of the body from the neck to the abdomen [LN].
  d. fut. act. indic. of βάπτω (LN 47.11) (BAGD 1. p. 132): 'to dip' [all translations], 'to dip in' [BAGD, LN]. This verb means to dip an object in a liquid [LN], or in something [BAGD].
  e. ψωμίον (LN **5.4**) (BAGD p. 894): 'piece of bread' [BAGD, Gdt, **LN**, WBC; CEV, NET, NIV, NJB, NRSV, Ph, REB], 'morsel' [HTC, NICNT2, NTC; NASB], 'morsel of food' [AB], 'bread' [NCV, NLT, TEV], 'sop' [KJV], 'bit of bread' [BAGD, LN]. This noun denotes a small piece or bit of bread [BAGD, LN].
QUESTION—What does the adverb οὕτως indicate?
  It literally means 'just as he was' or 'accordingly' or 'without more ado' [AB, HTC]. It means, He thus, that is, he, prompted by Peter's suggestion [Lns, Rd]. The translation 'as he was' may have the meaning that instead of turning around to speak to Jesus he just leaned back a little 'keeping the same attitude' [NICNT1]. It means he kept the same attitude of reclining in

JOHN 13:25–26 191

Jesus' bosom and leaned back a little [ICC]. He stayed as he was and threw his head back so he could speak to Jesus privately [TH].

QUESTION—Into what did Jesus dip the piece of bread?

He dipped it into the dish of sauce they were eating with the bread [AB, Bar, Car, CH, Kn, LN, Lns, My, NICNT2, NTC, TH, TRT, WBC; CEV, NCV, NET, NIV, NJB, NLT, NRSV, Ph, REB, TEV]: 'I will dip this piece of bread in the sauce' [CEV].

QUESTION—What words are emphasized in this verse?

The pronoun ἐγώ 'I' is emphatic [Lns, My]: '*I, for my part*' [My]. The pronoun ἐκεῖνος 'that one' is emphatic [Lns, TH]: '*He* for whom *I myself* shall dip' [Lns].

QUESTION—Is there any significance to Jesus' action of giving a piece of bread to Judas?

Giving food to a guest was a sign of honor [BECNT, Car, CH, Gdt, IVP, NICNT1], or hospitality [NICNT2, TH], or friendship [BECNT, Car, ICC, IVP, WBC], of favor [EGT, Kn, NICNT1, WBC], or love [Car, Kn]. As such it was an appeal [Gdt, NICNT1] to the conscience of Judas [Gdt]. Jesus' action is simply an answer to John's question, Who is it? and served as a warning to Judas of the enormity of his action—he was betraying the one from whose hand he had taken nourishment [HTC]. This act typically indicated who the guest of honor was [CH].

QUESTION—Did the other disciples hear what was said between John and Jesus?

Jesus' response must have been given quietly since the other disciples are not aware later of the reason of Judas's departure (27–30) [BECNT, Car, TRT]. Both the fact that John moved close to Jesus and that the disciples did not understand the meaning of Jesus' words to Judas (verses 28–29) may indicate that both John's question and Jesus' reply were quietly spoken [WBC]. The other disciples did not know why Judas left indicating that only Jesus and John were in on this dialogue [TRT]. Peter was too far removed to hear the quietly spoken words [IVP]. John leaned close to Jesus' breast so he could speak directly to him and be only heard by him [EGT, TH], or he leaned close as if to whisper in Jesus' ear [NICNT2]. He spoke in a whisper so others could not hear him [ICC, Lns, My, NICNT2]. The words were spoken quietly so only the beloved disciple knew the identity of the betrayer [IVP].

QUESTION—Should the text read 'Judas (son) of Simon Iscariot' or Judas Iscariot, (son) of Simon'?

1. The best reading is 'Judas, son of Simon Iscariot' [AB, Bar, BECNT, GNT, HTC, Lns, NICNT2, NTC, TH, WBC; CEV, NASB, NJB, NLT, NRSV, REB, TEV]. The phrase means, 'Judas, son of Simon (man of) Kerioth' [BECNT, Lns, NICNT1].
2. The best reading is 'Judas Iscariot, son of Simon' [Gdt; KJV, NCV, NET, NIV, Ph].

JOHN 13:27–28

DISCOURSE UNIT—13:27–30 [HTC]. The topic is Judas's departure.

13:27 After the piece-of-bread Satan[a] then entered[b] into that-one. So Jesus says to-him, "Do what you(sg)-do quickly.[c]" **13:28** But of-the-ones reclining no-one knew for what (purpose) he-spoke this to-him.

LEXICON—a. Σατανᾶς (LN 12.34) (BAGD p. 745): 'Satan' [BAGD, LN; all translations], 'Devil' [LN]. This noun is a borrowing from Aramaic, and is a title for the Devil. It literally means 'adversary'. He is the principal supernatural evil being. In a number of languages there is a well-known proper name for the Devil as the chief of all demons. In other instances, however, he is given a descriptive name, for example, 'the ruler of the evil spirits', 'the chief of the demons', 'the truly bad one', 'the left-handed one' (as the one who is opposed to all that is right or correct), 'the no-good one', 'the avaricious one'. In some instances a term for the Devil may be highly idiomatic as, for example, 'the barking one', a reference to the Devil's presumed activity in animal guise [LN]. In our literature his name means 'adversary' in a very special sense, the enemy of God and all of those who belong to God [BAGD]. This is the first time in the book of John that Satan is mentioned by name so it may be important to translate that he is 'the ruler over evil spirits' [TRT].

b. aorist act. indic. of εἰσέρχομαι (LN 15.93) (BAGD 1.b.β. p. 232): 'to enter' [BAGD, LN], 'to go into, to come into' [BAGD, LN], 'to move into' [LN]. The clause 'Satan entered into that one/him' [AB, Gdt, HTC, NICNT2, NTC, WBC; KJV, NASB, NET, NIV, NLT, NRSV, TEV] is also translated 'Satan entered him' [NCV, NJB, REB], 'Satan entered his heart' [Ph], 'Satan took control of Judas' [CEV]. This clause may be more clearly translated 'Satan took control of him' [TH, TRT] or 'Satan started to command him' [TH]. It indicates complete mastery by Satan [HTC], thorough possession [Car], complete spiritual possession [Lns]. This verb means to move into a space, either two-dimensional or three-dimensional [LN].

c. ταχύς (LN **67.110**) (BAGD 2.b. p. 807): 'quickly' [BAGD, **LN**; all translations except AB, NTC; NLT, Ph, TEV], 'more quickly' [Lns, NTC], 'hurriedly' [LN], 'without delay, at once' [BAGD]. This adverb is also translated as a verb or verbal phrase: 'Hurry (and do what you must/you're going to do)' [NLT, TEV], 'Be quick (and do)/(about your business!)' [AB; Ph]. This adverb describes an action as having very short extent of time. The emphasis is on the brief period of time before Judas is to do what he had set out to do [LN]. The form τάχιον may be a comparative similar to its use in verse 20:4 meaning to '(do) more quickly [Bar, Car, ICC, My, NICNT1, NTC] than you were planning' [Car, ICC, Lns, NICNT1].

QUESTION—What was the purpose of handing the piece of bread to Judas?
Jesus was only using the bread to indicate who was going to betray him and not to do sorcery on Judas. It is important that translations avoid this implication [TRT].

QUESTION—What information is implied in the phrase 'after the piece-of-bread'?
Different verbs are used to supply the implied information: 'After *he received* the piece of bread' [NRSV, similarly REB], 'as soon as *Judas took* the bread' [NCV, NIV, similarly Gdt, Lns, TRT; NET, NJB, Ph, TEV], 'when *Judas had eaten* the bread' [NLT, similarly TRT]. It was after Jesus *gave* the piece of bread [ICC, My].

QUESTION—What is indicated by the adverb τότε 'then'?
It points to the precise moment when Satan took control of Judas [Bar]. Or it stresses the moment of final decision [ICC], or the horribly tragic moment [My].

QUESTION—What is implied in the present tense of the verb 'what you do'?
It implies that Judas *was going to* do this [AB, HTC, WBC; NCV, NJB, NLT, NRSV], 'what *you are about to* do' [Bar; NET, NIV], 'what *you have to* do' [CEV, similarly REB], 'do what *you must*' [TEV], 'what you are doing' [NICNT2, NTC], 'what *you are bent on* doing/cannot leave undone' [Bar], 'what *you are occupied with*/what *you have begun*' [Lns], 'what *you purpose* to do' [My].

13:29 For some were-thinking,[a] since Judas had the money-box,[b] that Jesus says to-him, "Buy the-things-that we-have need (of) for the feast,[c]" or so-that he-should-give something to-the poor. **13:30** So having-taken the piece-of-bread that-one immediately[d] went-out. And it-was night.

LEXICON—a. imperf. act. indic. of δοκέω (LN 31.29): 'to think' [LN; all translations except AB, WBC; NASB, REB], 'to suppose' [LN, WBC; NASB, REB], 'to presume, to assume, to imagine, to believe' [LN]. The words 'some were thinking' is translated 'some had the idea' [AB]. This verb means to regard something as presumably true, but without particular certainty. In some languages the equivalent of 'to suppose' or 'to presume' is 'to think somewhat' or 'to think perhaps' or 'to think a little'. In some instances the lack of certainty is spelled out clearly as 'to think, but not with certainty' or 'to think, but not to know' or 'to think, but not to be sure' [LN].

b. γλωσσόκομον (LN **6.143**) (BAGD p. 162): 'moneybox' [BAGD, **LN**]. The clause 'since/because Judas had the money box' [HTC, NICNT2, NTC; NASB, NET] is also translated 'since Judas used to keep the money-box' [WBC], 'since Judas held the money box' [AB], 'since he was the one who kept the money box' [NCV], 'since Judas was in charge of the money box' [LN], 'because/as Judas had the bag' [Gdt; KJV], 'since Judas had the common purse' [NRSV], 'since/as Judas had charge of the money/purse/common purse' [NIV, Ph, REB], 'because/since Judas was in charge of the money/money bag' [CEV, TEV], 'since Judas had charge of the common fund' [NJB], 'since Judas was their treasurer' [NLT]. This noun denotes a box in which money was kept. It may be useful, however, in rendering John 13:29 to simply say 'Judas had charge of the money' or 'Judas was the treasurer of the group', since the Greek expression may be understood as an idiom [LN]. The idiom meant that Judas handled the joint funds of the group [TH]. Originally γλωσσόκομον meant a case for the mouthpiece or reed of a flute and then generally a case for anything at all [BAGD].

c. ἑορτή (LN **51.2**) (BAGD p. 280): 'feast' [AB, Gdt, HTC, BAGD, **LN**; NTC, WBC; KJV, NASB, NCV, NET, NRSV, Ph, REB, TEV], 'festival' [BAGD, LN, NICNT2; CEV, NJB], 'Feast' [NIV], 'celebration' [LN]. The words 'buy the things we have need of for the feast' is translated 'Jesus was telling him to go and pay for the food' [NLT]. This noun denotes the events associated with the celebration of a festival or feast [LN].

d. εὐθύς (LN 67.53) (BAGD p. 321): 'immediately' [BAGD, Gdt, HTC, LN, NICNT2, NTC; KJV, NASB, NCV, NET, NRSV], 'at once' [BAGD, WBC; NLT, TEV], 'right away' [LN], 'then' [LN], not explicit [CEV]. The sentence 'So having taken the piece of bread, that one immediately went out' is translated 'as soon as Judas had taken the piece of bread/the bread, he went out' [NIV, NJB, similarly AB; REB]. This adverb describes a point of time immediately subsequent to a previous point of time (the actual interval of time differs appreciably, depending on the nature of the events and the manner in which the sequence is interpreted by the writer) [LN].

QUESTION—What relationship is indicated by the conjunction γάρ 'for'?

It indicates that John is explaining with these guesses that no one knew what Jesus had meant by his words to Judas [Lns]. It indicates that this verse is the proof that they really did not know what Jesus' words to Judas had meant [My]. John uses this conjunction simply to introduce his own comment about what he has been writing [ICC].

QUESTION—What is implied by the words 'It was night'?

'Night' indicated for Judas the sphere of darkness into which he was entering [HTC]. It was night both outside the room and in the heart of Judas [NTC]. For Judas it was spiritual darkness that he entered [BECNT]. For Jesus too it was night—the hour when darkness reigns (Luke 22:53) [Car]. It marked the end of the 'day' the Father had given him in which he had to do the will of God [Rd].

QUESTION—What information is implied in the clause 'or so that he should give something to the poor'?

The words 'that he had said it' are implied [NTC]: 'or (that he had said it) in order that Judas might give something to the poor' [NTC].

DISCOURSE UNIT—13:31–17:26 [AB]. The topic is the last discourse.

DISCOURSE UNIT—13:31–16:33 [BECNT]. The topic is final instructions.

DISCOURSE UNIT—13:31–14:31 [BECNT, Car, CH, HTC, WBC]. The topic is the departure and return of Jesus [WBC], Jesus' departure and sending of the Spirit [BECNT], Jesus: the way, the truth and the life [CEV], farewell discourse [Car, HTC].

JOHN 13:31–32

DISCOURSE UNIT—13:31-38 [AB, Bar, BECNT, Car, WBC; NCV, NIV, NJB, NLT]. The topic is the last discourse [AB], transition to last discourses [Bar; NJB], Jesus' departure [BECNT], Jesus predicts Peter's denial [Car; NCV, NIV, NLT].

DISCOURSE UNIT—13:31-35 [HTC, IVP, NICNT1; CEV, NRSV, TEV]. The topic is the farewell discourse [IVP], announcement of Jesus' departure [HTC], the new commandment [NICNT1; CEV, NRSV, TEV].

13:31 So when he-went-out, Jesus says, "Now the Son-of-Man[a] is-glorified,[b] and God is-glorified in[c] him. **13:32** If[d] God is-glorified in[e] him, God will-glorify him in him (-self) and he-will-glorify him immediately.[f]

TEXT—In verse 32 some manuscripts omit εἰ ὁ θεὸς ἐδοξάσθη ἐν αὐτῷ 'if God has been glorified in him'. GNT includes this clause with a C decision, indicating difficulty in deciding whether or not to include it in the text.

TEXT—In verse 32 instead of the second occurrence of ἐν αὐτῷ 'in him', some manuscripts read ἐν ἑαυτῷ 'in himself'. GNT reads 'in him' with a B rating, indicating that the text is almost certain.

LEXICON—a. υἱὸς τοῦ ἀνθρώπου (LN 9.3) (BAGD 2.c. p. 835): 'Son of Man' [BAGD, LN; all translations]. This phrase is a title with Messianic implications used by Jesus concerning himself [LN]. The title 'Son of Man' served not only to affirm but also to hide Christ's Messianic role. In a number of languages there are serious complications involved in a literal translation of υἱὸς τοῦ ἀνθρώπου 'Son of Man'. In the first place, this is likely to be understood in a more or less literal sense of 'son of a man' and thus a denial of the virgin birth. Such is particularly true in languages which have two words for 'son' one meaning 'son of a man' and the other, 'son of a woman'. Under such circumstances, a literal translation would be a clear denial of the virgin birth [LN]. Jewish thought contemporary with Jesus knows of a heavenly being looked on as a 'Son of Man' or 'Man', who exercises Messianic functions such as judging the world. This concept is in some way connected with Daniel 7:13 [BAGD]. Outside of the NT the Son of Man is a figure of glory (Daniel 7:13). In the Synoptics he is a figure of suffering. John joins these two notions of glory and suffering in his depiction of the Son of Man [Bar].

b. aorist pass. indic. of δοξάζω (LN 87.24) (BAGD 2. p. 204): 'to be glorified' [AB, BAGD, Gdt, HTC, LN, NICNT2, NTC, WBC; KJV, NASB, NET, NIV, NJB, NRSV, REB], 'to be given glory' [CEV], 'to make gloriously great' [LN], 'to clothe in splendor' [BAGD]. The clause 'Now the Son of Man is glorified' is translated 'Now the Son of Man receives his glory' [NCV], 'Now comes the glory of the Son of Man' [Ph], 'Now the Son of Man's glory is revealed' [TEV], 'The time has come for the Son of Man to enter into his glory' [NLT]. This verb means to cause someone to have glorious greatness [LN]. The whole life of Jesus is depicted as a glorifiying of the Son by the Father [BAGD]. The aorist tense views the glorification as a completed whole and adds certainty to the statement [NICNT1]. It views the events as so certain that it speaks of them as already completed [TRT]. It reflects Hebrew usage to use an aorist to indicate prophetic anticipation of future events especially when the speaker is God [ICC].

c. ἐν (LN 89.119, 90.6): 'in' [LN (89.119); all translations except CEV, NCV, NLT, TEV], 'one with, in union with, joined closely to' [LN (89.119)], 'through' [NCV, TEV], 'because of' [NLT], 'by, from' [LN 90.6)]. The clause 'God is glorified in him' is translated 'he will bring glory to God' [CEV]. This preposition with the dative indicates close personal association [LN (89.119)]. Or it indicates an agent, often with the implication of the agent being used as an instrument, and in some instances relating to general behavior rather than to some specific event [LN 90.6].

d. εἰ (LN 89.30) (BAGD III. p. 219): 'if' [all translations except NICNT2; CEV], 'since' [BAGD, LN, TRT; NLT], 'because' [LN], not explicit [NICNT2]. The clause 'if God is glorified in him' is translated 'Then, after God is given glory because of him' [CEV]. This conjunction indicates cause or reason on the basis that an actual case is regarded formally as a supposition [BAGD, LN]. When εἰ is used with the indicative tense (as here) it indicates that the condition has been fulfilled [NICNT1].

e. ἐν (LN 89.119, 90.6): 'in' [LN (89.119); all translations except CEV, NCV, NLT, Ph, TEV], 'through' [NCV, Ph, TEV], 'because of' [CEV, NLT], 'one with, in union with, joined closely to' [LN (89.119)], 'by, from' [LN 90.6)], not explicit [CEV]. This preposition with the dative indicates close personal association [LN (89.119)]. Or it indicates an agent, often with the implication of the agent being used as an instrument, and in some instances relating to general behavior rather than to some specific event [LN 90.6]. God is not merely glorified 'by' Jesus, but 'in' Jesus' character and behavior [NTC]. The word ἐν here means 'in union with' and not merely through. Jesus' glorification is God's glorification. 'God was reconciling the world to himself in Christ' (2 Corinthians 5:19) [Lns].

f. εὐθύς (LN 67.53) (BAGD p. 321): 'immediately' [AB, BAGD, LN, NICNT2, NTC, WBC; NASB], 'at once' [BAGD, HTC; NIV, NRSV, TEV], 'quickly' [NCV], 'right away' [LN; NET], 'straightway' [Gdt; KJV], 'now' [REB], 'soon' [NLT], 'very soon' [CEV], 'without delay' [Ph]. This adverb describes a point of time immediately subsequent to a previous point of time (the actual interval of time differs appreciably, depending on the nature of the events and the manner in which the sequence is interpreted by the writer) [LN]. 'Immediately' refers to Gethsemane, Gabbatha, and Golgotha which were about to happen [NTC].

QUESTION—To what does the adverb νῦν 'now' refer?

It refers to the present situation that has been produced by the departure of Judas from the last supper [AB, EGT, Gdt, Lns, NICNT2, NTC]. Judas now goes to the police to set up the arrest and death of Jesus [AB]. Now that the betrayal is underway Jesus' glorification begins [NICNT1]. 'Now' refers to Jesus' hour when he would depart from this world to the Father (13:1), and includes the departure of Judas and Jesus' suffering [HTC]. The coming of the Greeks was the first signal that Jesus' hour of glorification had come (12:23), the departure of Judas is the second [BECNT, IVP, WBC].

QUESTION—Should the verb form ἐδοξάσθη be taken to mean 'is glorified' or 'has been glorified' or 'will be glorified'?

Although the aorist points to a past event, it seems best in view of the context to use a tense that will indicate the immediate future. For example, 'Now the Son of Man's glory is about to be revealed' [TH].

'Is glorified' [HTC, NICNT2; KJV, NASB, NCV, NET, NIV, REB, TEV].
'Has been glorified' [AB, Gdt, NTC, WBC; NJB, NRSV].
'Will be glorified' [CEV, Ph].

QUESTION—What is the glory of God and what does it mean to glorify God and Jesus?

God's glory means his own essential worth, greatness, power, and majesty. The supreme characteristic of God is his love which is revealed in Jesus' self-sacrificial love [IVP]. The cross was the supreme moment of God's self-disclosure in which his glory was revealed in the shame of the cross [Car]. True glory that has been realized in Jesus' person consists of humility and love [Gdt]. The cross shows people the heart of God and of Christ [NICNT1]. To glorify God is to reveal his love for humankind [WBC]. By his suffering and death Jesus made God's love, truth, and righteousness shine out for the world to see [Lns]. Jesus wanted to reveal his glorious love for his people by suffering and dying for them. It was his glory to protect them by allowing the wrath of God to descend on himself while keeping them safe [NTC]. Jesus' glorification is a clear reference to his death and resurrection [TH]. In some languages glory could be translated 'Now people are about to see how the Son of Man will be honored'. In others it might be expressed 'Now people will soon see how wonderful the Son of Man is' [TH].

QUESTION—How is/was the Son of Man glorified?

His suffering and death reveal the true glory of the Son of Man [ICC, Kn, NICNT2, TH]. In John Jesus' glorification is a euphemism for the events surrounding Jesus' crucifixion [BECNT]. Jesus sees himself glorified by Judas's action in setting off his suffering and death [Lns]. The aorist refers to the feet-washing in which the glory of Jesus has been revealed [Bar]. The aorist tense indicates that Jesus' death and resurrection were so certain to him that he considered them already accomplished [CH, My, TRT].

QUESTION—How is God glorified in Jesus?

God is glorified in Jesus' suffering and death [Car, ICC, IVP, Kn, NICNT1, NICNT2, TH]. God is glorified by Jesus' perfect obedience [Bar]. God is glorified by Judas's action [Lns].

JOHN 13:31–32

QUESTION—How will God glorify Jesus in himself?

He will glorify Jesus by honoring him in heaven [Gdt, IVP, NICNT1]. This glorification is the taking up of Christ into the Godhead by God [ICC]. He will glorify Jesus in his death which is imminent [Bar, Car, IVP, Lns, NICNT2, Rd]. This glory refers to Jesus' exaltation through his resurrection and ascension [Bar, Car, Gdt, Lns, My]. By the word 'immediately' he is possibly connecting Jesus' glorification and the betrayal of Judas [Kn].

QUESTION—To whom does the phrase 'in him (-self)' refer?

It refers to God the Father [Bar, Car, EGT, Lns, My, NICNT1]. It refers to Christ. 'God will glorify him in him' means that God will glorify him (Jesus) in him, that is in his death [NICNT2].

13:33 Little-children,[a] I-am with you(pl) yet (a) little[b] (while). You(pl)-will-look-for[c] me and as I-said to-the Jews I-say also to-you(pl) now, 'Where I go you(pl) are- not -able to-come'.

LEXICON—a. τεκνίον (LN 9.46) (BAGD p. 808): '(little) child' [BAGD], 'my child, my dear friend, my dear one' [LN]. The words 'little children' [HTC, NTC; KJV, NASB, NJB, NRSV] are also translated 'children' [NICNT2; NET], 'my children' [WBC; CEV, NCV, NIV, REB, TEV], 'oh my children' [Ph], 'dear children' [NLT], 'my little children' [AB Gdt]. This noun is an extended meaning of τέκνον 'child, offspring' and denotes a person of any age for whom there is a special relationship of endearment and association [LN]. It is a diminutive of τέκνον 'child' and is used by Jesus in familiar, loving address to his disciples, or by a Christian apostle or teacher to his spiritual children [BAGD], or by a Rabbi to his students [Rd, WBC]. It is a term of endearment or affection [BECNT, CH, HTC, IVP, Lns, NICNT1, NICNT2, NTC, TH, WBC], or tenderness [EGT, Gdt, ICC, My, NICNT1]. Use of this term implies that there is not necessarily a large gap in age between speaker and addressees [NICNT2]. The phrase 'My dear children' would not be an over-translation [Car]. In view of the fact that John uses τέκνον on three occasions, we should take the diminutive τεκνίον, expressing affection, seriously. Jesus is speaking like a father to his children [NICNT1].

b. μικρός (LN 67.106): 'a little while' [Gdt, HTC, LN, NTC; CEV, KJV, NASB, NET], 'a short time' [LN, NICNT2], 'for a little while, briefly' [LN]. The phrase 'yet a little while' is translated 'a little longer' [REB], 'only a little longer' [AB, WBC; NCV, NIV, NJB, NLT, NRSV], 'such a short time' [Ph], 'not…very much longer' [TEV]. This adverb describes an event as having a relatively brief extent of time [LN]. It is a relative term in that here it refers to an interval of a few hours while in 7:33 it referred to an interval of about six months [AB, TH]. This term can refer either to Jesus' departure in death or in his ascension [Bar, NICNT1].

c. fut. act. indic. of ζητέω (LN 27.41): 'to look for' [AB, LN, WBC; CEV, NCV, NET, NIV, NJB, NRSV, Ph, REB, TEV], 'to search for' [NLT], 'to seek' [Gdt, HTC, NICNT2, NTC; KJV, NASB], 'to try to learn where something is, to try to find' [LN]. This verb means to try to learn the location of something, often by movement from place to place in the process of searching [LN].

QUESTION—Were the disciples Jesus' children?

A literal translation may be understood to mean that the disciples were his sons. If so, it may be better to translate something like 'my dear ones' or 'my dear companions' or 'you whom I love' [TH], or 'my dear friends' [TRT].

QUESTION—What is implied by the words 'Where I go you are not able to come'?

This was a reference to Jesus death and departure to the Father [TH].

QUESTION—What word is emphasized in this verse?

The pronoun ὑμεῖς 'you(pl)' in the clause 'you are not able to come' is emphasized [Lns]: '*You on your part* cannot come' [Lns]. The pronouns ἐγώ 'I' and ὑμεῖς 'you(pl)' are in strong contrast [NICNT1]: Where *I, on my part* go, *you, on your part* are not able to come.

13:34 (A) new command[a] I-give to-you(pl), that you(pl)-love[b] each-other,[c] just-as[d] I-love you that you(pl) also love each-other. **13:35** By[e] this everyone will-know that you(pl)-are my disciples if you(pl)-have love among each-other.

LEXICON—a. ἐντολή (LN **33.330**) (BAGD 2.d. p. 269): 'command' [BAGD, NICNT2, WBC; CEV, NCV, NIV, Ph], 'commandment' [AB, BAGD, Gdt, HTC, **LN**; KJV, NASB, NET, NJB, NLT, NRSV, REB, TEV], 'precept' [NTC], 'order' [BAGD, LN]. This noun is derived from the verb ἐντέλλομαι 'to command' (33.329) and denotes that which is authoritatively commanded [LN].

b. pres. act. subj. of ἀγαπάω (LN **25.43**) (BAGD 1.a.α.; 1.c. p. 4): 'to love' [BAGD (1.a.α.), **LN**; all translations], 'to regard with affection' [LN], 'to cherish' [BAGD (1.a.α.)], 'to prove one's love' [BAGD (1.c.)]. This verb means to have love for someone or something, based on sincere appreciation and high regard [LN]. The present tense indicates that they are to keep on loving [Lns, NICNT1, NTC].

c. ἀλλήλων (LN 92.26) (BAGD p. 39): 'each other' [BAGD, LN, NICNT2; CEV, NCV, NLT], 'one another' [BAGD, LN; all translations except NICNT2; CEV, NCV, NLT]. This pronoun indicates a reciprocal reference between entities [LN].

d. καθώς (LN 64.14): 'just as' [LN, NICNT2, NTC; CEV, NET, NJB, NLT, NRSV, Ph], 'as' [AB, Gdt, WBC; KJV, NCV, NIV, REB, TEV], 'even as' [HTC; NASB], 'in comparison to' [LN]. This conjunction indicates similarity in events and states, with the possible implication of something being in accordance with something else [LN]. It is not so much a comparative sense but a motivating sense like 'according to the way in which' or 'because' [HTC]. It denotes the basis of their love for each other—a love based on Christ's love [Bar, My]. This signifies that the disciples' love for each other must be a love that is ready to sacrifice itself for its beloved [ICC].

e. ἐν (LN 89.76) (BAGD I.2. p. 258): 'by' [AB, BAGD, Gdt, HTC, LN, NICNT2, NTC, WBC; KJV, NASB, NET, NIV, NJB, NRSV], 'by means of, through' [LN]. The sentence 'By this everyone will know that you are my disciples if you have love among each other' is translated 'If you love each other, everyone will know that you are my disciples' [CEV, similarly TEV], 'All people will know that you are my followers if you love each other' [NCV], 'It is by your love for one another, that everyone will recognise you as my disciples' [NJB], 'Your love for each other will prove to the world that you are my disciples' [NLT], 'This is how all men will know that you are my disciples, because you have such love for one another' [Ph], 'If there is this love among you, then everyone will know that you are my disciples' [REB]. This preposition indicates the means by which one event makes another event possible [LN]. It is used to denote the object to which something happens or in which something shows itself, or by which something is recognized [BAGD]. The phrase 'by this' indicates that this love was to be the distinguishing mark of Jesus' disciples [NICNT1].

QUESTION—Was the command 'to love' a new command?

It was new in that it was patterned after Jesus' love for his disciples [BECNT, Car, ICC, IVP, Kn, Lns, NTC, TRT]. The command to love others had already been given in Leviticus 19:18—'love your neighbor as yourself'—but this love was new in its motive. They were to love each other for Christ's sake [EGT, NICNT1]. It was new in that it was as Jesus' loved. It was a love that revealed itself in washing each other's feet and giving itself in death [HTC]. It is new in two ways. It first focuses on one's fellow believer rather than on one's neighbor [EGT, ICC, NICNT2]. And second it is a love that is based on Jesus' love for his disciples [Bar, My, NICNT2]. It was a self-sacrificial, self-giving, selfless kind of love (15:12–13) [BECNT, TRT]. The disciples are to enter into the loving relationship that exists between the Father and the Son (15:10) [Bar, Car, IVP, TRT]. The command is new in that it is the ruling relationship between the Father and the Son. So when the disciples love in this way they are revealing the Father and the Son [Bar]. It was new because it had a new motive power—the love of Christ himself [My].

QUESTION—What relationship is indicated by the two conjunctions ἵνα 'that (you love)' and 'that (you also love)'?

They indicate that the following clauses are in apposition to the phrase 'a new command' [Lns]: A new command I give to you, *that is*, a command to love each other.

QUESTION—What words are emphasized in this verse?

The words ἐντολὴν καινὴν '(a) new command' is emphatic by its position in the Greek text [NICNT1, TRT]. The words ἐν τούτῳ 'by this' is emphatic. It was this alone that marked the Christian as a Christian [EGT].

The pronoun ἐμοί 'my' is emphatic [My, NTC]: You are *my* disciples. The pronouns ὑμᾶς '(I loved) you(pl)' and ὑμεῖς 'you(pl) (also love each other)' are emphatic [My]: as I loved *you*, that *you, on your part* also love each other.

DISCOURSE UNIT—13:36–14:31 [NICNT2]. The topic is the four questions.

DISCOURSE UNIT—13:36–14:4 [IVP]. The topic is Peter's denial predicted.

DISCOURSE UNIT—13:36–38 [HTC, NICNT1; CEV, NCV, NRSV, TEV]. The topic is Jesus predicts Peter's denial [HTC, NICNT1; NCV, NRSV, TEV], Peter's promise [CEV].

13:36 Simon Peter says to-him, "Lord, where do-you-go?" Jesus answered him, "Where I-go you(sg)-are- not -able to-follow me now, but later you(sg)-will-follow. **13:37** Peter says to-him, "Lord, why am-I- not -able to-follow you(sg) now? I-will-lay-down-my-life[a] for you." **13:38** Jesus answers, 'Will-you(sg)-lay-down your(sg) life for[b] me? Truly truly I-say to-you(sg), until (a) rooster by-no-means[c] crows you(sg)-will-deny[d] me three (times).

LEXICON—a. τὴν ψυχὴν τίθημι (LN **23.113**) (BAGD I.1.b.δ. p. 816): 'to lay down one's life' [BAGD, LN], 'to give up one's life' [BAGD], 'to die voluntarily, to die willingly' [LN]. The clause 'I will/would lay down my life for-you/for-your-sake' [AB, Gdt, NICNT2, WBC; KJV, NASB, NET, NIV, NJB, NRSV, Ph, REB] is also translated 'My life for you I will lay down' [NTC], 'I am ready to die for you' [**LN**; NCV, NLT, TEV], 'I would die for you' [CEV]. This phrase literally means 'to lay down one's life' and is an idiom meaning to die, with the implication of voluntary or willing action. Though in English the phrases 'to lay down one's life' or 'to give one's life' do suggest a voluntary dying, a literal rendering of such expressions in other languages would not necessarily imply the same. It may therefore be necessary to use such expressions as 'to die willingly' or 'to die without resisting'. In some languages 'willingly' is expressed primarily as a negation of objecting, for example, 'I will not object to dying' [LN].

b. ὑπέρ (LN 90.36) (BAGD 1.a.ε. p. 838): 'for' [BAGD, LN], 'on/in behalf of' [BAGD, LN], 'for the sake of' [BAGD, LN]. This preposition with a genitive object indicates a participant who is benefited by an event or on whose behalf an event takes place [LN]. See previous item for version evidence.

c. οὐ μή (LN 69.5): 'by no means, certainly not' [LN]. This phrase is indicates emphatic negation [LN]. See the following item for version evidence.

d. fut. mid. (deponent = act.) of ἀρνέομαι (LN 33.277) (BAGD 3.a. p. 108): 'to deny' [BAGD, LN], 'to disown, to repudiate' [BAGD]. The clause 'until a rooster by no means crows you will deny me three times' is translated 'the cock shall not crow, till you have denied me thrice' [Gdt;

KJV], 'a rooster will not crow until you deny me three times' [NASB], 'the rooster/cock will not crow until/till you have denied me three times' [HTC; NET], 'the rooster will certainly not crow until you have denied me three times' [NTC], 'the cock will not crow before you deny me three times' [AB, WBC], 'before the cock crows, you will have denied me three times' [NRSV, REB], 'before the rooster crows, you will disown me three times' [NIV], 'before the rooster crows, you will have disowned me three times' [NJB], 'before a/the rooster crows, you will say three times that you do not (even) know me' [CEV, NCV, TEV], 'before the rooster crows tomorrow morning, you will deny three times that you even know me' [NLT], 'you will disown me three times before the cock crows' [Ph], 'never will a rooster crow until you have denied me three times' [NICNT2]. This verb means to say that one does not know about or is in any way related to a person or event [LN].

QUESTION—What did Peter imply by his question 'Where do you go?'

Peter had walked on the water with Jesus and had been on the Mount of Transfiguration with him. His question 'Where are you going?' simply implies 'Can't I go with you?' [Gdt]. Peter's question is a sorrowful query 'Lord, why are you going? Why must you leave us?' [NICNT2].

QUESTION—What is implied by Jesus words 'Where I go you are not able to follow me now, but later you will follow'?

Jesus' is talking about Peter's death [Kn, My, TRT].

QUESTION—What is implied by Peter's question, 'Why am I not able to follow you now?'

The question amounts to an assertion that there is no reason why he cannot follow Jesus now [Lns, TRT]: 'What in the world is to prevent me from following you now?' [Lns]. It seems to imply that he wants to go with Jesus [TRT].

QUESTION—What is the function of the rhetorical question 'Will you lay down your life for me'?

Jesus' question expresses doubt that Peter is ready to lay down his life for him [HTC, NICNT2]. Jesus' reply is in effect 'Really?' [BECNT]. Jesus' reply is almost contemptuous as he uses Peter's own words to question him [Rd]. Jesus brings into question Peter's bold assertion [NICNT1]. Peter's question implies irony [AB, Car, TH]. This irony may be expressed in some languages as 'How is it that you say you are ready to die for me?' or 'How can you say that you are ready to die for me?' [TH].

QUESTION—When does the rooster crow?

The implied timing of the rooster crow is in the morning [TH; NLT]: 'before the rooster crows tomorrow morning, you will deny three times that you even know me' [NLT]. It was apparently usual for roosters to crow in Palestine about 12:30 a.m., 1:30 a.m., and 2:30 a.m. so that the term 'cockcrow' referred to the watch between midnight and about 3 a.m. [Car]. The implied timing was in the night [TRT].

QUESTION—Did Peter deny Jesus three times to one person or several?
To avoid implying that Peter denied Jesus to only one person three times, it may be necessary to supply the words, 'on three different occasions' or to translate 'will say to different people on three different occasions that you do not know me' [TH].

DISCOURSE UNIT—14:1–17:26 [Rd]. The topic is the farewell discourses.

DISCOURSE UNIT—14:1–31 [Bar, BECNT, Kn]. The topic is Jesus' departure and sending of the Spirit [BECNT], Jesus' return and presence [Kn], Jesus' departure a basis for hope [Bar].

DISCOURSE UNIT—14:1–26 [WBC]. The topic is the discourse proper.

DISCOURSE UNIT—14:1–14 [AB, BECNT; CEV, NCV, NET, NLT, NRSV, TEV]. The topic is Jesus, the way to the Father [BECNT; CEV, NLT, NRSV, TEV], Jesus comforts his followers [NCV, NET].

DISCOURSE UNIT—14:1–11 [Lns]. The topic is Jesus' departure is good.

DISCOURSE UNIT—14:1–7 [NICNT1; Ph]. The topic is Christ, the way.

DISCOURSE UNIT—14:1–6 [Kn; NASB]. The topic is going to the Father [Kn], Jesus comforts his disciples [NASB].

DISCOURSE UNIT—14:1–4 [Car; NIV]. The topic is Jesus' promise of a place in heaven [Car], Jesus comforts his disciples [NIV].

DISCOURSE UNIT—14:1–3 [HTC, WBC]. The topic is Jesus' departure and return.

14:1 **Do- not -let-be-troubled[a] your(pl) heart.[b] Believe/You(pl)-believe[c] in God also in me believe/you(pl)-believe.**
LEXICON—a. pres. pass. impera. of ταράσσω (LN 25.244) (BAGD 2. p. 805): 'to let be troubled' [BAGD], 'to be disturbed, to be stirred up, to be unsettled, to be thrown into confusion, to be frightened, to be terrified' [BAGD], 'to be caused great mental distress' [LN]. The clause 'Do not let your heart(s) be troubled' [AB; NASB, NCV, NIV, NJB, NLT, NRSV], is translated 'Let not your heart(s) be troubled' [Gdt, HTC; KJV], 'Let not your hearts any longer be troubled' [NTC], 'Do not let your hearts continually be in turmoil' [WBC], 'Do not let your hearts be distressed' [NET], 'Let no one's heart be shaken' [NICNT2], 'Set your troubled hearts at rest' [REB], 'You must not let yourselves be distressed' [Ph], 'Don't be worried' [CEV], 'Do not be worried and upset' [TEV]. This verb is a figurative extension of the meaning of ταράσσω 'to stir up' (16.3) and means to cause acute emotional distress or turbulence [LN]. It indicates mental and spiritual agitation and confusion [BAGD]. The present imperative indicates that they should stop doing an action that they were already doing [BECNT, Lns, NICNT1, NTC, WBC]. This verb

is also used to describe the troubling of Jesus' soul (11:33; 12:27; 13:21) [NICNT1].
- b. καρδία (LN 26.3) (BAGD 1.b.ε. p. 404): 'heart' [BAGD, LN; all translations except CEV, Ph, TEV], 'self' [Ph], 'inner self, mind' [LN], not explicit [CEV, TEV]. This noun is used figuratively in the NT to denote the causative source of a person's psychological life in its various aspects, but with special emphasis on thoughts. It is often possible to render καρδία by a number of different terms depending on the immediate context, for example, 'mind, intention, purpose', or 'desire'. In many languages it is quite impossible to use a term meaning 'heart', since such a term may not lend itself to figurative extension in meaning. Often the equivalent of καρδία is 'liver', while in a number of languages it is 'stomach' or 'bowels' [LN]. This noun indicates the heart as the seat of physical, spiritual, and mental life as the center and source of the whole inner life with its thinking, feeling, and volition, particularly of the emotions, wishes and desires. Here it refers to sorrow [BAGD].
- c. pres. indic. act./pres. impera. act. of πιστεύω (LN 31.85) (BAGD 2.a.β. p. 661): 'to believe' [BAGD, Gdt, HTC, LN, NICNT2, WBC; KJV, NASB, NET, NRSV, TEV], 'to trust' [BAGD, LN, NTC; NCV, NIV, NJB, NLT, REB], 'to have faith' [AB, LN; CEV], 'to hold onto one's faith' [Ph], 'to have confidence' [LN]. This verb means to believe to the extent of complete trust and reliance [LN]. It means 'to believe in, to trust' in regard to religious belief in a special sense, as faith in the God that lays special emphasis on trust in his power and his nearness to help, in addition to being convinced that he exists and that his revelations or disclosures are true [BAGD]. The present tense indicates that the action should be continuous [Lns, NICNT1, NTC, Rd, WBC]: 'Continue to trust in God, also in me continue to trust' [NTC].

QUESTION—To whom is Jesus speaking?

He is speaking to all his disciples and it may be important to make this explicit so that those listening to the text being read, may be aware of this change from just addressing Peter to addressing them all. Some make this explicit by pluralizing 'heart', others by adding a speech formula such as 'Jesus said to them' [TH, TRT; similarly AB, HTC, NICNT2, NTC, WBC; CEV, NCV, NET, NIV, NJB, NLT, NRSV, Ph, REB, TEV]: 'Do not be worried and upset, Jesus told them' [TEV], 'Do not let your hearts be troubled' [NIV].

QUESTION—Why was it necessary to tell them to not be worried and upset?

The disciples know that Jesus is going away and they cannot follow him and that separation looms ahead. They are understandably worried so he encourages them [Car, CH, ICC, IVP, Rd]. It also worried them that Jesus had predicted Peter's denial [Car, CH, ICC, IVP, NICNT1].

QUESTION—Are the two verbs πιστεύετε 'you(pl) believe', πιστεύετε 'you(pl) believe' best taken as commands or as statement plus a command?
1. It is best to interpret both verbs as commands [Bar, BECNT, Car, EGT, Gdt, HTC, ICC, Kn, Lns, My, NICNT1, NICNT2, NTC, WBC; CEV, NASB, NCV, NIV, NLT, NRSV, Ph, REB, TEV]: 'Have faith in God and have faith in me' [CEV]. In favor of this interpretation is the imperative form of the first verb, 'Do not let your heart be disturbed', suggesting that these two should also be imperatives [Bar, My, NICNT1, TH]. That both verbs should be taken the same is the fact that Jesus claimed that God had sent him and that to believe in him and to believe in God were the same (12:44) [Lns, NICNT2]. In view of their loss of Jesus through death, and Peter's denial it is imperative that they 'keep on believing in God' [WBC]. Almost all the Old Latin manuscripts take these two verbs as imperatives [Bar, Car] as well as many early Fathers [Bar]. Whatever interpretation is chosen, it is best to keep moods of the verbs the same, that is, imperative-imperative or indicative-indicative. Both verbs link Jesus with the Father as the supreme object of faith. However given the context the imperative is more likely [Kn].
2. It is best to interpret the first verb as a statement 'you(pl) believe', the second, as a command 'believe!' [AB, Rd; KJV, NET, NJB]: 'You trust in God, trust also in me' [NJB]. Jesus appeals to their faith in God as the grounds for believing in him [Rd].

QUESTION—What is the function of the chiastic arrangement of this verse?
The Greek of this verse is arranged in a chiastic form, ABBA, as follows:
(A) Believe
    (B) in God
    (B) also in me
(A) believe.
This arrangement puts the emphasis on the word 'believe' of the A members [Lns].

14:2 **In my Father's house**[a] **are many dwelling-places.**[b] **But if not would-I-have-told/I-would-have-told you(pl) that/because I-go to-prepare (a) place for-you(pl)? 14:3 And if**[c] **I-go and prepare (a) place for-you(pl), I-am-coming again and will-receive you(pl) to myself, so-that where I am you(pl) may-be also.**

TEXT—Some manuscripts omit ὅτι 'that/because (I-go)' in verse 2. GNT includes it with a B rating, indicating that the text is almost certain. [AB, Gdt; CEV, KJV, NCV, NIV, NJB] do not translate this word: 'otherwise I would have warned you. I am going off to prepare a place for you' [AB].

LEXICON—a. οἰκία (LN 7.3) (BAGD 1.b. p. 557): 'house' [BAGD, LN; CEV, all translations except NICNT2], 'household' [NICNT2], 'dwelling, home, residence' [LN]. This noun denotes a building or place where one dwells. In a number of languages it is important to distinguish clearly between various types of dwellings depending on their size and presumed importance. Accordingly, in rendering οἰκία it is necessary to use a number of different terms roughly equivalent to the English series 'cottage, house, official residence, palace, temple', etc. In a number of languages one must distinguish carefully between a house and a home. A term meaning 'house' would be used in referring to any dwelling as a construction, while a term meaning 'home' would be used in referring to the more or less permanent dwelling of a particular person [LN]. The Father's house is heaven [Bar, Car, Gdt, ICC, IVP, NICNT1, NICNT2, NTC, TH].

b. μονή (LN **85.76**) (BAGD 2. p. 527): 'dwelling place' [AB, BAGD, LN, NTC; NASB, NET, NRSV, REB], 'dwelling' [NICNT2, WBC], 'room' [BAGD, HTC; CEV, NIV, Ph, TEV], 'mansion' [Gdt; KJV], 'abode' [BAGD], 'place' [LN]. This noun is also translated as a phrase: 'place to live in' [NJB], 'more than enough room' [NLT]. This noun denotes a place where one may remain or dwell [LN]. It probably indicates some kind of permanent residence [Bar, BECNT, Car, HTC, ICC, Lns, NICNT1, TH]. The phrase 'many dwelling places' indicates that there is ample room in heaven [BECNT, Car, Gdt, Lns, NICNT1, NTC, TH]. The only other NT occurrence of this word is translated 'home' in 14:23 'Jesus replied, If anyone loves me, he will obey my teaching. My Father will love him, and we will come to him and make our *home* with him' [BECNT].

c. ἐάν (BAGD I.1.d. p. 211): 'if' [Gdt, NICNT2, WBC; KJV, NASB, NET, NIV, NRSV, REB], 'when' [AB, BAGD, HTC, NTC; NLT], 'after' [CEV, NCV, NJB, TEV], 'whenever' [BAGD]. The clause 'And if I go and prepare a place for you' is translated 'It is true that I am going away to prepare a place for you' [Ph], 'After I have done this' [CEV]. When used with the subjunctive (as here) this conjunction denotes what is expected to occur, under certain circumstances. At times the meaning approaches closely that of 'whenever' or 'when' [BAGD]. Since this word means 'when' in this context [Lns, TH, TRT], it important that the conjunction chosen rules out any doubt [TH, TRT].

QUESTION—It is possible to translate 'I would have told you' either as a statement or as a question. Also, the conjunction ὅτι is ambiguous meaning either 'that' or 'because'. Which is better and how should we translate ὅτι?

1. This conditional sentence should be taken as a statement [AB, Bar, EGT, Gdt, My, NICNT1, NICNT2, NTC, WBC; KJV, NASB, NET, REB, TEV]

1.1 With the following support clause introduced by ὅτι 'because' [Bar, EGT, My, NICNT1, NTC, WBC; NASB, NET, REB]: 'if it were not so I would have told you; *for* I go to prepare a place for you' [NASB, similarly REB], 'Otherwise, I would have told you, *because* I am going to make ready a place for you' [NET]. It may be best to take the words, 'if not, I would have told you' as a parenthesis as follows: 'In My Father's house are many rooms (if it were not so, I would have told you), for I go to prepare a place for you' [NICNT1, similarly Bar]. The ὅτι-clause gives the reason or proof of the many dwelling places in his Father's house, otherwise Jesus would not go away to prepare a place for the disciples in them [My].

   1.2 With the following clause introduced by 'that' [Lns, NICNT2, TH; TEV]: 'If not, I would have told you *that* I am going to prepare a place for you' [NICNT2], 'There are many rooms in My Father's house, and I am going to prepare a place for you, I would not tell you *this* if it were not so' [TEV]. The words 'if not' refers to the faith of the disciples in what Jesus had said, for example, 'But if not, i.e., if you had not believed this about the many mansions (as, however, I know that you have), I would have told you (as, however I have not needed to) that I am going to prepare a place for you' [Lns].

   1.3 Omitting the conjunction ὅτι [AB, Gdt, IVP; CEV, KJV, NCV, NIV, NJB]: 'if it were not so I would have told you. I am going...' [NIV], 'I wouldn't tell you this, unless it was true. I am going there to prepare a place for each of you' [CEV]. Taking all the possibilities into consideration, the translation without ὅτι makes the best sense [AB].

2. This conditional sentence should be taken as a question expecting a negative reply and the subordinate clause introduced by ὅτι 'that' [BECNT, GNT, HTC, ICC, Rd; NLT, NRSV, Ph]: 'If this were not so, would I have told you that I am going to prepare a place for you?' [NLT], 'If there were not many mansions, would I have said to you that I go to prepare a place for you?' [ICC]. If this is taken as a rhetorical question that expects a negative reply, it may be translated as a statement as follows, '(If not) I would not have told you that...' [TRT].

QUESTION—How should the present tense of come be understood?

It should be understood as a future tense 'I will come again' [ICC, Lns, TH; all translations except AB, NICNT2, NTC; Ph]. The present tense emphasizes the certainty of Jesus' return [ICC, TH]. This coming probably refers to Jesus second coming [AB, TRT].

QUESTION—What words are emphasized in verse 3?

The pronouns ἐγώ 'I' and ὑμεῖς 'you(pl)' are emphatic [Lns, TH]: 'in order that where *I, myself* am also *you, on your part* may be' [Lns].

DISCOURSE UNIT—14:4–11 [HTC]. The topic is admonition to believe.

DISCOURSE UNIT—14:4–6 [WBC]. The topic is Jesus the way to God.

DISCOURSE UNIT—14:5–14 [Car; NIV]. The topic is Jesus, the way to the Father.

DISCOURSE UNIT—14:5–7 [IVP]. The topic is Jesus, the way to the Father.

14:4 And you(pl)-know the way[a] where I go." **14:5** Thomas says to-him, "Lord, we-do- not -know where you(sg)-go. How[b] can-we know the way?"

TEXT—Instead of οἴδατε τὴν ὁδόν 'you know the way', some manuscripts read καὶ τὴν ὁδὸν οἴδατε 'and you know the way'. GNT reads 'the way' with a B rating, indicating that the text is almost certain. 'And you know the way' is read by Gdt, ICC; KJV, Ph.

LEXICON—a. ὁδός (LN 41.16): 'way' [all translations except Ph], 'road' [Ph], 'way of life, way to live' [LN]. This noun is also translated as a phrase: 'the way to the place' [NCV, NIV, NJB, NRSV], 'to the place (where I am going you know) the way' [NTC], 'the way that leads to the place' [TEV]. This noun denotes 'road' but is used here figuratively to mean a customary manner of life or behavior with some implication of goal or purpose [LN]. The way is not a literal road or path or a set of directions, but a 'way' to live, a commitment to follow Jesus [NICNT2]. It is the means by which people are brought to the Father [Lns, NTC].

b. πῶς (LN 92.16) (BAGD 1.d. p. 732): 'how?' [BAGD, LN; all translations], 'by what means?' [LN], 'in what way?' [BAGD]. This adverb indicates an interrogative reference to means [LN]. In rhetorical questions, as here, it calls an assumption into question or rejects it altogether, 'how (could or should)?' indicating 'by no means, it is impossible that' [BAGD].

QUESTION—Who was Thomas?

It may be necessary to translate 'Thomas' as 'his disciple, Thomas' so that reader will know who he was [TRT].

QUESTION—Is the question 'How can we know the way?' rhetorical and if so what is its function?

It is rhetorical and means that they think it is impossible for them to know the way [BAGD, ICC, NICNT1, TRT]. It could be translated 'how are we supposed to know the way?' or 'it's impossible for us to know/we can't possibly know the way to get there' [TRT]. Thomas' question expresses his perplexity [NICNT1]. Thomas emphasizes that they could not be expected to know the answer [ICC].

QUESTION—What word is emphasized in this verse?

The pronoun ἐγώ 'I' is emphasized [EGT, My]: 'Where *I, myself* go. The word ὁδός 'way' is placed last in the Greek for emphasis [Rd, WBC]: 'And *the way* to where I am going you know' [WBC].

14:6 Jesus says to-him, "I am the way[a] and the truth[b] and the life.[c] No-one comes to the Father except through[d] me.

LEXICON—a. ὁδός (LN 41.6) (BAGD 2.a. p. 554): 'way' [BAGD; all translations except Ph], 'road' [Ph], 'way of life, way to live' [LN]. This noun denotes 'road' but is used figuratively to indicate a customary manner of life or behavior, probably with some implication of goal or purpose [LN]. Here Jesus is the way—not a pathway, but a person. So both the way and the destination are persons [NICNT2].

b. ἀλήθεια (LN 72.2) (BAGD 2.b. p. 36): 'truth' [BAGD, LN; all translations]. This noun denotes the content of that which is true and thus in accordance with what actually happened [LN]. It denotes especially the content of Christianity as the absolute truth [BAGD].

c. ζωή (BAGD 2.a.β. p. 340): 'life' [BAGD; all translations]. This noun denotes the supernatural life belonging to God and Christ, that believers will receive in the future, but which they also enjoy here and now. Here it refers to Christ who received life from God [BAGD].

d. διά (LN 90.4): 'through' [AB, LN, NICNT2, WBC; NASB, NCV, NET, NJB, NIV, NLT, NRSV, Ph], 'by' [Gdt, HTC, LN, NTC; KJV, REB, TEV]. The sentence 'No one comes to the Father except through me' is translated 'Without me, no one can go to the Father' [CEV]. This preposition with the genitive case indicates an intermediate agent, with implicit or explicit causative agent [LN].

QUESTION—What word is emphasized in this verse?

The pronoun ἐγώ 'I' is emphasized [Lns, My]: '*I myself* am the way' [Lns], 'I (no other than I)' [My].

QUESTION—What is indicated by the Greek when the predicates of the verb (to be) all have their own definite article—I am *the* way, *the* truth, *the* life?

This construction indicates that both the subject and the predicates are interchangeable and identical. Jesus is the way, Jesus is the truth, and Jesus is the life and vice versa [Lns].

QUESTION—Are the words ἡ ὁδὸς καὶ ἡ ἀλήθεια καὶ ἡ ζωή 'the way and the truth and the life' in a coordinate relationship, or in some kind of subordinate relationship to each other?

1. 'Truth' and 'life' are subordinate to 'the way' and explain it or are the basis of it [AB, Bar, BECNT, Gdt, HTC, IVP, Kn, Lns, NICNT2, NTC, TH]: I am the way, *that is to say*, the truth and the life. In this passage, the topic has been 'the way'. Jesus introduces it in verse 4, Thomas continues the focus in verse 5 by his question, and the second clause of this verse focuses on Jesus being the way to the Father [AB]. The truth and life explain how Jesus is the way [AB, WBC]. He is the way because he is the truth or revelation of God and because God's life resides in him [WBC]. Jesus is saying that he is the means or way of coming to the Father in that he is the truth and the life [Gdt]. The way is the ruling predicate of the three. The words truth and life provide the benefits of the salvation to which the 'way' leads [NICNT2]. While all three serve equally to describe Jesus, in this context, the word 'way' predominates. It seems to mean that Jesus is the way because he is the truth and the life [AB, NTC]. The second half of this verse show us that the focus is on the way by which men come to God [Bar, TH]. The two terms, 'the truth' and 'the life' define 'the way' [Lns].

2. 'Truth' and 'life' modify 'the way' [TH]: the true way, the living way. This could be translated 'I am the true way, the way that gives people life', or 'I am the way that reveals the truth (about God) and gives life (to people)' [TH].

3. The three words 'the way', 'the truth', and 'the life' are simply in a coordinate relationship with each other [NICNT1]. The three nouns are all relevant pointing out the many sidedness of Jesus' saving work. 'Way'

indicates the link between man and God. 'Truth' indicates the complete dependability of Jesus in every aspect, and 'life' emphasizes that the only life worthy of the title is the life that Jesus brings, for He is life itself [NICNT1].

QUESTION—In what manner is Jesus 'the way'?

He is the way to the Father [AB, BAGD, Bar, BECNT, Car, CH, EGT, Gdt, HTC, IVP, Lns, NICNT1, NICNT2, Rd, NTC, TH, TRT]. In languages that cannot use 'way' or 'road' metaphorically to indicate the means to a goal, this could be translated 'I am the one by whom people know the truth about God and receive the life that God gives' [TH].

QUESTION—In what manner is Jesus 'the truth'?

He is the truth in that he reveals God to people [AB, BECNT, Gdt, IVP, My]. He is the reliable source of salvation [NTC]. He reveals the truth that leads to life [HTC]. He is the reliable one who is what he claims to be and does what he claims he will do [Rd]. He is reality [CH]. He is utter dependablility who brings us the saving truth of the Good News [NICNT1]. Jesus is the truth of God because he says and does just what the Father tells him to say and do [Car]. He is truth in that he is the revelation of God's character [Kn]. Since Jesus is the way to God who is the source of all truth and life, he himself then is the truth and life for men [Bar]. He is the source of the truth about God [TRT].

QUESTION—In what manner is Jesus 'the life'?

He is the source and giver of life to people [AB, CH, HTC, IVP, Kn, My, NICNT1, NTC, Rd, TRT]. He is the life in that he brings people salvation which is life in God [BECNT]. He is life in that he brings God to people [Gdt]. He is life because he has life in himself (5:26; 11:25) [Car].

QUESTION—How can the second clause 'No one comes to the Father except through me', be rendered positively?

It may be better in some languages to translate this verse positively such as 'All people must go to the Father by me' or 'I alone am the one by whom people go to the Father' [TH].

DISCOURSE UNIT—14:7–15 [NASB]. The topic is oneness with the Father.

DISCOURSE UNIT—14:7–14 [Kn]. The topic is revealing the Father.

DISCOURSE UNIT—14:7–11 [WBC]. The topic is Jesus the revelation of God.

14:7 **If[a] you(pl)-have-known[b] me, you(pl)-will- also -know the Father. And from now you(pl)-know him and have-seen him."**

TEXT—Instead of the perfect tense and a condition of fact εἰ ἐγνώκατέ με 'if you have known me', some manuscripts read the pluperfect tense and a condition contrary to fact εἰ ἐγνώκειτέ με 'if you had known me'. Another reads the aorist tense and a condition contrary to fact εἰ ἔγνωτέ με 'if you knew me'. GNT reads 'if you have known me' with a C rating, indicating

JOHN 14:7

difficulty in deciding which variant to place in the text. See first question below for version support.

TEXT—Instead of the future tense γνώσεσθε 'you will know', some manuscripts read the pluperfect tense ἐγνώκειτε ἄν 'you would have known', others read the pluperfect tense (with imperfect meaning) ἄν ἤδειτε 'you would be knowing', and still others read the perfect tense ἐγνώκατε 'you have known'. GNT reads 'you will know' with a C rating, indicating difficulty in deciding which variant to place in the text. See first question below for version support.

LEXICON—a. εἰ (LN 89.65) (BAGD): 'if' [LN; all translations except TEV], 'now' [TEV]. The sentence 'If you have known me you will know the Father also' is translated 'Now that you have known me…you will know My Father also' [TEV]. This conjunction indicates a condition, real or hypothetical, actual or contrary to fact [LN]. It is used here not conditionally but causally denoting a reality, 'since (you know me)' [Rd].

b. perf. act. indic. of γινώσκω (LN 27.18) (BAGD 1.b. p. 160): 'to know' [BAGD, LN; all translations], 'to become acquainted with, to be familiar with' [LN]. This verb means to learn to know a person through direct personal experience, implying a continuity of relationship [LN]. It is important to use a verb for 'know' that means more than just 'to get acquainted with'. A possible rendering would be 'Since you have come to know who I really am, you will therefore know who my Father really is' [TH]. This is a kind of knowing that comes by dialogue of one person with another [HTC].

QUESTION—Is the first sentence a statement of reality or a contrary to fact condition?

1. It is a statement of reality indicating a promise [Bar, BECNT, Car, HTC, Lns, TH, NICNT2, Rd, WBC; TEV]: 'Now that you have known me…you will know My Father also' [TEV]. This choice is almost demanded by the logic of Jesus' argument. He had already told them they knew the way (verse 4) and then explained that he was the way. In verse 9 he expresses surprise that Phillip does not know him. Further he has identified them with his sheep who know the Shepherd and his voice (10:4, 14) [NICNT2]. This interpretation fits better with the rest of the verse, 'from now you know him and have seen him'. It also fits well with the second part of verse 6 'no one comes to the Father except through me'. This positive statement is followed by 'if you have known me, you will know the Father also' [HTC]. That Jesus would deny that his disciples knew him as he did the unbelieving Jews (8:19) does not seem possible in view of the second part of this verse [Rd].

2. It is contrary to fact [AB, CH, Gdt, ICC, My, NTC, TRT; CEV, KJV, NASB, NCV, NLT, Ph]. The conditional sentence implies that the disciples have not really known Christ and have not known the Father [NICNT1]. In fact interpretation 2. fits better with the second half of the verse, but that may be the reason the scribes chose it. This interpretation is

therefore the more difficult reading and probably authentic [AB]. This reading seems to fit the context of verses 8 and 9 better [TRT]. Jesus' words are a reprimand. They did not know the Father because they had not yet learned to know the Son [ICC].

QUESTION—To what specific time does the phrase 'from now' refer?

It refers to the present time 'now, already' [HTC]. It does not refer to the moment Jesus is speaking but to the time of his suffering [AB, TH] and running through his ascension [AB]. It refers to the time during Jesus' ministry and includes his death and resurrection [Car]. It refers to the time when Jesus departs to his glory [Bar]. It refers to the time beginning from that very night and going through Jesus' death, resurrection, ascension to glory, and his sending of the Holy Spirit [Lns].

DISCOURSE UNIT—14:8–21 [IVP]. The topic is the relation of Jesus to the Father and the disciples to the Father.

DISCOURSE UNIT—14:8–14 [NICNT1; Ph]. The topic is the Father and the Son.

14:8 Philip says to-him, "Lord, show[a] us the Father, and it-is-enough[b] for-us." **14:9** Jesus says to-him, "I-am so-much[c] time with you(pl) and have-you(sg)- not -known me, Philip? The-one having-seen me has-seen the Father. How[d] do- you(sg) -say, Show us the Father?

LEXICON—a. aorist act. impera. of δείκνυμι (LN 28.47) (BAGD 1.a. p. 172): 'to show' [BAGD, LN; all translations], 'to make known' [BAGD, LN], 'to demonstrate' [LN], 'to point out' [BAGD]. This verb means to make known the character or significance of something by visual, auditory, gestural, or linguistic means [LN]. In some languages 'show us the Father' may be translated 'cause us to see your Father' or 'make us to see your Father with our own eyes' [TH].

   b. pres. act. impera. of ἀρκέω (LN 59.46) (BAGD 1. p. 107): 'to be enough, to be sufficient, to be adequate' [BAGD, LN]. The clause 'it is enough for us' [NICNT2; NASB] is also translated 'that will be/is enough for us' [AB, WBC; NIV], 'it suffices us' [Gdt, KJV], 'that is all we need' [CEV, NCV], 'we will/shall be content' [NTC; NET], 'we will/shall be satisfied' [HTC; NJB, NLT, NRSV, Ph]. This verb means to be sufficient or adequate for a particular purpose, with the implication of leading to satisfaction [LN].

   c. τοσοῦτος (LN 59.18) (BAGD 1.a.α. p. 823): 'so much, so great' [BAGD, LN], 'so long, so large' [BAGD], 'such a large' [LN]. The clause 'I am so much time with you' is translated 'I have been with you (for) a long time (now)' [CEV, NCV, similarly TEV], 'So long a time am I with you' [Gdt], 'such a long time I am with you all' [NICNT2], 'Have I been so long/such-a-long-time with you?' [NASB, similarly HTC, WBC; KJV, NET, Ph], 'Have I been with you all this time?' [NJB, NLT, NRSV, similarly REB], 'here I am with you all this time' [AB], 'after I have been among you such a long time' [NIV]. This adverb describes a thing as having a quantity considerably beyond normal expectations [LN].

d. πῶς (LN 92.16) (BAGD 1.c. p. 732): 'how?' [BAGD, LN; all translations except NCV, NLT, TEV], 'by what means?' [LN], 'in what way?' [BAGD]. The clause 'How do you say, Show us the Father?' is translated 'So why do you say, Show us the Father?' [NCV, similarly TEV], 'So why are you asking me to show him to you?' [NLT]. This interrogative particle interrogates by what means a thing occurs [LN]. It is used here in a question denoting disapproval or rejection 'with what right?, how dare you?' [BAGD].

QUESTION—What is implied by the rhetorical question 'I am so much time with you and have you not known me, Philip?'

It implies that Philip should have known him by now [TRT]. Jesus sharply corrects Philip—he should have known that the Father was seen in Jesus [HTC]. It is a gentle rebuke [BECNT, ICC, NICNT1, NICNT2, NTC, WBC]. Jesus' question implies his sadness at their lack of knowledge [Car, ICC]. It shows his surprise and regret at Philip's lack of knowledge [EGT, My]. He is deeply pained by Philip's lack of knowledge. Had his long association with the disciples been in vain? The poignancy of his question is brought out by the touching vocative at the end—'Philip?' [Lns].

QUESTION—What is indicated by the phrase 'have you not known me'?

The knowing is a spiritual kind of recognition of who Jesus was [NTC]. It indicates a lasting and real acquaintance [Rd].

QUESTION—What is implied by the rhetorical question 'How do you say, Show us the Father?'

It implies that there was no reason for him to say this [TRT]. It is a reproachful question [BECNT, WBC]. It implied disapproval or rejection 'with what right?, how dare you?' [BAGD].

QUESTION—What word is emphasized in verse 9?

The pronoun σύ 'you(sg)' is emphatic [ICC, NICNT1]: How do *you, on your part* say? Jesus means 'you who have followed me from the beginning' [ICC]. Philip was one of the apostolic band and one of Jesus' intimates—he should have known who Jesus was [NICNT1].

14:10 **Do-you(sg)- not -believe that I (am) in[a] the Father and the Father is in me? The words that I speak to-you(pl) I-do- not -speak of[b] myself, but the Father living in me does his works.[c] 14:11 Believe(pl) me that I (am) in the Father and the Father (is) in me. But if not, believe because-of[d] the works themselves.**

TEXT—Following the present imperative πιστεύετε 'believe' at the end of verse 11 some manuscripts add μοι 'me'. GNT rejects this addition with a B rating, indicating that the omission is almost certain. 'Believe me' seems to be read by AB, Gdt, HTC, Lns, NTC; CEV, KJV, NRSV.

LEXICON—a. ἐν (LN 89.119) (BAGD I.5.d. p. 259): 'in' [BAGD, LN; all translations except CEV], 'one with' [LN; CEV], 'in union with, joined closely to' [LN]. The phrase 'in the Father' is translated 'one with the Father' [CEV]. This preposition indicates a close personal association [BAGD, LN]. This relationship may be translated as 'my Father is united with me, and I am united with my Father' or 'my Father and I are just as though we were one' [TH].

b. ἀπό (LN 90.19) (BAGD V.5. p. 88): 'of' [BAGD, LN], 'by, on (the basis of), upon' [LN]. The phrase 'of myself' [Gdt, NTC; KJV] is also translated 'of my own accord' [WBC; NJB], 'on my own' [AB, NICNT2; CEV, NRSV], 'on my own initiative' [NASB, NET], 'on my own authority' [HTC], '(do not) come from me' [NCV, TEV], 'are not (just) my own' [NIV, NLT, Ph], 'I am not the source of (the words you hear me speak)' [REB]. This preposition indicates the one who is responsible for an event or state [LN]. It indicates cause, means, or outcome [BAGD]. In saying 'I do not speak from myself' he implies that what he says is derived from the Father [Lns].

c. ἔργον (LN 42.11) (BAGD 1.c.α. p. 308): 'work' [BAGD; all translations except CEV, NET], 'miraculous deed' [NET], 'deed' [BAGD, LN], 'act' [LN], 'action, accomplishment' [BAGD]. The phrase 'does his work' is translated 'does these things' [CEV]. This noun is derived from the verb ἐνεργέω 'to function, to work' (42.3), and denotes that which is done, with possible focus on the energy or effort involved [LN]. It is used here of the deeds of God, specifically the miracles [BAGD]. Jesus is referring to his supernatural works, his miracles [Car, Gdt, ICC, IVP, Lns, NICNT1, NTC, Rd, TH, TRT; NIV], or his signs [BECNT, Car, HTC, NICNT1, NTC, WBC].

d. διά (LN 89.26): 'because of' [LN; all translations except HTC; KJV, NIV, NJB, REB], 'for the sake of' [HTC; KJV], 'on the evidence of' [NIV, NJB], '(accept) the evidence of' [REB], 'on account of, by reason of' [LN]. This preposition indicates cause or reason, with focus on instrumentality, either of objects or events [LN].

QUESTION—What response is expected to the question 'Do you not believe…?'

The negative particle οὐ in a question indicates that a positive response is expected [Bar, Gdt, ICC, Lns, Rd, NICNT1, TRT, WBC]: 'You do believe, don't you, that I am in the Father?' [WBC], 'Certainly you believe that I am in the Father' [TRT].

QUESTION—What is indicated by the words 'I am in the Father and the Father is in me'?

They indicate the complete unity between Jesus and the Father [Car, HTC, IVP, WBC]. They indicate that the Father and the Son are one in essence or in all of their attributes and that they are essentially equal [NTC].

QUESTION—If the Father does his works in Jesus, does he also give him words to speak?

There is no contrast between Jesus' 'words' and the Father's 'works'. Jesus does what he sees the Father doing (5:19) [Rd], and included in the 'works' of the Father are the words and the miracles [ICC, Rd]. Both the words and the works of Jesus are given to him by the Father (5:19ff.; 8:28; 12:49) [Car].

QUESTION—Do the words πιστεύετέ μοι mean 'believe me' or 'believe in me'?
The meaning is not 'put your faith in me' but 'believe what I say to you' [NICNT1, TH].

QUESTION—What is indicated by the present tense of the command 'Believe me' in verse 11.
It indicates that the action is continuous or on-going [Lns, NTC]: 'Go on believing me' [Lns], 'Keep on believing me' [NTC].

QUESTION—What is implied by the words 'but if not'?
These elliptical words may be more fully translated 'If you do not believe what I say' or 'If you do not believe just because of what I say' [TH].

DISCOURSE UNIT—14:12–31 [Lns]. The topic is the peace of Jesus' disciples after his departure.

DISCOURSE UNIT—14:12–17 [HTC]. The topic is the Paraclete.

DISCOURSE UNIT—14:12–14 [WBC]. The topic is Jesus the power of the disciples' mission.

14:12 Truly truly I-say to-you(pl), the-one believing in me he-too[a] will-do the works[b] that I do he-will-do and/even[c] greater[d] than-these, because I go to the Father.

LEXICON—a. κἀκεῖνος (BAGD 2.b. p. 396): 'he too' [BAGD], 'he also' [BAGD, Gdt, NTC; KJV, NASB], 'the person...also' [NICNT2], not explicit [AB, HTC; CEV, NCV, NET, NJB, NIV, NLT, NRSV, Ph, REB, TEV]. This demonstrative pronoun is a combination of καί 'and' + ἐκεῖνος 'that one' and denotes the person or thing that is relatively closer [BAGD].

b. ἔργον (LN 42.11) (BAGD 1.c.α. p. 308): 'work' [BAGD; all translations except CEV, NCV, NET, NIV, Ph, TEV], 'thing' [CEV, NCV, Ph], 'miraculous deed' [NET], 'what (I have been doing)' [NIV, similarly REB, TEV], 'deed' [BAGD, LN], 'act' [LN], 'action, accomplishment' [BAGD]. This noun is derived from the verb ἐνεργέω 'to work, to function' (42.3), and denotes that which is done, with possible focus on the energy or effort involved [LN]. These works refer to Jesus' miracles [Car, Gdt, HTC, ICC, Kn, Lns, NTC, TH, WBC], but also to his signs [HTC, WBC].

c. καί (BAGD II.2. p. 393): 'and' [HTC, NICNT2, NTC; KJV, NASB, NET], 'even' [BAGD; CEV, NCV, NIV, NJB, NLT, Ph, TEV], 'and, in fact' [NRSV, TRT], 'and besides' [My], 'indeed' [My, WBC; REB]. This conjunction is also translated as an adjective: 'far (greater)' [AB], 'still (greater)' [Gdt]. It has an ascensive or intensifying sense here 'even' [BAGD, Rd].

d. μέγας (LN 78.2) (BAGD 2.a.γ. p. 497): 'great' [BAGD, LN]. The phrase 'greater than these' is also translated 'greater works than these' [HTC, NICNT2, NTC, WBC; KJV, NASB, NRSV], 'greater things than these'

[Gdt; NCV, NIV, Ph], 'greater deeds than these' [NET], 'greater works' [NJB, NLT], 'greater things' [CEV, REB, TEV], 'greater than these' [AB]. This comparative adjective describes the upper range of a scale of extent, with the possible implication of importance in relevant contexts [LN].

QUESTION—What is indicated by the present tense of the participle 'the one believing'?

It indicates that that person continues or keeps on believing [Lns, NTC]. The participle refers in general to 'whoever believes' and is not limited to the twelve apostles [BECNT, Car, IVP, WBC]. It indicates only the twelve apostles [My].

QUESTION—What words are emphasized in this verse?

The pronouns ἐγώ 'I' and κἀκεῖνος 'he too' are emphatic [Lns, My, NICNT1]: *that very one* also will do the works that *I myself* do. The pronoun ἐγώ 'I' is emphatic [NICNT2]. The words 'the works that I do' are placed forward with great emphasis [Lns].

QUESTION—How might the works of the disciples be greater than those of Jesus?

They would be greater in that they would encompass a greater geographical area than Jesus was able to reach [NICNT1, TH]. The book of Acts may show us what Jesus meant. It included some miracles but the stress is on the conversions to faith in Christ [Bar, EGT, ICC, Lns, My, NICNT1]. What Peter did at Pentecost and Paul did in his vast journeys are greater because they involve the work of the Holy Spirit who was only available after Jesus' glorification (7:39) [Gdt, My]. They included the missionary accomplishments of the disciples but beyond things that can be counted they indicate the increasing flow of God's power into the world [HTC]. It may be that greater meant more people, both Jews and Gentiles, would benefit from Jesus' death through the disciples. One prime example of a 'greater work' is the forgiveness of sins (20:22–23) [NICNT2]. Jesus' works were in the physical realm, the works of the disciples would be greater because they would be works in the spiritual realm—the conversion of Gentiles [NTC]. They are the conferring of the blessings and powers of God's kingdom on people that were made possible by the death and resurrection of Jesus [WBC]. They would be greater since Jesus' works were preliminary while the disciples' works would be based on Jesus' work on the cross—a more advanced stage in God's planning [BECNT]. The disciples would be giving to people the spiritual realities to which Jesus' works were merely pointing. They would be working in actual union with God and sharing in his very life as the result of Jesus' completed work [Car, IVP]. He certainly does not mean that the disciples would do greater works than raising Lazarus or giving sight to a man born blind [CH, Rd]. But in positions of authority over the kingdom that the Father had conferred on him, they would do greater works in the missionary mandate that he gave them [Rd], that is, in evangelism [CH].

QUESTION—What is indicated by the clause 'because I go to the Father'?
This probably has reference to Jesus' going to the Father and sending the Holy Spirit (7:39; 16:7) [Bar, Gdt, NICNT1, NTC, TRT]. It indicates indirectly the work of Jesus' cross, resurrection, and exaltation, following which Jesus would be able to work in and through his followers [BECNT]. It indicates that from His position of authority in Heaven he will do all that they ask in his name (verse 13) [My].

14:13 And whatever you(pl)-ask[a] in my name[b] this I-will-do, so-that the Father may-be-glorified[c] in the Son. **14:14** If you(pl)-ask me anything in my name I will-do (it).

TEXT—Instead of including verse 14 following verse 13, some manuscripts insert it following τοῦτο ποιήσω 'this I will do' in verse 13, others omit everything from ἵνα δοξασθῇ 'in order that (the Father) may be glorified' in verse 13 through all of verse 14, and still others omit it completely. GNT includes this verse following verse 13 with an A rating, indicating that the inclusion is certain.

TEXT—In verse 14, some manuscripts omit με 'me' and others read τὸν πατέρα 'the Father'. GNT reads 'me' with a B rating, indicating that the text is almost certain. The pronoun 'me' is omitted by Gdt, HTC, ICC; KJV, REB.

LEXICON—a. aorist act. subj. of αἰτέω (LN 33.163) (BAGD p. 26): 'to ask' [BAGD; all translations except NCV, NLT, TEV], 'to ask for' [BAGD, LN; NCV, NLT, TEV], 'to demand' [BAGD, LN], 'to plead for' [LN]. This verb means to ask for with urgency, even to the point of demanding [LN].

b. ὄνομα (LN 33.126) (BAGD I.4.c.γ. p. 572): 'name' [BAGD, LN]. The phrase 'you ask in my name' [all versions except CEV, NCV, NLT, TEV] is also translated 'you ask for…in my name' [NCV, similarly NLT, TEV], 'Ask me (and I will do whatever you ask)' [CEV]. This noun denotes the proper name of a person or object [LN].

c. aorist pass. subj. of δοξάζω (LN 87.24) (BAGD 2. p. 204): 'to be glorified' [AB, BAGD, Gdt, HTC, LN, NICNT2, NTC, WBC; KJV, NASB, NET, NJB, NRSV, REB], 'to be made gloriously great' [LN], 'to be clothed in splendor' [BAGD]. The clause 'so that the Father may be glorified in the Son' is translated 'so that the Father's glory will be shown through the Son' [NCV, TEV], 'so that/that the Son may/can bring glory to the Father' [NIV, NLT, Ph], 'this way the Son will bring honor to the Father' [CEV]. This verb means to cause someone to have glorious greatness [LN]. It is a favorite term in John in which the whole life of Jesus is depicted as a glorifying of the Son by the Father and, at the same time, of the Father by the Son [BAGD]. Being glorified refers to the visible display of God's presence [TH].

QUESTION—What is the function of καί 'and (whatever you ask)'?

It has the meaning of 'and thus' indicating that asking is the disciples' part in doing the greater works [Gdt, WBC]. It links this verse to the promise of 'greater works' in verse 12 in a causal relation. The disciples will do greater works because Jesus will hear their requests and do what they ask [Car, HTC]. The phrase 'this I will do' shows that what the disciples do, is Jesus' doing [EGT]. It indicates that this verse is also dependent on the word 'because' in verse 12—'*because* I go to the Father'. Jesus goes to the Father *and so*, being exalted to his position of power he will do all that the disciples ask in his name [My].

QUESTION—Who is the object of the verb 'to ask (in my name)' in verse 13?

The request is probably directed to the Father [EGT, Gdt, Lns, My; Ph]: 'Whatever you ask the Father in my name' [Ph]. The request is addressed to Jesus [CEV]: 'Ask me, and I will do whatever you ask' [CEV].

QUESTION—What does it mean to ask for something in someone's name?

It means to ask in a person's stead or on their part, as though recommended by that person and as though representing them [Gdt]. It may indicate 'Ask as if I were asking' or 'Ask what I would ask' [NICNT2]. It means: to ask for whatever is in harmony with what Jesus has revealed about himself [NTC], to ask with an appeal to Jesus [Rd], to pray in keeping with Jesus' character and interests [IVP, Kn], and in union with him [IVP, Kn, Lns], 'to ask as his representative [Bar, Gdt, Kn, TRT], to ask in keeping with all that Jesus' name stands for and with a desire to honor him [NICNT1], to ask as being those who have been sent by and are closely associated with Jesus [HTC]. The name of a person represents the person himself. Here the renderings 'because of your relation to me, because you are mine, because you are my followers, or on my authority' would be possible [TH].

QUESTION—What word is emphasized in verse 14?

The pronoun ἐγώ 'I' is emphasized [Bar, EGT, ICC, Lns, My, NICNT1, NICNT2, TRT]: '*I myself* will do it' [Lns]. This indicates that Jesus is not leaving the authority to do the greater works simply in the hands of his disciples. He is promising to continue to do greater works from Heaven in response to the prayers of the disciples [NICNT2].

DISCOURSE UNIT—14:15–31 [BECNT, Car; CEV, NCV, NLT, NRSV, TEV]. The topic is Jesus promises the Holy Spirit [BECNT; CEV, NCV, NLT, NRSV, TEV], Jesus' departure and coming of the Spirit [Car], teaching about the Holy Spirit [NET].

DISCOURSE UNIT—14:15–26 [Kn]. The topic is Jesus' coming and presence by the Spirit.

DISCOURSE UNIT—14:15–24 [AB]. The topic is the last discourse.

DISCOURSE UNIT—14:15–17 [NICNT1, WBC]. The topic is the coming of the Spirit.

DISCOURSE UNIT—14:16–31 [NASB]. The topic is the role of the Spirit.

14:15 If you(pl)-love[a] me, you(pl)-will-keep[b] my commands. **14:16** And-I will-ask[c] the Father and he-will-give you(pl) another Helper,[d] so that he-may-be with you(pl) forever.[e]

TEXT—Instead of the future indicative τηρήσετε 'you will keep', some manuscripts read the aorist subjunctive τηρήσητε '(if) you keep', and others read the aorist imperative τηρήσατε 'keep!'. GNT reads the future indicative 'you will keep' with a C rating, indicating difficulty in deciding which variant to place in the text. The subjunctive is read by AB: 'If you love me and keep my commandments'. The imperative is read by [Gdt; KJV, NLT]: 'If you love me, obey my commandments' [NLT].

LEXICON—a. pres. act. subj. of ἀγαπάω (LN 25.43) (BAGD 1.a.β. p. 4): 'to love' [BAGD, LN; all translations except Ph], 'to really love' [Ph], 'to regard with affection' [LN], 'to cherish' [BAGD]. This verb means to have love for someone or something, based on sincere appreciation and high regard [LN]. It means to have affection for [BAGD]. John defines love as being obedience in 1 John 5:3 'This is love for God: to obey his commands' [TRT]. This love is intelligent and purposeful [NTC]. The present tense indicates that the action is continuous and on-going [Lns, NICNT1]. This is the love of intelligent understanding and intentional devotion not merely of liking and personal preference [Lns].
  b. fut. act. indic. of τηρέω (LN **36.19**) (BAGD 5. p. 815): 'to keep' [AB, BAGD, Gdt, HTC, LN, NICNT2, NTC, WBC; KJV, NASB, NJB, NRSV, Ph], 'to obey' [LN; NCV, NET, NIV, NLT, REB, TEV], 'to observe, to pay attention to' [BAGD]. The clause 'you will keep my commands' is translated 'you will do as I command' [CEV]. This verb means to continue to obey orders or commandments [LN]. John ties the concepts of love and obedience together in 1 John 5:2 'This is how we know that we love the children of God: by loving God and carrying out his commands' [Car].
  c. ἐρωτάω (LN 33.161) (BAGD 2. p. 312): 'to ask' [BAGD; all translations except AB, Gdt, HTC, NTC; KJV], 'to pray' [Gdt, HTC; KJV], 'to request' [BAGD, LN; NTC], 'to ask for' [LN]. This verb is also translated as a noun: '(then at my) request' [AB]. This verb means to ask for, usually with the implication of an underlying question [LN]. It is important to note that Jesus is promising to ask for something rather than to inquire about a matter [TH, TRT].
  d. παράκλητος (LN 12.19) (BAGD p. 618): 'Helper' [BAGD, LN, NTC; NASB, NCV, TEV], 'Advocate' [NET, NLT, NRSV], 'advocate' [NICNT2; REB], 'Counselor' [HTC; NIV], 'Comforter' [KJV], 'Encourager' [LN], 'Mediator' [BAGD, LN], 'support' [Gdt], 'Paraclete' [AB, WBC; NJB]. This noun is also translated as a noun phrase: 'the Holy Spirit who will help you' [CEV], 'someone else to stand by you' [Ph]. This noun is a title for the Holy Spirit [BAGD, HTC, LN] and denotes one who helps, by consoling, encouraging, or mediating on behalf of someone. The principal difficulty encountered in rendering παράκλητος

is the fact that this term covers potentially such a wide area of meaning. The traditional rendering of 'Comforter' is especially misleading because it suggests only one very limited aspect of what the Holy Spirit does. A term such as 'Helper' is highly generic and can be particularly useful in some languages. In certain instances, for example, the concept of 'Helper' is expressed idiomatically, for example, 'the one who mothers us' or, as in one language in Central Africa, 'the one who falls down beside us', that is to say, an individual who on finding a person collapsed along the road, kneels down beside the victim, cares for his needs, and carries him to safety. A rendering based on the concept of legal advocate seems in most instances to be too restrictive. Furthermore, there may be quite unsatisfactory connotations associated with any word which suggests a lawyer, especially since in so many societies, a lawyer is thought of primarily as one who 'bribes the judges' or 'can speak two truths' or, as in one language, is 'a professional liar' [LN]. Παράκλητος denotes 'one who is called to someone's aid'. In the few places where the word is found in pre-Christian literature it has for the most part a more general meaning of 'one who appears in another's behalf, mediator, intercessor, helper'. In our literature the active sense of 'helper' or 'intercessor' is suitable in all occurrences of the word. In stating 'another Helper' it is implied that Jesus is also a παράκλητος [BAGD]. The role of the Holy Spirit is never seen as comforting the disciples. The general term 'Helper' is a better overall term [TH]. The idea of advocacy of one's cause is in focus [NICNT1]. The word παράκλητος literally means 'one who comes to (our) side when called on'. It is difficult to find one term that covers the meaning of this title because the Spirit's roles of comforting, helping, counselling, and consoling, also include the activities of advocating, exhorting and teaching [CH]. Jesus' role of strengthening and helping his disciples was now to be assumed by another [Car]. The KJV version's 'Comforter' is used in its original sense of 'strengthener' [EGT]. The phrase 'helping presence' may be the best way to render this concept [BECNT]. The ruling idea of this term is someone who offers assistance in a situation in which help is required [Rd].

e. εἰς τὸν αἰῶνα (LN 67.95) (BAGD 1.b. p. 27): This phrase is translated 'forever' [AB; LN, NICNT2, NTC, WBC; NASB NCV, NET, NIV, NRSV, TEV], 'for ever' [HTC; KJV, NJB, REB], 'always' [LN; CEV, Ph], 'eternally [BAGD, Gdt]. The clause 'he may be with you forever' is translated 'who will never leave you' [NLT]. This phrase indicates unlimited duration of time, with particular focus on the future and means 'forever, forever and ever' [LN], 'eternally' [BAGD, LN], 'to eternity, in perpetuity' [BAGD].

JOHN 14:15–16 221

QUESTION—What is implied by the conjunction ἐάν 'if'?
It implies that Jesus assumes that the disciples love him [Lns, Rd]: 'if you truly love me, as I know you do' [Rd]. It neither implies that they do love him or that they do not love him [Car].

QUESTION—What is implied by the adjective 'another'?
It implies that Jesus himself is also a παράκλητος 'Helper' [AB, BECNT, BAGD, Bar, Car, CH, EGT, Gdt, HTC, ICC, IVP, Lns, NICNT1, NICNT2, Rd, TH, WBC]. John calls Jesus a παράκλητος in 1 John 2:1 [Bar, Car, CH, EGT, Gdt, HTC, ICC, IVP, Lns, NICNT2, WBC]: 'But if anybody does sin, we have one who speaks to the Father in our defense—Jesus Christ, the Righteous One' [NIV]. The Spirit was going to replace Jesus' encouraging and strengthening presence with the disciples. When he does this it will be as though Jesus himself came and lived with them (14:18) [BECNT].

QUESTION—What word is emphasized in verse 16?
The pronoun ἐγώ 'I' in the contraction κἀγώ (καί + ἐγώ) 'and I' is emphasized [HTC, Lns, My, NICNT1]: 'And *I myself* will request the Father' [Lns]. After stating the part of the disciples, he emphatically introduces what he, on his part will do [My].

14:17 The Spirit[a] of truth,[b] whom the world[c] is- not -able to receive, because it- neither -sees[d] him nor knows (him). You(pl) know him, because he-remains with you(pl) and will-be in you(pl).

TEXT—Instead of μένει...ἔσται 'he remains (with you and) he will be (in you)', some manuscripts read μένει...ἐστιν 'he remains (with you and) he is (in you)', and others read μενεῖ...ἔσται 'he will remain (with you and) he will be (in you)'. GNT reads 'he remains (with you and) he will be (in you)' with a C rating, indicating difficulty in deciding which variant to place in the text. 'He remains (with you and) he is (in you)' is read by AB, ICC, NICNT2; CEV, NJB, TEV.

LEXICON—a. πνεῦμα (LN 12.18) (BAGD 5.e. p. 677): 'Spirit' [BAGD, LN; all translations except NLT], 'Holy Spirit' [My; NLT], 'Spirit of God' [LN]. This noun literally denotes 'spirit' and is a title for the third person of the Trinity [LN]. It denotes the spirit as that which differentiates God from everything that is not God, as the divine power that produces all divine existence, as the divine element in which all divine life is carried on, as the bearer of every application of the divine will. All those who belong to God possess or receive this spirit and hence have a share in his life. This spirit also serves to distinguish the Christians from all unbelievers. Here the Spirit is more closely defined by a genitive of the thing. The 'Spirit of Truth' is the Paraclete promised by Jesus on his departure [BAGD].
  b. ἀλήθεια (LN 72.2) (BAGD 2.b. p. 36): 'truth' [BAGD, LN; all translations except CEV, NLT, TEV. The phrase 'The Spirit of Truth' is translated 'The Spirit will show you what is true' [CEV], 'He is the Holy Spirit, who leads into all truth' [NLT], 'He is the Spirit, who reveals the

truth about God' [TEV]. This noun denotes the content of that which is true and thus in accordance with what actually happened [LN]. It refers to the content of Christianity as the absolute truth. The Spirit leads into truth [BAGD]. In verse 14:6 Jesus has described himself as the truth [Bar, NICNT1].

c. κόσμος (LN 9.23) (BAGD 7. p. 446): 'world' [BAGD; KJV, NASB, NCV, NET, NIV, NJB, NLT, NRSV, Ph, REB, TEV], 'cosmos, universe' [LN], 'people of the/this world' [LN, TH, TRT; CEV]. This noun literally means 'cosmos, universe', but is used figuratively to denote people associated with a world system and estranged from God [LN]. It denotes the world and everything that belongs to it, appearing as that which is hostile to God, that is, lost in sin, wholly at odds with anything divine, ruined and depraved [BAGD]. It refers to all humanity in opposition to God [Bar, WBC]. It is equivalent to 'unbelievers' [TH].

d. pres. act. indic. of θεωρέω (LN 32.11) (BAGD 2.b. p. 360): 'to see' [BAGD, LN; all translations except NLT], 'to look for' [NLT], 'to understand, to perceive, to recognize' [LN]. This verb means to come to understand as the result of perception [LN]. It refers to spiritual perception of the one sent by God, which is possible only to the believer [BAGD]. The word 'sees' is equivalent to 'perceives' [BAGD, NICNT1] and indicates that the world is unaware of the activities of the Spirit [Lns, NICNT1]. There is physical and spiritual sight. The world cannot physically see the Holy Spirit nor does it have the spiritual insight to detect his presence in the disciples [AB]. The world lacks the ability to see the Spirit. It has no spiritual eyes [My, HTC].

e. pres. act. indic. of γινώσκω (LN 27.18): 'to know' [LN; all translations except AB, NTC; NLT, Ph], 'to recognize' [AB, ICC; NLT, Ph], 'to acknowledge' [NTC], 'to become acquainted with, to be familiar with' [LN]. This verb means to learn to know a person through direct personal experience, implying a continuity of relationship [LN]. Knowing God indicates entering into communion with him [WBC]. The world has no personal relations with the Spirit [NICNT1]. This knowing indicates experiential knowledge of the Spirit [Lns].

QUESTION—What is the relationship of this verse to verse 16?

This verse is in apposition to verse 16 and serves to explain who the Helper is [Gdt, HTC, NTC, TRT; KJV, NASB, Ph]: '(Helper)...that is the Spirit of truth' [NASB].

QUESTION—How are the two nouns related in the genitive construction τὸ πνεῦμα τῆς ἀληθείας 'the Spirit of truth'?

The Spirit communicates the truth to people or guides them into the truth (16:3) [AB, Bar, Car, CH, EGT, Gdt, HTC, NICNT1, NTC, TH, TRT; CEV, NLT, TEV]: 'He is the Spirit, who leads into all truth' [NLT], 'He is the Spirit, who reveals the truth about God' [TEV]. It may also mean that the Spirit is truth [AB], or that the Spirit belongs to the truth [Lns]. It means that he both is the truth and as such guides people into the domain of truth

[HTC]. The Holy Spirit's teaching causes the divine truth to enter a person's soul and experience it [Gdt]. The Spirit reveals the reality about God [CH]. The Spirit communicates truth to people because he communicates the truth that Jesus is [Car]. This idea can be expressed as 'the Spirit who shows people what is true about God/what God is really like/who God really is' [TH], or 'who reveals the truth about God to people' [TRT].

QUESTION—How is it possible to receive a spirit?
Expressing this idea in some languages will require a verb that means more than just receiving an object. It not only means to welcome the Spirit into one's life but also to submitting to his control over oneself. Possible translations may be 'cannot receive him into their hearts' or 'cannot accept him as their helper' [TH].

QUESTION—Do the two verbs 'he remains (with you)' and 'will be (in you)' refer to the same or different times?
1. They refer to different times [Car, EGT, Gdt, IVP, Kn, Lns, My, NICNT1]. The Holy Spirit had been with the disciples in the presence of Jesus himself. He would be in them at Pentecost [Gdt, Kn, Lns]. The Spirit had been present with them in unique ways, but he would be in them after Jesus had been glorified and had sent the Spirit [Car].
2. They refer to the same time [Bar, ICC, NICNT2, NTC]. In the first verb, Jesus is speaking of the future event of Pentecost as though it were present. At which time the Holy Spirit would come to live in their midst and be within them [ICC, NTC]. Although the two verbs are in the present tense they refer to the same event in the future after Jesus has gone to the Father. At that time he will dwell beside them or be in them (the two verbs refer to the same reality [NICNT2].

QUESTION—What word is emphasized in this verse?
The pronoun ὑμεῖς 'you(pl)' is emphatic and contrasts the disciples with the world [Bar, Lns, NICNT1, TH]: the world…neither sees him nor knows him. *You, on your part* know him.

QUESTION—Does the phrase ἐν ὑμῖν '(he will be) in you(pl)' mean 'among you' or 'in you individually'?
It refers to the presence of the Holy Spirit in individual believers [Bar, HTC, ICC, My, WBC]. It refers not only to the Spirit's presence in the community but also to his inner presence in the individual disciples [HTC]. The two expessions 'with you' and 'in you' refer to the same experience [WBC].

DISCOURSE UNIT—14:18–24 [HTC, NICNT1]. The topic is Christ is revealed to the disciples [NICNT1], Jesus' return [HTC].

DISCOURSE UNIT—14:18–20 [WBC]. The topic is Jesus' coming at Easter.

14:18 I-will- not leave[a] you(pl) orphans,[b] I-am-coming to you(pl).
LEXICON—a. fut. act. indic. of ἀφίημι (LN 15.48) (BAGD 3.a. p. 126): 'to leave' [BAGD, LN; all translations except NET, NLT], 'to abandon' [BAGD; NET, NLT], 'to leave behind' [BAGD], 'to depart from' [LN].

This verb means to move away from, with the implication of a resulting separation [LN].

b. ὀρφανός (LN **34.21**) (BAGD 2. p. 583): 'orphan' [BAGD], 'helpless' [**LN**], 'friendless person' [LN]. The clause 'I will/shall not leave you orphans' [AB, Gdt, HTC, WBC] is also translated 'I will not leave you orphaned' [BAGD, NICNT2; NRSV], 'I will/shall not leave you as orphans' [BAGD; NASB, NIV, NJB], 'I won't leave you like orphans' [CEV], 'I will not leave you all alone like orphans' [NCV], 'I will not abandon you as orphans' [NET, NLT], 'I will not leave you helpless' [**LN**], 'I will not leave you comfortless' [KJV], 'I will not leave you desolate' [HTC], 'I will not leave you bereft' [REB], 'I am not going to leave you alone in the world' [Ph], 'When I go you will not be left all alone' [TEV], 'I will not leave you without a Helper and Friend' [ICC]. This noun literally denotes 'orphan' but is used figuratively to mean one who is without associates who may be of sustaining help [LN]. It literally denotes one who is deprived of one's parents [BAGD], or one who is fatherless [ICC, Kn], or 'one left without anyone to care for him' [TH].

QUESTION—Why does Jesus use the figure of an orphan?

It is not an unusual figure since the disciples of rabbis were called orphans on the death of their rabbi. For example, they called the disciples of Socrates 'orphans' after his death [AB, TH]. Also Jesus had referred to his disciples as 'Little children' at the beginning of this discourse (13:33) [AB, Gdt, NICNT1].

QUESTION—What is the function of the present tense 'I am coming'?

The present tense is used to refer to a future event [HTC, NTC; CEV, KJV, NASB, NCV, NET, NIV, NJB, NLT, TEV]: 'I will come back to you' [CEV]. It is used to give greater certainty to Jesus' return [NICNT1].

QUESTION—Do these words refer to Jesus' post-resurrection appearances, to his coming in the presence of the Holy Spirit, or to his Second Coming?

1. They refer primarily to the coming of the Holy Spirit [AB, CH, Gdt, ICC, Lns, My, NICNT2, NTC]. This refers to the time when the Spirit will be given, not to Jesus' second coming [ICC]. The lack of a connective at the beginning of this verse indicates a close tie with the thought about the Spirit's coming in the previous context (verses 16–17). So this promise of Jesus refers to his coming to the disciples through the Holy Spirit. In addition, the following passage, 19-23, builds on and develops the thought of this verse. The Spirit who comes at Pentecost is, in a sense, Jesus returning to his disciples [Gdt]. Both the immediately preceding and the immediately following contexts refer to the conferring of the Spirit [Gdt, ICC]. Jesus is referring to a more continued presence with the disciples than his post-resurrection appearances would provide [AB]. Jesus' promise to come to the disciples was fulfilled on the evening of the Resurrection when Jesus breathed on them and said 'Receive the Holy Spirit' (20:22) [CH, ICC]. It refers to the time when Jesus himself, only in a spiritual form comes to the disciples [My].

2. They refer primarily to Jesus' appearances after the Resurrection [Car, IVP, NICNT, Rd, TH, WBC]. Verse 18 shows that Jesus is referring here to his appearances after the Resurrection. In that verse he refers to his disciples seeing him again after a short time [Rd, WBC]. This thought is further expanded on in 16:20–30 [WBC]. Jesus' language in this and the following verse is personal—'I am coming to you...you will see me'. Moreover, the time when the disciples recognize that Jesus is in the Father and the Father in him is on *that* day (14:20), that is, when Jesus rises from the dead [Car]. While it can refer to either his post-resurrection appearances or to his return in the person of the Holy Spirit, in those cases where a specific verb aspect must be chosen, it is probably best to make reference to the resurrection since that would be the first fulfillment of Jesus' promise [TH].
3. They refer to both 1 and 2 [Kn]. It refers primarily to his post-resurrection appearance when he confers on them his Spirit (20:19–23), but implies that his presence with them will continue through the Spirit [Kn].
4. They refer to the post-resurrection appearances and/or the Second Coming of Jesus [Bar].

14:19 Yet^a (a) little-while^b and the world sees me no-longer,^c but you(pl) see me, because/that I live and you(pl) will-live.

LEXICON—a. ἔτι (LN 67.128) (BAGD 1.c. p. 316): 'yet' [BAGD, LN], 'still' [BAGD, LN]. The phrase 'yet a little while' [Gdt, HTC, NTC; KJV] is also translated 'yet a short time' [NICNT2], 'in a little while' [CEV, NCV, NET, NRSV, REB, TEV], 'in a very little while' [Ph], 'in just a little while' [AB], 'in a short time' [NJB], 'after a little while' [WBC; NASB], 'before long' [NIV], 'soon' [NLT]. This adverb indicates an extension of time up to and beyond an expected point [LN]. It indicates that a given situation is continuing 'a little while longer' [BAGD].
  b. μικρός (LN 67.106) (BAGD 3.e. p. 521): 'little while' [BAGD, LN], 'a short time' [BAGD, LN], 'for a short time' [LN]. This adjective indicates a relatively brief extent of time [LN]. See previous item for version evidence.
  c. οὐκέτι (LN 67.130) (BAGD 1. p. 592): 'no longer' [BAGD, LN, NICNT2, NTC, WBC; NASB, NJB, NLT, NRSV, REB], 'any longer' [NET], 'no more' [BAGD, Gdt, HTC; KJV, Ph, TEV], 'anymore' [AB; NCV, NIV], 'no further' [BAGD], not explicit [CEV]. This adverb indicates the extension of time up to a point but not beyond [LN].

QUESTION—To what does the word μικρός 'a little while' refer?
  It refers to the approaching death of Jesus [AB, Bar, Lns, NICNT1, TH].
QUESTION—To what does the word κόσμος 'world' refer?
  It refers to the people who are in the world—people associated with a world system and estranged from God [LN (9.23), TRT].

QUESTION—What is indicated by the present tenses 'the world no longer sees' and 'you(pl) see me'?

They refer to the future [AB, Gdt, EGT, ICC, My, NICNT2, rd, TH; CEV, NASB, NCV, NET, NIV, NJB, NLT, NRSV, Ph, REB, TEV]: the world *will see* me no longer but you *will see* me. The present tense is used proleptically here to indicate the certainty of the future [AB, ICC]. That the world would no longer see Jesus refers to the approaching crucifixion [ICC, TH].

QUESTION—Does the second verb 'to see' refer to physical sight or spiritual sight?

1. It refers to physical sight [Bar, BECNT, Car, CH, HTC, IVP, NICNT1, NICNT2, Rd, TH, WBC]. They will see him in his resurrection appearances [CH, NICNT1, NICNT2, WBC]. Even seeing him at his resurrection, they will see him with a new kind of perception with the eyes of faith [WBC]. The simplest explanation of these events is that the first refers to the crucifixion and the second to the resurrection [Bar].
2. It refers to spiritual sight [BAGD, Gdt, ICC, Lns, My, NTC]. The disciples will see Jesus in the spiritual realm enabled by the Holy Spirit [Gdt].

QUESTION—What words are emphasized in this verse?

The three pronouns ὑμεῖς 'you(pl)', ἐγώ 'I', and ὑμεῖς 'you(pl)' are all emphatic [NICNT1, TH]: but *you yourselves* see me, because *I myself* live, *you, on your part* also will live. The first ὑμεῖς 'you(pl)' contrasts the disciples with the world [NICNT1]. The 2nd occurrence of the pronoun ὑμεῖς 'you(pl)' and the pronoun ἐγώ 'I' are emphatic [Gdt, Lns]: because *I myself* live, *you, on your part* also will live.

QUESTION—What is the function of the clause 'because/that I live'?

1. It stands as the reason of the statement, 'you(pl) will live' [AB, BECNT, Car, CH, EGT, Gdt, IVP, Kn, Lns, NICNT1, NTC, TH, WBC; CEV, KJV, NASB, NCV, NET, NIV, NLT, NRSV, REB, TEV]: because I live, you also will live. This implies that Jesus is the source of the disciples' life in the same way that the Father was the source of his life (6:57) [TH]. This is a reason-result statement, the word ὅτι 'because' pointing forward to the clause 'you too will live' not backward. The pronouns 'I' and 'you(pl)' are also emphatic joining them together with the parallel verbs '(I myself) live' and '(you yourselves) will live' [Lns]. When Jesus rises from the dead, he imparts the Spirit to the disciples and they receive his resurrection life [Kn].
2. It stands as the cause of the previous clause, 'you(pl) see me' [Bar, HTC, My; Ph]: you will see me because I live. The disciples would see Jesus because he would be alive having risen from the dead and they would be alive too [Bar].

QUESTION—What is the function of the καί 'also/and' preceding the pronoun ὑμεῖς 'you(pl)' in the clause 'and you(pl) will live'?
1. It should be construed with 'you(pl)' to mean 'you also (will live)' [Gdt, HTC, Lns, NICNT2, NTC, WBC; KJV, NASB, NCV, NET, NIV, NJB, NLT, NRSV, Ph, REB, TEV].
2. It functions to coordinate the clause 'you(pl) will live', with the clause 'because I live' [AB, Bar, My]: 'because I have life and you will have life' [AB].

14:20 In that day[a] you(pl) will-know[b] that I (am) in[c] my Father and you(pl) (are) in me and-I (am) in you(pl).
LEXICON—a. ἡμέρα (BAGD 4.a. p. 347): 'day' [BAGD]. The phrase 'in that day' [NASB, Gdt, HTC, NICNT2, NTC] is also translated 'on that day' [AB, WBC; NCV, NIV, NJB, NRSV], 'at that day' [KJV], 'at that time' [NET], 'then' [CEV], 'when that day comes' [TH; Ph, REB, TEV], 'when I am raised to life again' [NLT]. Here 'day' refers to a longer period of time [BAGD].
b. fut. mid . ind. γινώσκω (BAGD 1.c. p. 161): 'to know' [BAGD, Gdt, HTC; CEV, KJV, NASB, NCV, NET, NJB, NLT, NRSV, REB, TEV], 'to come to know' [BAGD, NICNT2, WBC], 'to realize' [NIV, Ph], 'to recognize' [AB, NTC].
c. ἐν (LN 89.119) (BAGD I.5.d. p. 259): 'in' [BAGD, LN; all translations except CEV], 'one with' [LN; CEV], 'in union with, joined closely to' [LN]. The words 'I am in my father' are translated 'I am one with the Father' [CEV]. This preposition indicates close personal association [BAGD, LN].
QUESTION—To what specific time does the phrase 'in that day' refer?
1. It refers to the Resurrection [Bar, Car, CH, HTC, ICC, IVP, NICNT1, NICNT2, Rd, TH, WBC]. Although the primary reference is to the Resurrection, the thought also includes Christ's permanent presence with them [Bar, ICC, TH]. Jesus had said in verse 18 that he would come to them. It is this that is referred to [Bar]. The time referred to is the whole age in which the believers in Christ now live beginning with the Resurrection [NICNT2].
2. It refers to the Coming of the Holy Spirit at Pentecost [BECNT, Gdt, Lns, Kn, My, NTC]. That day begins with the outpouring of the Holy Spirit [Gdt, Lns, My, NTC]. It refers to the time that began when Jesus imparted the Spirit to the disciples [Kn]. It refers to the coming of Christ to the disciples in the Spirit [My, Rd], at Pentecost [Rd].
3. Other views [AB, EGT]. It refers to the new Christian era [AB, EGT]. This time was made possible by Jesus' suffering, death, and resurrection [AB].
QUESTION—What does it mean to be in another person?
This is a new teaching. The closest Jesus had come to expressing this was in 6:56, 'Whoever eats My flesh and drinks My blood remains in me, and I in

him'. He now draws the disciples right into the mutual indwelling of the Father and the Son [NICNT2]. This means that God and the believers are living in each other [CH]. It means that the Son and the Spirit will both be living in the disciples [IVP]. Jesus was in vital connection with the Father and the disciples were in vital connection with Jesus [EGT]. The idea may be expressed by such expressions as 'lives in, is united with', or 'is one with'. Jesus' words could be translated 'I and My Father are just like one person, and you and I are just like one person' [TH]. Or being in someone may be expressed as 'being in union with' a person, or 'having a very close relationship with' a person [TRT].

QUESTION—What words are emphasized in this verse?

The pronouns ἐγώ 'I' and ὑμεῖς 'you(pl)' are emphasized [Lns, TH]: '*you yourselves* in me and *I myself* in you' [Lns]. The second occurrence of the pronoun ὑμεῖς 'you(pl)' is emphasized [ICC, TH]: *you yourselves* will know.

DISCOURSE UNIT—14:21-24 [WBC]. The topic is Jesus' coming to the believer.

14:21 **The-one having^a my commands^b and keeping^c them that-one is the-one loving^d me. And the-one loving me will-be-loved by my Father, and-I will-love him and will-reveal^e myself to-him."**

LEXICON—a. pres. act. participle of ἔχω (LN 90.65) (BAGD I.2.i. p. 333): 'to have' [AB, BAGD, Gdt, HTC, LN, NICNT2, NTC, WBC; KJV, NASB, NET, NIV, NRSV], 'to know' [NCV, Ph], 'to accept' [NLT, TEV], 'to receive' [REB], 'to hold to' [NJB], 'to have as one's own, to possess [BAGD], 'to experience' [LN]. The sentence 'The one having my commands and keeping them is the one loving me' is translated 'If you love me, you will do what I have said' [CEV]. This verb means to experience a state or condition, generally involving duration [LN]. The present participle indicates continuous action [NTC].

b. ἐντολή (LN 33.330) (BAGD 2.d. p. 269): 'command' [BAGD, NICNT2, WBC; NJB, NIV, REB], 'commandment' [AB, BAGD, Gdt, HTC, LN; KJV, NASB, NET, NJB, NLT, NRSV, Ph, TEV], 'order' [BAGD, LN], 'precept' [NTC]. The phrase 'my commands' is translated 'what I have said' [CEV]. This noun is derived from the verb ἐντέλλομαι 'to command' (33.329) and means that which is authoritatively commanded [LN].

c. pres. act. participle of τηρέω (LN 36.19) (BAGD 5. p. 815): 'to keep' [AB, BAGD, Gdt, HTC, LN, NICNT2, NTC, WBC; KJV, NASB, NJB, NRSV], 'to obey' [LN; NCV, NET, NIV, NLT, Ph, REB, TEV], 'to do' [CEV], 'to observe, to fulfill, to pay attention to' [BAGD]. This verb means to continue to obey orders or commandments [LN]. The present participle indicates continuous action [NTC].

d. pres. act. participle of ἀγαπάω (LN 25.43) (BAGD 1.a.β. p. 4): 'to love' [BAGD, LN; all translations], 'to cherish' [BAGD], 'to regard with affection' [LN]. This verb means to have love for someone or something, based on sincere appreciation and high regard [LN]. The present participle indicates continuous action [NTC].

e. fut. act. indic. of ἐμφανίζω (LN **28.36**) (BAGD 1.b. p. 257): 'to reveal' [AB, BAGD, **LN**, NICNT2, WBC; NET, NJB, NLT, NRSV, TEV], 'to disclose' [LN; NASB, REB], 'to show' [NCV, NIV], 'to manifest' [Gdt, HTC, NTC; KJV], 'to make known' [LN; Ph], 'to make visible' [BAGD], 'to make plain, to bring to the light' [LN]. The statement 'I…will reveal myself to him' is translated 'I…will show you what I am like' [CEV]. This verb means to cause something to be fully known by revealing it clearly and in some detail [LN]. It is used figuratively here to indicate what transpires within one's soul [BAGD, Gdt].

QUESTION—Are the verbs 'having' and 'keeping' separate ideas or do they refer to a single event?

1. They refer to a single event [AB, Rd, TH; CEV]: 'If you love me you will do what I have said' [CEV]. It may be better to simply translate 'whoever obeys my commandments', or 'whoever does what I have commanded him to do' [TH]. The two verbs are parallel and are like the pair 'hearing' and 'keeping' in 12:47 or the pair 'hearing and believing' in 5:24 [Rd].
2. They are separate ideas [Bar, Car, EGT, ICC, Kn, My]. The verb 'to have' means more than 'to possess' [Car] and implies 'to grasp with the mind' [Bar, Car]. 'To have' means to have them in one's heart or to know them [EGT, ICC, My] and understand their meaning [ICC]. It appears to mean 'to make the commands one's own' or 'to take them into one's inner being' [NICNT1]. Jewish teachers used to argue whether knowing or doing took precedence, but eventually agreed on the need for both [Kn].

QUESTION—What word is emphasized in this verse?

The demonstrative pronoun ἐκεῖνός 'that one' is emphatic [Gdt, HTC, ICC, Lns, My, NTC; KJV, NIV, REB]: '*he it is* who loves me' [Gdt, HTC, NTC; REB]. The emphasis is exclusive [ICC, Lns, My, NTC]: 'he and he alone' [Lns].

QUESTION—Does the self-revelation of Jesus to the disciples mean his post resurrection appearances to them or an inner revelation of his character to them?

1. It refers to the post resurrection appearances to them [BECNT, CH, WBC]. For the disciples it refers to Jesus' post-resurrection appearances, but for subsequent believers it is the inner revelation of himself that is indicated [CH, WBC].
2. It refers to an inner revelation of his character to them [AB, BAGD, EGT, Gdt, HTC, ICC, Lns, NICNT1, NTC, TH, WBC; CEV]: 'I will show you what I am like' [CEV]. The revelation of Jesus is the disclosing of himself more and more to the disciple who loves him and is loved by the Father [HTC]. This is like the special revelation of God's person to Moses in Exodus 33:13 [AB, ICC, TH]. Here it is the revelation of Christ that will be given through the illumination of the Spirit (16:14) [ICC].

3. It includes both meanings [Bar, Car, CH, IVP, Rd, WBC]. This self disclosure of Jesus to his disciples is not limited to his appearances after his resurrection, but has a more general meaning and includes his progressive revealing of himself to them after his departure [IVP, Rd]. This self revelation will be accomplished through the Spirit [IVP]. The revelation here refers to Jesus' post-resurrection appearances but possibly includes his self-disclosures to his disciples in later times as well (14:22, 23) [Car].

DISCOURSE UNIT—14:22-31 [IVP]. The topic is how the disciples and the world relate to God.

14:22 **Judas,**[a] **not Iscariot,**[b] **says to-him, "And**[c] **Lord, what has-happened**[d] **that you-are-about-to**[e] **reveal yourself to-us and not**[f] **to-the world?**[g]**"**

TEXT—Instead of Ἰούδας, οὐχ ὁ Ἰσκαριώτης 'Judas, not Iscariot', some manuscripts read Ἰούδας, οὐχ ὁ ἀπὸ Καριώτου 'Judas, not the one from Kerioth', others read Ἰούδας ὁ Κανανίτης 'Judas the Canaanite', another reads Θωμᾶς 'Thomas', and still another reads Ἰούδας Θωμᾶς 'Judas Thomas'. GNT reads 'Judas, not Iscariot' with an A rating, indicating that the text is certain.

LEXICON—a. Ἰούδας (BAGD 5. p. 380): 'Judas' [BAGD; all translations]. 'Judas', an apostle, called...'son of Jacob' [BAGD].
  b. Ἰσκαριώθ (LN 93.181) (BAGD p. 381): 'Iscariot' [BAGD, LN; all translations]. The phrase 'Judas, not Iscariot' is translated 'Judas, not the Iscariot' [WBC], 'Judas, not Judas Iscariot' [AB; CEV, NCV, NET, NIV, NJB, TEV], 'Judas, not Judas Iscariot, but the other disciple with that name' [NLT], 'Judas...the other Judas, not Iscariot' [REB], 'Judas, not the one with the surname Iscariot' [HTC]. Ἰσκαριώθ is a name which is probably based on a place name [LN, Lns]. It is the surname of Judas and is usually taken to refer to the place of his origin, 'from Kerioth' (in southern Judea) [BAGD].
  c. καί (LN 91.12) (BAGD I.2.h.): 'and' [Gdt, NICNT2], 'but' [NCV, NIV], 'then' [LN; NASB], 'indeed, how is it then, yet' [LN], not explicit [all translations except Gdt, NICNT2; NASB, NCV, NIV]. This conjunction indicates emphasis, involving surprise and unexpectedness [LN]. It introduces an abrupt question, which may often express wonder, ill-will, or incredulity [BAGD]. It is an expression of surprise [Gdt]. The καί adds strength to the question 'Yes, but how is it?' [Bar].
  d. perf. act. indic. of γίνομαι (LN 13.107) (BAGD I.3.a. p. 158): 'to happen' [BAGD, LN], 'to occur' [LN], 'to take place' [BAGD], 'to come to be' [LN]. The question 'what has happened' [NTC; NET, NJB] is also translated 'whatever has happened' [WBC], 'what can have happened' [AB], 'what is come to pass' [Gdt], 'why' [NCV, NIV, NLT], 'how is it' [HTC; KJV, NRSV, Ph], 'how has it come about' [REB], 'how come' [NICNT2], 'how can it be' [TEV], 'what do you mean by saying' [CEV]. This verb means to happen, with the implication that what happens is

different from a previous state [LN]. The phrase 'what happened' means 'why is it that?' [BAGD], 'And for what reason is it? Why?' [Rd].

e. pres. act. indic. of μέλλω (LN 67.62) (BAGD 1.c.γ. p. 501): 'to be about to' [LN, NTC, WBC], 'to be going to' [AB, NICNT2; NASB, NET, NLT, Ph], 'to intend to' [BAGD; NIV, NJB], 'to plan to' [NCV], 'to mean to' [REB], 'to propose, to have in mind' [BAGD]. Other translations render this verb as indicating some kind of future action [Gdt, HTC; CEV, KJV, NRSV, TEV]: 'how can it be that you will reveal yourself' [TEV]. This verb means to occur at a point of time in the future which is subsequent to another event and closely related to it [LN]. Here it denotes an intended action [BAGD].

f. οὐχί (LN **69.4**) (BAGD 1. p. 598): 'not' [BAGD, LN], 'not indeed' [LN]. This negative particle indicates a somewhat more emphatically negativized proposition (than οὐ) [LN]. It is a strengthened form of οὐ 'not' [BAGD].

g. κόσμος (LN 9.23) (BAGD 5.a. p. 446): 'world' [BAGD; all translations except CEV, NCV, NLT], 'people of the/this world' [LN; CEV], 'the rest of the world' [NCV], 'the world at large' [NLT]. This noun is used as a figurative extension of the meaning of κόσμος a 'cosmos, universe' indicating people associated with a world system and estranged from God [LN]. Here it refers to the world as mankind [BAGD, TRT].

QUESTION—Why did Judas ask this?

Judas is probably expecting a visible glorious Messiah that everyone would see and he cannot understand that the world will not see him anymore [AB, Car, CH, Bar, EGT, Gdt, IVP, ICC, Lns, My, NICNT1, NICNT2, NTC, TH, WBC]. He imagines the revelation to be physical. The question he is asking emphasizes the phrase 'to us' and contrasts it with the strong negative οὐχί 'not' to the world. He seems to think that something has happened to change the Lord's program [NICNT1]. Judas expected that when Jesus came back 'every eye will see him' (Revelation 1:7), or the expectation expressed in Matthew 24:30 that when the sign of the Son of Man appeared in the sky, all the tribes would mourn for him and see him coming in the clouds with power and much glory. His question is legitimate [NICNT2]. Judas is puzzled because he is thinking of Jesus returning in a display of power and he thinks that it would be better for the world to see this as well as the disciples [CH, NTC, Rd].

QUESTION—What words are emphasized in this verse?

The phrase 'to us' stands first in its clause and is emphasized and so contrasts with the following phrase 'the world' [Bar, Lns, NICNT1, TH, TRT]: 'How is it that it is to *us* thou wilt manifest thyself, and not to *the world*?' [Bar]. The phrase 'to us' is exclusive and indicates 'only to us' [Lns, TRT; NLT]. The word οὐχί 'not' is an emphatic form of οὐ 'not' [BAGD, LN, NICNT1]: *not* to the world.

14:23 Jesus answered and said to-him, "If anyone loves me he-will-keep[a] my word[b] and my Father will-love him and we-will-come to him and will-make[c] (a) dwelling-place[d] with[e] him.

LEXICON—a. fut. act. indic. of τηρέω (LN 36.19) (BAGD 5. p. 815): 'to keep' [AB, BAGD, Gdt, HTC, NICNT2, NTC, WBC; KJV, NASB, NJB, NRSV], 'to obey' [LN; NCV, NET, NIV, TEV], 'to heed' [REB], 'to keep commandments' [LN], 'to observe, to fulfill, to pay attention to' [BAGD]. The statement 'he will keep my word' is translated 'they will obey me' [CEV], 'all who love me...will do what I say' [NLT], 'he follows my teaching' [Ph]. This verb means to continue to obey orders or commandments [LN].

b. λόγος (LN 33.98) (BAGD 1.b.β. p. 478): 'word' [AB, Gdt, HTC, LN, NICNT2, NTC, WBC; NASB, NET, NJB, NRSV], 'words' [KJV], 'teaching' [NCV, NIV Ph, TEV], 'what I say' [NLT, REB], 'saying, message, statement' [LN], not explicit [CEV]. This noun is derived from λέγω 'to say' and means that which has been stated or said, with primary focus on the content of the communication [LN]. It means 'speaking' in relation to revelation by God through Christ and his messengers [BAGD]. Here the word λόγος refers to Jesus' commands [NTC, TH]. It is used in the singular here to indicate the whole saving message of Jesus [Bar, ICC].

c. fut. mid. indic. of ποιέω (LN 90.45) (BAGD II.1. p. 683): 'to make' [BAGD, LN], 'to do' [BAGD, LN], 'to perform' [LN]. The statement 'we...will make a home with him' is translated 'we will make a dwelling right beside him' [NICNT2], 'we will...take up residence with him' [NET], 'we will...live in/with them' [CEV, TEV]. This verb in the middle voice means to make or do something for or of oneself [BAGD, Lns, My].

d. μονή (LN **85.76**) (BAGD 1. P. 527): 'dwelling place' [AB, **LN**], 'home' [NTC; HTC NCV, NIV, NJB, NLT, NRSV, Ph], 'dwelling' [NICNT2, WBC; REB], 'abode' [Gdt; KJV, NASB], 'residence' [NET], 'place' [LN], 'staying, tarrying' [BAGD], not explicit [CEV, TEV]. This noun denotes a place where one may remain or dwell [LN]. This is the same word translated 'dwelling places' at 14:3 [TH]. It refers to a permanent dwelling rather than a temporary one [Bar, NICNT1].

e. παρά (LN 89.111) (BAGD II.1.b.γ. p. 610): 'with' [LN; all translations except NICNT2; CEV, NJB, Ph], 'within' [Ph], 'in' [CEV, NJB], 'right beside' [NICNT2]. This preposition indicates association, with the implication of proximity to the so-called viewpoint character [LN]. It indicates a side-by-side, mutual activity as when two lovers make a home with each other [CH]. Verse 17 shows that παρά does not differ greatly from ἐν 'in'—'You know him, for he lives with (παρά) you and will be in (ἐν) you' (14:17) [NICNT1].

QUESTION—How does this verse answer the question of Judas?

Jesus is telling the disciples that his coming to them involves his Father also coming and taking up residence in them. This kind of revelation is reserved only for those believing in Him and obeying him and is not for the world [AB, Gdt, Lns]. And this revelation is intimate and personal [Lns]. Jesus' reply to Judas is love. He is telling him that he has not abandoned the world—the Father and the Son will come and live in all who will love him [NICNT1]. The world does not love or obey. It is not to the world that Jesus reveals himself [HTC].

QUESTION—What is indicated by the statement 'we will come to him'?

It indicates that Jesus' revelation of himself to the disciples did not mean his post resurrection appearances, or his Second Coming of the last days. Both the Father and the Son will come to him—it will be an inner experience [Bar]. The revelation is spiritual and is to the individual rather than being a public revelation [EGT]. It shows that Jesus plainly identifies himself with the Father as an equal [Bar, Gdt, ICC].

QUESTION—What words are emphasized in this verse?

The phrase 'to him' comes before the phrase 'we will come' in order to increase its prominence [TRT].

QUESTION—What is indicated by the statement 'we will…make a home with him'?

It indicates the invisible presence of the Father and the Son in the believer's heart made possible by the Holy Spirit [ICC, Lns]. The Father and Son will come like wanderers from their heavenly home and become house and table guests in the heart of believers [My].

14:24 The-one not loving me does- not -keep my words. And^a the word that you(pl)-hear is not mine but the Father's (who) sent me.

LEXICON—a. καί (LN 89.92): 'and' [Gdt, HTC, LN, NICNT2, NTC, WBC; KJV, NASB, NET, NJB, NRSV, REB, TEV], 'and remember' [NLT], 'indeed' [Ph], 'and indeed' [Gdt], not explicit [CEV, NCV, NIV]. Here καί has the meaning of καίτοι 'and yet' [ICC].

QUESTION—What is implied by this verse?

It indicates that the world that does not love Jesus or obey him is also not spiritually able to receive the spiritual revelation of the Father and Son. This is only given to those who love him [ICC].

QUESTION—What is indicated by the plural λόγους 'words'?

It indicates that there is no significant difference between this word and the singular λόγος 'word' of verse 23 [Bar, NICNT1]. It probably refers to the commands (ἐντολάς) of verse 21 [ICC, NICNT1].

QUESTION—What is implied by the words 'the word that you hear is not mine but the Father's who sent me'?

It implies that the Father and the Son are unified in what they do [Bar].

QUESTION—How are the two nouns related in the genitive construction ὁ λόγος...τοῦ...πατρός 'the word...of the...Father'?
The word *comes from* the Father [AB, TH, TRT; CEV, NCV, NLT, NRSV, Ph, TEV]: 'the teaching...comes from the Father, who sent me' [TEV]. The word *belongs to* the Father [NIV, TRT]. The implication of this phrase is that the Father is the authority behind Jesus' teaching [WBC]. Jesus' words are the Father's words [Car]. If this concept is difficult to translate in a given language, one could translate 'my Father told me to say/deliver this message' [TH].

DISCOURSE UNIT—14:25–31 [AB, HTC, NICNT1]. The topic is concluding words [HTC], the last discourse [AB], I go to the Father [NICNT1].

DISCOURSE UNIT—14:25–26 [WBC]. The topic is the Paraclete teacher.

14:25 I-have-told you(pl) these-things (while) remaining with you(pl). **14:26** But the Helper,[a] the Holy Spirit, whom the Father will-send in my name,[b] that-one will-teach you(pl) all-things and will-remind[c] you(pl) (of) all-things that I told you.

LEXICON—a. παράκλητος (LN **12.19**) (BAGD p. 618): 'Helper' [BAGD, **LN**, NTC; NASB, NCV, TEV], 'Advocate' [NICNT2; NET, NLT, NRSV], 'advocate' [REB], 'Counselor' [HTC; NIV], 'Comforter' [KJV], 'support' [Gdt], 'Encourager' [LN], 'Mediator' [BAGD, LN], 'Paraclete' [AB, WBC; NJB], 'one who appears in another's behalf, intercessor' [BAGD]. This noun is also translated as a clause: 'the Holy Spirit will come and help you' [CEV], 'the one who is coming to stand by you' [Ph]. See this word also at 14:16.
    b. ὄνομα (LN 33.126) (BAGD I.4.c.γ. p. 572): 'name' [BAGD,LN; all translations except CEV, NLT]. The words 'whom the Father will send in my name' is translated 'the Father will send the Spirit to take my place' [CEV], 'the Father sends the Advocate as my representative' [NLT]. This noun denotes the proper name of a person or object [LN]. When used of God or Jesus, this means 'with the mention of the name, while naming', or 'calling on the name'. Here it means 'whom the Father will send when my name is used' [BAGD].
    c. fut. act. indic. of ὑπομιμνῄσκω (LN **29.10**) (BAGD 1.a. p. 846): 'to remind' [AB, BAGD, LN, NICNT2, NTC, WBC; CEV, NJB, NIV, NLT, NRSV, REB], 'to bring to remembrance' [Gdt; KJV, NASB], 'to make (you) remember' [TEV], 'to cause to remember' [LN; NCV, NET], 'to bring to mind' [Ph], 'to cause to think about again' [LN]. This verb means to cause to recall and to think about again [LN].

QUESTION—What does it mean that the Father would send the Spirit in Jesus' name?
    1. It means that he would send him in Jesus' place or as his representative [EGT, ICC, TRT, WBC; CEV, NLT]: 'the Father will send the Spirit to take my place' [CEV]. Jesus had said (5:43) that he came in the name of

his Father, that is, as his representative. Here the Father sends the Spirit in the name of Jesus, that is, as his representative. Both Jesus and the Spirit come representing another [WBC].

2. It means that Jesus would ask the Father to send the Spirit [Car, HTC, NICNT2, Rd]. That this is the meaning is seen in verse 16, 'I will ask the Father and he will give you another Helper' [HTC, NICNT2]. Jesus promises to send the Helper from the Father (15:26) [Rd]. As Jesus, coming in the Father's name was the Father's ambassador, so the Spirit coming in Jesus' name, or at his request, is his ambassador [Car].
3. It may mean either 1 or 2 [Bar, NICNT1]. It may mean that Jesus will ask the Father to send the Spirit, or that the Spirit will be sent to continue Jesus' work—to be in his place [Bar, NICNT1].
4. It means that the Spirit was in union with Jesus and so was conformed to his character and mission [AB, IVP, My]. As Jesus came in God's name and revealed God to men, the Spirit comes in Jesus' name revealing Jesus to people [AB, IVP].

QUESTION—What word is emphasized in this verse?

The pronoun ἐκεῖνος 'that one' is emphatic [Gdt, HTC, NICNT1, NICNT2, NTC]: whom the Father will send in my name, *that very one* will teach you.... This pronoun emphasizes that the Holy Spirit is a person. The word πνεῦμα 'spirit' is neuter in the Greek, but the pronoun ἐκεῖνος is masculine and his activities such as teaching, reminding, testifying, coming, convincing, guiding, speaking, hearing, predicting, and so on, are all personal [NTC]. The pronoun ἐγώ 'I' is emphasized [AB, Bar, Lns, NICNT2, NTC]: 'that *I myself* said to you' [Lns]. These two pronouns are emphatic and frame the final clause—occurring one at the beginning and the other at the end of that Greek clause [NICNT2]: *that one* will teach you all things and will remind you of all things which told you *I*.

DISCOURSE UNIT—14:27-31 [Kn, WBC]. The topic is the gift of peace [WBC], encouragement for the disciples [Kn].

14:27 Peace[a] I-leave[b] to-you(pl), my peace I-give to-you(pl). I do- not -give to-you(pl) as the world gives. Do- not -let- your(pl) heart[c] -be-troubled[d] or let- (it) -be-cowardly.[e]

LEXICON—a. εἰρήνη (LN 25.248) (BAGD 3. p. 227): 'peace' [BAGD, LN; all translations except NLT], 'peace of mind and heart' [NLT], 'freedom from worry' [LN]. This noun denotes a state of freedom from anxiety and inner turmoil [Gdt, LN]. According to the prophets, peace will be an essential characteristic of the Messianic Kingdom. Christian thought also frequently regards εἰρήνη as nearly synonymous with Messianic salvation [BAGD]. This word does not indicate the absence of warfare or inner emotional tension [AB, NICNT1, TH]. It is not cessation of hostilities with one's enemies but the gift of calmness and trust that results from union with God [IVP]. It has a comprehensive meaning that includes the benefits of salvation that God has authored [AB, TH, WBC]. This peace includes a right relationship with God [BECNT, NICNT1]. It is a spiritual rather than an earthly peace [ICC]. The basic meaning of the Hebrew word *shalom* is 'prosperity'. So Jesus is leaving behind the entire prosperity of his work of salvation, including the peace of reconciliation with God [My]. The fact that peace here implies the absence of a troubled and fearful feeling is shown by the commands that follow to not be troubled or fearful [Bar, NTC].

b. pres. act. indic. of ἀφίημι (LN 85.62) (BAGD 3.a. p. 126): 'to leave' [BAGD, LN; all translations except AB, WBC; NJB, REB], 'to bequeath' [WBC; NJB], 'to leave behind' [Ph], 'to give' [CEV], 'to let remain' [LN], 'to let someone have something' [BAGD]. The words 'Peace I leave to you, my peace I give to you' are translated 'Peace is my parting gift to you' [REB], 'Peace is my farewell gift to you. My peace is my gift to you' [AB]. This verb means to permit something to continue in a place [LN]. It has the sense of 'to leave behind, to leave as a bequest' [Bar, BECNT, Car, EGT, ICC, NICNT1, WBC; NJB, Ph].

c. καρδία (LN 26.3) (BAGD 1.b.ε. p. 404): 'heart' [BAGD, LN; all translations except CEV, NLT, Ph, TEV], 'inner self, mind' [LN], not explicit [CEV, NLT, Ph, TEV]. This noun is used figuratively in the NT and denotes the causative source of a person's psychological life in its various aspects, but with special emphasis on thoughts [LN]. It denotes heart as the center and source of the whole inner life, with its thinking, feeling, and volition. Here it refers to the emotions, wishes, and desires [BAGD].

d. pres. pass. impera. of ταράσσω (LN 25.244) (BAGD 2. p. 805): 'to let be troubled' [Gdt, HTC, NTC; KJV, NASB, NCV NJB, NIV, NRSV], 'to let be distressed' [NET], 'to be troubled, to be stirred up, to be disturbed, to be unsettled, to be thrown into confusion, to be frightened, to be terrified' [BAGD], 'to be caused great mental distress' [LN]. The command 'Do not let your heart be troubled or let it be cowardly' is translated 'So don't be worried or afraid' [CEV], 'So don't be troubled or afraid' [NLT], 'You must not be distressed and you must not be daunted' [Ph], 'Set your troubled hearts at rest, and banish your fears' [REB], 'Do not be worried and upset; do not be afraid' [TEV], 'Let no one's heart be shaken, nor let it be fearful' [NICNT2], 'Stop letting your heart be disturbed, and don't let it be cowardly' [WBC]. This verb is a figurative extension of the meaning of ταράσσω 'to stir up' (16.3) and means to cause acute emotional distress or turbulence [LN]. The present tense imperative indicates that they should stop an action that was going on [NTC, WBC]: 'stop letting your hearts be disturbed' [WBC], 'Let not your hearts any longer be troubled' [NTC]. See this same command at 14:1 with its comment on the present imperative.

e. pres. act. impera. of δειλιάω (LN **25.267**) (BAGD p. 173): 'to let be cowardly' [BAGD, **LN**], 'to let be afraid' [CEV, NIV, NLT], 'to let be fearful' [NASB, NTC], 'to let be lacking in courage' [NET], 'to let be afraid' [Gdt, HTC; KJV, NCV NJB], 'to let be timid' [BAGD], 'to let lack courage' [LN]. This verb means to be fearful and cowardly [LN]. The addition of this command is significant. Jesus, himself, had been troubled (11:33; 12:27), but was never fearful, cowardly, or lacking in courage [NICNT2]. The noun δειλία 'cowardice, timidity', related to this verb, is never used in a good sense [NTC].

QUESTION—What words are emphasized in this verse?

The adjective 'my' is emphasized [My, NICNT1, Rd; CEV, TEV]: 'it is my own peace that I give you' [TEV], 'the kind of peace that only I can give' [CEV], 'my own peace I give to you' [NJB, similarly Ph, REB]. The phrase εἰρήνην τὴν ἐμὴν 'peace mine' lacks an article for the word 'peace' possibly meaning that the emphasis is on the quality of the peace. It is Christ's own peace [NICNT1]. The third occurrence of the pronoun ἐγώ 'I' is emphatic [Lns, TRT]: 'not as the world gives do *I on my part* give' [Lns]. There is emphasis on the word 'peace'. In the Greek, 'peace' comes before the words 'I leave to you', similarly the words 'my peace' come before the words 'I give to you'. This increases the prominence of this word [TRT].

QUESTION—Does the clause 'I do not give to you as the world gives' focus on what the world gives, or the way it gives?

1. It focuses on what they give [Bar, BECNT, Car, HTC, IVP, NICNT1, NICNT2, NTC, TH, TRT, WBC; CEV, NLT, Ph]: 'and the peace I give is a gift the world cannot give' [NLT], 'my peace is nothing like the peace of this world' [Ph]. It is the peace that is being compared, not the manner in which it is given [TH]. The world is powerless to give peace. But Jesus gives his peace to people, a peace that is not dependent on outward circumstances [Car, NICNT1]. Jesus was peaceful in the face of danger, suffering, and death [Car]. The world may offer peace in the sense of absence of conflict, but his peace was a quietness in their hearts despite persecution and outward circumstances [BECNT, NICNT2].

2. It focuses on contrasting the giving of the world with the giving of Jesus [Gdt, EGT, ICC, Lns, My, Rd]. Jesus makes this clear by omitting the object 'peace' from his following words 'I do not give to you as the world gives'. He is focusing on the manner of giving, not on the gift. Jesus actually gives peace, the world can only wish it and lacks the power to give it [Gdt, Lns]. The emphatic pronoun 'my' and the words 'I give' are further explained by the words 'not as the world gives do I give'. The world could wish someone peace but it lacked the ability to give it [Rd].

14:28 You(pl)-heard that I told you(pl), I-go and I-come to-you(pl). If you(pl)-loved me you(pl)- would-(have) -rejoiced[a] that/because I-go to the Father, because the Father is greater[b] than-I.

LEXICON—a. aorist pass. (deponent = active) indic. of χαίρω (LN 25.125) (BAGD 1. p. 873): 'to rejoice' [AB, BAGD, Gdt, LN, HTC, NICNT2, NTC, WBC; KJV, NASB, NRSV], 'to be glad' [BAGD, LN; CEV, NET,

NJB, NIV, Ph, REB, TEV], 'to be happy' [NCV, NLT]. This verb means to enjoy a state of happiness and well-being [LN].

b. μέγας (LN 87.22) (BAGD 2.b.α. p. 498): 'great' [BAGD, LN; all translations], 'important' [LN]. This adjective indicates being great in terms of status [LN]. It means great in terms of rank and dignity and occurs here as μείζων the comparative of μέγας. God is 'greater (than)' Jesus [BAGD].

QUESTION—When had Jesus said these things to the disciples?

He had told them that he was going to his Father's house to prepare a place for them (14:2(3,4)) [AB, Gdt, NICNT1, NICNT2, NTC], that because he was going to the Father, the person who believed on him would do greater works than he did (14:12), and that he would not leave them orphans but would come to them (14:18) [Gdt].

QUESTION—What was implied by Jesus' 'going away'?

He was indicating that he would die and return to his Father [Bar, Lns, TH, WBC].

QUESTION—What word in this verse is emphasized?

The pronoun ἐγώ 'I' in the clause 'You heard that I told you' is emphasized [Lns]: 'You heard that I myself said to you' [Lns]. Only Jesus could have said that he was going and meant it in the sense of his departure in death [Lns].

QUESTION—When did Jesus intend to return to them?

He would come to them in the sense of what he said in verses 18 and 23. This does not refer to his coming back in glory in the last days [Lns]. It refers to his return to them through the Spirit [ICC, Lns]. 'Come' should be translated: 'come back' [AB, WBC; CEV, NET, NIV, NLT, Ph, REB, TEV], 'come again' [HTC; KJV], 'return' [NJB].

QUESTION—What does the sentence mean 'If you loved me you would have rejoiced that I go to the Father'?

It is a contrary to fact condition indicating that the disciples did not love Jesus and that they are not glad that he is going [AB, Bar, BECNT, Car, EGT, IVP, Lns, NICNT1, NICNT2, NTC, TH]. Jesus is saying that their love is not genuine love. It is possessive rather than generous [AB]. He means that they did not love him for himself, but for themselves [Gdt], or that their love was not perfect [NICNT2]. If they had true love for Jesus, they would have been glad and understood that his departure was for their advantage [Bar, EGT]. Their love was lacking in that they failed to be glad about Jesus' coming exaltation [Lns].

QUESTION—Should the first occurrence of the conjunction ὅτι be translated 'that' or 'because'—'that I go' or 'because I go'?

1. It should be translated 'that' [AB, Lns, NICNT2, NTC, TH, TRT; CEV, NCV, NET, NJB, NIV, NLT, NRSV, REB, TEV]: you would have rejoiced *that* I go to the Father. The translation 'that' is preferable but the difference in meaning is slight [NICNT2].

2. It should be translated 'because' [Gdt, HTC, WBC; KJV, NASB, Ph]: you would have rejoiced *because* I go to the Father.

QUESTION—Why should the disciples have been happy at Jesus' departure?

He was going away to prepare a place for them but he would also return for them (14:2, 3). This should have been a reason for them to rejoice [Car, WBC]. Once Jesus was exalted, the disciples would be able to draw on the help of both Jesus and the indwelling Spirit of God [BECNT]. His departure would mean the beginning of a new dispensation, one that would exceed the limits of his physical presence with them on earth (14:12) [Rd]. Jesus' soon return to the Father filled him with joy. If the disciples loved Jesus, that is, wanted the best for him, they too would be happy for him [IVP]. Jesus was limited on earth as a man, but his return to the Father meant that all this limitation would cease. This should have resulted in joy for his disciples [Lns]. It was not Jesus' departure that should have made them happy, but his promised return—'I am coming to you' [Gdt].

QUESTION—In what way is the Father greater than Jesus?

When Jesus came into the world, he became limited as a human [BECNT, Bar, Car, ICC, Lns, NICNT1, TH]. The Father was greater in the sense that one who sends is greater than the one who is sent (13:16) [CH, Kn, TH]. But after Jesus was raised from the dead he would return to the position he knew before the world was created [AB, TH]. In ancient culture fathers were considered greater than their sons in rank [BAGD, Kn]. He is greater in the sense that the Father sent the Son and not the other way around. The Son does what he sees the Father doing, and says what he hears the Father saying. In this sense the Father is greater [ICC, NICNT2]. As Mediator between God and man Jesus was inferior [NTC]. Jesus is a Son who is eternally begotten of the Father. So the Father is greater in the sense that he is the eternal source of the Son [BECNT, Bar, IVP], but the Son is equal to the Father in the sense that they share the same nature [IVP]. The Father was the origin and end of all that he did on earth [EGT].

QUESTION—In what way is the Father's being greater than Jesus a reason for the disciples to rejoice?

Being greater meant that everything was under the Father's control and that he would carry out his benevolent purpose through the dreadful events of the coming days [WBC]. If they had truly loved Jesus they would have seen that his return to his home (away from his incarnate state and its limitations) was his gain and would have been glad for him [Car].

14:29 And now I-have-told you(pl) before it-happens, so-that when it-happens you(pl)-may-believe. 14:30 I-will- no-longer -speak many-things with you(pl), for the ruler[a] of-the world[b] comes and/but he-does- not -have[c] anything in-me.

LEXICON—a. ἄρχων (LN 37.56) (BAGD 3. p. 114): 'ruler' [BAGD, HTC, LN, NICNT2; CEV, NASB, NCV, NET, NLT, NRSV, TEV], 'prince' [Gdt, NTC, WBC; KJV, NJB, NIV, REB], 'Prince' [AB], 'governor' [LN], 'lord' [BAGD]. This noun is also translated as a noun phrase: 'the spirit that rules (this world)' [Ph]. This noun is derived from the verb ἄρχω 'to rule' (37.54) and denotes one who rules or governs [LN]. It is also used of evil spirits whose hierarchies resembled human political institutions. The world is ruled by the prince of the world, the devil [BAGD].

b. κόσμος (LN 41.38) (BAGD 7. p. 446): 'world' [BAGD, LN; all translations], 'world system, world's standards' [LN]. This noun denotes the system of practices and standards associated with secular society (that is, without reference to any demands or requirements of God) [LN]. It denotes the world and everything that belongs to it, appearing as that which is hostile to God, that is, lost in sin, wholly at odds with anything divine—ruined and depraved [BAGD]. It may refer to the people of the world who are not believers [TRT].

c. pres. act. indic. of ἔχω (LN 57.1) (BAGD I.7.a. p. 333): 'to have' [BAGD, LN], 'to own, to possess' [LN], 'to hold' [BAGD]. The clause 'he does not have anything in me' is translated 'he has nothing in me' [Gdt, NICNT2, NTC; KJV, NASB], 'he has no hold on/over me' [AB, BAGD; NIV, Ph], 'he has no power over me' [HTC; CEV, NCV, NET, NJB, NLT, NRSV, TEV], 'he has no rights over me' [REB], 'he has no claim over me' [WBC]. This verb means to have or possess objects or property (in the technical sense of having control over the use of such objects) [LN]. The idiom means that Satan has nothing in Jesus on which he can fasten [ICC]. It could be translated 'he is not able to control me' [TH]. It is an idiomatic translation of a Hebrew expression meaning 'he has no claim on me'. So rather than 'he has no power over me' it means that 'he has no legal claim on me' [Bar, BECNT, Car, Kn, WBC; REB]. This was because Jesus was sinless [BECNT, Car, Kn], and he was not of this world [Car]. Although Jesus would die, death would not be able to hold him [CH].

QUESTION—What specifically did Jesus mean that he had told them?

He had told them about going to the Father (14:26) and that he would send them the Holy Spirit (14:28) [TRT]. He had just told them about his going away and coming to them [CH, Lns, NICNT2]. He meant he had told them about his departure from them [EGT, HTC, ICC, My], and of the coming of the Holy Spirit who would convince them of his supernatural foreknowledge [ICC].

QUESTION—To what does the pronoun 'it' refer in the phrase 'it happens'?

It refers to his death, resurrection, (ascension) and the coming of the Spirit at Pentecost [AB, NTC]. It refers to his approaching death as he indicated in 13:19 [My, WBC].

QUESTION—What is the implied object of the verb 'believe'?

He means that they may believe in him [IVP, TRT; CEV, Ph]: 'your faith in me may not be shaken' [Ph]. Jesus means that they may believe him, that is, that what he had said to them was true [NICNT1, TH]. He means that they may believe that he was the person he claimed to be [CH]. He means that they may believe that he has gone to the Father [My].

QUESTION—Who is the 'ruler of this world'?

This refers to the devil or Satan [Bar, BAGD, BECNT, ICC, Kn, NICNT1, NICNT2, TRT].

QUESTION—What did Jesus mean by his claim, 'he does not have anything in me'?

He meant that because Jesus had committed himself to the Father's will in this struggle, now the Father was in control of all that was happening and would prevent the Prince of this world from gaining any control over Jesus [AB].

QUESTION—What relationship is indicated by the conjunction καί 'and/but' in the clause 'and/but he does not have anything in me'?

1. It indicates an adversative or contrastive relationship [Gdt, HTC, NTC; CEV]: '*and yet* in me he has nothing' [NTC].
2. It should be translated 'and' [NICNT2; KJV, NASB].
3. It does not need to be translated [WBC; NCV, NET, NJB, NIV, NLT, NRSV, Ph, REB, TEV].

QUESTION—What words are emphasized in this verse?

The double negative in the clause ἐν ἐμοὶ οὐκ ἔχει οὐδέν (literally) 'in me *not* he has *nothing*', emphasizes the negative holding of the Prince of this world over Jesus [BECNT, Lns]: 'he does not have anything on me at all' [BECNT]. The phrase ἐν ἐμοὶ 'in me' is fronted and emphasized [Lns, TRT]. The phrase 'of the world' is fronted and emphasized in contrast to the phrase 'in me'. Although Satan has dominion over the world, he has no dominion over Jesus [My].

14:31 But so-that[a] the world[b] may-know that I love the Father, and just-as the Father commanded me, so I-do. Rise, let-us-go from-here."

LEXICON—a. ἵνα (LN 89.59): 'so that' [LN; CEV, NASB, NLT, NRSV], 'in order that' [NTC], 'that' [Gdt, NICNT2; KJV], 'to' [Ph], 'in order to, for the purpose of' [LN]. The words 'so that the world may know that I love the Father' is translated 'I go on my way to show that world that I love the Father' [Ph]. This conjunction is also translated as an obligatory aspect: '(the world) must/should (know)' [AB, HTC, WBC; NCV, NJB, NIV, REB, TEV]. This conjunction indicates purpose for events and states (sometimes occurring in highly elliptical contexts). [LN].

b. κόσμος (LN 9.23): 'world' [all translations except CEV], 'everyone in the world' [CEV], 'people of the world' [LN, TH]. This noun denoting 'cosmos, universe' is used figuratively here to indicate people associated with a world system and estranged from God [LN].

QUESTION—What is indicated by the conjunction 'so that'?

1. It indicates that the purpose of Jesus' obeying the Father is so that the world may know that he loves the Father [NTC; CEV, NASB, NET, NLT,

NRSV]: 'I obey my Father, so that everyone in the world might know that I love him' [CEV].

1.1 It indicates that the purpose of rising and going from there is so that the world may know that he loves the Father and that he does what the Father commands [Gdt, Lns, My]: 'in order that the world may know that I love the Father, and that just as the Father gave me commission thus I do, arise, let us go hence' [Lns].

1.2 There is an implied statement after the word 'but' that supplies the means for the purpose of the following clauses [Bar, ICC; Ph]: 'But I go on my way to show the world that I love the Father and do what he sent me to do' [Ph]. The words that should be made explicit are '(but) I do these things (that)' [ICC], or 'these things are happening' or 'I am acting in this way' [Bar].

2. The conjunction should be translated as indicating an imperative aspect [AB, HTC, NICNT1, WBC; NCV, NJB, NIV, REB, TEV]: 'the world must recognize that I love the Father and that I act just as the Father commanded' [NJB].

2.1 The conjunction should be translated as providing an imperative aspect. However it is not coordinate but explanatory [NCV, TEV]: 'the world must know that I love the Father; that is why I do everything as he commands me' [TEV].

QUESTION—What specific command may Jesus have had in mind in saying 'Just as the Father commanded me, so I do'?

He was probably referring particularly to his approaching death on the cross [Bar, Car, EGT, NICNT1, NICNT2]. The supreme display of Jesus' love for the Father was his willingness to sacrifice his own life [Bar, Car].

DISCOURSE UNIT—15:1–16:33 [Car, WBC]. The topic is the true vine, the world's hatred, overcoming joy [WBC], the farewell discourse [Car].

DISCOURSE UNIT—15:1–16:4 [CH]. The topic is Jesus the True Vine.

DISCOURSE UNIT—15:1–16:4a [HTC]. The topic is an admonitory discourse.

DISCOURSE UNIT—15:1–17 [AB, Bar, BECNT, IVP, Lns, NICNT2, WBC; CEV, NCV, NET, NJB, NIV, NLT, NRSV, TEV]. The topic is the farewell discourses [AB], indwelling and command to love [NICNT2], the true vine [Bar, BECNT, IVP, WBC; CEV, NCV, NJB, NLT, NRSV, TEV], the vine and the branches [Lns; NET, NIV].

DISCOURSE UNIT—15:1–16 [Car, NICNT1; Ph]. The topic is the vine and the branches [Car, NICNT1], Jesus teaches union with himself [Ph].

DISCOURSE UNIT—15:1–11 [HTC; NASB]. The topic is the vine and the branches.

DISCOURSE UNIT—15:1–8 [Car, Rd]. The topic is the true vine.

DISCOURSE UNIT—15:1–7 [Kn]. The topic is the vine and the branches.

DISCOURSE UNIT—15:1–6 [IVP]. The topic is the vine and the branches.

15:1 **I am the true^a grapevine^b and my Father is the vinedresser.^c**

LEXICON—a. ἀληθινός (LN 70.3) (BAGD 3. p. 37): 'true' [LN; all translations except [AB, NTC; Ph, TEV], 'real' [AB, BAGD, LN, NTC; Ph, TEV], 'genuine' [BAGD]. This adjective describes a thing as being real and not imaginary [LN]. 'True vine' indicates a genuine vine in contrast to a false one [TH]. The image of Christ as the true vine probably contrasts with Israel as being the degenerate vine (Jeremiah 2:21 'I had planted you like a choice vine of sound and reliable stock. How then did you turn against me into a corrupt, wild vine?') [Bar, BECNT, Car, CH, EGT, IVP, NICNT1, Rd, WBC]. Jesus fulfills the goal God had for Israel as the true vine of God (Psalm 80:9–12, 14–17) [BECNT, Car, Rd]. While 'true' can contrast with others that are untrue, it also contrasts as 'true bread' contrasts with 'mere manna' [Kn]. 'True' is used not to contrast this vine with other vines, but to indicate that this vine is the embodiment of what every vine should be—chiefly the source of life to its branches [NICNT2].

b. ἄμπελος (LN **3.27**) (BAGD 2. p. 46): 'grapevine' [BAGD, **LN**; NLT], 'vine' [BAGD; all translations except NLT]. A rendering of ἄμπελος as 'vine' rather than as 'grapevine' in John 15:1 may cause serious misunderstanding, since it might refer merely to a vine which does not produce fruit. Accordingly, if there is no particular expression for 'grapevine' in a given language, it may be more satisfactory here to speak of 'fruit bush' or 'fruit plant'. A term in John 15:1 which would indicate only jungle vines would also result in complete misunderstanding of the function of pruning (see 43.12), since such jungle vines are never pruned and in fact are only useful when they have been cut down and used for building purposes [LN]. This word is used figuratively of Christ—he is the vine, they are the branches [BAGD]. If grapevines are an unknown plant, 'fruit vine' or 'fruit tree' [TRT], or 'tree that produces good fruit' could be substituted [TH].

c. γεωργός (LN 43.2) (BAGD 2. p. 157): 'vinedresser' [BAGD, Gdt, HTC, NTC, WBC; NASB, NJB, Ph], 'vinegrower' [NRSV], 'vinekeeper' [NICNT2], 'gardener' [AB, LN; CEV, NCV, NET, NIV, NLT, REB, TEV], 'farmer' [LN], 'husbandman' [KJV], 'tenant farmer' [BAGD]. This noun is derived from the verb γεωργέω 'to cultivate land' (43.1) and denotes one who engages in agriculture or gardening [LN]. It denotes 'one who tills the soil' [AB, BECNT, BAGD, Lns, NICNT1, NTC, Rd], but also includes the duties of a vine dresser [BECNT, Lns]. The context tells us that the action of the γεωργός is connected primarily to the vine [NICNT1].

QUESTION—What is the point of similarity in this metaphor of the vine?

The chief focus of the metaphor is the intimate union of Jesus and believers [IVP]. As the branch gets its life from the vine, so the disciples get their life from Jesus [AB, BECNT, Gdt, ICC, NICNT1, NICNT2, NTC]. As the vine produces fruit through its branches, so Jesus produces fruit through his disciples. The metaphor will develop the fact expressed in 14:20, 'You in me, and I in you' [Lns]. Jesus as the vine is the source of the branches and they are organically united to him [CH]. Just as the vine unifies and sustains its branches and produces fruit through them, so Christ is the source of the disciples' life and their ability to produce a harvest [NTC]. As the branches belong to the vine and are part of its makeup, so the disciples belong to Jesus and are incorporated into his community of people [Rd].

QUESTION—What is the point of similarity in this metaphor of the gardener?

The gardener is the supreme controller of the garden from its beginning to its finished products [Bar, BECNT]. Just as the gardener plants and cultivates the vine so God has sent Jesus and cares for him and those united to him [Car, Gdt]. He cares for the well-being and fruitfulness of the vine [EGT].

QUESTION—What words are emphasized in this verse?

The pronoun ἐγώ 'I' is emphasized [ICC, Lns, NTC]: 'I myself am the genuine vine' [Lns]. The word 'true' is strongly emphasized by being placed after the noun, ἡ ἄμπελος ἡ ἀληθινὴ 'the vine *the true*' [HTC, Lns].

15:2 Every branch[a] in me (that) does- not –bear-fruit[b] he-removes,[c] and every branch (that) does-bear fruit he-prunes[d] it so-that it-may-bear more[e] fruit.

LEXICON—a. κλῆμα (LN 3.50) (BAGD p. 434): 'branch' [BAGD, LN; all translations]. This noun denotes a more or less tender, flexible branch, as of a vine [LN]. It specifically refers to vine tendrils or shoots [Bar, BECNT, Car, EGT, LN, NICNT1, TH] but can refer to heavier branches in general [Bar, Car, TH]. It is typically used in the LXX to mean the 'shoot of a vine' [BECNT, ICC].

b. pres. act. participle of καρπὸν φέρω (LN 23.199) (BAGD 1.a. p. 404): 'to bear fruit' [BAGD, LN], 'to yield fruit' [BAGD], 'to produce fruit, to produce seed, to yield' [LN]. The phrase 'not bearing fruit' [Ph] is also translated 'does not bear fruit' [AB, NICNT2; KJV, TEV, NASB, NET], 'bears no/not fruit' [Gdt, HTC, NTC; NJB, NIV, NRSV], 'yields no fruit' [WBC], 'does not produce fruit' [CEV, NCV, NLT], '(any branch of mine that) is barren' [REB]. This phrase means to produce fruit or seed (of plants) [LN].

c. pres. act. indic. of αἴρω (LN 15.203) (BAGD 4. p. 24): 'to remove' [BAGD, LN; NRSV, Ph], 'to cut off' [AB, WBC; NCV, NIV, NLT], 'to take away' [BAGD, Gdt, HTC, LN, NICNT2, NTC; KJV, NASB, NET], 'to cut away' [CEV, NJB, REB], 'to break off' [TEV], 'to carry (away), to carry off' [LN]. This verb means to lift up and carry (away) [LN]. Although αἴρω can also mean 'to prop up', it is wrong to take that sense

here [BECNT]. Some cut off branches are like people such as Judas [CH, IVP, NICNT1, NICNT2]. They are not fruitful or clean (13:10) 'you are clean, though not every one of you' [NICNT1].
d. pres. act. indic. of καθαίρω (LN **43.12, 79.49**) (BAGD 1. p. 386): 'to prune' [BAGD, Gdt, **LN** (43.12); NASB, NET, NJB, NIV, NLT, NRSV, Ph], 'to prune clean' [REB], 'to prune…so that it will be clean' [TEV], 'to cleanse' [LN, (79.49), NTC], 'to clean' [LN (79.49)], 'to make clean' [BAGD, LN (79.49)], 'to trim clean' [AB, NICNT2; CEV], 'to trim and clean' [NCV], 'to cut clean' [WBC], 'to purge' [KJV], 'to take away, to cut off' [LN (43.12)], 'to clear' [BAGD]. This verb means to cut away or cut back unproductive branches or to cut back productive branches so they can produce better [LN (43.12)] or to cause something to become clean [LN (79.49)]. It means 'to make clean by pruning'. To translate as TEV has done has the advantage of bringing out the basic meaning of the verb καθαίρω, 'to make clean', and prepare for the reference to καθαρός 'clean' in verse 3 [TH]. The literal meaning of this verb is 'to clean' and brings out the fact that in this metaphor we have now moved into the spiritual sphere and what happens in the lives of people [NICNT1]. A vine is 'cleared' or 'pruned' by removing the superfluous wood [BAGD]. If the concept is foreign to a language the process could be translated 'to cut the branch short, to cut the branch back', or 'to cut off part of the branch' [TH]. Pruning has the function of concentrating the vigor of the vine on fruit production itself, not on peripheral activities [EGT].
e. πλέον (LN 78.28) (BAGD II.1.b. p. 689): 'more' [AB, BAGD, Gdt, HTC, LN, NICNT2, NTC, WBC; KJV, NASB, NET, NRSV TEV], 'even more' [LN; CEV, NCV, NJB, NIV, NLT], 'more than, to a greater degree' [LN]. The clause 'so that it may bear more fruit' is translated 'to increase its yield' [Ph], 'to make it more fruitful still' [REB]. This adjective is the comparative of πολύς 'many' (59.1) and describes a degree that surpasses in some manner a point on an explicit or implicit scale of extent [LN].

QUESTION—What words are emphasized in this verse?

The words 'every branch' are fronted in their clauses to emphasize them [Lns, TH]. The repeated reference to 'bearing fruit'—'not bearing fruit…bearing fruit…may bear more fruit'—highlights the fact that fruit-bearing is God's primary purpose in creation and salvation [BECNT].

QUESTION—What is the meaning of the phrase '(every branch) in me'?

It means that the branches are attached to the vine [AB, HTC, TH]. This could be translated 'every branch that is a part of me' or 'every branch that is attached to me' [TH].

QUESTION—Who are the branches symbolized by the ones not bearing fruit?

John is here using it to refer to apostate Christians [Bar, Gdt, HTC, Lns], or to 'lip-Christians' and those who say 'Lord! Lord' (Matthew 7:21) [My], or to nominal believers [BECNT]. To decide whether this refers to Jews who were once a part of God's vine but are now rejected, or to apostate Christians is to push the imagery too far. The clear purpose of the verse is that all true believers will bear fruit, an infallible mark of true Christianity [Car].

QUESTION—What is the point of similarity in this verse?

Just as a vine dresser cuts off branches that do not produce fruit, so the Father takes away those people who produce no spiritual fruit [NTC]. As the vinedresser prunes a vine to increase its production of grapes, so the Father purifies or disciplines believers to enable them to produce more spiritual fruit (Hebrews 12:4–11) [BECNT, Car, IVP, NTC]. The pruning refers to the cutting off of the shoots of their lives that paralyze the power of the Spirit [Gdt]. It is the false and arrogant life that must be pruned from the branch [ICC]. The pruning indicates growing in divine life, growing in union with Jesus and growing in love [AB]. The emphasis is on producing fruit [BECNT, Lns, NICNT1]—the only reason for growing a vine [NICNT1].

QUESTION—What 'fruit' does a believer produce?

'Fruit' probably refers to qualities of Christian character as seen in Galatians 5:22–23 'love, joy, peace, patience, kindness, goodness, faithfulness gentleness and self control', in Philippians 1:9–11, or in similar passages [Kn, Lns, NICNT1, NTC]. These fruits are: 'good motives, desires, attitudes, dispositions (spiritual virtues), words', and 'deeds' [NTC]. Bearing fruit refers to the production and development of the spiritual life in oneself or in others through the strength of Christ living within [Gdt]. In the context of 7–17, fruit is the possession of the life of God and its chief characteristics—knowing God and loving. From this comes both Christian witness and ethical qualities [IVP]. It is simply living as a Christian disciple, perhaps specifically loving each other [Bar]. Fruit-bearing most likely refers to bringing others to Christ [BECNT, NICNT1] as well as producing Christian character [NICNT1].

15:3 You are already clean[a] because-of[b] the word[c] that I-have-spoken to-you.

LEXICON—a. καθαρός (LN 53.29) (BAGD 3.a. p. 388): 'clean' [BAGD, LN; all translations except NLT, NRSV, Ph], 'pure' [BAGD, LN], 'free (from sin)' [BAGD]. The clause 'already you are clean' is translated 'you have already been pruned' [Ph], 'You have already been pruned and purified' [NLT], 'You have already been cleansed' [NRSV]. This adjective describes a thing as being ritually clean or pure. In a number of languages there is simply no relationship between physical cleanness and ritual acceptability or purity. Accordingly, it may be necessary to render καθαρός as 'acceptable to God' or 'good in God's eyes' or 'good as God thinks' [LN]. It indicates a moral and religious sense of being 'pure, free from sin' [BAGD].

b. διά (LN 89.76, 90.44): 'because of' [Gdt, LN (90.44), NICNT2, NTC; CEV, NASB, NCV, NET, NIV, REB], 'by' [HTC, LN (89.76); NLT, NRSV, Ph, TEV], 'by means of' [LN (89.76); NJB], 'on account of' [LN (90.44), WBC], 'thanks to' [AB], 'through' [LN (89.76); KJV]. This

preposition indicates the means by which one event makes another event possible [LN (89.76)]. It may also indicate a participant constituting the cause or reason for an event or state [LN (90.44)].
- c. λόγος (LN 33.260) (BAGD 1.b.β. p. 478): 'word' [AB, Gdt, HTC, NICNT2, NTC, WBC; KJV, NASB, NET, NJB, NIV, NRSV, REB], 'words' [NCV, Ph], 'message' [NLT], 'teaching' [TEV], 'what is preached, gospel' [LN]. The clause 'because of the word that I have spoken to you' is translated 'because of what I have said to you' [CEV]. This noun denotes the content of what is preached about Christ or about the good news [LN]. Here it means Christ's teaching in its entirety [AB, Car, EGT, ICC, My, NICNT1]. It denotes God's revelation to men through Christ and his messengers [BAGD].

QUESTION—What is implied by the word καθαρός 'clean'?
It implies that they had been justified [Lns, NTC] or made clean by having their sins forgiven [Lns]. It implies that they are clean from all that prevents fruit-bearing [AB], and are ready to produce fruit [CH, EGT, NICNT2, Rd] and that gradual cleansing would continue in their lives [NTC].

QUESTION—What words are emphasized in this verse?
The pronoun ὑμεῖς 'you' is emphasized [Lns, NICNT2, TH] making it clear that the disciples are the branches in the vine [NICNT2]: *you yourselves* are clean. 'You' contrasts the disciples with all those who are not yet in such a privileged position [Gdt]. It implies that many others will follow them as disciples [Lns, My].

15:4 Remain[a] in me, and-I in you. As the branch is- not -able to bear fruit by[b] itself unless it-remains in the vine, so neither (can) you unless you-remain in me.

LEXICON—a. aorist act. impera. of μένω (LN 68.11) (BAGD 1.a.β. p. 504): 'to remain' [AB, BAGD, LN, WBC; NCV, NET, NJB, NIV, NLT], 'to remain united (to)' [TEV], 'to stay joined (to)' [CEV], 'to abide' [BAGD, Gdt, HTC, NTC; KJV, NASB, NRSV], 'to dwell' [REB], 'to make one's dwelling' [NICNT2], 'to continue' [BAGD, LN], 'to stay' [BAGD], 'to keep on' [LN]. The command 'remain in me' is translated 'you must go on growing in me' [Ph]. This verb means to continue in an activity or state [LN]. It is used figuratively here of someone who does not leave the realm or sphere in which he finds himself [BAGD]. The aorist tense suggests that this action is an act of the will, a conscious decision to remain in one's present relationship with Jesus [NICNT2].

- b. ἀπό (LN 90.19) (BAGD V.5. p. 88): 'by' [AB, HTC, LN, WBC; NET, NIV, NRSV, REB, TEV], 'of' [BAGD, Gdt, LN, NTC; KJV, NASB], 'on (the basis of), upon' [LN], not explicit [CEV, Ph]. The phrase 'by itself' is translated 'all by (itself)' [NJB], 'on its own' [NICNT2], 'if it is severed from the vine' [NLT], 'alone' [NCV]. This preposition indicates the one who is responsible for an event or state [LN]. It indicates cause, means, or outcome. When a person does not come 'of himself', it means that someone else sent him/her [BAGD]. The phrase 'on its own' is reminiscent of the action of Jesus himself. He never acted 'on his own' but always in dependence on the Father (5:19) [NICNT2, TH].

QUESTION—There are two verbs 'to remain' in this verse. Are they both imperative or is one imperative and the other a future tense?

1. The first verb should be taken as an imperative, the second as a present or future tense [Gdt, EGT, Lns, My, NICNT2, NTC, WBC; CEV, NCV, NET, NIV, NLT, Ph, TEV]: 'Remain united to me and I will remain united to you' [TEV]. The two actions are equivalent. The disciples make their dwelling in Jesus and he makes his dwelling in them. This is God's doing not theirs but they will become aware of it at the Resurrection when he comes to them, and with the Father, makes his home with them. This is seen in 14:20 'On that day you will realize that I am in my Father, and you are in me and I am in you' [NICNT2]. Since the emphasis here is on Jesus it is likely that he is encouraging the disciples here 'Remain in me and be assured, I am remaining in union with you' [WBC].

    1.1 The first verb should be taken as an imperative, the second as a model [AB; NJB, NRSV, REB]: 'Remain in me, as I in you' [NJB].

    1.2 The first is an imperative to which the second is the result [BECNT, Car, Gdt]. The disciples must remain in Jesus so that Jesus will remain in them [BECNT]. Jesus' remaining in them is conditional on their remaining in him. 'If you remain in me, I will remain in you' [Car, Gdt]. Of the options, this choice has the slight edge, but the general thought is clear [Car].

2. The verbs of the two clauses should be taken as imperatives [Bar, IVP, NICNT1]: 'Abide in me and see that I abide in you' [NICNT1]. Jesus means that the disciples should so live that he will continue to abide in them [NICNT1]. Verse 5 suggests that the two balanced clauses should be very closely taken together meaning 'Let there be mutual indwelling' [Bar]. Both parties must be engaged. Jesus must take the initiative, making available the means and ability for the union to occur, but the disciples must also play their part [IVP].

QUESTION—What does it mean to 'remain' in Jesus?

Remaining in Jesus consists primarily in holding fast to his teaching (8:31) [BECNT]. To remain means 'to live in fellowship with', 'to live in union with', or 'to remain united with' [TH]. To remain or stay somewhere implies a continuing relationship, one that is already going on. Note, 'already you are clean' (13:10) [NICNT2]. Remaining involves more than believing in Jesus. It also consists of being united with him, sharing his thoughts, emotions, purposes, and power [IVP]. To remain means to adhere to Jesus as one's vital source of help and strength [Rd]. It has to do with continual dependence and reliance on him, obedience to him, and tenacious imbibing of his life [Car]. In this context it means continued and complete dependence for one's Christian life on the indwelling Christ [Gdt, Kn]. Remaining in Jesus is believing in him and taking in of his freely given grace over and over [Lns]. The phrase is a favorite of John to denote an inward, enduring personal communion. So of God in his relation to Christ, and of Christians in their relation to Christ [BAGD].

QUESTION—What is indicated by the present tense of the verbs 'unless it remains' and 'unless you remain'?

It indicates that the action of remaining is continuous [Lns].

QUESTION—What word is emphasized in this verse?

The pronoun ὑμεῖς 'you' is emphasized [NICNT2]: so neither can *you yourselves* unless you remain in me.

15:5 **I am the vine, you (are) the branches. He-who remains in me and-I in him this-one[a] bears much fruit, because you-can do nothing without[b] me.**

LEXICON—a. οὗτος (LN 92.29) (BAGD 1.a.ε p. 596): 'this one' [Gdt, LN], 'this' [BAGD, LN], 'he' [NICNT2; NASB, NIV], 'he it is that' [HTC, NTC], 'the same' [KJV], 'they' [NCV], not explicit [WBC; CEV, NET, NJB, NLT, NRSV, REB, TEV]. The clause 'this one bears much fruit' is translated 'It is the man…who proves fruitful' [Ph], 'He…is the one who bears much fruit' [AB]. This demonstrative pronoun refers to an entity regarded as a part of the discourse setting [LN]. It refers to someone comparatively near at hand and previously mentioned with special emphasis [BAGD].

b. χωρίς (LN 89.120) (BAGD 2.a.α p. 890): 'without' [BAGD, LN; CEV, KJV, NCV, TEV], 'apart from' [AB, Gdt, HTC, NICNT2, NTC, WBC; BAGD, LN; NASB, NET, NIV, NLT, NRSV, Ph, REB], 'cut off from (me)' [NJB], 'not with, no relationship to, independent of' [LN]. This preposition indicates negatively linked elements [LN]. When used with the genitive case of the person as here, it means 'separated from someone, far from someone, without someone' [BAGD]. 'Without me' can be translated 'only with my help'. For example, 'you cannot do anything except with my help' [TH].

QUESTION—Does 'nothing' mean 'absolutely nothing'?

It means nothing that is acceptable to God [Lns, NTC], or nothing that is honoring to him or that can be called fruit-bearing [EGT]. It means no spiritual achievement [NICNT1], or nothing that relates to the new life that Jesus brings and the command he gives [Rd].

QUESTION—What is the main point of this verse?

It is the total dependence of the believer on Jesus [NICNT2].

QUESTION—What words are emphasized in this verse?

The two pronouns ἐγώ 'I' and ὑμεῖς 'you' are emphatic and are contrasted [Lns, NICNT1]: 'I on my part am the vine, you on yours are the branches' [Lns]. The pronoun ὑμεῖς 'you' is emphasized as it is in verses 3 and 4 [NICNT2]. The phrase χωρὶς ἐμοῦ 'without me' is emphatic in the Greek [TH]. This phrase, 'without me', plus the double negative in the clause οὐ δύνασθε ποιεῖν οὐδέν (literally) 'you are *not* able to do *nothing*', emphasizes the futility of independent action apart from Christ. The positive of this statement is seen in Philippians 'I can do everything through him who gives me strength' [NICNT1]. The pronoun οὗτος 'this one' is emphatic [AB, BAGD, HTC, ICC, Lns, my, NTC; Ph]: 'he it is that (bears much fruit)' [ICC].

15:6 **If anyone does- not -remain in me, he-is-thrown[a] away like a branch and withers[b] and they-gather[c] them and throw (them) into the fire and they-are-burned.[d]**

LEXICON—a. aorist pass. indic. of βάλλω (LN 15.215) (BAGD 1.b. p. 131): 'to be thrown' [BAGD, LN]. The phrase 'he is thrown away' [NTC; NASB, similarly WBC; NCV, NJB, NIV, NLT, NRSV, REB] is also translated 'he is thrown out' [NICNT2; NET, TEV], 'he is cast forth' [Gdt, HTC; KJV], 'he is…cast off' [AB], 'you will be thrown away' [CEV]. The clause 'he is thrown away like a branch' is translated 'He becomes just like the dry sticks that men pick up and use (for firewood)' [Ph].

b. aorist pass. indic. of ξηραίνομαι (LN **79.81**) (BAGD 2.a. p. 548): 'to wither' [HTC, NTC; NJB, NIV, NLT, NRSV], 'to wither away' [Ph], 'to be withered' [AB, BAGD, Gdt, NICNT2; KJV, REB], 'to become withered' [WBC], 'to dry up' [**LN**; NASB, NET, TEV], 'to be dried up' [BAGD], 'to become dry' [BAGD, LN]. The word 'withers' is translated '(You) will be like dry branches' [CEV], '(and then) dies' [NCV]. This verb is derived from the adjective ξηρός 'dry' and means to become dry [LN].

c. pres. act. indic. of συνάγω (LN 15.125) (BAGD 1. p. 782): 'to gather' [Gdt, NICNT2, WBC; KJV, NASB], 'to gather up' [CEV, NET], 'to be gathered' [HTC; NLT, NRSV], 'to be gathered up' [REB, TEV], 'to pick up' [NCV, Ph], 'to be picked up' [NTC; NIV], 'to collect' [AB], 'to be collected' [NJB], 'to gather in' [BAGD], 'to gather together' [LN]. This verb means to cause to come together, whether of animate or inanimate objects [LN].

d. pres. pass. indic. of καίω (LN 14.63) (BAGD 2. p. 396): 'to be burned' [BAGD, LN; all translations except NICNT2, Gdt; NCV, NET, Ph], 'to be burned up' [BAGD, NICNT2; NET], 'to burn' [Gdt; NCV]. The verb phrase 'is burned' is translated '(that men pick up and) use for firewood' [Ph]. This verb means the process of burning [LN].

QUESTION—Who is the implied actor of the Greek phrase ἐβλήθη ἔξω 'he is thrown away'?

The implied actor is probably God, the gardener [HTC, Lns].

DISCOURSE UNIT—15:7–17 [IVP]. The topic is the image of the vine applied.

15:7 **If you-remain in me and my words remain in you, ask-for**[a] **whatever you-want,**[b] **and it-will-be-done for-you.**

LEXICON—a. aorist mid. impera. of αἰτέω (LN 33.163) (BAGD p. 26): 'to ask for' [AB, BAGD, LN; NJB, NLT, NRSV, Ph, TEV], 'to ask' [BAGD, Gdt, HTC, NICNT2, NTC, WBC; KJV, NASB, NCV, NET, NIV, REB], 'to pray for' [CEV], 'to demand' [BAGD, LN], 'to plead for' [LN]. This verb means to ask for with urgency, even to the point of demanding [LN].
   b. pres. act. subj. of θέλω (LN 25.1): 'to want' [AB, LN, NICNT2; CEV, NCV, NET, NLT, REB], 'to wish' [LN, WBC; NASB, NIV, NRSV, TEV], 'to will' [Gdt, HTC, NTC; KJV], 'to like' [Ph], 'to desire' [LN]. The clause 'ask for whatever you want' is translated 'ask for whatever you please' [NJB]. This verb means to desire to have or experience something [LN].

QUESTION—Is the verb 'to ask for' imperative, future, or another mood?
  1. It is an imperative [AB, Bar, EGT, Gdt, GNT, ICC, HTC, LN, Lns, NICNT2, NTC, WBC; NASB, NET, NIV, NRSV, REB]. The verb is peremptory or commanding. We are not merely permitted to ask for ourselves, we *must* ask [Lns].
  2. It is a future or some other mood [CEV, NCV, NJB, NLT, Ph, TEV]: 'you will ask/ask for' [KJV, TEV], 'you may ask for' [NJB, NLT], 'you can ask/ask for/pray for' [CEV, NCV, Ph].

QUESTION—How do Jesus' words remain in a person?
The words of Jesus remain in a person by his continually remembering them, and habitually meditating on them [AB]. They remain in a person by their act of committing themselves to obey them [BECNT, Car, HTC, NTC, Rd; NCV]. They take root or dwell in the person so as to govern his/her attitudes and actions [NICNT2]. The person both believes Jesus' words and obeys them so that they take complete control of him/her [NTC]. When Jesus' words remain in a person, they share his mind and will [IVP]. This action replaces the action of 'I in you' of verses 4 and 5 [Rd]. The words 'my words remain in you' explain what 'if you remain in me' (verse 4) means [Lns].

QUESTION—Why will a person who fulfills these two conditions get the requests he asks for?
They will receive them because such a person's requests will be in sync with God's will [Bar, BECNT, Car, ICC, IVP, NICNT1]. The person who stays in union with Jesus will ask for what will make Jesus' work fruitful (14:13) [HTC]. A person under the complete control of Jesus will always ask as he would ask—'Not my will, but yours be done' (Luke 22:42) and in harmony with the character of Jesus [NTC].

QUESTION—Who is the implied actor of γενήσεται 'it will be done'?
God is the implied actor [AB, HTC, Lns, NICNT2, TH, TRT]: 'it will be done for you by Him' [TRT]. Verse 16 states, '...the Father will give you whatever you ask in my name' [AB]. Matthew 18:19 states, '...anything you

ask for…will be done for you by my Father in heaven' [HTC]. See also Matthew 7:7 and Luke 11:9 [NICNT2].

QUESTION—What words are emphasized in this verse?

The words 'whatever you want' are placed forward in the clause to give them more prominence [Lns, My, TRT]: 'What you may will, ask for yourselves' [Lns].

DISCOURSE UNIT—15:8–17 [Kn]. The topic is the command to love.

15:8 My Father is-glorified[a] by this,[b] that[c] you-bear much fruit and become[d] my disciples.

TEXT—Instead of the aorist subjunctive γένησθε 'you may become', some manuscripts read the future indicative γενήσεσθε 'you will become', and one manuscript reads the present indicative γίνεσθε 'you are becoming'. GNT, along with Car, EGT, GNT, Lns, NICNT2, and Rd, reads 'you may become' with a C rating, indicating difficulty in deciding which variant to place in the text. The reading 'you will become' is taken by AB, Bar, EGT, Gdt, ICC, HTC, My, NICNT1, NTC.

LEXICON—a. aorist pass. indic. of δοξάζω (LN 87.24) (BAGD 2. p. 204): 'to be glorified' [AB, BAGD, Gdt, HTC, LN, NICNT2, NTC; KJV, NASB, NRSV, Ph, REB], 'to become glorified' [WBC], 'to bring (great) glory to' [NCV, NLT], 'to be honored' [CEV, NET], 'to be made gloriously great' [LN], 'to be clothed in splendor' [BAGD]. The clause 'My Father is glorified in this' is translated 'It is to the glory of my Father' [NJB], 'This is to my Father's glory' [NIV], 'My Father's glory is shown by (your bearing much fruit)' [TEV]. This verb means to cause someone to have glorious greatness [LN]. It means to reveal the Father's true glory [TH].

b. οὗτος (LN 92.29) (BAGD 1.b.β. p. 597): 'this' [AB, BAGD, LN, HTC, NICNT2, NTC WBC; NASB, NET, NIV, NRSV], 'herein' [Gdt; KJV], 'This is how' [Ph, REB]. The clause 'My Father is glorified in this' is translated 'When you become fruitful disciples of mine, my Father will be honored' [CEV], 'When you produce much fruit, you are my true disciples. This brings great glory to my Father' [NLT], 'You should produce much fruit and show that you are my followers, which brings glory to my Father' [NCV], 'It is to the glory of my Father that you should bear much fruit' [NJB], 'My Father's glory is shown by your bearing much fruit' [TEV]. This demonstrative pronoun indicates a reference to an entity regarded as a part of the discourse setting [LN]. It refers forward to what follows, especially before clauses that express a statement, purpose, result, or condition, which it introduces [BAGD].

c. ἵνα (LN 91.15) (BAGD II.1.e. p. 378): 'that' [Gdt, HTC, LN, NICNT2, NTC, WBC; KJV, NASB, NET, NJB, NIV, NRSV], 'namely' [BECNT, LN], 'namely that, that is' [LN], not explicit [AB; CEV, NCV, NLT, Ph, REB, TEV]. This conjunction indicates identificational and explanatory clauses [LN]. It denotes purpose, aim, or goal 'in order that, that'. But very often the purposive meaning of ἵνα is greatly weakened, or

JOHN 15:8

disappears altogether. Here it takes the place of the explanatory infinitive after the demonstrative pronoun 'this' [BAGD].
d. aorist. mid. subj. of γίνομαι (LN 13.48) (BAGD II.1. p. 160): 'to become' [LN], 'to be' [BAGD]. The clause 'and become disciples to me' is translated 'and become my disciples' [NICNT2, similarly AB, WBC; NJB, NRSV, Ph], 'and so be my disciples' [REB], 'so you shall/will become/be my disciples' [Gdt, NTC; KJV], 'and in this way you become my disciples' [TEV], 'and show that you are my followers/disciples' [NCV, NET], 'showing yourselves to be my disciples' [NIV], 'and so prove to be my disciples' [HTC; NASB], '(when you produce much fruit), you are my true disciples' [NLT]. This verb means to come to acquire or experience a state [LN].

QUESTION—Does οὗτος 'this' refer forward or back?

1. It refers forward to the conjunction 'that' following [AB, BAGD, Bar, BECNT, EGT, Gdt, IVP, Lns, NICNT1, NTC, Rd, TH, WBC; all versions]: 'My Father is honored by this, that you bear much fruit' [NET]. The demonstrative pronoun 'this' is followed by an explanatory conjunction ἵνα 'that' [AB, Bar, BAGD, Gdt]. It means, 'in this preeminently' that is, by your bearing much fruit [EGT].
2. It refers back to the previous verse [ICC, My]. 'In this' refers back to the disciples' abiding in Christ of verse 7 [ICC]. The Father is glorified in their receiving what they ask for as they abide in Christ [My].
3. It looks simultaneously forward and back [Car, NICNT2]. Looking back to verse 7 it relates to receiving answers to their prayers (see also 14:13) and forward to bearing fruit. Both result in bringing glory to the Father [NICNT2]. Success in prayer means glory to the Father as does fruit bearing [Car].

QUESTION—What is the relationship between the clause 'and you become my disciples' and the clause 'that you bear much fruit'?

1. They are in a coordinate relationship [AB, Lns, NICNT2, WBC; NCV, NET, NJB, NRSV, Ph]: 'This is how my Father will be glorified—in your becoming fruitful and being my disciples' [Ph].
2. They are in a means-result relationship [Gdt, ICC, NTC; KJV, NASB, REB, TEV]: '(My Father's glory is shown by) your bearing much fruit; and in this way you become my disciples' [TEV], 'you are to bear fruit in plenty and so be my disciples' [REB].
3. The bearing of fruit will show or prove that they are disciples [Bar, HTC; NASB, NCV, NET, NIV, NLT]: 'that you bear much fruit, showing yourselves to be my disciples' [NIV].

QUESTION—What word is emphasized in this verse?

The demonstrative pronoun οὗτος 'this' is emphasized [EGT]: 'In this preeminently' [EGT].

DISCOURSE UNIT—15:9–17 [Rd]. The topic is remain in my love.

DISCOURSE UNIT—15:9–16 [Car]. The topic is the metaphor explained.

15:9 Just-as[a] the Father loved[b] me, so-I[c] loved you. Remain[d] in my love.

LEXICON—a. καθώς (LN **64.14**) (BAGD 1. p. 391): 'just as' [BAGD, LN, NICNT2, NTC; CEV, NASB, NET, NJB, Ph, TEV], 'as' [AB, BAGD, Gdt, HTC, WBC; KJV, NCV, NIV, NRSV, REB], 'even as' [NLT], 'in comparison to' [LN]. The clause 'As the Father loved me' is translated 'the same way as the Father loved me' [**LN**]. This conjunction indicates similarity in events and states, with the possible implication of something being in accordance with something else [LN]. The construction καθώς...καί indicates 'as...so' or 'as...so also' [BAGD]. This indicates that the Father's love for Jesus is the basis of his love for his disciples, both as to origin and to intensity [AB]. It indicates that Jesus' love for his disciples was exactly like the Father's love for him [Lns, NTC].

b. aorist act. indic. of ἀγαπάω (LN 25.43) (BAGD 1.b.α. p. 4): 'to love' [BAGD, LN; all translations], 'to regard with affection' [LN], 'to cherish' [BAGD]. This verb means to have love for someone or something based on sincere appreciation and high regard [LN]. It means to have affection for someone [BAGD].

c. κἀγώ (BAGD 3.a. p. 386): 'so I' [AB, HTC, NICNT2, NTC, WBC; KJV, NIV, NRSV, REB], 'I also' [BAGD, Gdt; NASB, NET], 'I too' [BAGD], 'I' [CEV, NCV, NJB, NLT, Ph, TEV]. This complex form is a combination of καί + ἐγώ, 'and' + 'I' [BAGD].

d. aorist act. impera. of μένω (LN 68.11) (BAGD 1.a.β. p. 504): 'to remain' [BAGD, LN, WBC; NCV, NET, NIV, NJB, NLT, TEV], 'to abide' [BAGD, Gdt, HTC, NTC; NRSV], 'remain faithful to' [CEV], 'to remain on (in)' [AB], 'to live (in)' [Ph], 'to dwell' [REB], 'to make one's dwelling (in)' [NICNT2], 'to continue' [BAGD, LN; KJV], 'to stay' [BAGD], 'to keep on' [LN]. This verb means to continue in an activity or state [LN]. It is used figuratively here to mean to not leave the realm or sphere in which a person finds him/herself [BAGD]. The aorist tense may have been used to emphasize the command [Bar, TH]. It gives it a sense of authority [AB, ICC].

QUESTION—How does a person remain in Jesus' love?

They do so by obeying his commands (verse 10) [Car, CH, IVP]. They do so by staying in a close relationship with him so that they experience his love for them [TRT]. They do so by depending on his love for support and doing those things that please him [WBC]. The command to remain in Jesus' love means to make his love for them their very identity [NICNT2].

QUESTION—How are the two nouns related in the genitive construction 'my love'?

They indicate that Jesus loves his disciples [AB, Bar, BECNT, Gdt, HTC, IVP, Lns, My, NICNT1, NICNT2, NTC, TH]. This is clear from his just having said, 'I also loved you' [My].

QUESTION—How can the clause, 'remain in my love for you' be translated?
In some languages it may be difficult to translate 'remain in my love for you'. Alternatives could be: 'remain joined to me so that I may love you' or 'continue obeying me so that I may love you' [TH].

15:10 **If you-keep[a] my commands, you-will-remain in my love, just-as I have-kept my Father's commands and remain in his love.**
LEXICON—a. aorist act. subj. of τηρέω (LN 36.19) (BAGD 5. p. 815): 'to keep' [AB, BAGD, Gdt, HTC, LN, NICNT2, NTC, WBC; KJV, NASB, NJB, NRSV, Ph], 'to obey' [LN; CEV, NCV, NET, NIV, NLT, TEV], 'to heed' [REB], 'to observe, to fulfill, to pay attention to' [BAGD]. This verb means to continue to obey orders or commandments [LN]. Obedience to Jesus' commands is the means by which a person remains in his love [BECNT, Car, ICC, NICNT1, Rd, TH, WBC].
QUESTION—How can this verse be translated so as to be more easily understood?
In some languages it may be difficult to translate the idea of remaining in someone's love. It could be translated 'If you obey my commands, I will continue to love you, just as I have obeyed my Father's commands, and so he continues to love me' [TH].
QUESTION—What is an important fact that this verse teaches?
It teaches that his disciples should obey him out of a sense of love not out of obligation or fear [BECNT]. It teaches that love and obedience are mutually dependent—love springs from obedience, obedience from love [Bar]. It teaches that Jesus is subject to the same conditions as he demands of his followers [EGT].
QUESTION—What is indicated by the present tense 'I remain' in the clause '(I) remain in his love'?
It indicates that Jesus remains continually in the Father's love [NICNT1, NTC, TH, TRT; CEV]: 'I will keep on loving you, just as my Father keeps loving me' [CEV].
QUESTION—What word is emphasized in this verse?
In the pronoun ἐγώ 'I' coupled with the perfect τετήρηκα 'have kept' there is emphasis on Jesus' complete keeping of the Father's commands [TH].

15:11 **I-have-told you these-things so-that[a] my joy[b] may-be in you and (that) your joy may-be-made-full.[c]**
LEXICON—a. ἵνα (LN 89.59): 'so that' [LN, NICNT2; NASB, NCV, NET, NIV, NJB, NLT, NRSV, Ph, REB, TEV], 'that' [AB, Gdt, HTC, WBC; KJV], 'in order that' [NTC], 'to (make…happy)' [CEV], 'in order to, for the purpose of' [LN]. This conjunction indicates purpose for events and states (sometimes occurring in highly elliptical contexts) [LN]. 'So that' indicates purpose here [BECNT, NICNT1].
b. χαρά (LN 25.123) (BAGD 1. p. 875): 'joy' [BAGD, LN; all translations except CEV], 'gladness' [LN], 'great happiness' [LN]. This noun is also translated as an adjective: '(to make you as completely) happy (as I am)'

[CEV]. It denotes a state of joy and gladness [LN]. Johannine literature places emphasis on joy as brought to the highest degree [BAGD].
   c. aorist pass. subj. of πληρόω (LN 59.33) (BAGD 3. p. 671): 'to be made full' [BAGD; NASB], 'to be full' [HTC, NTC; KJV], 'to be made complete' [BAGD, LN], 'to be complete' [WBC; NET, NIV, NJB, NRSV, Ph, REB, TEV], 'to be fulfilled' [AB, Gdt, NICNT2], 'to be brought to completion, to be finished' [BAGD]. The clause 'so that your joy may be made complete' is translated 'so that your joy will be the fullest possible joy' [NCV], to make you as completely happy as I am' [CEV]. This verb means to make something total or complete [LN]. Ways of expressing this thought are: 'so that you may be completely joyful/happy', or negatively 'so that there may be nothing lacking in your joy' [TH].

QUESTION—What does it mean to have Jesus' love *in* someone?
   This idea is translated: 'so that you will be filled with my joy' [NLT], 'so that you can have the same joy I have' [TRT; NCV], 'so that you can have the same kind of joy that I have' [TH], 'so that you can share my joy' [Ph].

QUESTION—How are the nouns related in the genitive construction ἡ χαρὰ ἡ ἐμὴ 'my joy'?
   'My joy' is the joy that Jesus experiences as he obeys the Father and is the object of his love [AB, Bar, EGT, Gdt, Rd, TH]. 'My joy' is the joy that I have [My, TRT; NCV], or that I experience [EGT; CEV]. The phrase 'my joy' means 'the joy that I impart' [NTC]. Jesus wants his disciples to experience this same kind of joy as they obey him [EGT, Gdt, Rd].

QUESTION—Who is the implied actor in πληρωθῇ 'may be made full'?
   It is Jesus who will make the joy of the disciples full [Lns].

QUESTION—What words are emphasized in this verse and to what do they refer?
   The words 'these things' is placed first in the verse to make it more prominent [TRT]. By 'these things' Jesus is referring to the statement in verse 10 'if you keep my commands you will remain in my love' [ICC]. They refer to the previous 10 verses [Lns, NTC]. They may refer to what Jesus had just said in verses 7–10 or they may also include verses 1–6 or even chapter 14 and the rest of chapter 15 [TRT]. They include more than what he said in verse 10 because Jesus' love of verse 9 is the real basis of joy here [AB, TH]. They may also include verses 7 and 8 [TH].

DISCOURSE UNIT—15:12–17 [HTC; NASB]. The topic is love one another.

15:12 This is my command, that you-love[a] each-other as I-loved you. **15:13** No-one has greater love[b] than-this, that someone lay-down- his -life[c] for[d] his friends.[e]

LEXICON—a. pres. act. subj. of ἀγαπάω (LN 25.43) (BAGD 1.a.α. p. 4): 'to love' [BAGD, LN; all translations], 'to regard with affection' [LN]. This verb means to have love for someone or something, based on sincere appreciation and high regard [LN]. The present tense indicates that the

JOHN 15:12–13

action is continuous 'keep on loving each other' [AB, BECNT, ICC, Lns, NTC, TH], habitual [NICNT1], and lifelong [AB]. This love is not just a feeling, it is choosing to will the good of another and laying down one's life for that person [IVP].

b. ἀγάπη (LN 25.43) (BAGD I.2.a. p. 6): 'love' [BAGD, LN; all translations].

c. τὴν ψυχὴν τίθημι (LN 23.113) (BAGD I.1.b.δ. p. 816): 'to lay down one's life' [AB, BAGD, Gdt, HTC, LN, NICNT2; KJV, NASB, NET, NIV, NJB, NLT, NRSV, Ph, REB], 'to give one's life (for)' [BAGD; TEV], 'to die (for)' [CEV, NCV], 'to die voluntarily, to die willingly' [LN]. This idiom, literally 'to lay down one's life' means to die with the implication of voluntary or willing action. It may be necessary to use such expressions as 'to die willingly' or 'to die without resisting'. In some languages 'willingly' is expressed primarily as a negation of objecting, for example, 'I will not object to dying' [LN]. Here the sense of 'laying down' is 'to give up' [TH].

d. ὑπέρ (LN 90.36) (BAGD 1.a.ε. p. 838): 'for' [BAGD, LN; all translations except WBC], 'for the sake of' [BAGD, LN, WBC], 'on behalf of' [BAGD, LN]. This preposition indicates a participant who is benefited by an event or on whose behalf an event takes place [LN].

e. φίλος (LN 34.11) (BAGD 2.a.α. p. 861): 'friend' [BAGD, LN; all translations except AB]. This noun is also translated as a phrase: 'those he loves' [AB]. This noun denotes a male person with whom one associates and for whom there is affection or personal regard [LN]. This noun is derived from the verb φιλέω and means to love with affection, implying an affectionate, intimate relation [Lns].

QUESTION—In verse 12, what is the relationship between the conjunction ἵνα 'that' and the preceding pronoun αὕτη 'this'?

The word 'that' supplies the contents of the command to which the pronoun 'this' refers [BECNT, Lns, HTC]: *This* is my command *that* you love each other.

QUESTION—How does the clause 'as I loved you' define how they are to love each other?

They were not to love each other with just a faint notion of goodwill. If it was to be as he loved them, it would have to be a love that would pour itself out in sacrifice. How great that sacrifice would be is spelled out in the next verse [ICC].

QUESTION—To what other command is verse 12 similar?

John 13:34 states almost the same thought 'A new command I give you: Love one another. As I have loved you, so you must love one another' [Car, NICNT1].

QUESTION—In verse 13, what is the relationship between the conjunction ἵνα 'that (you love)' to the preceding phrase 'than this'?
  The clause introduced by 'that' explains the contents of 'this' [AB, Bar, BECNT, EGT, HTC, ICC]: *this* (love)...*that* someone lay down his life for his friends.
QUESTION—How does verse 13 relate to verse 12?
  It explains the way in which Jesus loves his disciples [TH]. It serves to clarify what Jesus meant by loving each other as he loved them—it meant for them to lay down their lives for each other [My, Rd].
QUESTION—How can verse 13 be translated positively?
  It could be translated 'If a man dies for his friends, that shows that he has the greatest love that anyone could have' [TH]. 'The greatest way that a person can show his friends that he loves them is to die for them' [TRT; similarly CEV] or 'there is no greater way for someone to show that he loves his friends than to give up his life to save them' [TRT]. 'The greatest love you can have for your friends is to give your life for them' [TEV].
QUESTION—What word is emphasized in verse 12?
  There is strong emphasis on the pronoun 'my' in the phrase ἡ ἐντολὴ ἡ ἐμή 'my command' [Lns].

15:14 You are my friends if[a] you-do what I command[b] you.
LEXICON—a. ἐάν (LN 89.67) (BAGD I.1.a. p. 211): 'if' [BAGD, LN; all translations except AB], 'when' [AB]. This conjunction indicates a condition, with the implication of reduced probability [LN]. It is used with the subjunctive to denote what is expected to occur, under certain circumstances, from a given standpoint in the present, either general or specific [BAGD]. The conjunction expects that they will do what he commands [Lns]. The condition has the sense of a first-class condition. It assumes that they are doing his commands. Or it has the sense of a participle 'You are my friends in doing what I command you'. They do not have to do this to become Jesus' friends, they already are his friends (verse 15) [NICNT2]. Obeying his commands is not what makes them his friends, it is what characterizes them as his friends [Car].
  b. pres. mid. or pass. (deponent = active) indic. of ἐντέλλομαι (LN 33.329) (BAGD p. 268): 'to command' [BAGD, LN; all translations except NTC; CEV, TEV]. The clause 'if you do the things that I command you' is translated 'if you obey me' [CEV], 'if you do what I tell you to do' [Ph], 'if you do what I bid you' [NTC]. This verb means to give definite orders, implying authority or official sanction [LN].
QUESTION—What is implied by this verse?
  It implies that doing his commands will prove that they are his friends and that he will die for them [My, TH]. It implies that to be a friend assumes common aims and outlook and so Jesus qualifies the clause 'you are my friends' with the condition 'if you do what I command' [NICNT1].

JOHN 15:14

QUESTION—Is the new status of the disciples as friends of Jesus significant?
In the time of Jesus, disciples of a rabbi were considered his servants [CH, TRT]. Jesus raised the disciples to a new level of relationship—friend to friend [CH].

QUESTION—What is indicated by the present tense of '(if) you do'?
It indicates that the action is continuous [Lns, NICNT2] or habitual [NICNT1]: 'You are my friends if you keep doing what I bid you' [Lns].

QUESTION—What words are emphasized in this verse?
The pronouns ὑμεῖς 'you' and ἐγώ 'I' are emphasized [BECNT, NICNT1, NICNT2]: *You yourselves* are my friends if you do what *I myself* command you. He means 'you, and not the world in general' and 'I and no other' [NICNT1].

15:15 I- no-longer -call[a] you servants,[b] because the servent does- not -know what his master[c] is-doing. But I-have-called you friends, because I-have-made-known to-you all that I-heard from my Father.

LEXICON—a. pres. act. indic. of λέγω (LN 33.131) (BAGD II.3. p. 470): 'to call' [AB, BAGD, LN; all translations except CEV, NICNT2], 'to name' [BAGD, LN]. The clause 'I no longer call you servants' is translated 'I no longer say that you are slaves' [NICNT2], 'I don't speak to you as my servants' [CEV]. This verb means to use a name in speaking of a person [LN].

b. δοῦλος (LN 87.76) (BAGD 4, p. 206): 'servant' [AB, Gdt, HTC, NTC, WBC; CEV, KJV, NCV, NIV, NJB, NRSV, Ph, REB, TEV], 'slave' [BAGD, LN, NICNT2; NASB, NET, NLT], 'bondservant' [LN]. This noun denotes one who is a slave in the sense of becoming the property of an owner (though in ancient times it was frequently possible for a slave to earn his freedom) [LN]. In the culture of the Jews, a rabbi's disciples were also considered his servants. In 12:26 and 13:13–16 Jesus implies that his disciples are his servants [TRT]. The word 'servant' is a better choice than 'slave' because the term 'slave' is derogatory [TH, TRT] and the disciples did not have the relationship with Jesus of slaves to an owner [TH].

c. κύριος (LN 57.12) (BAGD II.1.a.β. p. 459): 'master' [BAGD, LN, NTC, WBC; all translations except NICNT2; KJV], 'lord' [BAGD, LN, NICNT2; KJV], 'owner' [BAGD, LN]. This noun denotes one who owns and controls property, including especially servants and slaves, with important supplementary semantic components of high status and respect [LN].

QUESTION—What was the position of a servant to his master?
A servant was considered an instrument. He had no right to enter intelligently into the purposes of his master [NICNT2]. A servant was never given a reason for the work he was ordered to do [EGT, ICC, Lns, NTC]. A servant was expected to follow orders without understanding [AB, ICC] or without asking questions [Rd].

QUESTION—What words are emphatic in the Greek in this verse?
The object pronoun ὑμᾶς 'you' is emphatic [TH, TRT] being fronted (Greek order: '*you* I have called friends') to increase its prominence [TRT]: But *you, on your part*, I have called friends. The clause 'all that I heard from my Father' is emphatic [TH, TRT], being fronted (Greek order: 'all that I heard from my Father I have made known to you') to increase its prominence [TRT].

15:16 You did- not -choose[a] me, but[b] I chose you and appointed[c] you that you should-go and should-bear fruit and your fruit should-last,[d] so-that[e] whatever you-ask the Father in my name he-may-give to-you.

LEXICON—a. aorist act. indic. of ἐκλέγομαι (LN 30.92) (BAGD 2.a. p. 242): 'to choose' [BAGD, LN; all translations], 'to select' [BAGD]. This verb means to make a special choice based on significant preference, often implying a strongly favorable attitude toward what is chosen [LN]. It means 'to choose someone for oneself' [BAGD]. In the NT this term refers to setting a person apart for a specific ministry such as Paul's work as an apostle [BECNT, Car].

  b. ἀλλά (LN 89.125): 'but' [Gdt, HTC, LN, NICNT2, NTC, WBC; KJV, NASB, NET, NIV, NRSV, Ph], 'no' [NJB], 'on the contrary, instead' [LN], not explicit [AB; CEV, NCV, NLT, REB, TEV]. This conjunction indicates more emphatic contrast than δέ (89.124) [LN]. It is strongly adversative [BECNT, NICNT1].

  c. aorist act. indic. of τίθημι (LN **37.96**): 'to appoint' [AB, **LN**, Gdt, HTC, NICNT2, NTC; NASB, NET, NIV, NLT, NRSV, Ph, REB, TEV], 'to commission' [NJB], 'to ordain' [KJV], 'to give work to' [NCV], 'to set aside' [WBC], 'to send' [CEV], 'to give a task to, to designate, to assign' [LN]. This verb means to assign someone to a particular task, function, or role [LN].

  d. pres. act. subj. of μένω (LN 13.89) (BAGD 1.c.β. p. 504): 'to last' [BAGD, NICNT2; CEV, NCV, NIV, NRSV, REB], 'to remain' [AB, BAGD, Gdt, LN, WBC; KJV, NASB, NET, NJB], 'to endure' [TEV], 'to abide' [HTC, NTC], 'to persist, to continue to live' [BAGD], 'to continue, to continue to exist, to still be in existence' [LN]. This verb is also translated as an adjective 'lasting (fruit)' [NLT, Ph]. This verb means to continue to exist [LN].

  e. ἵνα (LN 89.49): 'so that' [AB, HTC, LN, NTC, WBC; NET, NJB, NRSV, REB], 'that' [Gdt, LN, NICNT2; KJV, NASB], 'then' [CEV, NCV, NIV], 'and so' [TEV], 'so as a result' [LN]. This conjunction indicates result, though in some cases implying an underlying or indirect purpose [LN].

QUESTION—How are the two ἵνα 'that'-clauses, '*that* you should go and should bear fruit', and '*that* whatever you ask the Father in my name he may give it to you' related?

  1. They are coordinate and both indicate purpose [AB, BECNT, Bar, Car, EGT, HTC, ICC, Lns, My, NICNT1, NICNT2, NTC, Rd, WBC; NET,

NJB, NRSV, Ph, REB]. The two purpose clauses refer back to the verb 'I appointed you to'. That is, the purpose of choosing and appointing the disciples is that they bear fruit and that they experience having their prayers answered [Bar, Lns, Rd]. It is impossible for the disciples to bear lasting fruit unless their requests are granted [EGT, HTC, My]. The purpose of fruit-bearing is so that their requests will be granted [ICC, NICNT1]. Jesus is reminding the disciples that success in fruit-bearing is gained only through answered prayer [Car, NICNT2, NTC]. Jesus desires that his disciples bear fruit so he promises them that their prayers will be answered [HTC].
2. The first indicates purpose and the second indicates that it is the result of it [Gdt, IVP, LN, TH; CEV, NCV, NIV, TEV]: 'I...sent you out to produce fruit....Then my Father will give you whatever you ask for in my name' [CEV]. The result of bearing fruit will be that their requests will be granted [IVP].

QUESTION—Does the verb ὑπάγω 'to go' have the meaning to go as to go on a mission, or is it just acting as an auxiliary to the verb 'bear fruit'?
1. The verb 'to go' refers to the disciples going out with the Good News commissioned by Jesus [Bar, Car, CH, EGT, Lns, My, WBC, NICNT1]. The first action is to act as Jesus' ambassadors, the second is that they bear fruit [NICNT1].
2. The verb 'to go' probably does not refer to missionary activity [AB, Rd; CEV]: 'I...sent you out to produce fruit' [CEV]. The combining of the verbs 'to go and bear fruit' reflects Semitic syntax in which the verb 'to go' is redundant. It could be omitted without loss of meaning [AB]. Since the primary meaning of bearing fruit is the disciples' love for each other, it is likely that 'to go' does not refer to missionary activity [Rd].

QUESTION—Does bearing fruit refer to bringing others to believe the Good News, or to the bearing of Christian character?
1. It refers primarily to success in winning others for Christ [BECNT, Gdt, Car, ICC, NICNT1]. There is an emphasis on going and bearing fruit. This indicates that fruit results from mission and the winning of new converts to the faith [Car]. If they do not go to lead others to the Lord, why else should they go? (4:36) [NICNT1]. It primarily refers to success in their apostolic labors, but also includes the perfecting of Christian character [ICC].
2. It refers primarily to the building of Christian character [HTC, IVP, NTC, Rd]. The primary focus is on producing Christian character, especially in the area of loving each other as seen in verse 17. However the idea that the disciples have been chosen may imply a certain missionary aspect [HTC]. It primarily refers to the fruits of the Spirit spoken about in Galatians 5:22–23. But in view of 4:36 and 12:24, where fruit refers to people saved for eternity, it is good to point out that bearing character fruit is not an end to itself, but is a means to bring others into God's Kingdom

[NTC]. The primary expression of fruit is love within the Christian community [IVP, Rd].
3. It refers to either or both 1 or 2 [CH, TRT]. This can refer either to the winning of new believers or to the fruit of the Spirit (Galatians 5:22–23) [CH]. Bearing fruit is the same as saying 'obeying Jesus' commands' (7–8, 10, 14). It includes loving each other (12, 17) and making disciples (4:35–38; 14:12) [TRT].

QUESTION—What does it mean to ask in Jesus' name?
It means either to ask as Jesus' representatives [Kn, TRT] and carrying out his work or to ask as being favored on the basis that they belong to him [Kn]. It means asking that is in keeping with all that Jesus' name stands for. Prayer that brings honor to him [NICNT1]. It means to ask on the basis of Christ's merits and in harmony with what he has revealed [NTC]. Asking in Jesus' name is asking in union with him and in keeping with his character and purposes [IVP]. It is perhaps best to understand 'in my name' to mean 'because you are my followers' [TH], or 'as my friends' [TRT]. See this question also at 14:13–14.

QUESTION—What words are emphasized in this verse?
Both ὑμεῖς 'you' and ἐγώ 'I' are emphatic [ICC, Lns, NICNT2, TH]: 'You on your part did not choose me, but I on my part did choose you' [Lns]. The pronoun ὑμεῖς 'you' is emphasized [AB, NICNT1; Ph]: 'It was not you who chose me' [AB], 'It is not that you have chosen me' [Ph]. The pronoun ἐγώ 'I' is emphatic [Bar, BECNT; Ph]: 'it is I who have chosen you' [Ph]. The word 'not' negates 'you' rather than 'chose'. 'It was not you that chose' [NICNT1]. The placing of the negative and positive side by side serves to strongly emphasize the statement [Lns].

DISCOURSE UNIT—15:17–16:4a [Car]. The topic is the world's opposition.

DISCOURSE UNIT—15:17–27 [Ph]. The topic is the world's hatred.

DISCOURSE UNIT—15:17–21 [NICNT1]. The topic is suffering for Christ.

15:17 These-things[a] I-command you, that[b] you-love each-other.

LEXICON—a. οὗτος (LN 92.29): 'this' [LN], 'this one' [LN]. The plural of this pronoun ταῦτα is translated 'these things' [NICNT2, NTC; KJV], 'these precepts/commands' [Gdt; NRSV], 'this' [AB, HTC, WBC; NASB, NCV, NET, NIV, NLT, Ph, REB, TEV], not explicit [CEV, NJB]. This pronoun denotes a reference to an entity regarded as a part of the discourse setting [LN].

b. ἵνα (LN 90.22) (BAGD II.1.a.δ. p. 377): 'that' [BAGD, Gdt, LN, NICNT2; KJV, NASB], 'to' [HTC; CEV, NET, NJB], 'so that' [NRSV], 'in order that' [NTC], not explicit [AB, WBC; NCV, NIV, NLT, Ph, REB, TEV]. This conjunction indicates the content of discourse, particularly if and when purpose is implied [LN]. Very often the purpose sense is greatly weakened or disappears altogether. In this case the ἵνα-construction serves as a substitute for an infinitive that supplements a verb or an accusative with an infinitive after verbs with the sense of 'to summon, to encourage, to order' [BAGD].

QUESTION—Does the pronoun ταῦτα 'these things' refer forward to the conjunction 'that', or back to what precedes?

1. It refers forward to the conjunction 'that' [AB, Bar, HTC, Lns, TH, WBC; CEV, NCV, NET, NIV, NJB, NLT, Ph, REB, TEV]: 'So I command you to love each other' [CEV]. The demonstrative pronoun 'these things' refers forward to the conjunction ἵνα 'that' which serves to explain the contents of 'these things' [AB, Bar, Lns]. It means that the commands he had given them were to the effect that they love each other [Bar]. The Greek is able to use the neuter plural 'these things' to refer to a single act which is that they keep loving each other [Lns].
2. It refers back to what precedes [EGT, Gdt, ICC, My, NICNT1, NTC; NRSV]: 'These things I bid you (to do) in order that you may keep on loving one another' [NTC]. The plural 'these things' proves that the reference is back to verses 1–16, but particularly to verses 12–16. (ἵνα must therefore be translated 'in order that' indicating the purpose of these commands). All that Jesus had commanded them amounted to 'love'. Love is the essential characteristic of God's Kingdom [Gdt]. The plural probably indicates that all the commandments in this teaching are for a single purpose—that the disciples continue to love each other [NICNT1]. 'These things' sum up all that precedes [NTC].

QUESTION—What is indicated by the present tense 'love each other'?

The present tense indicates that the action is continuous [Lns, NTC]: 'in order that you keep on loving one another' [NTC].

DISCOURSE UNIT—15:18–16:33 [BECNT; NET]. The topic is the Spirit and the disciples' witness [BECNT], the world's hatred [NET].

DISCOURSE UNIT—15:18–16:16 [NICNT2]. The topic is the world and the Advocate.

DISCOURSE UNIT—15:18–16:15 [IVP, Rd]. The topic is the world's hostility and the Paraclete's witness.

DISCOURSE UNIT—15:18–16:4 [Gdt, Kn, Lns; NIV, NLT]. The topic is the world's hatred [Kn; NIV, NLT], the disciples face the world [Lns].

DISCOURSE UNIT—15:18–16:4a [AB, BECNT, WBC; CEV, NCV, NRSV, TEV]. The topic is the hatred of the world [AB, BECNT, WBC; CEV, NRSV, TEV], Jesus warns the disciples [NCV].

DISCOURSE UNIT—15:18–27 [Bar, NTC; NASB, NCV, NET, NJB, NIV, Ph, TEV]. The topic is the world's hatred [Bar; NET, NIV, NLT, NRSV, TEV], the disciples' relation to the world [NASB, NJB], Jesus warns his followers [NCV].

DISCOURSE UNIT—15:18–25 [HTC, IVP]. The topic is the world's hostility.

15:18 If the world[a] hates[b] you, know/you-know[c] that it-has-hated me before (it hated) you.

LEXICON—a. κόσμος (LN 9.23) (BAGD 7. p. 446): 'world' [BAGD; all translations except CEV], 'people of the world' [LN; CEV]. This noun is a figurative extension of the literal meaning of κόσμος 'cosmos, universe' (1.1) and denotes people associated with a world system and estranged from God [LN]. It denotes 'the world' and everything that belongs to it, appearing as that which is hostile to God, that is, lost in sin, wholly at odds with anything divine, ruined and depraved [BAGD]. It means people opposed to God and aligned with the power of evil [TH]. It denotes people of the world who are not Jesus' followers [TRT].

b. pres. act. indic. of μισέω (LN 88.198) (BAGD 1. p. 522): 'to hate' [BAGD, LN; all translations], 'to detest' [BAGD, LN], 'to abhor, to persecute in hatred' [BAGD]. This verb means to dislike strongly, with the implication of aversion and hostility [LN]. The perfect tense 'it has hated' indicates that the hatred endures or is permanent [AB, Bar, NICNT1, TH].

c. pres. act. indic./impera. of γινώσκω (LN 28.1) (BAGD 6.c. p. 161): 'to know' [BAGD, Gdt, HTC, LN, NICNT2, NTC; KJV, NASB, Ph], 'to know well' [REB], 'to remember' [CEV, NCV, NLT, TEV], 'to be aware' [NET, NRSV], 'to keep in mind' [NIV], 'to bear in mind' [AB], 'to realize' [WBC; NJB], 'to know about, to have knowledge of, to be acquainted with' [LN]. This verb means to possess information about something [LN]. The present imperative indicates a continuous aspect [TH]: 'constantly bear in mind' [TH].

QUESTION—What is indicated by the conjunction εἰ 'if' with the indicative mood?

It indicates that the world does or will hate the disciples [AB, Bar, Car, EGT, HTC, Lns, NICNT1, NTC, TH, TRT]. It may be necessary to translate this sense as 'If the world hates you, and it does' or 'Since the world hates you' or 'The world hates you, (but you must remember…)' [TH], or 'the people in the world will definitely hate you but…' [TRT].

QUESTION—Should the verb 'to know' be taken as an imperative or as a statement?

1. It should be taken as an imperative [AB, Bar, Gdt, HTC, ICC, Lns, My, NTC, WBC; CEV, NCV, NET, NIV, NJB, NLT, TEV]: 'If the people of the world hate you, just remember that they hated me first' [CEV].
2. It should be taken as a statement [NICNT2; KJV, NASB, Ph, REB]: 'If the world hates you, you know that it hated me first' [Ph].

QUESTION—What words are emphasized in this verse?

The pronoun ἐμέ 'me' is emphatic both from its form and its position (literal Greek order: ('me before you it has hated') [NICNT1].

JOHN 15:19   265

15:19 If you-were of^a the world,^b the world^c would (have) loved^d its own. But because you-are not of the world, but I chose you out-of^e the world, because-of this the world hates you.

LEXICON—a. ἐκ (LN 89.3) (BAGD 3.b. p. 235): 'of' [Gdt, HTC, NTC; KJV, NASB], 'from' [BAGD, LN, NICNT2], 'out of' [BAGD]. The clause 'If you were of the world' is translated 'If you belonged to the world' [AB, WBC; CEV, NCV, NET, NIV, NJB, NRSV, Ph, REB, TEV, similarly NLT]. This preposition indicates the source from which someone or something is physically or psychologically derived [LN]. It indicates origin [BAGD, WBC] as to family, race, city, people, district, etc. [BAGD]. It indicates membership in a certain group [AB]. If 'belonging to the world' is difficult to translate, it could be expressed as 'to be a part of the world' or 'to be one with the people of the world', or 'to be the same as the people of the world' [TH].

  b. κόσμος (LN 41.38) (BAGD 7. p. 446–447): 'world' [BAGD; all translations], 'world system, world's standards' [LN]. This noun denotes the system of practices and standards associated with secular society (that is, without reference to any demands or requirements of God) [LN]. It denotes 'the world' and everything that belongs to it, appearing as that which is hostile to God, that is, lost in sin, wholly at odds with anything divine, ruined and depraved [BAGD].

  c. κόσμος (LN 9.23) (BAGD 7. p. 446): 'world' [BAGD; all translations except CEV], 'people of the world' [LN; similarly CEV]. This noun is a figurative extension of the meaning of κόσμος 'cosmos, universe' (1.1) and denotes people associated with a world system and estranged from God [LN]. Here 'world' is used in the sense of those who persecute Jesus and his disciples (verse 20) [HTC]. It is a society of rebels [Car].

  d. imperf. act. indic. of φιλέω (LN 25.33) (BAGD 1.a. p. 859): 'to love' [BAGD, LN; all translations except NTC], 'to have affection for' [BAGD, LN, NTC], 'to like' [BAGD]. This verb means to have love or affection for someone or something based on association [LN].

  e. ἐκ (LN 89.3) (BAGD 1.b. p. 234): 'out of' [AB; all translations except CEV, TEV], 'from' [BAGD, LN; TEV]. The clause 'I chose you out of the world' is translated 'I have chosen you to leave the world behind' [CEV]. This preposition indicates the source from which someone or something is physically or psychologically derived [LN]. Here ἐκ indicates separation from a group or company [BAGD, NICNT1].

QUESTION—What is implied by the conditional sentence 'If you were of the world'?

It is a contrary to fact condition and means that the disciples did not in fact belong to the world [AB, Bar, BECNT, Lns, NICNT1, TH, TRT]. It means 'if you were', but you are not, 'the world would love' you, but it does not' [Lns].

QUESTION—What is indicated by the present tense in the phrase 'the world hates you'?

The present tense indicates that the world continues to hate the disciples [Lns, NICNT1].

QUESTION—What word is emphasized in this verse?

The pronoun ἐγώ 'I' is emphasized [Lns, TH]: 'I on my part did choose you out of the world' [Lns]. Both the pronouns 'I' and 'you' in the clause 'I chose you' are emphasized [TH]. There is emphasis on the word 'world' that is repeated five times in this verse [My, NICNT1].

15:20 Remember/do-you-remember[a] the word that I told you, (A) servant is not greater-than his master. If they-persecuted[b] me, they-will- also -persecute you. If they-kept[c] my word, they-will- also -keep yours.

LEXICON—a. aorist act. indic./impera. of μνημονεύω (LN 29.7) (BAGD 1.a. p. 525): 'to remember' [BAGD, LN; all translations], 'to recall, to think about again' [LN], 'to keep in mind, to think of' [BAGD]. This verb means to recall information from memory [LN], but without necessarily implying that people have actually forgotten [LN, TH].

b. pres. act. indic. of διώκω (LN 39.45) (BAGD 2. p. 201): 'to persecute' [BAGD, LN; all translations except CEV, NCV], 'to mistreat' [CEV], 'to do wrong to' [NCV], 'to harass' [LN]. This verb means to systematically organize a program to oppress and harass people. In a number of languages the equivalent of 'to persecute' is simply 'to cause to suffer', but persecution is also expressed in terms of 'to be mean to' or 'to threaten' or 'to chase from place to place' [LN].

c. aorist act. indic. of τηρέω (LN 36.19) (BAGD 5. p. 815): 'to keep' [AB, BAGD, Gdt, HTC, NICNT2, NTC, WBC; KJV, NASB, NJB, NRSV], 'to obey' [LN, TH; NCV, NET, NIV, TEV], 'to observe, to fulfill, to pay attention to' [BAGD], 'to keep commandments' [LN]. The clause 'If they kept my word' is translated 'if they do what I say' [CEV], 'if they had listened to me' [NLT], 'if they have followed my teaching' [Ph, REB]. This verb means to continue to obey orders or commandments [LN].

QUESTION—Should the verb μνημονεύετε 'remember' be taken as indicative or imperative mood?

1. It should be taken as an imperative [AB, EGT, Gdt, HTC, Lns, NICNT1, NICNT2, NTC, TRT, WBC; all versions except NLT, Ph]: Remember the word that I told you.
2. It should be taken as an indicative [NLT, Ph]: 'Do you remember what I told you?' [NLT], 'Do you remember what I said to you..?' [Ph].

QUESTION—What is significant about the form of the saying that Jesus reminded his disciples about, 'A servant is not greater than his master' (13:16)?

It is said in the form of a litotes, two negatives indicating a positive [Lns, NTC]. It is a stronger way of affirming that a servant is always lower than his master [Lns].

QUESTION—What is implied by the conditional sentence, 'If they persecuted me, they will also persecute you'?

This is a first-class condition true to fact implying that they did persecute Jesus [AB, BECNT, Car, CH, Gdt, Lns, NICNT1, NICNT2, NTC, Rd, TH, TRT; NLT]: Since they persecuted me, naturally they will persecute you' [NLT]. This could be translated 'They persecuted me, so they will also persecute you' [TH, TRT], or 'they caused me to suffer, they will cause you to suffer too' [TH].

QUESTION—When Jesus said, 'If they kept my word, they will also keep yours', did he imply that they kept his word or that they did not keep it?

1. He was implying that they kept it [Bar, BECNT, Car, CH, Gdt, HTC, NTC, Rd, TH]. In this conditional sentence as well, the condition is assumed to be true, that is, 'they have kept my word' [NTC]. On the basis of the Greek sentence structure, it is difficult to assign a negative implication to this part of the verse. Jesus' words should be taken to mean that if some persecuted him, others also listened to him. Therefore some would persecute the disciples and others would listen to them [TH].
2. He meant that they did not keep it [AB, Lns, IVP, My, NICNT1, NICNT2; NLT]: 'If they had listened to me, they would listen to you' [NLT]. Although this sentence is also a first-class conditional sentence implying that they did keep Jesus' word, and since we know from verses 1:10–11, and 12:37–43 that the world did not accept Jesus, we must understand that Jesus is speaking ironically here. It appears to be a first-class condition but it is really a contrary to fact condition [NICNT2]. This basically indicates rejection, but the positive should also not be overlooked. He means that they will keep the word of the disciples to the extent that they kept Jesus' word [NICNT1].

QUESTION—What words are emphasized in this verse?

The objects in the 'if-then' sentences are emphasized '*me…you…my word…yours*'. In each sentence the object is placed before the verb for prominence (Greek order: if *me* they persecuted, also *you* they will persecute…if *my word* they kept, also *yours* they will keep) [Lns, TRT].

15:21 But[a] all these-things they-will-do to you on-account-of[b] my name,[c] because they-did- not -know him-who sent me.

LEXICON—a. ἀλλά (LN 89.125): 'but' [AB, Gdt, HTC, LN, NTC, WBC; KJV, NASB, NET, NJB, NRSV, TEV], 'no' [NICNT2], 'on the contrary' [LN, Lns], 'instead' [LN], not explicit [CEV, NCV, NIV, NLT, Ph, REB]. This conjunction indicates a more emphatic contrast than δέ (89.124) [LN].

b. διά (LN 90.44): 'on account of' [LN; NCV, NET, NJB, NRSV, REB], 'because of' [AB, HTC, LN; CEV, NIV, NLT, TEV], 'for the sake of' [Gdt, NICNT2, NTC; KJV, NASB], not explicit [WBC]. This preposition with accusative object indicates the participant that constitutes the cause or reason for an event or state [LN].

c. ὄνομα (LN 33.126) (BAGD I.4.c.α. p. 572): 'name' [AB, BAGD, Gdt, HTC, LN, NICNT2, NTC; KJV, NASB, NET, NRSV], not explicit [WBC]. The phrase 'because of my name' is translated 'on account of me' [NCV, similarly NJB, REB], 'because of me' [NIV, NLT], 'as my disciples' [Ph], 'because you belong to me' [CEV], 'because you are mine' [TEV]. This noun denotes the proper name of a person or object [LN].

QUESTION—What is implied information with the conjunction ἀλλά 'but'?

It implies that the disciples should take courage because it was on Jesus' account that they would have to suffer [EGT, Gdt]: but take courage…. They should not be surprised because people would treat them badly for Jesus' name's sake [NTC]: but don't be surprised…. The contrastive 'on the contrary' implies that the previous clause was negative, they did not keep my word and will not keep yours, on the contrary…. [Lns].

QUESTION—What is the antecedent of 'all these things'?

Jesus is referring to the persecution [HTC, NICNT2, NTC, TH, TRT] and hatred (verse 18) [NTC]. This could be made explicit as 'they will persecute you because you are mine' [TH]. It is all the things seen in verses 18–20 [WBC].

QUESTION—What is meant by 'because of my name'?

A person's name stands for the person himself, Jesus [Bar, Car, Gdt, ICC, IVP, Lns, NTC, Rd; NCV, NIV, NJB, NLT, REB]: 'because of me' [NIV, NLT]. The disciples will be persecuted because they belong to Jesus [TH]. The disciples belonged to Jesus [NICNT2, TH; CEV, Ph, TEV] or represented him [NICNT2]. This may imply that when people persecute Jesus' followers (because of his name) they, in fact, persecute Jesus (Acts 9:4) [NICNT1].

QUESTION—How does the clause 'because they did not know the one who sent me' stand as a reason for the people to hate and persecute the disciples?

The reasoning goes as follows: people oppose the disciples because they oppose Jesus. They oppose Jesus because they don't know the Father (15:23). So, they oppose the disciples because they do not know the Father [BECNT]. This lack of knowing God was at the root of the world's hatred [NICNT1, Rd].

QUESTION—What words are emphasized in this verse?

The phrase 'all these things' is placed before the verb to increase its prominence (Greek order: all these things they will do to you) [TRT].

DISCOURSE UNIT—15:22–25 [NICNT1]. The topic is Christ reveals people's sin.

15:22 If I-did- not -come and speak to-them, they-would- not -have[a] sin.[b] But now[c] they-have no excuse[d] for their sin. **15:23** He-who hates me hates my Father also.

LEXICON—a. imperf. act. indic. of ἔχω (LN 90.65) (BAGD I.2.e.β. p. 332): 'to have' [BAGD, LN], 'to have as one's own, to possess' [BAGD], 'to experience' [LN]. The clause 'they would not have sin' [HTC, NICNT2, NTC; NASB, NRSV] is also translated 'they had not had sin' [KJV], 'they would not be/have been guilty of sin' [AB, WBC; CEV, NCV, NET, NIV, Ph, REB, TEV], 'they would not be guilty' [NLT], 'they would have been blameless' [NJB]. This verb means to experience a state or condition, generally involving duration [LN]. The imperfect tense indicates that they are still guilty [AB]. The verb 'to have' implies that the sin stays as a personal possession of the one who commits it [NICNT1]. To have sin implies also the accompanying guilt of sin and it is better to include this sense in one's translation—guilty of sin [TH].

b. ἁμαρτία (LN 88.310): 'sin' [LN; all translations except NJB, NLT], 'guilt' [LN], not explicit [NJB, NLT]. This noun denotes the moral consequence of having sinned. A number of languages make a clear distinction between the active event of committing sin and the resulting moral effect of guilt, so that one must speak of 'committing sin' but of 'forgiving guilt.' The actual event of sinning often does not fit with such verbal expressions, since it is not the event itself that is eliminated but the moral consequences of such an event, namely, the guilt. [LN].

c. νῦν (BAGD 2. p. 546): 'now' [BAGD]. The phrase νῦν δέ 'but now' [Gdt, HTC, NTC, WBC; CEV, KJV, NASB, NCV, NLT, NRSV, REB] is also translated 'but now, as things are' [ICC], 'but as it is' [AB, My; NJB, Ph], 'as it is' [Bar, NICNT2; TEV], 'now, however' [NIV], 'but now in fact' [Bar, TH], 'but' [NET]. The phrase means 'in reality' [AB]. Often it is not so much the present time that is meant as much as the situation pertaining at a given moment 'as things now stand'. Not infrequently νῦν δέ 'but now' serves to contrast the real state of affairs with an unreal conditional clause 'but as a matter of fact' [BAGD].

d. πρόφασις (LN **33.437**) (BAGD 1. p. 722): 'excuse' [**LN**; all translations except NICNT2; KJV], 'cloak' [KJV], 'valid excuse' [BAGD], 'actual motive, reason' [BAGD]. This noun denotes what is said in defense of a particular action, but without real justification. In a number of languages 'to have no excuse' is rendered as 'to not be able to justify' or 'to not be able to give a good reason for' [LN]. It has a stronger meaning than 'excuse' and indicates 'pretense' or 'pretext' [Car]. To not have an excuse may be translated 'they now cannot say, "We did not know that what we did was sin" or "we did not know that our deeds were bad"' [TH].

QUESTION—What kind of question is this conditional sentence?

It is a contrary to fact condition, 'If I had not come (but I did come)…they would not have sin (but they do)' [AB, Bar, BECNT, Lns, NICNT2, TH].

QUESTION—Is there a specific sin that is in focus here?

This is evidently to be understood as the particular sin of rejecting Jesus (16:9) [AB, BECNT, Bar, CH, Gdt, HTC, IVP, NICNT2, NTC, WBC]. In rejecting Jesus the world is rejecting God himself [WBC]. By sin here is meant the most central and controlling sin—that of rejecting God and deciding to prefer darkness rather than light (3:19–21; 9:39–41)[Car]. The sin was in the rejection of the message that Jesus brought [TH].

QUESTION—What is implied by the phrase νῦν δέ 'but now'?

It implies 'But as it is', since 'I have appeared and spoken to them' [My].

QUESTION—What is indicated by the present tenses 'hates' and 'hates'?

They indicate that the hatred is continuous or enduring [Lns].

QUESTION—What words are emphasized in verse 23?

The pronoun ἐμέ 'me' and the phrase τὸν πατέρα μου 'my father' occur before the verbs to increase their prominence (Greek order: he who me hates also my Father hates) [NICNT1].

15:24 If I-did- not -do among them the works[a] that no-one else did, they- would- not -have[b] sin. But now they-have- both -seen and hated both me and my Father.

LEXICON—a. ἔργον (LN 42.11) (BAGD 1.c.α. p. 308): 'work' [AB, Gdt, HTC, LN, NICNT2, NTC, WBC; KJV, NASB, NCV, NJB, NRSV], 'thing' [CEV, Ph, TEV], 'miraculous signs' [NLT], 'deed' [BAGD, LN; REB], 'miraculous deeds' [NET], 'accomplishment' [BAGD], 'what' [NIV]. This noun is derived from the verb ἐνεργέω 'to function, to work' (42.3) and denotes that which is done, with possible focus on the energy or effort involved [LN]. It denotes the deeds of God and Jesus, specifically the miracles [BAGD]. While this noun includes miracles it also includes the whole of Jesus' life [NICNT1].

b. imperf. act. indic. of ἔχω (LN 90.65) (BAGD p. 331): 'to have' [BAGD, LN], 'to experience' [LN]. The clause 'they would not have/have had sin' [Gdt, HTC, NICNT2, NTC; NASB, NRSV] is translated 'they would not be/have been guilty (of sin)' [AB, WBC; CEV, NCV, NET, NIV, NLT, Ph, REB, TEV], 'they would be blameless' [NJB]. This verb means to experience a state or condition, generally involving duration [LN].

QUESTION—What kind of conditional sentence is this?

It is a contrary to fact condition, 'If I did not do among them the works that no one else did (but I did), they would not have sin (but they do)' [BECNT, Lns, NICNT2].

QUESTION—What is the object of the verb 'seen'?

1. The object of seen is works [AB, Bar, CH, Gdt, Rd; CEV, NCV, NET, NIV, NJB, NLT, TEV]: 'they have seen what I did and they hated both me and my Father' [TEV].

2. The object of seen is 'both me and my Father' [EGT, ICC, Lns, My, NICNT1, NICNT2, NTC, WBC; KJV, NASB, NRSV, Ph, REB]: 'they have both seen and hated both me and my Father' [NICNT2]. Jesus is evidently using 'seen' in the sense of his words to Phillip 'Anyone who has seen me has seen the Father' (14:9) [Car, EGT, ICC, NICNT1, NICNT2] and the more general principle 'When he looks at me he sees the one who sent me' (12:45) [NICNT2]. The world has seen God working in the person of the Son [WBC]. They may not have been

conscious of having seen the Father in Christ but they had actually done so (1:18) [EGT].

15:25 But so-that the word written in their law[a] may-be-fulfilled[b] They-hated me without-cause.[c]

LEXICON—a. νόμος (LN 33.56) (BAGD 4.b. p. 543): 'law' [BAGD, Gdt, HTC, NICNT2, NTC, WBC; KJV, NCV, NET, NRSV], 'Law' [AB; NASB, NIV, NJB, Ph, REB, TEV], 'Scriptures' [LN; CEV, NLT], 'holy writings, sacred writings' [LN]. This noun denotes the sacred writings of the OT [LN]. It denotes a collection of the holy writings precious to the Jews. In the wider sense it denotes the Holy Scripture generally, on the principle that the most authoritative part gives its name to the whole [BAGD]. The law refers to a larger section than just the Pentateuch because this quote is from the Psalms [AB]. 'Law' here is used to refer to the Jewish Scripture generally [BECNT, Car, CH, EGT, ICC, Kn, NICNT1, NICNT2, Rd, TH], or to the OT [WBC]. The likely Psalm cited is 35:19 or 69:4, 5 [AB, BECNT, Car, CH, Gdt, HTC, ICC, IVP, Kn, Lns, My, NICNT1, NICNT2, NTC, Rd, TH, WBC]. It is more likely from Psalm 69 since that is regarded as a Messianic Psalm by NT writers [Bar, Car, ICC].

b. aorist pass. subj. of πληρόω (LN 13.106) (BAGD 4.a. p. 671): 'to be fulfilled' [Gdt, LN, NICNT2, NTC; KJV], 'to be caused to happen, to be made to happen' [LN]. This passive verb is also translated actively: '(they have done this) to fulfill' [NASB, similarly AB, HTC; NET, NIV, NJB, NRSV], 'this fulfills (what is written)' [NLT, similarly Ph]. The clause 'the word…may be fulfilled' is translated '(that is why) the Scriptures are true' [CEV], 'what is written in their law would be true' [NCV], 'the saying that is written in their law had to come true' [WBC; similarly REB], 'what is written in their Law may come true' [TEV]. This verb means to cause to happen, with the implication of fulfilling some purpose [LN]. 'To be fulfilled' must be understood in the sense of 'to come true' [TH].

c. δωρεάν (LN **89.20**) (BAGD 2. p. 210): 'without (a) cause' [AB, Gdt, HTC, LN, NICNT2, NTC; KJV, NASB, NLT, NRSV, Ph], 'without reason' [BAGD, LN; NIV, NIV, NJB, REB], 'for no reason' [**LN**; CEV, NCV], 'for no reason at all' [TEV], 'undeservedly' [BAGD, Rd], 'for nothing' [WBC], 'groundlessly' [My]. This adverb describes a thing or event as having no cause or legitimate reason [LN]. Here it indicates the fulfillment of divine predictions or promises [BAGD].

QUESTION—What information is implied in the words ἀλλά ἵνα 'but so that'? The strong adversative ἀλλά 'but' seems to imply that the response of the Jews contrasts with what was reasonable to expect. The elliptical information could be: '(but) they did this' or '(but) this is' [NICNT1], '(but) this (has) happened' [BECNT, Gdt, similarly Bar, Rd], '(but) this must have happened' or '(but) there is nothing astonishing in this' [Gdt], '(but) it had to be' [Rd]. The following translations rendered this opening clause as: 'but (this happened) in order that the word written...' [NTC], 'however, this is to fulfill the text in their law...' [AB], 'but this is so, that the word may be fulfilled...' [Gdt], 'it is to fulfill the word that is written in their law...' [HTC], 'but the word that is written in their law must be fulfilled...' [NICNT2], 'however, the saying that is written in their law had to come true...' [WBC], 'that is why the Scriptures are true when they say...' [CEV], 'but this comes to pass, that the word might be fulfilled...' [KJV], 'but they have done this to fulfill the word...' [NASB], 'but this happened so that what is written...' [NCV], 'now this happened to fulfill the word that is written...' [NET], 'but this is to fulfill what is written...' [NIV], 'but all this was only to fulfill the words written...' [NJB], 'this fulfills what is written...' [NLT], 'it was to fulfill the word that is written...' [NRSV], 'yet this only fulfills what is written' [Ph], 'this text in their law had to come true...' [REB], 'this, however, was bound to happen so that what is written...' [TEV]. It is also possible to take 'but so that' as an imperative 'but let the word be fulfilled' [Bar, Car].

DISCOURSE UNIT—15:26–16:15 [HTC, NICNT1]. The topic is the work of the Holy Spirit.

DISCOURSE UNIT—15:26–27 [HTC, IVP, NICNT1]. The topic is the Spirit's witness about Jesus.

QUESTION—Why does Jesus shift from the hatred of the world to speaking about the Holy Spirit?

He is contrasting the hatred of the world (verse 25) with the witness of the Holy Spirit about himself [My, NICNT2, NTC].

15:26 When the Helper,[a] the Spirit of truth comes, whom I will-send to-you from the Father, who goes-out[b] from the Father, he will-testify[c] about[d] me.

LEXICON—a. παράκλητος (LN **12.19**) (BAGD p. 618): 'Helper' [BAGD, **LN**, NTC; NASB, NCV, Ph, TEV], 'Advocate' [NICNT2; NET, NLT, NRSV, REB], 'Counselor' [HTC; NIV], 'Comforter' [KJV], '(the) support' [Gdt], 'Paraclete' [AB, WBC; NJB], 'Mediator' [BAGD, LN], Intercessor' [BAGD], 'Encourager' [LN]. This noun is also translated as a clause: 'the Spirit will help you' [CEV]. It is a title for the Holy Spirit and denotes one who helps, by consoling, encouraging, or mediating on behalf of someone [LN]. It denotes 'one who is called to someone's aid' or 'one who appears in another's behalf'. In our literature the active sense of 'helper, intercessor' is suitable in all occurrences of the word [BAGD].

b. pres. mid. (deponent = active) indic. of ἐκπορεύομαι (LN **15.40**) (BAGD 1.b. p. 244): 'to go out' [BAGD, LN; NET, NIV], 'to proceed (from)' [Gdt, HTC, NTC; KJV, NASB], 'to go forth' [NICNT2], 'to issue (from)' [NJB, REB], 'to come forth (from)' [AB, WBC], 'to come (from)' [CEV, NCV, NLT, NRSV, Ph, TEV], 'to depart out of, to leave from within' [LN]. This verb means to move out of an enclosed or well-defined two- or three-dimensional area [LN].

c. fut. act. indic. of μαρτυρέω (LN 33.262) (BAGD 1.a. p. 492): 'to testify' [BAGD, Gdt, NICNT2, NTC; KJV, NASB, NET, NIV, NLT, NRSV], 'to bear witness' [AB, BAGD, HTC, WBC; REB], 'to tell (about)' [CEV, NCV], 'to speak (about)' [TEV], 'to speak plainly (about)' [Ph], 'to witness' [BAGD, LN]. This verb is also translated as a noun: '(he will be my) witness' [NJB]. This verb means to provide information about a person or an event concerning which the speaker has direct knowledge [LN]. It means to 'bear witness' or 'to testify concerning someone' [BAGD]. In some languages it may be important to identify the person spoken to 'he will speak to you about me' or 'he will speak to people about me' [TH].

d. περί (LN 90.24): 'about' [LN, NICNT2; CEV, NASB, NCV, NET, NIV, Ph, TEV], 'all about' [NLT], 'concerning' [LN, NTC, WBC], 'on behalf of' [AB; NRSV], 'of' [Gdt, LN; KJV]. The clause 'he will testify about me' is translated 'he will be my witness' [NJB], 'he will bear witness to me' [HTC; REB]. This preposition with the genitive case indicates the general content of a discourse or mental activity [LN].

QUESTION—What is significant about the term παράκλητος 'Helper'?

It is a title for the Holy Spirit so it may be important to indicate this when translating, 'the one who is called the Helper will come' [TH].

QUESTION—How are the two nouns related in the genitive construction 'Spirit of truth'?

The Spirit communicates truth [Bar, NICNT1; CEV]: the Spirit…shows what is true' [CEV]. The Spirit reveals the truth about God [TH, TRT; TEV]: 'he reveals the truth about Him to people' [TRT]. The Spirit speaks the truth and brings it home to the consciences of people [ICC].

QUESTION—The Spirit going out from the Father could either refer to the Spirit's coming to earth at Pentecost or it could refer to his eternal activity from within the Trinity. Which one is indicated in this verse?

1. The verb 'goes out' indicates a temporary event having to do with the mission of the Holy Spirit to the world [AB, BECNT, Bar, Car, EGT, HTC, ICC, IVP, NICNT1, TH, WBC]. Many Greek fathers reasoned that this referred to the Spirit's eternal procession from the Father. But here this verb parallels with the statement 'whom I will send' and refers to the mission of the Spirit to men [AB, HTC, WBC]. The passage is not dealing with eternal relations within the Trinity but with the Spirit's work in the world as a continuation of Jesus' ministry [NICNT1]. This action indicates the source from which the Spirit comes to the disciples [TH].

2. The verb 'goes out' indicates an eternal principle which is true of the Trinity [Gdt, Lns, NTC]. The tense of the verb 'send' is future and refers to a time in history, but the tense of 'goes out' is present indicating that the Spirit goes out or emanates eternally from the Father [Gdt]. The future tense 'I will send' looks forward to Pentecost, the present tense is a timeless present and refers to the intertrinitarian relationship of the Spirit which is eternal [NTC].

QUESTION—To whom does the Spirit testify?
1. He testifies to the world [AB, BECNT, Gdt, HTC, ICC, Lns, My, NICNT1, NICNT2, NTC, WBC]. The Spirit defends Christ's case before the world [NICNT1]. He will bear true witness about Christ to people of the world [ICC]. He will bear witness against the world [NTC]. The Spirit enlightens the minds of the hearers as to the truth of the message proclaimed by the disciples [BECNT].
2. He testifies to the disciples [CH, IVP, Rd, TH]. The Spirit will make Jesus real to the disciples [CH]. While the Spirit is sent to the disciples, they in turn would testify before the world [IVP]. The Spirit will reassure the disciples that they are not alone in their stand against the world. He will assist them in their stand for the truth concerning Jesus [Rd]. It is best to take the witness as meaning 'he will speak to you about me' [TH].

QUESTION—What word is emphasized in this verse?
The pronoun ἐγώ 'I' is emphatic [Lns, My, NICNT1]: *I myself* will send. The demonstrative pronoun ἐκεῖνος 'he' is emphatic [Gdt, ICC, Lns]: *he himself* will testify about me. This pronoun is masculine singular implying that the Spirit is personal [AB, BECNT, Bar, Car, ICC, NICNT1, TRT].

15:27 **And you also testify/must-testify, because you-are with me from (the) beginning.**

QUESTION—The form of the verb μαρτυρεῖτε 'you testify' can either be interpreted as an imperative or indicative mood. Which is the better choice?
1. The verb should be taken as a command [AB, BECNT, Car, NICNT2, NTC, WBC; NCV, NIV, NLT, NRSV]: 'And you also must testify' [NIV]. Following the future statement 'He will testify', the imperative seems more natural than the indicative [NTC].
2. The verb should be taken as a statement either present or future [Bar, Gdt, HTC, ICC, Lns, My, NICNT1; CEV, KJV, NASB, NET, NJB, Ph, REB, TEV]: 'You will also tell others about me' [CEV].

QUESTION—To what time does the phrase 'from the beginning' refer?
It refers to from the beginning of Jesus' public ministry [AB, BECNT, Car, CH, EGT, ICC, IVP, Lns, NICNT1, NICNT2, Rd, TH, WBC]. It could be translated 'from the time I began to teach' [TH].

QUESTION—What word is emphasized in this verse?
The pronoun ὑμεῖς 'you' is made prominent [Lns, NICNT1, TH]: And *you, yourselves* also testify/must testify.

DISCOURSE UNIT—16:1–15 [Bar, NTC; Ph]. The topic is Jesus' departure [Ph], the judgment of the world [Bar].

DISCOURSE UNIT—16:1–4 [IVP, NICNT1; NASB]. The topic is Jesus' warning of persecution [NICNT1; NASB], persecution from the Jews [IVP].

16:1 **I-have said these things to you so-that you-may- not -be-offended.**[a]
LEXICON—a. aorist pass. subj. of σκανδαλίζομαι (LN 25.180) (BAGD 1.a. p. 752): 'to be offended' [LN], 'to take offense' [LN]. The clause 'so

that/that you may/should not be offended' [Gdt; KJV] is also translated 'so that you will/may not fall away' [NET, NJB], 'to keep you from falling away' [HTC], 'so that you will not give up your faith' [TEV], 'so that your faith in me may not be shaken' [Ph], 'to prevent your faith from being shaken' [AB], 'to guard you against the breakdown of your faith' [REB], 'to prevent you from falling from faith' [WBC], 'so that you will not abandon your faith' [NLT], 'so that you will not go astray' [NIV], 'so that you will not be made to stumble' [NICNT2], 'so that you may be kept from stumbling' [NASB], 'to keep you from stumbling' [NRSV], 'to keep you from becoming afraid' [CEV], 'to keep you from giving up' [NCV], 'in order that you should not be caught unawares' [NTC]. This verb means to be offended because of some action [LN]. It basically means 'to cause to be caught' or 'to fall' i.e., 'to cause to sin' (the sin may consist in a breach of the moral law, in unbelief, or in the acceptance of false teachings). The absolute passive ('without an explicit agent') can also mean 'to let oneself be led into sin, to fall away' [BAGD].

QUESTION—To what things does the phrase 'all things' refer?

It refers to the things Jesus had said in 15:18–27 [AB, Bar, BECNT, CH IVP, My, NTC, TH, TRT]. Jesus is referring to the persecution that they will experience [CH, EGT, ICC, IVP, NICNT2] as well as the encouragements [EGT, ICC]. These were things about the hatred of the world for them [Bar, Lns, My, NICNT2, NTC].

QUESTION—What feature of 'being offended' is in focus in this verse?

The basic sense of σκανδαλίζομαι is surprise or unexpectedness [BECNT, CH, Lns, NICNT1, NTC], or being trapped [CH, NTC, WBC], or of stumbling over a σκάνδαλον, a 'stumbling block' that is placed in someone's path [AB, ICC, Rd, My, NICNT2; NASB, NRSV]. A σκάνδαλον is the stick in a trap which when touched by an animal causes the trap to spring shut [LN (6.25), Lns]. The result of 'being offended' is the loss of the faith of the disciples [AB, Bar, Gdt, HTC, ICC, Rd, TH, TRT, WBC; NLT, Ph, REB, TEV], or apostasy [BECNT, Car, EGT, HTC, NICNT2]. The cause of this apostasy or loss of faith is the hatred [Bar, Lns, Rd] and persecution of the world [Bar, Rd], or severe trials [NICNT1].

16:2 They-will-put you out-of-the-synagogues.[a] Indeed[b] (the) time comes when every one-who kills you will-think he-is-offering[c] service[d] to God. **16:3** And they-will-do these-things because they-did- not -know the Father nor me.

LEXICON—a. ἀποσυνάγωγος (LN 11.46) (BAGD p. 100): 'expelled from a/the synagogue' [BAGD, LN], 'excommunicated, put under the curse/ban' [BAGD]. The clause 'they/people will/shall put you out of the/their synagogue(s)' [Gdt, HTC, WBC; KJV, NCV, NET, NIV, NRSV] is also translated 'they will put you out of the synagogue' [NICNT2], 'they are going to put you out of the Synagogue' [AB], 'they will expel you from the synagogues' [NJB, similarly NLT, TEV], 'they will make you outcasts from the synagogue' [NTC; NASB], 'they will ban you from the synagogue' [REB], 'they will excommunicate you from their synagogues' [Ph], 'you will be chased out of the Jewish meeting places' [CEV]. This adjective indicates a state of having been excommunicated from membership in a synagogue [LN]. It meant the loss of all fellowship [NICNT1]. This was not a temporary discipline [NICNT2] but a definite break with the Jewish community [NICNT2, Rd]. This clause could be rendered 'they will no longer count you as members of their worship houses' or 'they will exclude you from worship in the synagogues' [TH]. Those experiencing this action would be seen by their former friends as worse than pagans [NTC].

b. ἀλλά (LN 91.2) (BAGD 5. p. 38): 'indeed' [HTC, NTC, Rd, WBC; NRSV, REB], 'and indeed' [NJB], 'yes' [Gdt, Lns; KJV, NCV, Ph], 'and yes' [NICNT2], 'in fact' [AB; NIV], 'and' [LN; CEV, NLT, TEV], 'yet' [LN; NET], 'but' [NASB]. This conjunction indicates a transition, with a slightly adversative implication in some contexts, often best left untranslated [LN]. It can be used to increase the force of a statement '(not only this) but rather' [BAGD, NICNT2]. Although ἀλλά is strongly adversative, here it introduces an event that is contrary to what may have been expected. It could be translated 'Nay, more'. Blass and Debrunner render it as 'not only this, but also' as emphatically introducing an additional point [NICNT1]. It means 'not only this, but you must expect what is worse' [Gdt], 'and not only so, but further' [Bar], 'indeed, furthermore' [ICC], 'nay, yet more' [My], 'not only that, but/besides that/in fact' [TRT].

c. pres. act. infin. of προσφέρω (LN 15.192) (BAGD 2.b. p. 720): 'to offer' [BAGD], 'to present' [BAGD], 'to carry to' [LN], 'to bring (to)' [BAGD, LN]. The clause 'will think he is/they are offering (a) service to God' [NCV, NET, NIV] is also translated 'will think they are doing a holy service for God' [NLT], 'will think/suppose (that) he is offering (a) service to God' [HTC, NTC, WBC; similarly NASB], 'will think that he is doing service to God' [Gdt; similarly KJV], 'will think thereby he is serving God' [Ph; similarly TEV], 'will think/suppose that he is serving God' [AB; REB], 'might think he is offering worship to God' [NICNT2; similarly NRSV], 'and think they are doing God a favor' [CEV]. This verb means to carry or bring something into the presence of someone, usually implying a transfer of something to that person [LN]. The object brought is offerings, gifts, and the like [BAGD]. The phrase 'offering service to God' could be rendered 'he is worshipping God by this means' or 'he is honoring God by doing what he does' [TH].

d. λατρεία (LN 53.14) (BAGD p. 467): 'service' [BAGD, Gdt, HTC, NTC; KJV, NASB, NCV, NET, NIV], 'worship' [BAGD, LN, NICNT2; NRSV], '(a) favor' [CEV]. This noun is also translated as a verb: '(he is) serving (God)' [AB; Ph, REB, TEV]. It denotes the service of offering worship to God [AB].

JOHN 16:2–3

QUESTION—What is meant by γινώσκω 'to know'?
It is important that the verb chosen to translate this not mean mere possession of information about God. Knowing here indicates intimate acquaintance with or knowledge based on close aquaintance with [TH].

16:4a But I-have-told you these-things so-that when their hour comes you-might-remember that I told you about-them.

TEXT—Instead of ἡ ὥρα αὐτῶν μνημονεύητε αὐτῶν 'their hour you may remember them' some manuscripts read ἡ ὥρα αὐτῶν μνημονεύητε 'their hour you may remember', others read ἡ ὥρα μνημονεύητε αὐτῶν 'the hour you may remember them', others read ἡ ὥρα μνημονεύετε αὐτῶν 'the hour you remember them', and still others read ἡ ὥρα μνημονεύετε 'the hour you remember'. GNT reads 'their hour you may remember of-them' with a B rating, indicating that the text is almost certain.

QUESTION—Does the possessive pronoun 'their (hour)' refer to the time of persecution or to the time of the disciples' enemies?
1. It refers to the time of persecution [CH, ICC, Lns, NICNT2, NTC; NJB, NLT, Ph, REB]: 'when they happen, you will remember' [NLT]. There are two demonstrative pronouns in this verse, 'their (αὐτῶν) (time comes) and '(I told you) 'of them (αὐτῶν)'. It is more likely that they both refer to the same things which in this case are the things Jesus had told them about—the hatred, persecution, excommunication and martyrdom (15:18–16:3). 'When their hour comes' is the same as saying 'When it happens'. This interpretation also agrees with the following statement (14:b) when Jesus again refers to 'these things' [NICNT2]. The plural pronoun ταῦτα 'these things' in verse 1, 3, and 4 and the two demonstrative pronouns αὐτῶν 'of them' in this verse all refer to Jesus' words in 15:18–16:3 centering around the hatred of the world [Lns].
2. It refers to the time of the disciples' enemies [AB, Bar, Car, HTC, NICNT1; TEV]: 'when the time comes for them to do these things' [TEV]. Although it could be understood to mean the hour for these things to happen, it is probably best to take it to mean the hour of Jesus' enemies. Jesus had said to the chief priests and the others, 'This is your hour' (Luke 22:53) [AB].

QUESTION—What words are emphasized in this verse?
The pronoun ἐγώ 'I' is emphatic [ICC, Lns, My, NICNT1]: 'that *I* told you' [NICNT1]. The emphatic pronoun indicates, 'I, the Person, with whom your faith is concerned' [My].

DISCOURSE UNIT—16:4b–33 [HTC, WBC]. The topic is the work of the Holy Spirit [HTC], joy over grief and trouble [WBC].

DISCOURSE UNIT—16:4b–15 [AB, BECNT, Car; CEV, NCV, NRSV, TEV]. The topic is the work of the Holy Spirit [BECNT, Car; CEV, NCV, NRSV, TEV], the coming of the Spirit [AB].

DISCOURSE UNIT—16:4b–11 [HTC]. The topic is the work of the Holy Spirit.

16:4b But I-did- not -say these-things to-you from (the) beginning, because I-was with you.

QUESTION—What beginning does Jesus refer to?

He refers to the beginning of his ministry [AB, TH]. It could be translated 'when you began to follow me' or 'when you first became my disciples' or 'when I first began to teach you' [TH].

QUESTION—How does Jesus' presence with them stand as a reason for not telling them about persecution.

Before this time the persecution was directed at him rather than at them [AB, BECNT, Car, CH, ICC, Lns, My, NICNT1, NICNT2, NTC, TH]. Also at the beginning he was present to protect them [Bar, BECNT, Car, Rd, TH].

QUESTION—What word is emphasized in this portion?

The pronoun ταῦτα 'these things' is placed forward in the Greek sentence to increase its prominence [TH]: *these things* I did not say to you. It refers to the approaching persecution Jesus spoke about in 15:18–16:3, 4a [AB, NTC, TH] or 15:18–25 [BECNT].

DISCOURSE UNIT—16:5–33 [CH, Kn]. The topic is Jesus and the Spirit [CH], the revelation of Jesus [Kn].

DISCOURSE UNIT—16:5–16 [NIV]. The topic is the work of the Holy Spirit.

DISCOURSE UNIT—16:5–15 [Gdt, IVP, Lns, NICNT1; CEV, NASB, NLT]. The topic is the work of the Holy Spirit [IVP, Lns, NICNT1; CEV, NLT], the Holy Spirit promised [NASB].

16:5 But now I-am-going to him who sent me, yet[a] none of-you asks me, Where are-you-going? **16:6** But sadness[b] has-filled- your -heart[c] because I-have-said these-things to-you.

LEXICON—a. καί (LN 91.12) (BAGD): 'yet' [AB, HTC, LN; NIV, NRSV, TEV], 'but' [NCV], 'and' [Gdt, NICNT2, NTC, WBC; CEV, KJV, NASB, NET, NLT], not explicit [NJB, Ph, REB]. This conjunction indicates emphasis, involving surprise and unexpectedness [LN]. It is used here in the sense of καίτοι 'and yet' [Lns, NICNT1], or in the sense of ἀλλά 'but' [ICC].

  b. λύπη (LN 25.273) (BAGD p. 482): 'sadness' [AB, LN; NCV, NET, TEV], 'sorrow' [BAGD, Gdt, HTC, LN, NTC; KJV, NASB, NRSV], 'grief' [BAGD, NICNT2; NIV, REB], 'anguish' [WBC], 'distress' [LN], 'pain (of mind or spirit), affliction' [BAGD]. This noun is also translated as an adjective: '(you are very) sad' [CEV, similarly NJB], and as a verb: '(you) grieve' [NLT], '(you are so) distressed' [Ph]. This noun denotes a state of mental pain and anxiety [LN].

  c. perf. act. indic. of πληρόω (LN 30.29). The clause 'sadness/sorrow/grief/anguish has filled your heart(s)' [Gdt, HTC, NICNT2, NTC, WBC;

KJV, NASB, NRSV] is also translated 'your hearts are filled with/full of sadness' [AB; NCV, NET, TEV], 'you are very sad' [CEV], 'you are sad at heart' [NJB], 'you are filled with grief' [NIV], 'you are plunged into grief' [REB], 'grief has caused you to think as you do' [**LN**], 'you grieve' [NLT], 'you are so distressed' [Ph]. The phrase 'to fill the heart' is an idiom that means to cause someone to think in a particular manner, often as a means of inducing some behavior 'to make think, to cause to decide' [LN]. The idiom indicates extreme grief or sadness [TRT].

QUESTION—To whom does the clause 'him who sent me' refer?

It refers to God the Father [ICC, Lns, TH, TRT]. In the case of misunderstanding it may be necessary to translate 'to my Father who sent me' [TH].

DISCOURSE UNIT—16:7–17 [IVP]. The topic is the image of the vine applied.

16:7 But^a I tell you the truth, it-is-to- your -advantage^b that I go-away. For if I-do- not -go-away, the Helper will- not -come to you. But if I-go, I-will- send him to you.

LEXICON—a. ἀλλά (LN 89.125): 'but' [Gdt, LN, WBC; CEV, NASB, NCV, NET, NIV, TEV], 'but, in fact' [NLT], 'nevertheless' [HTC, NTC; KJV, NRSV, REB], 'yet' [Ph], 'however' [NICNT2], 'still' [AB; NJB], 'instead, on the contrary' [LN]. This conjunction indicates a more emphatic contrast than δέ (89.124) [LN]. It means although you are filled with sadness [Lns].

b. pres. act. indic. of συμφέρω (LN 65.44) (BAGD 2.a. p. 780): 'to be of an advantage to someone, to be better off' [LN], 'to be advantageous' [BAGD, LN], 'to be good/profitable/useful/helpful (for someone)' [BAGD]. The clause 'it is to your advantage' [HTC, NICNT2, NTC WBC; NASB, NET, NRSV], is also translated 'it is better for you' [NCV, TEV], 'it is expedient for you' [Gdt; KJV], 'it is a good thing for you' [Ph], 'it is for your (own) good' [AB; NIV, NJB], 'it is best for you' [NLT], 'it is in your interest' [REB], '(I am going to do) what is best for you' [CEV]. This verb means to be of an advantage to someone [LN].

QUESTION—What is implied by the conditional sentence 'if I go, I will send him to you'?

This should not be translated as though Jesus would not go away [TH, TRT]. It may be better to translate something like 'my going away will benefit you. If I do not go away, the Helper will not come to you. That is why it will be better for you' [TH].

QUESTION—How is Jesus' departure advantageous for the disciples?

As long as Jesus was on earth, he was only *with* the disciples, but after his glorification through the crucifixion, resurrection and ascension (7:39), he would send the Spirit to them. Through the Spirit he would be present *in* each of his disciples [CH]. Jesus' departure would enable him to prepare a place for them (14:2), he would enable them to do greater works than

280   JOHN 16:7

himself (14:12), he would give them greater knowledge (14:20), and would be closer to them in the Spirit (14:28) [NTC].

QUESTION—What is the significance of the phrase 'to you' in the statement 'I will send him to you'?

It indicates that the work of the Spirit will be through the disciples. As Jesus prosecuted the world while he was on earth (3:20; 8:46), so the Spirit would continue that work through the preaching of the disciples [Kn].

QUESTION—What words are emphasized in this verse?

The pronoun ἐγώ 'I' is emphatic [Gdt, Lns, NICNT2]: 'I on my part (tell you the truth)' [Lns]. The emphatic pronoun stresses his knowledge of the true state of things in contrast to their ignorance [Gdt]. Both occurrences of ἐγώ 'I', '*I* tell you the truth' and '(it is to your advantage that) *I* go away' are emphasized [NICNT2]. The words 'I tell you the truth' serve to emphasize the words of Jesus that follow [Car, ICC, NICNT1, Rd].

DISCOURSE UNIT—16:8–17 [Kn]. The topic is the command to love.

16:8 And when- he -comes he-will-convict^a the world^b concerning^c sin^d and righteousness^e and judgment.^f

LEXICON—a. fut. act. indic. of ἐλέγχω (LN 33.417) (BAGD 2. p. 249): 'convict' [BAGD], 'to rebuke, to reproach' [LN], 'to convince someone of something, 'to point out something to someone' [BAGD]. This verb means to state that someone has done wrong, with the implication that there is adequate proof of such wrongdoing [LN]. For version evidence see the Question below.

b. κόσμος (LN 9.23): 'world' [all translations except CEV, NCV, REB], 'people of the world' [LN, TH, TRT; CEV, NCV, REB]. This noun is used with a figurative extension of the meaning of κόσμος 'cosmos, universe' (1.1) and denotes people associated with a world system and estranged from God [LN].

c. περί (LN 89.6): 'concerning' [LN; NASB, NET], 'about' [AB; CEV, NCV, NJB, NRSV, REB, TEV], 'with/in regard to' [LN; NIV], 'with respect to' [NTC, WBC], 'of' [Gdt, NICNT2; KJV, NLT, Ph], 'in relation to' [LN], not explicit [HTC]. This preposition indicates a relation, usually involving content or topic [LN].

d. ἁμαρτία (LN 88.289): 'sin' [LN; all translations]. This noun denotes an act contrary to the will and law of God [LN]. 'Concerning sin' could be translated 'what sin is' or 'what is involved when people do wrong' or 'what it really means when one sins' [TH].

e. δικαιοσύνη (LN 88.13) (BAGD 2.b. p. 196): 'righteousness' [BAGD, Gdt, HTC, LN, NTC; KJV, NASB, NET, NIV, NRSV], 'God's righteousness' [NLT], 'justice' [AB, NICNT2], 'God's justice' [CEV, REB], 'true goodness' [Ph], 'doing what God requires, doing what is right' [LN], 'uprightness' [BAGD]. This noun is also translated as a clause: 'being right with God' [NCV], 'who was in the right' [NJB], 'what is right' [TEV]. This noun denotes the act of doing what God

requires [LN]. It denotes the characteristics of the upright person in a moral and religious sense, that is, the characteristic required of men by God as the compelling motive for the conduct of one's whole life. Here it refers to the uprightness of Jesus [BAGD].
- f. κρίσις (LN 30.110) (BAGD 1.a.β. p. 452, 3. p. 453): 'judgment' [BAGD, LN; all translations except NLT, TEV], 'God's judgment' [TEV], 'the coming judgment' [NLT], 'judging' [BAGD], 'decision, evaluation' [LN]. This noun is derived from the verb κρίνω 'to judge' (30.108) and denotes the content of the process of judging [LN]. It refers to the activity of God or the Messiah as judge especially on the Last Day. The word often means 'judgment' that goes against a person, 'condemnation' and the 'punishment' that follows. It refers to 'judgment of (or on) this world' [BAGD (1.a.β.)]. Or it may refer to 'right' in the sense of 'justice, righteousness'. The meaning 'right, justice' may also play a role in 16:8 [BAGD (3)]. It means that God will judge or condemn the world for its sin [TH].

QUESTION—What is the meaning of sin?
In some languages it may be necessary to expand the word sin to: 'what sin is' or 'what is involved when people do wrong' or 'what it really means when one sins' [TH], or 'the fact that they have sinned' [TRT].

QUESTION—What word is emphasized in this verse?
The demonstrative pronoun ἐκεῖνος 'he' is emphatic [EGT; NASB]: 'And He, when He comes' [NASB]. The repetition of the preposition περί 'concerning' before each of the subjects (literal Greek, '*concerning* sin and *concerning* righteousness and *concerning* judgment') serves to bring each noun into prominence [Lns].

QUESTION—The verb ἐλέγχω 'to convict' is translated as follows:
    convict the world concerning/with respect to/of sin [NICNT2, NTC; NASB, NLT].
    convict the world of guilt in regard to sin [NIV].
    convince the world of sin [Gdt].
    convince the world of the meaning of sin [Ph].
    reprove the world of sin [KJV].
    expose the world with respect to sin [WBC].
    prove the world wrong concerning/about sin [AB; NET, NRSV, REB, similarly NJB, TEV].
    prove the world guilty (of) what sin is [HTC].
    show/prove to the people of the world the truth about sin [CEV, NCV].

16:9 Concerning sin because/that[a] they-do- not -believe in me.

LEXICON—a. ὅτι (LN 89.33, 90.21) (BAGD 1.c. / 3. p. 589): 'because' [BAGD (3), LN (89.33)], 'since' [BAGD (3), LN (89.33)], 'for, in view of the fact that' [LN (89.33)], 'that' [BAGD (1.c.), LN (90.21)], 'the fact that' [LN (90.21)]. The words 'concerning sin because/that' is translated 'of/concerning/in regard to/with respect to/about sin because' [Gdt,

NICNT2, NTC; CEV, KJV, NASB, NET, NIV, NRSV, REB, TEV], '(he will expose) their sin because' [Ph], 'about/with respect to sin in that' [AB, WBC; NJB], '(prove to them) that sin is (not believing in me)' [NCV], '(the world's) sin is that' [NLT, similarly HTC], 'concerning sin inasmuch as' [Lns]. This conjunction indicates cause or reason, based on an evident fact [LN (89.33)]. Or it indicates discourse content, whether direct or indirect [LN (90.21)].

QUESTION—What is indicated by the Greek conjunctions μέν...δέ...δέ beginning at this verse and proceeding to verses 10 and 11?

It indicates that the subjects sin, righteousness, and judgment are being addressed in order 'first (about sin)...then (about justice)...finally (about judgment)' [AB]. This does not indicate that one is more important than any of the others [Lns]. The three particles link these three nouns together in a deliberate triad [NICNT2].

QUESTION—What words are implied in the phrase 'concerning sin'?

The implied information is '*He will convict the world* (concerning sin)' [CEV, NCV, NLT, Ph, TEV]: 'The Spirit will show them that they are wrong about sin, because they didn't have faith in me' [CEV].

QUESTION—Although most versions keep the same meaning of convict from verse 8 to verse 9, some versions change the sense of the verb.

Verse 8, 'show the people of the world the truth about sin'. Verse 9, 'show them that they are wrong about sin' [CEV].

Verse 8 'prove to the people of the world the truth about sin'. Verse 9, 'prove to them that sin (is not believing in me)' [NCV].

Verse 8, 'convict the world of its sin'. Verse 9, 'The world's sin (is that it refuses to believe in me)' [NLT].

Verse 8, 'convince the world of the meaning of sin'. Verse 9, 'expose their sin' [Ph].

QUESTION—What is indicated by the present tense of the verb in the words 'they do not believe in me'?

It indicates a prolonged kind of unbelief [AB, TH; NJB, NLT, REB]: 'they refuse to believe in me' [AB].

QUESTION—What is the meaning of this verse?

1. It means that sin is defined as not believing in Jesus [AB, CH, HTC, Kn, NICNT2, WBC; NCV, NJB, NLT]: 'He will prove to them that sin is not believing in me' [NCV], 'the world's sin is that it refuses to believe in me' [NLT]. It is better to take the conjunction ὅτι to be explanatory rather than causative [AB, Kn]: 'about sin, in that they refuse to believe in me' [AB]. The Spirit will expose the world as sinful before God. Here 'sin' is defined as rejecting Jesus and his message [NICNT2].

2. It means that unbelief in Jesus is the chief or classic example of their sin [AB, Bar, BECNT, Gdt, NTC, IVP, NICNT1, NTC, Rd, TH]. Unbelief in Jesus is not their only sin, but it is the type and epitome of sin and so in reality the world's sin amounts to the crucifixion of Jesus [Bar]. Refusal to believe in Jesus is the fundamentally most important sin of the world

[AB, TH]. The Spirit will convict the world of its state of sin of which its unbelief in the Messiah is an evident case in point [Gdt]. Unbelief in Jesus is the one major sin that includes all others [NTC]. The Spirit's opposition to the world will be concentrated on faith in Jesus [Rd]. Unbelief in Jesus is not the only sin, but it is the type and crown of all sin, and so it amounts to the crucifixion of Christ [Bar].
3. It means that unbelief in Jesus is the cause or source of their sin [Car, EGT, Lns]. The world's conviction of sin is based on the fact that they do not believe in Jesus [EGT]. The Holy Spirit convicts the world of sin because they do not believe in Jesus. His conviction is designed to get people to see their need and turn to Jesus [Car].
4. Other views [Lns, My]. To believe is to have sin forgiven while to refuse to believe is to stay in one's sin. So the Spirit convicts the world of its incriminating unbelief [Lns]. The Spirit will convict the world of not believing in Jesus [My].

16:10 Concerning **righteousness** because I-go to the Father and you-will-no-longer -see me.

QUESTION—How will the Holy Spirit convict the world of righteousness?
1. The Spirit will show the world that Jesus was righteous [AB, Bar, BECNT, CH, EGT, Gdt, HTC, ICC, IVP, Kn, My, NICNT2, NTC, Rd, TH, WBC]. The Spirit will show the world that it was wrong to judge Jesus guilty because he was really innocent and just [AB]. That Jesus is righteous is shown by the fact that he is going to the Father where he will be justified by God. The fact of his presence with the Father is evidence that he has been accepted there and justified [HTC]. Jesus will be acquitted or shown to be innocent to the world in his resurrection and ascension [NICNT2]. Jesus, whom the world judged to be unrighteous, will go to the Father in victory and thereby be marked as the Righteous One (8:46; Acts 3:14; 7:52; 2 Corinthians 5:21; 1 Peter 3:18; 1 John 2:1 [NTC]. By exalting Jesus to heaven, the Father reversed the verdict of men and revealed Jesus' innocence [WBC]. Jesus' going to the Father proves his righteousness [Rd]. The death and glorification of Jesus proved the righteousness of both Jesus and God [Bar, TH].
2. The Spirit will show the world that it can be righteous only by believing in Jesus [Lns]. All true righteousness in the world is connected with Jesus. So the Spirit will prove to sinners that this righteousness is only available to them through believing in him [Lns].
3. Other views [Car, Lns, NICNT1]. Isaiah 64:5 states that 'all our righteous acts are like filthy rags'. One of Jesus' roles was to expose by his light the darkness of the world (3:19–21; 7:7; 15:22, 24). But now that Jesus is leaving the world, the Spirit will convict the world of its empty righteousness [Car]. The Spirit will show people that righteousness is not the gaining of merit that they assume it is, but it is the righteousness that depends on Christ's sacrificial work for them [NICNT1]. The Spirit will

convict sinners that true righteousness is only available to them through Jesus who has gone to the Father's side through the cross [Lns].

QUESTION—Is the translation 'convict of' as appropriate with the words 'righteousness' and 'judgment' as it was with 'sin'?

The word 'convict' is less appropriate for righteousness and judgment than it was with sin. The sense of 'prove wrong about' is more appropriate with 'righteousness' and 'judgment' [NICNT2]. The following versions changed the sense of how they translated 'convict' in verse 9 and how they translated it here with 'righteousness'.

Verse 9 'he will prove to them that sin is not believing in me'. Verse 10 'he will prove to them that being right with God comes from my going to the Father' [NCV].

Verse 9 'the world's sin is that it refuses to believe in me'. Verse 10 'righteousness is available because I go to the Father' [NLT].

Verse 9 'he will expose their sin because they do not believe in me'. Verse 10, 'he will reveal true goodness for I am going away' [Ph].

QUESTION—In what sense will the disciples no longer see Jesus?

He will be gone from them in his physical body but present with them in the person of the Helper [AB, Gdt, ICC, TH].

16:11 **And concerning judgment because the ruler^a of-this world has been judged.^b**

LEXICON—a. ἄρχων (LN 37.56) (BAGD 3. p. 114): 'ruler' [BAGD, HTC, LN, NICNT2, NTC; CEV, NASB, NCV, NET, NLT, NRSV, TEV], 'prince' [AB, Gdt, WBC; KJV, NIV, NJB, REB], 'governor' [LN]. This noun is also translated as a verb: '(the spirit which) rules (this world)' [Ph]. This noun is derived from the verb ἄρχω 'to rule' (37.54) and denotes one who rules or governs [LN]. Here it denotes an evil spirit, the devil, whose hierarchy resembles a human political institution [BAGD]. The phrase 'the ruler of this world' refers to the devil [AB, BAGD, Bar, My, NICNT2, TH].

b. perf. pass. indic. of κρίνω (LN 56.30) (BAGD 4.b.α. p. 452): 'to be judged' [Gdt, HTC, NICNT2, NTC, WBC; CEV, KJV, NASB, NCV, NLT, TEV], 'to be condemned' [AB, BAGD, LN; NET, NIV, NJB, NRSV, REB], 'to judge as guilty' [LN], 'to be punished' [BAGD]. This verb means to judge a person to be guilty and liable to punishment [LN, TRT]. Often the emphasis is unmistakably laid on that which follows the Divine Judge's verdict, on the condemnation or punishment [BAGD]. The perfect tense indicates that the judgment has taken place at the precise time when Jesus was exalted (12:31) [HTC].

QUESTION—In what sense of 'judged' had the ruler of this world been judged?

In this context the sense of 'to condemn' is correct [AB, BAGD, Gdt, LN, My, NICNT1, NTC; NET, NIV, NJB, NRSV, REB].

QUESTION—How will the Holy Spirit convict the world of judgment?

He will prove to the world that it was wrong about judging Jesus to be unrighteous [AB]. He will show the world that it was the ruler of the world that has been judged, not Jesus [NICNT2]. He shows to the world that it now has a new Master—Jesus, the Righteous One [Gdt]. He will show to people of the world that Jesus judged Satan by his death on the cross [CH], or by his glorification [IVP]. He will convict the world of its false judgment because it is the ruler of this world who stands condemned in the imminent victory of Christ [Car]. The condemnation of Satan reveals that the people of the world will also be judged [Bar, TRT]. The world will feel convicted of impending judgment by seeing what has already happened to the ruler of this world [Lns].

QUESTION—In what way had the ruler of the world been judged?

He was judged in his defeat at the cross of Christ [NICNT1, NICNT2, WBC]. In condemning Jesus who was welcomed by the Father, Satan had condemned himself [NTC]. He had been judged at the time when Jesus was exalted (12:31f 'Now is the time for judgment on this world; now the prince of this world will be driven out. But I, when I am lifted up from the earth, will draw all men to myself') [HTC, WBC].

QUESTION—Who is the implied actor of κέκριται 'has been judged'?

If it is necessary for this verb to be changed to active mood, God would be the agent [TH, TRT; CEV]: 'God has already judged the ruler of this world' [CEV].

DISCOURSE UNIT—16:12–15 [HTC]. The topic is the work of the Holy Spirit among the disciples.

16:12 I- still -have many-things to-tell you, but you-can- not -bear[a] (them) now.

LEXICON—a. pres. act. indic. of βαστάζω (LN **31.55**) (BAGD 2.b.β. p. 137): 'to bear' [AB, BAGD, Gdt, HTC, NICNT2, NTC; KJV, NASB, NET, NIV, NJB, NLT, NRSV, Ph, TEV], 'to accept' [**LN**], 'to endure' [BAGD, WBC], 'to receive' [LN]. The clause 'you cannot bear them now' is translated 'it would be more than you could understand' [CEV], 'they are too much for you now' [NCV], 'the burden would be too great for you now' [REB]. This verb means to accept, but with the implication of the truth being difficult to comprehend or to respond to properly [LN]. It is used figuratively here of being able to bear words of divine mysteries [BAGD].

QUESTION—In what sense were the disciples not able to bear what Jesus had to tell them?

They were unable to understand those things [AB, BECNT, Gdt, HTC, ICC, IVP, My, Rd, TRT]. If Jesus were to tell them the meaning of the events that were happening to him at the moment, the disciples would not have been able to grasp it [Rd]. He was referring to the hatred and persecution they would have to face and endure to remain faithful [AB, NICNT2]. It probably refers to the inability of the disciples to put into practice what the further revelation would teach them [NICNT1].

16:13 But when the Spirit of truth comes, he will-lead[a] you in all the truth, for he-will- not -speak from[b] himself, but he-will-speak what he will-hear and he-will-tell[c] you things to-come.

TEXT—Instead of ὁδηγήσει ὑμᾶς ἐν τῇ ἀληθείᾳ πάσῃ 'he will guide you in all the truth', some manuscripts read ἐκεῖνος ὑμᾶς ὁδηγήσει ἐν τῇ ἀληθείᾳ πάσῃ 'that one will guide you in all the truth', others read ὁδηγήσει ὑμᾶς εἰς πᾶσαν τὴν ἀλήθειαν 'he will guide you into all the truth', and still others read διηγήσεται ὑμῖν τὴν ἀλήθειαν πᾶσαν 'he will tell you all the truth'. GNT reads 'he will guide you in all the truth' with a B rating, indicating that the text is almost certain.

LEXICON—a. fut. act. indic. of ὁδηγέω (LN 27.17) (BAGD 2. p. 553): 'to lead' [BAGD, **LN**], 'to guide' [BAGD, LN], 'to conduct' [BAGD]. The clause 'he will guide you in all the truth' is translated 'he will guide/lead you into all (the) truth' [Gdt, HTC, NTC; KJV, NASB, NET, NIV, NLT, NRSV, REB], 'he will lead/guide you in the entire/in all the truth' [NICNT2, WBC], 'he will guide you into everything that is true' [Ph], 'he will guide you into the full truth' [CEV], 'he will lead you to (the) complete truth' [**LN**; NJB], 'he will guide you along the way of all truth' [AB]. This verb is a figurative extension of the meaning of ὁδηγέω (15.182) to guide or to direct, with the implication of making certain that people reach an appropriate destination [LN]. The clause 'he will guide you into all the truth' may be expressed 'he will cause you to know all the truth' [TH]. It is significant that the Spirit does not drive the believer, but he leads him [NTC].

b. ἀπό (LN 90.15) (BAGD 1.a. p. 212): 'from' [LN], 'by' [LN]. The phrase 'from himself' is translated 'on his own' [AB, NICNT2; CEV, NIV, NLT, NRSV], 'on his own initiative' [NASB], 'on his own authority' [HTC; NET, REB, TEV], 'of his own accord' [Ph], 'his own words' [NCV], 'of himself' [Gdt, NTC; KJV]. This preposition in the genitive case indicates the source of an implied event [LN]. The idiom λαλεῖν ἀφ' ἑαυτοῦ 'to speak from oneself' means 'to speak on one's own authority' [BAGD].

c. fut. act. indic. of ἀναγγέλλω (LN 33.197) (BAGD 2. p. 51): 'to tell' [LN; NCV, NET, NIV, NLT, TEV], 'to announce' [BAGD, Gdt, LN, NICNT2, NTC], 'to declare' [AB, HTC; NRSV], 'to inform' [LN; Ph], 'to disclose' [BAGD; NASB], 'to make known' [REB], 'to reveal' [NJB], 'to let someone know' [CEV], 'to show' [KJV], 'to proclaim' [BAGD]. This verb means to provide information, with the possible implication of considerable detail [LN].

QUESTION—What specific time is referred to when the Spirit will come?
This refers to his coming at Pentecost [Lns].

QUESTION—How are the nouns related in the genitive construction τὸ πνεῦμα τῆς ἀληθείας 'the Spirit of truth'?

The Spirit reveals the truth [TH, TRT; CEV, TEV]: 'the Spirit...who reveals the truth about God' [TEV]. The Spirit belongs to the truth [Lns].

QUESTION—What is meant by 'the truth'?

'All truth' does not mean what is true about all areas of knowledge [ICC, IVP, NICNT1, NICNT2], but refers to the truth about Jesus and his teachings and actions [ICC, IVP, NICNT1]. It refers to the truth that the Father has given to Jesus to make known [NICNT2]. It refers to the complete corpus of revelation about salvation [NTC]. The truth is Jesus himself (14:6) [Gdt].

QUESTION—From whom does the Spirit hear what to say?

He hears from the Father [Bar, EGT, Gdt, ICC, My, NICNT2, NTC, TH]. As Jesus only tells the world what he hears from the Father (8:26), so the Spirit hears from the Father [TH]. He will hear from God about Christ (15:26) [Gdt]. He hears from Jesus [AB, BECNT, Kn, TRT, WBC]: 'he hears me tell him' [TRT]. There is no significant difference whether he hears from the Father or the Son [NICNT1]. There is no reason to restrict the speaker to the Father or the Son for both of them send out and give the Spirit (14:16; 15:25; 16:7) [Lns].

16:14 He will-glorify[a] me, because he-will-receive[b] of mine and tell (it) to-you.

LEXICON—a. fut. act. indic. of δοξάζω (LN 87.24) (BAGD 2. p. 204): 'to glorify' [AB, BAGD, Gdt, HTC, LN, NICNT2, NTC, WBC; KJV, NASB, NET, NJB, NRSV, REB], 'to bring glory to' [CEV, NCV, NIV, NLT, Ph], 'to give glory to' [TEV], 'to make gloriously great' [LN], 'to clothe in splendor' [BAGD]. This verb means to cause someone to have glorious greatness [LN]. This could be translated 'he will show you how wonderful/glorious I really am' [TH].

b. fut. mid. (deponent = active) indic. of λαμβάνω (LN 57.125): 'to receive, to accept' [LN]. The words 'he will/shall receive of mine' [KJV, NASB], is also translated 'he will receive from me what is mine' [NET], 'he will receive what is from me' [WBC], 'whatever he receives from me' [NLT], 'he will take (of/from) what is mine' [Gdt, HTC, NICNT2, NTC; NRSV, REB], 'he will take what I (have to) say' [NCV, TEV], 'by taking from what is mine' [NIV], '(all he reveals) will be taken from what is mine' [NJB], 'by taking my message' [CEV], 'he will draw on my truth' [Ph], 'it is from me that he will receive what he will declare to you' [AB]. This verb means to receive or accept an object or benefit for which the initiative rests with the giver, but the focus of attention in the transfer is on the receiver [LN].

QUESTION—What is indicated by the phrase '(he will receive) of mine'?

'Of mine' indicates what Jesus has said, or his message (14:26) [TH, TRT; CEV, NCV, Ph, TEV]. It indicates that the Spirit will take Christian truth and reveal it to people [ICC]. It indicates the truth that Jesus embodies [Lns].

QUESTION—What words are emphasized in this verse?

The pronoun ἐμέ 'me' is emphasized as seen by both its form and its position in the clause (Greek = 'that one me will glorify') [Lns, My, NICNT1, TRT]. There is also emphasis on ἐκεῖνος 'he' [NICNT1, TRT].

16:15 **All things-that the Father has are mine. That-is-why I-said that he-receives from mine and will-tell (it) to you.**

QUESTION—What is the significance of this verse?

It is included to eliminate the wrong thought that what belonged to Jesus was his exclusively apart from the Father. All that Jesus possessed was 'whatever the Father has' [Lns]. It highlights the mutual interdependence of the Persons of the Trinity [CH].

QUESTION—What is indicated by 'all things that the Father has (are mine)'?

This refers to all the truth that the Father possesses [My]. It refers to the truth that Jesus teaches [AB, TH] as is seen in the final clause of the verse—'he receives from mine and will tell it to you' [TH]. Since the Spirit takes what belongs to Jesus and all that the Father has belongs to Jesus, it puts at the Spirit's disposal all the limitless fullness of the Godhead [EGT].

QUESTION—Does the phrase διὰ τοῦτο 'that is why' refer to what precedes or to what follows?

It refers to the words that precede as being the reason why Jesus said what he did [AB, ICC].

DISCOURSE UNIT—16:16–33 [AB, Car, Gdt, IVP, NICNT1, Rd; CEV, NLT]. The topic is sorrow into joy [AB, Car, IVP, Rd; CEV, NLT], difficulties solved [NICNT1].

DISCOURSE UNIT—16:16–24 [BECNT, HTC, Lns, NTC; NCV, NRSV, Ph, TEV]. The topic is sorrow into joy [BECNT, HTC, Lns; NCV, NRSV, TEV], the confusion of the disciples [Ph].

DISCOURSE UNIT—16:16–22 [NASB]. The topic is death and resurrection foretold.

DISCOURSE UNIT—16:16–21 [IVP]. The topic is sorrow into joy.

DISCOURSE UNIT—16:16–18 [NICNT1]. The topic is the perplexity of the disciples.

16:16 **(A) little-while[a] and you-will- no-longer -see me, and again (a) little-while and you-will-see me."**

TEXT—Following ὄψεσθέ με 'you will see me', some manuscripts add ὅτι ὑπάγω πρὸς τὸν πατέρα 'because I am going to the Father', others add ὅτι ἐγὼ ὑπάγω πρὸς τὸν πατέρα 'because I am going to the Father'. GNT rejects both of these with an A rating, indicating that the omission is certain.

LEXICON—a. μικρός (LN 67.106) (BAGD): 'a little while' [BAGD, HTC, LN, NTC, WBC; KJV, NASB, NRSV, REB]. This word is also translated 'in a little while' [AB; NET, NIV, NLT, Ph, TEV], 'for a little while'

[LN; CEV], 'after a little while' [NCV], 'yet a little while' [Gdt], 'a short time' [BAGD, LN, NICNT2], 'in a short time' [NJB]. This pronominal adjective pertains to a relatively brief extent of time [LN]. It may be necessary to translate the general phrase 'a little while' with a more specific phrase 'in a few days' [TH].

QUESTION—What event would occur that would prevent the disciples from seeing Jesus after a little while?

This 'little while' probably refers to Jesus' approaching death [BECNT, Car, CH, EGT, Gdt, HTC, ICC, IVP, Kn, Lns, NICNT1, NTC, Rd, TH, TRT]. It may refer to his burial or to his ascension [Bar].

QUESTION—When would the disciples again see Jesus?

They would see Jesus after his resurrection [BECNT, Car, CH, EGT, HTC, ICC, IVP, Kn, Lns, NICNT1, NTC, Rd, TH, TRT], or at Pentecost when Jesus would be in their hearts in the presence of the Holy Spirit [Gdt, My, NTC] and they would see him in the miracles he would perform through the Holy Spirit [My, NTC].

DISCOURSE UNIT—16:17-33 [Bar, NICNT2; NIV]. The topic is sorrow into joy [NIV], the disciples' response [NICNT2], the future [Bar].

16:17 So some-of his disciples said to each-other, "What is this that he-tells us, '(A) little-while and you-do- not -see me, and again (a) little-while and you-will-see me?' And 'Because/that I-am-going to the Father'?"

QUESTION—What is the function of the conjunction οὖν 'so'?

It indicates a logical, not a temporal connection with the preceding [AB, Gdt, Lns, TRT, WBC; Ph]: 'At this some of his disciples remarked to each other' [Ph].

QUESTION—What is implied by the question 'What is this that he tells us?'?

It implies that they are asking each other about the meaning of what Jesus had just said [AB, Gdt, NTC, TH; CEV, NCV, NET, NIV, NJB, NLT, NRSV, REB, TEV]: 'What is the meaning of what he is saying?' [NET]. There were two things that puzzled them. First if Jesus was going to found his Messianic Kingdom, why go away? Second, if not, why return? [BECNT, Gdt, ICC, NICNT1].

QUESTION—What information is implied in the clause 'and because I am going to the Father'?

The versions translated this differently: 'and he also says, "It is because I am going to the Father"' [TEV], 'And what does he mean when he says, "Because I am going to the Father"?' [NCV, similarly CEV], '(What does he mean by this)…and by this: "Because I am going to the Father"?' [REB], 'he also says, "Because I am going to the Father"' [AB], 'and that other word: Because I go to the Father' [Gdt].

QUESTION—Does the conjunction ὅτι introduce a causal clause 'because' or a direct or indirect quotation 'that'?

1. It probably introduces a causal clause [AB, Gdt, NICNT1, NICNT2, NTC, WBC; KJV, NASB, NCV, NET, NIV, NRSV, Ph, REB, TEV]: 'And what

does he mean when he says, "Because I am going to the Father"' [NCV]. It is unlikely that ὅτι introduces a quote here because the previous quote in this verse is not introduced with a ὅτι [AB]. Jesus will again be seen by the disciples through the Holy Spirit because he returns to the Father [Gdt]. The words are referring to Jesus' words in 16:10 'because I go to the Father and you will no longer see me' [NICNT1].
2. It probably introduces a quotation [BAGD (2. p. 589), HTC, Lns, My; CEV, NJB, NLT]: 'What does he mean when he says…"I am going to the Father"?' [NLT].

16:18 So they-were-saying, "What is this that he-says 'A little while'? We- do- not -know what he-is-talking-about."

TEXT—Some manuscripts omit ὃ λέγει 'that he says'. GNT includes it with a C decision indicating difficulty in deciding whether or not to include it in the text.

QUESTION—What is indicated by the imperfect tense ἔλεγον, 'they were saying'?

It may indicate a continuous aspect [AB, Lns, NICNT1, NTC, WBC; NET, NIV]: 'So they kept on repeating' [NET].

QUESTION—What is indicated by the inclusion of the article before 'little while' (Greek literally: what is this that he says *the* little while)?

It points to the one word that was troubling them [ICC, NICNT1]. Even without the article the question bothering them was, 'Will his absence really last only a little while?' [AB].

QUESTION—How to translate a quote within a quote?

It may be difficult in some languages to put quotations in direct speech. If so this may be translated 'What does Jesus mean when he says the words, a little while?

DISCOURSE UNIT—16:19–24 [NICNT1]. The topic is the joy of the disciples.

16:19 Jesus knew that they-wanted to-ask him, and he-said to-them, "Are- you-asking each-other about what I-said, 'A-little-while and you-will- not - see me, and again a-little-while and you-will-see me'? **16:20** Truly[a] truly I- say to-you that you will-weep and mourn,[b] but the world will-rejoice. You will-be-grieved,[c] but your grief[d] will-become joy.

LEXICON—a. ἀμήν (LN 72.6): 'truly, indeed, it is true that' [LN]. The clause 'truly truly I say to you' [HTC; NASB] is also translated 'Amen, amen, I say to/tell you' [NICNT2, WBC], 'Verily, verily I say to you' [Gdt; KJV], 'Very truly I tell you' [NRSV], 'I tell you truly' [Ph], 'I tell you the truth' [NCV, NIV, NLT, similarly TEV], 'In all/very truth I tell you' [NJB, REB], 'I tell you the solemn truth' [NET], 'Truly I assure you' [AB], 'I most solemnly assure you' [NTC], 'I tell you for certain' [CEV]. This particle indicates strong affirmation of what is declared [LN]. John uses this doubled expression 25 times in this Gospel [NICNT1].

b. fut. act. indic. of θρηνέω (LN 25.141) (BAGD 1.a. p. 363): 'to mourn' [BAGD, NICNT2; NIV, NLT, NRSV, REB], 'to go into mourning' [AB], 'to lament' [BAGD, Gdt, HTC, LN; KJV, NASB], 'to make lamentation' [WBC], 'to weep' [TEV], 'to wail' [LN, NTC; NET, NJB], 'to be sad' [CEV, NCV], 'to be sorry' [Ph]. This verb means to weep or cry, especially in mourning for the dead [EGT, LN].

c. fut. pass. indic. of λυπέομαι (LN 25.274) (BAGD 2.a. p. 481): 'to be grieved' [NICNT2], 'to grieve' [NASB, NIV, NLT], 'to be plunged in grief' [REB], 'to be plunged into anguish' [WBC], 'to be sad' [AB, LN; CEV, NCV, NET, TEV], 'to become sad' [BAGD], 'to be sorrowful' [Gdt, HTC, NTC; KJV, NJB], 'to become sorrowful' [BAGD], 'to have pain' [NRSV], 'to be deeply distressed' [Ph], 'to be distressed' [LN], 'to become distressed' [BAGD]. This word means to be sad as the result of what has happened or what one has done [LN].

d. λύπη (LN 25.273) (BAGD p. 482): 'grief' [BAGD, NICNT2; NASB, NIV, NLT, REB], 'sorrow' [BAGD, Gdt, HTC, LN, NTC; KJV, NJB], 'sadness' [AB, LN; NCV, NET, TEV], 'pain' [BAGD, NRSV, Ph], 'anguish' [WBC], 'distress' [LN]. This noun is also translated as a verb: 'to be sad' [CEV]. This noun denotes a state of mental pain and anxiety [LN]. In the NT it denotes anguish of mind and spirit [AB, BAGD].

QUESTION—In verse 19, is Jesus telling the disciples that they were asking each other, or is he asking them if they were?
1. Jesus is telling them that they were asking each other [AB; CEV, NJB]: 'Jesus…said: "You are wondering what I meant when I said…"' [CEV].
2. Jesus is asking them if they were asking each other [GNT; all other translations]: 'Jesus…said to them, "Are you deliberating together about this?"' [NASB].

QUESTION—What is significant about the two verbs 'weep' and 'mourn'?
They refer to the loud weeping and wailing that was typical in the Near East on the occasion of a death [AB, ICC, TH]. The first verb κλαύσετε 'to weep' implies mourning for the dead. The second verb θρηνήσετε 'to mourn' implies a formal ritual of mourning [NICNT2]. The first verb indicates loud unrestrained weeping, the second indicates wailing cries for the dead [Lns].

QUESTION—To whom does the term κόσμος 'world' refer?
It refers to the people of the world [TH, TRT]. It refers to the Jews who were seeking to have him crucified [ICC, NTC]. It refers to the unbelieving people in the world [HTC, TRT].

QUESTION—What is indicated by the contrastive conjunction ἀλλά 'but' in the statement 'but your grief will be come joy'?
It marks a strong contrast with the preceding clause—'You will be grieved' [Gdt]. It indicates that there is something special in the joy that follows their grief. Their joy is not replaced by joy, but rather turns into it. [NICNT1]. The cross would cause them sadness but afterwards it would become a source of joy [Lns, NICNT1, NTC].

QUESTION—What words are emphasized in verse 20?

The first occurrence of the pronoun ὑμεῖς 'you(pl)', '*you* will weep and mourn' is emphatic and contrasts with the world [NICNT1]. It is conspicuously placed at the end of its clause [Lns, My, NICNT2]. The second occurrence is emphasized in the statement '*you* will be grieved' where it contrasts with the world [Lns, My, TH]: *you, yourselves* will be grieved. Here it emphasizes that it is they themselves who will be grieved [ICC, NICNT1]. Both occurrences are emphatic and contrast the disciples with the world [Bar, NICNT2]. The phrase 'truly, truly (I tell you)' places emphasis on what Jesus is telling them [Car, Lns, Rd].

16:21 The woman has[a] pain when she-gives-birth,[b] because her hour[c] has-come. But when she-gives-birth-to[d] the child, she- no-longer -remembers the suffering[e] because-of the joy that (a) man[f] was-born into the world.

LEXICON—a. pres. act. indic. of ἔχω (LN 90.65) (BAGD I.2.e.β. p. 332): 'to have' [BAGD, LN], 'to experience' [LN]. The clause 'the woman has pain' is translated 'the woman...has grief' [NICNT2], 'a woman...has sorrow' [Gdt, HTC; KJV], 'she is sad' [AB; TEV], 'she has pain/distress' [NASB, NCV, NET, NRSV, similarly NIV], 'she has anguish' [WBC], 'she knows...pain' [Ph], 'a/any woman...is in pain' [NTC; REB], 'a woman...suffers' [NJB, similarly NLT], 'she is in great pain' [CEV]. This verb means to experience a state or condition, generally involving duration [LN]. It is used here generally of conditions, characteristics, capabilities, emotions, and inner possessions of body and soul [BAGD].

b. pres. act. subj. of τίκτω (LN 23.52) (BAGD 1. p. 816): 'to give birth (to)' [BAGD, LN, NICNT2; CEV, NCV, NET, NIV, Ph], 'to be about to give birth' [TEV], 'to bear' [BAGD, LN], 'to be in labor' [AB, NTC, WBC; NASB, NRSV], 'to be in travail' [Gdt, HTC; KJV]. The verb is also translated as a phrase: '(a woman) in childbirth' [NJB], '(a woman) suffering the pains of labor' [NLT], '(a woman) in labor' [REB]. This verb means to give birth to a child. All languages have expressions for human birth, though these are frequently in idiomatic forms, for example, 'to drop a child' or 'to cause a baby to pass between the legs'. A number of languages have a variety of terms referring to giving birth, and some of these may involve unfortunate connotations. One must therefore be careful about the selection of appropriate expressions [LN].

c. ὥρα (LN 67.1) (BAGD 3. p. 896): 'hour' [BAGD], 'time' [LN], 'occasion' [LN], not explicit [CEV, NLT]. The phrase 'her hour' [AB, Gdt, HTC, NICNT2, NTC, WBC; KJV, NASB, NRSV] is also translated 'her hour of distress/suffering' [My; TEV], 'her time' [NCV, NET, NIV, NJB, Ph, REB]. This noun denotes points of time consisting of occasions for particular events [LN]. Here it denotes the time for a woman to give birth or to suffer something [BAGD].

d. aorist. act. subj. of γεννάω (LN 23.52) (BAGD 2. p. 155): 'to give birth (to)' [LN; NASB, NJB, Ph], 'to bear' [BAGD, LN], 'to be delivered of'

[KJV], not explicit [CEV]. The clause 'when she gives birth to the child' is translated 'when/once the/her baby/child is born' [AB, NICNT2, WBC; NCV, NET, NIV, NLT, NRSV, REB, TEV], 'when she has brought forth the child' [Gdt], 'when she is delivered of the child' [HTC], 'whenever she has given birth to the little one' [NTC]. This verb means to give birth to a child [BAGD].

e. θλῖψις (LN 22.2) (BAGD 1. p. 362): 'suffering' [AB, LN; NET, NJB, TEV], 'pain' [BAGD; NCV], 'anguish' [Gdt, HTC, NTC, WBC; KJV, NASB, NIV, NLT, NRSV, REB], 'agony' [Ph], 'trouble and suffering' [LN], 'distress' [NICNT2], 'birth-pangs' [BAGD]. This noun denotes trouble involving direct suffering [LN].

f. ἄνθρωπος (LN 9.1) (BAGD 1.a.α. p. 68): 'man' [BAGD, Gdt, HTC; KJV, Ph], 'human being' [BAGD, LN, NICNT2, NTC, WBC; NET, NJB, NRSV], 'child' [AB; CEV, NASB, NCV, NIV, REB], 'baby' [TEV], 'new baby' [NLT], 'person, individual' [LN]. This noun denotes a human being [LN], or man as a class of beings [BAGD].

QUESTION—In this metaphor, the Image is a woman's anguish while her child is being born and her joy afterward, the Topic is the disciples' sorrow at Jesus' death and their joy after the Resurrection, what is the Point of Similarity?

The point of similarity is that pain before an event is followed by joy afterward causing a person to forget the pain [Lns]. It is the contrast between the woman's state of mind before versus after the birth. During the birth she is in great distress, but after she forgets her pain [NICNT1]. It is the shift from sorrow or anxiety to joy in both cases [EGT, Gdt, HTC, NTC]. Pain is frequently the needed antecedent to the supreme joys of life [ICC].

QUESTION—What is indicated by the definite article ἡ γυνὴ 'the woman'?

It is a generic article marking the woman as representing womankind in general [Bar, EGT, ICC, Lns, My, NICNT1, NICNT2]: 'a woman' [TEV]. The definite article 'the' is a reflection of Semitic parabolic style. For example, in 12:24 'a *grain* of *wheat*' is literally 'the grain of wheat' [AB, TH].

QUESTION—Is it pain or sadness that a woman experiences in childbirth?

1. She experiences pain [NICNT2; NTC, TRT, WBC; CEV, NASB, NCV, NIV, NJB, NLT, NRSV, Ph, REB]. A woman in childbirth experiences actual physical pain. The gloss 'grief' may be kept simply to keep to consistency in translating in verses 20–22 [NICNT2].
2. She experiences sadness [AB, Gdt, HTC; KJV, TEV]. A woman experiences sadness before giving birth because she is anxious about the future [TH].

DISCOURSE UNIT—16:22–28 [IVP]. The topic is the joy explained.

16:22 **So also you have grief[a] now, but I-will-see you again and your hearts will-rejoice,[b] and no-one takes your joy from you.**

TEXT—Instead of the present tense ἔχετε 'you have', some manuscripts read the future tense ἕξετε 'you will have'. GNT reads 'you have' with a B rating, indicating that the text is almost certain.

TEXT—Instead of the present tense αἴρει 'takes', some manuscripts read the future tense ἀρεῖ 'will take', and one manuscript reads ἀφαίρει 'takes away'. GNT reads 'takes' with a B rating, indicating that the text is almost certain.

LEXICON—a. λύπη (LN 25.273) (BAGD p. 482): 'grief' [BAGD; NASB], 'sorrow' [BAGD, LN], 'sadness, distress' [LN], 'pain, affliction' [BAGD]. The phrase 'you have grief now' [NICNT2] is also translated 'now is your time of grief' [NIV], 'you have sorrow now' [Gdt, HTC; KJV, NET, NLT], 'you now have anguish' [WBC], 'you are now in sorrow' [NTC], 'now you are sad' [AB; NCV, NJB, TEV], 'you are now very sad' [CEV], 'for the moment you are sad' [REB], 'you have pain now' [NRSV], 'now you are going through pain' [Ph]. This noun denotes a state of mental pain and anxiety [LN] or pain of mind or spirit' [BAGD].

b. fut. mid. (deponent = active) indic. of χαίρω (LN 25.125) (BAGD 1. p. 873): 'to rejoice' [BAGD, LN], 'to be glad' [BAGD, LN]. The phrase 'your hearts will rejoice' [AB, HTC, NTC; NET, NRSV] is also translated 'your heart will/shall rejoice' [Gdt, NICNT2; KJV, NASB], 'your hearts will be full of joy' [NJB], 'your hearts will thrill with joy' [Ph], 'your hearts will be filled with gladness' [TEV], 'your heart will be gladdened' [WBC], 'you will be joyful' [REB], 'you will rejoice' [NIV, NLT], 'you will be happy' [CEV, NCV]. This verb means to enjoy a state of happiness and well-being [LN].

QUESTION—What is indicated by the conjunction καί 'also' in the clause 'So *also* you have grief now'?

It is used here to draw a parallel between the figure of a woman giving birth and the experience of the disciples [HTC, TH]: 'That is how it is with you now' [TEV].

QUESTION—To what event(s) is Jesus referring when he says, 'I will see you again'?

He is referring to his appearances to the disciples after his resurrection [BECNT, EGT, ICC, Lns, NICNT1, WBC]. It refers to the time when the exalted Christ sees the disciples in the person of the Holy Spirit [Gdt, My]. It refers to both the resurrection and to the presence of the Holy Spirit among them [NTC].

QUESTION—What is indicated by the present tense 'no one *takes* your joy from you'?

The present is probably used to express the certainty of the future [AB, ICC, My]. The present tense is used to anticipate the future [CH]. The following versions render this present as a future [Gdt, HTC, NTC, WBC; NASB, NCV, NET, NIV, NJB, NRSV, REB]. Others translate it as 'no one can take your joy' [AB; CEV, NLT, Ph, TEV].

QUESTION—What word is emphasized in this verse?

The pronoun ὑμεῖς 'you pl.' is emphatic [TH]: *you yourselves* have grief.

DISCOURSE UNIT—16:23–33 [NASB]. The topic is prayer promises.

16:23 And on that day you-will- not -ask[a] me anything. Truly truly I-say to-you, whatever you-ask[b] the Father in my name he-will-give (it) to-you.

TEXT—Instead of ἐν τῷ ὀνόματί μου δώσει ὑμῖν 'in my name he will give you', some manuscripts read δώσει ὑμῖν ἐν τῷ ὀνόματί μου 'he will give you in my name', and one manuscript reads δώσει ὑμῖν 'he will give you'. GNT reads 'in my name he will give you' with a C rating, indicating difficulty in deciding which variant to place in the text.

TEXT—Instead of ἄν τι 'whatever', some manuscripts read ὅτι ὃ ἐάν 'that whatever', others read ὅ τι (or ὅτι) ἐάν 'whatever', and still others read ὅτι ὅσα ἄν 'that as many things as'. GNT reads ἄν τι 'whatever' with a B rating, indicating that the text is almost certain.

LEXICON—a. fut. act. indic. of ἐρωτάω (LN 33.161) (BAGD 1. p. 312): 'to ask' [BAGD, LN, NICNT2; KJV, NET, NIV, REB], 'to ask about' [BAGD; CEV, NASB], 'to ask a question' [BAGD; NJB, Ph], 'to put questions to someone' [AB, WBC], 'to question' [Gdt], 'to inquire of' [NTC], 'to ask of' [HTC; NRSV], 'to ask for' [LN; NCV, NLT, TEV], 'to request' [LN]. This verb means to ask for, usually with the implication of an underlying question [LN].

b. aorist act. subj. of αἰτέω (LN 33.163) (BAGD 1. p. 26): 'to ask' [BAGD, Gdt, NTC, WBC; KJV, NET, NIV, NLT, Ph], 'to ask for' [BAGD, LN; CEV, NASB, NCV, REB], 'to ask from' [NJB], 'to ask of' [AB, HTC, NICNT2; NRSV, TEV], 'to demand' [BAGD, LN], 'to plead for' [LN]. This verb means to ask for with urgency, even to the point of demanding [LN]. It has the sense of 'to ask someone for something' [BAGD].

QUESTION—To what time does the phrase 'in that day' refer?

It refers to the time of Jesus' resurrection and following [BECNT, Car, CH, EGT, HTC, ICC, Kn, NICNT1, NICNT2, Rd]. It refers to the time when Jesus will be present with the disciples through the Spirit [Lns, My].

QUESTION—What sense of the first verb ἐρωτάω 'to ask' is indicated?

1. It is used here in the sense of requesting information about something [AB, BAGD, BECNT, Bar, CH, EGT, Gdt, IVP, Lns, My, NICNT1, NICNT2, NTC, Rd, TH, WBC; CEV, NASB, NJB, Ph, REB]: 'you will not question me about anything' [NASB]. The verb ἐρωτάω is the verb of interrogation. In this case it refers back to the questions of the disciples in verses 17–19 concerning a lack of understanding. In this Gospel, ἐρωτάω is only used when referring to Jesus' prayers, not to the prayers of the disciples. When the disciples are the actors, the verb normally means 'to ask questions' (see 9:2; 16:5, 19) [NICNT2]. Up to this point the disciples had not prayed to Jesus, so the sense of 'to ask questions' here is the most likely meaning intended [NICNT1, Rd]. The presence of the solemn words 'Truly, truly' following this, suggests a change of subject and supports a different meaning for 'ask' here than the αἰτέω verb that follows [AB, NICNT1, TH]. The disciples will not need to ask Jesus anything because the Holy Spirit will guide them into all truth [AB, Bar, My, NICNT1, NTC, TH].

2. It is used here in the sense of asking for something in prayer [ICC; NCV, NLT, TEV]: 'you will not ask me for anything' [NCV]. The emphatic position of the pronoun 'me' before the verb suggests that it contrasts with the Father in the next clause. Jesus would be taken away but they would have direct access to the Father and could ask of him [ICC].

QUESTION—The phrase 'in my name' can either be connected with 'ask', as in 'ask in my name' or it can be connected with 'he will give', as in 'he will give in my name'.
1. The phrase 'in my name' should be construed with 'whatever you ask' [BECNT, Car, CH, ICC, IVP, Kn, NICNT1, NICNT2, Rd, TH; CEV, KJV, NASB, NCV, NIV, NRSV, REB, TEV]. The clause in verse 24, 'Until now you have asked nothing in my name', supports this interpretation showing that 'asking in Jesus' name is to be preferred [Rd].
2. It should be construed with the verb phrase 'he will give' [AB, Gdt, GNT, HTC, Lns, My, NTC; NJB, NLT, Ph]: 'he will give it to you in my name' [Gdt]. The Father will give you your requests in virtue of my name, that is because you have prayed in my name [My]. The Father will give on the basis of his love for the Son and on the basis of the Son's sacrifice [NTC].

QUESTION—What does it mean to ask 'in Jesus' name'?
It means to ask in view of the fact that the person asking belongs to Jesus or to ask 'in Jesus' place' [HTC]. If the reference is to asking in Jesus' name it means to ask for Jesus' sake and glory. If the reference is to the Father giving in Jesus' name, it means giving by virtue of the salvation that Jesus made possible and by virtue of the believers' relationship to him [WBC].

QUESTION—What words are emphasized in this verse?
The pronoun ἐμέ 'me' is emphatic [Gdt, ICC, My, NICNT1, NICNT2, TRT]. Both the form of the pronoun and its forward position in the sentence indicate that it is emphasized [NICNT1]. The emphatic position of the pronoun 'me' before the verb suggests that it contrasts with the Father in the next clause [ICC].

16:24 Until now you-have- not -asked-for[a] anything in my name. Ask and you-will-receive, that your joy may-be made-full.[b]

LEXICON—a. aorist act. indic. of αἰτέω (LN 33.163) (BAGD p. 26): 'to ask for' [BAGD, LN, NICNT2; CEV, NASB, NCV, NET, NIV, NRSV, TEV], 'to ask' [AB, Gdt, HTC, NTC, WBC; BAGD; KJV, NJB, NLT, Ph, REB], 'to demand' [BAGD, LN], 'to plead for' [LN]. This verb means to ask for with urgency, even to the point of demanding [LN].

b. perf. pass. participle of πληρόω (LN 59.33) (BAGD 3. p. 671): 'to be made full' [NASB], 'to be made complete' [BAGD, LN], 'to be brought to completion' [BAGD]. The clause 'that your joy may be made full' [NASB] is also translated 'that your joy may be full' [AB, HTC, NTC; KJV], 'that your joy may/might be fulfilled' [Gdt, NICNT2], 'so that your joy will be the fullest possible joy' [NCV], 'so that/that your joy may/will be complete' [NET, NRSV, REB], 'and so your joy will be complete'

[NCV], 'that your gladness may be complete' [WBC], 'and your joy will be complete' [NIV], 'so that your happiness may be complete' [TEV], 'that your joy may be overflowing' [Ph], 'so that you will be completely happy' [CEV], 'and you will have abundant joy' [NLT]. This verb means to make something total or complete [LN].

QUESTION—What does it mean to ask for something in Jesus' name?
It means to ask as if the person asking were Jesus' himself [Gdt], to ask on the basis of the merits of Jesus and in harmony with his message of salvation [NTC], appealing to Jesus' authority and power in his new role as one glorified by the Father [Rd], to ask as a representative of Jesus [Kn].

QUESTION—What is indicated by the present tense imperative 'Ask!'?
It indicates that the action is to be persistent or continuous [AB, BECNT, ICC, Lns, NICNT1, NTC, TH]: 'Keep asking, and you shall receive' [Lns].

QUESTION—What relationship is indicated by the conjunction ἵνα 'that' in the clause '*that* your joy may be made full'?
The purpose of asking and receiving is that their joy may be made complete [Lns, My, NICNT1, NTC; CEV, NASB, NCV, NET, NRSV, TEV]. In the present context it seems to indicate result [TH; NIV, NJB, NLT]: 'and your joy will be complete' [NIV].

QUESTION—What does it mean to have one's joy made full?
It means that what is lacking in the believers' joy will be supplied until their cup of joy is filled up to the brim [NTC].

QUESTION—Who is the implied giver of λήμψεσθε 'you will receive'?
If it is necessary to supply an agent to 'you will receive' one could translate 'God will give it to you' [TH, TRT].

QUESTION—Who is the implied actor of ᾖ πεπληρωμένη 'may be made full'?
Their joy will be made full by the Father who answers their prayers [Lns].

DISCOURSE UNIT—16:25–33 [BECNT, HTC, Lns, NTC; NCV, NRSV, Ph, TEV]. The topic is peace for the disciples [NRSV], victory over the world [BECNT, Lns; NCV, TEV], future matters [HTC; Ph].

DISCOURSE UNIT—16:25–30 [NICNT1]. The topic is the disciples' faith.

16:25 I have-spoken these-things to-you in figures-of-speech.[a] (An)-hour is coming when I-will- no-longer -speak to you in figuratives-of-speech, but I-will-speak plainly[b] to-you about the Father.

LEXICON—a. παραβολή (LN **33.15**) (BAGD 2. p. 629): 'figure of speech' [AB, **LN**; NLT, NRSV, REB, TEV], 'figurative language' [NASB], 'figure' [BAGD, HTC, LN], 'proverb' [KJV], 'parable' [LN, NICNT2; Ph], 'similitude' [Gdt], 'allegory' [LN], 'dark saying' [BAGD]. The phrase 'in figures of speech' is translated 'in obscure figures of speech' [NET], '(speaking) figuratively' [NIV], 'in the obscure speech of metaphor' [WBC], '(I have used) examples (to explain)' [CEV], 'in veiled sayings' [NTC], 'in veiled language' [NJB], '(I have told you these things) using stories that hide the meaning' [NCV]. This noun denotes a relatively short narrative with symbolic meaning. In almost all languages there is some way of speaking about parables or allegories. The equivalent in some languages may be 'a likeness story' or 'a story that teaches' or 'a story that points the way' or 'words that have another meaning' or 'words that are saying something else important' [LN]. John uses this term to indicate 'dark sayings' or 'figures' of speech in which especially lofty ideas are concealed [BAGD]. This is the same word translated 'parable' in 10:6 that describes Jesus' teaching about the Good Shepherd [TH, TRT].

b. παρρησία [BAGD 1. p. 630]: 'plainly' [BAGD; all translations except AB, Gdt, NTC; NCV, NJB, REB], 'openly' [BAGD, Gdt, NTC]. This noun is also translated as a phrase: 'in plain words' [AB; NCV, NJB, REB]. This noun denotes 'outspokenness, frankness, plainness of speech' that conceals nothing and passes over nothing [BAGD].

QUESTION—What is indicated by the pronoun ταῦτα 'these things'?

Although it may also refer to the images of the Vine (15:1) and of the Woman in Labor (16:21), and other parables of Jesus' ministry, the primary reference is to what he had just said in verses 15–18 [ICC]. It may refer to everything that Jesus has so far taught his disciples [Bar, EGT, IVP, NTC, TH], including the last group of teachings that Jesus delivered [Bar]. It refers to verses 16–17 where Jesus speaks of 'a little time' and his departure to the Father as well as the figure of the woman in labor [BECNT, HTC, My, NICNT2, WBC]. It includes the whole teaching of 16:4b–33 [BECNT, Car, NICNT1, WBC] as well as the last discourses of Jesus [WBC]. Jesus is referring to the things that puzzled the disciples (16:18) as well as his reference to the Father [Rd].

QUESTION—What kind of speech is figurative speech?

Figurative language is language that is difficult to understand [Bar, NICNT1]. Examples of figurative speech could be the woman in childbirth (16:21), washing the disciples feet (13:8–11), the vine and branches (15:1–17), the shepherd and the sheep (10:1–18) [TH]. It is not limited to merely the parables that Jesus used, but to all teaching about God that men do not understand that must be revealed to them by the Spirit [Gdt].

QUESTION—In what way did Jesus speak plainly to his disciples?

In John 11:14 Jesus told the disciples figuratively that Lazarus was merely sleeping, but because they did not understand, he told them *plainly* that Lazarus was dead [NICNT2]. The Jews wanted Jesus to tell them plainly if he was the Christ (10:24) instead of speaking about sheep and shepherds [NICNT2]. To paraphrase the word 'plainly', one could translate 'I will speak to you about the Father in such a way that you will clearly understand' [TH].

QUESTION—To what specific time was Jesus referring by the coming hour?

He was referring to the time after the resurrection when the Holy Spirit was given [AB, Bar, Car, Gdt, ICC, IVP, NICNT1, NTC, Rd, TRT]. Jesus would speak plainly to them about the Father after his resurrection and the Spirit would continue this revelation after that [Car, Kn]. It refers to the time when

Jesus would be withdrawn from them and the Holy Spirit would begin to teach the disciples plainly about the Father [ICC, Lns, My]. This time cannot be limited to the teaching of Jesus after his resurrection in chapters 20 and 21, but must include the character of the preaching that began at that time and was explained by Jesus' death and resurrection [NICNT2].

QUESTION—What word is emphasized in this verse?

The word ταῦτα 'these things' is emphatic by its fronted initial position in the Greek sentence [TH, TRT]: *These things* I have spoken to you.

16:26 In that day you-will-ask[a] in my name and I-do- not -tell you that I will-request[b] the Father on-your-behalf.[c] **16:27** For the Father himself[d] loves[e] you, because you have-loved me and have-believed that I came from God.

TEXT—Instead of τοῦ θεοῦ 'God', (in the words 'I came from God') some manuscripts read θεοῦ 'God', others read τοῦ πατρός 'the Father'. GNT reads τοῦ θεοῦ 'God' with a C rating indicating difficulty in deciding which variant to place in the text. HTC, NTC; NASB appear to accept the reading 'the Father'.

LEXICON—a. fut. mid. indic. of αἰτέω (LN 33.163) (BAGD p. 26): 'to ask' [BAGD, LN; all translations except NCV, Ph, REB], 'to ask for' [BAGD, LN; NCV], 'to make a request (to)' [Ph, REB], 'to demand' [BAGD, LN], 'to plead for' [LN]. This verb means to ask for with urgency, even to the point of demanding [LN].

b. fut. act. indic. of ἐρωτάω (LN 33.161) (BAGD 2. p. 312): 'to request (of)' [BAGD, LN; NASB], 'to make request of' [NTC], 'to ask' [BAGD, NICNT2, WBC; CEV, NCV, NET, NIV, NLT, NRSV, TEV], 'to pray (to)' [Gdt, HTC; KJV, NASB, REB], 'to plead to' [Ph], 'to petition' [AB], 'to ask for' [LN], 'to beseech' [BAGD]. This verb means to ask for, usually with the implication of an underlying question [LN].

c. περί (LN 90.39): 'in behalf of' [LN, NICNT2, WBC; NASB, NET, NIV, NLT, NRSV, TEV], 'for' [AB, Gdt, HTC, NTC; CEV, KJV, NCV, NJB, Ph, REB]. This preposition indicates events that are indirectly involved in a beneficial activity [LN].

d. αὐτός (LN 92.37) (BAGD 1.e. p. 122): 'himself' [BAGD, LN; all translations except CEV]. The phrase 'the Father himself' is translated 'God the Father' [CEV]. This pronoun serves as a marker of emphasis by calling attention to the distinctiveness of the lexical item with which it occurs (used for all persons, genders, and numbers) [BAGD, LN].

e. pres. act. indic. of φιλέω (LN 25.33) (BAGD 1.a. p. 859): 'to love' [BAGD, LN; all translations], 'to have affection for' [BAGD, LN], 'to like' [BAGD]. This verb means to have love or affection for someone or something based on association [LN].

QUESTION—To what time does the phrase 'In that day' refer?

It refers to the time of Pentecost and after [Bar, ICC]. It refers to the same time as the phrase 'an hour' of verse 25 [AB, EGT, NICNT2, TH].

QUESTION—Who is the implied object of the verb 'you will ask'?
>The prayer is addressed to the Father [Gdt, TH, TRT; CEV, NCV, Ph, TEV]: 'You will ask the Father in my name' [CEV].

QUESTION—What is implied in the clause 'you will ask in my name'?
>In the light of verse 14:13, 'Whatever you ask in my name this I will do', it is implied that their requests would be granted [AB, TH].

QUESTION—What may be implied by the sentence 'I do not tell you that I will request the Father on your behalf'?
>In some languages a literal translation may imply the idea 'I say that I will *not* ask him on your behalf'. To avoid this it may be advisable to translate something like 'I will not need to ask him on your behalf' [TH]. It implies that there is now no need for Jesus to present their requests to the Father for them because now they have direct access to the Father in Jesus' name [Car, IVP]. Jesus would not need to approach the Father for them because they are in Christ and their prayers offered to the Father in Jesus' name are virtually His prayers [ICC].

QUESTION—What is indicated by the conjunction γάρ 'for (the Father himself loves you)'?
>It indicates the reason why Jesus will not need to take their requests to the Father for them, because the Father himself loves them [IVP, Lns, NICNT1]. It indicates the reason why the disciples may be bold in prayer [ICC].

QUESTION—What is implied by the perfect tenses 'you have loved' and 'you have believed'?
>The perfect tenses imply that this was their continuous attitude [AB, NICNT1, TH]. They indicate that these are traits that now characterized them, 'you are become those who love me and believe' [Gdt]. They imply that their love still continues and that they do not stop believing [NTC].

QUESTION—What words are emphasized in these verses?
>In verse 26, the pronoun ἐγώ 'I' ('I, on my part will request the Father') is emphatic stressing the fact that intercession for them will not be needed because the disciples' prayers would be in Jesus' name [My]. In verse 27 the presence of the pronoun αὐτός 'himself' preceding the phrase 'the Father' serves to emphasize the Father [AB, BAGD, Bar, LN, Lns, NICNT1]: 'the Father himself has affection for you' [Lns]. It indicates that it is the Father, and no one other than he, who loves them [NICNT1]. Also in verse 27 the two pronouns ὑμεῖς 'you' and ἐγώ 'I' are emphasized [Lns, My, TH]: '*you on your part* have had affection for me and have believed that *I on my part* came forth from the Father' [Lns]. This emphasizes the contrast between them and the hostile world [Lns]. The pronouns ὑμεῖς 'you' and ἐμέ 'me' are emphasized in the phrase 'you have loved me' [ICC, TH].

16:28 **I-came[a] from the Father and I-have-come into the world.[b] Again[c] I am-leaving the world and going to the Father.**

TEXT—Instead of ἐξῆλθον παρὰ τοῦ πατρός 'I came from the Father', some manuscripts read ἐξῆλθον ἐκ τοῦ πατρός 'I came from the Father', others read παρὰ τοῦ πατρός 'from the Father', and still others omit this clause. GNT reads ἐξῆλθον παρὰ τοῦ πατρός 'I came from the Father' with a C rating, indicating difficulty in deciding which variant to place in the text.

LEXICON—a. aorist act. indic. of ἐξέπχομαι (LN 15.40) (BAGD 1. a. γ. p. 274): 'to come' [HTC; CEV, NCV, NET, NIV, NJB, NLT, NRSV, Ph, REB, TEV], 'to come forth' [AB, NICNT2, WBC; Gdt, KJV, NASB], 'to come out' [BAGD], 'to go out' [BAGD, LN, NTC], 'to depart out of, to leave from within' [LN]. This verb means to move out of an enclosed or well-defined two or three-dimensional area [LN].

b. κόσμος (LN 1.39) (BAGD 4.c. p. 446): 'world' [BAGD, LN; all translations], 'earth' [BAGD, LN]. This noun denotes the surface of the earth as the dwelling place of mankind, in contrast with the heavens above and the world below [LN]. It denotes 'the world' as the earth, the planet on which we live [BAGD].

c. πάλιν (LN 89.129): 'again' [HTC, NICNT2, NTC, WBC; KJV, NASB, NRSV], 'and again' [Gdt], 'now' [AB; NCV, NIV, Ph], 'and now' [NJB, NLT, REB, TEV], 'but' [CEV], 'but in turn' [LN; NET], 'on the other hand, however' [LN]. This adverb indicates a contrast, with the implication of a sequence [LN]. It indicates what is next in a sequence [AB, LN].

QUESTION—What is indicated by the aorist tense 'I came (from the Father)'?

It probably refers to Jesus' incarnation that took place at a particular time in history [AB, TH].

QUESTION—To what do the four clauses of this verse correspond in Jesus' life?

They correspond to his pre-existence/self-renunciation, incarnation, death, and ascension [Gdt, ICC, NTC].

DISCOURSE UNIT—16:29–33 [IVP]. The topic is preparation for Jesus' departure.

16:29 His disciples said, "Look[a] now you-are-speaking plainly and are no-longer speaking in-figures-of-speech.[b] **16:30** Now we-know that you-know all-things and you-have no need (for) anyone to-question[c] you. By[d] this we-believe that you-came from God."

LEXICON—a. ἴδε (LN 91.13) (BAGD 1. p. 369): 'look' [LN, NICNT2, WBC; NET], 'lo' [Gdt; KJV, NASB], 'ah' [HTC, NTC], 'yes' [NRSV], 'there' [AB], '(you) see' [BAGD], 'listen, pay attention, come now, then' [LN], not explicit [CEV, NCV, NIV, NJB, NLT, Ph, REB, TEV]. This particle is a prompter of attention [BAGD, LN], that serves also to emphasize the following statement [LN]. It is an interjection of astonished admiration [ICC, My].

b. παροιμία (LN 33.15) (BAGD 21. p. 629): 'figure of speech' [AB, BAGD, LN; NASB, NIV, NRSV, REB, TEV], 'obscure figures of speech' [NET], 'veiled language' [NJB], 'veiled saying' [NTC], 'obscure language' [WBC], 'figure' [HTC, LN], 'story that is hard to understand'

[NCV], 'parable' [LN, NICNT2; Ph], 'allegory' [LN], 'example' [CEV], 'proverb' [KJV], 'similitude' [Gdt]. This noun is also used as an adverb: '(you are speaking plainly and not) figuratively' [NLT]. This noun denotes a relatively short narrative with symbolic meaning [LN]. It is a 'dark saying' or 'figure of speech' in which especially lofty ideas are concealed [BAGD].

c. pres. act. subj. of ἐρωτάω (LN 33.180) (BAGD 1. p. 311): 'to question' [BAGD, Gdt, WBC; NASB, NLT, NRSV], 'to ask' [BAGD, Gdt, LN, NICNT2; KJV, NET, REB], to ask a question' [AB, BAGD, LN; NIV, TEV], 'to inquire of' [NTC]. The clause 'you have no need for anyone to question you' [NASB] is also translated 'no more questions are needed' [Ph], 'we have no more questions' [CEV], 'you...need not wait for questions to be put into words' [NJB], 'you can answer a person's question even before it is asked' [NCV]. This verb means to ask for information [LN].

d. ἐν (LN **89.26**) (BAGD III.3.a. p. 261): 'because of' [BAGD, **LN**], 'on account of' [BAGD, LN], 'by reason of' [LN]. The clause 'by this we believe' [HTC, NICNT2, TRT, WBC; NASB, NRSV] is also translated 'but this we believe' [KJV], 'from this we believe' [NLT], 'for this we believe' [Gdt], 'because of this we believe' [AB, **LN**; NET, NJB, REB], 'for this reason we believe' [NTC], 'this is the reason we believe' [BAGD], 'that's why we believe' [TRT], 'this makes us believe' [NCV, NIV, TEV], 'this makes us sure' [Ph], 'now we believe' [CEV]. This preposition indicates cause or reason [BAGD, LN], with focus on instrumentality, either of objects or events [LN].

QUESTION—To what event does the adverb νῦν 'now' in verse 29 refer?

It refers to the present time in which the disciples believe that the promise of verse 25 that he would no longer speak in figures, was already being fulfilled [AB, Bar, Car, Gdt, ICC, Lns, My, NICNT2, NTC, Rd].

QUESTION—How do the disciples know that Jesus did not need to have people question him?

Verse 19 states that Jesus knew what they were wanting to ask him and he proceeded to suggest to them the very questions they were desiring to ask [Bar, Gdt, ICC, Lns, My, NICNT1, NTC, Rd, TH]. Rather than verse 19, verses 2:24–25 are the basis for their confidence that Jesus did not need to have people question him [Car]. The disciples apparently believe that the promise of verse 23a has been fulfilled when Jesus told them, 'And on that day you will not ask me anything' [AB, BECNT].

QUESTION—What does 'you have no need for anyone to question you' mean?

It is a semantically compact sentence and for some languages it may be necessary to expand it to 'in order to know what questions people have in their minds, it is not necessary for you to ask them what they are thinking' [TH]. In Jewish thinking the ability to anticipate questions before they were asked was a mark of the divine [AB, BECNT, IVP].

QUESTION—To what does the phrase ἐν τούτῳ 'by this' refer?
It refers back to Jesus knowing everything and his ability to anticipate questions [AB].

DISCOURSE UNIT—16:31–33 [NICNT1]. The topic is the disciples' peace.

16:31 Jesus answered them, "Do-you- now -believe? **16:32** Look[a] an-hour is-coming and has- (already) -come when you-will-be-scattered[b] each to (his) own-home[c] and you-will-leave me alone. Yet[d] I-am not alone, because the Father is with me.

- LEXICON—a. ἰδού (LN 91.13) (BAGD): 'look' [LN, NICNT2, NET], 'behold' [Gdt; KJV, NASB], 'listen' [LN, WBC; NJB], 'listen to me' [NCV], 'note well' [NTC], 'pay attention' [LN], 'I warn you' [REB], 'why' [AB], not explicit [HTC; CEV, NIV, NLT, NRSV, Ph, TEV]. This particle is a prompter of attention that serves also to emphasize the following statement [LN].
- b. aorist pass. subj. of σκορπίζω (LN **15.135**) (BAGD 1. p. 757): 'to be scattered' [BAGD, **LN**; all translations], 'to be dispersed' [BAGD], 'to be caused to disperse' [BAGD, LN]. This verb means to cause a group or a gathering to disperse or scatter [LN].
- c. ἴδιος (LN 57.4) (BAGD 3.b. p. 370): 'own home' [BAGD; NASB], 'one's own' [LN], 'one's property' [LN]. The phrase 'each/each one/every one to his/his own home' [Gdt, NICNT2, NTC; NCV, NET, NIV, NRSV, REB] is also translated 'each of you will go back home' [CEV], 'each of you to your own home' [TEV], 'every one of you going home' [Ph], 'each to his own place' [WBC], 'each on his own' [AB], 'every man to his own' [KJV], 'each/every man for himself' [HTC, Lns], 'each/each one going his own way' [NJB, NLT]. This pronoun pertains to being the exclusive property of someone [LN].
- d. καί (LN 91.12): 'yet' [AB, HTC, LN, NTC; NASB, NET, NIV, NLT, NRSV, Ph, REB], 'and yet' [NICNT2, WBC; KJV, NASB, NJB], 'but' [Gdt; CEV, NCV, TEV], 'then, indeed, how is it then' [LN]. This conjunction marks emphasis, involving surprise and unexpectedness [LN]. Καί here has the adversative sense of 'and yet' [Bar, EGT, Gdt, ICC, NICNT1].

QUESTION—Are the words Ἄρτι πιστεύετε 'Do you now believe?/You now believe', a statement or a question?
  1. This is really meant as a question—at least in form [AB, Bar, EGT, HTC, NICNT1, NTC, TRT; all translations except Gdt, NICNT2; NIV]. The question is rhetorical and functions: to throw doubt on the adequacy of the disciples' faith [AB, Bar, NICNT1], to express doubt [HTC], to warn against over-confidence and stress the imperfect character of their faith [NTC], to mildly rebuke and express exasperation [BECNT], to inform them that the time to speak so confidently (16:13) has not yet come [Rd]. It is as though Jesus is saying, 'I believe that your confession is genuine and that your faith is real; but is it full-grown?' [NTC]. Jesus is not

questioning the reality of the disciples' faith [Bar, BECNT, Gdt, IVP, My, NICNT1, NICNT2, NTC].
2. They are meant to be a statement, not a question [Car, Gdt, ICC, IVP, Lns, My, NICNT2: NIV]: 'You believe at last!' [NIV]. Jesus is expressing his confidence in their faith. This is shown by his statement in the next chapter (17:8), 'They knew with certainty that I came from you, and they believed that you sent me' [Lns]. For Jesus this is a moment of complete happiness and fulfillment. It is as though he were saying, 'Now at last you have reached the point to which I have been laboring to lead you: you have recognized me for what I am, and have received me as such' [Gdt]. The emphasis is on the word ἄρτι 'now' [ICC, My, NICNT1] and the words must be taken, not interrogatively, but concessively meaning 'Now, just now, ye believe, but how soon will ye become vacillating!' Their faith did not in fact disappear, but did not pass the test of self-denial [My]. Although taken as a statement, it is ironical (the meaning is opposite of what is stated). Their faith is real but it is temporary ('now'). He implies that it would not stand the test of time and persecution [NICNT2]. He informs them that their celebrations are premature. They have not yet taken the final exam [IVP]. The irony of Jesus' reply is better expressed as an exclamation of strong exasperation [Car]. He warns them that their faith will not stand the test [ICC].
3. Whether a question or a statement, it functions to indicate the inadequacy of the disciples' faith [TH].

QUESTION—What is the implied object of the verb 'believe'?

The object is Jesus [CEV]: 'Do you really believe me?' [CEV]. The object could be 'in me' ('You/Do you now believe in me!?' [TRT; Ph], or 'that I came from God [Lns, TRT], '(You/Do you now believe that I came from God?!' [TRT], or 'that I am God's representative?' [EGT].

QUESTION—In what way could the hour be coming and have already arrived?

In one sense what Jesus was referring to was future since they had not yet crossed the Kidron Brook or encountered the enemy. But in another sense the hour had arrived for even at that time Judas was on his way to betray him [Lns, NTC]. The expression 'a time is coming and has come' emphasizes the imminence of this event [NICNT1]. The hour refers to the events of Jesus' arrest and crucifixion [TH].

QUESTION—Of what Scripture is the scattering of the disciples a fulfillment?

It fulfills Zechariah 13:7 'Strike the Shepherd, and the sheep will be scattered' [Bar, BECNT, Car, CH, HTC, IVP, Kn, Lns, NICNT2, NTC, Rd, TH, WBC].

QUESTION—Who is the actor of the passive verb σκορπισθῆτε 'you will be scattered'?

A vicious, hostile power will scatter the disciples [Lns]. The actors are the soldiers and the ones accompanying them, but the verb phrase could be expressed as 'all of you will run away' [TH].

QUESTION—The phrase εἰς τὰ ἴδια 'to his own things' can either mean 'to his own home' or more generally, 'to his own things'. Which one is intended here?
1. It means 'to his own home' [AB, Bar, BECNT, Gdt, ICC, Kn, My, NICNT1, NICNT2, NTC, Rd; CEV, NASB, NCV, NET, NIV, NRSV, Ph, REB, TEV]. The use of this same phrase in 19:27 indicates that the meaning 'to *his own home*' is preferable [NICNT1, ICC, My, NTC, TH]. It probably refers to their temporary homes in Jerusalem rather than their homes in Galilee [BECNT, NTC]. It is more likely that the disciples returned to their homes in Galilee [Bar, TH].
2. It has a more general meaning of 'to one's own things' [EGT, HTC, Lns, WBC; KJV, NJB, NLT]. The phrase εἰς τὰ ἴδια 'to his own things' should not be taken to mean to his own home but rather means that they would now be concerned for their own safety, not with that of Jesus [HTC]. It is better to translate 'to his own' since it includes 'to his own interests/pursuits/familiar surroundings/private affairs' or all of these together [EGT]. Here the phrase means that each disciple looked out for his own safety wherever he could find cover for himself [Lns, HTC].

QUESTION—What words are emphasized in these verses?

The pronoun με 'me' is emphasized [Lns, NTC, TRT]: and *me* you will leave alone. Jesus emphasizes his own suffering. He will soon enter the environment of isolation until at last even the Father will forsake him [NTC].

16:33 I-have-said these-things to-you so-that you-might-have peace[a] in me. In the world[b] you-will-have tribulation,[c] but take-courage,[d] I have-overcome[e] the world.[f]

LEXICON—a. εἰρήνη (LN 25.248) (BAGD 3. p. 227): 'peace' [BAGD, LN; all translations], 'freedom from worry' [LN]. This noun denotes a state of freedom from anxiety and inner turmoil [LN]. It is thought of as being nearly synonymous with messianic salvation [BAGD].
b. κόσμος (LN 1.39) (BAGD 7. p. 447): 'world' [BAGD, LN; all translations except NLT], 'earth' [LN; NLT]. This noun denotes the surface of the earth as the dwelling place of mankind, in contrast with the heavens above and the world below [LN].
c. θλῖψις (LN 22.2) (BAGD 1. p. 362): 'tribulation' [BAGD, Gdt, HTC, NTC; KJV, NASB], 'trouble' [WBC; NCV, NIV, Ph], 'trouble and suffering' [LN; NET], 'suffering' [AB, LN; REB], 'distress' [NICNT2], 'trials and sorrows' [NLT], 'hardship' [NJB], 'persecution' [BAGD, LN], 'affliction, oppression' [BAGD]. This noun is also translated as a verb: 'you will have to suffer' [CEV], '(the world) will make you suffer' [TEV], 'you face persecution' [NRSV]. This noun denotes trouble involving direct suffering [LN]. It denotes great and pressing affliction, not some mild trouble [NICNT1]. The Greek term primarily means 'pressure' [NTC].
d. pres. act. impera. of θαρσέω (LN **25.156**) (BAGD p. 352): 'to take courage' [NICNT2; NASB, NET, NRSV], 'to be of good courage' [Gdt,

NTC], 'to be courageous' [BAGD, LN; NJB], 'to have courage' [AB, BAGD, **LN**], 'to take heart' [WBC; NIV, NLT, REB], 'to be brave' [NCV, TEV], 'to cheer up' [CEV], 'to be of good cheer' [HTC; KJV], 'to be cheerful' [BAGD], 'to be bold' [LN]. The phrase 'take courage' is translated 'never lose heart' [Ph]. This verb means to have confidence and firmness of purpose in the face of danger or testing [LN].
  e. perf. act. indic. νικάω (LN 39.57) (BAGD 2.a. p. 539): 'to overcome' [BAGD, Gdt, HTC, NICNT2; KJV, NASB, NIV, NLT], 'to conquer' [AB, BAGD, LN, NTC, WBC; NET, NJB, NRSV, Ph, REB], 'to defeat' [CEV, NCV, TEV], 'to be victorious over' [LN], 'to vanquish' [BAGD]. This word means to win a victory over [LN]. Jesus means that by his death he has rendered the world's opposition pointless [Car]. He promises them that evil will not prevail in the end for believers [Kn]. The perfect tense indicates that Jesus' victory has been won and its results continue [NICNT1].
  f. κόσμος (LN 41.38) (BAGD 7. p. 447): 'world' [BAGD, LN; all translations], 'world system, world's standards' [LN]. This noun denotes the system of practices and standards associated with secular society (that is, without reference to any demands or requirements of God) [LN]. It includes everything that belongs to the world and is hostile to God, i.e., lost in sin, wholly at odds with anything divine, ruined and depraved [BAGD].

QUESTION—To what does the pronoun ταῦτα 'these things' refer?
  It probably refers back to the whole of chapter 16 [Bar, EGT, TH, TRT], and may include everything he had said that evening [NTC, TRT]. It probably refers to the promises of verses 26–27, and possibly to some earlier ones in this chapter [AB]. It seems to refer to the dispersion of the disciples after Jesus' arrest that he had spoken about in verse 32 [ICC].

QUESTION—What relationship is indicated by the conjunction ἵνα 'so that'?
  It indicates that Jesus' purpose is that the disciples have peace [Car, EGT, ICC, Lns, NICNT1].

QUESTION—What does the phrase '(you might have peace) in me' mean?
  It means 'in union with me' [CH, HTC, TH: TEV]: 'you will have peace by being united to me' [TEV]. It means living in vital fellowship with Jesus [My, TH]. It is peace in the life they share with Jesus [HTC]. It could mean 'you might have peace in your hearts because of me' [CEV], or 'in your hearts because of your faith in me/as my followers' [TRT].

QUESTION—In what sense has Jesus overcome the world?
  He has conquered the world in the sense that the ruler of this world has been judged (16:11) and will be cast out (12:31) [Lns]. Jesus has defeated the world in the same way that he defeated the prince of this evil world [Car]. The 'evil one' is behind the world [HTC]. It is not the Prince of the world that is in focus here, but the principle of evil that is in the world that is defeated and destroyed [Bar]. It is the world force or world system that he has conquered [TH, TRT]—its anti-Messianic power [My].

QUESTION—What words are emphasized in this verse?
The phrase 'peace in me' occurs before the verb 'you might have' to increase its prominence [TRT]: 'peace in me you might have'. The pronoun ἐγώ 'I' in the phrase 'I have conquered' is emphatic [EGT, Gdt, My, NICNT1]: 'I, none else, have overcome' [NICNT1].

DISCOURSE UNIT—17:1–26 [BECNT, Car, CH, GNT, IVP, Kn, NICNT1, NICNT2, Rd, WBC; CEV, NCV, NLT, NRSV, Ph, TEV]. The topic is the prayer of Jesus.

DISCOURSE UNIT—17:1–12 [NASB]. The topic is the high priestly prayer.

DISCOURSE UNIT—17:1–8 [AB, ICC]. The topic is Jesus prays for glory [AB], Jesus prays for himself [ICC].

DISCOURSE UNIT—17:1–5 [BECNT, Car, HTC, IVP, Kn, NICNT1, NTC, Rd, WBC; NET, NIV]. The topic is Jesus prays for glory [Car, HTC, IVP, NICNT1, NTC, Rd, WBC; NET], Jesus prays for himself [BECNT; NIV], the Father and Son share glory [Kn].

17:1 Jesus said these-things and lifting-up-his-eyes[a] to heaven said, "Father, the hour[b] has-come, glorify[c] your Son, so-that the Son may-glorify you,

TEXT—Instead of ὁ υἱός 'the Son (may glorify)', some manuscripts read ὁ υἱός σου 'your Son', and others read καὶ ὁ υἱός σου 'your Son also'. GNT reads 'the Son' with a B rating, indicating that the text is almost certain. KJV, NET, NIV, NJB seem to accept the reading 'your Son' and Gdt accepts the reading 'your Son also'.

LEXICON—a. aorist act. participle of ἐπαίρω (LN 24.34, 15.105) (BAGD 1. p. 282): 'to lift up, to hold up' [BAGD], 'to raise' [LN (15.105)], 'to notice, to look' [LN (24.34)]. The phrase ἐπαίρω τοὺς ὀφθαλμούς 'to lift up the eyes' [Gdt, HTC, NICNT2, NTC; KJV, NASB] is also translated 'to raise the eyes' [NJB, Ph, WBC], 'to look up' [AB, BAGD; CEV, NLT, NRSV, REB, TEV], 'to look upward' [NET], 'to look (toward)' [LN; NCV, NIV], 'to notice' [LN]. This verb when used with eyes is an idiom, (literally 'to lift up the eyes') meaning to direct one's attention to something by looking closely at it [LN (24.34)], or it means to cause to move up [LN (15.105)]. It is important to avoid implying that Jesus literally looked into heaven by using a translation such as 'he looked up toward heaven' [TH]. Before this, Jesus had been looking at his disciples while speaking to them. But now the act of looking up towards heaven indicated that he was praying to the Father [Gdt]. To lift up one's eyes to heaven was a common gesture of prayer [BECNT, NICNT1, NTC], heaven being where God's throne is [NTC].

b. ὥρα (LN 67.1) (BAGD 3. p. 896): 'hour' [AB, Gdt, HTC, NICNT2, NTC; KJV, NASB, NJB, NLT, NRSV, Ph, REB, TEV, WBC], 'time' [BAGD, LN; CEV, NCV, NET, NIV], 'occasion' [LN]. This noun denotes a point of time consisting of an occasion for a particular event [LN]. It denotes the time when something took place, is taking place, or will take place [BAGD].

c. aorist act. impera. of δοξάζω (LN 87.24) (BAGD 2. p. 204): 'to glorify' [BAGD, LN; all translations except CEV, NCV, TEV], 'to bring glory to' [CEV], 'to give glory to' [NCV, TEV], 'to make gloriously great' [LN], 'to clothe in splendor' [BAGD, Car]. This verb is a favorite term in John in which the whole life of Jesus is depicted as a glorifying of the Son by the Father and at the same time of the Father by the Son [BAGD]. It means to cause someone to have glorious greatness [LN].

QUESTION—What does the pronoun ταῦτα 'these things' refer to?

It refers to the teachings of chapters 13–16 [Bar, TH], or chapters 14–16 [Car, HTC].

QUESTION—Is it culturally appropriate in other languages for Jesus to address the Father as just 'Father'?

In some languages it may be more appropriate to rather address a person's Father as 'my Father' or some other culturally appropriate form of address to one's father [TH, TRT]. Also it is important that Jesus' address to the Father sound polite and not rude [TRT].

QUESTION—To what specific time does the noun ὥρα 'hour' refer?

It refers to the time when Jesus will reveal his true glory to the world by means of his death on the cross [Gdt, HTC, Kn, My, NICNT1, NICNT2, TH]. The hour began with the first indication of the process that would lead to Jesus' death and ended with his return to the Father [AB]. The hour began when the Greeks were trying to find Jesus (12:20) and it was described as having come in (12:23, 27–28, 31–32; 13:1, 31) [Car]. The hour includes Jesus' death, resurrection, ascension and coronation in the Father's presence [BECNT, Car, EGT, Lns, NTC].

QUESTION—What did Jesus mean by his request that the Father glorify him?

The primary focus of 'glorify' here is on revealing the true glory of the Son and the Father rather than on giving glory to them [TH]. The primary sense is to 'clothe in splendor'. Jesus is asking here that the Father reverse the self-emptying that he experienced in the incarnation and to restore the glory he knew before the world began. So the cross became the glorification of the Son [Car]. It seems that he was asking to be reunited with the Father as seen by what he says in verse 5. On the other hand, the Father is glorified by the Son's giving eternal life to those given to him (verse 2) [NICNT2]. Jesus is asking that the Father give him his own honor and that all would recognize it. The honor is God's saving love and power [WBC]. To glorify Jesus is to reveal something that has been partially hidden. The Father would glorify Jesus in his resurrection enabling him to give eternal life to believers [CH]. To glorify someone is to show him as deserving of honor or praise. So Jesus is asking that God reveal to people Jesus' own honor—that he is one with God. This will be done through Jesus' death which will reveal the love of both the Father and the Son [IVP]. Jesus was asking for the glory that he already had on earth (12:28), which he had as the Word made flesh (1:14; 2:11), and by which he had glorified the Father (11:4, 40; 9:3) [Rd]. He was requesting that the Father now speed up the cross and reveal his love for and devotion to the Father [Kn]. Part of Jesus' request for glory was for support in his suffering and death. But more than this it was asking for the acceptance of his sacrifice by the Father, sealing his mission as being complete [ICC]. Jesus was glorified when the Father invested his human nature with the full use of the divine attributes [Lns].

QUESTION—What is indicated by the conjunction ἵνα 'so that'?

It indicates that Jesus' *purpose* in asking for the Father to glorify him is that this would in turn be a means to glorify the Father [Bar, EGT, Gdt, HTC, Lns, NICNT1].

QUESTION—To whom does the phrase 'your Son' refer?

It is important to make sure that the phrase '(glorify) your Son' refers to Jesus and not to some other third person. If this is not understood one could translate something like, 'Please glorify me as your Son' [TRT]. Similarly, it may be important to continue this first person reference in the final clause by translating 'that I may show people how wonderful you are' [TH, TRT].

QUESTION—What word is emphasized in this verse?

The pronoun ταῦτα 'these things' occurs before the phrase 'Jesus said' to increase its prominence [TRT].

17:2 even as^a you-gave him authority^b over-all flesh,^{c} so-that he-may-give eternal-life^d to-all whom you-have-given him.

LEXICON—a. καθώς (LN 89.34) (BAGD 3. p. 391): 'even as' [NTC; NASB], 'for' [NIV, NLT, Ph, REB, TEV], 'since' [BAGD, HTC; NRSV], 'because' [LN], 'inasmuch as' [**LN**; AB], 'just as' [NICNT2; NET, NJB], 'according as' [WBC], 'as' [BAGD, Gdt; KJV], 'in so far as' [BAGD], 'and' [CEV], not explicit [NCV]. This conjunction is used here in a causal sense, especially as a conjunction beginning a sentence [BAGD]. It indicates cause or reason, often with the implication of some implied comparison [LN].

b. ἐξουσία (LN 37.35) (BAGD 3. p. 278): 'authority' [BAGD, NICNT2, NTC, WBC; NASB, NET, NIV, NLT, NRSV, Ph, TEV], 'power' [AB, Gdt, HTC; CEV, KJV, NCV, NJB], 'authority to rule, right to control' [LN], 'absolute power, warrant' [BAGD]. The clause 'you gave him authority' is translated 'you made him sovereign' [REB]. This noun denotes the right to control or govern over [LN].

c. σάρξ (LN 9.11) (BAGD 3. p. 743): 'flesh' [Gdt, HTC, NICNT2, NTC, WBC; KJV, NASB], 'human being' [LN], 'a man of flesh and blood' [BAGD]. The phrase '(over) all flesh' is translated '(over) all people' [CEV, NCV, NIV, NRSV, TEV], '(over) all humanity' [NET, NJB], '(over) all mankind' [REB], '(over) all men' [AB; Ph], '(over) everyone' [BAGD; NLT], '(over) every person' [BAGD]. This noun is a figurative extension of the meaning of σάρξ 'flesh (8.63) and denotes humans as physical beings [LN].

d. ζωή αἰώνιος (LN **67.96**) (BAGD 3. p. 28): 'eternal life' [**LN**; all translations except NICNT2, NTC], 'life eternal' [NICNT2], 'everlasting life' [NTC]. This adjective describes an unlimited duration of time. The most frequent use of αἰώνιος in the NT is with ζωή 'life'. In combination with ζωή there is evidently not only a temporal element, but also a qualitative distinction [LN, IVP]. In such contexts, αἰώνιος evidently carries certain implications associated with αἰώνιος in relationship to divine and supernatural attributes. If one translates 'eternal life' as simply 'never dying', there may be serious misunderstandings, since persons may assume that 'never dying' refers only to physical existence rather than to 'spiritual death'. Accordingly, some translators have rendered 'eternal life' as 'unending real life', so as to introduce a qualitative distinction [LN]. The phrase 'eternal life' is a significant one in John and occurs 17 times at these references: 3:15, 16, 36; 4:14, 36; 5:24, 39; 6:27, 40, 47, 54, 68; 10:28; 12:25, 50; 17:2, 3.

QUESTION—What is the function of the conjunction καθώς 'even as'?

It indicates that this verse explains the request 'Glorify me'. He is reminding the Father of what gives him the right to ask the Father to glorify him [Gdt]. Jesus is declaring that his request for glory is in harmony with God's own decree 'As thou hast given him power over all flesh...' [EGT, Gdt, Lns]. The καθώς clause is a repetition and clarification of the clause 'that your son may glorify you' [HTC]. It indicates that the giving of authority to Jesus is comparable to the glorification of Jesus [IVP]. It serves to continue the thought of glory by indicating that the giving of eternal life is the outworking of that glory [NICNT1].

QUESTION—To whom does 'him' refer?

It is important to keep the pronouns consistent. If 'your Son' was translated 'me, your Son' in verse 1, it should be continued in this verse as well, 'You gave me authority over all mankind so that I might give eternal life to all those you gave me' [TH].

QUESTION—How does a person give authority to another person?

In some languages it may be difficult to express this concept. If so, translations like 'assigned me to command', 'allowed me to give orders to', or 'placed me in front of all men/above all men' would be acceptable [TH].

QUESTION—Does the conjunction ἵνα 'so that' in this verse act as the purpose of the Father glorifying Jesus (glorify your Son *so that* he may give eternal life), or to the fact that the Father gave the Son authority over all flesh (you gave him authority *so that* he may give eternal life)?

1. The purpose clause depends on the request 'Glorify me!' of verse 1 [Gdt, HTC, ICC, IVP, NICNT2; NJB]: 'glorify your Son...so that, just as you have given him power over all humanity, he may give eternal life to all those you have entrusted to him' [NJB]. The Son will glorify the Father by giving eternal life to believers [IVP, NICNT2]. The intervening καθώς

clause is a repetition and clarification of the clause 'that your son may glorify you'. It makes clear that Jesus received authority over all men by virtue of his being glorified by the Father. Note that John 13:34 also has an intervening καθώς clause between two purpose clauses which argues for this interpretation, 'A new command I give to you, *that* you love each other, *just as* I love you *that* you also love each other' [HTC]. The clause 'so that the Son may glorify you' is parallel to the clause 'so that he may give eternal life'. Giving eternal life is the true means of glorifying the Father [Gdt]. The καθώς clause is parenthetical and this purpose clause, 'so that he may give eternal life' is simply a repetition or another way of saying 'so that the Son may glorify you' [ICC].

2. The purpose clause rather depends on the clause, 'you have given him authority' [Bar, Car, Lns, My, NICNT1, Rd; CEV, NCV, NIV]: 'you gave him power over all people, *so that* he would give eternal life to everyone you give him' [CEV]. The Father gave Jesus authority to the end that he might give eternal life to believers [Car, NICNT1, Rd]. It is possible that the purpose clause depends on the request 'Glorify me', but that request is more remote and so it is less probable that this clause depends on it [Bar]. This clause supplies the contents of the authority given to Jesus. He has authority to give eternal life to those the Father gives to him [Lns].

3. The purpose clause depends on both verbs [AB]. It is probably better to recognize that the granting of eternal life is the goal of the authority over all men that has been given to the Son. At the same time the giving of eternal life also stands as the purpose for which the Son asks to be glorified. It is the means by which the Son glorifies the Father [AB].

QUESTION—How can a person be given to another person?

If the clause, 'so that he may give eternal life to all whom you have given him' is difficult to express in a language, the concept may be expressed as 'those whom you caused to be my followers', or 'those whom you put in my charge', or 'those whom you sent to me' [TH].

QUESTION—What does it mean to give eternal life to someone?

It may be necessary to express this concept as 'he may cause everyone you have given him to live forever' [TRT].

QUESTION—What words are emphasized in this verse?

The clause 'to everyone whom you have given him' occurs before the clause 'he may give eternal life' to increase its prominence [TRT].

17:3 And this is eternal life that[a] they-may-know[b] you the only[c] true[d] God and Jesus Christ[e] whom you-sent.

LEXICON—a. ἵνα (LN 91.15) (BAGD I.3./II.1.3. p. 377/378): 'that' [AB, BAGD, Gdt, HTC, LN, NICNT2, NTC, WBC; KJV, NASB, NCV, NET, NIV, NRSV], 'that is, namely, namely that' [LN]. The statement 'this is eternal life, that they may know you' is translated 'Eternal life is (this:) to know you' [CEV, NJB, similarly Ph, REB], 'this is the way to have eternal life—to know you' [NLT], 'eternal life means to know you'

[TEV]. This conjunction indicates that the following clause is explanatory or identificational [LN]. It may indicate purpose, aim, or goal (I.3) or as a substitute for an infinitive that supplements the verb (II.1.3) [BAGD].

b. pres. act. subj. of γινώσκω (LN **27.18**) (BAGD 1.b. p. 160): 'to know' [BAGD, **LN**; all translations], 'to come to know' [BAGD], 'to become acquainted with, to be familiar with' [LN]. This verb means to learn to know a person through direct personal experience, implying a continuity of relationship. In translating γινώσκω in John 17:3, it is important to avoid an expression which will mean merely 'to learn about'. Here the emphasis must be on the interpersonal relationship which is experienced [LN]. The present tense indicates an ever-increasing kind of knowing [ICC, NICNT1].

c. μόνος (LN 58.50) (BAGD 1.a.δ. p. 527): 'only' [BAGD; all translations except AB], 'one' [AB], 'alone' [BAGD, LN], 'only one' [LN]. This adjective describes a thing or person as being the only entity in a class [LN].

d. ἀληθινός (LN **70.3**) (BAGD 3. p. 37): 'true' [LN; all translations], 'real' [BAGD, LN], 'genuine' [BAGD]. This adjective is also translated as an adverb: 'the only one who is really God' [**LN**]. This adjective describes something/someone as being real and not imaginary [LN]. It contrasts God with other gods, who are not real [BAGD]. The phrase, 'the only true God' may be translated in some languages as 'the only one who is really God' [TH, TRT], 'the only God who actually exists' [TRT].

e. Χριστός (LN 93.387) (BAGD 2. p. 887): 'Christ' [BAGD, LN; all translations]. This noun is the Greek translation of the Hebrew and Aramaic word 'Messiah' and is a proper name for Jesus [LN].

QUESTION—What is indicated by the conjunction ἵνα 'that' in the clause 'that they may know you…'?

It should be taken as indicating apposition to or explanation of eternal life [AB, Bar, BECNT, ICC, IVP, LN, Lns, NICNT1, Rd, TH; probably most translations]: 'eternal life, that is, knowledge of the Father and the Son' [IVP]. If it is taken to indicate purpose it may be translated 'this is the purpose of eternal life, namely, for people to know the only true God and Jesus Christ'. If it is taken to indicate means or cause it may be translated 'through knowing the only true God and Jesus Christ, one acquires eternal life', or 'knowing the only true God and Jesus Christ causes one to live eternally' [TH].

QUESTION—What is meant by the verb 'to know'?

The Greek and Hebrew words for 'to know' have the sense of immediate experience and intimacy and involve a life of obedience to God and loving fellowship with fellow believers [AB]. It means to know someone personally [IVP, Kn, TRT], to live in fellowship with someone [CH], to have intimate personal experience of someone [LN, Lns]. It goes beyond intellectual knowledge to include relationship and fellowship with the Father and the Son [BECNT, WBC]. When said of the relationship between two people, it indicates the perfect intuition that each has of the moral being of the other [Gdt]. Knowing God includes fellowship, trust, personal relationship, and faith [Car].

QUESTION—Is the phrase 'Jesus Christ' used here as a name or does it describe Jesus as being the Messiah?

1. 'Jesus Christ' is used here as a name identifying the person in the clause 'whom you have sent' [AB, BAGD, EGT, HTC, Kn, LN, NICNT1, NICNT2, NTC, TH; all translations]. The name 'Jesus Christ' was in common use in Apostolic times [EGT]. To take this as meaning 'know Jesus as Christ' seems to be straining the meaning of the Greek [NICNT1].

2. The phrase 'Jesus Christ' should rather mean 'Jesus, who is the Christ, the Messiah in the Hebrew language' [Gdt, Lns, My]. Up until this time, Jesus had avoided calling himself the Messiah. Now, however, just before the beginning of the proclamation of Jesus as Messiah by the disciples, it was necessary that they hear this outright claim to Messiahship from Jesus' own lips [Gdt].

QUESTION—What do the words 'this is eternal life' mean?

They do not define eternal life, but describe what receiving and possessing it mean [Lns], or they indicate how wonderful it is [NTC]. There may be an ellipsis in the statement 'this is eternal life'. Adding the implied information would yield, 'this is the result of receiving eternal life' [CH], 'This is the way to have eternal life—to know you' [NLT], 'Eternal life means to know you' [Lns; TEV, similarly TRT], 'Eternal life consists in this: that they know you' [AB, similarly EGT, Lns, My, WBC].

17:4 **I glorified you on the earth having-finished the work that you-have-given me to-do.**

QUESTION—What is the relationship between the clauses 'I glorified you on the earth' and 'having finished the work you have given me to do'?

The second clause is the means by which Jesus glorified the Father [AB, Bar, CH, Lns, NICNT2, TH, TRT, WBC; CEV, NET, NIV, NJB, NLT, NRSV, REB]: 'I have brought glory to you here on earth *by doing* everything you gave me to do' [CEV]. The participle (having glorified) should be translated 'by finishing the work...' [Bar].

QUESTION—How did Jesus glorify the Father?

He could glorify the Father in the sense of giving glory to him or by revealing His glory to others. In this context it is best to understand that Jesus revealed the Father's glory to others [Gdt, ICC, Lns, TH].

QUESTION—Does the word ἔργον 'work' refer to physical labor or to more general activity?

In some languages the word 'work' may only refer to physical labor in which cases it may be necessary to translate something like 'I finished doing what you told me to do' [TH].

QUESTION—What is indicated by the conjunction ἵνα 'that' in the clause 'work you have given me *that* I should do'?
   The conjunction can be taken in the sense of purpose, 'work you have given me *with the intention that* I should do it' or complement 'work you have given me, *consists in doing* (your will)'. Probably it is best to not press the distinction of one to the exclusion of the other [AB]. The conjunction serves to explain what the work was [Bar].
QUESTION—What word is emphasized in this verse?
   The pronoun ἐγώ 'I' is emphatic [Lns, My, NICNT1, NICNT2, NTC]. The placing of the personal pronouns 'I' and 'you' side by side in verses 4 and 5 shows that they are emphasized (literally, (verse 4) ἐγώ σε ἐδόξασα 'I you glorified', (verse 5) δόξασόν με σύ 'glorify me you') [Lns, NICNT2]. The emphasis is on ἐγώ 'I' and σε 'you' [My].

DISCOURSE UNIT—17:4b–33 [HTC, WBC]. The topic is the work of the Holy Spirit [HTC], joy over grief and trouble [WBC].

17:5 **And now Father, glorify[a] me with[b] yourself with-the glory that I had with you before the world existed.[c]**
LEXICON—a. aorist act. impera. of δοξάζω (LN **87.24**) (BAGD 2. p. 204): 'to glorify' [BAGD, LN], 'to make gloriously great' [LN], 'to clothe in splendor' [BAGD]. The sentence 'glorify me' [AB, Gdt, HTC, **LN**, NICNT2, NTC, WBC; KJV, NASB, NET, NIV, NJB, NRSV, REB] is also translated 'give me glory' [NCV, TEV], 'give me back the glory' [CEV], 'give me that glorious greatness' [**LN**], 'bring me into the glory (we shared…)' [NLT], 'honor me' [Ph]. This verb means to cause someone to have glorious greatness. In some languages the equivalent of this expression may be 'raise me up high' or 'give me great glory in the eyes of' [**LN**].
   b. παρά (LN 89.111) (BAGD II.1.b.γ. p. 610): 'with' [BAGD, LN], not explicit [NJB, NLT]. The phrase 'with you/yourself/your own self' [Gdt; CEV, KJV, NASB, NCV] is also translated 'in your (own) presence' [AB, HTC, NICNT2, NTC; NIV, NRSV, Ph, REB, TEV], 'with your own glory' [**LN**], 'at your side' [NET], 'alongside yourself' [WBC]. This conjunction indicates association, with the implication of proximity to the so-called viewpoint character [LN]. With the dative (nearly always of the person) it denotes nearness in space 'at' or 'by (the side of), beside, near, with', according to the standpoint from which the relationship is viewed [BAGD].
   c. pres. act. infin. of εἰμί (LN **13.69**) (BAGD I.1. p. 223): 'to exist' [AB, BAGD, **LN**, NTC; NJB, NRSV], 'to be' [BAGD, Gdt, NICNT2; KJV, NASB], 'to begin' [NIV, NLT, REB]. This active verb is also translated passively: 'to be created' [CEV, NET], 'to be made' [HTC; NCV, Ph, TEV]. It means to exist, in an absolute sense [LN].

QUESTION—What does the phrase 'and now' refer to?

It resumes the request that the Father glorify him that Jesus had made in verse 1 [AB, NTC, TH] and emphasizes it [TH].

QUESTION—In what way is Jesus asking to be glorified?

1. He is asking to be glorified in his approaching suffering on the cross [BECNT, Gdt, IVP, NICNT1]. The glory that Jesus requests includes the crucifixion—the place where the Father glorifies ('lifts up') the Son, as well as the glory awaiting him in the Father's presence [BECNT]. The Father will glorify Jesus with true glory in the cross, the last place people of the world would expect to look for it [NICNT1].
2. He is asking to be glorified in his exaltation and ascension to heaven [Bar, Car, CH, HTC, ICC, Kn, NICNT2, NTC, Rd]. Jesus wants to return to the position he knew before his incarnation [Bar]. There is a contrast between what Jesus was saying about glorifying the Father in verse four and his request for glory in this verse. In verse four he includes all the work that brought glory to the Father, including his own death, resurrection, and exaltation. Here he is asking to be given glory in Heaven [Car]. The glory Jesus requests in this verse supercedes the glory in his suffering that Jesus requested in verse 1. Now he is requesting a heavenly glorification [ICC]. Jesus is anticipating the reward for his mediatorial work. He longs to go home to his Father [NTC].

QUESTION—What words are emphasized in this verse?

The pronouns and σε 'you' and με 'me' are emphasized [NICNT2, TH]. The emphasis is on σε 'you' [My].

DISCOURSE UNIT—17:6–26 [NIV]. The topic is Jesus prays for his disciples.

DISCOURSE UNIT—17:6–24 [Kn]. The topic is Jesus prays for the disciples.

DISCOURSE UNIT—17:6–19 [BECNT, Car, NICNT1, NTC; NET]. The topic is Jesus prays for the disciples.

DISCOURSE UNIT—17:6–11a [Car, HTC, WBC]. The topic is the reason Jesus prays for the disciples.

DISCOURSE UNIT—17:6–10 [IVP, Rd]. Jesus prays for the disciples.

17:6 I-revealed[a] your name[b] to-the men you-gave me out-of-the world. They-were yours and you-gave them to-me and they-have-kept[c] your word.

LEXICON—a. aorist act. indic. of φανερόω (LN 28.36) (BAGD 1.a. p. 852): 'to reveal' [AB, BAGD, NICNT2; NET, NIV, NJB], 'to make known' [BAGD, LN; NRSV, REB, TEV], 'to make plain, to bring to the light, to disclose' [LN], 'to show' [BAGD]. The sentence 'I (have) manifested your name to the men' [Gdt, HTC, NTC, WBC; KJV, NASB] is also translated 'I have shown your self to the men' [Ph], 'I have shown them what you are like' [CEV], 'I showed what you are like to those you gave me' [NCV], 'I have revealed you to those whom/the ones you gave me'

[NIV, NLT], 'I have made you known to those you gave me' [TEV]. This verb means to cause something to be fully known by revealing clearly and in some detail [LN]. It means to make known by word of mouth, 'teach' (though here the teaching is accompanied by a revelation that comes through actions) [BAGD].

b. ὄνομα (LN 33.265) (BAGD I.4.b. p. 572): 'name' [AB, BAGD, Gdt, HTC, NICNT2, NTC, WBC; KJV, NASB, NET, NJB, NRSV, REB], 'reputation' [LN], not explicit [CEV, NCV, NIV, NLT, Ph, TEV]. This noun denotes that which is said about a person on the basis of an evaluation of the person's conduct [LN]. A person's name is often practically inseparable from the being who bears it. Here the name appears nearly as representative of the Godhead as a tangible manifestation of his nature [BAGD].

c. perf. act. indic. of τηρέω (LN 36.19) (BAGD 5. 815): 'to keep' [AB, BAGD, Gdt, HTC, NICNT2, NTC, WBC; KJV, NASB, NJB, NRSV], 'to obey' [LN; CEV, NCV, NET, NIV, REB, TEV], 'to accept' [Ph], 'to keep commandments' [LN], 'to observe, to fulfill, to pay attention to' [BAGD]. The sentence 'they have kept your word' is translated 'they have obeyed you' [CEV]. This verb means to continue to obey orders or commandments [LN]. It means to adhere to God's word and to try to live in its light [WBC].

QUESTION—What is indicated by a person's name?

It is the same as referring to the person himself [Bar, BECNT, Car, CH, EGT, HTC, ICC, IVP, Kn, NICNT1, NICNT2, NTC, Rd, TH, TRT, WBC; CEV, NCV, NIV, NLT, Ph, TEV]: 'I have made *you* known' [TEV]. To reveal someone's name to someone else is the same as telling them what the other person is like [CEV, NCV]. Here it means to reveal the essential nature of God to people [BECNT, ICC, NICNT1, WBC], or to reveal his character to them [BECNT, Car, Gdt, Kn, WBC].

QUESTION—In what sense did God give these men to Jesus?

In this case, God chose the disciples who would belong to and serve Jesus [WBC]. He could have put them in his care or entrusted them to him [TRT]. Care must be taken to avoid the idea that God removed the disciples physically from the world [TH].

QUESTION—What does it mean to keep God's word?

It means to obey God himself [CEV], or his teachings [NCV], or commands [REB]. The disciples kept God's word in the sense that they kept Jesus' word because Jesus taught them the message he received from his Father God [TH].

17:7 Now[a] they-have-known[b] that everything you-have-given me is from you. **17:8** For/that[c] I-have-given them the words that you-gave me, and they-received[d] (them) and knew truly that I-came from you, and they-believed that you sent me.

LEXICON—a. νῦν (LN 67.38) (BAGD 1.a.β. p. 545): 'now' [BAGD, LN; all translations], 'at the present time' [BAGD]. The word 'now' means 'now at the end of my ministry' [Bar, Car, Rd, TH]. This word has a temporal sense here indicating that now, at this stage in their development, the disciples have come to know [HTC]. He may be thinking that now, at last, they have come to know [NICNT1]. This adverb indicates a point of time simultaneous with the event of the discourse itself [LN].

b. perf. act. indic. of γινώσκω (LN 28.1) (BAGD 1.c. p 161): 'to know' [BAGD, Gdt, HTC, LN, NICNT2; CEV, KJV, NCV, NIV, NLT, NRSV, REB, TEV], 'to come to know' [AB, BAGD, WBC; NASB], 'to come to acknowledge' [NTC], 'to understand' [NET], 'to recognize' [NJB], 'to realize' [Ph], 'to know about, to have knowledge of, to be acquainted with' [LN]. This verb means to possess information about something [LN].

c. ὅτι (LN 89.33, 90.21): 'for' [AB, Gdt, HTC, LN (89.33), NTC, WBC; KJV, NASB, NIV, NJB, NLT, NRSV, REB], 'because' [LN (89.33), NICNT2; NET], 'that' [ICC, LN (90.21); Ph], 'the fact that' [LN (90.21)], 'since, in view of the fact that' [LN (89.33)], not explicit [CEV, NCV, TEV]. This conjunction indicates cause or reason, based on an evident fact [LN (89.33)], or it indicates discourse content, whether direct or indirect [LN (90.21)].

d. aorist act. indic. of λαμβάνω (LN 31.50) (BAGD 1.e.β. p. 464): 'to receive' [BAGD, LN, Gdt, HTC, NICNT2, NTC, WBC; KJV, NASB, NRSV, REB, TEV]. 'to accept' [AB, LN; CEV, NCV, NET, NIV, NJB, NLT, Ph], 'to come to believe' [LN]. This verb means to come to believe something and to act in accordance with such a belief [LN]. It means to receive someone's words and to use them as a guide [BAGD].

QUESTION—Can words be given to another person?

In some languages it is strange to give words to someone. In such cases it would be better to say 'I told them what you told me' [TH].

QUESTION—Is it possible to receive words?

It may be strange in some languages to say that they received words. In such cases it would be better to translate something like, 'they listened eagerly to the words' or 'they believed the words' [TH].

QUESTION—Does the conjunction ὅτι in the clause 'For/that I have given them the words that you gave me', indicate cause 'for/because', or an indirect quote 'that'?

1. It indicates cause [AB, Gdt, HTC, Lns, My, NICNT2, NTC, WBC; KJV, NASB, NIV, NJB, NLT, NRSV, REB]: '(they have known that all things you have given me are from you), *because* the words that you gave me I

have given to them' [NICNT2]. The disciples know the truth on the basis of the fact that Jesus has given it to them [Bar]. This is the better alternative of the two [AB].
2. It indicates a further fact or an indirect quote [ICC; Ph]: 'they realize that all that you have given me comes from you—*and that* every message that you gave me I have given them' [Ph].

QUESTION—What words are emphasized in this verse?

The pronoun σύ 'you', in the words 'you sent me' is emphatic [Lns, NICNT1, NICNT2; CEV, NJB]: 'they have believed that *it was you* who sent me' [NJB], 'they believed that *it was none less than you...*' [NICNT1]. The repetition of the emphatic personal pronouns in verses 6–8 is remarkable: 'your name' (verse 6), 'yours they were' (verse 6), 'your word' (verse 6), 'from you...from you' (verses 7–8), 'you sent me' (verse 8). Jesus is focusing attention on the Father, not on himself [NICNT2]. The adverb νῦν 'now' is emphatic meaning 'now, at the end of my ministry' [TH]. The pronoun αὐτοί 'they' is emphasized [Lns]: '*they on their part* did receive them' [Lns]. In contrast to the many who spurned Jesus' words, *they* accepted them [Lns].

DISCOURSE UNIT—17:9–19 [AB]. The topic is Jesus prays for believers.

DISCOURSE UNIT—17:9–16 [ICC]. The topic is Jesus prays that the disciples may be protected.

17:9 I pray[a] for[b] them. I do- not -ask for the world[c] but for the-ones you-have-given to-me, because they-are yours.

LEXICON—a. pres. act. indic. of ἐρωτάω (LN 33.161) (BAGD 2. p. 312): 'to pray' [AB, Gdt, HTC, WBC; CEV, KJV, NCV, NET, NIV, NJB, Ph, REB, TEV], 'to ask' [BAGD, NICNT2; NASB, NRSV], 'to ask for' [LN], 'to make request' [NTC], 'to request' [BAGD, LN], 'to beseech someone on someone's behalf' [BAGD]. This verb is also translated as a noun: '(My) prayer' [NLT].

b. περί (LN 90.39): 'for' [Gdt, HTC, NTC, WBC; CEV, KJV, NCV, NIV, NJB, NLT, Ph, REB, TEV], 'on behalf of' [AB, LN, NICNT2; NASB, NET, NRSV]. This preposition (with the genitive) indicates events that are indirectly involved in a beneficial activity [LN].

c. κόσμος (LN 9.23) (BAGD 7. p. 447): 'world' [BAGD; all translations except CEV, NCV], 'people in the world' [NCV], 'those who belong to this world' [CEV], 'people of the world' [LN]. This noun is a figurative extension of meaning of κόσμος 'cosmos, universe' denoting people associated with a world system and estranged from God [LN]. It indicates the world and everything that belongs to it, appearing as that which is hostile to God, that is, lost in sin, wholly at odds with anything divine, ruined and depraved [BAGD].

QUESTION—To what part of the verse does the clause 'because they are yours' stand as a reason or explanation?

The clause tells why Jesus is praying for His disciples, not why God gave them to Jesus [Bar, EGT, ICC, Lns, My, TH, TRT; CEV]: 'My followers belong to you and I am praying for them' [CEV]. It may be necessary to make this clear by translating 'I pray for them because they belong to you' [TH]. It explains both why Jesus prays for the disciples and why he says that it was the Father who gave them to him [AB].

QUESTION—What words are emphasized in this verse?

The pronoun ἐγώ 'I' is emphatic [Lns, My]: 'I on my part make request concerning them' [Lns]. Both ἐγώ 'I' and the phrase περὶ αὐτῶν 'for them' are emphatic, the latter in that it is highlighted, first negatively, 'not for the world', and then positively, 'but for those you have given to me' [My].

17:10 And all things (that are) mine are yours and your things (are) mine, and I-have-been-glorified in^a them.

LEXICON—a. ἐν (LN 90.6, 83.13): 'in' [LN (83.13)], 'by, from' [LN (90.6)]. The statement 'I have been/am glorified in them' [Gdt, HTC, NICNT2, NTC, WBC; KJV, NASB, NRSV, similarly AB; NJB] is also translated 'I have been glorified by them' [NET], 'they will bring glory to me' [CEV, similarly NLT], 'my glory is shown through them' [NCV, TEV], 'through them my glory is revealed' [REB], 'glory has come to me through them' [NIV], 'they have done me honor' [Ph]. This preposition (with the dative) indicates an agent, often with the implication of the agent being used as an instrument, and in some instances relating to general behavior rather than to some specific event [LN (90.6)], or it indicates that a thing is within certain limits [LN (83.13)]. The preposition seems to refer to the location where Jesus is glorified, that is, in his disciples, but perhaps it is instrumental as well [Bar].

QUESTION—To what does the phrase 'all things that are mine' refer?

Although the phrase 'all things' is neuter, it refers to the disciples [HTC, NICNT2, TH] about whom he had just spoken in verse 9. This same feature of having a neuter pronoun refer to animate beings can be seen in verse 2 'so that he may give eternal life to everyone whom (literally, everything which) you have given him' [TH]. It shows that not only are the disciples indicated but also brings out the fact that between the Father and the Son there is a complete mutuality of possessions and interests [Bar, EGT, HTC].

QUESTION—What is indicated by the statement 'I have been glorified in them'?

It indicates that Jesus' glory was revealed through his disciples [TH]. They have become entrusted with the glory of the Son [Gdt]. In contemporary terms it means that the disciples are his pride and joy [NICNT2]. The virtues that beautify believers who have been transformed from darkness into light reveal Jesus' forgiving love and power to the world. Paul called the believers at Philippi, 'my joy and crown' (Philippians 4:1), and the believers at

Thessalonica 'our glory and joy' (1 Thessalonians 4:1). In the same way, Jesus received glory from the salvation of his disciples [NTC]. In 15:8 Jesus says that the Father is glorified when the disciples bear much fruit [BECNT].

DISCOURSE UNIT—17:11–19 [IVP, Rd]. The topic is Jesus prays for the disciples [IVP], prayer for preservation and sanctification [Rd].

17:11 And I-am no-longer in the world, but/and[a] they are in the world, and-I am-coming to you. Holy[b] Father keep[c] them in/by[d] your name that you-have-given to-me, so-that they-may-be one[e] as we (are).

TEXT—Instead of ᾧ δέδωκάς μοι 'that you have given me', some manuscripts read ὅ δέδωκάς μοι 'that you have given me' (a Greek word difference). Others read ᾧ ἔδωκάς μοι 'that you gave me', while others read οὓς δέδωκάς μοι 'those whom you have given me'. Still others omit all from ᾧ δέδωκάς μοι 'that you have given me' through ἡμεῖς 'we' at the close of the verse. GNT reads ᾧ δέδωκάς μοι 'that you have given me' with a B rating, indicating that the text is almost certain.

LEXICON—a. καί (LN 89.93, 91.12): 'but' [all translations except NICNT2; NASB], 'yet' [LN (91.12)], 'and yet' [NASB], 'and' [LN (89.93), NICNT2]. This conjunction indicates an additive relation [LN (89.93)], or it indicates emphasis involving surprise and unexpectedness [LN (91.12)]. The καί here in this contrasted context has the force of 'but' [NICNT1].

b. ἅγιος (LN 88.24) (BAGD 1.b.δ. p. 9): 'holy' [BAGD, LN; all translations], 'most holy' [AB], 'pure' [LN], 'divine' [LN]. This adjective pertains to being holy in the sense of superior moral qualities and possessing certain essentially divine qualities in contrast with what is human [LN].

c. aorist act. impera. of τηρέω (LN 37.122) (BAGD 2.b. p. 815): 'to keep' [BAGD, Gdt, HTC, NICNT2, NTC, WBC; KJV, NASB, Ph], 'to keep safe' [AB; CEV, NCV, NET, TEV], 'to protect' [NIV, NLT, NRSV, REB], 'to guard' [LN], 'to keep true (to)' [NJB], 'to keep watch' [LN]. This verb means to continue to hold in custody [LN]. It means 'to keep someone (unharmed) by' or 'through something' [BAGD].

d. ἐν (LN 89.119): 'in' [Gdt, HTC, LN, NICNT2, NTC, WBC; KJV, NASB, NET, NRSV], 'by' [Ph], 'by the power of' [CEV, NCV, NIV, NLT, REB, TEV], 'with' [AB], 'through' [KJV], 'to' [NJB], 'in, one with, in union with, joined closely to' [LN]. The phrase 'in your name' is translated 'by your power' [Ph]. This preposition indicates close personal association [LN].

e. εἷς (LN 63.4) (BAGD 1.b. p. 230): 'one' [BAGD, LN; all translations except CEV, NLT], 'one with each other' [CEV]. This pronoun is also translated as a verb: '(they will be) united' [NLT], '(they may) constantly be one' [NTC]. This word denotes that which is united as one in contrast with being divided or consisting of separate parts [LN]. It denotes the whole unit in contrast to the parts of which the whole consists [BAGD].

JOHN 17:11

QUESTION—What is the best order for the first three clauses of this verse?

Since the first and third clauses speak about Jesus' position in relation to the Father, it may be better to keep them together [TH, TRT; CEV, NCV, TEV]: 'And now I am coming to you; I am no longer in the world, but they are in the world' [TEV].

QUESTION—What is the sense intended by ἐν 'in/by (your name')?

1. The preposition ἐν has a local sense of 'within' or 'inside of' [Car, Gdt, HTC, ICC, Lns, My, NTC, WBC; probably NASB, NET, NJB, NRSV]: 'keep those you have given me true to your name' [NJB]. Jesus meant that the Father would guard the disciples so that they would continue to stay faithfully within the sphere of His name. That is, that they would continue to know and believe in Him [My]. The locative interpretation is more closely tied to the context of verses 6–8 where Jesus revealed God's name to the disciples [Car, WBC]. 'God's name' refers to the revelation of his character. So he is requesting that they would be kept loyal to Him and fully adhere to his character [Car]. The name of the Father is his Word, so Jesus is asking that the Father keep the disciples in his Word [Lns], or under his fatherly protection [ICC]. He asks that they be preserved in the knowledge of the Father's name [EGT]. Jesus has revealed the Father's name to the disciples in verse 6. Since he is now leaving them, he requests that they be kept and strengthened in the teaching he has given them [Car, HTC].

2. It has an instrumental sense of 'by' or 'through' [BECNT, CH, IVP, TH; CEV, KJV, NCV, NIV, NLT, Ph, REB, TEV]: 'keep them safe by the power of the name that you have given me' [CEV]. The 'name' of God implies his power, so a translation such as 'keep them safe by your power' would be appropriate [TH]. The name of God indicates the presence of the Father himself. While Jesus was with the disciples, he protected them by his own divine presence. He was the 'I AM' of the Father among them. He is now asking that the Father protect them by his own presence through the Spirit [IVP]. To be kept in the Father's name is to be kept by God's power (Psalm 20:1; 54:1; Proverbs 18:10) [CH].

3. It probably has both a locative and an instrumental sense [AB, Bar, Kn]. It may mean that Jesus is asking that the disciples be kept as God's own property or it may have an instrumental sense [Bar]. Jesus is asking that God keep them with his name as the 'I AM'. The Jews recognized the protective power of God's name as seen in Proverbs 18:10 'The name of the LORD is a strong tower; the righteous run to it and are safe'. The power of this name is also seen in John 18:5–8 where those who come to arrest Jesus, fall down powerless when he says the words 'I am' [AB].

4. The name of God points to his whole revealed character. So Jesus is asking that the Father, acting within his character, protect the disciples from evil [NICNT1].

QUESTION—From what did the disciples need to be protected?
> Jesus probably wanted them protected or kept from evil [BECNT, CH, Lns, NICNT1], or from the world's temptations and hostility [Car].

QUESTION—What is meant by the noun ὄνομα 'name' of God and how was that given to Jesus?
> It indicates God's revealed character that was given to Jesus [Bar, ICC].

QUESTION—What is the meaning of the purpose clause, 'so that they may be one'?
> It means that they may be united in heart, mind, and will, that they become a harmony of love [NICNT1], or a unity of love [Bar]. He wanted them to be united in will, purpose, and spiritual fellowship [ICC]. Jesus revealed the name of the Father to the disciples through the words he had spoken to them. Only as they are kept adhering to that revelation can they be one as the Father and Son are one [WBC]. He wants their unity to be one that would be seen in their cooperation with each other [NTC]. The present tense of 'may be' has a continuative aspect indicating 'continue to be' one [Lns, NICNT1, NTC].

DISCOURSE UNIT—17:11b–16 [Car, HTC, WBC]. The topic is Jesus' prayer for protection.

17:12 When I-was with them I was-keeping them in your name that you have-given to-me, and I-guarded[a] (them), and none of them was-lost[b] except the son[c] of destruction,[d] so-that the Scripture might-be-fulfilled.

TEXT—Instead of ᾧ δέδωκάς μοι, καί '(name) that you have given me, and', some manuscripts read οὕς δέδωκάς μοι 'those-whom you have given me', and others simply read καί 'and'. GNT and the majority of translations read '(name) that you have given me, and' with a B rating, indicating that the text is almost certain. Gdt; KJV, and NJB support the reading 'those whom you have given me'.

LEXICON—a. aorist act. indic. of φυλάσσω (LN 37.120) (BAGD 1.c. p. 168): 'to guard' [BAGD, HTC, NICNT2, NTC, WBC; NASB, NLT, NRSV, Ph], 'to guard closely' [LN], 'to protect' [BAGD; NCV, NIV, TEV], 'to keep safe' [CEV, REB], 'to watch over' [Gdt; NET, NJB], 'to keep watch' [AB], 'to keep' [KJV]. This verb means to hold someone in close custody [LN].

b. aorist mid. (deponent = active) indic. of ἀπόλλυμι (LN 20.31) (BAGD 2.a.α. p. 95): 'to be lost' [Gdt, HTC, NICNT2, WBC; CEV, KJV, NCV, NET, NIV, NJB, NLT, NRSV, REB, TEV], 'to perish' [AB, BAGD, NTC; NASB], 'to be destroyed' [LN; Ph], 'to be ruined' [LN], 'to die' [BAGD]. This verb means to destroy or to cause the destruction of persons, objects, or institutions [LN]. Here the meaning of lost in the sense of eternal death is in focus [BAGD].

c. υἱός (LN 9.4, 58.26) (BAGD 1.c.δ. p. 834): 'son' [BAGD]. This noun (followed by the genitive of class or kind) denotes a person of a class or kind, specified by the following genitive construction 'son of..., person of..., one who is...'. In most languages it is difficult, if not impossible, to represent adequately the meaning of such expressions consisting of the formula 'son of...' without making some significant adjustments. For example, 'your sons (sons of you)' in Matthew 12:27 may be rendered as 'your followers'. In Acts 13:10 'son of the Devil' may be rendered as 'you are like the Devil,' while in Luke 16:8 'sons of this age' may be readily translated as 'people who are typical of this age'. In Matthew 23:15 'son of Gehenna' may be rendered as 'you who deserve to go to hell', and in Mark 3:17 'sons of thunder' may be rendered as 'men who are like thunder' or 'thunderous persons' [LN (9.4)]. Or it denotes a kind or class of persons, with the implication of possessing certain derived characteristics 'son of, offspring of, child of, kind of, one who has the characteristics of, person of' [LN (58.26)]. It is used figuratively here to denote one who shares in this thing or who is worthy of it, or who stands in some other close relation to it, often made clear by the context. It refers here to Judas [BAGD].

d. ἀπώλεια (LN **20.31**) (BAGD 2. p. 103): 'destruction' [BAGD, LN]. The phrase 'the son of destruction' [NICNT2; Ph] is also translated 'the one bound for destruction' [**LN**], 'the one worthy of destruction' [NCV], 'the one destined for destruction' [NET], 'the one doomed to destruction' [NIV], 'the one headed for destruction' [NLT], '(the) one who was destined to be lost' [NJB, NRSV, WBC, similarly REB], 'the man who was bound to be lost' [TEV], 'the one who had to be lost' [CEV], 'the one destined to perish' [AB], 'the son of perdition' [Gdt, HTC, NTC; KJV, NASB]. This noun is derived from the verb ἀπόλλυμι meaning to destroy or to cause the destruction of persons, objects, or institutions [LN]. It denotes the 'destruction' that one experiences, 'annihilation' both complete and in process, 'ruin' [BAGD].

QUESTION—What is indicated by the expression 'son of ...'?

It denotes one who shares in this condition or who is worthy of it, or who stands in some other close relation to it [BAGD]. It can either refer to the person's character or his destiny [BECNT, Car]. In this context, destiny is in focus [Bar, Car]. He was destined or foreknown for this role [Kn]. This expression refers to one's character rather than one's destiny [IVP, NICNT1]. It means that the person indicated was characterized by 'lostness' rather than that he was predestined to be lost [NICNT1]. 'Son of destruction' refers to one who belongs to the domain of damnation and is destined to destruction. The identical phrase is used to describe the antichrist in 2 Thessalonians 2:3 [AB]. The Hebraistic expression 'son of...' indicates the principle that determines the tendency of the person so designated [Gdt]. It can either indicate 'one who belongs to' or 'one who is controlled by' [Rd]. It indicates one who is going to be eternally lost [TH].

QUESTION—To what particular Scripture does this refer?

Here is a list of possible scriptures that might have been referred to: Psalm 41:9–10; 55:12–15; 69:25; 109:4–13; Isaiah 57:12–13.

QUESTION—What is meant by the clause 'so that the Scriptures might be fulfilled'?

It may be necessary to add some information like: '*this happened/all this had to happen* so that the Scripture/scripture might come true' [TH, TRT].

QUESTION—What word is emphasized in this verse?

The pronoun ἐγώ 'I' in the phrase 'I kept them' is emphasized [ICC, Lns]: '*I myself* kept guarding them' [Lns]. The pronoun contrasts Jesus who has kept the disciples, with the Father who will keep them in the future [Gdt].

DISCOURSE UNIT—17:13–21 [NASB]. The topic is the disciples in the world.

17:13 And now I-am-coming to you and I-say[a] these-things in the world so-that they-may-have my joy made-complete[b] in themselves.

LEXICON—a. pres. act. indic. of λαλέω (LN 33.70): 'to say' [AB, Gdt, LN, WBC; CEV, NET, NIV, NJB, Ph, TEV], 'to speak' [HTC, LN, NICNT2, NTC; KJV, NASB, NRSV, REB], 'to pray' [NCV], 'to tell' [NLT], 'to talk' [LN]. This verb means to speak or talk, with the possible implication of more informal usage (though this cannot be clearly and consistently shown from NT contexts) [LN]. It also carries the connotation of speaking out loud [EGT, Gdt, ICC, Lns].

b. perf. pass. participle of πληρόω (LN 59.33) (BAGD 3. p. 671): 'to be made complete' [BAGD, LN], 'to have something brought to completion' [BAGD]. The statement 'that/so that they may have my joy completed/made complete in themselves' [WBC; NRSV] is also translated 'that/in order that they may/might have my joy fulfilled/made full in themselves' [Gdt, HTC, NICNT2, NTC; KJV, NASB], 'so they may experience my joy completed in themselves' [NET, similarly Ph], 'so that they may have the full measure of my joy within them' [NIV], 'so that my followers will have the same complete joy that I do' [CEV], 'so that my followers can have all of my joy in them' [NCV], 'that they may share my joy to the full' [AB; similarly NJB], 'so they would be filled with my joy' [NLT], 'so that they may have my joy within them in full measure' [REB], 'so that they might have my joy in their hearts in all its fullness' [TEV]. This verb means to make something total or complete [LN]. Jesus' purpose could be expressed as 'that my joy may be as fulfilling to them as it is to me' [CH].

QUESTION—What is the sense of δέ 'but/and' (now I am coming)?

The better sense is 'but' [AB, Gdt, HTC, Lns, NICNT2, NTC, WBC; NASB, NET, NJB, NRSV]. The δέ signals a contrast to the time when Jesus was with them on earth [Bar, HTC, Lns, NICNT2, Rd]. The better sense is 'and' [KJV, Ph, TEV]. It is best to leave it untranslated [CEV, NCV, NIV, NLT, REB].

QUESTION—To what does the pronoun ταῦτα 'these things' refer?

It probably refers to the words of Jesus' prayer in this chapter [My, TH, TRT, WBC]. It probably refers to the earlier part of Jesus' prayer [AB]. It refers both to his current prayer and to his teaching before it [NICNT2]. It probably refers to his complete farewell address [BECNT, Car, Kn].

QUESTION—How are the nouns related in the genitive construction τὴν χαρὰν τὴν ἐμὴν 'the joy of me (my joy)'?

This joy fills the heart of Jesus [Lns]. Jesus experiences this joy himself [TH]. Jesus gives this joy to the disciples [NTC].

QUESTION—Where had Jesus spoken of having the joy of the disciples made full?

Jesus had spoken of their having fullness of joy in 15:11 and 16:20–22, 24 [HTC, ICC, NICNT2, Rd, TH].

17:14 I have-given them your word[a] and the world[b] hated[c] them, because they-are not of[d] the world just-as I am not of the world.

TEXT—Some manuscripts omit the clause καθὼς ἐγὼ οὐκ εἰμὶ ἐκ τοῦ κόσμου 'just as I am not of the world'. GNT includes it with an A rating, indicating that the text is certain.

LEXICON—a. λόγος (LN 33.98) (BAGD 1.b.β. p. 478): 'word' [AB, BAGD, LN; KJV, NASB, NET, NIV, NJB, NLT, NRSV, Ph, REB, TEV], 'message' [LN; CEV], 'teaching' NCV], 'saying, statement' [LN]. This noun is derived from the verb λέγω 'to say' (33.69), and denotes that which has been stated or said, with primary focus on the content of the communication [LN]. It denotes God's revelation through Christ and his messengers [BAGD]. It denotes the entire teaching that Jesus has given the disciples [NICNT1].

b. κόσμος (LN 9.23) (BAGD 7. p. 446): 'world' [BAGD; all translations except CEV], 'people of the world' [LN, TRT; CEV]. This noun is a figurative extension of the meaning of κόσμος 'cosmos, universe', and denotes people associated with a world system and estranged from God [LN]. It denotes the world and everything that belongs to it, appearing as that which is hostile to God, that is, lost in sin, wholly at odds with anything divine, ruined and depraved [BAGD].

c. aorist act. indic. of μισέω (LN 88.198) (BAGD 7. p. 446): 'to hate' [BAGD, LN; all translations], 'to detest' [BAGD, LN], 'to persecute in hatred, to abhor' [BAGD]. This verb means to dislike strongly, with the implication of aversion and hostility [LN].

d. ἐκ (LN 89.3) (BAGD 3.b. p. 235): 'of' [BAGD], 'from' [LN]. The words 'they are not of the world' [Gdt, HTC, NTC; KJV, NASB, NIV] is also translated 'they are not from the world' [NICNT2], 'they do not belong to this/the world' [AB, WBC; CEV, NCV, NET, NLT, NRSV, TEV, similarly NJB], 'they are no more sons of the world than I am' [Ph], 'they are strangers in the world' [REB]. This preposition indicates the source from which someone or something is physically or psychologically derived [LN]. It indicates origin as to family, race, city, people, district, etc. [BAGD]. 'Of' indicates that the disciples were not the same nature, kind, and quality as the world [Lns].

QUESTION—What is the relation between the clause 'I have given them your word' and the clause 'the world hated them'?

The clause 'the world hated them' is *the result* of the clause 'I have given them your word' [Car, Gdt, HTC, Lns, NTC, TH, TRT]. This could then be translated 'I told them what you told me, *and as a result*, the people of the world hated them' [TH]. It is a contrastive relationship 'but' [CEV], or an additive relationship 'and' [all translations except CEV].

QUESTION—What is indicated by the preposition ἐκ 'of' in the phrase 'not of the world'?

The disciples did not *belong to* the world [AB, HTC, NICNT1, NTC, WBC; CEV, NCV, NET, NJB, NLT, NRSV, TEV]. The disciples did not derive their character from the world [NTC]. The disciples were spiritually reborn or born again (1:12–13; 3:3–8) [AB, Bar, BECNT, IVP, NICNT1]. They were not of the world in the sense that they had been chosen out of the world (15:19) [Bar, Car].

QUESTION—What words are emphasized in this verse?

The pronoun ἐγώ 'I' in the words 'I have given them your word' is emphasized [TH].

17:15 I-do- not -ask that you-take them out-of the world, but that you-keep them from the evil.ᵃ 17:16 They-are not ofᵇ the world just as I am not of the world.

LEXICON—a. πονηρός (LN 12.35) (BAGD 2.b. p. 691): 'evil' [BAGD, Gdt; KJV], '(the) evil one' [HTC, NTC, WBC; CEV, NASB, NET, NIV, NLT, NRSV, Ph, REB], '(the) Evil One' [AB, LN, NICNT2; NCV, NJB, TEV], 'wicked person, evil-intentioned person, evil doer' [BAGD], 'He who is evil' [LN]. This adjective used as a noun with the definite article denotes a title for the Devil, literally 'the evil one', the one who is essentially evil or in a sense personifies evil [LN].

b. ἐκ [LN 89.3], (BAGD): 'of' [Gdt, HTC, NTC; KJV, NASB, NIV], 'from' [LN, NICNT2]. The clause 'they are not of the world' [Gdt, HTC, NTC; KJV, NASB, NIV] is also translated 'they do not belong to this/the world' [AB, WBC; CEV, NCV, NET, NJB, NLT, NRSV, TEV], 'they are no more sons of the world (than I am)' [Ph], 'they are strangers in the world' [REB]. This preposition indicates the source from which someone or something is physically or psychologically derived [LN].

QUESTION—Should the adjective 'evil' be taken as an abstract noun or a personal noun?

1. It should be taken as having a personal reference [AB, BAGD, Bar, BECNT, Car, CH, HTC, ICC, IVP, Kn, Lns, My, NICNT1, NTC, Rd, TH, TRT, WBC; all translations except Gdt; KJV]: 'keep them safe from the evil one' [CEV]. It is probably best to be taken as a personal noun referring to the devil (see 1 John 2:13–14; 3:12; 5:18–19) [AB]. The evil one referred to is Satan or the Devil [AB, BAGD, BECNT, Car, HTC, NICNT1, NICNT2, NTC, TH]. It may be necessary to indicate that 'the

evil one' is a title so one could translate 'keep them safe from the one who is known as the Evil One' or '…is called the Evil One' [TH].
2. It should be taken as an abstract noun indicating evil in general [Gdt; KJV]; 'keep them from the evil' [KJV]. The preposition ἐκ 'from' refers to a domain from which a person is kept rather than a person from whose power one is kept [Gdt].

QUESTION—What words are emphasized in verse 16?
The phrase ἐκ τοῦ κόσμου 'of the world' is emphasized by being placed first in verse 16. He strongly stresses that the disciples are not of the world just as he is not of the world [HTC, My, NTC].

DISCOURSE UNIT—17:17–19 [Car, HTC, ICC, WBC]. The topic is Jesus prays that the disciples may be sanctified.

17:17 Sanctify[a] them in/by[b] the truth.[c] Your word is truth.

LEXICON—a. aorist act. impera. of ἁγιάζω (LN 88.26) (BAGD 2. p. 8): 'to sanctify' [BAGD, Gdt, HTC, NTC; KJV, NASB, NIV, NRSV], 'to consecrate' [AB, BAGD, NICNT2, WBC; NJB, REB], 'to set apart' [NET], 'to dedicate' [BAGD; TEV], 'to make holy' [LN; NLT, Ph]. The sentence 'Sanctify them in/by the truth' is translated 'let this truth make them completely yours' [CEV], 'Make them ready for your service through the truth' [NCV], 'Dedicate them to yourself by means of the truth' [TEV]. This verb means to cause someone to have the quality of holiness [LN]. It means to include in the inner circle of what is holy [BAGD].

b. ἐν (LN 89.76): 'in' [AB, HTC, NICNT2, NTC, WBC; NASB, NET, NJB, NRSV], 'by' [Gdt, LN; NIV, NLT, Ph, REB], 'by means of' [LN; TEV], 'through' [LN; KJV, NCV]. This preposition indicates the means by which one event makes another event possible [LN].

c. ἀλήθεια (LN 72.2) (BAGD 2.b. p. 36): 'truth' [BAGD, LN; all translations]. This noun denotes the content of that which is true and thus in accordance with what actually happened [LN]. It denotes the content of Christianity as the absolute truth. God's word is truth [BAGD].

QUESTION—What does the word ἁγιάζω 'to sanctify' mean here?
1. It means 'to set someone apart for special use' [Bar, Car, EGT, IVP, Kn, Lns, NICNT1, Rd, TH, WBC]. This verb means to set the apostles apart for God. Then the disciples would become separate from common or profane work and be devoted solely to God [Lns]. Jesus asks the Father to set apart the disciples for a mission in the world [Bar]. It is the dedication of something to the exclusive service or possession of God [TH].
2. It means to make someone holy [AB, BECNT]. There is an allusion in this command to the address 'Holy Father' in verse 11 implying that Jesus wants the Father to make the disciples holy or God-like. The Father consecrated Jesus and sent him into the world (10:36). Now Jesus wants the Father to consecrate the disciples so they may serve as apostles—sent ones [AB].

3. It means both 'to set someone apart for special use' and 'to equip or enable them to carry out that assignment' [Gdt, NTC]. Jesus requests for them a will that is committed to God and His service [Gdt]. The consecration by the Father means that the disciples will be set apart from the world, resulting in making them begin to think, speak, and act more and more in sync with the will of God [NTC].
4. It means to equip a person to carry out an assignment [ICC, Me]. The focus of ἁγιάζω is not so much on his/her selection for a specified work as on the equipping and enabling them to carry it out [ICC]. It means that the Father would enlighten, empower, inspire, and fill them with courage, joy, and love to carry out their assignments [My].

QUESTION—What is the primary sense of the preposition ἐν 'in/by' here?
1. 'In' has either an instrumental or agentive meaning [Bar, Car, EGT, Gdt, IVP, Kn, NTC, TH; CEV, KJV, NCV, NIV, NLT, Ph, REB, TEV]: 'Dedicate them to yourself *by means of* the truth' [TEV]. The *means by which* the Father will sanctify, or set apart the disciples to God's service, is the truth. The Father will immerse them in the revelation of himself in Jesus and he will send them the Holy Spirit to guide them into all the truth (15:13) [Car]. In some languages it may be difficult to have an abstract noun as the means of doing something, so a translation like 'sanctify them by means of your words, which are true' would be acceptable [TH].
2. It has rather a local sense of 'within' [BECNT, HTC, ICC, Lns, My, NICNT1, Rd]. The realm in which the making holy is to be realized is the truth of God's word [BECNT, NICNT1]. The Spirit of God would be the agent of the disciples' dedication, while the truth would be *the medium* in which it would take place [ICC, Lns].
3. Both 1 and 2 above are intended [AB]. 'Truth' is both the agent of the consecration and the realm into which the disciples are consecrated [AB].

17:18 As you-sent[a] me into the world, I-also sent them into the world.

LEXICON—a. aorist act. indic. of ἀποστέλλω (LN 15.66) (BAGD 1.c. p. 98): 'to send' [LN; all translations], 'to send out, to send away' [BAGD]. This verb means to cause someone to depart for a particular purpose [LN]. Their mission is to announce the message of salvation through Christ [NTC].

QUESTION—In what sense had Jesus sent the disciples into the world?
He is using the aorist tense 'sent' as anticipating the future when he will send them into the world (see John 20:21–22) [AB, Car, CH]. The use of the aorist to imply a future event adds an aspect of certainty to the actual future event itself [ICC, NICNT1]. In fact Jesus had just now sent them when he asked the Father to sanctify them or set them apart for a mission [NICNT2]. He uses the aorist 'I sent' because they had actually already served as apostles, that is, of being sent ones in 4:38 (see also Mark 3:14) [EGT, ICC]. The aorist refers historically to the first appointment of the Twelve [Lns]. 'I sent' could be translated 'I am sending' [TRT; CEV, NLT].

QUESTION—How does the sending of the disciples parallel the Father's sending Jesus into the world?

The Father had sanctified the Son and sent him into the world (10:36), so here having asked the Father to sanctify the disciples Jesus sends them into the world [BECNT, HTC, NICNT1, NICNT2].

QUESTION—If the disciples were already in the world, in what sense did Jesus send them into the world?

Jesus had raised the disciples to a higher sphere of life than the life of the world. It is from there that he now sends them back into that world [Gdt]. Jesus had loved his disciples and had commanded them to love each other. Their mission then was to invite the world through their witness to join this circle of prayer and love [Bar].

QUESTION—What words are emphasized in this verse?

The pronouns ἐμέ 'me' [NICNT1, TRT] and κἀγώ 'I also' are emphasized [NICNT1].

17:19 And I sanctify^a myself for- their -sake^b, so-that they also may-be sanctified in truth.^c

LEXICON—a. pres. act. indic. of ἁγιάζω (LN 88.26, 53.44) (BAGD 2. p. 9): 'to sanctify' [BAGD, Gdt, HTC; KJV, NASB, NIV, NRSV], 'to consecrate' [BAGD, LN (53.44), NTC, NICNT2, WBC; NJB, Ph, REB], 'to dedicate to God' [LN (53.44); TEV], 'to dedicate' [BAGD], 'to make holy' [LN (88.26)]. The words 'I sanctify myself for their sake' is translated 'I have given myself completely for their sake' [CEV], 'For their sake, I am making myself ready to serve' [NCV], 'I set myself apart on their behalf' [NET], 'I give myself as a holy sacrifice for them' [NLT]. This verb means to dedicate someone to the service of God and to loyalty to him [LN (53.44)], or to cause someone to have the quality of holiness [LN (88.26)]. It means to consecrate, to dedicate, sanctify, that is, to include in the inner circle of what is holy [BAGD].

b. ὑπέρ (LN 90.36): 'for the sake of' [LN; all translations except NICNT2; NET, NIV, NLT], 'on behalf of' [LN, NICNT2; NET], 'for' [LN; NIV, NLT]. This preposition with the genitive case indicates a participant who is benefited by an event or on whose behalf an event takes place [LN].

c. ἀλήθεια (LN **70.4**, 72.2) (BAGD 3. p. 36): 'truth' [LN (72.2); CEV], 'reality' [BAGD]. The phrase 'in (the) truth' [Gdt, HTC, NICNT2, WBC; NASB, NJB, NRSV] is also translated 'through the truth' [KJV], '(they may belong completely) to the truth' [CEV], '(so that they can be ready for their service) of the truth' [NCV], '(be made holy) by the/your truth' [NLT, Ph, REB]. This noun is also translated as an adverb: 'truly (dedicated)' [**LN** (70.4); TEV], 'truly (set apart) [NET], 'truly (sanctified)' [NIV], 'truly (consecrated ones)' [NTC]. The idiom ἐν ἀληθείᾳ (literally 'in truth', 'upon truth', and 'according to truth') pertains to being a real or actual event or state. It means 'really, actually' [LN], 'truly, indeed' [BAGD].

QUESTION—What does Jesus mean when he says that he sanctifies himself?

The preposition ὑπέρ 'for' may suggest death. Note the following uses of this word that indicate the laying down of Jesus' own life (11:51; 10:11, 17–18; 15:13; Romans 8:32). Jesus is thinking here of offering himself as a sacrifice to death for the disciples [AB, Bar, Car, BECNT, EGT, HTC, ICC, IVP, Lns, My, NICNT1, NICNT2, NTC, Rd, WBC]. The offering of himself as a sacrifice also includes going to the Father, being glorified, sending the Spirit, being spiritually with them and finally receiving them to himself [Lns]. This interpretation is supported by OT references in which a sacrificial animal is 'consecrated' or 'set apart' for death (Deuteronomy 15:19, 21) [Car, HTC]. Sanctify here has its classical meaning of taking what is common or profane and dedicating it to God's service [Gdt].

QUESTION—In what sense are the disciples 'sanctified'?

They are sanctified in the sense that they are set apart for a mission of salvation to the world [BECNT, Car, HTC, Lns, NICNT1, NICNT2, NTC, Rd, WBC]. They are consecrated in the sense of being kept in holiness and experiencing an increase in holiness so that they may become agents of sanctification to the world [Gdt]. Sometimes the pursuance of this mission resulted in a martyr's death [NICNT1]. Part of the sanctification of the disciples is their sacrificial living and even dying as martyrs [IVP].

QUESTION—What does the phrase 'in truth' mean here?

1. The phrase 'in truth' means simply 'truly' or 'really' [BAGD, BECNT, Car, CH, Gdt, LN, My, NICNT1, NTC, Rd; NET, NIV, TEV]: 'in order that they too may be *truly* dedicated to you' [TEV]. The phrase 'in truth', without the article, must have the adverbial sense indicating 'in a true way' [Gdt, Rd] as opposed to the false consecration of the Pharisees and Levites [Gdt], or as opposed to a ceremonial or outward consecration [NTC].
2. It means 'by means of truth', with truth as instrument or agent [TH; KJV, NLT, Ph, REB]. The phrase 'in truth' (without an article) here is similar to the phrase 'in the truth' in verse 17. If the phrase 'in truth' occurred in isolation it would be natural to translate it as 'truly'. However, it seems best in the present to take this phrase as being the same as it was in verse 17 and translate it as 'by means of the truth' [TH].
3. It means 'in the realm of' or 'in the sphere of the truth' [AB, HTC, ICC]. The meaning of the phrase 'in truth' is virtually the same as its meaning in verse 17 except that here the focus is on the realm of the disciples' consecration and Jesus is the agent of it [AB]. The truth is the full revelation of the Father in which the disciples are consecrated [ICC].
4. It includes the meanings of both 2 and 3 above [EGT]. Jesus consecrated himself to bring the truth *by* and *in* which the disciples could be consecrated [EGT].

QUESTION—What word is emphasized in this verse?

The pronoun ἐγώ 'I' is emphasized [AB, Gdt, ICC, Lns]: '*I on my part* sanctify myself' [Lns]. The two pronouns 'I' and 'myself' reveal the stress that Jesus placed on himself in order to realize the sanctification of his disciples [Gdt]. There is also emphasis on the pronoun αὐτοί 'they' [Lns, My; NASB]: 'that *they themselves* also may be sanctified in truth' [NASB].

DISCOURSE UNIT—17:20–26 [AB, BECNT, ICC, NICNT1, NTC; NET]. The topic is Jesus prays for future believers.

DISCOURSE UNIT—17:20–24 [IVP]. The topic is prayer for future believers.

DISCOURSE UNIT—17:20–23 [Car, HTC, Rd, WBC]. The topic is prayer for unity [HTC, Rd, WBC], Jesus prays for future believers [Car].

17:20 **I-do- not -ask for these alone, but also for those believing in me because-of their word.**
QUESTION—What is indicated by the present participle 'believing'?
1. It should be taken as indicating a future time [My, TRT, WBC; CEV, KJV, NCV, NIV, NJB, NLT, NRSV, Ph]: 'all those who will believe in me through their message' [Ph].
2. It should be translated as a present tense [AB, Gdt, HTC, NICNT2, NTC, TRT; TEV, NASB, NET, REB]: 'for those who believe in me through their word' [NICNT2].

QUESTION—The phrase εἰς ἐμέ 'in/to/about me' in the Greek follows the phrase 'their word' and could be taken as modifying that phrase, that is, 'their word about me'. Most however translate it as modifying 'believing' (in me)? Which is correct?
1. It modifies the verb 'believing' [AB, Bar, Car, CH, Gdt, HTC, ICC, Lns, My, NICNT1, NICNT2, NTC, WBC; all translations except CEV]. It should probably be construed with the verb 'believing' although the Greek order favors it being construed with 'their word'. If this is chosen the meaning would be 'their word of testimony to me' [Bar].
2. It modifies the phrase 'their word' [CEV]: 'everyone else who will have faith because of what my followers will say *about me*' [CEV].

17:21 **That they- all -may-be one,**[a] **as you, Father, (are) in me and-I (am) in you, that they also may-be in us, that the world**[b] **may-believe that you sent me.**
TEXT—Instead of ὦσιν 'they may be (in us)', some manuscripts read ἓν ὦσιν 'they may be one (in us)'. GNT reads 'they may be' with a B rating, indicating that the text is almost certain. AB; CEV, KJV, and NCV seem to accept the reading 'they may be one (in us)'. AB accepts it but includes the word 'one' in brackets.
LEXICON—a. εἷς (LN 63.4) (BAGD1.b. p. 230): 'one' [BAGD, LN; all translations except CEV], 'one with each other' [CEV]. This noun denotes that which is united as one in contrast with being divided or consisting of separate parts [BAGD, LN].
b. κόσμος (LN 9.23): 'world' [all translations except CEV], 'people of the/this world' [LN; CEV], 'people in the world' [TRT]. This noun is a

figurative extension of the meaning of κόσμος 'cosmos, universe' (1.1), and denotes people associated with a world system and estranged from God [LN]. It indicates mankind in need of being saved [NTC].

QUESTION—What is implied by the first word ἵνα 'that (they may be one)'?

It implies that the words 'I ask' from verse 20 are to be understood—'I ask (that…)' [Bar, Lns, TH, TRT; CEV, NCV, NLT, TEV]: '*Father, I pray that they can be one*' [NCV].

QUESTION—In what sense does Jesus want his disciples to be one?

He wants them to be: unified in mind, effort, and purpose [NTC], unified in brotherly love [HTC], united in their commitment to Jesus and to the Father [NICNT2], alike in purpose, in love, and in behavior [Car, My], one in the Word [Lns]. It could be expressed by 'I pray that they may act together just as though they were one person' [TH]. He wants them to be one unit, one body, one spiritual whole [Lns]. It is a unity that must be observable to people of the world [Car, ICC].

QUESTION—Should the clause 'as you, Father, are in me and I am in you' be construed with the previous clause 'that they all may all be one' or with the following clause 'that they may be in us'?

1. It should be construed with the previous clause 'that they all may be one' [AB, Car, CH, ICC, Lns, My, NTC, NICNT2, WBC; all translations except NCV, NRSV, Ph, TEV]: 'that they all be one *even as* thou, Father, art in me and I in thee' [Lns]. In verse 11 the clause 'so that they may be one, as we are' parallels this interpretation [Lns].

2. It should be construed with the following clause 'that they may be in us' [Gdt, NICNT1; NCV, NRSV, Ph, TEV]: 'As you are in me and I am in you, I pray that they can also be one in us' [NCV]. Jesus first prays that the disciples may be one. But then he prays that the disciples would be in the Father and the Son, just as the Father and Son are in each other [NICNT1]. The clause 'as you, Father…' looks forward to the following 'that'. 'That, as thou, Father art in me and I in thee, they also may be in us' [Gdt].

QUESTION—If interpretation 1 above is chosen, how does the clause 'as you, Father, are in me and I am in you' stand as a model for the unity of the disciples with each other?

Since the Father lives in the Son and the Son lives in the Father, so Jesus living in the disciples unites them closely with each other [Gdt]. The unity of the Father and the Son is a unity of mutually indwelling each other (10:30, 38; 14:9–11), so the unity of the believers consists in the mutual indwelling of each believer with the Father, Son, and Spirit. This is seen in the vine and the branches (chapter 15). The branches are unified with each other by virtue with their vital relationship to the vine [CH].

DISCOURSE UNIT—17:22–26 [NASB]. The topic is the future glory of the disciples.

17:22 **And-I have-given them the glory**[a] **that you-have-given me, so-that they-may-be one just-as we (are) one.**

LEXICON—a. δόξα (LN 87.4) (BAGD 1.b.α. p. 203): 'glory' [all translations except CEV, Ph], 'honor' [LN; Ph], 'respect, status' [LN], 'brightness, splendor, radiance' [BAGD]. This noun is also translated as a verb: '(I) have honored (my followers)' [CEV]. This noun denotes honor as an element in the assignment of status to a person [LN]. It denotes the state of being in the next life as described as participation in the radiance or glory. It is also meant of Christ in his preexistence [BAGD].

QUESTION—To whom does the pronoun 'them' refer?

It refers to those who believe in Jesus, not to the people of the world [TRT].

QUESTION—What is indicated by the perfect tense of the verbs 'have given' in this verse?

The perfect tense 'have given' indicates that just as Jesus continues to possess the glory the Father had given him, so the disciples continue to possess the glory that he has given to them [AB, HTC, TH].

QUESTION—What is the 'glory' that Jesus has given to the disciples?

1. Glory consisted in Jesus' and the Father's presence in the disciples here on earth [ICC, IVP, Lns, NTC]. 'Glory' here is the revelation of God's nature in man. Jesus revealed that glory in his earthly ministry and now has given it to the disciples so that now they have become participants in the divine nature (2 Peter 1:4) [ICC, Lns]. Believers are in Christ and Christ is in them. This is their glory. The Father had revealed himself in the Son. Now Jesus revealed himself in the disciples (1 John 3:2; 2 Corinthians 3:18; Hebrews 12:10; 2 Peter 1:4) [NTC]. This glory was the Father's presence in the disciples [IVP]. As such it was the participation in the eternal life of the Father (Exodus 33:18–23) [IVP].

2. Glory is something believers will receive in the future [BAGD, EGT, HTC, My]. The word δόξα points to the fullness of divine life that will only be fully realized in Heaven (see verse 24) [HTC]. This glory could not be completely given until the event of verse 24 when the disciples would be with Jesus in heaven and see his glory there [EGT, My].

3. Other views [Bar, Car, Gdt, Kn, NICNT1, NICNT2, Rd]. Verse 24 informs us that the glory of Jesus was being the object of the Father's love. This then is the glory Jesus gave to his disciples, that they also have become the objects of the Father's love (verse 23), have been adopted into the same family [Gdt]. In John, Jesus' glory was something the disciples could observe but not share in (1:14; 2:11; 11:4, 40). Now he gives his glory to the disciples as he dedicates himself as a sacrifice so that they may be dedicated in truth (verse 19). So the glory he has given them is the mission on which he sends them—a mission to reveal the Father as he had done [NICNT2]. The glory the Father gave to Jesus was the authority and power he exhibited in his mission to the world. He now gives this ability to the disciples promising them his assistance and that they would do even greater things than he had done (14:12–14; 20:21–23) [Rd]. Glory refers

to God's character when it is revealed through a person. Jesus now has given the disciples this glory in that he has fully revealed the character of his Father to the disciples [Car, Kn]. True glory for Jesus was to walk the path of humble service leading to the cross that the Father had given him. Similarly for the disciples, true glory lay in following this humble pathway wherever it led them [NICNT1]. Jesus' glory was most clearly expressed in his crucifixion. Similarly the disciples express this glory in obedience, humiliation, poverty, and suffering [Bar].

QUESTION—How would the disciples' possession of glory result in their unity?

The disciples now shared the glory of being indwelt by the Father with Christ and with each other. This would result in spiritual union with each other such as the Father and Son enjoyed [ICC, Lns, NTC].

QUESTION—What word is emphatic in this verse?

The pronoun ἐγώ 'I' is emphatic [Gdt, Lns, My, NICNT1, TH]: 'And the glory which thou hast given me *I on my part* have given to them' [Lns].

17:23 I in them and you in me, so-that they-may-be perfected[a] into one, so-that the world may-know that you sent me and loved them as you-loved me.

LEXICON—a. perf. pass. participle of τελειόω (LN **13.18**) (BAGD 2.e.α. p. 810): 'to be made perfect' [BAGD], 'to attain, to become' [LN]. The clause 'so that/that they may/might be perfected into one' [NICNT2, WBC] is also translated 'so that/that they may become/will be/may be completely one' [CEV, NCV, NET, NRSV, TEV], 'that/in order that they may become perfectly one' [HTC, NTC, similarly REB], 'that they may be made perfect in one' [KJV], 'in order that they might in the end become one' [**LN**], 'that they may grow complete into one' [Ph], 'that they may be brought to completion as one' [AB], 'in order that they might attain perfect unity' [BAGD], 'that they may be perfected in unity' [NASB], 'that their unity might be perfect' [Gdt], 'may they be brought to complete unity' [NIV], 'may they be so perfected in unity (that the world...)' [NJB], 'may they experience such complete unity (that the world...)' [NLT], 'that they may become full grown into one' [NICNT1]. This verb means to attain a state as a goal [LN]. The perfect tense indicates an action that is brought to a state of completion and continues there indefinitely [Lns].

QUESTION—What is the relationship between this verse and the previous one?

This verse explains the meaning of being one as the Father and Jesus are one (verse 22) [TH].

QUESTION—Who is the implied actor of τετελειωμένοι 'they may be perfected (into one)'?

Jesus is the implied actor of this passive verb. He is the one who intends to bring the disciples into complete oneness [Lns].

QUESTION—What does it mean for Jesus to be *in them* and the Father *in him*?
  This expression explains the meaning of the words of verse 22 'so that they may be one as we are one'. If this is difficult to translate it could also be expressed as: 'just as I am united with them, and you are united with me' [TH], 'I am one with them, and you are one with me' [CEV], 'I live in them and you live in me' [Gdt, NICNT1].
QUESTION—How are the disciples perfected into one and what does this phrase mean?
  Since the Father is in Jesus, and Jesus is in the disciples, they are completely filled with God's presence and in this way joined together as one [HTC]. It means that they will be united [Gdt, My, TH, TRT; NASB, NIV, NJB, NLT]: 'may they be so perfected in unity that the world will recognize that it was you who sent me' [NJB].
QUESTION—When will the disciples be perfected into one?
  It appears that they will be perfected in this life in view of the fact that this perfection is to have an effect on the world [AB].
QUESTION—The purpose clause 'that the world may know that you sent me…' could refer back to the reason Jesus gave glory to his disciples in verse 22, or it could refer to the disciples becoming perfected into one in this verse. Which one is more likely?
  1. It probably refers back to the disciples becoming perfected into one [AB, Car, CH, EGT, Gdt, HTC, IVP, Lns, NICNT1, NICNT2, NTC, Rd, TH]. The unity of believers is meant to impress the world just as it was in verse 21, 'That they all may be one… that the world may believe that you sent me' [NICNT1].
  2. It refers back to verse 22. This is the final result of Jesus' giving glory to the disciples [ICC].
QUESTION—In what sense is the word 'world' being used in this verse?
  It is being used to refer to the people who live in the world [TRT; CEV]: 'Then *this world's people* will know that you sent me' [CEV].
QUESTION—Whom does αὐτούς 'them' in the phrase 'loved them' refer to?
  1. It refers to believers, not to the people of the world [AB, NICNT1, NICNT2, TH, TRT; probably all translations]: 'They will know that you love *my followers* as much as you love me' [CEV].
  2. It refers to the world [ICC]. When the world realizes that the Father sent Jesus it will also come to know that he loves it as he loved the Son [ICC].

DISCOURSE UNIT—17:24–26 [Car, HTC, Rd, WBC]. The topic is prayer for the fulfillment of the disciples [HTC], prayer for their perfection in glory [Car, WBC], prayer for reunion of believers with himself [Rd].

17:24 Father, I-desire that they-also whom you-have-given me may-be with me where I am, so-that they-may-see my glory which you-have-given me because[a] you-loved me before (the) foundation[b] of- (the) -world.

TEXT—Instead of ὃ δέδωκάς μου 'that which you have given me' (not reflected in the above rendering of this verse), some manuscripts read οὓς δέδωκάς μου 'those whom you have given me', and some patristic quotations omit this clause. GNT reads 'that which you have given me' with a B rating, indicating that the text is almost certain. Gdt supports the reading 'those whom you have given me'. (Note that although the GNT reading is considered correct by most, all translations translated the neuter 'that which' as being personal).

LEXICON—a. ὅτι (LN 89.33, 91.14): 'because' [LN (89.33); CEV, NCV, NET, NIV, NJB, NLT, NRSV, REB, TEV], 'for' [KJV, NASB, NTC, Ph], 'since, in view of the fact that' [LN (89.33)], 'that, namely, that is, namely that' [LN (91.14)]. This conjunction indicates cause or reason, based on an evident fact [LN (89.33)], or it indicates an identificational or an explanatory clause [LN (91.14)].

b. καταβολή (LN 42.37) (BAGD 1. p. 409): 'foundation' [BAGD, Gdt, NICNT2, NTC, WBC; KJV, NASB, NJB, NRSV], 'creation' [AB, LN; NET, NIV], 'beginning' [BAGD]. This noun is also translated as a verb: '(before the world) was created' [CEV], '(before the world) was made' [NCV, TEV], '(before the world) began' [NLT, Ph, REB]. This noun denotes creation, particularly of the world, with focus on the beginning phase [LN].

QUESTION—If the reading 'that which you have given me' refers to believers, what is the purpose of the neuter pronoun to refer to them?

It may emphasize the unity of the people in the group [AB, CH, Gdt, ICC, IVP, NTC, TH]. The neuter 'that which' points to all believers as one collective unity that has been given as a gift from the Father (see 6:37, 39; 10:29; and 17:2) [CH]. The neuter singular is often used in John when believers are referred to as a group [Car, Lns].

QUESTION—To what place does the clause 'where I am' refer?

It refers to where he will be in the next life rather than in this (14:3) [Bar, Gdt, HTC, IVP, Kn, Lns, NICNT1, NICNT2, Rd, TH]. If in some languages 'where I am' refers to where Jesus is at the time of his prayer, it may be necessary to translate 'may be with me where I will be' [TH, TRT].

QUESTION—What is the glory that the disciples will see?

It is the glory of Jesus in the Godhead—his glory as God [Bar]. The disciples had seen Jesus' glory in his miracles and in the cross and resurrection but not in its unveiled splendor [Car]. While Jesus may be referring to the majesty and splendor he will have in the life to come, he may be asking that the disciples will be able to know what true glory is and recognize that lowly service is truly glorious [NICNT1].

JOHN 17:24   337

QUESTION—What is indicated by the conjunction ὅτι 'because/that is (you loved me)'?
1. It indicates that the Father's love for the Son is the reason he gave him glory [AB, Bar, BECNT, EGT, NTC, Rd, TH, TRT; probably all translations]: 'that they may see my glory which you have given me *because* you loved me before the creation of the world' [AB]. The Father's love for the Son is the basis of the glory that he possessed before the creation of the world (17:5) [AB].
2. It indicates specifically what that glory was [Gdt, ICC]. It should be translated 'that is', indicating that his glory consisted in being the object of the Father's love [Gdt].

QUESTION—What words are emphasized in this verse?
The words 'those whom you have given me' are emphatic being placed forward in the Greek sentence order [AB, Lns, HTC, My, NICNT1, NTC, TH, WBC]: 'Father, *they are your gift to me*; and where I am, I wish them also to be with me' [AB]. The pronoun ἐγώ 'I' in the clause 'where I am' [Lns, NICNT1] and the pronoun κἀκεῖνοι 'they also' in the clause 'they also whom you have given me' are emphatic [Lns]: 'I will that where *I myself* am *also they on their part* may be with me' [Lns].

DISCOURSE UNIT—17:25–26 [IVP, Kn]. The topic is the conclusion of Jesus' prayer.

17:25 **Righteous**[a] **Father, although**[b] **the world did- not -know you, yet I knew you, and these knew that you sent me.**

LEXICON—a. δίκαιος (LN 88.12) (BAGD 2. p. 196): 'righteous' [BAGD, Gdt, HTC, LN, NICNT2, NTC, WBC; KJV, NASB, NET, NIV, NLT, NRSV, REB, TEV], 'Upright One' [NJB], 'most just' [AB], 'just' [BAGD, LN], 'good' [CEV]. This adjective is also translated as a clause: 'you are the One who is good' [NCV], and as a phrase: '(Father) of goodness and truth' [Ph]. This adjective pertains to being in accordance with what God requires [LN]. It means 'just' or 'righteous' with reference to his judgment of men and nations [BAGD]. The adjective 'righteous, just' is used to describe the Father here possibly because the context is speaking about judging the world and acquitting believers [AB, Bar, BECNT, Car, CH, Gdt, ICC, NICNT1, TH].
b. καί (BAGD I.6. p. 393): 'although' [BAGD, WBC; NASB, NET, REB], 'though' [NTC; NIV], 'and yet' [NICNT2], 'even if' [NET], 'while' [AB], not explicit [all other translations]. This conjunction is also translated as a clause: '(Righteous Father, the world) it is true (has not known thee)' [Gdt]. The conjunction combination καί…καί indicates a contrast 'although…yet' [BAGD].

QUESTION—The Greek text contains three conjunctions in this verse, καί…δέ…καί, and the versions have translated them in different ways. Two commentaries and one version support the translation of the three as 'although…yet…and' respectively [BECNT, Car; NASB]. If the combination καί…καί bracketing the δέ clause, is taken to mean 'both…and', the intervening clause with δέ should either be taken to be parenthetical [AB, Bar, ICC, NICNT1], or it contrasts Jesus with the world [Lns].

NOTE—Here's how the translations rendered these three conjunctions:
'*although* (the world)…*yet* (I have known you)…*and* (these)' [WBC; NASB].
'…(the people of this world)…*but* (I know you)…*and* (my followers)' [CEV, similarly HTC; KJV, NCV, NASB, NLT, NRSV, Ph, TEV].
'*though* (the world)…(I know you)…*and* (they)' [NIV, similarly NTC].
'*and yet* (the world)…*but* (I knew you)…*and* (these)' [NICNT2].
'*although* (the world)…(I know you)…*and* (they)' [REB].
'*even if* (the world)…(I know you)…*and* (these)' [NET].
'*while* (the world)…(though I knew you)…(these men)' [AB].
'(the world) *it is true*…*but* (as for me, I)…*and* (these)' [Gdt].

QUESTION—To whom does the pronoun οὗτοι 'these' refer?
It refers to Jesus' followers [CH, Gdt, HTC, IVP, Lns, My, NICNT2, Rd, TH, TRT; CEV]. This is shown by the fact that they are the ones who knew that the Father sent Jesus [Rd]. Although it refers here to the eleven, it applies similarly to all believers [Lns].

QUESTION—There are three verbs 'to know' in this verse all in the aorist tense. How should they be translated? (It is valid to render the aorist as a present indicating timelessness [TH]).
Here is how the translations rendered these tenses:
'know…know…know' [CEV, NCV, NET, NIV, NLT, NRSV, REB, TEV].
'has known…have known…have known' [Gdt, NTC, WBC; KJV, NASB, NJB].
'has known…have known…know' [HTC; Ph].
'did know…knew…came to know' [AB].
'did know…knew…knew' [NICNT2].

QUESTION—What word is emphasized in this verse?
The pronoun ἐγώ 'I' is emphasized and contrasts Jesus with the world [Lns].

17:26 I-made- your name[a] -known[b] to-them and will-make (it) -known, so-that the love (with) which you-loved me may-be in[c] them, and-I in[d] them."

LEXICON—a. ὄνομα (LN 9.19, 33.265) (BAGD I.4.b. p. 572): 'name' [AB, BAGD, Gdt, HTC, LN (9.19), NICNT2, NTC, WBC; KJV, NASB, NET, NJB, NRSV, REB], 'reputation' [LN (33.265)]. The clause 'I made your name known to them' is translated 'I have made your self known to them' [Ph], 'I have made/made you known to them' [NIV, TEV], 'I have revealed you to them' [NLT], 'I told them what you are like' [CEV], 'I showed them what you are like' [NCV]. This noun is a figurative extension of the meaning of ὄνομα 'name' and it denotes a person with the possible implication of their existence or relevance as an individual [LN (9.19)], or it denotes that which is said about a person on the basis of an evaluation of the person's conduct [LN (33.265)]. A person's name is

often practically inseparable from the person who bears it. When used of God it is representative of the Godhead as a tangible revelation of his nature [BAGD]. The word 'name' refers to what a person is and so it may be translated by the pronoun 'you' [TH].
- b. aorist act. indic. of γνωρίζω (LN 28.26) (BAGD 1. p. 163): 'to make known' [AB, Gdt, HTC, LN, NICNT2, NTC, WBC; NASB, NET, NIV, NJB, NRSV, Ph, REB, TEV], 'to reveal' [BAGD; NLT], 'to declare' [KJV], 'to tell' [CEV], 'to show' [NCV]. This verb means to cause information to be known by someone [LN]. There is no meaning difference between this verb and the verb φανερόω 'to reveal' at verse 6 [AB, Bar, ICC, Lns].
- c. ἐν (LN 89.119): 'in' [LN; all translations except CEV, NCV], 'one with, in union with, joined closely to' [LN]. The clause 'the love (with) which you loved me may be in them' is translated 'the love that you have for me will become a part of them' [CEV], 'they will have the same love that you have for me' [NCV], 'the love which you have had for me may be in their hearts' [Ph]. This preposition in the dative case indicates close personal association [LN].
- d. ἐν (LN 89.119): 'in' [LN; all translations except CEV], 'one with, in union with, joined closely to' [LN]. The clause 'and I in them' is translated 'and I will be one with them' [CEV], 'I will live in them' [NCV], 'I may be there also' [Ph]. This preposition in the dative case indicates close personal association [LN]. Here ἐν has both senses of being 'in' and 'among' the disciples. He did not go to the Father to leave his disciples as orphans but so that he might live in them individually and among them as a group [Bar].

QUESTION—How will Jesus continue to make the Father known to the disciples?

This may refer to the revelation of the Father in the cross [EGT, NICNT1], or it may refer to the work of the Holy Spirit whom He has promised to send (15:26) [Bar, BECNT, EGT, Gdt, HTC, ICC, My, NICNT2, TRT]. In view of the reference to love that follows it may more likely indicate that the cross is in focus [NICNT1]. He means that he will continue to make the Father known to them as part of his work in Heaven [Rd].

QUESTION—Does the clause 'so that the love with which you loved me may be in them' mean that God may love them as he does Jesus or that they may have his love in their hearts for others?

1. It means that God may love them as He loves Jesus [CH, EGT, Gdt, ICC, Lns]. Jesus is asking the Father to love the disciples with the same love that the Father had for him [CH]. Before creating the world the Son was the object of the Father's love. Now Jesus is asking that the disciples too be the object of the Father's love [Gdt]. Jesus intends that the Father's love will fill them like a rich treasure that they can experience constantly [Lns]. The meaning is that they may be keenly aware of God's love in their hearts [ICC].

2. It means that the disciples may have God's love in their hearts for others, that is, that they may love others in the same way that the Father loves the Son [TH].
3. Both 1 and 2 are intended [Bar, Car, NICNT1, TRT]. This love probably has a double effect to be both 'in' their hearts and 'among' them as they are enabled to love each other [NICNT1]. If God's love is *within* each of them, it cannot fail to be the same relation that exists *between* them as well [Bar].

DISCOURSE UNIT—18:1–21:25 [NICNT2]. The topic is Jesus reveals himself in his suffering and resurrection.

DISCOURSE UNIT—18:1–20:31 [Kn, Lns, WBC]. The topic is Jesus' death and resurrection.

DISCOURSE UNIT—18:1–19:42 [AB, BECNT, Car, Gdt, IVP, Kn, NICNT1, Rd, WBC; REB]. The topic is Jesus' arrest, trial, crucifixion, and burial [AB, BECNT, Car, Gdt, Kn, Rd, WBC; REB], the climax of Jesus' glorification begins [IVP], the crucifixion [NICNT1].

DISCOURSE UNIT—18:1–27 [AB, HTC, NICNT2]. The topic is the arrest and questioning of Jesus.

DISCOURSE UNIT—18:1–12 [NICNT1, Rd]. The topic is the arrest.

DISCOURSE UNIT—18:1–11 [AB, Bar, BECNT, Car, Gdt, GNT, HTC, IVP, Kn, Lns, WBC; CEV, NASB, NCV, NET, NIV, NJB, NLT, NRSV, Ph, TEV]. The topic is the arrest of Jesus [AB, Bar, BECNT, Car, Gdt, HTC, IVP, Lns, WBC; NCV, NIV, NJB, Ph, TEV], betrayal and arrest [GNT, Kn; NET, NLT, NRSV], Judas betrays Jesus [NASB].

18:1 **When- Jesus -had-said these-things he-went-out[a] with his disciples across[b] the Kidron[c] Valley[d] where there-was (a) garden,[e] which he and his disciples entered.**

LEXICON—a. aorist act. ind. of ἐξέρχομαι (LN 15.40) (BAGD 1.a.β. 274): 'to go out (of)' [AB, Gdt, BAGD, LN, NICNT2, NTC, WBC; NRSV, Ph, REB], 'to go forth' [HTC; KJV, NASB], 'to come out, to go away' [BAGD], 'to depart out of, to leave from within' [LN]. The clause 'he went out with his disciples across the Kidron valley' is translated 'he went with his disciples across the Kidron Valley' [NCV, NET], 'he and his disciples crossed the Kidron Valley' [CEV, similarly NLT], 'Jesus left with his disciples and crossed the Kidron Valley' [NIV, NJB], 'he left with his disciples and went across the Kidron Brook' [TEV]. This verb means to move out of an enclosed or well-defined two or three-dimensional area [LN]. It means to go away in such a way that the place from which one goes is not expressly named, but can be supplied from the context. For example, 'to go away from' a region or house [BAGD].

b. πέραν (LN 83.43) (BAGD 2.a. p,. 643): 'across' [AB, NICNT2, NTC; NCV, NET, NRSV, Ph, REB, TEV], 'beyond' [Gdt], 'across from, opposite' [LN], 'on/to the other side' [BAGD, HTC, LN, WBC], 'over' [KJV, NASB]. This preposition indicates a position opposite another position, with something intervening [LN]. They probably crossed the stream/valley by a bridge [Gdt, TH].

c. Κεδρών (LN 93.500) (BAGD p. 426): 'Kidron' [BAGD, LN, AB, HTC, NICNT2; CEV, NASB, NCV, NET, NIV, NJB, NLT, NRSV, TEV], 'Kedron' [NTC, WBC; REB], 'Cedron' [Gdt; KJV, Ph]. This noun denotes a valley between Jerusalem and the Mount of Olives [LN]. It denotes the Kidron valley, a wadi or watercourse (dry except in the rainy season), adjoining Jerusalem on the east and emptying into the Dead Sea [BAGD].

d. χείμαρρος or χειμάρρους (LN **1.52, 1.77**) (BAGD p. 879): 'valley' [AB, NICNT2; CEV, NCV, NET, NIV, NJB, NLT, NRSV, Ph], 'ravine' [BAGD, **LN** (1.52); NASB, REB], 'brook' [AB, HTC, **LN** (1.77); KJV, TEV], 'winter-brook' [NTC], 'winter stream, rainy-season stream' [LN (1.77)], 'torrent' [WBC], 'winter torrent' [BAGD], 'wadi' [BAGD, LN (1.52)]. This noun denotes a ravine or narrow valley in which a stream flows during the rainy season, but which is normally dry during the dry season. In desert areas of the world designations for such ravines or valleys are common enough. What is important, however, in the biblical context in which χείμαρρος occurs is not the intermittent nature of the stream so much as the fact that this is a relatively narrow valley (compare χείμαρρος 'a seasonal stream' (1.77) [LN (1.52)]. Or it denotes a stream or river that flows only during the rainy season (in Palestine this would be during the winter months) or when melting snow from the mountains, provides running water for a relatively short period of time. The reference in John 18:1 is probably to the narrow valley, not to the stream itself, as noted in (1.52) [**LN** (1.77)]. It denotes a stream of water that flows abundantly in the winter [BAGD]. This stream or valley stands between Jerusalem and the Mount of Olives [ICC, Lns, NICNT2, NTC].

e. κῆπος (LN 1.97) (BAGD p. 430): 'garden' [BAGD, LN; all translations except NET, NIV, NLT], 'orchard' [LN; NET], 'olive grove' [NIV], 'grove of olive trees' [NLT]. This noun denotes a field used for the cultivation of herbs, fruits, flowers, or vegetables [AB, LN, TH], as well as trees [AB, TH]. The garden was probably an olive grove [BECNT, Car, IVP, Lns, NTC, TRT; NIV, NLT]. The verbs 'entered' and 'went/came out' (verse 4) suggest an enclosed place [ICC] or a walled enclosure [Bar, BECNT, Car, NICNT1].

QUESTION—Does the verb 'went out' imply that he left the city or simply the house where they had just been?

1. It probably means that he left the city with his disciples [EGT, Gdt, ICC, Lns, My, NTC, TRT]. The fact that the phrase 'went out' is followed by 'across the Kidron Valley' indicates that he left the city [Lns].
2. It probably means that he left the house where they had been eating together [Bar, NICNT1, WBC].

18:2 Now Judas who betrayed[a] him also knew the place, because Jesus often[b] met there with his disciples.

LEXICON—a. pres. act. participle of παραδίδωμι (LN 37.111) (BAGD 1.b. p. 614): 'to betray' [BAGD, Gdt, HTC, LN, NTC; CEV, KJV, NASB, NET, NIV, NRSV, Ph], 'to hand over' [BAGD, LN, NICNT2], 'to turn against' [NCV], 'to turn over (to)' [BAGD, LN], 'to give up (a person)' [BAGD]. This verb is also translated as a noun: '(Judas) the traitor' [NJB, TEV], 'the/his betrayer' [AB, WBC; NLT, REB]. This verb means to deliver a person into the control of someone else, involving either the handing over of a presumably guilty person for punishment by authorities or the handing over of an individual to an enemy who will presumably take undue advantage of the victim. As is the case in English, a number of languages make a clear distinction between legitimate handing over of a presumably guilty person to a civil authority and the betrayal of a person in the in-group to someone in the out-group [LN]. The present participle indicates 'who was betraying him' (that is, at that moment) [BECNT, ICC, Lns, NICNT1, NICNT2, NTC; NASB].

b. πολλάκις (LN **67.11**) (BAGD p. 686): 'often' [BAGD, LN; all translations except KJV, NET, TEV], 'many times' [**LN**; NET, TEV], 'ofttimes' [KJV]. This adverb indicates a number of related points of time [LN].

QUESTION—What did Judas' betrayal consist of?

It consisted of telling or showing the Jewish authorities the place where Jesus could be found and arrested [Bar].

18:3 Then Judas took the detachment-of-soldiers[a] and some officers[b] of the chief priests and the Pharisees, (and) came there with lanterns[c] and torches[d] and weapons.[e]

LEXICON—a. σπεῖρα (LN **55.9**) (BAGD p. 761): 'detachment of soldiers' [AB, WBC; NIV, NRSV, REB], 'group of (Roman) soldiers' [**LN**; NCV, TEV], 'band of soldiers' [LN, NICNT2], 'squad of soldiers' [NET], 'troop of soldiers' [HTC], 'contingent of Roman soldiers' [NLT], 'Roman soldiers' [CEV], 'band (of men)' [KJV], 'Roman cohort' [NASB], 'cohort' [BAGD, Gdt, LN, NTC; NJB], 'guard' [Ph]. This noun denotes a Roman military unit of about 600 soldiers called a cohort, though even a part of such a cohort was often referred to as a cohort [LN]. In our literature it probably always was a cohort, the tenth part of a legion, that is, 600 men, but the number varied [BAGD]. This term could also refer to a 'maniple' of only 200 men [Car, WBC], but even the entire maniple may not have been present [Car]. Although a full cohort was probably not employed, still the number was a significant one [IVP, NTC].

b. ὑπηρέτης (LN 35.20) (BAGD 842): 'officer' [BAGD, Gdt, LN, NICNT2, NTC; NASB, NET, Ph], 'official' [NIV], 'police' [AB, WBC; NRSV], 'temple police' [CEV, REB], 'Temple guard' [NLT, TEV], 'guard' [NCV, NJB], 'servant' [BAGD, HTC, LN; KJV], 'helper, assistant' [BAGD].

This noun is derived from ὑπηρετέω 'to serve' (35.19) and so denotes a person who renders service [LN]. Here it refers to the servants of the Sanhedrin [BAGD], or the temple police [Bar, BECNT, ICC, Kn, Lns; CEV, REB].
  c. φανός (LN **6.103**) (BAGD p. 853): 'lantern' [AB, BAGD, Gdt, **LN**, NICNT2, WBC; KJV NASB, NCV, NET, NJB, NRSV, REB, TEV], 'torch' [HTC, Lns, My, NTC; CEV, NCV, NIV, Ph], 'blazing torch' [NLT], 'lamp' [BAGD]. This noun denotes a small fire which was carried about for the sake of its light and which had some type of protection from wind and weather. Though φανός in earlier Greek meant a 'torch', by NT times it appears to have been used primarily to identify a type of lamp used outdoors [LN].
  d. λαμπάς (LN **6.102**) (BAGD p. 465): 'torch' [AB; BAGD, Gdt, **LN**, NICNT2, WBC; CEV, KJV, NASB, NCV, NET, NJB, NRSV, REB, TEV], 'lantern' [HTC, Lns, My, NTC; CEV, NCV, NIV, NLT, Ph]. This noun denotes a stick or bundle of sticks carried about as a light [LN]. It consisted of resinous strips of wood tied together and set afire [BECNT, NICNT1].
  e. ὅπλον (LN **6.29**) (BAGD 2.a. p. 575): 'weapon' [BAGD, **LN**; all translations except TEV]. This noun is also translated as a verb: 'they were armed' [TEV]. It denotes an instrument used in fighting, whether offensive or defensive [LN], and specifically indicated swords and clubs (see Matthew 26:47) [Lns, NTC, TRT].
QUESTION—In what way did Judas 'take' the detachment of soldiers?
  He was not in authority over them, he simply took them in the sense that he was their guide to Jesus [AB, Bar, BECNT, Car, CH, NTC, Rd, WBC].
QUESTION—What is indicated by the definite article before 'detachment of soldiers'?
  It indicated that it was the well-known cohort [Gdt, HTC, NICNT2] and had a definite size [HTC]. It indicated the band of soldiers that kept guard at the Roman fortress known as Antonia [EGT, Lns, My, NICNT1, NTC].
QUESTION—How are the nouns related in the genitive construction 'some officers *of* the chief priests and the Pharisees'?
  The chief priests and Pharisees sent the officers [Gdt, NICNT1, NTC, TH, TRT; CEV, NJB, TEV]. The chief priests and Pharisees gave the officers to Judas [WBC; NASB, NLT], provided officers for him [Ph, REB], or supplied officers to him [AB].
QUESTION—What is the significance of the present tense 'comes' in the statement 'Judas…came (literally 'comes') there with lanterns…'?
  It is a dramatic present and serves to highlight the arrival of Judas [Lns].
QUESTION—Who sent the Roman soldiers?
  The soldiers were probably placed at the disposal of the chief priests or Sanhedrin by Pilate [AB, Gdt, NTC], perhaps indicating that he was afraid of an insurrection [AB]. The chief priests and Pharisees gave Judas both the detachment of soldiers and the officers [CH, WBC].

18:4 Therefore[a] **Jesus knowing all that-would come**[b] **upon him went-out**[c] **and says to-them, "Who are-you-looking-for?"**

LEXICON—a. οὖν (LN 89.50): 'therefore' [Gdt, LN, Lns, My; KJV], 'then' [HTC, NICNT2, NTC; NET, NRSV], 'so' [LN; NASB, NLT, TEV], 'consequently, accordingly, so then' [LN], not explicit [AB, WBC; CEV, NCV, NIV, NJB, Ph, REB]. This conjunction indicates result, often implying the conclusion of a process of reasoning [LN].

    b. pres. mid. or pass. (deponent = active) participle of ἔρχομαι (LN 15.81) (BAGD I.2.c. p. 311): 'to come' [BAGD, LN]. The clause 'Jesus knowing all that would come upon him' is translated 'Jesus...knowing all things that should come upon him' [KJV, similarly Gdt; NASB, WBC], 'Jesus knew everything that was going to happen to him' [AB, NICNT2, NTC; CEV, NCV, similarly NET, NIV, NJB, NLT, NRSV, Ph, REB, TEV], 'Jesus, knowing all that was to befall him' [HTC]. When ἔρχομαι is used with ἐπί 'on, upon' (as here) it indicates serious misfortune coming over someone [BAGD]. This verb means to move toward or up to the reference point of the viewpoint character or event [LN]. It may be necessary to be more specific about the impending events that would happen, by using a translation such as 'all that they were going to do to him' or 'how they were going to treat him' [TH].

    c. aorist act. indic. of ἐξέρχομαι (LN 15.40) (BAGD 1.a.β. p. 274): 'to go out (of)' [BAGD, HTC, LN, WBC; NCV, NIV], 'to step forward' [NLT, REB, TEV], 'to go forward' [Ph], 'to come forward' [NJB, NRSV], 'to go forth' [Gdt; KJV, NASB], 'to come out' [AB, BAGD, NTC], 'to come' [NET], 'to depart out of, to leave from within' [LN], not explicit [CEV]. This verb means to move out of an enclosed or well defined two or three-dimensional area [LN]. It almost always implies a personal actor. It can be used in such a way that the place from which one goes is not expressly named, but can be supplied from the context, for example 'go away' from a region or a house [BAGD].

QUESTION—What relationship is indicated by the conjunction οὖν 'therefore/then'?

    1. It indicates that Jesus went out *because* he knew what was going to happen to him [My, NICNT1, WBC]. The appearance of Judas sparked Jesus' action because he knew what was about to happen and had no intention of retreating from it [My]. His thorough knowledge of the situation dictates Jesus' action [NICNT1]. This 'hour' had been ordained by the Father so Jesus takes the initiative [WBC].

    2. It simply indicates a transition to the next event or has no significant meaning [TRT; probably AB, WBC; CEV, NCV, NIV, NJB, Ph, REB who do not translate this word].

QUESTION—What is the place that Jesus went out from?

He went out from the garden where he had been with his disciples [Bar, Car, Gdt, ICC, Lns, My, NICNT1, NICNT2]. Although Jesus may have stepped out of the garden, he still did not separate himself from his disciples (see verse 8) [Rd]. He went out from the group of his disciples [EGT]. It could mean that he went out of the garden or simply that he stepped forward [TRT].

QUESTION—What is indicated by Jesus' question 'Who are you looking for'?

Jesus wished to focus attention on himself so as to prevent an attack on his disciples [EGT, Gdt], and so provide for their safety by surrendering himself [Gdt]. Jesus was voluntarily accepting his arrest in that he did not wait to be identified [ICC].

18:5 **They-answered him, "Jesus the Nazarene."[a] He-said to them, "I am[b] (he)." Now Judas also who was-betraying him stood with them.**

TEXT—Instead of Ἐγώ εἰμι 'I am (he)' some manuscripts read ὁ Ἰησοῦς, Ἐγώ εἰμι 'Jesus, I am (he)', and others read Ἐγώ εἰμι Ἰησοῦς 'I am Jesus'. GNT reads 'I am (he)' with a C rating, indicating that the Committee had difficulty making the decision.

LEXICON—a. Ναζαρηνός (LN 93.537) (BAGD p. 532): 'Nazarene' [BAGD, LN]. The phrase 'the Nazarene' [NTC; NASB, NET, NJB, NLT] is also translated 'from Nazareth' [CEV, NCV], 'of Nazareth' [Gdt, HTC; KJV, NIV, NRSV, Ph, REB, TEV], 'the Nazorean' [AB, NICNT2], the Nazarean' [WBC]. This word is derived from the noun Ναζαρέθ 'Nazareth' (93.536) and indicates a person who lives in or is a native of Nazareth. It has an alternative spelling Ναζωραῖος (93.538) [LN]. It is applied only to Jesus and indicates 'coming from Nazareth' or 'inhabitant of Nazareth' [BAGD]. It may be necessary to specify the town Nazareth by translating something like 'Jesus whose hometown is Nazareth' or 'Jesus who comes from Nazareth' (see Matthew 2:23) [TH]. This term may have a derogatory connotation [BECNT].

b. pres. act. indic. of εἰμί (LN 13.4) (BAGD II.5, p. 224): 'to be' [BAGD, LN]. The phrase Ἐγώ εἰμι 'I am [he]' [KJV] is also translated, 'I am he' [AB, Gdt, EGT, HTC, ICC, Lns, NICNT2, NTC, WBC; NCV, NET, NJB, NRSV, REB, TEV], 'I AM he' [NLT], 'I am He' [NASB], 'I am Jesus' [CEV], 'I am the man' [Ph]. The formula Ἐγώ εἰμι 'I am' is often used in the gospels in such a way that the predicate must be understood from the context [BAGD]. This verb means that one thing is identical with another [LN].

QUESTION—What is indicated by Jesus' reply, 'I am'?

It was intended to identify himself as the one they were looking for [Bar, HTC, Lns, NICNT1, NICNT2, TH, WBC]. But it may also have been Jesus' claim to be God himself [BECNT, IVP, Kn, NICNT1, WBC]. Jesus identifies himself as the man from Galilee and at the same time claims to be God [IVP]. By this term Jesus identifies himself as one sent by God with absolute authority [Rd].

QUESTION—What is indicated by the conjunction δέ 'now/and/but' in the clause that begins 'Now Judas…'?

It indicates that the statement following it is parenthetical or is included as an extra comment [AB, Lns; NCV, NET, NIV, NLT, Ph].

QUESTION—Who does the pronoun αὐτῶν 'them', in the phrase 'Judas stood…with them', refer to?

It refers to the soldiers and guards [Bar, BECNT, Lns, HTC, NICNT1, NICNT2, NTC, Rd, TH, TRT]. The phrase shows that Judas is now allied with Jesus' enemies [Lns, NICNT1]. It may be necessary to make this explicit by translating 'was standing there with the soldiers and guards' [TH].

18:6 So[a] when he-said to-them, "I am [he]," they-went[b] back[c] and fell[d] to-the-ground.[e] **18:7** So he-asked them again, "Whom-do-you-seek?" And they said, "Jesus the Nazarene."

LEXICON—a. οὖν (LN 89.50): 'so' [LN; NASB, NET], 'therefore' [BAGD, Gdt, LN, WBC], 'then' [LN, NICNT2, NTC], 'consequently, accordingly, so then' [LN], not explicit [AB, HTC; CEV, KJV, NCV, NIV, NJB, NLT, NRSV, Ph, REB, TEV]. This conjunction indicates result, often implying the conclusion of a process of reasoning [LN].

  b. aorist act. indic. of ἀπέρχομαι (LN **15.37**) (BAGD 4. p. 84): 'to go away' [LN], 'to depart, to leave' [LN]. The statement ἀπῆλθον εἰς τὰ ὀπίσω (literally 'they went into the behind') 'they went backward' [Gdt; KJV] is also translated 'they drew back' [BAGD, HTC, NICNT2; NASB, NIV, NLT, REB], 'they moved back/backward' [**LN**, WBC; NCV, NJB, TEV], 'they stepped back' [AB; NRSV], 'they retreated' [NET, Ph], 'they lurched backward' [NTC], 'they all backed away' [CEV]. This verb means to move away from a reference point with emphasis on the departure, but without implications as to any resulting state of separation or rupture [LN].

  c. ὀπίσω (LN 83.40) (BAGD 1.a. p. 575): 'back' [AB, HTC, LN (15.37), NICNT2; NASB, NCV, NIV, NJB, NLT, REB, NRSV, TEV], 'backward' [Gdt, NTC, WBC; KJV], 'behind' [BAGD, LN], 'in back of' [LN]. This adverb indicates a position behind an object or other position [LN]. When used as an adverb with the verb 'to go back' it means 'to shrink back' [BAGD].

  d. aorist. act. indic. of πίπτω (LN 15.119) (BAGD 1.b.α. p. 659): 'to fall' [LN; all translations], 'to fall down' [LN], 'to fall down (violently), to fall to the ground' [BAGD]. This verb means to fall from a standing or upright position down to the ground or surface [LN]. It is used of something or someone that, until recently, had been standing [BAGD].

  e. χαμαί (LN 1.45) (BAGD 2. p. 875): 'to the ground' [BAGD, LN; all translations except NJB], 'on the ground' [BAGD, LN; NJB]. This adverb indicates a location on the surface of the earth [LN].

QUESTION—To whom does the pronoun 'he' refer in the phrase 'he said'?

It may be advisable to use the name Jesus rather than the pronoun since the last person named was Judas [TH, TRT; NCV, NET, NIV, NJB, NLT, NRSV, REB, TEV].

JOHN 18:6–7

QUESTION—Does the action of drawing back and falling to the ground indicate something miraculous or not?
1. Their response was due to a miraculous cause [AB, BECNT, CH, IVP, Kn, Lns, My, NICNT2, NTC]. Their reaction was not merely spontaneous astonishment. Jesus' enemies fall down prostrate before his majesty. But he uses the divine name not to his own advantage, but to protect his beloved disciples [AB]. By making his enemies experience his power Jesus intended to show them that it would be unwise to go beyond their orders and arrest the disciples as well [Gdt]. No other miracle recorded in John exceeds the significance of this event. It highlights the words of Jesus, 'I lay down my life—only to take it up again. No one takes it from me, but I lay it down of my own accord'. *No one* takes his life, he lays it down freely and voluntarily [NICNT2]. Roman soldiers do not fall to the ground without some tremendous show of strength. Yet this falling was their response to Jesus' simple reply, 'I am he' [Lns]. This was the miraculous result of the power of Jesus [My]. This display of Jesus' power shows that he could have used it to foil his arrest [CH].
2. Their response was a natural reaction to Jesus reply [EGT, ICC, NICNT1]. The effect of Jesus' fearless bearing produces fear and awe. It may be that those in front of the crowd recoiled from Jesus' advance and bumped into those behind making them fall [NICNT1]. His enemies were so overcome by his moral supremacy that they recoiled in fear [ICC].

QUESTION—Why does Jesus ask them the second time who it was they were looking for?
He wanted to focus the attention of the arresting party on himself and away from his disciples [NICNT1, NTC].

18:8 Jesus answered, "I-told you that I am [he]. So if you-are-looking-for[a] me, let these-men go."

LEXICON—a. pres. act. indic. of ζητέω (LN 27.41): 'to look for' [LN, NTC, WBC; CEV, NCV, NET, NJB, NIV, NRSV, Ph, TEV], 'to want' [AB; NLT, REB], 'to seek' [Gdt, HTC, NICNT2; KJV, NASB], 'to try to learn where something is, to try to find' [LN]. This verb means to try to learn the location of something, often by movement from place to place in the process of searching [LN].

QUESTION—What is implied by the conditional clause 'if you seek me'?
It implies that this condition is actually true, that is, 'if you seek me (as is the case)' [NICNT1; NLT]: 'And since I am the one you want, let these others go' [NLT].

QUESTION—Who are referred to by the pronoun τούτους 'these men'?
It refers to the disciples [ICC, TH]. Since the disciples have not been mentioned since verse 1, it may be necessary to translate something like 'these followers of mine' [TH].

QUESTION—What is the implied response of the arresting party?

They comply with Jesus' orders and do not arrest the disciples [Lns, NICNT2, TRT]. They apparently obeyed Jesus' command to let them go. This is seen in verse 9 that assumes that they were not lost [NICNT2].

QUESTION—What word is emphasized in this verse?

The pronoun ἐμέ 'me' is emphasized [AB, ICC, TH; CEV, NJB, NLT, Ph, REB]: 'If I am the one you are looking for' [CEV].

18:9 **This was to fulfill[a] the word that he-said "I-did- not -lose one of those whom you-have-given me."**

LEXICON—a. aorist pass. subj. of πληρόω (LN 13.106) (BAGD 4.a. p. 671): 'to fulfill' [BAGD, LN], 'to cause to happen, to make happen' [LN]. The words 'This was to fulfill the word(s)' [AB, HTC; NJB, NRSV] (literally 'in order that the word may-be-fulfilled) is also translated 'that the word/saying might be fulfilled' [Gdt; KJV], 'so that the word...might be fulfilled' [NICNT2], 'This was in order that the saying...might be fulfilled' [WBC], 'This happened in order that the word...might be fulfilled' [NTC; similarly NIV], '(He said this) to fulfill the word' [NASB, NET], 'He did this to fulfill his own statement' [NLT], 'Thus fulfilling his previous words' [Ph], 'He said this so that what he had said might come true' [TEV], 'this happened so that the words...would come true' [NCV], 'Then everything will happen just as the Scriptures say' [CEV], 'This was to make good his words' [REB]. This verb means to cause to happen, with the implication of fulfilling some purpose [LN]. It means to fulfill a divine prediction or promise. Here one of Jesus' predictions is fulfilled [BAGD].

QUESTION—Is this verse parenthetical?

The following translations use parentheses around this verse [AB, TH; Ph, REB, TEV].

QUESTION—What relationship is indicated by the conjunction ἵνα 'this (was to fulfill)' (literally '*in order that* (the word may be fulfilled))'?

The conjunction indicates a relationship of purpose [AB, Lns, NTC; NCV]: '(This happened) in order that the word...might be fulfilled' [NLT]. This verse shows the intention Jesus had in mind when he gave the command to his captors to 'let these men go'. He saw the danger his disciples were in and acted so that none of them would be lost [Lns].

QUESTION—What saying of Jesus is referred to here?

The saying referred to is probably verse 17:12, 'While I was with them, I protected them and kept them safe by that name you gave me. None has been lost...' [AB, BECNT, Bar, Car, CH, EGT, Gdt, ICC, IVP, Kn, Lns, My, NICNT2, NTC, Rd, TH, TRT, WBC]. Other references that might have been referred to are 6:39 [Bar, BECNT, Car, CH, HTC, ICC, IVP, NICNT2, NTC], and 10:28 [BECNT, HTC, ICC, IVP, NICNT2, NTC, WBC].

QUESTION—In what sense did the Father give the disciples to Jesus?

He gave them to him in the sense that he committed/put them to/in his care, or told him to care for them [TH, TRT], or entrusted them to him, or chose them to be his disciples [TRT].

QUESTION—Does the verb 'to lose' refer to saving them merely from arrest or saving them from giving up their faith completely?

Here it means saving them from arrest, but doing so also keeps them from being lost eternally [Gdt, NICNT1]. Jesus' intention is to keep them from being eternally lost, but the immediate crisis that he avoids for them is their physical arrest [EGT, ICC, IVP, Lns, NTC] which might have proved to be a too severe test of their faith [IVP, Lns, NTC]. Their physical safety at this time is symbolic of their eternal salvation [Bar, Car].

QUESTION—What words are emphasized in this verse?

The words 'those you have given me' are placed first in the Greek clause in order to highlight them [HTC].

18:10 Then Simon Peter having (a) sword^a drew^b it and struck^c the high-priest's servant and cut-off^d his right ear. The servant's name was Malchus.

LEXICON—a. μάχαιρα (LN 6.33) (BAGD 1. p. 496): 'sword' [LN; all translations except NTC; REB], 'short sword' [Lns, NTC], 'sword he was wearing' [REB], 'dagger' [LN], 'saber' [BAGD]. This noun denotes a relatively short sword (or even dagger) used for cutting and stabbing [LN]. It is a short sword or a large knife [BECNT, NICNT1, TRT] since there is a different word (ῥομφαία) that refers to a long sword [TRT]. It was a kind of dagger [HTC]. It may have been a weapon about the size of a dagger [AB] or short sword [BECNT] that could be concealed [AB, BECNT].

b. aorist act. indic. of ἕλκω (LN **15.212**) (BAGD 1.a. p. 251): 'to draw' [BAGD, **LN**; all translations except AB; CEV, NCV, NET], 'to pull out' [AB; CEV, NCV, NET], 'to drag' [BAGD, LN], 'to pull' [LN]. This verb means to pull or drag, requiring force because of the inertia of the object being dragged [LN].

c. aorist act. indic. of παίω (LN 19.1) (BAGD 1. p. 605): 'to strike' [BAGD, LN; all translations except AB; CEV, KJV, NLT, Ph, REB], 'to strike at' [AB; CEV, REB], 'to slash at' [Ph], 'to smite' [KJV], 'to hit, to wound' [BAGD, LN], 'to beat' [LN], not explicit [NLT]. This verb means to strike or hit an object, one or more times [LN].

d. aorist act. indic. of ἀποκόπτω (LN 19.18) (BAGD 1. p. 93): 'to cut off' [BAGD, LN; all translations except NLT], 'to slash off' [NLT], 'to cut down, to cut in two' [LN]. This verb means to cut in such a way as to cause separation [LN]. These two words 'struck' and 'cut off' together indicate a single action, not two separate ones [TH].

QUESTION—What did Peter draw the sword out of?

He drew it out of its sheath or scabbard [HTC, NTC, TRT].

QUESTION—What is indicated by the definite article before the word 'servant' (literally '*the* servant of the high priest')?

It probably indicates that this servant held a place of honor among the High Priest's servants [HTC]. It may be that he was known by believers of that time as 'the servant' in this well-known story [NICNT2]. He was the one who was especially chosen by the High Priest to accompany the arresting party [Lns].

QUESTION—What is indicated by the naming of Malchus as the servant of the High Priest?

It probably indicates that the author was known to the High Priest and so was familiar with such details (see verses 15 and 16) [EGT, IVP, Lns, NICNT2]. In verse 26 John records that he also knows that the servant mentioned there was a relative of Malchus [Lns].

QUESTION—If Peter was right handed, how could he have cut off the servant's right ear?

It may have been that the servant jumped to the side to avoid getting hit [ICC, IVP, Kn, NTC]. Peter may have been left handed [IVP].

18:11 So Jesus said to Peter, "Put the sword into the sheath.[a] Should-I-not[b] -drink-the-cup[c] that the Father has-given me?"

LEXICON—a. θήκη (LN **6.119**) (BAGD 2. p. 360): 'sheath' [BAGD, LN; all translations except AB; CEV, NCV, NIV, REB, TEV], 'scabbard' [NJB], 'receptacle' [BAGD, LN], 'chest' [LN]. The command 'Put the sword into/in the sheath' [NICNT2, NTC; NASB] is also translated 'Put the sword back into its sheath' [WBC], 'Put up the sword into the sheath' [Gdt], 'Put your sword (back) into its sheath/scabbard' [HTC; NET, NJB, NLT, NRSV, Ph], 'Put back that sword' [AB], 'Put your sword back' [NCV], 'Put your sword away' [CEV, NIV, similarly REB], 'Put your sword back in its place' [TEV]. This noun is also translated as a verb: 'Sheathe your sword' [Lns]. This noun denotes a receptacle into which an object is customarily placed for safekeeping. In this one occurrence of θήκη in the NT, the reference is to a 'sheath' for a sword, which may be rendered in some languages as 'a leather bag for a sword' or 'a covering for a sword' or 'something in which a sword is carried' [LN].

b. οὐ μή (LN **69.13**) (BAGD D.1. p. 517): 'not' [BAGD, LN; all translations except CEV]. This negative phrase implies a strongly emphatic affirmative response to a question [LN]. In a rhetorical question when an affirmative answer is expected, it is the most decisive way of negating something in the future [BAGD]: 'I must drink from the cup' [CEV].

c. πίνω ποτήριον (LN **24.81**) (BAGD 2.b.α. p. 658): 'to drink the cup' [BAGD, LN], 'to undergo a difficult experience, to suffer' [LN]. The question 'should/shall/am I not (to) drink the cup' [AB, Gdt, HTC, **LN**, NTC, WBC; KJV, NASB, NCV, NET, NIV, NJB, NLT, NRSV, Ph, REB] is also translated 'I must drink from the cup' [CEV], 'Do you think that I will not drink the cup of suffering' [TEV], 'shall I not suffer (in the way in which the Father has indicated to me)?' [**LN**], 'Shall I refuse the lot appointed me by the Father?' [EGT]. This idiom (literally 'to drink a cup') means to undergo a trying, difficult experience [LN], or to submit to a severe trial or death [BAGD]. In a number of languages it is not possible to use the phrase 'to drink the cup' since this will almost inevitably refer to the drinking of a poison cup as a means of proving innocence in an ordeal. Even if one uses a literal rendering of the idiom 'to drink the cup', it is usually necessary to have some explanation as to the significance of the idiom [LN]. A person cannot literally drink a cup, only its contents, so to translate this idiom literally would be meaningless. The metaphor must be dropped and the meaning translated as 'Do you think that I am not willing to suffer in the way in which my Father has ordained that I should suffer?' [TH] or 'Should I not/Do you think that I should not/Don't you know that I must go through whatever suffering the/My Father has decided I must go through/suffer the way that the/My Father has decided I must suffer' [TRT].

c. ποτήριον [BAGD 2. p. 695]: 'cup' [BAGD, LN; all translations except NLT], 'cup of suffering' [TRT; NLT, TEV], 'drinking-vessel' [BAGD]. This noun is used in the OT figurative of one's destiny in both good and bad senses. Here it refers to drinking a cup of suffering as undergoing a violent death [BAGD]. It is a cup of death [BECNT, CH, HTC, My]. The cup is the same as the hour, that is, the anticipation of suffering and death [NICNT2]. It symbolized the drinking of God's judgment for the world's sins [CH].

QUESTION—How does this verse illustrate the figure of metonomy?
The cup is named for what it contains [Lns, TH].

QUESTION—What response is expected to this rhetorical question?
It indicates that a positive reply is expected [BAGD, LN, NICNT1, TH, TRT; CEV]: 'I must drink from the cup' [CEV]. The question indicates Jesus' readiness to drink the cup [Bar, IVP, WBC], his determination/resolve/comitment to drink the cup [Car, CH, Kn], that it was imperative that he drink the cup [Rd; CEV], the necessity of drinking from the cup while the emphatic negative οὐ μή leaves no room for doubt [NICNT1].

QUESTION—What words are emphasized in this verse?
The words 'the cup that the Father has given me' are placed first in the Greek question to increase its prominence (literally 'the cup that the Father has given me should I not drink it?') [Lns, TRT].

DISCOURSE UNIT—18:12–27 [BECNT, Bar, Gdt, HTC, IVP, Kn, Lns, NJB, WBC]. The topic is Jesus' trial before the Sanhedrin [Gdt], the Jewish trial and Peter's denial [BECNT, Bar, HTC, IVP, Kn, Lns, NJB, WBC].

DISCOURSE UNIT—18:12–24 [NASB, Ph]. The topic is Jesus before the priests [NASB], Peter denies Jesus [Ph].

352   JOHN 18:12

DISCOURSE UNIT—18:12-14 [BECNT, Car, GNT, HTC, IVP; CEV, NCV, NET, NIV, NLT, NRSV, TEV]. The topic is Jesus before the High Priest.

DISCOURSE UNIT—18:12-13 [AB]. The topic is Jesus is taken from the garden to Annas [AB].

18:12 Then the detachment-of-soldiers[a] and their commanding-officer[b] and the officers of-the Jews arrested[c] Jesus and tied- him -up.[d]

LEXICON—a. σπεῖρα (LN 55.9) (BAGD p. 761): 'detachment of soldiers' [WBC; NIV], 'band of soldiers' [HTC, LN, NICNT2], 'squad of soldiers' [NET], 'Roman soldiers' [TEV], 'soldier(s)' [AB; NCV, NLT, NRSV], 'troop(s)' [REB], 'cohort' [BAGD, Gdt, LN, NTC; NJB], 'Roman cohort' [NASB], 'band' [KJV], '(The Roman officer and his) men' [CEV], 'guard' [Ph]. This noun denotes a Roman military unit of about six hundred soldiers [BAGD, LN], though only a part of such a cohort was often referred to as a cohort [LN]. The exact number varied [BAGD].

b. χιλίαρχος (LN **55.15**) (BAGD p. 882): 'commanding officer' [**LN**; NET, NLT, TEV], 'commander' [NTC, WBC; NASB, NCV, NIV, REB], 'Roman officer' [CEV], 'officer' [NRSV], 'captain' [HTC, NICNT2; KJV, Ph], 'tribune' [AB, BAGD, Gdt; NJB], 'general, chiliarch' [LN]. This noun denotes a military officer, normally in command of a thousand soldiers [BAGD, LN], or a military tribune, or the commander of a cohort [BAGD].

c. aorist act. indic. of συλλαμβάνω (LN 37.109) (BAGD 1.a.α. p. 776): 'to arrest' [AB, BAGD, LN, NICNT2; CEV, NASB, NCV, NET, NIV, NLT, NRSV, REB, TEV], 'to seize' [BAGD, Gdt, HTC, LN, NTC, WBC; NJB], 'to take' [LN; KJV], 'to take hold of' [Ph], 'to catch [LN], 'to grasp, to apprehend' [BAGD]. This verb means to seize and to take along with [LN]. It means to take a prisoner into custody [BAGD].

d. aorist act. indic. of δέω (LN 18.13) (BAGD 1.b. p. 177): 'to tie up' LN; CEV, NET, NLT, TEV], 'to bind' [AB, BAGD, Gdt, HTC, NICNT2, NTC, WBC; KJV, NASB, NIV, NJB, NRSV], 'to tie' [BAGD, LN; NCV], 'to tie (his) hands together' [Ph], 'to secure' [REB], 'to tie together' [LN]. This verb means to tie objects together [LN]. It is used of the actual binding and imprisonment of prisoners [BAGD].

QUESTION—To whom does the phrase 'the Jews' refer?

It refers to the Jewish authorities or the Sanhedrin [Car, HTC, Lns, TRT; NET]: 'the Jewish leaders' [NET]. The phrase 'the officers of the Jews' simply means 'Jewish officers/officials' [NIV, Ph], 'Jewish guards' [NCV, NJB, TEV], 'Temple guards' [NLT], Jewish police' [AB, WBC; NRSV, REB], 'temple police' [CEV].

QUESTION—Who arrested Jesus?

The soldiers seized Jesus at the command of their commanding officer [Lns, NTC]. Since the detachment of soldiers and their commanding officer are mentioned first, they were probably the ones who took the lead in arresting Jesus [NTC]. The temple police made the arrest while the soldiers made sure there was no trouble arising from it [Car, WBC]. The temple police took the leading role in arresting Jesus as seen in the fact that they took him first to Annas and then to the High Priest Caiaphas while the Roman soldiers probably retired to their barracks having prevented trouble [Car].

QUESTION—What part of Jesus did they tie up?

They probably tied up his hands [EGT, ICC, Lns, TH, TRT; Ph]: 'tied his hands together' [Ph]. They tied his hands behind his back [EGT, ICC, TH, TRT] or in front of him [TRT].

DISCOURSE UNIT—18:13–27 [NICNT1, Rd]. The topic is Jesus before Pilate and Peter's denials.

DISCOURSE UNIT—18:13–14 [NICNT1]. The topic is Jesus before Annas.

18:13 First they-took[a] him to Annas,[b] for he-was (the) father-in-law of Caiaphas,[c] who was high-priest that year.

TEXT—Instead of verses 13–27 being in sequential order, one version manuscript has the order 13, 24, 14–15, 19–23, 16–18, 25b–27. Another manuscript, some version manuscripts, and one patristic quotation have the order 13, 24, 14–23, 24 (*again*), 25–27. Still another manuscript has the order 13a, 24, 13b–23, 24 (*again*), 25–27. GNT has the sequence 13–27 with an A rating, indicating that the text is certain.

LEXICON—a. aorist act. indic. of ἄγω (LN 15.165): 'to take' [AB, WBC; CEV, NJB, NLT, NRSV, REB, TEV], 'to lead' [Gdt, HTC, LN, NICNT2, NTC; KJV, NASB, NCV], 'to lead off' [Ph], 'to bring' [LN; NET, NIV]. This verb means to direct or guide the movement of a person or object, without special regard to the point of departure or goal [LN].

b. Ἅννας (LN 93.28) (BAGD p. 70): 'Annas' [BAGD, LN; all translations]. Annas was a Jewish high priest [LN]. He had been appointed High Priest by the Roman ruler Quirinius in A.D. 6 and deposed by Valerius Gratus in A.D. 15 [AB, BECNT, Kn]. That he was a powerful leader is seen by the fact that after him five of his sons became High Priest as well as his son-in-law Caiaphas [AB, BECNT, NICNT1, WBC].

c. Καϊάφας (LN 93.205) (BAGD p. 393): 'Caiaphas' [BAGD, LN; all translations]. This name indicates the high priest who played a prominent role in the condemnation of Jesus [LN].

QUESTION—What relationship is indicated by the conjunction γάρ 'for'?

It indicates the reason why Jesus was taken first to Annas. It was because it was necessary that a preliminary non-formal examination be done preceding the trial before the High Priest Caiaphas [My].

QUESTION—What was the office of the high priest and the relationship between Annas and Caiaphas?

The High Priesthood under Mosaic law was supposed to be a lifetime office (see Numbers 35:25) [AB, Car, BECNT, Kn, NICNT1, TRT]. Ultra orthodox Jews may have refused to recognize the Roman deposition of High Priests since the Jewish High Priesthood was for life [AB]. It may have been that Annas was not considered High Priest at the time because he had been deposed by the Romans in A.D. 15. It may also have been that Annas was the effective high priest holding the power while his relatives merely held the title [AB]. Many men may have maintained that Annas was the real High Priest in view of this lifetime appointment although Caiaphas held the official position [BECNT, Car, NICNT1]. Luke records that both Annas and Caiaphas were High Priest (see Luke 3:2) [BECNT]. Annas may have continued to be considered High Priest after he was deposed [Lns, Rd].

QUESTION—Does the reference to 'that year' indicate that the office of the High Priesthood lasted only for one year?

The phrase 'that year' does not mean that the office of High priest was a yearly appointment [NICNT2, TH]. The phrase is better translated more generally as 'at that time' [NICNT1, TRT; NLT], 'during that memorable year' [Car, TH, TRT], 'that fateful year' [Car, NICNT1], or 'that year of all years' [NICNT1].

DISCOURSE UNIT—18:14–27 [AB]. The topic is the questioning of Jesus.

18:14 Now Caiaphas was the one-who had-advised[a] the Jews that it-was-better[b] (for) one man to-die for the people.

LEXICON—a. aorist act. participle of συμβουλεύω (LN **33.294**) (BAGD 1. p. 777): 'to advise' [AB, BAGD, **LN**, NTC; NASB, NET, NIV, NRSV, Ph, REB, TEV], 'to give counsel to' [Gdt, HTC, WBC; KJV], 'to counsel' [LN, NICNT2; NJB], 'to tell' [CEV, NCV, NLT]. This verb means to tell someone what he or she should plan to do [LN], 'to give advice to' [BAGD]. This event was recorded in 11:50 [TH, TRT].

b. pres. act. indic. of συμφέρω (LN 65.44) (BAGD 2.a. p. 780): 'to be better' [BAGD, LN; CEV, NCV, NJB, NLT, NRSV, TEV], 'to be expedient' [Gdt, HTC, NTC; KJV, NASB], 'to be (more) advantageous' [AB, BAGD, LN, NICNT2], 'to be to someone's advantage' [LN, WBC; NET], 'to be to one's interest' [REB], 'to be good' [BAGD; NIV], 'to be a good thing' [Ph], 'to be useful, to be helpful' [BAGD]. This verb means to be of an advantage to someone [LN]. The implied information of this verse is that it would be better for one man to die *than it would be for many people to die* [TRT].

QUESTION—Is this verse parenthetical?

The following translations either enclose it in parentheses or consider it parenthetical [AB, Lns, NTC; NET]. John may have recalled this prophecy to indicate that Jesus could not expect much justice from such a judge since he had already spoken in favor of his captive's death [NICNT1].

DISCOURSE UNIT—18:15–18 [BECNT, Car, GNT, HTC, IVP, NICNT1; CEV, NCV, NET, NIV, NLT, NRSV, TEV]. The topic is Peter denies Jesus.

18:15 Simon Peter and another disciple were-following Jesus. Now that disciple was known[a] to-the high-priest and he-entered-with Jesus into the courtyard[b] of-the high-priest.

- LEXICON—a. γνωστός (LN **34.17**) (BAGD 1.b. p. 164): 'known' [BAGD], 'acquaintance' [BAGD, LN], 'friend' [BAGD, **LN**], 'intimate' [BAGD]. The statement 'that/this disciple was known to the high priest' [AB, HTC, NTC; KJV, NASB, NIV, NRSV, similarly AB, NICNT2; NJB, REB] is also translated 'one other disciple who was known personally to the high priest' [Ph, TRT], 'that other disciple was well known to the high priest' [TEV], 'that disciple knew the high priest' [CEV similarly NCV], 'the/that other disciple was acquainted with the high priest' [NET, NLT], 'that disciple was a friend of the High Priest' [**LN**, TRT, WBC]. This adjective pertained to being a friend or acquaintance of someone, and thus enjoying certain privileges as a result of such a relation. It is clear that in John 18:15 γνωστός implies much more than simply being 'well known by'. To have been simply well known by the High Priest could have been a source of danger for the disciple. It was the fact of a relationship of friendship which made it possible for the disciple to view the proceedings [LN]. In the Septuagint translation of Psalm 55:13, this word is translated to mean 'close friend' [Car, TH], or 'familiar friend' [Bar]. The term indicates that he was a member of the High Priest's circle and may have been of priestly birth and related to the High Priest. At least he was in some way intimately related to the high priestly family [NICNT1]. It is significant that even the servants knew John [Lns].
- b. αὐλή (LN 7.56) (BAGD 1. p. 121): 'courtyard' [HTC, LN, NICNT2, WBC; CEV, NCV, NET, NIV, NLT, NRSV, Ph, REB, TEV], 'court' [Gdt, NTC; NASB], 'palace' [AB; KJV, NJB]. This noun denotes a walled enclosure either to enclose human activity or to protect livestock [LN]. It was an enclosed space, open to the sky, near a house, or surrounded by buildings [BAGD].

QUESTION—Who was the other disciple?
1. It was probably the disciple Jesus loved [BECNT, Car, CH, EGT, IVP, Lns, My, NTC, Rd, TRT, WBC]. It was the disciple whom Jesus loved, the apostle John [BECNT, Car, CH, EGT, IVP, Lns, My, TRT]. This disciple also accompanied Peter (as did the disciple whom Jesus loved) (13:23–26; 20:2–10; 21:7, 21ff). Further, the disciple whom Jesus loved is designated by a similar phrase in verse 20:2 where he is called 'the other disciple' [Rd].
2. It was probably some other disciple than the disciple whom Jesus loved [Bar, HTC, Kn, NICNT1, NICNT2]. If the author had meant 'the disciple Jesus loved' he would have so named him [Kn]. Peter's companion is probably intentionally vague here [NICNT2].

QUESTION—Who was the High Priest?
1. The High Priest referred to here was Annas [AB, BECNT, Car, Gdt, IVP, Lns, My, Rd]. Annas had been and still had the title of High Priest [Gdt, Lns, My]. The reference to Caiaphas (verses 13 and 14) was merely an aside [My]. The two residences may have shared the same courtyard [Car, Gdt, Lns].
2. He was Caiaphas [EGT, NTC]. Caiaphas occupied the official palace of the High Priest [EGT], but it seems that Annas had apartments there [EGT, NTC]. It is implied that he was Caiaphas in Matthew 26:57 [NTC].

18:16 **But Peter stood[a] outside at the door.[b] So the other disciple who was-known to-the high-priest went-out and spoke[c] to-the doorkeeper[d] and brought- Peter -in.**

LEXICON—a. pluperfect act. indic. of ἵσταμαι (LN 17.1) (BAGD II.2.α. p. 382): 'to stand' [BAGD, Gdt, HTC, LN, NICNT2, NTC; KJV, NASB, NET, NRSV, Ph], 'to stay' [CEV, NJB, NLT, REB, TEV], 'to wait' [NCV, NIV]. This verb is also translated as a phrase: 'to be left standing' [AB], 'to remain standing' [WBC]. This verb means to be in a standing position [LN].
b. θύρα (LN 7.49) (BAGD 1.a. p. 365): 'door' [BAGD, Gdt, HTC, LN, NICNT2; KJV, NASB, NCV, NET, NIV, NJB, Ph, REB], 'gate' [AB, LN, NTC, WBC; CEV, NLT, NRSV, TEV]. This noun denotes the door to a house or building (often occurring in plural form and designating double doors or gates) [LN].
c. aorist act. indic. of λέγω (LN 33.69): 'to speak (to)' [LN; all translations], 'to say, to talk, to tell' [LN]. This verb means to speak or talk, with apparent focus on the content of what is said [LN].
d. θυρωρός (LN **46.8**) (BAGD p. 366): 'doorkeeper' [BAGD, **LN**, NICNT2; NASB, NJB, Ph]. This noun is also translated as a phrase: 'the girl at the gate/door' [AB; CEV, NCV, TEV], 'the maid that/her-who kept the door' [Gdt, HTC; KJV], 'the girl who kept the gate' [NTC, WBC], 'the slave girl who watched the door' [NET], 'the girl on duty there/at the door' [NIV, REB], 'the woman watching at the gate' [NLT], 'the woman who guarded the gate' [NRSV]. This noun denotes one who guards the door giving access to a house or building [LN].

QUESTION—Why is 'the other disciple' identified again here as the one known to the high priest?
The Greek repeats the same identification of this disciple as in verse 15 to emphasize his identity [TH].

QUESTION—Who is the actor of the verb 'brought (Peter) in'?
1. The disciple himself brought Peter in [AB, Lns, My, NICNT2; probably all translations]. The disciple is the subject of the two previous verbs, so it follows that he is the actor here as well. Also to say that the girl is the actor does not explain why she is reintroduced in the next verse

[NICNT2]. To say it was the girl who did it is to introduce an unnecessary change of subject [My].
2. The girl is the actor [CEV, NLT]: 'She let Peter go in' [CEV].
3. It is ambiguous and could be either the disciple who did it or the doorkeeper [Bar, BECNT, ICC, NICNT1, TRT]. It can be understood either that 'he brought Peter in' or that 'she admitted Peter' [Bar, NICNT1].

18:17 Then the servant girl who kept the door says to-Peter, "You also are not^a one-of this man's disciples, are you?" He says, "I-am not."

LEXICON—a. μή (LN 69.15) (BAGD): 'not' This particle indicates that a negative response is expected to a question [LN].

QUESTION—What is implied by the girl's question?
1. Her question expects the negative reply, 'No, I am not' [CH, ICC, LN, My, NICNT1; NASB, NET, NIV, NLT, NRSV]: 'You are not also one of this man's disciples, are you?' [NASB]. The force of her question is 'You aren't one of the disciples of this man too, are you?' and implies that he is not [NICNT1]. Her question implies that she expected a 'No!' reply. But she feels that otherwise she should not have admitted him [My].
2. Her question expects rather the positive reply, 'Yes, I am' or suggests doubt about who Peter was [Bar, BECNT, EGT, Lns, NTC, Rd, TH]. The normal meaning of μή in a question is to indicate that a 'No' answer is expected [Bar, NTC, Rd, TH]. Although the maiden asks the question in a form that expects a negative reply, she herself knew better. She was speaking ironically because she knew in her heart that Peter was Jesus' disciple [NTC]. Perhaps because of the 'you too' phrase indicating you and the other disciple who is known to the High Priest, the μή rather indicates a cautious assertion that perhaps he might be a disciple too [Bar]. The particle μή probably indicates deliberation or doubt as to what her question implied [Rd]. In view of the fact that the third question in verse 26 definitely expects a 'Yes' reply, it may be best to translate these preceding two questions as expecting a 'Yes' reply as well [TH].
3. Her question was simply asking for information [NICNT2].

QUESTION—What other person or persons are implied in the phrase 'You too'?
1. She probably intended 'you and the other disciples' [AB, NICNT2, Rd]. Since Mark 14:67 ("'You also were with that Nazarene, Jesus,' she said"), shows that the girl there was asking about Peter and those who were with Jesus, it probably means that this was her intention here too [AB].
2. She probably intended 'you and this disciple who is known to the High Priest' [Bar, BECNT, Gdt, ICC, Lns, My, NTC]. Since it was John who had requested Peter's admission, she seemed to indicate that Peter was a disciple like John [NTC].

QUESTION—To whom does the phrase 'this man's (disciple)' refer?

Since 'this man' could possibly be taken to refer to the other disciple, it may be best to translate it as 'this man Jesus' disciples' or something similar to remove the ambiguity [TH, TRT]. The phrase 'this man' connotes a feeling of contempt toward him [ICC, Lns, My].

18:18 Now the servants and the officers had made (a) charcoal-fire,[a] because it-was cold,[b] and they-were-standing and warming-themselves. And Peter also was standing and warming-himself[c] with them.

LEXICON—a. ἀνθρακιά (LN **2.6**) (BAGD p. 67): 'charcoal fire' [BAGD, **LN** all translations except Gdt, HTC, WBC; KJV, NCV, NIV], 'fire of charcoal/coals' [Gdt; KJV], 'coal fire' [HTC, WBC], 'fire' [NCV, NIV]. This noun denotes a pile of burning charcoal [BAGD], or glowing charcoal [HTC]. This was not a wood fire, but a fire of coals that did not give off a lot of smoke. This would not be suitable in a courtyard [TH]. This noun only occurs here and in 21:9 [Bar].

b. ψῦχος (LN **79.75**) (BAGD p. 894): 'cold' [BAGD, LN; all translations]. This noun pertains to being cold, as of weather conditions [LN]. Jerusalem was about 24-2500 feet above sea level so nights were chilly during this time of year [EGT, ICC, TRT].

c. pres. mid. (deponent = active) participle of θερμαίνομαι (LN 79.73) (BAGD p. 359): 'to warm oneself' [BAGD, LN; all translations except REB]. This verb is also translated: 'to share the warmth' [REB]. It means to cause oneself to become warm [BAGD, LN], at a fire [BAGD].

QUESTION—What is indicated by the conjunction δέ 'now' that introduces this verse?

It indicates that this verse is like a parenthesis that adds details to the main point of the passage [Lns; NET].

QUESTION—Who were the servants and the officers?

The servants were the servants of the high priest [Bar, BECNT, EGT, Gdt, My, NICNT1, Rd, TH]. The officers were the temple guards [Bar, BECNT, Gdt, ICC, Lns, NICNT1, TH, TRT], or the official servants/police of the Sanhedrin [EGT, Gdt, Lns, Rd].

QUESTION—Why did Peter stand with the servants and officers?

He stood with them so that he could be as inconspicuous as possible and still observe all that was happening [Rd].

DISCOURSE UNIT—18:19–24 [BECNT, Car, GNT, HTC, IVP, NICNT1; CEV, NCV, NET, NIV, NLT, NRSV, TEV]. The topic is the High Priest questions Jesus.

18:19 Then high-priest questioned[a] Jesus about his disciples and his teaching.

LEXICON—a. aorist act. indic. of ἐρωτάω (LN 33.180) (BAGD 1. p. 312): 'to question' [AB, BAGD, HTC, NTC, WBC; CEV, NASB, NET, NIV, NJB, NRSV, REB, TEV], 'to ask a question' [BAGD, LN; NCV], 'to ask'

[BAGD, Gdt, LN, NICNT2; KJV, NLT], 'to interrogate' [Ph]. This verb means to ask for information [LN].

QUESTION—What is indicated by the conjunction οὖν 'then'?

It indicates that Annas was now resuming his interrogation of Jesus from verse 12–14 [BECNT, Lns, My].

QUESTION—Who was the High Priest mentioned here?

1. The High Priest was Annas [AB, BECNT, Car, CH, HTC, IVP, ICC, Lns, My, NICNT1, NTC, Rd, TH, TRT, WBC]. Since verse 24 records that it was Annas who sent Jesus to Caiaphas, the high priest here must have been Annas [AB, NICNT1]. It was appropriate to call an official 'high priest' after he was removed from office (Mishnah, Horayot 3.1-2, 4) [BECNT].
2. The High Priest was Caiaphas [Gdt, NICNT2]. When the officer asks Jesus in verse 22, 'Is this the way you answer the high priest?', it is natural to think that he referred to the actual high priest that year, Caiaphas who was so identified in verses 13 and 14 [Gdt]. It is better to maintain consistency in the identity of the High Priest. In verse 13 it was Caiaphas and so it is better to understand Caiaphas here as well [NICNT2].

QUESTION—Was it legal to question Jesus before they had heard testimony against him?

A Jewish judge was not supposed to question the accused himself but to question witnesses about the accused [BECNT, IVP, NICNT1, WBC], see Sanhedrin 6.2 [BECNT]. No trial in history was more shockingly illegal than this one. It was illegal on several points. First a trial at night was not permitted. Secondly Jesus' arrest was the result of a bribe. Thirdly Jesus was asked to incriminate himself. Fourthly in cases involving capital punishment it was not permitted to pronounce sentence until the day after the prisoner had been convicted [NTC]. If this phase of questioning was part of a formal trial, it was illegal, but if it was merely an informal information gathering, direct questioning may have been permitted [Bar]. Apparently Annas was trying to convict Jesus of being a false prophet, one who secretly enticed people or led them astray [BECNT, Car, IVP, WBC]. Jesus sees through Annas' attempt and declares that he had taught in public places—in the temple and synagogues [WBC]. The fact that Jesus is questioned suggests that this was not a formal hearing [BECNT].

QUESTION—What was the High Priest asking about the disciples and Jesus' teaching?

He may have been asking about how many disciples Jesus had [Car, Lns] and the potential for a conspiracy [Car], or what they did and what was expected of them [NICNT1], or who they were and why they were following Jesus [ICC], or on what terms Jesus made disciples—simply as a rabbi, or as Messiah [EGT]. Some languages may require these indirect questions to be made direct. If so, one could translate, 'Who are your disciples?' [TH, TRT] and 'Why do you teach them what you do?' [TRT], or 'What do you teach?' [TH].

18:20 Jesus answered him, "I have-spoken openly[a] to-the world.[b] I always taught in synagogues and in the temple,[c] where all the Jews gather, and I-said nothing in secret.[d] **18:21** Why do-you-question me? Question those who-heard what I-said to-them. Look,[e] they know what I said."

LEXICON—a. παρρησία [BAGD 2. p. 630]: 'openly' [AB, Gdt, HTC, NTC, WBC; KJV, NASB, NCV, NIV, NJB, NRSV, REB], 'quite openly' [Ph], 'publicly' [BAGD, Bar, Lns, NICNT2; NET, TEV], 'in public' [BAGD], 'freely' [CEV]. The clause 'I have spoken openly to the world' is translated 'Everyone knows what I teach' [NLT]. This adverb indicates 'outspokenness, frankness, plainness' of speech that conceals nothing and passes over nothing. It sometimes develops into 'openness to the public', before whom speaking and actions take place [BAGD]. It means 'without reserve' [EGT, My].

b. κόσμος (LN 9.23) (BAGD 5.a. p. 446): 'world' [BAGD, LN], 'people of the world' [LN]. The phrase 'to (all) the world' [AB, Gdt, HTC, NICNT2, NTC, WBC; KJV, NASB, NET, NIV, NRSV, Ph], is also translated 'in front of everyone' [CEV], 'to everyone' [NCV, TEV], 'for all the world to hear' [NJB, REB], 'everyone knows (what I teach)' [NLT]. This noun is a figurative extension of the meaning of κόσμος 'cosmos, universe' meaning people associated with a world system and estranged from God [LN]. It means here 'the world' as mankind [BAGD].

c. ἱερόν (LN 7.16): 'temple' [Gdt, HTC, LN, NICNT2, NTC, WBC; CEV, KJV, NASB, NIV, NRSV, REB], 'Temple' [NCV, NJB, NLT, Ph, TEV], 'temple courts' [NET], 'temple precincts' [AB]. This noun denotes a temple or sanctuary (ναός, 7.15) and the surrounding consecrated area. With the exception of ἱερόν in Acts 19:27 (a reference to the temple of Artemis in Ephesus), ἱερόν in the NT refers to the Temple in Jerusalem, including the entire Temple precinct with its buildings, courts, and storerooms [LN]. Here in John 'temple precincts' or 'temple courts' is what is meant [BECNT].

d. κρυπτός (LN 28.69, 28.71) (BAGD 2.b. p. 454): 'secret' [BAGD, LN (28.69)], 'hidden, not able to be made known' [LN (28.69)], 'secretly' [BAGD, LN (28.71)], 'in secret, in private, privately' [LN (28.71)], 'in a secret place' [BAGD]. The idiom ἐν κρυπτῷ is translated: 'in secret' [Gdt, NICNT2, NTC, WBC; CEV, KJV, NASB, NCV, NET, NIV, NJB, NLT, NRSV, Ph, REB, TEV], '(there was nothing) secret (about what I said)' [AB], '(I have said nothing) secretly' [HTC]. This noun pertains to not being able to be known, in view of the fact that it has been kept secret [LN (28.69)]. The phrase ἐν (τῷ) κρυπτῷ (as it is here) is an idiom meaning literally 'in the hidden'. It pertains to not being able to be known by the public, but known by some in-group or by those immediately involved [LN (28.71)].

e. ἴδε (LN 91.13) (BAGD 1. p. 369): 'look' [LN, NICNT2], 'behold' [Gdt; KJV], 'surely (they know) [WBC; NIV], 'Obviously (they are the ones who know)' [Ph], 'Obviously, (they should know what I said)' [AB], 'Of course, (they know what I said)' [NTC], 'listen, pay attention, come now' [LN], not explicit [HTC; CEV, NASB, NCV, NET, NJB, NLT, NRSV, REB, TEV]. This particle is a prompter of attention that also serves to emphasize the following statement [LN]. It is properly the imperative of εἶδον 'to see' and is used to point out something to which the speaker wishes to draw attention [BAGD].

QUESTION—Did Jesus always speak in public?
The point is not that Jesus never spoke in private, but that whether in public or private his message was the same [BECNT, Car].

QUESTION—Why does Jesus ask the high priest 'Why do you question me?'
Jesus is asking that his trial be carried out legally, with proper witnesses [NTC, TH, WBC]. That a man's testimony about himself was suspect was a recognized principle of law [ICC]. The rule that it was illegal to have the accused incriminate himself may have been already in force at that time [AB, Bar, BECNT, Car, CH, IVP, Lns, TH, WBC].

QUESTION—What words are emphasized in these verses?
The pronouns ἐγώ 'I' [BECNT, ICC, Lns, NICNT1] are emphatic '*I on my part* have spoken openly...*I on my part* always teach in synagogue...these know what *I on my part* said' [Lns]. The pronouns οὗτοι 'they' and ἐγώ 'I' (verse 21) are placed at opposite ends of this final clause in the Greek stressing both and contrasting them ('*they* know what *I* said')[NICNT1, NTC]. In the Greek the words 'in secret' are placed before the words 'I said nothing' (in verse 20) to emphasize them [TRT].

18:22 Now (when) he had-said these-things one of-the officers standing-by slapped[a] Jesus, saying, "Is-that-how[b] you-answer the high-priest?"

LEXICON—a. ῥάπισμα (LN **19.4**) (BAGD p. 734): 'a blow with a club, rod, or whip' [BAGD]. The words ἔδωκεν ῥάπισμα τῷ Ἰησοῦ '(the officer) gave Jesus a slap in the face' [NJB] is translated '(the officer) slapped Jesus' [**LN**; TEV], '(the officer)...slapped Jesus in the face' [NTC; similarly NLT], '(the police)...gave Jesus a slap in the face' [AB, similarly NICNT2, WBC], '(the officer)...struck Jesus on the face' [NASB, NET, NIV, NLT, NRSV, REB], '(the officer)...struck Jesus with the palm of his hand' [KJV], '(the officer)...struck Jesus with his hand' [HTC; similarly Ph], '(the temple police) hit him' [CEV, similarly NCV], '(the officer)... struck him with a rod' [Gdt]. The verb ῥαπίζω 'to slap, to hit, to whip, to beat' (from which this noun is derived) means to hit or strike with the open hand, the fist, or an instrument (for example, club, rod, or whip) [LN]. The phrase διδόναι ῥάπισμα τινι means 'to give someone a slap in the face' [BAGD]. This noun denoted a sharp blow with the flat of one's hand [AB, Bar, BECNT, Car, Lns], on one's cheek [AB, Bar, ICC, Lns]. The slap was intended as an insulting rebuke to Jesus [ICC].

b. οὕτως (LN 61.9) (BAGD 1.b. p. 597): 'in this manner' [BAGD], 'thus' [BAGD, LN], 'so' [BAGD, LN], 'so shamelessly' [BAGD]. The question 'Is that how you answer the high priest?' [NRSV] is also translated 'Is that/this the way you answer the high priest?' [NASB, NCV, NET, NJB, NIV, NLT, similarly Ph, REB], 'Answerest thou the high priest so?' [KJV], 'That's no way to talk to the high priest!' [CEV], 'How dare you talk like that to the high priest!' [TEV]. This adverb refers to that which precedes [BAGD, LN].

QUESTION—What is the function of the rhetorical question 'Is that how you answer the high priest'?

His question is meant as a scornful reprimand to Jesus [NTC]. The officer is expressing his indignation at Jesus' reply [Lns]. He is reminding Jesus of the respect he should give to a ruler of Israel [Gdt]. An attitude of appropriate behavior toward authority was implied in Exodus 22:28 'Do not blaspheme God or curse the ruler of your people' [AB, BECNT]. Several versions change the question to a statement: 'How dare you talk like that to the High Priest!' [TRT; TEV]. 'That's no way to talk to the high priest!' [CEV], 'It's wrong for you to answer the high priest like that!' [TRT].

QUESTION—Was it legal to hit a prisoner in a formal trial?

In a formal trial this action was considered illegal [BECNT, ICC, Kn, NICNT1].

QUESTION—What is implied by the word οὕτως 'thus (is that how)?

The question of the officer implies: 'In so unbecoming a manner (do you reply to the high priest)?' [ICC, My].

18:23 Jesus answered him, "If I-spoke wrongly[a] testify about the wrong.[b] But if (I spoke) rightly,[c] why do-you-strike[d] me?"

LEXICON—a. κακῶς (LN **72.22**) (BAGD 2. p. 398): 'wrongly' [BAGD], 'badly' [BAGD, NICNT2], 'wickedly' [BAGD], 'incorrect, wrong' [LN], 'evil' [Gdt; KJV]. The clause 'If I spoke/have spoken wrongly' [HTC, NTC, WBC; NASB, NRSV] is also translated 'If I said/have said something/anything wrong' [AB, **LN**; NCV, NET, NIV, NLT, Ph], 'If I have done something wrong' [CEV, TEV], 'if there is some offense in what I said' [NJB], 'If I was wrong to speak what I did' [REB]. This adverb pertains to being incorrect or inaccurate, with the possible implication of also being reprehensible [LN]. It means 'to speak wrongly' or 'wickedly' in the moral sense [BAGD].

b. κακός (LN **72.22**) (BAGD 1.c. p. 397): 'wrong' [**LN**, HTC, NTC, WBC; NET, NIV, NRSV], 'evil' [Gdt; KJV], 'bad' [NICNT2], 'incorrect' [LN]. The words 'testify about/to the wrong' [NASB, NRSV] are also translated 'you must give evidence about it' [Ph, similarly AB; REB], 'say so' [CEV], 'then show what it was' [NCV], 'point it out' [NJB], 'tell everyone here what it was' [TEV], 'you must prove it' [NLT]. This pronominal adjective pertains to being incorrect or inaccurate, with the possible implication of also being reprehensible [LN]. It means 'bad' or 'evil' in the moral sense. Here it pertains to what is contrary to law or is a crime or sin [BAGD].

c. καλῶς (LN 72.12) (BAGD 4.b. p. 401): 'rightly' [BAGD], 'correctly' [BAGD, LN; NET], 'well' [BAGD, Gdt; KJV], 'true' [NCV], 'accurate, right' [LN]. The clause 'if I spoke/have spoken rightly' [HTC, WBC; NRSV] is also translated 'if rightly' [NTC; NASB], 'if I spoke the truth' [NIV, similarly NLT, Ph], 'if I was right' [AB; REB, similarly TEV], 'if well' [NICNT2], 'if not' [CEV, NJB]. This adverb pertains to being accurate and right, with the possible implication of being commendable [LN].

d. pres. act. indic. of δέρω (LN 19.2) (BAGD p. 175): 'to strike' [LN, HTC, NICNT2, NTC; NASB, NET, NIV, NJB, NRSV, Ph, REB], 'to hit' [AB, WBC; CEV, NCV, TEV], 'to smite' [Gdt; KJV], 'to beat' [BAGD, LN; NLT], 'to whip' [LN]. This verb means to strike or beat repeatedly [LN].

QUESTION—What does Jesus imply by his reply?

Jesus is implicitly denying the fact that he has violated Exodus 22:28. He has said nothing wrong and challenges the high priest to prove him wrong [AB, Lns, TH]. He implies that what Annas was doing was illegal and unwarranted [CH]. Jesus is asking for a just trial [Car, WBC]. His remarks are a challenge to the High Priest to prove him guilty [TH].

QUESTION—To whom does Jesus direct his question?

1. He directs his question to the officer who hit him [Gdt, HTC, IVP, Lns, NICNT1]. Jesus invites the guard to testify to any wrong he may have done [NICNT1].

2. He directs his question to the high priest [TH]. It was probably to the High Priest that Jesus speaks since the guard would not likely have been the person to witness against Jesus nor would he have spoken like this unless the high priest told him to. So Jesus challenges the high priest to produce the evidence that would prove him guilty. A better translation would be 'Why do you cause me to be hit?' [TH].

QUESTION—Is Jesus question 'Why do you hit me?' rhetorical and if so, what is its function?

The question is rhetorical and implies 'it was wrong for you to hit me' [NTC, TRT]. Jesus denies that he has violated the law [AB, BECNT, Lns, NTC, TH]. Jesus' reply is a tacit reprimand to his questioner [Gdt]. He corrects the officer's accusation showing that justice was rather on his (Jesus') side [HTC].

QUESTION—What is the force of using the present tense 'do you strike'?

The translation of the present 'do you strike' must convey the fact that Jesus has just been slapped and that it does not refer to some previous time to this [TH, TRT].

QUESTION—Was it legal to hit an accused man in an informal hearing?

This action was forbidden by the law (see Acts 23:3) [Kn].

18:24 Annas then sent him tied-up[a] to Caiaphas the high-priest.

LEXICON—a. perf. pass. participle of δέω (LN 18.13): 'to be tied up, to be tied, to be tied together, to be bound' [LN]. The participle 'tied up' is translated 'still tied up' [CEV, NET, TEV], 'still tied' [NCV], 'with his hands still tied' [Ph], 'bound' [AB, Gdt, HTC, NICNT2, NTC, WBC; KJV, NASB, NJB, NRSV, REB], 'still bound' [NIV]. This passive participle is also translated actively: 'then Annas bound Jesus' [NLT]. This verb means to tie objects together [LN].

QUESTION—What is indicated by the conjunction οὖν, 'then'?
1. It has a continuative meaning pointing out the next event in a chronological order [NICNT1]. This word is translated by the versions as 'then' [AB, HTC, NTC; NCV, NIV, NJB, NLT, NRSV, Ph, TEV].
2. The meaning may be 'so/therefore' [AB, Gdt, Lns, probably NICNT2, WBC; NASB, REB]. Οὖν means 'accordingly', that is, when this hearing proved to be unsuccessful [Lns]. The interrogation was getting nowhere and Jesus was asking for a formal hearing [AB].

QUESTION—Why do some versions translate 'bound' as 'still bound'?
Some versions translate 'bound' as 'still bound' because Jesus had been bound when he was first arrested (verse 12). Others either translate literally 'bound' or believe that Jesus was unbound before the hearing and was again bound before he was sent [BECNT]. Jesus had been untied before his hearing by Annas [ICC].

DISCOURSE UNIT—18:25–27 [BECNT, Car, GNT, HTC, IVP, NICNT1; CEV, NASB. NCV, NET, NIV, NLT, NRSV, Ph, TEV]. The topic is Peter denies Jesus again.

18:25 **Now Simon Peter was standing and warming-himself. So they-said to him, "You also are not^a one-of his disciples, are you?" He denied^b (it) and said, "I-am not."**

LEXICON—a. μή (LN 69.15): 'not' [LN; all translations except AB, NICNT2; REB]. This particle is a marker of a negative response to a question [LN].
b. aorist mid. (deponent = active) indicative of ἀρνέομαι (LN 33.277) (BAGD 3.a. p. 108): 'to deny' [BAGD, LN; all translations except NCV], 'to repudiate, to disown' [BAGD]. The words 'he denied it' are translated 'Peter said it was not true' [NCV]. This verb means to say that one does not know about or is in any way related to a person or event. In translating ἀρνέομαι, one can often use an equivalent phrase such as 'to say that one does not know' or 'to say that one has nothing to do with' [LN].

QUESTION—What is the function of the conjunction δέ 'now'?
It seems that John is now turning back to inform us what was happening while Jesus was being interrogated [AB]. The translations rendered this particle as follows: 'in the meantime' [AB, BECNT; Ph], 'meanwhile' [WBC; NET, NLT, REB], 'now' [HTC, NTC; NASB], 'and' [Gdt, NICNT2; KJV], not explicit [CEV, NCV, NIV, NJB, NRSV, TEV].

QUESTION—Who does the pronoun 'they (said)' refer to?
It refers to those standing by the fire with Peter [Bar, EGT, My, TH, TRT]. It probably refers to the servants and police mentioned in verse 18 [AB, EGT, HTC, NTC, WBC]. Probably the girl at the door told one of her friends

about Peter. She in turn denounced him to the other servants there. It was then from this group that the question to Peter came [Gdt]. The plural refers to the fact that first one and then another would take up the question to Peter [NICNT1]. It should be kept indefinite, 'someone' [CEV, NJB], 'some of them' [Ph], 'the others' [TEV].

QUESTION—What reply is expected to the question introduced by the particle μή?
1. The question expects the answer 'No' [CH, HTC, ICC, LN, NICNT1, NTC, WBC; probably CEV, KJV, NASB, NET, NIV, NJB, NLT, NRSV, TEV]: 'You surely are not one of his disciples, are you?' [NTC]. John expresses the first two questions in a way that almost implied that Peter should reply 'No!' In this way he gives a less severe account of Peter's infidelity than the Synoptics do [ICC].
2. The question expects the answer 'Yes' [BECNT, Lns, TH, TRT; Ph]: 'Surely you too are one of his disciples, aren't you?' [Ph], 'Certainly, you, too, are one of the disciples?' [Lns]. The particle here, rather than expecting a negative reply, may indicate a cautious assertion that he was a disciple [BECNT].

18:26 One of the servants of-the high-priest, being (a) relative[a] of-the-man-whose ear Peter had-cut-off asked, "Did- I not[b] -see you with him in the garden?"

LEXICON—a. συγγενής (LN 10.6) (BAGD p. 772): 'relative' [AB, LN; CEV, NASB, NCV, NET, NIV, NLT, NRSV, TEV], 'relation' [NJB, REB, Ph], 'kinsman' [Gdt, HTC, LN; KJV]. This pronominal adjective denotes a person who belongs to the same extended family or clan [LN]. As an adjective it means 'related to' or 'akin to' but in our literature it is only used as a substantive [BAGD].
b. οὐ (LN 69.11): 'not' [LN; all translations]. This interrogative particle marks a question that expects a positive reply [LN].

QUESTION—What reply is expected to the question of the servant?
A positive reply is expected [HTC, Lns, LN, NTC, NICNT1, NICNT2, NTC, Rd, TH, TRT, WBC; probably all translations]: 'I saw you in the garden with him, didn't I?' [WBC]. The question expects an affirmative reply [NTC]. The servant's question to Peter is an accusation [NICNT2].

QUESTION—To whom does the pronoun '(with) him' refer?
Since the pronoun 'him' could refer to the man whose ear had been cut off, it might be advisable to use the name 'Jesus' here [TH, TRT; NLT]: 'Didn't I see you out there in the olive grove with Jesus?' [NLT].

QUESTION—What words are emphasized in this verse?
The pronoun ἐγώ 'I' is emphatic [HTC, ICC, Lns, My]: 'Did not I myself see you in the garden with him?' [Lns], 'I, with my own eyes' [ICC]. Both 'I' and 'you' are emphasized as if to say, '*I*—did not *I* see *you*—yes, *you*—in the garden with him?' [NICNT2].

18:27 Then Peter again denied (it), and at-once[a] (a) rooster crowed.

LEXICON—a. εὐθέως (LN 67.53): 'at once' [HTC; NCV, NJB, TEV], 'at that moment' [NIV, NRSV, REB], 'immediately' [Gdt, LN, NICNT2, WBC; KJV, NASB, NET, NLT, Ph], 'instantly' [NTC], 'just then' [AB], 'right then' [CEV], 'right away, then' [LN]. This adverb indicates a point of time immediately subsequent to a previous point of time (the actual interval of time differs appreciably, depending upon the nature of the events and the manner in which the sequence is interpreted by the writer) [LN]. In John εὐθέως always indicates *immediate* consecutiveness [ICC].

QUESTION—Where did Jesus predict Peter's denial?

In John 13:38 Jesus foretold this would happen, 'Then Jesus answered, "Will you really lay down your life for me? I tell you the truth, before the rooster crows, you will disown me three times!"' [Bar, EGT, TH, TRT].

DISCOURSE UNIT—18:28–19:16 [Bar, IVP, NICNT1]. The topic is Pilate interrogates Jesus [IVP], Jesus, Pilate, and the Jews [Bar], the Roman trial [NICNT1].

DISCOURSE UNIT—18:28–19:16a [AB, BECNT, Car, Gdt, HTC, Rd, WBC; NCV]. The topic is Jesus' trial before Pilate.

DISCOURSE UNIT—18:28–19:15 [NICNT2]. The topic is Jesus, Pilate, and the Jews.

DISCOURSE UNIT—18:28–40 [AB, Lns; NASB, NIV, NJB, NLT]. The topic is the trial before Pilate.

DISCOURSE UNIT—18:28–38a [GNT, Kn; CEV, NRSV, TEV]. The topic is Pilate interrogates Jesus.

DISCOURSE UNIT—18:28–32 [Car, HTC, NICNT1, WBC; NET]. The topic is Jesus is handed over to Pilate [HTC, NICNT1, WBC; NET], Pilate questions the accusers [Car].

18:28 Then they-led[a] Jesus from Caiaphas to the governor's-residence.[b] It-was early-in-the-morning.[c] They did- not -enter the governor's-residence, so-that they- not -be-defiled[d] but might-eat the Passover.[e]

LEXICON—a. aorist act. indic. of ἄγω (LN 15.165) (BAGD 2. p. 14): 'to lead' [Gdt, HTC, LN, NICNT2, NTC; KJV, NASB, NCV, NIV, NJB, Ph], 'to lead away' [BAGD], 'to bring' [LN; NET], 'to take' [AB, WBC; NRSV]. This active verb is also translated passively: 'to be led' [REB], 'to be taken' [CEV, TEV]. This verb means to direct or guide the movement of an object, without special regard to the point of departure or goal [LN]. It refers here the transport of a prisoner [BAGD].

b. πραιτώριον (LN 7.7) (BAGD p. 697): 'governor's residence' [NTC, WBC; NET], 'building where the Roman governor stayed' [CEV], 'governor's palace' [TEV], 'Roman governor's palace' [CH, IVP; NCV, similarly NIV], 'palace' [LN; Ph], 'headquarters of the Roman governor'

[BECNT, Car, Rd; NLT], 'governor's headquarters' [REB], 'Pilate's headquarters' [NRSV], 'fortress' [LN], 'hall of judgment' [KJV], 'praetorium' [AB, BAGD, Gdt, HTC, NICNT2; NASB, NJB]. This noun denotes a governor's official residence [AB, BAGD, Bar, EGT, HTC, ICC, My, NICNT1, NICNT2, NTC, Rd, TH]. In the Gospels it is satisfactory to translate πραιτώριον as 'the palace where the governor lived' or 'the large dwelling where the ruler lived'. In a number of languages a term for 'palace' often suggests a military fortification, and this would also be quite appropriate for NT usage [LN]. Originally it referred to the praetor's tent in camp, with its surroundings. The word also came to designate the Roman governor's official residence in Jerusalem. This is the meaning of the word in the gospels. But it is a matter of dispute whether it refers to the Palace of Herod in the western part of the city, or to the fortress Antonia northwest of the temple area [BAGD].

c. πρωΐ (LN 67.187) (BAGD p. 724): 'early in the morning' [BAGD; CEV, NCV, NRSV, TEV], 'early-morning' [LN, NICNT2; NIV, Ph, REB], 'very early morning' [NET], 'early' [BAGD, Gdt, HTC, NTC, WBC; KJV, NASB], 'daybreak' [AB], 'morning' [NJB]. This adverb indicates the early part of the daylight period [LN]. As the fourth watch of the night, it is the time from three to six o'clock [BAGD, Gdt]. It probably referred to the time around 6 a.m. [AB, Bar, Car, BECNT, HTC, Kn, Lns, NICNT1, Rd, TH, TRT]. Since the law stated that a death sentence could not be decided at night, and the day began at 6 a.m., it was likely that the Jews held this session of the Sanhedrin sometime after 6 a.m. to give it some semblance of legality [NICNT1].

d. aorist pass. subj. of μιαίνω (LN **53.34**) (BAGD 1. p. 520): 'to be defiled' [BAGD, Gdt, HTC, **LN**, NICNT2, NTC; KJV, NASB], 'to become defiled' [WBC; NJB], 'to be ceremonially defiled' [NET], 'to be contaminated' [Ph], 'to be stained' [BAGD, LN]. This verb is also translated actively: 'it would defile them, (and they wouldn't be allowed to celebrate the Passover)' [NLT], 'to avoid defilement, (so that they could eat the Passover meal)' [REB], '(they had to avoid) 'ritual impurity' [AB], '(they did not want to) make themselves unclean' [NCV], '(they wanted) to keep themselves ritually clean' [TEV], 'so as to avoid ritual defilement (and to be able to eat the Passover)' [NRSV], 'to avoid ceremonial uncleanness' [NIV]. The words 'so that they not be defiled but might eat the Passover (meal)' are translated 'Any of them who had gone inside would have become unclean and would not be allowed to eat the Passover meal' [CEV]. This verb means to cause something to be ceremonially impure [BAGD, LN], with the implication of serious defilement [LN]. In Mishnah *Oholoth* 18.7 it is stated, 'The dwelling-places of gentiles are unclean' [Bar, BECNT, Car, IVP, Kn, NICNT1, NICNT2, WBC].

e. πάσχα (LN 51.7) (BAGD 2. p. 633): 'Passover' [BAGD, Gdt, NICNT2, NTC; NASB, NIV, NJB, NLT, Ph], 'passover' [HTC; KJV], 'Passover meal' [LN; CEV, NCV, NET, REB, TEV], 'Passover supper' [AB], 'passover lamb' [WBC], 'Pascal lamb' [BAGD]. This noun denotes a Passover meal eaten in connection with the Passover festival [LN].

QUESTION—To whom does the pronoun 'they' refer?

It refers in general to the Jews [Bar, TH]. It refers to the Jewish authorities [Car, NICNT1, Rd, TH, TRT] though some Roman soldiers may have been included [NICNT1, TH]. It probably refers to some of the authorities of the Sanhedrin [AB, EGT, HTC, NTC], and/or their temple police [NTC, WBC]. It refers to the chief priests and officers (see 19:6) [NICNT2].

QUESTION—The phrase 'from Caiaphas' in Greek is literally 'from the of Caiaphas'. How should it be understood?

This was translated variously by the versions and commentaries: 'from the house of Caiaphas' [NJB, similarly NCV, TEV], 'from the ecclesiastical court over which Caiaphas presided' [ICC], 'from Caiaphas' presence' [Ph], 'from Caiaphas' [AB, Gdt, HTC, NICNT2, NTC, WBC; CEV, KJV, NASB, NET, NIV, NRSV, REB]. It could mean from the high priest's palace or from the meeting place of the Sanhedrin [AB].

QUESTION—Do the words 'eat the Passover' refer to the eating of a single meal or are they figurative of celebrating the Passover in general?

1. The words refer to eating the Passover lamb or meal [AB, EGT, ICC, IVP, My, WBC; CEV, NCV, NET, REB, TEV]: 'they wanted to eat the Passover meal' [NCV]. The words 'eat the Passover', in the whole NT, refer only to the eating of the paschal meal [My]. They must refer to eating the Passover meal itself (see Mark 14:12; Matthew 26:17) [EGT].

2. The words refer to general participation in the Passover Festival, or to eating meals during the Passover Festival [BECNT, Car, Gdt, NTC, TH, TRT; probably NLT]: 'they wouldn't be allowed to celebrate the Passover' [NLT]. The meaning of the phrase is probably 'celebrate the feast' (see 2 Chronicles 30:21) [BECNT]. The word Passover was used to indicate the entire week of the festival (see 2:23 and 18:3). This included the celebration of *Chagigah*, a feast of joy. It was this feast that the Jewish leaders did not want to miss [Lns]. If a Jew became ritually unclean he would have to postpone celebrating Passover for a month (see Numbers 9:9–11). This phrase may be translated 'to have a share in the Passover festival' or 'to be a part of the Passover festival' [TH].

QUESTION—What words are emphasized in this verse?

The pronoun αὐτόι 'they' is emphatic [AB, Gdt, HTC, Lns, NICNT2, NTC; KJV, NASB, NJB, NRSV, Ph, REB]: 'they themselves did not go into the praetorium' [NICNT2, similarly AB, Gdt, HTC, NTC; KJV, NASB, NJB, NRSV], 'they on their part' [Lns], 'the Jews themselves' [Ph, REB].

18:29 So[a] Pilate[b] went outside to them and said, "What charge[c] do-you-bring against this man?"

LEXICON—a. οὖν (LN 89.50) 'so' [AB, HTC, LN; NCV, NET, NIV, NJB, NLT, NRSV, Ph, REB, TEV], 'therefore' [Gdt, LN, NICNT2, WBC;

NASB], 'then' [LN, NTC; KJV], 'accordingly' [LN, Lns], 'consequently, so then' [LN], not explicit [CEV]. This conjunction indicates result, often implying the conclusion of a process of reasoning [LN].
b. Πιλᾶτος (LN 93.297) (BAGD p. 657): 'Pilate' [BAGD, LN; all translations]. This noun denotes the governor of Judea 26–36 AD who gave the order to crucify Jesus [LN]. This was Pontius Pilate, the procurator of Judea who played a decisive role in Jesus' trial and gave the order for his crucifixion [AB]. Since John assumes that Pilate is known to his readers and this is the first mention of him in John, it may be good to identify him in translation as 'Governor Pilate went outside to them' or 'Pilate, who was governor, went outside to them' [TH].
c. κατηγορία (LN 33.428) (BAGD p. 423): 'charge' [LN, NICNT2, NTC; CEV, NCV, NIV, NJB, NLT, Ph, REB], 'accusation' [AB, BAGD, Gdt, HTC, LN, WBC; KJV, NASB, NET, NRSV]. This noun is also translated as a verb: 'what do you accuse this man of?' [TEV]. This noun is derived from κατηγορέω 'to accuse' (33.427) and denotes the content of the accusation or charge made against someone [LN]. It was the word by means of which a trial was begun [Rd]. Pilate's question about the 'charge' formally opened the court proceedings [Car, EGT, ICC].

QUESTION—What relationship is indicated by the conjunction οὖν?
It indicates the reason that Pilate came out to them [Car, Gdt, ICC, NICNT1, NICNT2].

18:30 They answered him, "If this-man were not doing evil,[a] we-would- not -have-handed- him -over[b] to-you."

TEXT—Instead of κακὸν ποιῶν 'doing evil', some manuscripts read κακοποιῶν 'evil-doing', and others read κακοποιός '(an) evildoer'. GNT reads 'doing evil' with a B rating, indicating that the text is almost certain. Most translations seem to follow the reading '(an) evildoer' [AB, Gdt, HTC, NTC; CEV, NASB, NCV, KJV, NASB, NET, NIV, NJB, NLT, NRSV, Ph, REB].

LEXICON—a. κακός (LN 88.106) (BAGD 1.c. p. 397): 'evil' [BAGD, LN, WBC], 'bad' [LN]. This adjective is also translated as a noun: 'criminal' [CEV, NCV, NET, NIV, NJB, NLT, NRSV, REB], 'evildoer' [Gdt, HTC, NTC; NASB, Ph], 'malefactor' [KJV]; or as a clause: 'what is bad' [NICNT2]. The clause 'If this man were not doing evil' is translated 'if he had not committed a crime' [TEV]. This pronominal adjective pertains to being bad, with the implication of harmful and damaging [LN]. It means what is contrary to law [BAGD].
b. aorist act. indic. of παραδίδωμι (LN 37.111) (BAGD 1.b. p. 614): 'to hand over (to)' [AB, BAGD, HTC, LN, NICNT2, NTC, WBC; NET, NIV, NJB, NLT, NRSV, Ph], 'to bring (to/before)' [CEV, NCV, REB, TEV], 'to deliver (to/up to)' [Gdt; KJV], 'to turn over (to)' [BAGD, LN], 'to give up (a person)' [BAGD]. This verb means to deliver a person into the control of someone else, involving either the handing over of a

presumably guilty person for punishment by authorities or the handing over of an individual to an enemy who will presumably take undue advantage of the victim [LN]. It is a technical term of police and courts meaning 'to hand over into (the) custody (of)' [BAGD].

QUESTION—What is implied by the reply of the accusers?

They imply that they want Pilate to agree with their findings (not stated) and have Jesus executed [EGT, Gdt, Lns, NTC, WBC]. The reply reveals that they wanted him to take their word for the verdict and not begin his own investigation [IVP]. They want to continue in their role as judges and give Pilate the role of executioner [Gdt]. Their response shows that they are unable to bring a water-tight charge against Jesus [BECNT, HTC, NICNT1]. They imply that Jesus is a criminal [NICNT2; CEV, NCV, NET, NIV, NJB, NLT, NRSV, REB]. Pilate should trust them [NICNT1]. The Jews understood that their real case against Jesus—his claim to be the Messiah and the Son of God which was blasphemy—would not convince Pilate that he deserved the death penalty [Rd]. Their reply shows that the Jews were 'petulant' [HTC], 'insolent' [Car, ICC], 'impudent' [Bar, NTC], 'indignant' [Rd], or 'upset' [IVP].

QUESTION—What kind of condition is this reply?

It is a contrary to fact condition [Lns, TH] indicating 'Only if he had done something that is a crime would we bring him to you' [TH], 'He's a criminal! That's why we brought him to you' [CEV], 'Since there is no question about his being an evildoer, we have delivered him up to you' [Lns], 'The only reason we would bring him to you is that he is an evildoer' [TRT].

QUESTION—What is implied by the pronoun οὗτος 'this man'?

It is probably being used in a contemptuous way [AB, NICNT1]: 'this fellow' [AB]. It reveals indifference [My].

18:31 So Pilate said to-them, "You take him and try[a] him by your law." The Jews said to-him, "It-is- not -permitted[b] for-us to-put- anyone -to-death."[c]

LEXICON—a. impera. act. indic. of κρίνω (LN 56.20) (BAGD 4.a.α. p. 451): 'to try (a case)' [**LN**; NJB, REB, TEV], 'to judge' [BAGD, Gdt, HTC, NICNT2, NTC, WBC; CEV, KJV, NASB, NCV, NIV, NLT, Ph], 'to pass judgment on' [AB; NET], 'to decide a legal question, to act as a judge, making a legal decision, to arrive at a verdict' [LN], 'to decide, to hale before a court, to condemn' [BAGD]. This verb means to decide a question of legal right or wrong, and thus determine the innocence or guilt of the accused and assign appropriate punishment or retribution [LN].

b. pres. act. indic. of ἔξεστι [BAGD 2. p. 275]: 'it is permitted' [AB, BAGD, Gdt, WBC; NASB, NLT, NRSV], 'it is allowed' [CEV, NCV, NJB, Ph, REB], 'it is lawful' [HTC, NICNT2; KJV], 'it is possible, it is proper' [BAGD]. The words 'It is not permitted for us' are translated 'We cannot legally (put anyone to death)' [NET], 'we have no right to' [NTC;

NIV], 'only the Romans are permitted to' [NLT]. If the passive expression 'It is not permitted for us' is not allowed in some languages and needs to be changed into an active form, it could be expressed as 'the Roman government will not allow us' [TH].
- c. aorist act. infin. of ἀποκτείνω (LN 20.61) (BAGD 1.a. p. 94): 'to put to death' [AB, Gdt, HTC, WBC; CEV, KJV, NASB, NCV, NET, NJB, NRSV, Ph, REB], 'to kill' [BAGD, LN, NICNT2], 'to execute' [NTC; NIV, NLT]. This verb means to cause someone's death, normally by violent means, with or without intent and with or without legal justification [LN]. It refers to any means of depriving a person of life [BAGD].

QUESTION—To which of 'the Jews' does this phrase refer?

It refers to the Jewish authorities [AB; NET, NLT]: 'the Jewish leaders' [NET, NLT].

QUESTION—What does the reply of the Jews reveal?

Their reply reveals that they were after the death penalty for Jesus [Bar, Gdt, HTC, ICC, IVP, Lns, NICNT1, NTC, Rd].

QUESTION—What words are emphasized in this verse?

The pronoun ὑμεῖς 'you pl.' is emphasized [AB, Bar, Gdt, HTC, ICC, Lns, My, NICNT1, NTC, TH, WBC; NASB, NCV, NET, NIV, NJB, NRSV, Ph, REB, TEV]: 'you yourselves (take him and try him)' [TEV]. The word ἡμῖν 'for us' is placed first in its clause serving to emphasize it [BECNT, ICC, TRT], and serving to contrast themselves with Pilate [BECNT].

18:32 (This happened) to fulfill the word that Jesus had-spoken, indicating[a] by-what-kind-of[b] death he-was-about to-die.

LEXICON—a. pres. act. participle of σημαίνω (LN 33.153) (BAGD): 'to indicate' [AB; NET, NIV, NJB, NRSV, REB, TEV], 'to signify' [Gdt, NICNT2, NTC, WBC; KJV, NASB], 'to show' [HTC], 'to indicate clearly, to make clear' [LN]. This verse is also translated, 'And so what Jesus said about his death would soon come true' [CEV], 'This fulfilled Jesus' prediction about the way he would die' [NLT], 'thus fulfilling Christ's prophecy of the method of his own death' [Ph]. This verb means to cause something to be both specific and clear [LN].
- b. ποῖος (LN 58.30) (BAGD 1.a.γ. p. 684): 'what kind of' [LN; NASB, NET, NIV, NRSV, REB, TEV], 'what sort of' [LN], 'what' [Gdt; KJV], not explicit [CEV]. The words 'by what kind of death' is translated 'by what death he was to/going to/was about to die' [HTC, NICNT2, NTC], 'how he would die' [NCV], 'the way he was going to die' [NJB, similarly NLT], 'the method of his own death' [Ph], 'the sort of death he was to die' [AB, similarly WBC]. This interrogative adjective queries the class or kind of a thing [LN].

QUESTION—This verse begins with the conjunction ἵνα 'to/in order to/so that'. What information is left implicit?
The translations handled this in the following ways: 'This happened so that/to/in order to/in order that' [NTC, TRT; NCV, NET, NIV, TEV], 'This was to' [AB, HTC; NJB, NRSV], 'This (fulfilled)' [NLT], 'thus (fulfilling)' [Ph], 'Thus they (fulfilled)' [REB], 'let the word (be fulfilled)' [NICNT1].

QUESTION—Where did Jesus predict the kind of death he would die?
John may have been thinking about John 12:32–33 'I, when I am lifted up from the earth, will draw all men to myself. He said this to show the kind of death he was going to die' [AB, similarly most other commentaries]. Other passages are 3:14 and 8:28 [NICNT2]. The phrase 'lifted up' was a euphemism for crucifixion [BECNT].

QUESTION—How did this indicate that Jesus would have to die by crucifixion?
Since the Jews were not permitted to put anyone to death, then it would have to be by the Romans and that meant by crucifixion [AB, Gdt, TH].

QUESTION—Why did the Jews want Jesus put to death by crucifixion?
It may have been because they were unsure what the people would do if they themselves killed Jesus by stoning [NICNT2]. Death by crucifixion would place the responsibility on the Romans and not on themselves [CH]. They wanted to show that Jesus was under God's curse as Deuteronomy 21:23 states, '…anyone who is hung on a tree is under God's curse' [NICNT1].

DISCOURSE UNIT—18:33–40 [NICNT1; NET, Ph]. The topic is Jesus before Pilate.

DISCOURSE UNIT—18:33–38 [Rd]. The topic is the first interrogation: Jesus' kingship.

DISCOURSE UNIT—18:33–38a [AB, Car, HTC, WBC]. The topic is Pilate questions Jesus.

18:33 **So Pilate went back[a] into the governor's-residence and summoned[b] Jesus and said to him, "Are you the king of the Jews?"**

LEXICON—a. πάλιν (LN 67.55) (BAGD 1., 2. p. 606): 'back' [AB, BAGD (1); CEV, NCV, NET, NIV, NJB, NLT, Ph, REB, TEV], 'again' [BAGD (2), Gdt, HTC, LN, NICNT2, WBC; KJV, NASB, NRSV], 'once more, anew' [BAGD (2)]. The words 'Pilate went back into the Praetorium' are translated 'Pilate re-entered the governor's residence' [NTC]. This adverb indicates a subsequent point of time involving repetition [LN]. It means 'back' with verbs of going, sending, turning, calling [BAGD (1)]. It means 'again' when someone repeats something he has already done or an event takes place in the same manner as before, or a state of being recurs in the same way as at first [BAGD (2)]. In this context, the meaning of 'back' is in focus [Bar, BECNT, ICC, NICNT1, TRT].

b. aorist act. indic. of φωνέω (LN 33.307) (BAGD 2.b. p. 870): 'to summon' [AB, BAGD, LN, NICNT2, NTC; NASB, NET, NIV, NRSV,

REB], 'to call (someone) to (oneself)' [BAGD; NCV, NJB, Ph], 'to call for (someone) to be brought' [NLT], 'to call over' [CEV], 'to call' [Gdt, HTC, LN; KJV, TEV], not explicit [WBC]. This verb means to communicate directly or indirectly to someone who is presumably at a distance, in order to tell such a person to come [LN].

QUESTION—What is the function of the conjunction οὖν 'so/then/therefore'?
This conjunction is rendered as follows by the translations: 'so' [NET, NJB, Ph], 'then' [AB, NICNT2, NTC; CEV, KJV, NCV, NIV, NLT, NRSV, REB], 'therefore' [Gdt, WBC; NASB], not explicit [HTC; TEV].

QUESTION—What information has been left implicit in John's account?
John has omitted mentioning before Pilate Jesus' claim to be king. This claim was included in all three of the other Gospels [Gdt, NTC, NICNT1, NICNT2]. For example 'We found this man perverting our nation, forbidding us to pay taxes to the emperor, and saying that he himself is the Messiah, a king' Luke 23:2 [Gdt, NTC].

QUESTION—What is Pilate's attitude as he asks this question?
Pilate is incredulous [AB, ICC, Lns, My, NICNT1, Rd]. He is astonished [EGT, Rd, WBC]. Pilate is mocking Jesus [Lns, My, TRT]. Pilate, seeing Jesus as he was, may have been amazed that he claimed to be the king of the Jews [AB]. He expected a straight forward negative response to his question [Gdt]. He may mean, 'You, a prisoner, deserted even by your friends, are a king, are you?' [BECNT], or 'Are you, (whose appearance so belies it), the king of the Jews?' [EGT]. His question could be rephrased 'Do you (of all people/really) claim to be the King of the Jews?' [TRT]. The question is a serious and straightforward investigative opening [IVP]. Pilate needed to know if Jesus posed a political threat to Roman power [BECNT].

QUESTION—What word is emphasized in this verse?
The pronoun σύ 'you' is emphatic [AB, BECNT, ICC, Lns, NICNT1, NTC, TH, TRT]: 'You! Are You the king of the Jews?' [ICC]. Both the presence of the explicit pronoun and its fronted position make it emphatic [TRT]. Pilate may have spoken this word scornfully [BECNT, Car, EGT, TH], or intending ridicule not toward Jesus but toward those who would bring such lofty charges against such a prisoner [NTC]. In all four Gospels this question is the first one Pilate asked Jesus, and in each the pronoun 'you' is emphatic [NICNT1].

18:34 Jesus answered, "Do- you -say this from yourself, or did- others -tell you about me?"
QUESTION—What is Jesus requesting to know from Pilate?
Jesus cannot answer the question until he knows what precisely is being asked [BECNT, Bar, Car]. What Jesus needs to know before he replies to Pilate is what does Pilate mean by the word 'king'. If he means political earthly king, Jesus' answer will be 'No!' But if he means 'king' in the religious sense, that is, 'Messiah' as every believing Jew understood the term, then Jesus must accept this no matter what the consequences [Gdt,

NICNT1, NTC, TRT]. The Jews have given Pilate the impression that Jesus claims to be a political king [Lns].

QUESTION—To whom does the term 'others' refer?

It refers to the Jews [BECNT, Car, EGT, Gdt, HTC, Lns, NICNT2, NTC, Rd, TH, WBC]. Pilate takes it to refer to the Jews as seen in his reply in the next verse, 'Am I a Jew?' [HTC].

QUESTION—What did the question 'Do you say this from yourself?' mean?

This question could be framed, 'Are you the one who thought of this question?' [TH], or 'Did you yourself have reason to ask this question?' [TH], or 'Is that/this your own question?' [TRT; NCV, NLT, REB].

18:35 Pilate answered, "I am not[a] (a) Jew, (am I)? Your people[b] and the chief-priests handed- you -over[c] to-me. What have-you-done?"

LEXICON—a. μήτι (LN 69.16) (BAGD p. 520): 'not' [BAGD, LN]. This question is translated 'I am not a Jew, am I?' [WBC; NASB, NET, NRSV], 'Am I a Jew?' [Gdt, HTC, NICNT2; KJV, NIV NJB, NLT, REB], 'Do you think I am a Jew?' [Ph, TEV], 'Surely you don't think I am a Jew?' [AB], 'I surely am not a Jew, am I?' [NTC], 'I am not Jewish' [NCV], 'You know I am not a Jew!' [CEV], 'What do I have to do with your Jewish subtleties?' [Gdt]. This interrogative particle is a marker of a somewhat more emphatic negative response [LN]. It marks a question as expecting a negative reply [BAGD].

b. ἔθνος (LN 11.55): 'people' [LN; CEV, NCV, NET, NIV, NJB, NLT, Ph, TEV], 'nation' [AB, Gdt, HTC, LN, NICNT2, NTC, WBC; KJV, NASB, NRSV, REB]. This noun denotes the largest unit into which the people of the world are divided on the basis of their constituting a socio-political community [LN].

c. aorist act. indic. of παραδίδωμι (LN 37.111) (BAGD 1.b. p. 614): 'hand (someone) over (to)' [AB, BAGD, HTC, LN, NICNT2, NTC, WBC; NCV, NET, NIV, NJB, NRSV, Ph, TEV], 'to bring (someone) to/before (for trial)' [CEV, NLT, REB], 'to deliver (someone) to' [Gdt; KJV, NASB], 'to turn over (to)' [BAGD, LN], 'to give up (a person)' [BAGD]. This verb means to deliver a person into the control of someone else, involving either the handing over of a presumably guilty person for punishment by authorities or the handing over of an individual to an enemy who will presumably take undue advantage of the victim [LN]. It is a technical term of the police and courts meaning 'to hand over into (the) custody (of)' [BAGD].

QUESTION—What response was expected to Pilate's question 'I am not a Jew, am I?' And what is his attitude?

The question with the interrogative particle μήτι expected a negative reply [AB, BAGD, Bar, CH, Car, Gdt, ICC, LN, Lns, My, NICNT1, NICNT2, NTC, TH, TRT, WBC; CEV, NASB, NCV, NET, NRSV]: 'You know I am not a Jew! [CEV], 'I surely am not a Jew, am I?' [NTC], 'You certainly do not suppose that *I* am a Jew!' [Lns]. With μήτι a question expects a strong

JOHN 18:35

negative response [Car, NICNT1]. Pilate's question is rhetorical and forcefully dissociates himself from 'the Jews' [NICNT2]. There is profound contempt in his question 'I...a Jew?' [Gdt]. The question shows Pilate's contempt [Car, EGT, Gdt, NTC, WBC], disdain [NTC], indignation [Car, WBC], exasperation [BECNT], irritation [Rd]. He denies asking the question from the perspective of a Jew [NTC]. He is claiming that he knows nothing of Jesus besides what the Jewish authorities have told him [AB, TH, WBC].

QUESTION—What is Pilate asking in his question 'What have you done?'

He wants to know on what charges Jesus stands before him [Gdt, NICNT2, Rd, WBC]. Pilate wants to know if Jesus had simply offended the Jews, or if his crime was one that the Romans must address [WBC]. He is not satisfied with the charges of the Sanhedrin against Jesus. There must be something more behind their strong animosity [Car].

QUESTION—What word is emphatic in this verse?

The pronoun ἐγώ 'I' is emphatic [Lns, My, NICNT1]: 'you do not surely suppose that *I*, I your procurator, am a *Jew*?' [My]. The pronoun 'I' is spoken with Roman pride [Lns, My] with scorn on the phrase 'a Jew'. He implies that only a Jew would even think of charging Jesus of desiring to be a king [Lns].

18:36 Jesus answered, "My kingdom[a] is not of[b] this world. If my kingdom were of this world, my servants[c] would-fight[d] so-that I-might- not -be-delivered-over to-the Jews. But now[e] my kingdom is not from-here."

LEXICON—a. βασιλεία (LN 37.64): 'kingdom' [All translations except HTC, NICNT2, NTC], 'kingship' [HTC, NICNT2, NTC], 'rule, reign' [LN]. This noun is derived from the verb βασιλεύω 'to rule, to reign, to be a king' meaning to rule as a king, with the implication of complete authority and the possibility of being able to pass on the right to rule to one's son or near kin. As a noun it denotes 'rule' or 'reign' [LN]. The sense of this noun probably focuses more on the meaning of 'reign, rule' or possibly 'kingship' rather than on the sense of 'realm' [Car, HTC, NICNT1, NICNT2, NTC, WBC]. Kingship refers to Jesus' rule in the hearts of his followers [NTC].

b. ἐκ (LN 90.16, 89.3): 'of' [Gdt, HTC, NTC, WBC; KJV, NASB, NIV, NJB], 'from' [LN (90.16, 89.3), NICNT2; NET, NRSV]. The words 'is not of this world' are translated 'does not belong to this world' [AB; CEV, NCV, REB, TEV], 'is not an earthly kingdom' [NLT], 'is not founded in this world' [Ph]. This preposition indicates the source of an activity or state, with the implication of something proceeding from or out of the source [LN (90.16)], or it indicates the source from which someone or something is physically or psychologically derived [LN (89.3)]. Here it indicates the source or origin from which something emerges [AB, Car, Gdt, HTC, Lns, NICNT1, NTC, TH, WBC]. It also serves to contrast the nature of Jesus' kingdom with earthly kingdoms [AB, EGT, Gdt, HTC].

The words 'not of this world' indicate that Jesus' kingdom is from heaven [NICNT2].
c. ὑπηρέτης (LN 35.20) (BAGD p. 842): 'servant' [BAGD, Gdt, HTC, LN; KJV, NASB, NCV, NET, NIV, Ph], 'follower' [CEV, NLT, NRSV, REB, TEV], 'attendant' [NTC], 'officer' [NICNT2], 'subject' [AB, WBC], 'men' [NJB], 'assistant, helper' [BAGD]. This noun is derived from ὑπηρετέω 'to serve' (35.19) and denotes a person who renders service [LN]. It denotes a person who serves a master or a superior. Here it denotes someone who belongs to a king's entourage [BAGD].
d. imperf. (deponent = active) indic. of ἀγωνίζομαι (LN **39.29**) (BAGD 2.a p. 15): 'to fight' [BAGD, **LN**; all translations], 'to struggle' [BAGD, LN]. This verb means to engage in intense struggle, involving physical or nonphysical force against strong opposition [LN].
e. νῦν (LN 67.38) (BAGD 2. p. 546): 'now' [BAGD, Gdt, LN, NICNT2, NTC; KJV, NIV], 'as it is' [AB, WBC; NASB, NET, NJB, NRSV], 'as things now stand' [BAGD, EGT, ICC], 'in fact' [Ph], not explicit [HTC; CEV, NCV, NLT, REB, TEV]. This adverb indicates a point of time simultaneous with the event of the discourse itself [LN]. Often it is not so much the present time that is meant as much as the situation pertaining at a given moment [BAGD]. It should be taken in the logical sense rather than the temporal sense [AB, Gdt, Lns]. The phase 'but now' contrasts the real situation from the one presupposed by Pilate [AB, TH].

QUESTION—What is one thing Jesus is implying in this verse?
He is admitting that he is a king [Bar, BECNT, Car, CH, EGT, Gdt, Kn, My, NICNT1, NICNT2, NTC, Rd, TH], but he immediately eases the suspicion that his kingship is of the kind that competes with Rome [Bar, CH, HTC, Rd].

QUESTION—What kind of condition is Jesus statement, 'If my kingdom were of this world, my servants would fight'?
It is a contrary to fact condition in which both the conditional and the consequence clauses are not true (Jesus' kingdom was *not* from this world and his servants did *not* fight) [AB, Lns, NICNT2]. The consequence indicates that they 'would fight/would be fighting' [AB, HTC, Lns, NICNT1, NICNT2, WBC; KJV, NASB, NCV, NET, NIV, NLT, NRSV, REB, TEV), or that they 'would have fought/would have been fighting' [Gdt, NTC; CEV, NJB, Ph].

QUESTION—What did Jesus mean by the word ὑπηρέται 'servants'?
Jesus was referring to angels in the sense of Matthew 26:53 'Do you think I cannot call on my Father, and he will at once put at my disposal more than twelve legions of angels?' [ICC, TRT]. His servants are his disciples [Bar, CH, IVP, Kn, My, TRT; CEV, NLT, NRSV, REB, TEV], not the angels [My]. They are an imaginary force [Lns, NICNT1, Rd], not angels, or disciples since Jesus was speaking hypothetically [Lns, Rd]. They are officers like the officers of the chief priests [BECNT, NTC, NICNT2] in addition to his disciples [NICNT2].

QUESTION—What words are emphasized in this verse?
The possessive pronoun ἐμή 'my' is emphasized [IVP, Lns, My, NTC]: 'the kingship that is mine' [Lns]. The triple mention of 'my kingdom' not being 'of this world' serves to emphasize the fact [My].

18:37 So Pilate said to-him, "So- you are (a) king -then?"[a] Jesus answered, "You say that I-am (a) king. For[b] this I have-been-born and for this I-have-come into the world that I-might-bear-witness to-the truth. Everyone who is of[c] the truth listens-to[d] my voice."[e]

LEXICON—a. οὐκοῦν (LN **69.12**) (BAGD 2. p. 592): 'so then' [BAGD], 'so' [BAGD], 'not' [**LN**]. Pilate's question is translated as follows: 'So you are a king' [CEV], 'So you are a king?' [HTC, NTC; NASB, NLT, NRSV], 'So you are a king!' [NICNT2; NCV, NET], 'So then, you are a king?' [AB; NJB], 'You are a king, then!' [NIV, REB], 'So you are a king, then?' [WBC], 'Are you a king, then?' [Gdt; KJV, TEV], 'So you are a king, are you?' [Ph], 'are you not a king?' [**LN**]. This conjunction indicates that a somewhat more emphatic affirmative response is expected to a question [LN]. When this word is used in a question it indicates that the question has inferential force [BAGD]. This is the only occurrence of this word in the NT. It serves to return the conversation to its main theme after a gap [AB, TH], back to Pilate's question 'Are you the king of the Jews?' [TH].

b. εἰς (LN **89.57**) (BAGD 4.f. p. 229): 'for the purpose of' [BAGD, **LN**], 'in order to' [BAGD, LN], 'to' [BAGD]. The statement 'For this I have been born' [NASB, similarly HTC, NICNT2; NJB, NRSV] is also translated 'For this purpose I came into the world' [**LN**; similarly NTC, WBC; TEV], 'The reason why I have been born' [AB; similarly NET, NIV], 'the reason for my birth' [Ph], 'I was born…to (tell about the truth)' [CEV, similarly Gdt; NLT], 'to this end was I born' [KJV], 'this is why I was born' [NCV], 'My task is to (bear witness to the truth). For this I was born' [REB]. This preposition is a marker of intent, often with the implication of expected result [LN]. It indicates the goal or purpose of an action [BAGD].

c. ἐκ (LN 89.3): 'of' [Gdt, HTC, NTC, WBC; KJV, NASB, NCV, NET] 'from' [LN, NICNT2]. The words 'Everyone who is of the truth' are translated 'all who are not deaf to the truth' [REB], 'Everyone who belongs to the truth' [AB; CEV, similarly NRSV, TEV], 'Everyone on the side of truth' [Car; NIV, similarly NJB], 'All who love the truth' [NLT, similarly Ph]. This preposition indicates the source from which someone or something is physically or psychologically derived [LN]. The phrase 'to be of' indicates 'to belong to' [AB, EGT, NICNT2, TH; CEV, NRSV, TEV], or 'to owe one's spiritual origin to' [Lns, My, NTC]. It indicates the moral propensity to receive the truth and put oneself under its authority [Gdt].

d. pres. act. indic. of ἀκούω (LN 31.56): 'to listen to' [AB, LN, NTC, WBC; NCV, NET, NIV, NJB, NRSV, REB, TEV], 'to hear' [Gdt, HTC, NICNT2; KJV, NASB], 'to know' [CEV], 'to recognize' [NLT, Ph], 'to obey' [EGT], 'to accept, to listen and respond, to pay attention and respond, to heed' [LN]. This verb means to believe something and to respond to it on the basis of having heard [LN]. It means to listen with understanding and acceptance [AB], or to hear with appreciation and obedience [ICC].

e. φωνή (LN 33.103) (BAGD 2.a. p. 871): 'voice' [BAGD, LN; all translations except NCV, NIV, NLT, TEV]. The following translated the noun 'voice' as indicating its speaker 'listens to me' [NCV, NIV, TEV], 'recognize that what I say is true' [NLT]. This noun denotes the human voice as an instrument of communication [LN]. The expression 'to listen to someone's voice' means 'to follow someone' [BAGD].

QUESTION—What is implied by Pilate's question 'So you are a king then'?

The question expects an affirmative reply [Bar, EGT, Gdt, HTC, ICC, My, NICNT1, NICNT2, Rd, TH, TRT, WBC; CEV, KJV, NASB, NCV, NET, NJB, NRSV, Ph, REB, TEV]: 'So you are a king' [CEV]. There is a note in it of, incredulity [ICC, Lns], irony [NICNT1], surprise [Gdt, Lns, My, NTC], or arrogant scorn [My]. He means to say, 'It is, then, not false, the claim that is imputed to you?' [Gdt].

QUESTION—What did Jesus mean by his reply to Pilate, 'You say that I am a king'?

1. He is not denying that he is a king but it is not his choice of word to describe his role [AB, ICC, IVP, NICNT1, NICNT2; NCV, REB]: '"King" is your word' [REB], 'You are the one saying I am a king' [NCV, similarly NJB]. It is as though he were saying, 'It is you who say it, not I' [AB]. Jesus does not warm to Pilate's suggestion nor does he completely deny it [NICNT1]. Jesus admits to a kingship, but not to the word 'king' as Pilate uses it—this was too loaded with misunderstanding [IVP]. He adds his own explanatory words [ICC].

2. He is agreeing with Pilate [Car, CH, EGT, Gdt, Lns, NTC, Rd, WBC; NASB, NIV, Ph]: 'You are right in saying I am a king' [NIV], 'Indeed I am a king' [Ph], 'You say it well, that I am a king' [Gdt]. After admitting his role as king, he goes on to define that role more specifically [CH]. He meant, 'Yes, indeed; it is even as you have just now affirmed' [NTC]. Jesus' response is unambiguously positive, but he goes on to describe the nature of his reign [Car].

QUESTION—What does 'truth' mean?

It refers to the domain of pure eternal reality in contrast to what is merely transient [Bar]. It is an account of what actually happened in any particular case [LN], or refers to anything that has spiritual reality [CH]. The Greek term ἀλήθεια meant a correct perspective on reality. The Romans thought of the word *veritas* as meaning an accurate, factual account of the facts. The Hebrew Bible portrayed truth as being God's faithfulness to his covenant of redemption. Jesus intended the meaning to be the revelation of God's covenant character—that which was fully shown in his own life and ministry [Kn].

QUESTION—What words are emphasized in this verse?

The pronoun 'you' is emphasized in the question 'So *you* are a king, then?' [ICC, Lns, My, NICNT1, TH]. This pronoun is spoken with contempt [ICC, My], and incredulity, '*you*, poor prisoner' [ICC]. The pronoun 'you', in the statement 'You say that I am a king', is emphasized [NICNT1, TH; NJB]: 'It is you who say I am a king' [NJB]. The pronoun 'I' in the statement, 'For this I have been born' is emphatic [ICC, Lns, My, NICNT1]: 'I for my part have been born to this end' [Lns]. The pronoun 'I (have been born)' of Jesus' reply stands out in sharp contrast with the pronoun 'you (say)' referring to Pilate [NICNT1]. The emphatic repetition of the phrase 'for this (I have been born)…for this (I have come)' [Lns, My, NICNT2, Rd, TRT] makes it the most definite statement of Jesus' mission in the NT [NICNT2].

DISCOURSE UNIT—18:38–40 [IVP]. The topic is Pilate finds Jesus innocent.

18:38a Pilate said to him, "What is truth?"

QUESTION—What is the function of this rhetorical question?

Pilate is turning away from the truth [AB]. He is indifferent [Gdt, Lns, Rd] and frivolously skeptical of the truth [Gdt]. He dismisses the subject [BECNT, IVP, NICNT1, NICNT2] and ends the conversation [NICNT2]. He is cynical [Car, NTC] and skeptical [Lns, NTC] and no longer interested in the subject [Kn, NTC]. He does not believe that anyone can give a satisfactory answer to his question [WBC]. He is flippant and his reply may show his disappointment and possibly his bitterness [BECNT]. He may be wistful [CH, ICC, NICNT1] or jesting [NICNT1]. His question reveals his contemptuous depreciation of the question [My].

DISCOURSE UNIT—18:38b–19:16 [Kn]. The topic is Pilate and the people.

DISCOURSE UNIT—18:38b–19:16a [GNT; CEV, NRSV, TEV]. The topic is Jesus sentenced to die.

DISCOURSE UNIT—18:38b–40 [AB, Car, HTC, WBC]. The topic is Pilate tries to release Jesus [AB, HTC], Pilate declares that Jesus is innocent [WBC], Barabbas [Car], Jesus is sentenced to death [CEV, NRSV, TEV].

18:38b After he-had-said this he-went-out again to the Jews and told them, "I find[a] no guilt[b] in him.

LEXICON—a. pres. act. indic. of εὑρίσκω (LN 27.27) (BAGD 2. p. 325): 'to find' [BAGD, LN; all translations except NLT], 'to discover' [BAGD, LN], not explicit [NLT]. This verb figuratively means to discover based on reflection, observation, examination, or investigation. When speaking of the result of judicial investigation it means 'to find a cause for putting to death' [BAGD].

b. αἰτία (LN **56.4, 88.315**) (BAGD 2.a. p. 26): 'guilt' [**LN** (88.315); NASB], 'case (against)' [AB, LN (56.4); NJB, NRSV, REB], 'crime' [HTC, NTC; NLT], 'reason for condemning' [LN (88.315); TEV], 'reason for an accusation' [**LN** (56.4)], 'basis for an accusation' [LN (56.4); NET], 'probable cause' NICNT2, 'ground for a charge' [WBC], 'fault' [KJV], 'cause' [LN (56.4)], 'wrongdoing' [LN (88.315)], 'charge, ground for complaint' [BAGD]. The statement 'I find no guilt in him' is translated 'I don't find this man guilty of anything!' [CEV], 'I find in him no fault (at all)' [KJV], 'I find nothing against this man' [NCV], 'I find no basis for a charge against him' [NIV], 'I cannot find any reason to condemn him' [TEV]. This noun is also translated as an adjective: 'He is not guilty of any crime' [NLT], 'I find nothing criminal about him at all' [Ph]. This noun is a technical legal term and denotes the basis of or grounds for an accusation in court [LN (56.4)], or it denotes guilt as a basis or reason for condemnation [LN (88.315)]. It indicates 'the crime of which the prisoner is charged' [AB].

QUESTION—What words are emphasized in this verse?

The pronoun ἐγώ 'I' is emphatic [AB, EGT, Gdt, Lns, NICNT2; REB]: 'For my part, I find no case against this man' [AB, similarly Lns], 'As for me I find no crime in him' [Gdt]. He meant, '*I* find none, but perhaps *you* might' [NICNT2]. The adjective οὐδεμίαν 'no (guilt)' is emphatic [NICNT1, NICNT2, NTC; KJV, Ph]: 'no crime whatever do I find in him' [NTC], 'no fault (at all)' [KJV], 'I find nothing criminal about him at all' [Ph]. It means 'no cause whatsoever' [NICNT2]. It is placed forward in the Greek for emphasis [NICNT1].

DISCOURSE UNIT—18:39–40 [Rd]. The topic is Jesus or Barabbas?

18:39 But you have (a) custom[a] that I-should-release one-man for-you at the Passover. So do-you-want me-to-release to-you the king of-the Jews?"

LEXICON—a. συνήθεια (LN 41.25) (BAGD 2.b. p. 789): 'custom' [BAGD, LN; all translations except CEV, Ph], 'arrangement' [Ph], 'habit, usage' [BAGD, LN]. The statement 'you have a custom' is translated 'I usually (set a prisoner free for you)' [CEV], 'I have an arrangement (with you)' [Ph]. This noun denotes a pattern of behavior more or less fixed by tradition and generally sanctioned by the society [LN].

QUESTION—Was this a custom of the Jews or of Pilate?

Since a literal translation may imply that the Jews themselves released the prisoner, it may be necessary to translate, 'It is customary for me to set free a prisoner for you during the Passover' [TH].

QUESTION—Is there a problem between the identity of the pronoun 'you' and the title 'King of the Jews' in Pilate's question 'do you want me to release to you the King of the Jews'?

Since the pronoun 'you' refers to the Jews as does the phrase in the title 'King of the Jews', it may be necessary to translate, 'Do you want me to do you the favor of setting free your king?' Otherwise readers may assume that Pilate was addressing a group of non-Jews [TH].

QUESTION—What is Pilate's attitude as he asks this question?
He uses the term 'King of the Jews' ironically [Gdt, WBC] and sarcastically [Gdt, IVP] but he is addressing the Jews, not Jesus whom he respects [Gdt]. He mocks the Jews [BECNT, ICC, Lns, My, NTC, Rd] thinking that it was ridiculous to suggest that this prisoner, bound and helpless, was the only king they could put forward [NTC]. Pilate thinks that the charge of the Jews against Jesus was absurd [BECNT, Rd]. He was trying to antagonize the Jewish authorities [Car]. He thought that the use of the full title 'King of the Jews' would serve to sway the Jews in Jesus' favor [NICNT1].

18:40 **Then they-shouted^a back/again,^b "Not this-man but Barabbas."^c Now Barabbas was (a) robber.^d**

LEXICON—a. aorist act. indic. of κραυγάζω (LN 33.83) (BAGD 2.a. p. 449): 'to shout' [AB, LN, WBC; NCV, NET, NIV, NJB, NLT, NRSV, REB], 'to shout out' [Ph], 'to cry out' [BAGD, Gdt, HTC, LN, NICNT2, NTC; NASB], 'to cry' [KJV], 'to scream' [BAGD, LN]. This verb is also translated as a phrase: '(They answered him) with a shout' [TEV]. This verb means to shout or cry out, with the possible implication of the unpleasant nature of the sound [LN].
   b. πάλιν (LN 67.55): 'back' [AB; NCV, NET, NIV, NLT, REB], 'again' [Gdt, HTC, LN, NICNT2, WBC; KJV, NASB, Ph], 'once more' [NTC], not explicit [CEV, NJB]. This adverb is also translated as a phrase: '(they shouted) in reply' [NRSV], or a verb: 'They answered (him)' [TEV].
   c. Βαραββᾶς (LN 93.59) (BAGD 1. p. 133): Barabbas' [BAGD, LN; all translations]. This noun denotes a prisoner released by Pilate at the request of the Jews during the trial of Jesus [LN].
   d. λῃστής (LN **39.37**) (BAGD 2. p. 473): 'robber' [Gdt, HTC, NICNT2; KJV, NASB, NCV], 'bandit' [AB; NJB, NRSV, Ph, REB, TEV], 'revolutionary' [BAGD, Kn, Rd; NET, NLT], 'insurrectionist' [BAGD, BECNT, Kn, LN], 'terrorist' [Car, NICNT2; CEV], 'rebel' [LN, Rd; WBC], 'brigand' [NICNT1]. This noun is also translated as a verb phrase: '(Barabbas) had taken part in a rebellion' [NIV]. It is derived from the noun στάσις 'insurrection' (39.34), and denotes a person who engages in insurrection [LN]. The literal meaning of λῃστής is 'one who seizes plunder' [BECNT, Car, WBC]. This word may have been used to describe guerrilla fighters [Car, Kn, TH] who were involved in subversive activity against the Roman government [TH]. This term does not always mean 'robber' but simply a violent man in general [Gdt]. Mark and Luke record that he had taken part in an insurrection [Gdt, IVP, NICNT2] in which murder had been committed [Gdt, NICNT2].

QUESTION—What attitude is understood of the term τοῦτον 'this (man)'?
It is probably spoken with disrespect [NTC, TRT] or contempt [TRT]. It was a derogatory reference to Jesus. The crowd will not tarnish their lips by speaking his name [Lns].

QUESTION—What is indicated by the presence of the article with the name τὸν Βαραββᾶν '(not this man but) *the* Barabbas'?
The definite article indicates that he was 'the well-known Barabbas' [ICC].
QUESTION—What is indicated by the conjunction δέ 'now'?
It indicates that the statement ('Barabbas was a robber') is parenthetical [AB, Lns; NCV, NET, NLT, TEV], or an aside [NICNT2].
QUESTION—Does the word πάλιν have its usual meaning of 'again' or 'back' as, 'in reply'?
1. It means 'back' or 'in reply' [AB, NICNT2; NCV, NET, NIV, NLT, NRSV, REB, TEV]: 'They shouted in reply' [NRSV], 'They answered him with a shout' [TEV]. The probable meaning is that they shouted back in response [NICNT2].
2. It means that they cried out a second time [EGT, Gdt, HTC, ICC, Lns, My, NICNT2, NTC, WBC; KJV, NASB, Ph]: 'They cried out *once more*' [NTC]. It presupposes a previous outcry by the crowd [ICC, Lns, My].
3. Probably the best interpretation is that this word is a translation of the Aramaic inferential conjunction *tubh* meaning 'thereupon' [NICNT1].

DISCOURSE UNIT—19:1–42 [CH]. The topic is Jesus' crucifixion and burial.

DISCOURSE UNIT—19:1–16 [Lns; Ph]. The topic is Pilate's efforts to save Jesus.

DISCOURSE UNIT—19:1–16a [AB, BECNT, Car; NASB, NET, NIV, NLT]. The topic is the trial of Jesus before Pilate [AB], Pilate tries to release Jesus [NET], Jesus is sentenced to be crucified [BECNT, Car; NIV, NLT].

DISCOURSE UNIT—19:1–15 [NASB]. The topic is the crown of thorns.

DISCOURSE UNIT—19:1–6a [NICNT1]. The topic is behold the man.

DISCOURSE UNIT—19:1–5 [Rd]. The topic is here is the man.

DISCOURSE UNIT—19:1–3 [HTC, IVP, Kn, WBC]. The topic is scourging and crowning with thorns.

19:1 So then[a] Pilate took[b] Jesus and whipped[c] him.
LEXICON—a. τότε (LN 67.47) (BAGD 2. p. 824): 'then' [AB, BAGD, Gdt, HTC, LN, NICNT2, NTC, WBC; KJV, NASB, NCV, NET, NJB, NIV, NLT, NRSV, Ph, TEV], 'now' [REB], not explicit [CEV]. This adverb indicates a point of time subsequent to another point of time [AB, LN]. It introduces that which follows in time. The phrase τότε οὖν means '(so) then' [BAGD]. The phrase indicates that what now happens is sequentially next in the narrative [NICNT1].
    b. aorist act. indic. of λαμβάνω (LN 18.1) (BAGD 1.a. p. 464): 'to take' [All translations except CEV, NCV, NJB, NLT], 'to take hold of, to grasp' [BAGD, LN], 'to grab' [LN], 'to take in the hand' [BAGD], not explicit [CEV, NLT]. This active verb is also translated passively: '(Pilate ordered that Jesus) be taken away' [NCV], 'Pilate…had Jesus taken away'

[NJB]. This verb means to take hold of something or someone, with or without force [LN]. Here the combination 'to take and whip' means that 'he had Jesus scourged' [BAGD]. As in the following verb Pilate did not do this himself, but caused it to be done [BAGD, Lns, NTC].

c. aorist act. indic. of μαστιγόω (LN **19.9**) (BAGD 1. p. 495): 'to whip' [LN], 'to scourge' [Gdt, HTC, NTC; KJV, NASB], 'to beat with a whip' [LN]. This active verb is also translated passively: '(Pilate)...had him whipped' [**LN**; TEV], '(Pilate) gave orders for Jesus to be beaten with a whip' [CEV], '(Pilate) ordered that Jesus...be whipped' [NCV], '(Pilate)...had him flogged' [NICNT2, WBC; NIV, similarly NLT, NRSV, REB, Ph], '(Pilate)...had him flogged severely' [NET], '(Pilate)...had Jesus/him...scourged' [AB; NJB]. This verb means to beat severely with a whip [LN]. It refers to the beating given those condemned to death [BAGD]. The μαστιγόω was severe but not fatal [CH]. There were three Roman forms of bodily punishment, the *fustigatio* or 'beating', the *flagellatio* or 'flogging', and the *verberatio* or 'scourging' [AB, BECNT]. The latter two were more severe and were a part of capital punishment [AB]. This type, the *fustigation*, was the least severe form [BECNT, Car, IVP]. Pilate ordered this done rather than do it himself (see verse 2) [AB, CH, Gdt, ICC, IVP, Lns, My, NTC, TH, TRT]. Jesus was again whipped after the sentence of crucifixion was given and that time with the most severe form, the *verberatio* [BECNT, Car]. The *verberatio* was so severe that it sometimes killed the prisoner [EGT, Car, CH, Gdt, IVP, Kn, NICNT1, NTC]. The whip used in this punishment was made up of several thongs. To each one of these was attached pieces of bone or metal. It could lay open a man's back making it a bleeding pulp [NICNT1].

QUESTION—What is indicated by the statement 'Pilate took Jesus'?

The action puts the responsibility for what happens to Jesus on Pilate. He had told the Jews to *take* Jesus and try him by their law (18:31). He tries to do the same in 19:6. Finally in 19:16 the Jews *take* him to be crucified. The responsibility for the crucifixion belonged to both Pilate and the Jews, but most heavily on the Jews [HTC]. This verb may mean 'to take away' in the sense that Pilate ordered the soldiers to take Jesus away and whip him. If it is not taken passively like this, it is redundant and could be rendered 'Then Pilate had Jesus whipped' [TH].

QUESTION—Why was Jesus whipped?

In the Roman penal code, scourging necessarily preceded crucifixion. Jesus also predicted this sequence in Matthew 20:19 and Luke 18:33 [Gdt]. Pilate was hoping to appeal to the sympathy of the people and so avert having to have Jesus crucified [Car, EGT, Gdt, ICC, IVP, Lns, My, NICNT1, NTC, Rd, WBC]. Pilate was not using the whipping as a prelude to crucifixion [Lns, NTC, WBC], because he still tries to release Jesus in 19:12. In 19:5 he seems to be trying to arouse sympathy for Jesus. Pilate was trying to avoid the crucifixion and at the same time appease Annas, Caiaphas and the others

[NTC]. He was proposing the whipping as an alternative to crucifixion not as an accompaniment [WBC].

19:2 And the soldiers wove[a] (a) crown[b] of thorns[c] (and) put- (it) -on his head and put-on[d] him (in a) purple[e] robe.[f] **19:3** They were-coming-up to him saying, "Hail,[g] King of-the Jews!" And they-were-giving- him -slaps[h] (in the face).

LEXICON—a. aorist act. participle of πλέκω (LN 49.27) (BAGD p. 667): 'to weave' [AB, BAGD, LN, NICNT2, WBC; NLT, NRSV], 'to braid' [LN; NET], 'to plait' [BAGD, Gdt, HTC, NTC; REB], 'to twist (something) into' [NJB, Ph], 'to twist together' [NASB, NIV], 'to platt' [KJV]. The statement 'The soldiers wove a crown of thorns' is translated 'The soldiers made a crown out of thorn branches' [CEV, similarly NCV, TEV]. This verb means to interlace strands (of material) either by braiding or weaving [LN].

b. στέφανος (LN 6.192) (BAGD 1. p. 767): 'crown' [BAGD, LN; all translations], 'wreath' [BAGD, LN]. This noun denotes a wreath consisting either of foliage or of precious metals formed to resemble foliage and worn as a symbol of honor, victory, or as a badge of high office [LN]. The crown or wreath was of thorny branches rather than of thorns themselves [TH; NCV, TEV]. It may be helpful to translate 'wove some thorny branches into the shape of a ring that looked like a king's crown' [TRT].

c. ἄκανθα (LN 3.17) (BAGD p. 29): 'thorn' [BAGD, Gdt, HTC, LN; all translations except CEV, NCV, Ph, TEV], 'thorny branches' [NCV, TEV], 'thorn branches' [CEV], 'thorn-twigs' [Ph], 'thorn plant' [BAGD, LN], 'thistle, brier' [LN]. This noun denotes any kind of thorny plant [BAGD, LN], especially the common weed Ononis spinosa, cammock [BAGD]. Others site the Spina Christi or Palinrus Shrub [NTC], the Poterium Spinosum L [AB], the Lycium spinosum that grows profusely around Jerusalem [Gdt], the acanthus shrub [Kn], or de morte Christi [EGT]. These thorns may have been from the date palm that had thorns near the base [BECNT, Car, IVP]. The thorns could have been up to 12 inches long [BECNT, Car, IVP]. Thorns and thistles were the result of the curse (Genesis 3:18) and Jesus is here shown bearing the curse that weighs down humanity [NTC].

d. aorist act. indic. of περιβάλλω (LN 49.3) (BAGD 1.b.δ. p. 646): 'to put (something) on (someone)' [BAGD; CEV, KJV, NASB, NLT, TEV], 'to throw (something) around (someone)' [AB, BAGD, NTC; Ph], 'to put (something) around (someone)' [BAGD, WBC; NCV], 'to wrap (something) around (someone)'[NICNT2], 'to clothe' [LN; NET, NIV], 'to dress' [NJB, NRSV], 'to array' [Gdt, HTC], 'to robe' [REB]. This verb means to put on clothes, implying the clothing being completely around someone or something [LN].

e. πορφυροῦς (LN **79.38**) (BAGD p. 694): 'purple' [BAGD, **LN**; all translations except AB], 'royal purple' [AB]. This adjective indicates the color purple (having the symbolic value of royal status). Here the use of πορφυροῦς may refer more to the symbolic value of the color than to the color itself. Therefore, it may be important to include some marginal note indicating the significance of the color [LN]. It is important that the robe resembled a king's robe. If the receptor language does not have a word for purple, you could say 'a robe like a king's robe' [TRT]. In some languages there may be no specific word for purple in which case 'dark red' or 'bluish red' may be used [TH].

f. ἱμάτιον (LN 6.172) (BAGD 2. p. 376): 'robe' [BAGD, Gdt, HTC, LN; all translations except AB, WBC; REB], 'cloak' [AB, BAGD, LN, WBC; REB], 'coat' [LN], 'garment' [BAGD]. This noun denotes any type of outer garment [BAGD, LN]. This garment may have been the cloak worn by military officers [ICC, Lns, NICNT1] known as the *chlamys* [NICNT1].

g. pres. act. impera. of χαίρω (LN 33.22) (BAGD 2.a. p. 874): 'hail' [BAGD, LN; all translations except AB; CEV, TEV], 'All hail' [AB], 'Long live!' [TEV], 'Hey, you!' [CEV], 'greetings' [LN]. This verb means to employ a formalized expression of greeting, implying a wish for happiness on the part of the person greeted [LN]. It is used as a formula of greeting or address, often on meeting people, 'welcome, good day, hail (to you), I am glad to see you, how do you do' or even 'hello'. Here it is used as a sarcastic greeting as to a king [BAGD]. This greeting was an imitation of the salutation given to the Roman Emperor, *Ave, Caesar* [BECNT, EGT, ICC, IVP, Kn, WBC]. 'Hail King of the Jews' may require different translations such as 'May you, the King of the Jews, be prosperous!', 'May you, as the King of the Jews, rule forever!', 'May you, the King of the Jews, conquer all your enemies!', or 'King of the Jews, may your right arm always be strong!' [TH].

h. imperf. act. indic. of δίδωμι ῥάπισμα (BAGD p. 193, 734): 'to give (someone) a slap in the face' [AB, BAGD (p. 734), NICNT2; NASB], 'to slap (someone) in/across the face' [NTC; NJB, NLT], 'to strike (someone) in/on the face' [NET, NIV, NRSV, REB], 'to hit in the face' [NCV], 'to slap (someone)' [BAGD (p. 193); TEV], 'to slap with open hands' [Ph], 'to hit (someone) with the fist' [CEV], 'to smite (someone) with the hand' [KJV], 'to strike with the hand' [HTC], 'to strike with rods' [Gdt]. The imperfect aspect indicates repeated action [AB, BECNT, Kn, Lns, NICNT2, NTC, TH, TRT, WBC; NCV, NET, NJB, NRSV, Ph, REB]: 'they struck him repeatedly' [NET], or inceptive action [NASB]: 'they began...to give him slaps in the face' [NASB]. The hitting is apparently done with the hands [EGT, Lns, HTC, ICC, NICNT1; KJV, Ph].

QUESTION—Was the action of the soldiers sincere or mocking?

The soldiers intended to mock Jesus as a king even though he was a criminal condemned to crucifixion [AB, Bar, Car, CH, EGT, ICC, Gdt, HTC, Kn,

Lns, NICNT1, NICNT2, NTC, Rd, TRT, WBC]. The whole scene was a parody more on Jewish royalty and less on Jesus personally [EGT, Gdt, NICNT1] whom the soldiers did not know [Gdt]. The mocking was aimed at both Jesus and the Jews [NICNT2]. Pilate thinks it ridiculous that the pitiful beaten figure of Jesus could actually be the king of the subjugated Jewish people [NICNT2]. Their mockery in reality is reversed since Jesus is the very person they sarcastically claim that he is [Kn].

QUESTION—Of what was the crown of thorns symbolic?

It was symbolic of a king's crown [AB, BECNT, Car, CH, IVP, WBC], the laurel wreath worn by the emperor [AB, TH, TRT], or a victor's wreath [NICNT1]. It was a mockery of Jesus' royal dignity [Rd]. It symbolized the radiate crown worn by rulers [Bar]. In some languages that lack a term for crown this may be translated as 'thorny branches woven into a circle' or 'twisted into a circle' [TH].

QUESTION—Of what was the purple robe symbolic?

It was symbolic of the royal robes of a king [AB, BECNT, Car, CH, Gdt, Lns, NICNT1, NTC, Rd, TH, TRT, WBC]: 'cloak of royal purple' [AB].

QUESTION—What is the significance of the definite article and the nominative case with the title 'King of the Jews' (literally, Hail *the* King of the Jews)?

It indicates that they are mocking and expressing contempt [NICNT1]. The article before the word 'King' suggests derision [ICC]. It could be rendered, 'Hail, you "King"!' [AB, Bar, NICNT1].

DISCOURSE UNIT—19:4–8 [IVP]. The topic is Pilate declares Jesus innocent.

DISCOURSE UNIT—19:4–7 [HTC, Kn, WBC]. The topic is Pilate's presentation of Jesus [HTC, WBC], rejecting God's son [Kn].

19:4 Pilate went out again and said to-them, "Look I-bring him out to-you so-that you-may-know that I-find no[a] fault in him."

LEXICON—a. οὐδεμία (LN 92.23) (BAGD): 'no' [KJV, NASB], 'none, nothing' [LN]. The statement 'I find no fault/guilt in him' [KJV, NASB] is also translated 'I find no case against him' [AB; NJB, NRSV, REB], 'I find no crime in him' [Gdt, HTC, NTC], 'I do not find him guilty' [CEV, similarly NLT], 'I find nothing against him' [NCV], 'I find no reason for an accusation against him' [NET], 'I find no basis for a charge against him' [NIV], 'I find in him no probable cause' [NICNT2], 'I find nothing criminal about him at all' [Ph], 'I cannot find any reason to condemn him' [TEV], 'I find no ground for complaint against him' [WBC]. This adjective indicates a negative reference to an entity, event, or state [LN]. This was Pilate's second 'not guilty' decision (see 18:38) [AB, Bar, HTC, IVP, NICNT1, NICNT2, TH].

QUESTION—Where did Pilate come out of?

He came out of the praetorium [Car, Gdt, ICC, TRT].

QUESTION—What is the function of the particle ἴδε 'Look'?
    It is used to draw the attention of the listeners [BAGD (1. p. 369), TH] so it may be better to translated this as 'Listen!' [TH].
QUESTION—What was Pilate's intention in presenting Jesus like this?
    He was hoping to arouse pity for him among the Jews [ICC, My, NTC]. He wanted to gain the Jews' approval to release Jesus [WBC]. He wanted to convince them of the absurdity of their accusation against him [BECNT, Lns, My, NICNT1, Rd]. He meant to go no further with this case [Gdt].
QUESTION—What word is emphasized in this verse?
    The adjective οὐδεμία 'no' is emphatic [Lns; Ph]: 'I find nothing criminal about him at all' [Ph]. Pilate did not find *a single fault* against Jesus to support the death sentence [Lns].

19:5 So Jesus came-out, wearing^a the crown of-thorns^b and the purple robe. Pilate said to them, "Here-is^c the^d man."

LEXICON—a. pres. act. participle of φορέω (LN 49.11) (BAGD 1. p. 865): 'to wear' [BAGD, LN; all translations except NTC], 'to still wear' [NTC]. This verb means to put on and to wear clothes [LN]. It means 'to bear for a considerable time' or 'regularly', hence 'to wear' [BAGD].
  b. ἀκάνθινος (LN 3.18) (BAGD p. 29): 'of thorns' [LN; all translations except AB, NICNT2, NTC; Ph], 'thorny' [AB, BAGD, LN, NICNT2, NTC], 'thorn' [Ph]. This adjective is derived from ἄκανθα 'thorn plant', pertaining to being made or consisting of thorns [LN].
  c. ἰδού (LN 91.13) (BAGD 2. p. 371): 'here is' [BAGD, HTC; CEV, NCV, NIV, NJB, NRSV, REB], 'look, here is' [NET, NLT, Ph, TEV], 'look' [LN, NICNT2, NTC, WBC], 'behold' [AB, Gdt; KJV, NASB]. This particle functions as a prompter of attention [LN, TH], that serves also to emphasize the following statement [LN].
  d. ὁ (LN 92.24) (BAGD II.1.a.α. p. 550): 'the' [BAGD, LN; all translations]. This article indicates a reference to an entity, event, or state, clearly identified by the linguistic or non-linguistic context of the utterance [LN]. The individualizing article stands before a common noun which, in a given situation, is given special attention as the only or obvious one of its kind. Here it means 'here is this (wretched) man' [BAGD].
  e. ἄνθρωπος (LN 9.24) (BAGD 4.b. p. 69): 'man' [BAGD, LN; all translations]. This noun denotes an adult male person of marriageable age [LN]. Here it connotes contempt [BAGD].
QUESTION—What did Pilate mean by his statement, 'Here is the man'?
    Pilate wanted to show the harmlessness of Jesus [Car, Lns, My, TRT, WBC]. He is still trying to arouse sympathy for Jesus [CH, ICC, NTC]. He meant: 'See the poor fellow!' [ICC], 'Here is the man in all of his absurd unworthiness and dejection, [Rd], how can he be a threat to the empire?' [Car, Rd]. He says, 'Look! The man!' as though asking, 'Has he not suffered enough [CH, NTC], 'Is it really necessary to inflict more punishment on him? And does *he* look like a dangerous rebel?' [NTC]. He says it with a

mix of respect and pity for Jesus but at the same time expressing sarcasm at the absurd attitude of the Jews toward Jesus. It is as though he were saying, 'There is the wretched being against whom you are enraged' [Gdt]. He probably meant to call attention to Jesus as mock-king. He says it with a bit of scorn as if to say, 'Here is the man whom you accuse of claiming the thone' [HTC]. He meant to say, 'Look, here is *the man* you were looking for....Now what are you going to do with him?' [NICNT2]. Pilate's words are heavy with irony [Car]. He asks if they can't see that he is harmless and rather ridiculous as king [Car, Lns]. He may have been speaking contemptuously [BAGD, EGT, NICNT1]. He wanted the crowd to see that Jesus as he stood there could never have been a candidate for kingship and that the only right action would be to just release him [NICNT1, TH]. Pilate means that it would be ridiculous to charge such a figure with treason [EGT].

DISCOURSE UNIT—19:6–11 [AB, Rd]. The topic is the second interrogation.

DISCOURSE UNIT—19:6b–16a [NICNT1]. The topic is Pilate's final decision.

19:6 Therefore[a] when the chief-priests and the officers saw him they-shouted,[b] "Crucify[c] crucify." Pilate said to-them, "You- take him -yourselves and crucify (him), for I find no fault in him."
LEXICON—a. οὖν (LN 89.50) (BAGD 5. p. 593): 'therefore' [BAGD, Gdt, LN, WBC; KJV], 'so' [LN, NICNT2; NASB], 'then' [LN, NTC], 'consequently, accordingly, so then' [LN], not explicit [AB, HTC; CEV, NCV, NJB, NIV, NLT, NRSV, REB, TEV]. This conjunction is also translated as a clause: 'The sight of him made (the chief priests and the Jewish officials shout)' [Ph]. Seeing Jesus like this goads them on [My]. This conjunction indicates result, often implying the conclusion of a process of reasoning [LN].
  b. aorist act. indic. of κραυγάζω (LN 33.83) (BAGD 2.a. p. 449): 'to shout' [AB, WBC; LN; NCV, NIV, NJB, NLT, NRSV, REB, TEV], 'to cry out' [BAGD, Gdt, HTC, NICNT2, NTC; KJV, NASB], 'to shout out' [NET], 'to shout at the top of one's voice' [Ph], 'to yell' [CEV], 'to scream excitedly' [BAGD], 'to scream' [LN]. This verb means to shout or cry out, with the possible implication of the unpleasant nature of the sound [LN]. It denotes a loud shout [NICNT1].
  c. aorist act. impera. of σταυρόω (LN 20.76) (BAGD '1. p. 765): 'to crucify' [BAGD, LN; all translations except CEV], 'to nail (someone) to a cross' [BAGD; CEV]. This verb means to execute by nailing to a cross. It is rare that one can find in receptor languages a technical term or phrase meaning specifically 'to crucify'. In general, a phrase must be employed, since this type of execution is no longer practiced. One can, for example, use such expressions as 'to nail to a cross bar' or 'to nail up on wood' or even 'to nail up high' [LN]. If some languages have no term for 'crucify' it could be rendered as 'Execute him on a cross' [TH, TRT], or 'Kill him

by nailing him to a cross', or 'Kill him on a cross' [TH, TRT]. The word cross itself may be rendered, 'crossed sticks' or 'crossed boards' [TRT]. The Jews may have wanted Jesus crucified since this form of death was known to incur a curse (see Deuteronomy 21:23) [IVP].

QUESTION—What is indicated by the repetition of the definite article before both *the* chief priests and *the* officers?

It brings out that they were two separate groups instead of a uniform whole [AB, NICNT1]. It shows that the opposition to Jesus lay with these leaders, not with the people themselves [EGT, Rd].

QUESTION—What is the effect of repeating the shout 'Crucify, crucify'?

It indicates the intensity of their demand [AB, HTC, TH].

QUESTION—If Pilate knew that the Jews were not allowed to crucify anyone, why did he tell the Jews to do this?

He intended to taunt them [Bar, Car, Lns, TRT]. His reply showed his exasperation [AB, IVP, My, NICNT1, NTC], or his anger and disgust with them [Car, WBC]. He was rejecting their request, telling them to do what both he and they knew was impossible [AB]. He was indignant and vexed and by their reply told them to do it themselves because it was impossible for him to have a part in such a murder [Gdt]. Pilate's reply is said sarcastically [BECNT, Car, HTC] and as a provocation [HTC]. He was simply refusing to crucify Jesus [My, NICNT2]. He was not serious because both he and they knew that his challenge to them was impossible [NICNT2].

QUESTION—What is indicated by the third repetition of Pilate that Jesus was innocent (see 18:38; 19:4; 19:6)?

He was stressing that in Jesus there was no cause for indictment [NTC].

QUESTION—What words are emphasized in this verse?

The pronoun ὑμεῖς 'you (pl.)' is emphatic [AB, Bar, Car, EGT, Gdt, HTC, ICC, Lns, NICNT1, NICNT2, NTC, TH, TRT, WBC; NASB, NCV, NJB, NLT, NRSV, REB]: 'Take him yourselves and crucify him' [NASB]. The pronoun ἐγώ 'I' is emphatic [Car, EGT, Lns, NICNT1, NICNT2, NTC, TH, TRT]: 'I on my part do not find an indictment in his case' [Lns]. The 'I' is spoken in emphatic contrast to the pronoun 'you' [Lns, NICNT1, NICNT2].

19:7 The Jews answered him, "We have (a) law and according-to the law he-ought to-die because he-made[a] himself (the) Son of-God."

LEXICON—a. aorist act. indic. of ποιέω (BAGD I.1.b.ι. p. 682): 'to make someone or something (into) something, to claim that someone is something, to pretend that someone is something' [BAGD]. The clause 'He made himself (the) Son of God' [Gdt, HTC, NICNT2, NTC, WBC; KJV] is also translated 'He made himself out to be the Son of God' [Bar; NASB, Ph], 'He claimed/has claimed to be the Son of God/God's Son' [CEV, NET, NIV, NJB, NRSV, REB, TEV], 'He said he is the Son of God' [NCV], 'he called himself the Son of God' [NLT], 'he pretended to be God's Son' [AB].

QUESTION—To whom does the phrase 'the Jews' refer?
>It refers to the chief priests [HTC, ICC] or especially the leaders of the Jews [Car, IVP, NTC, Rd, WBC; NET, NLT, TRT].

QUESTION—What specific law do they refer to?
>They are referring to Leviticus 24:16 'anyone who blasphemes the name of the LORD must be put to death. The entire assembly must stone him. Whether an alien or native-born, when he blasphemes the Name, he must be put to death' [AB, Bar, BECNT, Car, EGT, HTC, ICC, IVP, My, NICNT1, NICNT2, NTC, TH, TRT], (see also John 10:36) [AB].

QUESTION—Why did the Jews cite their law?
>They cited their law because the real reason they wanted Jesus to be put to death was the fact that he claimed to be the Son of God [AB, Car, Gdt, Lns, My, NICNT1, NICNT2, Rd, TH, WBC]. This charge has been their complaint against Jesus from the beginning (see 5:18; 10:33, 36) [Rd].

QUESTION—What were the Jews implying by citing their law?
>They were demanding Pilate to respect their law and order the execution of Jesus [Lns]. The Romans permitted conquered nations to continue to observe their own laws [Gdt, ICC, Lns, My, NTC].

QUESTION—What kept the Jews from accepting Pilate's challenge to crucify Jesus?
>It was probably because they feared the reaction of the crowd and so they want Pilate to do it for them [NICNT2].

QUESTION—What words are emphasized in this verse?
>The pronoun ἡμεῖς 'we' is emphatic [Lns, My, NICNT1, NICNT2, TH]: 'We on our part have a law' [Lns]. By this emphasis they imply, 'Whatever be the case with you Romans!' [Lns, My, NICNT1]. The phrase 'Son of God' is fronted in Greek emphasizing it (literally, '*Son of God* himself he made') [NICNT1].

DISCOURSE UNIT—19:8–12 [HTC, WBC]. The topic is second examination by Pilate.

DISCOURSE UNIT—19:8–11 [Kn]. The topic is true authority.

19:8 **So when Pilate heard this, he-was- more**[a] **-afraid.**[b]

LEXICON—a. μᾶλλον (LN **78.28**) (BAGD 1. p. 489): 'more' [BAGD, LN], 'even more, to a greater degree (than)' [BAGD, LN], 'more than' [LN], 'now more than ever' [BAGD]. The clause 'He was (the) more afraid' [Gdt, HTC, NTC; KJV] is also translated 'He was all the more afraid' [NICNT2], 'He was even more afraid' [**LN**; NASB, NCV, NIV, TEV], 'he was more afraid/frightened than ever' [AB; NET, NLT, NRSV, REB], 'his fears increased' [NJB], 'he became much more uneasy' [Ph], 'He became yet more afraid' [WBC], 'He was terrified' [CEV]. This comparative adverb indicates a degree which surpasses in some manner a point on an explicit or implicit scale of extent [LN].

b. aorist pass. indic. of φοβέομαι (LN 25.252): 'to be afraid, to fear' [LN]. This verb is derived from the noun φόβος 'fear' (25.251) and means to be in a state of fearing [LN]. (See a. above for translations).

QUESTION—To what does the phrase 'this' (literally, τοῦτον τὸν λόγον 'this word') refer?

It refers to the claim that Jesus 'made himself the Son of God' [CH, IVP, Lns, NICNT2, NTC, TRT, WBC].

QUESTION—Does the word μᾶλλον 'more' necessarily imply a preceding event? And if so, what might Pilate have been previously afraid of?

1. It implies that Pilate was indeed previously afraid [AB, BAGD, EGT, Gdt, ICC, IVP, NICNT1, My, NTC, Rd, TH, WBC; all translations except CEV]. He may have felt fear when he heard his wife's dream and warning: 'Don't have anything to do with that innocent man' (Matthew 27:19) [AB, CH, ICC, Lns, NICNT1, NTC]. He may have been afraid by observing the bearing of Jesus himself [EGT, Lns, Gdt, NICNT1, Rd, WBC]. He had heard about Jesus' miracles, his teachings, and his character [Gdt]. He intuitively sensed that Jesus may have been more than just a human being, something the Jews were blind to [CH]. Now he hears about Jesus' claim to be the Son of God and he is gripped with fear even more [Gdt, IVP, Lns]. The term 'God's Son' may have aroused superstitious feelings about Jesus' magical powers [AB, BECNT, CH, Gdt, HTC, Lns, NICNT1, Rd, WBC]. Coupled with this was the fear of possible reprisals from his just having had Jesus flogged [BECNT, Lns, WBC]. His reticence to condemn Jesus (18:38; 19:4,6) may have been the result of fear [TH]. Pilate may have been afraid that his failure to respect Jewish religious customs would be reported to Rome [BECNT]. He had felt an increasing uneasiness about how the Jews were cornering him and he was having trouble in extricating himself [Rd]. To the fear of conscience that he may be wrong to allow Jesus to be crucified was added the fear of what the Jewish God might do to enact vengeance on him [My].

2. It has no reference to previous experience. The word μᾶλλον here has an intensive meaning indicating that 'he was very much afraid' [Bar; CEV]: 'he was terrified' [CEV]. It is probably better to interpret μᾶλλον as the comparative of μάλα 'very, exceedingly' meaning that Pilate was very much afraid [Bar].

3. It has no reference to previous experience and means 'rather', presenting an alternative [NICNT2]. Since fear has not yet been mentioned in relation to Pilate, this word is more likely to mean 'rather' as introducing an alterntive. That is, Pilate's bearing was not as it had been before, 'rather he became afraid' (for other places where this word means 'rather' see 3:19 and 12:43) [NICNT2].

4. It may mean either 2 or 3 above [Car]. It is doubtful that Pilate was fearful before this point. But since many senior officers were deeply superstitious, on hearing this new turn in the trial, he may have become

afraid *rather than* complying with the Jewish hopes of executing Jesus. Or the word μᾶλλον may have indicated intensity and meant that Pilate was 'very much afraid' [Car].

QUESTION—Of what may Pilate have been afraid?

Some languages may require the information of what Pilate feared. If so, one could translate 'he was all the more afraid to condemn Jesus' [TH, TRT], or 'he was all the more afraid to pass judgment on Jesus' [TH].

DISCOURSE UNIT—19:9–11 [IVP]. The topic is Jesus speaks of power and guilt.

19:9 And he entered the governor's-residence again and said to Jesus, "Where- are you -from?"[a] **But Jesus gave him no answer.**

LEXICON—a. πόθεν (LN 84.6) (BAGD 1. p. 680): 'from where?' [BAGD, LN], 'whence' [BAGD, Gdt, LN; KJV]. The question 'Where are you from' [HTC, NICNT2, NTC, WBC; CEV, NASB, NLT, NRSV] is also translated 'Where do/have you come from?' [AB, NCV, NET, NIV, NJB, Ph, REB, TEV]. This interrogative pronoun indicates extension from a source, with an incorporated interrogative point of reference [LN]. It refers here to locality as in 'from what place' [BAGD].

QUESTION—Is Pilate asking about Jesus' physical or his spiritual origin?

1. Pilate here was asking about Jesus' ultimate Heavenly origin [AB, EGT, Gdt, HTC, ICC, IVP, Kn, Lns, My, NICNT1, WBC]. Pilate already knew Jesus was from Galilee [Gdt, ICC]. He was inquiring whether Jesus came from Heaven or was human [AB, Gdt, IVP, Lns, My, WBC]. His real question was, 'Are you an earth-born man or some god?' [IVP]. This explains Jesus' silence since if the Jews themselves could not understand how he had come 'from above' neither could a Roman [AB, BECNT].

2. Pilate is asking about his earthly home with possibly a secondary meaning as to his ultimate origin [Bar, TH, TRT]. The question refers to which part of Palestine Jesus came from (see Luke 23:6), but John also wanted his readers to understand the larger question of Jesus' ultimate origin—Heaven [TH]. He may have been asking if Jesus were a god or if he were from a different province so that someone else could judge the case [TRT].

QUESTION—Why did Jesus remain silent?

He remained silent because he had already told Pilate, 'My kingdom is not of this world…my kingdom is from another place' (18:36–37) [Lns, My, NICNT2, NTC]. Pilate did not deserve an answer because he had given the order for Jesus to be scourged even though he knew that he was innocent and had said so [NTC]. He did not reply because he knew that Pilate would not be able to comprehend his real origin and his relationship to God [BECNT, Car, My, WBC]. The charge on which Jesus was being tried was that he had claimed to be the king of the Jews. This charge had been settled and Pilate had judged him innocent. Jesus refused to prolong the procedure [EGT].

QUESTION—What Scripture predicted the silence of Jesus?
Isaiah 53:7 describes the Messiah as remaining silent before his judges, 'He was oppressed and afflicted, yet he did not open his mouth; he was led like a lamb to the slaughter, and as a sheep before her shearers is silent, so he did not open his mouth' [AB, BECNT, IVP, NICNT1, TH, WBC].

QUESTION—What word is emphasized in this verse?
The pronoun σύ 'you' is emphatic [NICNT1, NICNT2]. Pilate may have been incredulous saying to himself, 'This man son of God!' Then he asks Jesus, '*How could you possibly be* (Son of God)?' [NICNT1].

19:10 So Pilate said to-him, "Do-you not -speak[a] to-me? Do-you- not -know that I-have authority[b] to-release[c] you and I-have authority to-crucify you?"

LEXICON—a. pres. act. indic. of λαλέω [LN 33.70]: 'to speak, to say, to talk, to tell' [LN]. The question 'Do you not speak to me?' is translated 'To *me* you do not speak?' [NTC], 'Are you not speaking to me?' [NICNT2], 'Are you not going to talk to me?' [WBC], 'You do/will not speak to me?' [HTC; NASB, TEV], 'You/do you refuse to speak to me?' [AB; NCV, NET, NIV, NRSV, REB, similarly NJB], 'Won't you speak to me?' [Ph], 'Why won't you answer my question?' [CEV], 'Why don't you talk to me?' [NLT], 'Speak you not to me?' [Gdt; KJV]. This verb means to speak or talk, with the possible implication of more informal usage (though this cannot be clearly and consistently shown from NT contexts) [LN].

b. ἐξουσία (LN 37.35) (BAGD 3., 4. p. 278): 'authority' [BAGD (3); NASB, NET, REB, TEV], 'power' [CEV, NCV, NIV, NJB, NLT, NRSV, Ph], 'absolute power, warrant' [BAGD (3)], 'authority to rule, right to control' [LN], 'ruling power, official power' [BAGD (4)]. This noun denotes the right to control or govern over [LN]. It denotes the power exercised by rulers or others in high position by virtue of their office [BAGD (4)]. Some languages may not have a specific word for 'authority'. In these cases it could be translated 'the government has made me able to set you free' [TH].

b. aorist act. infin. of ἀπολύω (LN 37.127) (BAGD 1. p. 96): 'to release' [BAGD, LN; KJV, NASB, NET, NJB, NLT, NRSV, REB], 'to set free' [BAGD, LN; NCV, Ph, TEV], 'to let go free' [CEV], 'to free' [NIV], 'to pardon' [BAGD]. This verb means to release from control, to set free (highly generic meaning applicable to a wide variety of circumstances, including confinement, political domination, sin, sickness) [LN].

QUESTION—What is Pilate's attitude as he now questions Jesus again?
His dignity is insulted [ICC]. He is proud and considers Jesus' silence an insult [Lns]. Pilate was irritated by Jesus' silence [Bar, BECNT, Car, IVP, Kn, Lns, Rd, TRT, WBC]. He feels that Jesus means his silence to be critical of him and he reasserts his proud authority as judge [Gdt]. He is indignant [EGT, NTC] and begins to boast [NTC]. He is hostile [Kn], incredulous [NICNT1], surprised [TH, TRT]. He thinks either Jesus is stupid or is baiting him with his sullen silence [Car]. Pilate secretly fears Jesus [HTC, NTC].

QUESTION—What did Pilate mean by his question 'Do you not speak to me?'
This is a rhetorical question [TRT]. Some suggested renderings are: 'You're not answering me!', 'Aren't you going to answer me?', 'You should answer me!', 'How dare you not answer me!' [TRT], similarly [NTC].

QUESTION—What did Pilate mean by his question 'Do you not know that I have authority to release you and I have authority to crucify you'?
This is a rhetorical question [CH, IVP, Kn, Lns, NICNT1, TRT, WBC]. Pilate reminds Jesus that he has authority to release him [BECNT, CH, NICNT1, WBC]. Pilate threatens Jesus by appealing to his power [IVP]. Some suggested renderings are: 'You act like you don't know/Let me remind you that I have the authority to set you free and the authority to have you crucified' [TRT], 'Remember, I have the authority to set you free and also to have you crucified' [TEV], 'Surely you know that I have authority to release you, and authority to crucify you' [REB, similarly NJB]. Pilate boasts about his tremendous authority [Lns].

QUESTION—What word is emphasized in this verse?
The pronoun ἐμοί 'me' is emphasized [Gdt, HTC, ICC, Lns, My, NICNT1, NICNT2, NTC, TRT]: 'To *me* you do not speak?' [NTC]. He implies, 'How dare you? Don't you know who I am?' [NTC]. In the Greek the pronoun is placed first in the sentence to emphasize it [HTC, ICC, NICNT2, NTC, TRT]. The emphatic phrase 'to me' shows that Pilate is angry that Jesus treats his question with silence [Lns]. This emphasis is shown in the following repetition of the phrase '*I* have authority...*I* have authority' [Gdt, My].

19:11 Jesus answered him, "You-would-have no authority over me at-all[a] unless it-had-been given you from-above.[b] Therefore he-who delivered- me -over to-you has (the) greater sin."

LEXICON—a. οὐδεμία (LN 92.23): 'at all' [AB, Gdt, NICNT2, NTC, WBC; CEV, KJV, REB, NET, NJB, NLT, Ph, REB], 'anything at all' [CEV], 'no one, none, nothing' [LN], not explicit [HTC; NASB, NCV, NIV, NRSV, TEV]. The statement 'you would have no authority over me at all' is translated 'you couldn't do anything at all to me' [CEV]. This adjective indicates a negative reference to an entity, event, or state [LN].

b. ἄνωθεν (LN **84.13**) (BAGD 1. p. 77): 'from above' [AB, Gdt, NICNT2, NTC, WBC; BAGD, **LN**], 'from the top of' [LN]. The clause 'unless it had been given you from above' [NASB, similarly all translations except CEV, NCV, TEV] is also translated 'If God had not given you the power (you couldn't do anything at all to me)' [CEV], '(The only power you have over me) is the power given to you by God' [NCV], '(You have authority over me) only because it was given to you by God' [TEV]. This adverb indicates an extension from a source which is above [LN]. Here it is a figure of speech meaning 'from God' [BAGD, Bar, BECNT, Car, CH, EGT, ICC, IVP, Kn, Lns, My, NICNT1, Rd, TH; CEV, NCV, TEV].

JOHN 19:11

QUESTION—To whom does the pronoun ὁ 'he who' refer?
1. It refers to Caiaphas [BECNT, Car, CH, EGT, ICC, Lns, My, NICNT1, NTC, TH, WBC]. This must refer to the person who was ultimately responsible for delivering Jesus to Pilate, and that was the High Priest, Caiaphas [NICNT1]. Caiaphas was the official representative of the Sanhedrin who delivered Jesus to Pilate, so he is the one referred to here [ICC]. The singular 'he who' refers more naturally to an individual, that is, to Caiaphas. He had initiated Jesus' death (11:49–53), had elicited the charge that Jesus was King of the Jews and so was a blasphemer (Mark 4:61–64), and had delivered him to Pilate [WBC].
2. It refers to the Jews who have handed Jesus over to Pilate [Kn, Rd]. Specifically it refers to the Jewish leaders who handed Jesus over to Pilate [Kn].
3. It refers to Caiaphas and/or to the Jews and/or their leaders [AB, Gdt, IVP]. Although the singular could indicate a reference to Caiaphas, the singular may be a generalizing reference to the Jews [AB]. It refers to the Sanhedrin, the official representative of the Jews [Gdt].
4. Other views [Bar, HTC, NICNT2]. It refers to Judas the tool of Satan [Bar]. It refers all the way back to Satan himself [NICNT2]. It refers to all who were instrumental in handing Jesus over—Judas, the chief priests, and Caiaphas, [HTC].

QUESTION—How is 'the one who delivered (Jesus) over' guilty of a greater sin than Pilate?
1. That one's sin was greater because he acted willfully but Pilate had not [AB, Lns, NTC, TH, WBC]. Pilate had been given a role in the crucifixion by God and so was acting unknowingly or unwillfully. The other party however was acting deliberately [AB]. Caiaphas had abused his authority over Jesus handing him over on false charges to obtain his death. Therefore his guilt was greater than Pilate's [WBC].
2. That one's sin was greater because Pilate's authority was God-given, his was not [Go, HTC, My, NTC]. The conjunction 'therefore' (literally 'because of this') points back to the word 'given'. Pilate was *given* authority over Jesus by God so was guilty of a lesser sin. But the Sanhedrin had arrogated authority to themselves, so their sin was greater. They were making an illegal use of Pilate's legitimate authority [Gdt]. Caiaphas had condemned Jesus and delivered him up to Pilate to be crucified without authorization from God [NTC].
3. Other views [Car, IVP, Rd]. Pilate had judicial authority over Jesus because God had given it to him (it was 'from above'). Pilate's role was relatively passive. But the one who had delivered Jesus to him took the initiative himself and so was guilty of a greater sin [Car]. The Jews were much more to blame because they were more deeply involved in this trial not only because they instigated it, but also because it was in their presence that Jesus spoke and performed miracles and their own law contained everything by which they could have recognized Jesus as being

sent from God [Rd]. The sin of the Jews is greater because they had been the recipients of greater gifts from God and still they rejected Jesus [IVP].

QUESTION—What word is emphasized in this verse?

The negative adjective οὐδεμία '(no authority)...at all' is very emphatic [Bar].

DISCOURSE UNIT—19:12–16 [IVP, Kn]. The topic is the Jews reject Jesus [IVP], handing over the Jewish king [Kn].

DISCOURSE UNIT—19:12–16a [AB, Rd]. The topic is Jesus condemned.

19:12 Because-of/from[a] this Pilate tried[b] to-release him. But the Jews shouted, "If you-release this-man, you-are not Caesar's friend. Everyone who makes himself (a) king opposes[c] Caesar."

LEXICON—a. ἐκ (LN **89.25**, 67.131) (BAGD 3.f. p. 235): 'because of' [BAGD, **LN** (89.25)], 'as a result of' [BAGD, Lns], 'since, from' [LN (67.131)], 'by reason of' [BAGD]. The phrase ἐκ τούτου 'because of/from this' is translated 'as a result of this' [NTC; NTC], 'upon this' [HTC], 'from this time' [Gdt, NICNT2], 'from thenceforth' [KJV], 'from then on' [NIV, NRSV], 'from this point on' [NET], 'from this moment on' [WBC; similarly NJB, Ph, REB], 'after this' [AB; NCV], 'when Pilate heard this' [TEV], 'then' [CEV, NLT]. This preposition indicates cause or reason, with focus on the source [LN (89.25)] or it indicates the extent of time from a point in the past [LN (67.131)]. It indicates the reason that is a presupposition for something [BAGD]. Here the phrase ἐκ τούτου 'because of this' means 'for this reason, therefore' [BAGD].

b. imperf. act. indic. of ζητέω (LN 68.60): 'to try to' [LN, WBC; NCV, NET, NIV, NLT, NRSV], 'to try hard to' [Ph, REB], 'to try to find a way to' [TEV], 'to make efforts to' [NTC; NASB], 'to be eager to' [AB], 'to be anxious to' [NJB], 'to seek to' [LN, Gdt, HTC, NICNT2; KJV], 'to want to' [CEV]. This verb means to seek to do something, but without success [LN]. The imperfect tense indicates that he did this repeatedly [AB, Gdt, HTC, IVP, My, NICNT1, NICNT2, NTC, Rd]: 'Pilate kept seeking to release him' [NICNT2].

c. pres. act. indic. of ἀντιλέγω (LN 33.455) (BAGD 2. p. 74): 'to oppose' [BAGD, LN; KJV, NIV], 'to speak against' [BAGD, Lns; KJV], 'to speak in opposition to' [LN], 'to refuse, to contradict' [BAGD]. The words 'opposes/is opposing Caesar' [Gdt; NIV, REB] are also translated 'is in opposition to Caesar' [WBC], 'is an enemy of the Emperor' [CEV], 'is defying Caesar' [NJB], 'is anti-Caesar' [Ph], 'sets himself against Caesar' [HTC], 'you are no friend of Caesar' [NCV, similarly AB, NICNT2; NRSV], 'rebels against the emperor' [NTC; similarly NLT, TEV]. This verb means to speak against something or someone [LN]. In addition to meaning 'to contradict' it also can mean 'to resist' [Rd].

QUESTION—What is indicated by the phrase ἐκ τούτου 'as a result of/from this'?
1. This preposition is logical indicating cause or result [BAGD, Gdt, HTC, LN, Lns, My, NICNT2, NTC; NASB]: 'as a result of this' [NTC; NASB]. The phrase 'from this' means 'on this ground' referring to Jesus' last words [Lns, My]. The reference is to Jesus' claim to belong to another world. This caused Pilate to try to release Jesus [HTC].
2. The preposition is temporal [ICC; all translations except NTC; NASB]: 'From this point on' [NET].
3. The phrase is ambiguous. It could be either temporal or causal [Bar, Car, EGT, NICNT1, TH, TRT]. Both causal and temporal senses are in focus here [EGT].

QUESTION—What is implied by the pronoun τοῦτον 'this (man)' when referring to Jesus?

It implied contempt for him [AB, TRT].

QUESTION—What figure of speech is the phrase 'not Caesar's friend'?

It is a kind of *litotes* in which 'not a friend' indicates 'an enemy' [Lns, TRT].

QUESTION—What is indicated by the phrase φίλος τοῦ Καίσαρος 'friend of Caesar'?

The title (*amicus Caesaris*) was given to all Roman senators by virtue of their office but was also awarded to other outstanding men [HTC]. It was a title of honor that was conferred on men for special service to their Emperor [TH]. The Emperor awarded this title to loyal subjects, so Pilate did not want the Emperor to hear that he was unable to govern Israel [CH]. It is not certain that Pilate enjoyed this status or was merely hoping to attain to it [NICNT2]. The phrase is best understood on its face value that a person claiming to be king is not a friend of the Emperor [Bar, EGT, ICC, My]. Tiberius, the Emperor at that time, was suspicious of anything opposing his position [EGT, Rd]. This charge of the Jews implied treason against the Emperor and they could report to him that Pilate had not dealt firmly with a man guilty of this offense [ICC, NICNT1]. The title may have been in force in Jesus' day [BECNT, NTC]. This phrase as a technical title may not have been in force at this time [NICNT1, NTC, WBC]. The title was probably not in use until the time of Vespasian (AD 69–79) [ICC]. Whether or not this title was valid at this time, the accusation was a very strong weapon against Pilate [Rd].

DISCOURSE UNIT—19:13–16a [HTC, WBC]. The topic is the condemnation of Jesus.

19:13 **So when- Pilate -heard these words he brought Jesus out and sat-down on (the) judgment-seat[a] at (a) place called (the) Stone-Pavement,[b] but in-Hebrew[c] Gabbatha.[d]**

TEXT—Instead of verses 13–27 being in sequential order, one manuscript has the order 13, 24, 14–15, 19–23, 16–19, 25b–27. Other manuscripts, and one patristic quotation have the order 13, 24, 14–23, 24 (*again*), 25–27. Still another manuscript has the order 13a, 24, 13b–23, 24 (*again*), 25–27. GNT has the sequence 13–27 with an A rating, indicating that the text is certain.

LEXICON—a. βῆμα (LN **7.63**) (BAGD 2. p. 140): 'judgment seat' [Gdt, HTC, LN, NTC; KJV, NASB, NLT, Ph], 'judge's seat' [**LN**, WBC; NCV, NIV, TEV], 'judge's bench' [AB, NICNT2; CEV, NRSV], 'chair of judgment' [NJB], 'tribunal' [BAGD; REB], 'judgment place' [LN], 'judicial bench' [BAGD]. This noun denotes a raised platform [EGT, LN, Lns, NTC] mounted by steps [LN, Lns, NTC] and usually furnished with a seat, used by officials in addressing an assembly, often on judicial matters. The association of a βῆμα with judicial procedures means that there is almost always an important component of judicial function associated with this term. Therefore in translating βῆμα, it is often best to use a phrase such as 'a place where a judge decides' or 'a place where decisions are made' or 'a judge's seat' [LN].

b. λιθόστρωτον (LN **7.71**) (BAGD p. 474): 'stone pavement' [AB, BAGD, **LN**, NICNT2, WBC; CEV, NCV, NET, NIV, NRSV, TEV], 'pavement' [BAGD, Gdt, HTC; KJV, NASB, NJB, Ph, REB], 'stone platform' [NTC], 'mosaic' [BAGD]. The phrase 'a place called the stone pavement' is translated 'the platform that is called the Stone Pavement' [NLT]. This noun denotes an area in Jerusalem, paved with flat blocks of stone and forming a kind of courtyard (not a thoroughfare). In some languages one may describe 'The Stone Pavement' as 'a court covered with large blocks of flat stone' or 'a stone-paved courtyard' [LN]. It denotes 'place paved with stones/tiles' [Gdt, Rd]. Probably large stones are indicated [BECNT, LN, TH].

c. Ἑβραϊστί (LN **33.6**) (BAGD p. 213): 'in Hebrew' [AB, BAGD, Gdt, HTC, LN, NICNT2; KJV, NASB, NJB, NLT, NRSV, Ph, REB, TEV], 'in Aramaic' [BAGD, NTC; CEV, NET, NIV], 'in the Hebrew language' [LN], 'in the language of the Jews' [WBC; similarly NCV]. The form of the word Γαββαθα shows that Aramaic is indicated [Bar, EGT, NICNT1, TH].

d. Γαββαθα (LN **93.437**) (BAGD p. 149): 'Gabbatha' [BAGD, LN; all translations]. This noun denotes the Aramaic name for a paved area outside the residence of Pontius Pilate and the setting for the public trial of Jesus [LN]. Its Greek equivalent was λιθόστρωτον 'stone pavement' [BAGD].

QUESTION—To what does the phrase τῶν λόγων τούτων 'these words' refer?

It refers to what the Jews had just said, 'If you release this man, you are not Caesar's friend. Everyone who makes himself a king opposes Caesar' [AB, Gdt, IVP, Lns]. It was the mention of the name 'Caesar' that triggered Jesus fate [NICNT1]. Pilate could not allow the information that he had released a prisoner who was accused of making himself a king to be reported to the emperor [ICC].

QUESTION—Out of what place did Pilate bring Jesus?
He had him brought out of the governor's residence or the Praetorium [Gdt, ICC].

QUESTION—What was indicated by Pilate's sitting down on the judgment seat?
It indicated that he was ready to proclaim an official decision or pass sentence [BECNT, EGT, CH, Kn, Lns, NICNT2, NTC, WBC]. It was only from this place that a governor would issue a formal condemnation in a case involving capital punishment [Kn]. This action indicated that he was opening the trial [BAGD 2.a.α. p. 390].

QUESTION—What is the relationship of the two terms 'stone pavement' and 'Gabbatha'?
They do not mean the same thing but are simply different names for the same place [EGT, Lns, My, NICNT1].

DISCOURSE UNIT—19:14–27 [AB]. The topic is the questioning of Jesus.

19:14 Now it-was (the) day-of-preparation[a] of-the Passover. It-was about (the) sixth hour.[b] He said to-the Jews, "Look[c] your King."

LEXICON—a. παρασκευή (LN 67.201) (BAGD p. 622): 'day of preparation' [BAGD, LN], 'Friday' [LN, Rd], 'preparation' [BAGD]. The phrase 'the day of Preparation of/for (the) Passover' [AB, HTC; NASB, NET, NLT, NRSV, REB, similarly WBC] is also translated 'the preparation (day) of the Passover' [Gdt, NICNT2, NTC; KJV, Ph], 'the day of Preparation of Passover Week' [NIV], 'Preparation Day of Passover week' [NCV], 'the day before (the) Passover' [CEV, TEV], 'the Day of Preparation' [NJB]. This noun denotes a day on which preparations were made for a sacred or feast day. The identification of παρασκευή with Friday became so traditional that it eventually came to be the present-day Greek term for 'Friday' [LN]. It refers to a definite day, as the 'day of preparation' for a festival. According to Jewish usage it was Friday, on which day everything had to be prepared for the Sabbath, when no work was permitted. Here it means 'day of preparation for the Passover (or Friday of Passover week)' [BAGD].

b. ὥρα (LN 67.199) (BAGD 2.b. p. 896): 'hour' [BAGD, LN]. The phrase 'the sixth hour' [Gdt, HTC, NICNT2, NTC; KJV, NASB, NIV, NJB] is also translated 'noon' [AB, BAGD; CEV, NCV, NET, NLT, NRSV, REB, TEV], 'midday' [WBC; Ph]. This noun denotes the twelfth part of a day, measured from sunrise to sunset (in any one day the hours would be of equal length, but would vary somewhat depending on the time of the year) [LN]. It denotes a moment of time that takes its name from the hour that has just passed [BAGD].

c. ἴδε (LN 91.13) (BAGD 3. p. 369): 'look' [LN, NICNT2, NTC, WBC], 'Look, here is/Look, here's' [AB; NET, NLT, Ph], 'here is' [BAGD, HTC; NCV, NIV, NJB, NRSV, REB, TEV], 'look at' [CEV], 'behold' [Gdt; KJV, NASB], 'listen, pay attention' [LN]. This particle functions as a prompter of attention, that serves also to emphasize the following statement [LN, TH].

QUESTION—What is the meaning of the phrase 'the day of Preparation of the Passover'? This is difficult to understand because of the possible misunderstanding of the meaning of the word Passover. It can either refer to Passover day or Passover week—the whole festival.

1. It meant the day of preparation for the Sabbath in the Passover week [BAGD, BECNT, Car, EGT, Gdt, ICC, Lns, My, NICNT1, NTC, Rd, TH, TRT; NCV, NIV]. The expression simply means that it was the Friday preceding Passover-week [Car, EGT, ICC, Lns, NICNT1, NTC]. The phrase 'day of preparation' does not refer simply to the ordinary Sabbath, but to the whole Passover celebration [EGT]. It usually referred to the day before the sabbath (Friday), but with the addition of the phrase 'of the Passover', it referred to the Friday before the Passover celebration [Rd].
2. It meant the day of preparation for the Passover feast [AB, Bar, NICNT2]. This must refer to Passover eve, the day before the 14th of Nisan [Bar]. It refers to the day before Passover in preparation for the Passover meal [NICNT2].

QUESTION—What time of day is the sixth hour?

1. The sixth hour indicates about 12 o'clock noon [AB, BAGD, BECNT, Car, EGT, Gdt, ICC, Kn, My, NICNT1, NICNT2, TH, TRT, WBC; CEV, NCV, NET, NLT, NRSV, Ph, REB, TEV]. John was computing time from daylight (6 a.m.) rather than midnight. This would put the time at noon [AB]. Since Jesus was brought before Pilate around daybreak (see 8:28), it seems impossible for him to have done all that he did by 6:00 a.m. [Gdt, ICC, Kn, NICNT2, TRT].
2. The sixth hour indicates about 6:00 a.m. [NTC]. John was using the Roman method of computing time that began the day at midnight (see 1:39; 4:6; 4:52) putting the sixth hour at about six in the morning. Considering that the morning meeting of the Sanhedrin may have been very early and that the intent of the Jews was to rush Pilate to a decision, the interpretation of 6 a.m. for Pilate's presentation of Jesus to the crowd seems most reasonable [NTC].

QUESTION—To whom does the pronoun 'he' refer in the words 'he says to the Jews'?

Since Jesus was the last proper name mentioned in the context, it may be advisable to make explicit the name Pilate here to avoid confusion on the part of the readers [TH, TRT; CEV, NCV, NET, NIV, NJB, NLT, Ph, REB, TEV]: 'Pilate said to the people' [TEV].

QUESTION—What was Pilate thinking as he presented Jesus as the King of the Jews?

He was ridiculing them. This was *their* king, a bloody, weak, defenceless monarch, now presented at *their own* request [NTC]. He is mocking the Jews [Bar, BECNT, Car, EGT, ICC, IVP, Lns]—this helpless prisoner was the only king they were likely to have [Bar, BECNT, Car]. He was bitter [EGT,

My], angry [EGT], sarcastic [TRT]. He is responding to the threat of the Jews that he was no friend of Caesar. He was saying in effect, 'How dare you threaten me! He is *your* king after all!' He emphasizes the pronoun 'your'. He means that if Jesus is the King of the Jews in any sense, then it is the Jews who are disloyal to Caesar, not he [NICNT2].

19:15 Then[a] they shouted, "Away[b] away, crucify[c] him." Pilate says to-them, "Shall-I-crucify your king?" The chief-priests answered (him), "We-have no king but Caesar."

LEXICON—a. οὖν (LN 89.50, 89.127): 'then' [LN (89.50), NICNT2, NTC], 'so' [LN (89.50); NASB], 'at this' [AB], 'at which' [Ph], 'but' [LN (89.127); KJV, NIV, NJB], 'therefore, consequently, accordingly' [LN (89.50)], not explicit [Gdt, HTC, WBC; CEV, NCV, NET, NLT, NRSV, REB, TEV]. This conjunction indicates result, often implying the conclusion of a process of reasoning [LN (89.50)], or it is a marker of relatively weak contrast [LN (89.127)].

b. aorist act. impera. of αἴρω (LN 20.65) (BAGD 4. p. 24): 'to take away, to remove' [BAGD], 'to kill, to execute' [LN]. The verb ἆρον 'away' is translated 'Away with him!' [AB, Gdt, HTC, NTC; similarly KJV, NASB, NET, NJB, NLT, NRSV, REB], 'Take him away!' [WBC; NCV, NIV, Ph], 'Take!' [NICNT2], 'Kill him!' [CEV, TEV]. This verb means to deprive a person of life, with the implication of this being the result of condemnation by legal or quasi-legal procedures [LN]. Here it implied 'taking away by force', even by killing [BAGD]. Although the basic meaning of this verb is 'to lift up' here it has the extended meaning of 'to kill' by 'lifting up' or 'taking away' [TH]. It is an idiom that means 'to kill' or 'to execute' [TRT].

c. aorist act. subj. of σταυρόω (LN 20.76) (BAGD 1. p. 765): 'to crucify' [BAGD, LN; all translations except CEV], 'to nail to a cross' [CEV]. This verb means to execute by nailing to a cross. It is rare that one can find in receptor languages a technical term or phrase meaning specifically 'to crucify'. In general, a phrase must be employed, since this type of execution is no longer practiced. One can, for example, use such expressions as 'to nail to a cross bar' or 'to nail up on wood' or 'to nail up high' [LN], or 'to execute on a cross' [TRT].

QUESTION—What is Pilate's attitude as he says, 'Shall I crucify your king?'

He is mocking the Jews [Bar, Car, ICC]. He was being sarcastic [EGT]. He feigns surprise that the Jews are not calling for him to release their Messianic King [Lns]. His words are a rhetorical question and could be translated, 'Certainly you don't want me to crucify your King!' [TRT].

QUESTION—What is meant by the Jews' statement, 'We have no king but Caesar'?

In pledging their allegiance to Caesar, they were rejecting God who was their true king (see Judges 8:23; 1 Samuel 8:7; 12:12) [Bar, Car, CH, IVP, NICNT1, TRT], and rejecting Jesus as their Messiah [Car, ICC].

QUESTION—What words are emphasized in this verse?
The pronoun ἐκεῖνοι 'they (literally 'these ones (cried out'))' is emphatic [ICC, Lns, NICNT1]. As such the Jews emphatically contrast with Pilate [NICNT1]. The antecedent of 'they' is 'the Jews' [Lns, NICNT1, TRT]. The phrase 'your king' is placed first in Pilate's reply emphasizing it [EGT, ICC, NICNT1, NTC, TRT, WBC]: '*Your* king! Am I to crucify *him*?' [WBC], 'Your king shall I crucify?' [Lns]. The three imperatives 'Away, away, crucify him' express the impatience of the Jews to end the matter quickly [Gdt]. These three demands are highly authoritative and dictatorial [Lns].

DISCOURSE UNIT—19:16–42 [NICNT2]. The topic is the crucifixion and burial.

DISCOURSE UNIT—19:16–30 [IVP; NASB]. The topic is Jesus is crucified [IVP], the care of Jesus' body [NASB].

DISCOURSE UNIT—19:16–18 [IVP]. The topic is the crucifixion.

19:16a Then therefore[a] he-handed- him -over[b] to-them to-be-crucified.

LEXICON—a. οὖν (LN 89.50, 89.127): 'therefore' [ICC; KJV], 'so' [ICC, LN, NICNT2, NTC; NASB, NCV], 'at this' [AB; Ph], 'at that' [NJB], 'then, consequently, accordingly' [LN (89.50)], not explicit [Gdt, HTC, WBC; CEV, NET, NLT, NRSV, TEV]. The two words τότε οὖν 'then therefore' are translated 'then at last (to satisfy them)' [AB; REB], 'finally' [NIV]. This conjunction indicates result, often implying the conclusion of a process of reasoning [LN (89.50)], or it may serve as a type of transition [LN (89.127)]. Pilate was afraid of the demands of the crowd and not all that interested in what would happen to this unpopular fanatic, *so* he gave in to their demands [ICC].
  b. aorist act. indic. of παραδίδωμι (LN 37.111) (BAGD 1.b. p. 615): 'to hand over (to)' [BAGD, LN; all translations except Gdt; KJV], 'to deliver (to)' [Gdt; KJV], 'to turn over (to), 'to give up (a person)' [BAGD]. This verb means to deliver a person into the control of someone else, involving either the handing over of a presumably guilty person for punishment by authorities or the handing over of an individual to an enemy who will presumably take undue advantage of the victim [LN]. Here it is a technical term of police and courts 'to hand over into (the) custody (of)' [BAGD]. This action was clearly a judicial sentence to the penalty of crucifixion [WBC].

QUESTION—To whom does the pronoun 'he' refer?
It refers to Pilate [AB, BECNT, NICNT1, TH; CEV, TEV NCV,NET, NIV, NJB, NLT, Ph].

QUESTION—To whom did Pilate hand Jesus over?
  1. He handed Jesus over to the Jews or their leaders [AB, CH, Gdt, HTC, ICC, IVP, Kn, Lns, My, NICNT1, NICNT2, NTC, Rd]. It either refers to the Jews or to the chief priests. But now there is a new reality, the Jews have made themselves true Romans in their choice of Caesar as their king

[NICNT2]. The handing over was to them a surrendering to their wishes, not for crucifixion [Lns, NICNT1, NTC]. He was handed over to the will of the Jews who were desiring his death (Luke 23:25), but in reality to the soldiers for crucifixion [Kn, NICNT1]. The verb does not mean that Pilate put Jesus into their hands, but that he granted the Jews what they were asking [Rd]. Although the Jews did not carry out the crucifixion, in saying that he handed him over to them, he completes the cycle of guilt—they had handed Jesus over to Pilate, now he hands him over to them. Both Jews and Gentiles have rejected Jesus [IVP]. It was the soldiers who crucified Jesus but the final responsibility for his death belonged to the Jews [CH].

2. He handed Jesus over to the Roman soldiers [BECNT, Car, NICNT1, Rd, WBC]. Pilate would not hand Jesus over to the Jews to crucify since they did not have authority to crucify prisoners. Matthew 27:26 and Mark 15:15 note that immediately following the 'hand over' the Roman soliders took Jesus into custody [TH]. It was primarily to the soldiers but also indicates that he was handed over to satisfy the Jews [BECNT, Car].

DISCOURSE UNIT—19:16b–42 [BECNT, HTC, Lns, NICNT1, WBC]. The topic is Jesus is put to death [NICNT1], the passion [HTC], the crucifixion and burial of Jesus [BECNT, Lns, WBC].

DISCOURSE UNIT—19:16b–30 [AB, Car, HTC; NASB, NRSV]. The topic is the crucifixion of Jesus.

DISCOURSE UNIT—19:16b–27 [BECNT, HTC, Rd; CEV, NCV, NET, NIV, NLT, TEV]. The topic is Jesus is crucified.

DISCOURSE UNIT—19:16b–22 [NICNT1]. The topic is Jesus is crucified.

DISCOURSE UNIT—19:16b–18 [WBC]. The topic is the crucifixion.

DISCOURSE UNIT—19:17–37 [Kn]. The topic is Jesus' crucifixion.

DISCOURSE UNIT—19:17–30 [Bar]. The topic is the crucifixion.

DISCOURSE UNIT—19:17–24 [Ph]. The topic is the crucifixion.

NOTE: The following include verse 16b, 'So they took Jesus', with the next section [AB, BECNT, Car, Gdt, HTC, NICNT1, NTC, Rd, TH; CEV, NASB, NCV, NET, NIV, NLT, NRSV, Ph, REB, TEV]. So following them we have joined verse 16b and verse 17 in this section division.

19:17 So they-took Jesus, and he-went-out carrying[a] the cross[b] by-himself to the (place) called (the) Place of-(the)-Skull,[c] which is-called in-Hebrew[d] Golgotha.[e]

TEXT—Instead of παρέλαβον οὖν τὸν Ἰησοῦν 'So they took Jesus', some manuscripts read παρέλαβον οὖν τὸν Ἰησοῦν καὶ ἤγαγον 'So they took Jesus and led', others read Οἱ δὲ παραλαβόντες τὸν Ἰησοῦν ἀπήγαγον 'And they/and the ones having taken Jesus led (him) away', others read Οἱ δὲ παραλαβόντες αὐτὸν ἤγαγον καὶ ἐπέθηκαν αὐτῷ τὸν σταυρόν 'And they (or And the ones) having taken him led (him) and placed on him the cross', and still others read Παραλαβόντες οὖν τὸν Ἰησοῦν ἀπήγαγον εἰς τὸ πραιτώριον 'Then having taken Jesus they led (him) away into the Praetorium'. GNT reads 'So they took Jesus' with a B rating, indicating that the text is almost certain.

LEXICON—a. pres. act. participle of βαστάζω (LN 15.188) (BAGD 2.a. p. 137): 'to carry' [BAGD, LN; all translations except Gdt, HTC, NICNT2; KJV, NASB], 'to bear' [LN, Gdt, HTC, NICNT2; KJV, NASB]. This verb means to bear or carry a relatively heavy or burdensome object [LN]. It was customary for the condemned man to carry the cross to the place of execution [BAGD, EGT, Lns, NICNT2, TRT] or just the crossbeam on his shoulder [EGT, NICNT1, TH]. Plutarch, (*The Divine Vengeance*, 554 A/B) records that 'Each criminal as part of his punishment carries his cross on his back' [Car, ICC].

b. σταυρός (LN 6.27) (BAGD 1. p. 765): 'cross' [BAGD, LN; all translations]. This noun denotes a pole stuck into the ground in an upright position with a crosspiece attached to its upper part. Because of the symbolism associated with the cross, translations of the NT in all languages preserve some expression which will identify the cross, not only as a means of capital punishment, but as having a particular form, namely, an upright pole with a crossbeam. In some receptor languages the term for a cross means simply 'crossbeam'. In other instances it is composed of a phrase meaning 'crossed poles'. It is important, however, to avoid an expression which will suggest crossed sticks in the form of X rather than a cross consisting of an upright with a horizontal beam [LN]. In our literature it denotes an instrument by which the capital punishment of crucifixion was carried out, a stake sunk into the earth in an upright position. A cross-piece was often attached to its upper part, so that it was shaped like a 'T' [BAGD], or with the crosspiece intersecting the stake slightly below its top [BAGD, Lns]. The artists are correct, the cross had more the shape of a dagger or a Latin cross since the title was written above Jesus' head [IVP, NTC] (see Matthew 27:37; Luke 23:38) [NTC]. This is not necessarily correct as the man's body would sink down to allow a title to be attached above his head [NICNT1]. It seems that the 'cross' here referred to just the crossbeam [AB, BECNT, Car, CH, IVP, Kn, WBC] or *patibulum* since the upright stake (about nine feet high) was usually left in the ground as a permanent part of the place of execution [AB, BECNT]. The height of the upright stake varied between 6 to 10 feet [Kn]. The assumption that the complete cross was too heavy to carry and that a prisoner only carried the crossbeam is not correct. Crosses were not as heavy as is so often depicted [TRT]. It seems that Jesus carried both the stake and the crossbeam [Lns, NTC].

c. κρανίον (LN 8.11, **93.453**a) (BAGD p. 448): 'skull' [BAGD, LN]. The phrase Κρανίου Τόπος '(the) Place of the/a Skull' [AB, Gdt, HTC, NTC;

NASB, NCV, NET, NIV, NJB, NLT, NRSV, TEV] is also translated 'Skull Place' [Bar, **LN** (93.453a), NICNT2], 'Skull Hill' [Ph], 'the place (that is called a) skull' [BAGD], 'the place (called) The Skull' [WBC; REB], 'a place (known as) "The Skull"' [CEV], 'the Place of a Skull' [NASB, similarly KJV]. There is a small knoll just outside the north wall of Jerusalem having two hollow caves in its face roughly resembling a skull [EGT]. In rendering κρανίου τόπος 'place of the skull,' it may be necessary to indicate clearly the relationship between 'place' and 'skull.' A literal rendering of such a phrase might simply mean 'a place where there was a skull.' However, the meaning of Golgotha has been interpreted generally as 'a hill resembling a skull,' and therefore κρανίου τόπος may be more satisfactorily rendered as 'a place resembling a skull' or 'a hill looking like a skull' [LN (8.11)].

d. Ἑβραϊστί (LN 33.6) (BAGD p. 213): 'in Hebrew' [BAGD, Gdt, HTC, LN, NICNT2; KJV, NASB, NJB, NLT, NRSV, Ph, REB, TEV], 'in the Jewish language' [NCV], 'in the Jews' language' [WBC], 'in the Hebrew language' [LN], 'in Aramaic' [NTC; CEV, NET, NIV]. The statement 'called in Hebrew Golgotha' is translated 'Golgotha being its Hebrew name' [AB].

e. Γολγοθᾶ (LN 93.453) (BAGD p. 164): 'Golgotha' [BAGD, LN; all translations]. This noun denotes the Aramaic name of a hill near Jerusalem where executions took place [LN]. The Aramaic word γολγοθᾶ means 'skull' [AB, Bar, CH, Gdt, HTC, Lns, NTC, TH], or 'head' [Bar, TH]. The Latin equivalent was *calvaria*, 'Calvary' [Car, IVP, Lns].

QUESTION—To whom does the pronoun 'they' refer in the words 'they took Jesus'?

1. 'They' refers to the soldiers [AB, BECNT, Car, HTC, NICNT1, NTC, Rd, TH, TRT, WBC; NCV, NIV]. It probably refers to the soldiers even though grammatically it would refer to the chief priests [NICNT1].
2. 'They' refers to the Jews or the Jewish authorities [EGT, Gdt, Lns, My, NICNT2]. It was the Jews who executed Jesus by the hands of the Roman soldiers [Gdt, Lns]. Jesus himself had told the Jews that they would 'lift up the Son of Man' (8:28). Also these leaders are Jews no longer but true Romans recognizing only Caesar as their king [NICNT2]. No change of subject is indicated in the context, not even in verse 18 [Lns].

QUESTION—Out of which place did Jesus go?

He went out of the city [AB, EGT, Gdt, ICC, Kn, Lns, NICNT2, NTC, Rd, TH, TRT]. The place of the crucifixion was outside the city (see verse 20) [AB]. Hebrews 13:12 records that Jesus 'suffered outside the city gate' [NTC]. He went out of the *praetorium* (see 18:28) [Car].

QUESTION—What is the best translation of the dative pronoun ἑαυτῷ 'by himself'?

The translations rendered this pronoun 'by himself' [AB, NTC; NLT, NRSV], 'his own (cross)' [HTC; NASB, NCV, NET, NIV, NJB], 'his (cross)' [Gdt; CEV, KJV, TEV], '(carrying the cross) himself' [Ph, REB], 'for himself' [Lns, NICNT2, WBC].

QUESTION—What word is emphasized in this verse?

The pronoun ἑαυτῷ 'by himself' is emphatic [Bar, NICNT1] and should be translated 'alone' [Bar].

19:18 There they-crucified him and two others with him on-either-side,^a and Jesus in-the-middle.^b

LEXICON—a. ἐντεῦθεν (LN 84.9) (BAGD 1. p. 268): 'from here' [BAGD, LN]. The phrase ἐντεῦθεν καὶ ἐντεῦθεν (literally, 'from here and from there') 'on either side' [AB, Gdt, HTC, NICNT2; KJV, NASB, NJB, NLT, NRSV, Ph, REB] is also translated 'on each side' [BAGD, WBC; CEV, NCV, NET, NIV, TEV], 'on this side and on that' [NTC]. This adverb indicates an extension from a source, with the point of reference near the speaker [LN].

c. μέσος (LN 83.10) (BAGD 1. p. 507): 'in the middle' [AB, BAGD, LN, NICNT2, NTC, WBC; NCV, NET, NIV, NJB, Ph], '(Jesus) between (them)' [BAGD, HTC; NLT, NRSV, TEV], 'in between' [NASB, REB], 'in the midst' [Gdt, LN; KJV], 'middle' [BAGD], not explicit [CEV]. This adverb indicates a position in the middle of an area (either an object in the midst of other objects or an area in the middle of a larger area) [LN].

QUESTION—To whom does the pronoun 'they' refer?

1. 'They' refers to the soldiers [ICC, NTC]. Verse 19:23 indicates that the pronoun refers to the soldiers [NTC].
2. 'They' refers to the Jews [Lns, My, NICNT2]. It was the Jews who did this by means of the soldiers. The Jews were the real agents who had already caused Pilate to do their will [Lns]. The Jews crucified Jesus even though it was the Roman soldiers who drove the nails [NICNT2].

QUESTION—How was a crucifixion carried out?

The subject was either nailed or tied to the crossbeam with his hands outspread. The crossbeam was then raised into place on the upright post. The man's body was able to rest on a peg on the post and the feet were either nailed or tied [AB, TH]. A block of wood was attached to the vertical shaft which the victim straddled. This reduced strain on the nails in the hands which might otherwise be torn by the body's weight [Gdt]. This block, the *sedecula* partically supported the weight of the body and so prolonged both life and agony [Car]. The nails were driven through the man's wrists or forearms, not his hands since they could not hold his weight and would tear out [NICNT1]. Luke 24:24 implies that they also nailed Jesus' feet [NTC]. The feet may have rested on a wooden slab attached to the upright post close to the ground [NTC]. The nails used were typically five to seven inches long [Kn]. The prisoner was either raised up to the seat or he climbed up by himself with the possible assistance of the executioners [Lns].

QUESTION—Who were the two others crucified with Jesus?
Matthew 27:38 and Mark 15:27 describe them as 'bandits' [AB, BECNT, TH], while Luke 23:33 describes them as 'criminals' [AB, TH]. They were probably guerrilla fighters [Car]. That Jesus was crucified with these men was the fulfillment of Psalms 53:12, 'he...was numbered with the transgressors' [AB, Car, Lns].

DISCOURSE UNIT—19:19-22 [HTC, IVP, WBC]. The topic is the title on the cross.

19:19 Pilate also wrote[a] (an) inscription[b] and put[c] (it) on the cross. It read, "Jesus the Nazarene[d] the King of-the Jews."

LEXICON—a. aorist act. indic. of γράφω (LN 33.61) (BAGD 4. p. 167): 'to write' [HTC, LN, NICNT2, WBC; KJV, NASB, NCV, TEV], 'to write out' [NJB], 'to compose' [BAGD], not explicit [NLT]. This active verb is also translated as a passive: 'Pilate ordered the charge against Jesus to be written on a board' [CEV], 'Pilate also had a notice/inscription/title/placard written/prepared' [AB, NTC; NET, NIV, NRSV, Ph, REB], 'Pilate also caused an inscription to be made' [Gdt]. The sense intended is that Pilate caused this to be done for him [AB, Bar, BECNT, Car, Gdt, HTC, Lns, My, NICNT1, NICNT2, NTC, Rd, TH; CEV, NIV, NRSV, Ph, REB].

b. τίτλος (LN **33.46**) (BAGD p. 820): 'inscription' [BAGD, **LN**, Gdt, WBC; NASB, NRSV, REB], 'title' [HTC, NICNT2, NTC; KJV], 'notice' [AB, BAGD; NET, NIV, NJB, TEV], 'sign' [NCV, NLT], 'placard' [Ph], 'writing' [LN], not explicit [CEV]. This noun denotes a brief notice used primarily for identification [LN]. The notice gave the reason for the condemnation [BAGD]. This presumably was written on a board that had been whitened with gypsum and attached to the cross [BECNT, EGT, NICNT1].

c. aorist act. indic. of τίθημι (LN 85.32) (BAGD I.1.a.β. p. 816): 'to put' [HTC, LN; KJV, NASB, NCV], 'to place [BAGD, LN, NICNT2], 'to post' [NLT], not explicit [WBC]. This verb is also translated passively: 'Pilate ordered the charge...to be...put above the cross' [CEV], 'Pilate also had a notice...fastened to the cross' [NET, NIV, similarly REB], 'Pilate...had it fixed to the cross' [NJB], 'Pilate also had an inscription...put on the cross' [AB, NTC; NRSV, similarly Ph, TEV]. It is causal in sense [Gdt, HTC, My, NICNT2, TH, TRT]: 'Pilate also caused an inscription...to be put on the cross' [Gdt]. This verb means to put or place in a particular location [LN]. Matthew 27:37 records that the inscription was placed over Jesus' head [AB], and Luke 23:38 records that it was placed over him [AB].

d. Ναζωραῖος (LN 93.538) (BAGD p. 532): 'Nazarene' [BAGD, LN, WBC; NASB, NET, NJB], 'of Nazareth' [Gdt, HTC, NTC; CEV, KJV, NCV, NIV, NLT, NRSV, Ph, REB, TEV], 'Nazorean' [AB, NICNT2]. This word is an alternative form of Ναζαρηνός (93.537), which is derived from Ναζαρέθ 'Nazareth' (93.536). It means a person who lives in or is a native of Nazareth [LN].

QUESTION—What was Pilate's motive in writing this?

He meant it to get his revenge on the Jews [Car, Lns, NICNT1, WBC] and to anger them [WBC]. Pilate was paying the Jews back for forcing him to act counter to his will in condemning Jesus. Now he reasons that, if Jesus were so dangerous that he deserves to be crucified, then the whole world will know what his crime was [Rd]. He intended to stigmatize the Jews [Gdt] or humiliate them [Car, HTC] by announcing that this malefactor was their King [Gdt]. He was insulting [EGT, NTC], or mocking them [ICC]. The mention of Nazareth may have been a further insult aimed at the Jews [BECNT].

QUESTION—What is indicated by the addition of the word 'also' in the phrase 'also wrote'?

It probably indicated that he wrote this title in addition to the other indignities that he had already shown to the Jews [EGT, NICNT1].

19:20 So many of-the Jews read this inscription, for the place where Jesus was-crucified was near the city. And it-was written in-Hebrew,[a] in-Latin,[b] (and) in-Greek.[c]

LEXICON—a. Ἑβραϊστί (LN 33.6) (BAGD p. 213): 'in Hebrew' [BAGD, LN; all translations except NTC; NCV, NET, NIV], 'in Aramaic' [BAGD, NTC; NET, NIV], 'in the Hebrew language' [LN], 'in the Jewish language' [NCV].
b. Ῥωμαϊστί (LN **33.7**) (BAGD p. 738): 'in Latin' [BAGD, **LN**; all translations], 'in the Latin language' [BAGD, LN].
c. Ἑλληνιστί (LN **33.5**) (BAGD p. 252): 'in Greek' [**LN**; all translations], 'in the Greek language' [BAGD, LN].

QUESTION—How did the proximity of the crucifixion site to Jerusalem insure that many Jews read the inscription?

Since it was Passover celebration many Jews were flowing into Jerusalem from every direction to observe the festival [HTC].

QUESTION—What is the significance of having the inscription in these three languages?

It insured that the title could have been read by a wide audience since anyone who could read would have known one of these langauges. Aramaic was the language of Palestine and so would have been understood best by the Jews. Latin was the official language, and Greek was the common language of communication for the whole Roman world. The three languages may also account for the differences between the Gospels as to what exactly was written [NICNT1]. The Latin language assured that the Romans would understand it [WBC]. Greek would have been understood by the Gentiles as well as most of the Jews of the Diaspora [BECNT]. It was Pilate's desire that the title be given the greatest possible publicity [Gdt]. John wanted to announce Jesus' kingship to the world [HTC]. It was God's intention that the whole world be able to read this title (Romans 11:15) [NTC].

QUESTION—How many times was the inscription written?

In order to avoid the misunderstanding that the inscription was written in a mixture of three languages, it may be necessary to translate something like, 'It was written three times, first in Hebrew, then in Latin, and then in Greek' [TRT; TEV].

QUESTION—What word is emphasized in this verse?

The word 'inscription' is placed first in its clause to emphasize it [TRT].

19:21 So the chief-priests of-the Jews said to-Pilate, "Do- not[a] -write, 'The King of the Jews,' but that, 'That-one said, I-am (the) King of-the Jews.'"

19:22 Pilate replied, "What I-have-written, I-have-written."

LEXICON—a. μή (BAGD A.III.3.b. p. 517): 'not' [BAGD]. This negative particle is used in a prohibitive sense in independent clauses, to express a negative wish or a warning. When used with the present tense it functions to bring to an end a condition now existing. As such 'do not write (any longer)' means, it must no longer stand written [BAGD].

QUESTION—What is indicated by the imperfect tense of 'said' (literally, '(the chief priests)...were saying')?

It indicates that they were trying to tell Pilate this [AB]: 'the chief priests...tried to tell Pilate' [AB]. The imperfect describes the attempt that failed [Gdt].

QUESTION—What is indicated by the negative particle μή in the verb phrase 'Do *not* write'?

The present imperative with μή means to prohibit activity that is on-going and so indicates, 'Do not leave it written' or perhaps, 'Alter what you have written' [AB, BAGD, Bar].

QUESTION—What is indicated by the pronoun ἐκεῖνος 'that one'?

It may have been used contemptuously to refer to Jesus [AB, BECNT, TH, TRT].

QUESTION—Why does no article precede the word 'King' in the statement (in Greek), 'That one said, I am King of the Jews'?

E.C. Colwell has shown that definite nouns that precede the verb (as here, Βασιλεύς εἰμι 'King I am') typically lack the article [AB, NICNT1]. The meaning is 'the King' [NICNT1]. (NOTE: AB, NICNT1, NICNT2; NCV, TEV all include the definite article in Jesus' statement.)

DISCOURSE UNIT—19:23–24 [HTC, IVP, NICNT1, WBC]. The topic is soldiers divide Jesus' clothing.

DISCOURSE UNIT—19:23–24b [HTC]. The topic is distribution of Jesus' clothing.

19:23 Then when (the) soldiers had-crucified Jesus, they-took his clothes[a] and made four parts, (a) part for-each soldier. (They) also (took) his tunic.[b] Now the tunic was seamless,[c] woven from the top through (the) whole.

LEXICON—a. ἱμάτιον (LN 6.162, 6.172): 'clothes' [AB, LN (6.162), WBC; NCV, NET, NIV, NLT, NRSV, Ph, REB, TEV], 'garment' [Gdt, HTC,

NICNT2, NTC; KJV], 'outer garment' [NASB], 'clothing' [LN (6.162); NJB], 'apparel' [LN (6.162)], 'cloak, coat, robe' [LN (6.172)]. This noun denotes any kind of clothing [LN (6.162)], or any type of outer garment [LN (6.172)].

b. χιτών (LN 6.176) (BAGD p. 882): 'tunic' [AB, Gdt, HTC, LN, NICNT2, NTC, WBC; NASB, NET, NRSV, REB], 'robe' [LN (48.6); NLT, TEV], 'shirt' [BAGD, LN; Ph], 'undergarment' [NIV, NJB], 'long shirt' [NCV], 'outer garment' [CEV], 'coat' [KJV]. This noun denotes a garment worn under the ἱμάτιον 'cloak' [ICC, LN]. This was a garment worn next to the skin [AB, BAGD, Car, HTC, IVP, NTC, TH] by both sexes [BAGD]. It was a long undergarment which was common and not especially costly [HTC, TH]. It was short-sleeved like a long T-shirt reaching to the knees. It could have been worn in public. It should not be translated either 'robe' or 'underwear' [TRT].

c. ἄραφος (LN **48.6**) (BAGD p. 104): 'seamless' [BAGD, LN, NICNT2, NTC, WBC; NASB, NET, NIV, NJB, NLT, NRSV, Ph, REB], 'without (a) seam' [Gdt, HTC, **LN**; KJV, TEV]. The statement 'the tunic was seamless' is translated 'the robe consisted of a single piece of cloth' [**LN**], 'it did not have any seams' [CEV, similarly AB], 'which was all one piece of cloth' [NCV]. This noun is derived from ῥάπτω 'to sew together', that is, being without a seam or without being sewn together [LN].

QUESTION—What is indicated by the conjunction οὖν 'then' at the beginning of the verse?

It indicates that the narrative is resuming from where it left off at verse 18 [Lns, My].

QUESTION—When were Jesus' clothes taken from him?

It was customary to remove a man's clothing from him before the crucifixion. This refers to all the clothes he was wearing [TH].

QUESTION—Why did the soldiers divide Jesus' clothes among them?

It was customary for the soldiers to divide up the clothes of a condemned prisoner [AB, Bar, Car, CH, EGT, Gdt, HTC, ICC, Kn, Lns, NICNT1, NTC, Rd, TH, WBC]. According to Roman law the condemned man's clothing became the property of the executioners [Gdt, ICC, TH].

QUESTION—How were the parts of Jesus' clothing divided?

The pieces of apparel were divided in such a way that each soldier received one portion. The pieces were not torn or cut in any way to make the portions equal [NTC, TRT]. The pieces may have been head covering, sandals, belt, and outer garment [AB, BECNT, Car, EGT, Lns, NTC, WBC]. If the sandals were not included, the fourth item may have been an undershirt, or *haluq*, worn under the tunic [AB].

QUESTION—What is indicated by the conjunction δέ 'now (the tunic was seamless)'?

It indicates that this is a further explanation about the tunic [Lns].

QUESTION—What is the implied verb for the phrase 'also his tunic'?
The verb ἔλαβον '(the soldiers) took' at the beginning of the verse provide the implied verb of the phrase 'also his tunic' [Bar, HTC, TH; TEV]: 'They also took his robe' [TEV].

DISCOURSE UNIT—19:24c–27 [HTC]. The topic is words to Mary and the disciple with her.

19:24 So they-said to each-other, "Let-us- not -tear[a] it, but let-us-cast-lots[b] for it (to see) whose it-will-be." So-that[c] the Scripture might-be-fulfilled [that says], "They divided my garments[d] among them, and they-cast lots[e] for my clothing."[f] So[g] the soldiers did these things.

TEXT—Some manuscripts omit the words ἡ λέγουσα 'that says'. GNT includes it with a C decision, and follows NA in enclosing this phrase in brackets, indicating difficulty in making the decision. Gdt, NICNT2, WBC; CEV, KJV, NET, NIV, NLT, NRSV, and Ph also include these words.

LEXICON—a. aorist act. subj. of σχίζω (LN 19.27) (BAGD 1.a. p. 797): 'to tear' [HTC, LN, NICNT2, NTC, WBC; NASB, NET, NIV, NJB, NLT, NRSV, Ph, REB, TEV], 'to tear up' [AB], 'to tear into parts' [NCV], 'to rip' [CEV], 'to rend' [Gdt; KJV], 'to split, to divide, to tear apart, to separate, to tear off' [BAGD]. This verb means to split or to tear an object into at least two parts [LN].

b. aorist. act. subj. of λαγχάνω (LN **30.104**) (BAGD 3. p. 462): 'to cast lots' [BAGD, Gdt, HTC, NTC, WBC; KJV, NASB, NRSV], 'to throw dice' [NET, NLT, TEV], 'to throw lots to determine/see' [**LN**; NCV], 'to decide by lot' [NIV], 'to gamble' [NICNT2; CEV], 'to toss' [AB; REB], 'to draw lots' [Ph], ' to throw dice to decide' [NJB], 'to choose by lot, to decide by gambling' [LN]. This verb means to choose by lot, probably by the use of marked pebbles or pieces of pottery [LN].

c. ἵνα (LN 89.59) (BAGD II.2. p. 378): 'so that, in order to, for the purpose of' [LN]. The clause 'so that/that/in order that the Scripture might be fulfilled' [Gdt, NICNT2, NTC, WBC; KJV] is also translated 'this happened that the scripture might be fulfilled' [NIV, similarly Ph], 'this happened so that the Scriptures would come true' [CEV, similarly NCV, TEV], 'thus the text of scripture came true' [REB], 'this was to fulfill the scripture' [HTC; similarly NASB, NLT, NRSV], 'this took place to fulfill the scripture' [NET], 'in this way the words of scripture were fulfilled' [NJB], 'the purpose of this was to have the Scripture fulfilled' [AB]. This conjunction marks the purpose for events and states (sometimes occurring in highly elliptical contexts) [LN]. Here it functions as a substitute for the infinitive of result. In Jewish thought, purpose and result are identical in declarations of the divine will. The formula ἵνα πληρωθῇ 'in order that it may be fulfilled', is so to be understood, since the fulfilment is according to God's plan of salvation [BAGD].

d. ἱμάτιον (LN 6.162): 'garment' [Gdt, HTC, NICNT2, NTC; NET, NIV, NJB, NLT, Ph, REB], 'clothes' [AB, WBC; CEV, NCV, NRSV, TEV],

'raiment' [KJV], 'outer garment' [NASB], 'apparel, clothing' [LN]. This noun in the plural denotes any kind of clothing [LN]. Here the plural of this word is used [TRT].
- e. κλῆρος (LN 6.219) (BAGD 1. p. 435): 'lot' [LN]. The phrase ἔβαλον κλῆρον 'they cast lots' [Gdt, HTC, NICNT2; KJV, NASB, NIV, NJB, NRSV, Ph, REB, WBC] is also translated 'they cast lot' [NTC], 'they threw lots' [NCV], 'they threw dice' [NET, NLT], 'they rolled dice' [AB], 'they…gambled' [CEV, TEV]. This noun denotes a specially marked pebble, piece of pottery, or stick employed in making decisions based on chance. Both in form as well as in function, the closest equivalent of κλῆρος is frequently a term which refers to 'dice' [LN]. A κλῆρος was a pebble or a small stick [BAGD]. One way to do this was to put the lots in a helmet and shake them until one flew out. Another was to reach in and draw one out [Lns].
- f. ἱματισμός (LN 6.162) (BAGD p. 376): 'clothing' [AB, BAGD, HTC, LN, WBC; NASB, NCV, NET, NIV, NLT, NRSV, REB], 'garment' [NICNT2; CEV], 'vesture' [Gdt; KJV, Ph], 'vestment' [NTC], 'clothes' [NJB], 'robe' [TEV], 'apparel' [BAGD, LN]. This noun in the plural denotes any kind of clothing [LN]. Here the singular of this word is used [TRT].
- g. μὲν οὖν (BAGD 1.a.α. p. 502; 5. p. 593): 'so' [AB, HTC, NICNT2; NCV, NET, NIV, NLT], 'then' [CEV], '(now) indeed' [BAGD, NTC], 'therefore' [Gdt, WBC; KJV, NASB], not explicit [NJB, NRSV, Ph, REB, TEV]. Here this combination means '(now) indeed' (the soldiers did this) and contrasts it with the conjunction δέ 'but' that begins the next verse [BAGD].

QUESTION—Who does the pronoun 'they' refer to?
It refers to the soldiers [TH, TRT; CEV, NCV, NET, TEV].

QUESTION—What particular Scripture is being referred to here?
The Scripture is Psalms 22:18/19, 'They divide my garments among them and cast lots for my clothing' [AB, Bar, Car, CH, EGT, IVP, Lns, My, NTC, TH, WBC].

QUESTION—What is the significance of the two words for clothing the first of which is plural, the second singular?
1. The first word refers to the clothing soldiers divided up among themselves, the second to the tunic for which they cast lots [Gdt, ICC, Lns, NICNT2]. Hebrew parallelism is not a mere repetition of two items, but the second adds a new sense to the first [Gdt, Lns]. The LXX has the words ἱμάτια (plural) and ἱματισμόν (singular) for the two words just as here in this verse. John meant that the garments were divided, but that lots were cast for the tunic [ICC]. The Hebrew words *begadim* 'garments' and *lebush* 'vesture' do not refer to the same clothing. The word 'vesture' refers to the tunic of Jesus. Also the Psalm records that for this piece of clothing a single lot (κλῆρος) was cast [Lns].
2. There is no difference in sense intended between the two words [Bar, NTC, WBC]. The Psalm does not distinguish between two different kinds of clothing [WBC]. The parallelism of Hebrew poetry that considers the

two lines of poetry synonymous, requires us to consider the singular noun to be a collective synonym for garments [NTC].
3. It may be that the two words for clothing in the Psalm both refer to the tunic itself, and the two verbs, 'divided' and 'cast lots', refer to the same action [Car].

QUESTION—What is indicated by the conjunction οὖν 'So (the soldiers did these things)'?
1. It indicates that the reason they did them was *because* in doing so they unwittingly fulfilled the prophecy in Psalm 22:18 [Kn, NICNT1]. This shows that God was controlling all that was done so that it was His will that was being accomplished and not the will of men [NICNT1].
2. It indicates that the narrative is resuming after the quote [AB, Bar].
3. Together with the particle μέν it indicates a contrast between what the soldiers did with what was happening with Jesus' mother and friends around the cross introduced by δέ 'but' (see note in Lexicon above) [BAGD].

DISCOURSE UNIT—19:25–30 [Ph]. The topic is Jesus provides for his mother.

DISCOURSE UNIT—19:25–27 [HTC, IVP, NICNT1, WBC]. The topic is Jesus provides for Mary.

19:25 But/now^a standing by the cross of Jesus (were) his mother and his mother's sister, Mary the (wife) of Clopas^b and Mary Magdalene.^c

LEXICON—a. δέ (LN 89.136) (BAGD 1.a.α. p. 502): 'but' [BAGD, HTC, WBC; NASB], 'now' [Gdt, Lns, NICNT2, NTC; KJV, NET], 'meanwhile' [AB; NRSV, REB], 'while (the soldiers were doing this)' [Ph], not explicit [CEV, NCV, NIV, NJB, NLT, TEV]. The combination μέν...δέ (μέν in verse 24, δέ here) are markers of sets of items in contrast with each other 'on the one hand ... but on the other hand' [LN]. The women may have provided the very clothing over which the soldiers were gambling [NICNT1].
b. Κλωπᾶς (LN 93.217) (BAGD p. 436): 'Clopas' [BAGD, LN; all translations except KJV], 'Cleophas' [KJV]. This noun denotes the husband of Μαρία, one of the women at the crucifixion [LN].
c. Μαγδαληνή (LN 93.242) (BAGD p. 484): 'Magdalene' [BAGD, LN; all translations except NJB, Ph, REB], '(Mary) of Magdala' [NJB, Ph, REB]. This noun is derived from Μαγδαλά (93.523) (a town on the west side of the Lake of Galilee) and denotes a woman of Magdala [LN]. It was about a twenty minute walk from Tiberias [BAGD]. Mary Magdalene may be translated 'Mary from Magdala' [TH].

QUESTION—What is indicated by the conjunction δέ 'but/now'?
1. It indicates a contrast of these women with the soldiers of verse 24 [Bar, BAGD, BECNT, Car, CH, EGT, HTC, Kn, WBC]. The soldiers are occupied with dividing Jesus' clothes but the women are watching and waiting with devotion and prayer. But the contrast further extends to Jesus

who is taking care of the relationships of his loved ones [WBC]. The construction μέν...δέ from verse 24 to here support the interpretation of a contrast [Car, Kn]. If a contrast is indicated it is not a sharp one, but simply distinguishes between the two groups [BECNT]. The soldiers are occupied with dividing Jesus' clothing but the women are watching devotedly in prayer [WBC].

2. It indicates a resumption of the narrative or a transition to the next event [Lns, IVP, Rd]. No contrast is intended, δέ simply indicates continuation [Lns].

QUESTION—How are the two nouns related in the genitive construction τῷ σταυρῷ τοῦ Ἰησοῦ 'the cross of Jesus'?

The cross did not belong to Jesus but was the instrument on which he was crucified [TH, TRT].

QUESTION—How are the two nouns related in the genitive construction Μαρία τοῦ Κλωπᾶ 'Mary of Clopas'?

Mary is probably the 'wife' of Clopas [NICNT2; all translations except NICNT2], although she could have been his mother, daughter, or sister [NICNT2]: 'Mary of Clopas' [NICNT2].

QUESTION—How many women are referred to here?

1. There are four women named here [AB, BECNT, Bar, EGT, HTC, ICC, IVP, NICNT1, NICNT2, NTC, Rd, TH, WBC; probably all translations except Gdt]: 'Jesus' mother was standing near the cross with her sister, and with them Mary, the wife of Clopas, and Mary of Magdala' [Ph]. We take the four women to be likely to be: 1) Jesus' mother, 2) her sister, Salome (see Matthew 27:56; Mark 15:40; 16:1), 3), Mary, the wife of Clopas, and 4) Mary Magdalene [BECNT, Car, ICC, IVP, NICNT1, NTC]. To indicate only 3 women would mean that Jesus' mother had a sister also named Mary which was unlikely [AB, My, NICNT2, NICNT1, NTC, TH].

2. There are three women named here [Lns]. The three would be 1) Jesus' mother, 2) her sister, the wife of Clopas, and 3) Mary Magdalene. That both Jesus' mother and her sister were named Mary can be explained in that they may have been so named from former marriages [Lns].

19:26 Then when- Jesus -saw his mother and the disciple whom he-loved standing-nearby,[a] he-said to his mother, "Woman,[b] look[c] your son!"

LEXICON—a. perf. act. participle of παρίσταμαι (LN **17.3**) (BAGD 2.b.α. p. 628): 'to stand nearby' [**LN**; NASB, NCV, NIV], 'to stand near' [BAGD, HTC, LN; NJB, WBC], 'to stand by' [BAGD, NICNT2; KJV], 'to stand there' [NTC; NET, TEV], 'to be present (with) someone' [BAGD]. The phrase 'standing by' is also translated '(his...disciple) with her' [CEV], '(his mother) there with (the disciple)' [AB], 'standing there beside (the disciple)' [NLT], '(his mother) and beside (her)' [Gdt], 'standing beside (her)' [NRSV, REB], 'standing by her side' [Ph]. This verb means to stand near or alongside of someone, either with friendly or hostile intent [LN].

b. γυνή (LN 9.34) (BAGD 1. p. 168): 'woman' [AB, BAGD, Gdt, HTC, LN, NICNT2, NTC; KJV, NASB, NET, NJB, NRSV, TEV], 'dear woman' [NIV, NLT], 'Mother' [WBC; REB], not explicit [CEV, NCV, Ph]. This noun denotes an adult female person of marriageable age. As a form of address, γυνή was used in Koine Greek in speaking politely to a female person. In John 2:4 Jesus uses it to address his mother courteously. In a number of languages it would be totally impossible to have Jesus address his mother merely as 'woman'. To do so would imply that he was denying that Mary was his mother. In other languages, such an expression would imply that Jesus was calling his mother a prostitute or evil person. Accordingly, in a number of languages there is simply no other way in which Jesus could address his mother than as 'mother' or 'my mother' [LN]. The vocative of 'woman' is by no means a disrespectful form of address [BAGD, Gdt, ICC, Lns]. NIV prefixes the modifier 'dear' to erase any harshness the word may have implied [NICNT1]. It may be necessary to follow TEV and not make this word explicit in the translation in order to avoid the impression that Jesus was being impolite to her [TH]: 'he said to his mother, "He is your son"' [TEV].

c. ἴδε (LN 91.13) (BAGD 3. p. 369): 'look' [LN, NICNT2, NTC, WBC], 'here is' [AB, BAGD; NCV, NIV, NLT, NRSV], 'look, here/there is' [NET, Ph], 'there is' [REB], 'this is' [NJB], 'he is' [TEV], 'behold' [Gdt, HTC; KJV, NASB], 'listen, pay attention' [LN]. The statement 'Look, your son' is translated 'This man is now your son' [CEV]. This particle is a prompter of attention, that serves also to emphasize the following statement [LN].

QUESTION—To whom does the participle 'standing nearby' refer? That is, who was standing by whom?

1. The participle is masculine indicating that the disciple was standing by Jesus' mother [EGT, Gdt, Lns, NTC, TH, TRT, WBC; CEV, NJB, NRSV, Ph, REB]: '…seeing his mother and beside her the disciple whom he loved…' [Gdt].
2. Jesus' mother is standing with the disciple [AB; NLT]: '…saw his mother there with the disciple whom he loved…' [AB].

QUESTION—To whom do the words 'your son' in the statement, 'Look, your son' refer?

They refer to the disciple, not to Jesus [AB, EGT, Lns, TRT; NCV, NIV, NLT, NRSV, Ph, REB, TEV]: 'he is your son' [TEV].

QUESTION—What was implied in the statement 'Look, your son'?

It was intended to put Jesus' mother into the care and responsibility of the beloved disciple [Car, CH, ICC, IVP, Kn, Lns, My, NICNT1]. Since the beloved disciple was not in reality Jesus' mother's physical son, it may be better to translate something like, 'Consider him as your son' [TH, TRT].

Jesus wants John to look after his (Jesus') mother as though she were his own mother [TRT].

QUESTION—Why may Jesus not have committed his mother to one of his own brothers?

Verse 7:5 informs us that his own brothers did not believe in him [ICC, NICNT1], though later they joined the apostles [NICNT1].

19:27 Then[a] he-said to-the disciple, "Look your mother!" And from that hour the disciple took her into his-own-home.[b]

LEXICON—a. εἶτα (LN 67.44) (BAGD 1. p. 233): 'then' [BAGD, Gdt, HTC, LN, NICNT2, NTC, WBC; CEV, KJV, NASB, NCV, NET, NJB, NRSV, TEV], 'and' [NIV, NLT, REB], 'and then' [Ph], 'in turn' [AB], 'afterwards, later' [LN], 'next' [BAGD]. This adverb indicates a point of time following another point [LN].

b. ἴδιος (LN Index supplement **7.3a**) (BAGD 3.b. p. 370): 'home' [BAGD, LN]. The phrase εἰς τὰ ἴδια is translated 'into/to his (own) home' [all translations except AB; CEV, NASB] is also translated 'into his own household' [CEV, NASB], 'into his care' [AB]. The phrase τὰ ἴδια here denotes 'home' [BAGD, BECNT, Lns].

QUESTION—What did Jesus imply by his words, 'Look, your mother'?

It implies: 'Consider this woman to be as your own mother' or 'Take care of my mother as (if she were) your own mother' [TRT]. Jesus was asking the disciple to take care of her [AB, Lns, My, NICNT2]. Jesus was asking the disciple to take responsibility for her as a person should for his/her own parents [NTC]. The disciple is to take over the rights and duties of a mature son toward Mary [WBC]. In these two statements, Mary receives back what she was giving up [Rd]. Two translations rendered these words as follows: 'She is (now) your mother' [CEV, TEV].

QUESTION—Should the word 'hour' be taken literally?

It is better to translate this as a more general reference to time—'From that time' [Lns, TH; CEV, NCV, NET, NIV, NLT, Ph, REB]. The 'hour' may have reference to the event of the crucifixion [Bar, My, NICNT1, NICNT2].

QUESTION—What is implied by the action, 'took her into his own home'?

It means that he not only gave her a place to live but that he also took responsibility for her [NICNT1]. This could be translated, 'considered her a member of his family' or 'treated her as a member of his own household' [TH].

DISCOURSE UNIT—19:28–37 [BECNT, Rd; NCV, NET, NIV, NLT]. The topic is the death of Jesus.

DISCOURSE UNIT—19:28–30 [HTC, IVP, NICNT1, WBC; CEV, TEV]. The topic is the death of Jesus.

19:28 After this Jesus knowing that all-things had- now[a] -been-completed,[b] so-that the Scripture might-be-fulfilled[c] said, "I-thirst."
LEXICON—a. ἤδη (LN 67.20) (BAGD p. 344): 'now' [AB, BAGD, Gdt, HTC, NTC, WBC; CEV, KJV, NIV, NJB, NLT, NRSV, Ph, REB], 'already' [BAGD, LN, NICNT2; NASB], 'by now' [TEV], 'by this time' [BAGD; NET], not explicit [NCV]. This adverb indicates a point of time preceding another point of time and implying completion [LN]. The word 'now' refers to Jesus' time on earth not to our present time. It could be translated 'at that time' [TRT].

b. perf. pass. indicative of τελέω (LN 68.22) (BAGD 1. p. 810): 'to be completed' [BAGD, LN; NET, NIV, NJB, NRSV, Ph, TEV], 'to be finished' [AB, BAGD, Gdt, HTC, LN, NICNT2, NTC; NLT], 'to be accomplished' [LN, WBC; KJV, NASB], 'to be done' [NCV], 'to come to an appointed end' [REB], 'to be ended' [LN], 'to be brought to an end' [BAGD]. This verb is also translated actively: '(Jesus knew that) he had now finished (his work)' [CEV]. This verb means to bring an activity to a successful finish [LN].

c. aorist pass. subj. of τελειόω (LN **13.126**) (BAGD 1; 2.c. p. 210): 'to be fulfilled' [LN], 'to be made to happen, to be accomplished, to be brought to fruition' [LN], 'to be brought to an end, to be brought to its goal or accomplishment' [BAGD (2.c)]. The clause 'to/in order to fulfill the Scripture' [HTC; NASB, NET, NLT, NRSV] is also translated 'that/in order that/so that the scripture might/would/should be (completely) fulilled' [Gdt, WBC; KJV, NIV, NJB], 'so that the scripture might be completed' [NICNT2], 'in order that the scripture might be accomplished' [NTC],'in order that what was written in the Scripture might happen' [**LN**], 'in order that the Scripture might receive its final fulfilment' [BAGD (1)], 'in order to bring the Scripture to its complete fulfillment' [AB],'in order to make the Scriptures come true' [CEV], 'so that the Scripture would come true' [NCV], 'fulfilling the saying of scripture' [Ph, similarly REB]. This verb means to cause to happen for some end result [LN]. It means 'to be brought to an end' in the sense of the overcoming or supplanting of an imperfect state of things by that which is free from objection. Here it refers to the fulfilling of a prophecy or promise that is not satisfied until it is fulfilled [BAGD (2.c)].

QUESTION—How much time is indicated by the phrase 'after this'?
It refers to an indefinite, but brief sequence of time [NICNT1, TH]. It merely indicates that an interval passed between the former and the following events [ICC, Lns]. Considering the other Gospel accounts, a period of three hours may have occurred between verses 25–27 and verses 28–30 [ICC, TRT].

QUESTION—What is indicated by the word πάντα 'all things'?
It indicates all that the Father had given the Son to do [AB, Bar, TH, TRT]. It indicates all that was involved in his work as Redeemer [Gdt].

QUESTION—Who is the actor in the passive construction 'had now been completed'?

This may better be expressed actively as follows, 'Jesus had done everything that he should have done' [TH], 'Jesus knew that he had now finished his work' [CEV], 'He had now accomplished everything that His Father had sent Him to do' [TRT].

QUESTION—What specific Scripture does this refer to?

It refers to Psalm 69:21/22 'They put gall in my food and gave me vinegar for my thirst' [Bar, BECNT, Car, CH, EGT, HTC, ICC, IVP, NICNT1, Rd, TH, WBC]. The prophecy of both Psalm 69:21 and of Psalm 22:15 'My strength is dried up like a potsherd, and my tongue sticks to the roof of my mouth; you lay me in the dust of death' may be referred to [NTC, TRT]. It may also refer to the entire Psalm 69 [BECNT, Rd].

QUESTION—The words 'to fulfill the Scripture' can refer forward to Jesus' words, 'I thirst', or back to the words 'all things had been completed'. Which is considered correct?

1. The words 'in order to' refer forward to the words 'He said, "I thirst"' [BECNT, Car, Gdt, ICC, IVP, NTC, TH; probably all translations]. Even with reference to Jesus' thirst, prophecy was being fulfilled [NTC].
2. These words refer back to the words that 'all things had been completed' [Lns, My]. Jesus knew that all things were now accomplished in order to fulfill the Scriptures. The action he refers to that had been accomplished was the bitter agony that occurred during the three hours of darkness in which he experienced the Father's rejection [Lns]. Since all things had been completed there was nothing still lacking that needed to happen. So the connection to the following 'He said' is excluded. Also, John never makes the purpose clause ('to fulfill the Scripture'), precede the fulfillment clause [My].
3. It could grammatically refer either forward or backward [AB, NICNT1]. If it refers back it means that all things were now finished in order that the Scripture might be brought to fulfillment. However, most grammarians cite this as an example where the purpose clause refers forward to Jesus' saying that he was thirsty. Perhaps the two interpretations should not be distinguished [AB].

19:29 (A) jar[a] full of-sour-wine[b] was[c] (there). So they-put- (a) sponge full of-(the)-sour-wine -on[d] (a)-hyssop-branch[e] (and) held-(it)-to[f] his mouth.

TEXT—Instead of σπόγγον οὖν μεστὸν τοῦ ὄξους ὑσσώτῳ περιθέντες 'so they put a sponge full of sour wine on hyssop', some manuscripts read οἱ δὲ πλήσαντες σπόγγον ὄξους καὶ ὑσσώτῳ περιθέντες 'and they having filled a sponge with sour wine and having put (it) on hyssop', others read οἱ δὲ πλήσαντες σπόγγον ὄξους μετὰ χολῆς καὶ ὑσσώτῳ περιθέντες 'and they having filled a sponge with sour wine with gall and having put (it) on hyssop', and still others read οἱ δὲ πλήσαντες σπόγγον τοῦ ὄξους μετὰ χολῆς καὶ ὑσσώτῳ καὶ περιθέντες καλάμῳ 'and they having filled a sponge with sour wine with gall and hyssop, and having put (it) on a reed'. GNT reads 'so they put a sponge full of sour wine on hyssop' with an A rating, indicating that the text is certain.

LEXICON—a. σκεῦος (LN 6.118) (BAGD 1.a.b. p. 754): 'jar' [AB, BAGD, LN, WBC; CEV, NASB, NCV, NET, NIV, NJB, NLT, NRSV, REB], 'vessel' [BAGD, Gdt, LN, NICNT2, NTC; KJV], 'bowl' [HTC; Ph, TEV], 'container' [LN], 'dish' [BAGD]. This noun denotes a highly generic term for any kind of jar, bowl, basket, or vase [LN]. In general it can mean a thing or object used for any purpose at all [BAGD].

b. ὄξος (LN 6.201) (BAGD): 'sour wine' [BAGD, LN, NICNT2; NASB, NET, NJB, NLT, NRSV, Ph, REB], 'vinegar' [Gdt, HTC, NTC; KJV, NCV], 'cheap wine' [WBC; CEV, TEV], 'common wine' [AB], 'wine vinegar' [BAGD; NIV]. This noun denotes a cheap, sour wine (evidently a favorite beverage of poorer people and relatively effective in quenching thirst). Sometimes it is translated as 'bitter wine' or 'sour juice' [LN]. This relieved the thirst more effectively than water and, because it was cheaper than regular wine, it was a favorite beverage of the lower ranks of society and of those in moderate circumstances [BAGD]. It was like the sour wine that the soldiers drank [Bar, Car, EGT, ICC, Kn, Lns, My, NTC, TH, TRT]. It was the Roman *posca* [ICC, NICNT1], a vinegar diluted with water [NICNT1]. It was vinegar specifically provided for the condemned criminals and not the wine the soldiers drank [Gdt].

c. imperf. mid. or pass. (deponent = active) indic. of κεῖμαι (LN **85.3**) (BAGD 1.b. p. 426): 'to be (there)' [Gdt, **LN**; CEV, NCV, NET, NIV, TEV], 'to stand (there)' [BAGD, HTC, WBC; NASB, NJB, NRSV, Ph, REB], 'to lie (there)' [BAGD, LN, NTC], 'to be set (there)' [NICNT2; KJV], 'to be (at hand)' [AB], 'to sit (there)' [NLT]. This verb means to be in a place, frequently in the sense of 'being contained in' or 'resting on' [LN]. When used of vessels, it means 'to stand (there)' [BAGD]. The verb 'set there' seems to indicate that the wine was provided for the use of the crucifixion [NICNT1].

d. aorist act. participle of περιτίθημι (LN 85.39) (BAGD 1. p. 652): 'to put on/upon' [BAGD, Gdt, HTC, NICNT2, WBC; KJV, NASB, NCV, NET, NIV, NJB, NLT, NRSV, Ph, TEV], 'to stick on/around' [AB, NTC], 'to fix on' [REB], 'to surround' [LN], 'to put around' [BAGD, LN], 'to place on/around' [BAGD], not explicit [CEV]. This verb means to place something around an object or area [LN]. Here it means 'to put a sponge on a reed' [BAGD].

e. ὕσσωπος (LN **3.26**) (BAGD p. 848): '(a) hyssop branch' [NLT, similarly NASB, NET, NRSV], '(a) branch of hyssop plant' [NCV], '(a) stem of the hyssop plant' [CEV], '(a) stalk of hyssop' [Gdt, NICNT2; similarly NIV, TEV], 'hyssop' [AB, BAGD, HTC, **LN**; KJV, REB], 'hyssop plant' [WBC; CEV], '(a) hyssop stick' [NTC; NJB], '(a) spear' [Ph]. This noun denotes a small aromatic bush, the branches of which were often used by the Jews in religious ceremonies. The hyssop bush may reach a height of three feet and has a number of woody stems. In some translations a term for hyssop is borrowed with a classifier such as 'plant', for example, 'a branch of a plant called hyssop' [LN]. The hyssop is a small bush with blue flowers and highly aromatic leaves. It is used in purification sacrifices. Here the hyssop appears as a plant with a long, firm stem or stalk [BAGD]. It may have been the *marjoram* (Origanum maru) that has woody stalks suited to this use [NTC]. The stems of the hyssop plant were about 18 inches long [Lns, My]. It was doubtless a plant with sufficiently long stems for the purpose for which it was used here [NICNT1]. It needed to have been only 2 or 3 feet long [EGT] since the crucified men were only slightly elevated [EGT, Lns, My]. There is a textual variant reading of ὑσσός 'javelin' that is adopted by ICC [AB]. (Note also Ph).

  f. aorist act. indic. of προσφέρω (LN 15.192) (BAGD 1.b. p. 719): 'to hold to/up to' [BAGD, HTC; CEV, NJB, NLT, NRSV, REB], 'to bring to/up to' [BAGD, Gdt, LN, NICNT2, NTC, WBC; NASB], 'to lift to/up to' [NCV, NET, NIV, TEV], 'to push up towards' [Ph], 'to raise to' [AB], 'to put to' [KJV], 'to offer to' [BAGD], 'to carry to' [LN]. This verb means to carry or bring something into the presence of someone, usually implying a transfer of something to that person [LN]. Here it means that they held the sponge to Jesus' mouth [BAGD].

QUESTION—How did the sponge get filled with wine?

 The soldiers or an undefined 'they' or 'someone' apparently soaked the sponge in the wine [CH, Gdt; CEV, KJV, NIV, NLT, Ph, REB, NCV]: 'the soldiers soaked a sponge in it' [NCV].

QUESTION—To whom does the pronoun 'they' refer in the words '*they*...held it to his mouth'?

 It probably refers to one of the soldiers [AB, CH, EGT, Gdt, Lns, My, NICNT2, NTC; NCV], or the women [NICNT2]. The use of the plural 'they' may include the centurion in charge who gave his consent to the action [Lns]. Or it refers to an unspecified person—'someone' [TRT; CEV].

19:30 **So when Jesus received the sour-wine he-said, "It-is-finished,"**[a] **and he-bowed**[b] **his head and gave-up**[c] **his spirit.**

LEXICON—a. perf. pass. indic. of τελέω (LN 68.22) (BAGD 1. p. 811): 'to be finished' [BAGD, LN; all translations except WBC; CEV, NJB, NET, REB], 'to be accomplished' [LN, WBC; REB], 'to be completed' [BAGD, LN; NET], 'to be ended' [LN], 'to be brought to an end' [BAGD]. The words 'It is finished' are translated 'Everything is done' [CEV], 'It is fulfilled' [NJB]. This verb means to bring an activity to a successful finish [LN]. Here it refers to divine ordinances contained in the Scriptures as being finished [BAGD]. The perfect tense indicates action completed in the past with continuing effects into the present [Kn].

  b. aorist act. participle of κλίνω (LN **16.16**) (BAGD 1.a. p. 436): 'to bow' [BAGD, **LN**; all translations except Ph], 'to bow down (the head)' [LN], 'to incline' [BAGD, LN], 'to bend' [BAGD]. The words 'he bowed his head' is translated 'his head fell forward' [Ph]. This verb means to cause something to incline [LN]. Since the bowing of the head came before the giving up of his spirit, and since especially in this Gospel the Passion is a voluntary act of Jesus to the very last, the bowing must not be regarded as a sign of weakness. The Crucified One acted of his own accord [BAGD].

c. aorist act. indic. of παραδίδωμι (LN 23.110) (BAGD 1.a. p. 614): 'to give up' [BAGD, **LN**], 'to hand over' [AB, BAGD, NICNT2, WBC], 'to give over' [BAGD, LN], 'to deliver, to entrust' [BAGD]. The idiom 'he gave up his spirit' [Gdt, HTC, NTC; NASB, NET, NIV, NJB, NRSV, REB, TEV] is also translated 'he gave up the ghost' [KJV], 'he released his spirit' [NLT], 'he died' [**LN**, TRT; CEV, NCV, Ph]. The words παραδίδωμι τὸ πνεῦμα, literally 'to give over the spirit' are an idiom meaning 'to die', with the possible implication of a willing or voluntary act [LN].

QUESTION—How did Jesus 'receive' the wine?

Since his hands were nailed to the cross, Jesus must have sucked the wine from the sponge and swallowed it [TH].

QUESTION—How did Jesus speak the words 'It is finished'?

He probably spoke in a loud voice (see Matthew 27:50; Mark 15:37; Luke 23:46) [Car, CH, Lns, NICNT1; Ph]: 'he cried, "It is finished!"' [Ph]. Jesus needed the wine to moisten his throat so he could shout the final proclamation 'It is finished' [CH].

QUESTION—What was Jesus referring to that was finished?

He was referring to the work that his Father had given him to complete on earth (see 4:34; 14:31; 17:4) [Car, EGT, HTC, Kn, My, NICNT1, NICNT2, WBC]. The complete work of redemption was finished (see 1:29) [Kn, Lns, NICNT1, NTC]. To make sure that Jesus' work was what was finished and not the wine he had just drank, it may be necessary to translate something like, 'My work is finished' [TRT].

QUESTION—To whom did Jesus 'give up' his spirit?

He gave or committed his spirit to the Father (see Luke 23:46, "Father, into your hands I commit my spirit") [AB, Car, EGT, Kn, Lns, NICNT2].

QUESTION—What is implied by the words 'he bowed his head'?

They imply that he did so voluntarily [BAGD, Gdt]. The words imply that until that point he had held his head erect [Gdt, Lns]. It is noteworthy that the verb 'bowed' is active not passive [Bar].

QUESTION—What is implied by the idiom 'he gave up his spirit'?

It is implied that he gave up his life voluntarily [BAGD, CH, ICC, Kn, LN, NICNT1, NICNT2, NTC, TRT]. The act of giving up his spirit fulfilled his words of 10:18, 'No one takes it from me, but I lay it down of my own accord. I have authority to lay it down and authority to take it up again. This command I received from my Father' [Gdt, ICC, WBC]. The words 'to give up one's spirit' is an idiom that means 'to die' [TRT]. The departure of a person's spirit was a common Jewish expression of death [Kn].

QUESTION—What did Jesus mean by the term πνεῦμα 'spirit'?

1. He meant his own human spirit [AB, Car, HTC, ICC, Lns, NICNT1, NTC, TH, TRT, WBC; probably all translations except NICNT2]. It refers

to the spirit of Jesus himself while the giving of the Holy Spirit belongs to the activity of Jesus after the resurrection (see 20:22) [WBC].
2. He meant the Holy Spirit of God [NICNT2]. Jesus had received the Holy Spirit at his baptism (1:32) and had kept this Spirit until this moment. That he handed over his Spirit here means that he stopped breathing but his breath was the Holy Spirit [NICNT2].

DISCOURSE UNIT—19:31–42 [AB, Bar, HTC, IVP; NASB, Ph]. The topic is the burial of Jesus [AB, Bar, HTC, IVP; NASB], the care of the body of Jesus [NASB, Ph].

DISCOURSE UNIT—19:31–37 [Car, HTC, NICNT1, WBC; CEV, NRSV, TEV]. The topic is the piercing of Jesus' side.

19:31 Therefore/then because[a] it-was (the) day-of-preparation,[b] (and) so-that the bodies would- not -remain on the cross on the Sabbath,[c] for that Sabbath was (a) special[d] day), the Jews asked Pilate that their legs might-be-broken and (that they) might-be- taken-away.[e]

LEXICON—a. ἐπεί (LN 89.32) (BAGD 2. p. 284): 'because' [BAGD, Gdt, LN, NICNT2, WBC; KJV, NASB NET, NIV, NLT, REB, TEV], 'since' [AB, BAGD, HTC, LN, NTC; NCV, NJB, NRSV], 'for' [BAGD, LN; KJV], 'as' [Ph], 'inasmuch as' [LN]. This causal relationship was also translated as a result relationship: '(It was a special day)…So (they asked Pilate)' [CEV]. This conjunction indicates cause or reason [BAGD, LN], often with the implication of a relevant temporal element [LN].

b. παρασκευή (LN 67.201) (BAGD p. 622): 'day of preparation' [AB, BAGD, HTC, LN; NASB NET, NIV, NJB, NLT, NRSV], 'day of Preparation for the Passover' [Ph], 'Preparation Day' [WBC; NCV], 'the eve of the sabbath' [REB], 'Friday' [LN; TEV], '(the) P/preparation' [Gdt, NICNT2, NTC; KJV]. This noun is translated 'The next day would be both a Sabbath and the Passover. It was a special day for the Jewish people' [CEV]. This noun denotes a day on which preparations were made for a sacred or feast day [LN]. In Jewish literature only it was a definite day, as the 'day of preparation' for a festival. It was Friday [AB, BAGD, Bar, Car, CH, EGT, HTC, LN, Lns, ICC, NICNT1, NTC, TH, TRT; TEV], on which day everything had to be prepared for the Sabbath when no work was permitted [BAGD]. This was the day of preparation before the Jewish Sabbath covering the time between 6 p.m. on Thursday and 6 p.m. on Friday when the Sabbath began [AB, Bar, TH].

c. σάββατον (LN 67.184) (BAGD 1.a. p. 739): 'S/sabbath' [BAGD, LN; all translations except KJV, NCV], 'S/sabbath day' [KJV, NCV], 'Saturday' [LN]. This noun denotes the seventh or last day of the week (religiously the most important since it was consecrated to the worship of God) [LN]. The seventh day of the week in the Jewish calendar was marked by rest from work and by special religous ceremonies [BAGD]. Here it refers to the Sabbath day that begins a festival period [BAGD 2b.β. p. 498]. The

Sabbath began in the evening during which no activities like buying, cooking, and cleaning were permitted [Lns].
- d. μέγας [BAGD 2.b.β. p. 498]: 'special' [CEV, NCV], 'high' [Gdt, HTC; KJV, NASB, NIV], 'great' [BAGD; NICNT2, NTC, WBC], '(a) very special' [NLT], 'especially important' [NET], 'particularly important' [Ph], 'especially holy' [TEV], '(a day) of special/great solemnity' [NJB, NRSV, REB], 'solemn' [AB], 'sublime, important' [BAGD].
- e. aorist pass. subj. of αἴρω (LN 15.203): 'to be taken away' [AB, Gdt, HTC, LN, NICNT2, WBC; KJV, NASB, NCV, NJB], 'to be taken down' [NET, NIV, NLT, REB], 'to be removed' [LN, similarly NTC; NRSV, Ph], 'to be carried (away), to be carried off' [LN]. The passive 'They...might be taken away' is also translated actively: '(they asked Pilate to) take their bodies down' [CEV, similarly TEV]. This verb means to lift up and carry (away) [LN].

QUESTION—What relationship is indicated by the conjunction οὖν 'so'?

It indicates that what follows is a conclusion from what precedes—Jesus had already died, 'therefore' [Gdt, Lns, My; KJV], 'accordingly' [WBC]. It simply indicates a sequence to the next event 'then' [NTC; NASB, NET, TEV]. Other translations either rendered this word 'now' or left it implicit.

QUESTION—What made this Sabbath so important?

It was a significant day not only because the first day of the Passover festival was a holy day, but also because that Passover began on a Sabbath [AB]. It was the Sabbath of the seven-day Passover Feast [CH, EGT, Lns, NTC, TH, TRT, WBC; CEV]. It was not only a Sabbath but the first day of the Passover Festival [BAGD, Bar, Kn, My]. This Sabbath not only happened during the Passover Feast but it also coincided with the second paschal day that was devoted to the very significant sheaf offering (see Leviticus 23:11) [Bar, Car]. It was doubly significant because it synchronized with the first day of unleavened bread and this was a 'great' day [ICC].

QUESTION—What was significant about the day of preparation?

Since it was the preparation for the Sabbath, it meant that it was the time of the killing of the lamb for the Passover meal which followed preparation day [Gdt].

QUESTION—Why was it so urgent to remove the bodies from the crosses so quickly?

Deuteronomy 21:22–23 states 'If a man guilty of a capital offense is put to death and his body is hung on a tree, you must not leave his body on the tree overnight. Be sure to bury him that same day, because anyone who is hung on a tree is under God's curse' (see also Joshua 8:29; 10:26) [AB, Bar, CH, EGT, Gdt, ICC, Lns, My, NICNT1, NICNT2, NTC, TRT, WBC]. To leave the bodies on the crosses would defile the Sabbath [TRT].

QUESTION—To whom does the phrase 'the Jews' refer?

It refers to the Jewish authorities [AB, Car, HTC, ICC, Kn, Lns, NTC, TH, TRT, WBC; NET, NLT, TEV], or specifically to the chief priests [AB, NTC, TH].

QUESTION—Where was Pilate at this time and did he grant their request?
Pilate was probably not present at the crucifixion so it was necessary for the Jews to leave Golgotha and to go to him [AB, TRT]. It is implied that Pilate granted their request [EGT, HTC, ICC, Lns, NICNT2, NTC].

QUESTION—Why was it necessary to break the legs of the men on the crosses?
The reason they broke their legs was to speed up their deaths [AB, BAGD (p. 409), Car, CH, EGT, Gdt, HTC, ICC, Lns, My, NICNT1, NICNT2, NTC, TH, TRT, WBC]. The Passover supper was to follow at 6 p.m. and the bodies needed to be removed before that began [Gdt]. Once their legs were broken they could no longer hold themselves up to breathe [TRT]. The legs of the men were broken with an iron mallet (known as the *crurifragium*). As well as causing shock and loss of blood, it prevented the man from using his legs to push himself up to open his chest cavity to allow him to breathe and asphyxia soon followed [Car].

19:32 So the soldiers came[a] and broke the legs of-the first and of-the other who had-been-crucified-with[b] him.

LEXICON—a. aorist act. indic. of ἔρχομαι (LN 15.81): 'to come' [LN; all translations except CEV, Ph, TEV], 'to go' [Ph, TEV], not explicit [CEV]. This verb means to move toward or up to the reference point of the viewpoint character or event [LN].

b. aorist pass. participle of συσταυρόω (LN 20.78) (BAGD 1. p. 795): 'to be crucified (together) with' [BAGD, LN; all translations except CEV, NCV], 'to be nailed there' [CEV]. This word is also translated '(broke the legs of the first man) on the cross beside Jesus' [NCV]. This verb means to crucify someone at the same time that another person is being crucified [BAGD, LN].

QUESTION—What is indicated by the conjunction οὖν 'so/then'?
It implies that Pilate had granted the request of the Jews and as a result the soldiers did this [AB, ICC, NICNT1, TRT]. The translations rendered this word as follows: 'therefore' [Gdt, Lns, WBC; NIV], 'so' [HTC, NICNT2, NTC; NASB, NCV, NET, NLT, Ph, TEV], 'consequently' [NJB], 'accordingly' [AB; REB], 'then' [KJV, NRSV].

QUESTION—What is indicated by the verb 'came'?
The definite article '*the* soldiers' indicates that it was the very soldiers who were doing the crucifying who came [Lns, My]. The verb 'came' indicates that these soldiers had been especially sent from some other location with the necessary instruments for this task [Gdt].

QUESTION—How were the legs of the men broken?
They were broken by a severe blow with some kind of heavy instrument, probably a large mallet, sledge hammer, or club [TH]. They broke the leg bones by a hammer or iron [NTC]. It was sometimes done with an iron club [Kn].

19:33 But coming (to) Jesus, when they-saw (that) he had- already -died, they-did- not -break his legs. **19:34** But one of-the soldiers pierced[a] his side with- (a) -spear,[b] and at-once there-came-out[c] blood and water.

LEXICON—a. aorist act. indic. of νύσσω (LN **19.15**) (BAGD p. 547): 'to pierce' [BAGD, Gdt, HTC, **LN**, NTC, WBC; KJV, NASB, NET, NIV, NJB, NLT, NRSV, Ph], 'to puncture' [NICNT2], 'to stick into' [CEV, NCV], 'to thrust into' [REB], 'to plunge into' [TEV], 'to stab (at)' [AB, BAGD], 'to prick' [BAGD, LN]. This verb means 'to prick, to pierce' (normally not as serious a wound as is implied by ἐκκεντέω ('to pierce') 19:37). Although νύσσω in John 19:34 and ἐκκεντέω in John 19:37 refer to the same event, this does not necessarily mean that the two words have precisely the same meaning. This shift in close synonyms is characteristic of Johannine style [LN]. This kind of action may also be used to indicate a more serious wound [Gdt, TH] like one intended to kill the person. The context here suggests this kind of wound [TH].

b. λόγχη (LN **6.34**) (BAGD p. 479): 'spear' [BAGD, **LN**; all translations except AB, WBC; NJB, REB], 'lance' [AB, BAGD, WBC; NJB, REB], 'spear point' [BAGD, LN]. This noun denotes a long weapon with sharpened end used for piercing by thrusting or as a projectile by hurling [LN]. The common Roman *hasta* had an iron head that was oblong and about a hand's breadth at the widest point (see 20:25) [EGT]. Verse 20:25 indicates that the spear wound was a large one [ICC].

c. aorist act. indic. of ἐξέρχομαι (LN 15.40) (BAGD 2.a. p. 275): 'to come out' [BAGD, Gdt, HTC, NICNT2, NTC, WBC; CEV, KJV, NASB, NCV, NJB, NRSV], 'to flow out' [AB, BAGD; NET, NLT], 'to pour out' [TEV], 'to go out of, to depart out of, to leave from within' [LN]. The statement 'at once there came out blood and water' is translated 'bringing a sudden flow of blood and water' [NIV], 'there was an outrush/a flow of blood and water' [Ph, REB]. This verb means to move out of an enclosed or well-defined two or three-dimensional area [LN].

QUESTION—What relationship is indicated by the conjunction ὡς 'when (they saw that he had already died)'?

Here its meaning is almost causal, meaning 'since' or 'because' [Lns; NJB, NLT, TEV]: 'they saw that he had already died *so* they didn't break his legs' [TEV].

QUESTION—Why did the soldier do this?

He did this to make sure that Jesus had really died [AB, Car, CH, EGT, Gdt, HTC, ICC, IVP, Lns, My, NTC, Rd, TRT, WBC], and in case he had not died, to put him to death [EGT, Gdt, My]. A crucified person can hang on the cross several days without dying [AB, Bar, ICC]. In Mark 15:44 it is recorded that Pilate was surprised that Jesus was dead so soon [ICC].

19:35 He who-saw (it) has-testified and his testimony is true,[a] and he[b] knows that he-is-telling (the) truth, so-that you also may-believe.

LEXICON—a. ἀληθινός (LN **72.1**) (BAGD 2. p. 37): 'true' [BAGD, **LN**; all translations except NTC, WBC; NLT, REB], 'accurate' [NLT], 'authentic' [WBC], 'genuine' [ICC, Lns, NTC], 'reliable' [NICNT1, TRT], 'valid, certain' [TRT], 'in accordance with truth, dependable' [BAGD], 'trustworthy' [ICC]. This adjective is also translated as a verb phrase: 'to be trusted' [REB]. It indicates that a thing or event is in accordance with historical fact [LN]. It means that this testimony is both sufficient and true. It is sufficient when it is from a competent eyewitness [EGT, NICNT1].

b. ἐκεῖνος (LN 92.30) (BAGD 1.b/c/e. p. 239): 'he' [BAGD (1.b.); all translations except NICNT2; CEV], 'that one' [LN, Lns; NICNT2], 'that person' [BAGD], not explicit [CEV]. This demonstrative pronoun refers to an entity regarded as relatively absent in terms of the discourse setting [LN]. It may refer back to and resume a word immediately preceding and is often weakened to 'he, she, it'. Here it perhaps is referring to the eyewitness (just mentioned), who then, to be sure, would be vouching for his own credibility and love of the truth [BAGD (1.b.)]. Or it may refer to well-known or notorious personalities. Many scholars also refer the ἐκεῖνος here to Jesus [BAGD (1.c.)]. In indirect discourse the speaker refers to himself as ἐκεῖνος. Is it possible to see in this an indication that the narrator of this Gospel (who could no more use the 'I'-form than could the speaker in indirect discourse), is designating himself by ἐκεῖνος, and by what he says is seeking to corroborate the statement of another? [BAGD (1.e.)].

QUESTION—Who is the person who has seen this?
1. The eyewitness is probably the Beloved Disciple, John, or the Author [AB, Bar, BECNT, Car, EGT, Gdt, HTC, ICC, Kn, Lns, My, NICNT1, NTC, Rd, TH, TRT, WBC]. In the light of verse 21:24 it seems best to see this as a reference to the beloved disciple [Bar, Car, CH, HTC, ICC, Kn, NICNT1, WBC] considering the fact that apart from Jesus' mother, he was the only disciple who was reported to have been present at the crucifixion (see verses 26–27) [AB, NICNT1, Rd, TH]. John was referring to himself [CH, EGT, Gdt, ICC, Lns, Kn, My, NICNT1, NTC, TRT].
2. The eyewitness may have been one of the four Roman soldiers at the cross [NICNT2].

QUESTION—What is indicated by the perfect tense μεμαρτύρηκεν 'he has testified'?
The perfect tense indicates this is now a permanent record of the event [NICNT1], or that what John saw stays clearly in his vision even though many years have gone by since it happened [Lns].

QUESTION—What is it that he has seen and testifies about?

He was testifying about seeing the blood and water that flowed out of Jesus' side [Bar, Car, ICC, Kn, My, NTC] that proved that he was human and had actually died [NTC]. The outflow of blood and water was the incredible thing about which he was testifying [My]. He was not only a witness to Jesus' death but also to his escape from having his legs broken [Car]. He had witnessed the definite death of Christ [EGT].

QUESTION—To whom does the pronoun ἐκεῖνος 'he (knows)' refer?

1. It probably refers to the eyewitness of the previous question [AB, Bar, BECNT, Car, Gdt, HTC, My, NICNT1, Rd, WBC; probably all translations]. Grammatically, ἐκεῖνος 'he' refers back to the previous pronoun '*his* (testimony)' [Bar, Car, ICC]. This pronoun refers back to the eyewitness himself, the beloved disciple. This conclusion is also supported in John 21:24 where the beloved disciple is identified by the context [BECNT, Car, Rd].
2. It refers to Christ [Lns, NTC]. John appeals to Jesus who supports the fact that his witness is true [NTC].
3. It refers back to the eyewitness himself, that is to one of the soldiers who saw Jesus die, or to an anononymous witness [NICNT2].

QUESTION—To what does the purpose clause 'so that you also may believe' refer?

The statement 'He who saw it has testified' is the means to which this purpose clause refers [TH; TEV]: 'The one who saw this happen has spoken of it, so that you may believe' [TEV]. Rather, the words 'he speaks the truth', immediately precede this clause and are the means to which it refers [My].

QUESTION—To whom does the pronoun 'you' in the clause 'so that you also may believe' refer?

It refers to the readers of this Gospel [Bar, BECNT].

QUESTION—What is the implied object of the verb '(so that) you also may believe'?

The implied object is 'in Jesus' or, 'on Jesus the Son of God' [BECNT, Gdt, My, TRT]. The object is that Jesus is the Son of God (see 20:31) [Bar, NICNT2]. It is the death of Jesus and its effects that are to be believed [AB]. It is the veracity of the Gospel that they should believe [CH]. The object is both the record of this eyewitness and in Jesus and his revelation [EGT].

QUESTION—GNT reads πιστεύ[σ]ητε, which is either present subjunctive (without σ) meaning something like 'you may go on believing', or aorist subjunctive (including σ) meaning something like 'may you begin to believe'. Is the verb 'to believe' in the present subjunctive or aorist tense?

1. It is present subjunctive indicating that they are already believers [AB, CH, ICC, My, NICNT1, NTC]: 'in order that you also may continue to believe' [NTC]. The present subjunctive has the best textual attestation [AB]. He calls them not to an entrance into faith, but to a stronger and

higher degree of faith [My]. Many manuscripts also read the aorist, so the point should not be insisted on [NICNT1].
2. It is the aorist subjunctive indicating a definite final kind of believing [Lns; probably CEV]: 'Now you can have faith too' [CEV].

QUESTION—What words are emphasized in this verse?

The demonstrative pronoun ἐκεῖνος 'he/that one (knows)' is emphasized [Gdt, ICC, Lns, My]. The adjective 'genuine' emphatic [Lns, My]—it was a competent witness in that he saw it with his own eyes [Lns]. It is placed first in its clause for emphasis [Lns, My]: 'genuine is his testimony' [Lns].

19:36 **For these-things happened so that the Scripture might-be-fulfilled, "Not (a) bone of-his will-be-broken."**

QUESTION—What relationship is indicated by the conjunction γάρ 'for'?

It indicates that what follows is the scriptural grounds or basis for the words 'so that you may believe' [BECNT, My]. It gives a reason to believe since they may identify Jesus as the Messiah from the Scripture itself [EGT].

QUESTION—To what does the word ταῦτα 'these things' refer?

It refers to the two facts just mentioned that Jesus' legs were not broken (verse 33), and that his side was pierced by a spear (verse 34) [AB, Lns, My, NICNT1, Rd, TH]. These things refer to the events in verses 31–33 [Car]. In this verse reference is made to the first fact that his legs were not broken [TH].

QUESTION—What Scriptures supported the fact that Jesus' legs would not be broken?

1. It is best to take Exodus 12:46, 'It must be eaten inside one house; take none of the meat outside the house. Do not break any of the bones' Exodus 12:46, and Numbers 9:12 'They must not leave any of it till morning or break any of its bones. When they celebrate the Passover, they must follow all the regulations', as the Scriptures referred to here [Bar, BECNT, Car, CH, EGT, Gdt, ICC, IVP, Kn, Lns, My, NICNT1, NTC, TH, TRT]. The Passover lamb was the type of which Jesus was the fulfillment [Lns, My]. This choice may be valid since Jesus died at the time of the Passover sacrifice [Bar]. There may be a reference to Psalm 34:20, 'he protects all his bones, not one of them will be broken', about a righteous man [Bar, IVP, Rd].
2. The Scripture quoted is Psalm 34:20 about a righteous man, 'he protects all his bones, not one of them will be broken' [EGT, NICNT2, TRT].
3. It may be that both of the above alternatives are the source of this reference [WBC].

19:37 **And again another Scripture says, "They-will-look[a] at him-whom they-pierced."**

LEXICON—a. fut. mid. (deponent = active) indic. of ὁράω (LN 24.1) (BAGD 2.a. p. 578): 'to look (on/upon/at/to)' [BAGD; all translations except NICNT2; CEV], 'to see' [LN, NICNT2; CEV]. This verb with the preposition εἰς (as here) means 'to look on/at' [BAGD]. Here the look is one of contrition, reverence, awe and possible horror at the one they treated with such violence [Rd]. It is a look of mourning [IVP].

QUESTION—To what Scripture does this refer?

It probably refers to Zechariah 12:10, 'And I will pour out on the house of David and the inhabitants of Jerusalem a spirit of grace and supplication. They will look on me, the one they have pierced, and they will mourn for him as one mourns for an only child, and grieve bitterly for him as one grieves for a firstborn son' [AB, Bar, BECNT, Car, CH, EGT, Gdt, HTC, ICC, Kn, Lns, NICNT1, NTC, TH, TRT]. It is of interest that in the Psalm it is Yahweh himself who is pierced [AB, BECNT, Car, IVP, Lns, Rd].

QUESTION—Does the Scripture speak?

For languages that cannot understand how the Scripture can speak, one could translate something like, 'there is another Scripture in which one can read' [TH].

QUESTION—To whom does the pronoun 'they' refer in the phrase 'They will look'?

This is a general reference to people in general [BECNT, CH, Rd, TH, TRT]. It refers to the Jews [Gdt, ICC]. It probably refers to the soldiers and Jewish leaders who would look at him on the day after his death [Kn]. In the context of the verse in Zechariah it is the 'inhabitants of Jerusalem' who will look, but it may also be a reference to those who will look and be saved as well as those who look in unbelief [IVP].

DISCOURSE UNIT—19:38–42 [BECNT, Car, HTC, Kn, NICNT1, Rd, WBC; CEV, NCV, NET, NIV, NLT, NRSV, TEV]. The topic is Jesus is buried.

19:38 Now after these-things Joseph from Arimathea,[a] (who) was (a) disciple[b] of-Jesus but secretly for fear of-the Jews, asked Pilate that he-might-take-away the body of Jesus, and Pilate gave- (him) -permission. So he-came and took-away his body.

LEXICON—a. Ἀριμαθαία (LN 93.413) (BAGD p. 106): 'Arimathea' [BAGD, LN; all translations]. This noun denotes a city in Judea [BAGD, LN], Joseph's home [BAGD]. Others refer to it as a town [AB, TH, TRT; TEV].

b. μαθητής (LN 36.38): 'disciple' [LN; all translations except NCV, TEV], 'follower' [LN; NCV, TEV]. This noun is derived from μαθητεύω 'to follow, to be a disciple of' (36.31) and denotes a person who is a disciple or follower of someone [LN].

QUESTION—What is indicated by the phrase μετὰ ταῦτα 'after these things'?

It simply indicates that this event follows the ones before it [AB]. The length of intervening time indicated is general and indefinite [HTC, NICNT1]. The phrase introduces a new section in the narrative [ICC, TH].

QUESTION—Who was Joseph?

He was a wealthy man (Matthew 27:57) and a member of the Sanhedrin (Mark 15:43) [AB, BECNT, Car, CH, EGT, ICC, IVP, Lns, NICNT1, NICNT2, NTC, TRT, WBC], but he had not agreed to the decision to condemn Jesus (Luke 23:51) [AB, CH, ICC, IVP, Lns, NICNT2, NTC, TRT, WBC].

QUESTION—Why was Joseph afraid of the Jews?
He was afraid he would be dismissed from the Sanhedrin since the Jews had agreed to excommunicate or put anyone out of the Synagogue if they confessed that Jesus was the Messiah (9:22) [Lns, NTC].

QUESTION—What is indicated by the phrase 'the Jews'?
This is a reference to the Jewish authorities [Car, Kn, TH, TRT].

QUESTION—What did Joseph intend to do with Jesus' body?
Since 'take a body' could imply bad intentions, it may be necessary to translate something like 'take the body of Jesus to bury it/place it in a tomb' [TH].

QUESTION—Of what Scripture may Joseph's action have been a fulfillment?
It may have been a fulfillment of Isaiah 53:9, 'He was assigned a grave with the wicked, and with the rich in his death, though he had done no violence, nor was any deceit in his mouth' [BECNT, Lns, NICNT1].

QUESTION—How did Joseph 'take away' the body of Jesus?
In some languages it may be necessary to be specific about whether he himself carried it or had it carried away (he probably had some servants do most of the work) [TRT]. Also his method of carrying may have to be indicated. It is likely that it was carried on some kind of stretcher [TH].

19:39 **Nicodemus, who had- first**[a] **-come to him by-night, also came bringing (a) mixture**[b] **of myrrh**[c] **and aloes,**[d] **(weighing) about seventy-five pounds.**[e]

TEXT—Instead of μίγμα 'mixture', some manuscripts read ἕλιγμα 'package', others read σμίγμα 'perfumed ointment', and still others read σμῆγμα 'ointment'. GNT reads 'mixture' with a B rating, indicating that the text is almost certain.

LEXICON—a. πρῶτος (LN 60.46) (BAGD 2.a. p. 726): 'first' [AB, BAGD, LN; NASB, NJB], 'at (the) first' [Gdt, HTC, WBC; KJV, NRSV, TEV], 'previously' [NET], 'earlier' [BAGD; NCV, NIV], 'at the beginning' [Ph], 'in the first place, before, to begin with' [BAGD], not explicit [CEV, NLT, REB]. The phrase τὸ πρῶτον 'the first' is translated 'at an earlier occasion' [NTC]. This adjective indicates the first in a series involving time, space, or set [LN]. When it occurs with the article as here, it means, 'the first time' [BAGD].

b. μίγμα (LN **63.11**) (BAGD p. 521): 'mixture' [BAGD, **LN**; all translations except CEV, NCV, NLT], 'compound' [BAGD], not explicit [NCV]. The phrase 'a mixture of myrrh and aloes' is translated 'spices made from myrrh and aloes' [CEV], 'perfumed ointment made from myrrh and aloes' [NLT]. This noun is derived from μίγνυμι 'to mix, to mingle' (63.10) and denotes that which has been mixed [LN]. It is a compound or mixture of an ointment [BAGD]. The use of these two substances here was not for embalming but to keep it smelling sweet for a time and to combat putrification [Car, Kn, WBC]. The mixture was used to overcome the stench of putrefaction [BECNT, CH, TRT].

c. σμύρνα (LN **6.208**) (BAGD p. 758): 'myrrh' [BAGD, **LN**; all translations]. This noun denotes the fragrant resin of certain bushes [BECNT, Car, ICC, LN, Lns, Rd, WBC]. It is the resinous gum of the *balsamodendron myrrha* bush [BAGD, Lns, NTC]. Myrrh was used by the Egyptians as an embalming element [AB, Bar, BECNT, TH, WBC].

d. ἀλόη (LN **6.209**) (BAGD p. 41): 'aloes' [BAGD, **LN**; all translations]. This noun denotes an aromatic resin [HTC, LN, NTC] of a lily-like plant [LN], often used for embalming a corpse [LN, TH]. It is the strongly aromatic, quick-drying sap of a tree [BAGD, Rd], the *Aquillaria* [BAGD]. It is from a large tree, the *Agallocha* [NTC]. It is powdered fragrant sandalwood [AB, BECNT, Car, TRT, WBC] used in perfuming clothing or bedding [AB, Bar, TH]. It was probably used to counteract the odor [AB, TRT, WBC] and retard decay [AB]. It is a sweet-smelling wood [Gdt, HTC].

e. λίτρα (LN 86.4) (BAGD p. 475): 'pound' [BAGD, LN], 'pint' [LN]. The phrase ὡς λίτρας ἑκατόν '(weighing) about seventy-five pounds' [CEV, NCV, NET, NIV] is also translated 'seventy-five pounds' [NLT], 'weighing about one hundred pounds' [AB; NJB, NRSV, Ph, similarly Gdt, HTC, NICNT2, NTC, WBC; KJV, NASB, TEV], 'more than half a hundredweight' [REB]. This noun denotes a Roman pound, weighing about twelve ounces [BAGD, LN], about 325 grams [LN] or 327.45 grams [BAGD]. In translating λίτρα in the NT, one need not identify the pound as being 'a Roman pound'. It is better to employ a common term for pound (normally weighing sixteen ounces) or to provide a rounded-off equivalent of the amount in metric units [LN].

QUESTION—To whom does the pronoun 'to him' refer?

It refers to Jesus and the following translations make that explicit [ICC, TH, TRT; all translations except HTC, NICNT2, NTC, WBC; Ph].

QUESTION—How much did λίτρας ἑκατόν 'one-hundred pounds' weigh?

The word λίτρα signifies a Roman pound, 100 of which weighed about seventy-five of our pounds [AB, BAGD, Bar, Kn, LN, NICNT1, NICNT2, TRT; CEV, NCV, NET, NIV, NLT], or seventy-two of our pounds [NTC], or 65.45 of our pounds [BECNT, Car, WBC]. This much perfume is an extraordinarily large amount [AB, BECNT, Car, CH, EGT, HTC, IVP, Lns, My, NICNT2, NTC, WBC], and reveals great respect such as would be given to royalty [CH, HTC, Kn, Lns, NICNT1, NICNT2, Rd, WBC]. The large amount implies that Nicodemus may also have been wealthy [Car, ICC, IVP, NICNT1]. The large amount may have been a weatlhy man's expression of devotion or the amount needed to cover Jesus' body and its wrappings [EGT]. If the woman's gift in 12:3 had been worth 300 denarii, Nicodemus's was perhaps worth 30,000. He honored Jesus lavishly [Kn].

19:40 So they-took the body of-Jesus and wrapped[a] it in-linen-cloths[b] with the spices,[c] as is (the) burial[d] custom of-the Jews.

LEXICON—a. aorist act. indic. of δέω (BAGD 1.a. p. 177): 'to wrap' [Gdt; CEV, NCV, NET, NIV, NLT, NRSV, REB, TEV], 'to bind' [AB, BAGD, HTC, NICNT2, NTC, WBC; NASB, NJB], 'to wind' [KJV], 'to wind (something) round' [Ph], 'to tie' [BAGD].

  b. ὀθόνιον (LN **6.154**) (BAGD p. 555): 'linen cloth' [BAGD, Gdt, HTC, **LN**, NICNT2; CEV, KJV, NCV, NJB, NRSV, TEV], '(a) strip of linen (cloth)' [NET, NIV, REB], '(a) linen strip' [Ph], '(a) long sheet of linen cloth' [NLT], '(a) linen wrapping' [NASB], '(a) linen bandage' [BAGD; NTC], '(a) cloth wrapping' [AB, WBC]. This noun denotes a piece or strip of linen cloth used in preparing a corpse for burial [BAGD, LN].

  c. ἄρωμα (LN 6.207) (BAGD p. 114): 'spices' [BAGD; all translations except AB, NTC; NET], 'aromatic spices' [NET], 'aromatics' [NTC], 'aromatic oil' [AB, BAGD, LN], 'aromatic salves' [BAGD, LN], 'perfumed ointment' [LN], 'perfumery' [BAGD]. This noun denotes aromatic oils or salves used especially in embalming the dead [BAGD, LN]. The Jews customarily used oil in burial preparation, so if the meaning here is 'aromatic oils', it may be that this is a third element indicated here [AB]. Here it clearly refers back to the myrrh and aloes of verse 39 [WBC].

  d. pres. act. infin. of ἐνταφιάζω (LN **52.6**) (BAGD; p. 268): 'to prepare for burial' [BAGD, LN], 'to bury' [BAGD]. The clause 'as is the burial custom of the Jews' (literally, 'as is the custom of the Jews to bury') [NASB], is also translated 'as the manner of the Jews is to bury' [KJV], 'as is the custom of the Jews in preparing (a body) for burial' [**LN**; similarly Ph, TEV], 'This was in accordance with Jewish burial customs' [NIV, similarly AB, Gdt, HTC, NTC; NASB, NET, NJB, NLT, NRSV, REB], 'which was/is how the Jewish people buried/bury their dead' [CEV, NCV]. This verb means to prepare a body for burial [LN].

QUESTION—Who are the ones who took Jesus' body?

They were Joseph and Nicodemus [BECNT, HTC, ICC, NICNT2, TRT, WBC; CEV, NCV, NIV, TEV]: 'The two men took Jesus' body' [TEV]. Other persons in addition to Joseph and Nicodemus may have been included in the plural pronoun 'they' [Rd].

QUESTION—What was the burial custom of the Jews?

They would wash the body, anoint it with aromatic oil and clothe it [AB]. It was not like the Egyptian custom of embalming by removing the internal organs [AB, My, NTC, Rd]. It was not injected with myrrh and aloes to embalm it, rather the myrrh and aloes were put around Jesus' body and between the layers of the burial cloths [TRT].

QUESTION—Does the word ὀθόνιον mean a shroud-like linen cloth or strips of cloth?

  1. It probably means strips of linen cloth bandages [Bar, BECNT, EGT, HTC, ICC, Lns, My, NTC, NICNT1; probably NET, NIV, Ph, REB]. The

word refers to long, bandage-like strips and not to a shroud. The spices were distributed between the folds of cloth [NICNT2].
2. It means that both a shroud-like cloth and strips of linen cloth were used [Gdt]. The body was covered with a shroud while part of it was cut into bandages to wrap the arms and legs separately [Gdt].
3. The question is too obscure to make a firm decision either way [AB, Car, IVP, TH]. The discussion is sufficiently obscure that a general translation is preferable like 'cloth wrappings' [AB], or 'linen cloths' [TH]. The plural could refer to a single sheet or in general to 'grave clothes' [IVP].

19:41 Now in the place where he-was-crucified there-was (a) garden, and in the garden[a] (a) new tomb[b] in which no-one had yet[c] been laid.[d]

LEXICON—a. κῆπος (LN 1.97) (BAGD p. 430): 'garden' [BAGD, LN; all translations], 'orchard' [LN]. This noun denotes a field used for the cultivation of herbs, fruits, flowers, or vegetables [LN]. It denotes a large garden, orchard, or plantation [Bar].
b. μνημεῖον (LN 7.75) (BAGD 2. p. 524): 'tomb' [BAGD, LN; all translations except Gdt; KJV], 'sepulchre' [Gdt; KJV], 'grave' [BAGD, LN]. This noun denotes a construction for the burial of the dead [LN]. Almost certainly it was a man-made cave [Car]. It means a tomb in a cave into which a person can enter [BAGD]. These tombs were expensive and were typically hewn out of the solid rock having the entrance closed with a heavy stone. This stone ran in a groove and so served as a door over the entrance [NICNT1].
c. οὐδέπω (LN 67.129) (BAGD p. 592): 'not yet' [LN], 'still not' [LN]. The words 'a new tomb in which no one had yet/ever yet been laid' [NICNT2, NTC, WBC; NASB, Ph] is also translated 'a new tomb, in which/where no one had ever been laid' [HTC; NIV, NRSV], 'a new tomb where/in which no one had yet/ever been buried' [AB; NET, TEV, similarly NJB], 'a new sepulchre, wherein no one had ever yet been laid' [AB; similarly KJV], 'a (new) tomb that had never been used (before)' [CEV, NCV, similarly NLT], 'a new tomb, not yet used for burial' [REB]. This adverb indicates the negation of extending time up to and beyond an expected point [LN]. The combination οὐδέπω οὐδείς 'not yet anyone' indicates 'no one ever' [BAGD].
d. perf. pass. participle of τίθημι (LN 85.32) (BAGD I.1.a.β. p. 816): 'to be laid' [BAGD, Gdt, HTC, NICNT2, NTC, WBC; KJV, NASB, NIV, NRSV, Ph], 'to be buried' [AB; NET, NJB, TEV], 'to be put, 'to be placed' [BAGD, LN], not explicit [CEV, NCV, NLT]. This verb is also translated as a verbal noun: 'not yet used for burial' [REB]. This verb means to put or place in a particular location [LN].

QUESTION—What is indicated by the preposition ἐν 'in' in the phrase 'in the place'?

The fact that the garden was '*in* the place' where Jesus was crucified indicates that the garden was close by [NICNT1, TH].

QUESTION—Why may it have been important to note that the tomb was new and had not yet been used?

The Resurrection was likely in the writer's mind. If the tomb was empty on the third day, one person only could have been resurrected from it [AB, Car]. The Jews provided a special burial place for criminals but did not allow the bodies of criminals to be buried in family tombs lest they defile the bodies already put there [Car].

QUESTION—What words are emphasized in this verse?

The double negative in the literal phrase 'no one…not yet' puts emphasis on the fact that no one had yet been buried there [BECNT, NICNT1].

19:42 So[a] **because-of the Jewish Preparation-day, since the tomb was nearby, they-laid Jesus there.**

LEXICON—a. οὖν (LN 89.50): 'so' [LN, HTC, NICNT2], 'and so' [AB; NET, NLT, NRSV], 'therefore' [LN, WBC; KJV, NASB], 'accordingly' [NTC], 'and' [REB], 'consequently, accordingly, then, so then' [LN], not explicit [BAGD, Gdt; CEV, NCV, NIV, NJB, Ph, TEV]. This conjunction indicates result, often implying the conclusion of a process of reasoning [LN].

QUESTION—Why does the fact of the Jewish preparation day and the nearness of the tomb stand as a reason to bury Jesus there?

Haste was required since sundown was near when the Preparation day would end and the Sabbath would begin. So the burial had to be completed before that [Bar, Car, CH, EGT, Gdt, HTC, ICC, My, NICNT1, NICNT2; CEV]: 'The tomb was nearby, and since it was the time to prepare for the Sabbath, they were in a hurry to put the body of Jesus there' [CEV]. Mishnah *Sabbath* 23:4–5 states that burial would not have been permitted on the Sabbath day [AB]. Verse 31 already stated that haste was required because of the day of Preparation [HTC].

QUESTION—What word is emphasized in this verse?

The word ἐκεῖ 'there' occurs first in the verse giving it emphasis [Gdt, HTC, NICNT2, NTC; REB]: '*It was there* that they laid Jesus' [Gdt], 'So there…they laid Jesus' [NICNT2], 'There, accordingly…they laid Jesus' [NTC], 'and there…they laid Jesus' [REB].

DISCOURSE UNIT—20:1–31 [Car, CH, WBC; REB]. The topic is the resurrection of Jesus.

DISCOURSE UNIT—20:1–29 [AB, BECNT, IVP, Kn, NICNT1]. The topic is Jesus' resurrection [AB, Kn, NICNT1], Jesus' resurrection and appearances to the disciples [BECNT, IVP].

DISCOURSE UNIT—20:1–23 [Ph]. The topic is the risen Lord.

DISCOURSE UNIT—20:1–18 [AB, Bar, Kn, NICNT2; NASB, NCV]. The topic is Mary at the tomb [Kn], at the tomb [AB], 'the empty tomb' [NASB, NCV], the empty tomb and appearance to Mary [Bar, NICNT2].

DISCOURSE UNIT—20:1-10 [AB, BECNT, HTC, ICC, IVP, Lns, NICNT1, NTC, Rd, WBC; CEV, NLT, NRSV, TEV]. The topic is the empty tomb [AB, Rd, BECNT, NICNT1; TEV], the resurrection [NLT, NRSV], Mary's report of the empty tomb and the disciples' visit [HTC, ICC, IVP, WBC], the linen wrappings—empty! [Lns], Jesus is alive [CEV].

DISCOURSE UNIT—20:1-9 [Car; NET, NIV]. The topic is the empty tomb [Car; NIV], the resurrection [NET].

20:1 Now on-the-first-day of-the-week[a] Mary Magdalene[b] came to the tomb early[c] while-it-was still dark and saw (that) the stone had-been-taken-away[d] from the tomb.

LEXICON—a. σάββατον (LN **67.177**) (BAGD p. 2.b. p. 739): 'week' [BAGD, LN; all translations except CEV, NLT, TEV]. The phrase 'on the first day of the week' is translated 'on Sunday morning' [CEV, NLT, TEV]. This plural noun denotes a period of seven days [LN]. The word σάββατον 'Sabbath' occurs here in the plural indicating 'week' [TH]. Since the phrase 'first day of the week' may not indicate the same day to all cultures, it may be better to translate a specific day of the week in its place [TH]. It refers to Sunday [Kn, NTC, TH, TRT; CEV, NLT, TEV].

b. Μαγδαληνή (LN 93.242) (BAGD p. 484): 'Magdalene' [BAGD, LN; all translations except NJB, Ph, REB], 'of Magdala' [NJB, Ph, REB]. This noun is derived from Μαγδαλά (93.523) and denotes a woman of Magdala [LN]. Magdala was a town located about twenty minutes walk from Tiberias on the west side of the Lake of Gennesaret [BAGD]. Magdala, a fishing village north of Tiberias, is now known as Mejdel [EGT].

c. πρωΐ (LN 67.187) (BAGD p. 724): 'early' [BAGD; all translations except CEV, NCV, NET, NIV, NJB], 'very early' [NET, NJB, Ph], 'early (in the) morning' [BAGD, LN], not explicit [CEV, NCV]. This adverb indicates the early part of the daylight period [LN]. As the fourth watch of the night it is the time from three to six o'clock [AB, BAGD, TH].

d. perf. pass. participle of αἴρω (LN 15.203) (BAGD 3. p. 24): 'to be taken away' [Gdt, HTC, LN, NICNT2; KJV, NASB, Ph, TEV], 'to be removed' [BAGD, LN, NTC, WBC; NIV, NRSV], 'to be moved away' [AB; NCV, NET, NJB, REB], 'to be rolled away' [CEV, NLT], 'to be carried (away/off)' [LN], 'to be (lifted up and) carried away' [BAGD]. This verb means to lift up and carry (away) [LN]. It is implied that the stone was removed by supernatural means [Bar, TH]. Matthew 28:2 states that 'an angel of the Lord came down from heaven and, going to the tomb, rolled back the stone and sat on it' [TRT].

QUESTION—Was Mary alone?

Apparently other women were with her since the pronoun in verse 2, 'we (do not know where they have put him)', indicates the presence of others [EGT, Gdt, Kn, Lns, NTC, Rd, TRT, WBC]. It was also unlikely that the disciples would have allowed a woman to travel alone [Kn].

QUESTION—What stone does this refer to?

Since this is the first mention of this stone in John it might be advisable to translate something like, 'a stone which had been at the entrance to the tomb had been taken away' [TH]. The stone was disk shaped and at least three feet in diameter [TRT].

QUESTION—What is implied by the phrase 'from the tomb'?

It is implied that the stone was taken away from the *entrance* to the tomb. The tomb was probably one that was entered horizontally, that is from the side, rather than vertically, that is one going down into the ground [AB, CH, HTC].

20:2 So[a] she-ran and went to Simon Peter and the other disciple whom Jesus loved[b] and said to-them, "They-have-taken the Lord[c] out-of the tomb and we-do- not -know where they-have-laid[d] him."

LEXICON—a. οὖν (LN 89.50): 'so' [AB, HTC, LN, NICNT2, NTC, TRT, WBC; NASB, NET, NIV, NRSV], 'then' [LN; KJV], 'at this' [Ph], 'therefore' [TRT, Gdt], 'consequently, accordingly, so then' [LN], not explicit [CEV, NCV, NJB, NLT, REB, TEV]. This conjunction indicates result, often implying the conclusion of a process of reasoning [LN]. This word occurs more frequently in the accounts of Jesus' death and resurrection than in any other parts of the Gospel, contributing to the dramatic tension [TH].

b. imperf. act. indic. of φιλέω (LN 25.33) (BAGD 1.a. p. 859): 'to love' [BAGD, LN; all translations except CEV], 'to have affection for' [BAGD, LN], 'to like' [BAGD]. The phrase 'the other disciple whom Jesus loved' is translated 'Jesus' favorite disciple' [CEV]. This verb means to have love or affection for someone or something based on association [LN]. This verb is used synonymously with ἀγαπάω 'to love' in similar expressions (see 13:23; 19:26; and 21:20) [BECNT, Rd].

c. κύριος (LN 12.9) (BAGD 2.c.β p. 459): 'Lord' [BAGD, LN; all translations except WBC; NLT], 'Master' [BAGD, WBC], 'Lord's body' [NLT], 'lord' [BAGD], 'Ruler, One who commands' [LN]. This noun is a title for God and for Christ and denotes one who exercises supernatural authority over mankind. The most common equivalent of 'Lord' is a term meaning 'chief' or 'leader', but frequently this cannot be employed as a title for 'God'. One may, however, combine such an expression with a term for 'God' and employ a phrase meaning 'God our leader' or 'God our chief'. In some instances, however, a term for 'Lord' is related to a verb meaning 'to command' or 'to order', and therefore 'Lord' is rendered as 'the one who commands us' and combined with 'God' may form a phrase such as 'God, the one who commands us' [LN].

d. aorist act. indic. of τίθημι (LN 85.32) (BAGD I.1.a.α. 815): 'to lay' [Gdt, HTC, NICNT2, NTC; KJV, NASB, NRSV, REB], 'to put' [AB, BAGD, LN, WBC; CEV, NCV, NET, NIV, NJB, NLT, Ph, TEV], 'to place'

[BAGD, LN], 'to lay away, to put away, to bury' [BAGD]. This verb means to put or place something in a particular location [LN].

QUESTION—The preposition πρός 'to (Simon Peter)' in Greek occurs both before Simon Peter and before the other disciple. Some commentaries say this inplies that they must have been living in different places while others disagree.

1. The repeated preposition may mean that Peter and the other disciple lived in different places [BECNT, Gdt, ICC, IVP, NICNT2, NTC]. The more natural interpretation of the original is that each disciple had his own separate home in Jerusalem [NTC].
2. There is no special significance to the repetition [Lns, TH]. Here it may indicate that she turned first to one and then to the other as she told them her news [Lns]. That the two disciples set off for the tomb from the same place may imply that they were staying together (see also verse 19) [TH].

QUESTION—To whom does the pronoun 'they' refer in the phrase 'they have taken the Lord out of the tomb'?

She may have meant grave robbers [Bar, BECNT, Car, NICNT1, WBC], or enemies in general [Bar, NICNT1, NTC, WBC], or the Jewish leaders [Lns, NICNT1, TRT], or the Romans [TRT], or it may be an impersonal plural equivalent to our passive [AB, Bar, TH, TRT]. It is best taken as an indefinite 'somebody' [HTC].

QUESTION—Was it *the Lord* whom they took away or *his body*?

In case taking the Lord out of the tomb implies that he was not necessarily dead, it may be better to specify that it was his body, rather than the Lord himself, that was taken away [TH, TRT; NLT]: 'They have taken the Lord's body out of the tomb' [NLT].

QUESTION—To whom does the pronoun 'we' refer in the phrase 'we know'?

1. It probably refers to Mary and some other women who were with her [BECNT, CH, EGT, Gdt, ICC, IVP, Lns, NICNT1, TRT, WBC]. The other Gospels refer to the presence of several women (see Matthew 28:1; Mark 16:1; and Luke 24:1, 10, 24) [Gdt, TRT]. The fact that it was still dark supports the fact that she did not go alone especially during religious festivities when visitors of dubious character were present in Jerusalem [BECNT, NICNT1].
2. Other views [My, NICNT2]. The plural indicates that she included also the disciples to whom she was speaking as well as the others who loved the Lord as she did [My]. It probably refers to an indefinite 'we' that includes the larger community of believers [NICNT2].

20:3 So Peter and the other disciple went-out and they-were-going to the tomb. **20:4** The two of-them were-running[a] together, but the other disciple ran-ahead[b] faster-than[c] Peter and reached the tomb first. **20:5** And stooping-down[d] he-saw the linen-cloths[e] lying (there), but he-did- not -go-in.

LEXICON—a. imperf. act. indic. of τρέχω (LN 15.230) (BAGD 1. p. 825): 'to run' [BAGD, LN], 'to rush' [LN]. This verb means to run, with emphasis

on relative speed in contrast with walking [LN]. For verson evidence see next item b. just below.
- b. aorist act. indic. of προτρέχω (LN **15.235**) (BAGD p. 722): 'to run ahead (of)' [BAGD, LN; NASB], 'to run in front of' [LN]. The phrase προέδραμεν τάχιον 'ran ahead faster than (Peter)' [NASB] is also translated 'started to run ahead, faster than (Peter)' [NTC], 'ran ahead more speedily than (Peter)' [WBC], 'ran faster than (Peter)' [NICNT2; CEV, NCV, NET, Ph, REB, TEV similarly NJB], 'ran more quickly than (Peter)' [Gdt], 'outran (Peter)' [HTC; KJV, NIV, NLT, NRSV], 'being faster, outran (Peter)' [AB]. This verb means to run ahead of someone else, with the implication of arriving at a destination sooner [LN].
- c. ταχύς (LN 67.110) (BAGD p. 806): 'quickly' [BAGD, LN], 'hurriedly' [LN]. This comparative adverb indicates a very short extent of time [LN]. As a comparative it means 'more quickly, faster than' [BAGD]. For version evidence see item b. above.
- d. aorist act. participle of παρακύπτω (LN 17.31) (BAGD 1. p. 619): 'to stoop down (and look in)' [KJV], 'to stoop and look in(side)' [NASB, NLT, Ph], 'to stoop to look in' [HTC], 'to bend down/over and look in' [NCV, NIV], 'to bend down to look/peer in' [AB, WBC; NRSV], 'to stoop down' [Gdt, LN, NICNT2], 'to stoop' [NTC], 'to bend down' [NET, NJB], 'to bend over' [BAGD, LN; CEV, TEV], 'to peer in' [REB]. This verb means to bend over or stoop down, with the implication of looking into something [BAGD, LN]. (See this same action about Mary at verse 11.)
- e. ὀθόνιον (LN 6.154) (BAGD p. 555): 'linen cloth' [BAGD, Gdt, HTC, LN, NICNT2; KJV, NCV, NJB, Ph, TEV], 'linen wrapping' [WBC; NASB, NLT, NRSV, REB], 'cloth wrapping' [AB], 'strip of linen cloth' [CEV, NET], 'strip of linen' [NIV], 'linen bandage' [NTC], 'bandage' [BAGD]. This noun denotes a piece of linen cloth [LN].

QUESTION—What does the verb παρακύπτω mean?
1. This verb contains the two components of 'stooping' and 'looking' [AB, BAGD, HTC, LN, My, NICNT1, TH, TRT, WBC; KJV, NASB, NCV, NIV, NLT, NRSV, Ph]: 'stooping and looking in, he saw' [NASB]. Several translations indicated that the sense of *looking* served as the purpose of bending down [AB, BECNT, HTC, My, NICNT1, TRT, WBC; NRSV]: 'He bent down to peer in (and saw)' [AB].
2. This word denotes only the act of stooping [Gdt, NICNT2, NTC; CEV, NET, NJB, TEV]: 'He bent down and saw' [NET]. Although the original meaning of the verb does not always require the sense of 'stooping', when it is used with the verb 'to see' (as here), this is its most natural meaning. Since the entrance was probably low, one had to first stoop down and then they were able to look inside [NTC].
3. This word denotes only the act of 'looking' [Bar, ICC, Lns, TRT; REB]: 'He peered in and saw' [REB]. Although in its primary sense the verb meant 'to stoop down for the purpose of looking', it is seldom used as

such anymore. In the LXX it *always* has the sense of 'to peep' as through a door or window—no stooping is implied [ICC]. The verb means a glance that required that the head be inclined [Bar].

QUESTION—What was the significance of seeing 'the linen cloths lying there'?

They were evidence that Jesus' body had not been simply moved [Bar, BECNT, EGT, Car, Gdt, ICC, Lns, WBC]. Robbers would not have left behind expensive linen wrappings or spices [BECNT, Car, Kn, WBC] or they would not have left the tomb so orderly [NICNT1]. It indicated that they were lying there *without* the body [Kn, Lns, NTC]. Jesus' body had passed through the grave cloths [Bar, Car, Kn].

20:6 Then Simon Peter also came following him and entered the tomb, and saw[a] the linen-cloths lying (there), **20:7** and the face-cloth,[b] that had-been on his head, not lying with the linen-cloths but rolled-up[c] in one place by-itself.[d]

LEXICON—a. θεωρέω (LN 24.14) (BAGD 1. p. 360): 'to see' [BAGD, HTC, WBC; CEV, KJV, NASB, NCV, NET, NJB, NIV, NRSV, REB, TEV], 'to observe' [AB, BAGD, LN, NTC], 'to notice' [NLT, Ph], 'to look at' [BAGD, LN, NICNT2], 'to behold' [Gdt], 'to be a spectator (of)' [BAGD, LN]. This verb means to observe something with continuity and attention, often with the implication that what is observed is something unusual [LN]. It implies seeing with one's physical eyes [BAGD].

b. σουδάριον (LN 6.159) (BAGD p. 759): 'face cloth' [LN; NASB, NET], 'cloth' [NICNT2; NCV, NJB, NLT, NRSV, TEV], 'piece of cloth' [AB; CEV], 'napkin' [Gdt, HTC, LN, WBC; KJV, REB], 'handkerchief' [BAGD, LN; Ph], 'sweatband' [NTC], 'burial cloth' [NIV], 'towel' [KJV]. This noun denotes a small piece of cloth used as a towel, napkin, or face cloth [LN]. It is a 'face cloth' or 'handkerchief' to wipe off perspiration [BAGD]. It is derived from the verb *sudo*, 'I sweat' [EGT]. It was probably about the size of a small towel or a large napkin [AB]. It may have been tied around his face and functioned to keep his mouth from falling open [AB, BECNT, NICNT1, TH].

c. perf. pass. participle of ἐντυλίσσω (LN **79.120**) (BAGD 2. p. 270): 'to roll up' [AB, Gdt, HTC, **LN**, NICNT2, WBC; CEV, NASB, NET, NJB, NRSV, Ph, REB, TEV], 'to fold up' [BAGD, NTC; NCV, NIV, NLT], 'to make into a roll' [LN], 'to wrap together' [KJV]. This verb means to cause something to be in the shape of a roll [LN], or to fold up [BAGD].

d. χωρίς (LN **63.31**) (BAGD 1. p. 890): 'by itself' [AB, BAGD, Gdt, HTC, **LN**, NTC; CEV, KJV, NASB, NET, NJB, NRSV, Ph, REB, TEV], 'separate, by itself' [WBC; similarly NIV], 'separately' [BAGD, LN, NICNT2], 'apart' [BAGD; NLT]. The phrase 'in one place by itself' is also translated 'in a different place' [NCV]. This adverb pertains to something which occurs separately or by itself [LN].

QUESTION—In this description, verse five tells us that John 'saw' (βλέπω), but here in this verse that Peter 'saw' (θεωρέω). Are the verbs being used synonymously or is there a distinction intended?
1. The meaning of 'see' in this verse is not different from that of 'see' in verse five [AB; CEV, KJV, NASB, NCV, NET, NJB, NIV, NRSV, Ph, REB, TEV]. There is no contrast between Peter and John's observations. Peter's look was not more leisurely or more thorough than John's [AB].
2. The meaning of 'see' here is different from that of 'see' in verse five [EGT, Gdt, Lns, My, (probably also LN)]. John had merely 'noticed' the linen cloths, but Peter observed them and saw more clearly than John [NTC]. The verb is probably used here in the sense of 'seeing to draw a conclusion' [EGT]. John had only seen from the entrance. Peter went inside and not only saw but continued to look and reflect on what he saw [Gdt]. John had merely 'seen', but Peter stood there looking and looking at those linen cloths [Lns].

QUESTION—What was the condition of the linen cloths?
They were lying there collapsed but probably retaining the shape of the body due to the spices [IVP].

QUESTION—What is implied by the 'face cloth' being rolled up in a place by itself?
It implies that Jesus' body was not removed by robbers. If they had done this, they would not have taken the time to roll or fold up the facecloth but would have kept the body as it was [BECNT, CH, Kn, NICNT2, TRT]. It also implies that the disciples did not steal Jesus' body as they would not have left the facecloth and linen wrappings there [BECNT]. It implied that Jesus was calmly awakened rather than quickly removed [Gdt], or that there was no haste involved in what had happened there [EGT, My]. Apparently Jesus put things in order before leaving [IVP].

20:8 So then the other disciple who had-come to the tomb first also went-in, and he-saw and believed, 20:9 for they-did- not-yet -understand the Scripture that he must^a rise^b from (the) dead.^{c}

LEXICON—a. δεῖ (LN 71.34) (BAGD 1. p. 172): '(one) must' [BAGD, LN; all translations except AB, Gdt; CEV], 'one has to' [AB, BAGD; NIV], 'to be necessary' [BAGD, LN], not explicit [Gdt; CEV]. This verb means to be that which must necessarily take place, often with the implication of inevitability [LN]. It denotes compulsion of any kind. Here it is used of divine destiny [BAGD, BECNT, My, TH] or unavoidable outcome [BAGD]. It means that the resurrection was willed by God [AB].
b. aorist act. infin. of ἀνίσταμαι (LN 23.93) (BAGD 2. p. 70): 'to rise' [BAGD], 'to stand up, to get up' [BAGD], 'to come back to life, to live again, to be resurrected' [LN]. This verb means to come back to life after having once died [LN]. See next item for version evidence.
c. νεκρός (LN 23.121) (BAGD 2.a. p. 535): 'dead' [BAGD, LN], 'lifeless' [LN]. The phrase 'Jesus/he must rise from the dead' [HTC, NICNT2,

NTC, WBC; NCV, NET, NJB, NLT, NRSV, Ph, REB] is also translated 'he must rise from death' [TEV], 'Jesus had to rise from the dead' [AB, NIV], 'he must rise again from the dead' [KJV, NASB], 'Jesus would rise to life' [CEV], 'he should rise from the dead' [Gdt]. This adjective pertains to being dead [LN]. When used as a noun, as here, it means a 'dead person'. In the plural and without the article again as here, it means all the dead, all those who are in the underworld [BAGD].

QUESTION—What did this disciple see?

It must be that he saw the linen cloths and face cloth [BECNT, Gdt, IVP, NICNT1, NICNT2, NTC, Rd, TRT, WBC] or that he saw that Jesus' body was gone [TRT]. He saw an empty tomb [IVP, Rd].

QUESTION—What did this disciple believe?

He believed that Jesus had risen from the dead [AB, BECNT, Car, CH, EGT, Gdt, HTC, ICC, Lns, My, NICNT1, NTC, TH, TRT]. Also he believed that Jesus was the Messiah, the Son of God [NTC]. He believed that Jesus had gone to the Father as he had said he would (see John 14:28) [NICNT2].

QUESTION—What is indicated by the conjunction γάρ 'for (they did not yet understand)'?

Here it only introduces a comment, not a reason for that disciple's faith [TRT]. Here it means, 'You must remember that...' [ICC]. The disciple believed because he saw the empty tomb, not that he understood the Scripture [Bar, BECNT, EGT].

QUESTION—What particular Scripture is being referred to here?

This probably refers to the OT in general [Bar, BECNT, Car, IVP, TH, TRT, WBC]. Some specific Scriptures that speak of Jesus' resurrection might be Psalm 16:10–11; 110:1, 4; 118:22–24; Isaiah 53:10–12; Hosea 6:2; Jonah 1:17 [BECNT, CH, Gdt, IVP, NTC, TRT].

DISCOURSE UNIT—20:10–18 [Car; NET, NIV]. The topic is Jesus appears to Mary.

20:10 Then they went[a] back[b] to their-homes.[c]

LEXICON—a. ἀπέρχομαι (LN 15.37) (BAGD 2. p. 84): 'to go' [AB, BAGD, HTC; CEV, NCV NET, NJB, NLT, NIV, REB, TEV], 'to go away' [LN NICNT2; KJV, NASB], 'to go back' [NTC; Ph], 'to depart, to leave' [LN]. The phrase ἀπῆλθον οὖν πάλιν 'Then they went away again' is translated 'Then/So the disciples returned' [Gdt, WBC; NRSV]. This verb means to move away from a reference point with emphasis on the departure, but without implications as to any resulting state of separation or rupture [LN].

b. πάλιν (LN 67.55): 'back' [AB, HTC; CEV, NCV NET, NJB, NIV, TEV], 'again' [LN, NICNT2 NTC; KJV, NASB, Ph, REB], not explicit [Gdt, WBC; NLT, NRSV]. This adverb indicates a subsequent point of time involving repetition [LN].

c. αὐτός (LN 92.11) (BAGD 1.i. p. 212): 'he, him, she, her, it, they, them' [LN]. The phrase πρὸς αὐτούς 'to their homes' [HTC, NTC, WBC;

NET, NIV, NRSV, Ph] is also translated 'to their own home(s)' [Gdt; KJV, NASB], 'home' [AB, BAGD; NCV, NJB, NLT, REB, TEV], 'to the other disciples' [CEV], 'to themselves' [NICNT2]. This pronoun is a reference to a definite person or persons spoken or written about [LN].

QUESTION—Does the phrase πρὸς αὐτούς mean 'to their homes' or to some other place?

1. It means 'to their homes/home' [AB, BAGD, BECNT, Car, EGT, Gdt, HTC, ICC, Lns, My, NICNT1, NICNT2, NTC, WBC; all translations except CEV]. It means 'to their lodgings' [EGT]. Although literally it means 'to themselves' it probably has the sense of returning to the place where they were previously staying [NICNT2].
2. It means 'to the other disciples' [CEV]: 'So the two of them went back to the other disciples' [CEV].

QUESTION—If the phrase πρὸς αὐτούς is taken to mean 'to their homes', to which place does this refer, Jerusalem or Galilee?

It probably refers to their homes in Jerusalem rather than Galilee [AB, TH, TRT].

DISCOURSE UNIT—20:11–29 [NICNT1]. The topic is the appearances.

DISCOURSE UNIT—20:11–18 [AB, BECNT, HTC, ICC, IVP, Lns, NICNT1, NTC, Rd, WBC; CEV, NLT, NRSV, TEV]. The topic is Jesus appears to Mary Magdalene.

20:11 But Mary stood weeping[a] outside the tomb. Then as she-was-weeping, she-stooped-to-look[b] into the tomb **20:12** and saw two angels in white sitting, one at the head and one at the feet, where the body of-Jesus had-lain.

LEXICON—a. pres. act. participle of κλαίω (LN 25.138) (BAGD 1. p. 433): 'to weep' [AB, BAGD, Gdt, HTC, LN, NTC; KJV, NASB, NET, NJB, NLT, NRSV, REB], 'to cry' [BAGD, NICNT2, WBC; CEV, NCV, NIV, Ph, TEV], 'to wail, to lament' [LN]. This verb means to weep or wail, with emphasis on the noise accompanying the weeping [LN].

b. aorist act. indic. of παρακύπτω (LN **17.31, 24.13**): 'to stoop and look into' [LN (24.13)], 'to stoop down' [LN (17.31)], 'to bend over' [LN (17.31)]. The words 'she stooped to look into the tomb' [HTC, NTC] is also translated 'she stooped/stooped down and looked into the tomb' [**LN** (24.13); NASB, 'she stooped down to look into the sepulchre' [Gdt], 'she stooped down (and looked) into the sepulchre' [KJV], 'she bent over and looked in the tomb' [**LN** (17.31); TEV], 'she bent down and looked inside/into the tomb' [NCV, NET], 'she stooped to look inside' [NJB], 'she bent over/down to look/peer into the tomb' [AB, WBC; NIV, NRSV], 'she stooped and looked in' [NLT], 'she looked/peered into the tomb' [Ph, REB], 'she stooped down (and saw)' [CEV], 'she stooped down (into the tomb)' [NICNT2]. This verb means to look into something by stooping down [LN 24.13], or it means to bend over or stoop down, with the implication of looking into something [LN 17.31]. The sense of 'looking' is definitely implied [TH]. See this verb also at 20:5.

QUESTION—What is indicated by the conjunction δέ 'but'?

It indicates a contrast 'but' [BECNT, Car, NICNT1] with the action of Peter and John [Car, NICNT1]. Version evidence is as follows: 'but' [Gdt, HTC, NTC, WBC; KJV, NASB, NCV, NET, NJB, NIV, NRSV, Ph, REB], 'meanwhile' [AB], 'now' [NICNT2], not explicit [CEV, NLT, TEV].

QUESTION—What characterized her weeping?

It was not a quiet sobbing but a noisy lamentation [BECNT, Lns, NICNT1]. The verb implies unrestrained weeping [ICC, Lns, NICNT1, NTC]. Her sobbing was continual [NTC, Rd]. It was helpless and hopeless [EGT].

QUESTION—What is implied by the phrase '(two angels) in white'?

It implies that the two angels *were dressed* in white clothing [My, TRT; CEV, NCV, NLT, TEV]: 'two white-robed angels' [NLT].

20:13 They-said to-her, "Woman, why are-you-weeping?" She-said to-them "They-have-taken-away my Lord, and I-do- not -know where they-have-laid him."

QUESTION—What is indicated by the vocative γυνή 'Woman'?

As a form of address, this word was used in Koine Greek in speaking politely to a female person [Car, LN, TH]. It is a term of respect [AB, Bar, NICNT1, TH] and is the same term as was used in 2:4 and 19:26 [TH].

QUESTION—What does the question of the angels imply?

It implies that this was no time for weeping [Car, Kn, Lns, NTC], it was a time for joy [Kn, NTC]. It is a gentle reproof [Car]. Mary should be ashamed of her unbelief in the teaching of Jesus regarding his death and resurrection [NTC]. The question serves to urge Mary to forget her sorrow and realize that Jesus is alive [BECNT].

QUESTION—Does the conjunction ὅτι 'that/because' ('she says to them *that*/she says to them *because*') mark Mary's words as a quote, or is it part of Mary's reply?

1. It marks Mary's reply as a quote [Lns, NICNT2, NTC, WBC; CEV, NCV, NET, NJB, NIV, NRSV, REB, TEV]: 'She answered, "They have taken away my Lord's body!"' [CEV].
2. It is part of her reply [AB, Gdt, HTC; KJV, NASB, NLT, Ph]: 'She said to them, "Because they have taken away my Lord"' [NASB].

20:14 Having said this she-turned-around[a] and saw Jesus standing (there) but she-did- not -know[b] that it-was Jesus.

LEXICON—a. aorist pass. indic. of στρέφομαι (LN 16.13) (BAGD 2.a.α. p. 771): 'to turn around, to turn toward' [BAGD, LN]. The phrase ἐστράφη εἰς τὰ ὀπίσω (literally, 'she turned around into the back') is translated 'she turned herself back' [Gdt; KJV], 'she turned back' [WBC], 'she turned (a)round' [AB, BAGD, HTC, NICNT2, NTC; CEV, NASB, NCV, NET, NJB, NIV, NRSV, REB, TEV], 'she turned' [Ph], 'she turned to

leave' [NLT]. This verb means to turn around to or toward someone or something [LN].
- b. pluperfect act. indic. of οἶδα (LN 28.1): 'to know' [Gdt, HTC, LN, NICNT2, NTC, WBC; CEV, KJV, NASB, NCV, NET, NRSV, TEV], 'to realize' [AB; NJB, NIV, Ph], 'to recognize' [NLT, REB], 'to know about, to have knowledge of, to be acquainted with' [LN]. This verb means to possess information about [LN].

QUESTION—What might explain why Mary did not recognize Jesus?

She did not recognize him because of the character of his new resurrected body (see also Matthew 28:17; Mark 16:12; Luke 24:16, 37; John 21:4; 1 Corinthians 15:35ff.) [Car, EGT, Gdt, IVP, Lns, My, NICNT1, WBC]. Her failure to recognize Jesus may have been due to the fact that she did not expect to see him alive [AB, Gdt, Lns, My] and her grief blinded her eyes [Lns]. She may have been prevented from recognizing him (see 21:4; Luke 24:16) [NICNT2, WBC]. She supposed that he was the gardener (see verse 15) [BECNT].

20:15 Jesus said to-her, "Woman, why are-you-weeping? Who are-you-looking-for?" Thinking[a] he-was the gardener[b] she-said to-him, "Sir,[c] if you have-carried- him -away,[d] tell me where you-have-laid him, and-I will-take-him -away.

LEXICON—a. pres. act. participle of δοκέω (LN 31.29): 'to think' [AB, LN, NICNT2, NTC, WBC; CEV, NCV, NET, NLT, NIV, REB, TEV], 'to suppose' [Gdt, HTC, LN; KJV, NASB, NJB, NRSV, Ph], 'to presume, to assume, to imagine, to believe' [LN]. This verb means to regard something as presumably true, but without particular certainty [LN].
- b. κηπουρός (LN **43.20**) (BAGD p. 430) 'gardener' [BAGD, **LN**; all translations]. This noun denotes one who takes care of a garden or orchard [LN]. This person is a keeper of a κῆπος 'garden' [Bar, BECNT].
- c. κύριος (LN 87.53) (BAGD 1.b. p. 459): 'sir' [BAGD, LN; all translations], 'mister' [LN], 'lord, Lord, master' [BAGD]. This noun is a title of respect used in addressing or speaking of a man [LN]. It is a designation of any person of high position. Here it means 'sir' and is a form of address to repected persons generally [BAGD].
- d. aorist act. indic. of βαστάζω (LN **15.201**) (BAGD 3.a. p. 137): 'to carry away' [BAGD, Gdt, **LN**, NTC, WBC; NASB, NET, NIV, NRSV, Ph], 'to take away' [LN; CEV, NCV, NJB, NLT, TEV], 'to carry off' [AB, NICNT2], 'to remove' [BAGD, LN; REB], 'to bear hence' [Gdt; KJV]. This verb means to carry away from a place, with the probable implication of something that is relatively heavy [LN]. In other places this verb is used in the context of disposing of a corpse [BECNT].

QUESTION—What may have caused Mary to not recognize Jesus?

Since she did not expect or believe that he would come back to life, such a thought was absurd to her in her present state of mind [Gdt, NTC]. Either she was blinded by her tears or his appearance had changed dramatically after the resurrection [CH]. No one else but a gardener would have been likely to have been there at that time of the morning [EGT, ICC, My].

QUESTION—What may have been the purpose of Jesus' question, 'Why are you weeping'?

It may be a mild reprimand [BECNT, Car] or a sympathetic way of showing Jesus' care for her grief [BECNT]. He was drawing her attention to himself [WBC].

QUESTION—What may have been the purpose of Jesus' next question, 'Who are you looking for'?

It is a rhetorical question that leads to an invitation as it does in 1:38–39 ('Come and you will see') [Kn]. It may have been a reprimand that she should not have been looking for a living person among the dead and that she should remember that he had power to take his life back again and in fact had predicted that he would do so [NICNT1]. It served to cause her to consider the kind of Messiah she was expecting and to show her that her estimate of who he was, was still far too small [Car]. Jesus was directing Mary's attention away from herself [BECNT]. He was beginning to turn her attention away from something (a corpse) to someone (τίνα 'whom' not 'what' are you looking for) [Lns, NTC]. Jesus wanted to open Mary's eyes to reality [Lns].

QUESTION—What may have been Mary's intention in taking the body of Jesus away?

She probably intended to give him a proper burial [Car, Kn, My, NICNT1, TRT] or return his body to the tomb [TH].

QUESTION—What word is emphasized in this verse?

The pronoun σύ 'you' is emphasized in the words 'if you have carried him away' [Bar, My]. The pronoun ἐκεῖνος 'she' (literally, 'that one') is emphasized, and highlights Mary's dialogue with Jesus (see the same pronoun in verse 16, '*she* turned') [NICNT2]. The pronoun in the compound word κἀγώ (καί ἐγώ) 'and I' is emphatic [Lns].

20:16 Jesus said to-her, "Mary."ᵃ She turned (and) said to-him in-Hebrew,ᵇ "Rabboni!"ᶜ (which means Teacher).ᵈ

LEXICON—a. Μαριάμ (LN 93.254, 93.253) (BAGD 2. p. 492): 'Mary' [LN (93.253); all translations except NTC], 'Miriam' [NTC]. Μαριάμ is an alternative form of Μαρία [BAGD, LN (93.254)]. The name refers to Mary Magdalene [BAGD, NICNT2, Rd]. Mary's own name spoken directly to her in well known tones reveals to her who the speaker is [ICC].

b. Ἑβραϊστί (LN 33.6) (BAGD p. 213): 'in Hebrew' [AB, BAGD, Gdt, HTC, LN, NICNT2, WBC; NRSV, NJB, NRSV, Ph, TEV], 'in Aramaic' [BAGD, NTC; NET, NIV], 'in the Jewish language' [NCV], 'in the Hebrew language' [LN], not explicit [KJV]. The phrase 'in Hebrew' means 'in Aramaic' (see 5:2; 19:13, 17, 20) [AB, BECNT, HTC, ICC, Lns, NICNT2, NTC, Rd, TH, TRT; CEV, NET, NIV]. These words could also be translated 'she said "Rabboni" (this is a word in the Hebrew language that means "Teacher")' [TH].

c. ραββουνι (LN 33.247) (BAGD p. 733): 'Rabboni' [Gdt, HTC, LN, NTC; CEV, NASB, NCV, NET, NLT, NIV, TEV], 'Robbouni' [NICNT2, WBC; NRSV], 'Rabbuni' [AB; REB], not explicit [Ph]. The words '"Rabboni" (which means Teacher)' are translated '"Rabboni." The Aramaic word "Rabboni" means "Teacher"' [CEV], '"Rabboni/Rabbuni!" (which is Hebrew for "Teacher")' [NLT, REB]. This word is an Aramaic transcription [Car, LN, NICNT1, NICNT2, Rd] meaning 'my teacher' [LN, NICNT2, Rd], and is an honorific title for a teacher of the Jewish Scriptures, implying an important personal relationship [LN]. It no longer means 'my teacher' but may be simply the same as the normal vocative 'rabbi' [EGT, HTC, ICC, NTC]. It means 'my Master' [BAGD, Rd], or 'my Lord' [BAGD]. The expression 'Rabboni' expresses Mary's recognition, surprise, joy, and relief [EGT]. John translates both titles, 'Rabbi' and 'Rabboni', as διδάσκαλος 'teacher' (see 1:38 and 20:16) [Car].

d. διδάσκαλος (LN 33.243) (BAGD p. 191): 'teacher' [AB, LN; all translations except Gdt; KJV, NJB, Ph], 'master' [Gdt; KJV, NJB, Ph], 'instructor' [LN]. This noun is derived from the verb διδάσκω 'to teach' (33.224), and denotes one who provides instruction [LN].

QUESTION—Why did Mary turn *again*?

Apparently she had turned back toward the tomb after she had first turned to speak to him [Bar, Gdt, ICC, My, NICNT1]. She turned again because something in the way her name was spoken caught her attention [NICNT1]. The Greek word στραφεῖσα 'turned' rather means 'leaned forward' as it does in Luke 9:55 and 20:23. She had not turned back but was looking at the gardener awaiting his reply. On hearing his response, 'Mary', she leaned forward and exclaimed 'Rabbuni' [Lns].

20:17 **Jesus said to-her, "Do- not**[a] **-hold-on-to**[b] **me, for I-have- not-yet -ascended to the Father. But go to my brothers**[c] **and tell them, 'I-am- ascending to my Father and your Father and (to) my God and your God.'"**

LEXICON—a. μή (LN 69.3) (BAGD A.III.3.b. p. 517): 'not' [BAGD, LN; all translations except NASB]. This particle marks a proposition as being negative [LN]. It functions here to bring an end to a condition now existing [BAGD, WBC].

b. pres. mid. impera. of ἅπτομαι (LN **18.6**) (BAGD 2.a. p. 101): 'to hold on to' [**LN**], 'to cling to, to touch, to hold, to take hold of' [BAGD], 'to retain in the hand, to seize' [LN]. The words 'Do not/don't hold on to me' [**LN**; CEV, NCV, NIV, NRSV, TEV], are also translated 'Stop holding on to me' [Kn, TRT], 'Do not cling to me' [AB; NJB, NLT, REB], 'Stop clinging to me' [BAGD, BECNT, Lns, NICNT1, TRT; NASB], 'Do not keep clinging to me' [NTC], 'Do not keep on trying to hold me' [WBC], 'No!...Do not hold me (now)' [HTC; Ph], 'Don't take hold of me'

[NICNT2], 'Touch me not' [Gdt; KJV]. This verb means to hold on to an object [LN].

c. ἀδελφός (LN 11.23) (BAGD 2. p. 16): 'brother' [BAGD; all translations except CEV], 'disciple' [CEV], 'fellow believer, Christian brother' [LN]. This noun denotes a close associate of a group of persons having a well-defined membership (in the NT ἀδελφός refers specifically to fellow believers in Christ). Though in a number of languages it is possible to use a corresponding term meaning 'brother' or 'brothers' in the sense of fellow believers, in some languages this cannot be done, and one must employ other types of expressions. In some instances it is possible to generalize a term meaning 'relative' and therefore to address or to speak of fellow Christians as 'relatives' rather than specifically 'brothers and sisters'. In most instances, however, one may only employ a phrase such as 'those who also believe' or 'those who believe in Christ even as we do' [LN]. Jesus calls everyone who is devoted to him 'brother' [BAGD]. Jesus' brothers are his disciples [AB, Bar, BECNT, CH, HTC, Kn, Lns, My, NICNT1, NICNT2, NTC, TH, TRT, WBC; CEV]. If in some languages it is not possible to translate 'brothers' without indicating 'blood brothers', it could be translated 'those who believe in me' [TH], or 'spiritual brothers/my disciples who are like brothers to me' [TRT].

QUESTION—Does the verb ἅπτομαι mean 'to touch' or rather 'to hold on to or cling to'?

1. It has the sense of holding on to or clinging to someone [AB, BAGD, BECNT, Car, HTC, Kn, Lns, NICNT1, NTC, Rd, TH, TRT, WBC; CEV, NASB, NCV, NIV, NJB, NLT, Ph, REB, TEV]. Here it means 'Stop clinging to me' [BAGD, BECNT, NICNT1, NTC, TRT; NASB]. The present tense plus a negative means to 'Stop doing something' not 'Start doing something' [AB, BAGD, Lns, NICNT1, WBC]. In Matthew 28:9 Mary Magdalene and the other Mary 'clasped (κρατέω) his feet and worshiped him' [Car, HTC, NICNT1, TH, TRT, WBC]. The question remains that if Jesus told Mary not to touch him why did he later encourage Thomas to do so [NTC].
2. It here has the meaning of 'to touch' or 'to try to take hold of' in the sense of forbidding an action not yet begun or being attempted [Bar, EGT, Gdt, My, NICNT2; KJV]. It could either mean 'Let go of me' or more likely 'Do not attempt to hold on to me' [NICNT2].
3. It has either the meaning 'to touch' or to hold on to' [IVP]. Whichever meaning is in focus, the sense of the present tense in this context indicates that she is to stop doing what she is doing [IVP].
4. A different verb should be read here [ICC]. It is likely that the verb phrase Μή μου ἅπτου is a corruption of μή πτόου 'do not be frightened' [ICC].

QUESTION—What is indicated by the conjunction γάρ 'for' in the statement 'for I have not yet ascended to the Father'?

It indicates the reason that Mary should not try to hold on to him or keep him to herself because he was now in the process of going to the Father [IVP,

Rd]. Jesus is telling Mary that this meeting with her was not the real fulfillment of his promise that she would see him again. In order to come back in a real and permanent way he must first ascend to the Father [Gdt].

QUESTION—Does Jesus mean only 'my brothers' or 'my brothers and sisters'?

He spoke the words to Mary as to all who would believe either male or female [NICNT2].

QUESTION—What is the significance of the present tense 'I am ascending'?

It indicates that Jesus was in the process of going to the Father but had not yet arrived there [TH].

QUESTION—Do Jesus' words 'my Father' and 'your Father', 'my God' and 'your God' indicate that believers have the same relationship with the Father and with God as Jesus does, or do they indicate a different kind of relationship?

1. By these words Jesus is indicating that the disciples now enjoy the same relationship with God as He does [AB, Car, EGT, HTC, IVP, My, NICNT2, Rd, TH, TRT]. These words stress what Jesus and his disciples have in common. God is Jesus' Father and the disciples' Father. He is Jesus' God and their God. They are now brought into the closest possible relationship to the Father [Rd]. The phrase 'my brothers', occurring only here in John (see also Matthew 28:10), also supports this interpretation [AB, Rd]. The conversation between Ruth and Naomi in Ruth 1:16 is a parallel to this passage. Ruth says to Naomi, 'Your people will be my people and your God my God'. She was identifying with Naomi and her people in which her relationship to God would be the same as Naomi's. In the same sense, Jesus' words indicate identification with his disciples not disjunction from them. This same concept is shown in Romans 8:29 where it is said of Jesus that 'he might be the firstborn among many brothers' [AB]. While there is a distinction between Jesus, the only son of the Father, and believers who share his sonship through the Spirit, it is not the difference but the similarity that is in focus here [WBC]. Jesus' relationship to the Father is unique, but the emphasis here is on the shared privileges of sonship that believers now have (see Romans 8:15–16; Hebrews 2:11–12) [Car].

2. By these words Jesus is indicating a distinction between his relationship to the Father, and that of the disciples [Bar, BECNT, Gdt, ICC, Lns, NICNT1, NTC]. Here Jesus is accenting a different sense in which God is his Father and the sense of which he is the Father of his followers [BECNT]. He is reminding them that although God was his and their father, there was a difference in the relation. Note that he does not say 'our Father'. Still God is theirs as well as his God (see Romans 15:6) [ICC]. God was Jesus' Father by nature, but theirs by freely given favor. He was Jesus' God in that Jesus was a man, but the disciples' God in the sense that Jesus was the one who acted a Mediator for them [Lns]. While highlighting the closeness of fellowship between himself, the Father, and

the disciples, Jesus is making a distinction here—his sonship differs from theirs [NTC].

20:18 Mary Magdalene went (and) told the disciples, "I-have-seen the Lord,"—and (that) he-had-said these-things to-her.

QUESTION—What is indicated by the use of present tenses (literally), 'Mary Magdalene *comes telling* to the disciples, "I have seen the Lord," and he said these things to her'?

The present tenses preserve the vividness of the surprise that the announcement produced in the disciples [Gdt]. The present tense focuses attention on the significant words and stress Mary's experience [NICNT1]. They paint a vivid picture—Mary is changed! Her grief, fear, and tears are all replaced by pure joy [Lns].

QUESTION—How should this combination of direct and indirect quotes be translated?

It is best to either have both as direct speech, 'Mary Magdalene told the disciples, "I have seen the Lord and he said these things to me"' [TH], or both as indirect speech [Gdt, TH; CEV, KJV, TEV], 'Mary Magdalene then went and told the disciples that she had seen the Lord. She also told them what he had said to her' [CEV]. If the direct and indirect speech combination is kept, it may be best to translate something like 'Mary Magdalene told them, "I have seen the Lord." She also told them what he had told her to tell them' [AB, HTC, NTC, TRT, WBC; NCV, NET, NIV, NLT, NRSV, Ph, REB].

QUESTION—What was the response of the disciples to Mary's words?

The disciples did not believe her (see Mark 16:9–11; Luke 24:10–11) [Car, CH, ICC, WBC].

DISCOURSE UNIT—20:19–31 [Bar, NICNT2]. The topic is the appearance to the disciples and Thomas.

DISCOURSE UNIT—20:19–29 [Kn; CEV, NASB]. The topic is appearances to the disciples.

DISCOURSE UNIT—20:19–23 [AB, BECNT, Car, HTC, ICC, IVP, Lns, NICNT1, NTC, Rd, WBC; NCV, NET, NLT, NRSV, TEV]. The topic is Jesus appears to the disciples.

20:19 So on-the evening^a of that day the first (day) of-the-week^b the doors being-locked^c where the disciples were for^d fear of-the Jews, Jesus came and stood among (them) and said to them, "Peace^e (be) to-you."

TEXT—Instead of μαθηταί 'disciples', some manuscripts read μαθηταί συνηγμένοι 'disciples gathered together', and others read μαθηταί αὐτοῦ συνηγμένοι 'his disciples gathered together'. GNT reads 'disciples' with an A rating, indicating that the text is certain.

LEXICON—a. ὄψιος (LN 67.76) (BAGD 2. p. 601): 'evening' [BAGD; all translations except NICNT2; NLT, REB, TEV], 'Sunday evening' [NLT], 'late' [BAGD, LN; REB], 'late in the day' [LN]. The words 'on the evening of that day' are translated 'It was late that Sunday evening' [TEV], 'it was late on that first day' [NICNT2]. This adjective indicates a point near the end of a day (normally after sunset but before night) [LN]. It was late in the evening [ICC, LN, Lns, NICNT2, NTC; REB, TEV]. The context often makes it easier to decide just what time is meant, whether before or after sundown. In our literature this word is mostly used as a noun [BAGD]. Note that Luke places this meeting after the return of the two from Emmaus, probably around 8 p.m. [ICC].

b. σάββατον (LN 67.177) (BAGD 2.b. p. 739): 'week' [BAGD, LN; all translations except CEV, NLT, TEV]. The words 'So on the evening of that day the first day of the week' is translated 'on the evening of that same Sunday' [CEV], 'that Sunday evening' [NLT, TEV]. This noun in the plural denotes a period of seven days. For the expression 'the first day of the week', there may be a number of complications, especially since in present day usage Monday is often regarded as 'the first day of the week'. For the NT, of course, the Sabbath Day, or 'Saturday', marked the seventh day of the week and the next day would be regarded as 'the first day of the week', namely, Sunday. [LN].

c. perf. pass. participle of κλείω (LN 79.112) (BAGD 1. p. 434): 'to lock' [AB, BAGD, BECNT, Kn, Lns, NICNT2, NTC, WBC; CEV, NCV, NET, NIV, NRSV, Ph, REB, TEV], 'to shut' [BAGD, Gdt, HTC, LN; KJV, NASB], 'to close' [BAGD, LN; NJB], 'to bar' [BAGD], 'to make shut' [LN]. This passive verb is also translated actively: 'They locked themselves in a room' [CEV], 'The disciples had locked the doors of the place where they were' [AB]. Κλείω means to cause something to be shut [LN].

d. διά (LN 89.26): 'for' [AB, HTC, NICNT2, WBC; KJV, NASB, NIV, NJB, NRSV, Ph, REB], 'because of' [Gdt, LN], 'out of' [NTC], 'on account of, by reason of' [LN]. The phrase 'for fear of the Jews' is translated 'because they were afraid of the Jews/Jewish leaders/authorities' [NCV, NET, NLT, TEV, similarly CEV]. This preposition in the accusative indicates cause or reason, with focus on instrumentality, either of objects or events [LN].

e. εἰρήνη (LN 25.248) (BAGD 2. p. 227): 'peace' [LN; all translations except CEV], 'welfare, health' [BAGD], 'freedom from worry' [LN]. The words 'Jesus...said to them, "Peace be to you"' are translated 'He greeted them' [CEV]. This noun denotes a state of freedom from anxiety and inner turmoil' [LN]. We should understand that these words from Jesus carried more than the conventional greeting [NICNT1]. These words complemented his words 'It is finished' spoken on the cross. It indicated reconciliation with and life from God [Car, WBC]. It denoted the unqualified well-being of believers in the new Kingdom of God that had just dawned [Car]. In some languages the greeting 'Peace be to you' is expressed 'I wish you well' or 'I pray that all may be well with you'. The disciples were in a state of fear from what the Jewish leaders might do and Jesus' greeting was intended to relieve them of this anxiety [TH]. The Hebrew salutation *shalom lekem* 'peace be to you', is a common Jewish greeting still used today [BECNT, IVP, WBC].

QUESTION—To which day does the phrase 'that day' refer?

It refers to the day mentioned in verse 20:1 when Mary Magdalene visited the tomb [AB, Bar, HTC, Lns, NICNT2, NTC].

QUESTION—What may be indicated by the phrase 'the doors being locked' and which doors are being referred to?

It may indicate the miraculous nature of Jesus' sudden appearance among the disciples [Car, Bar, BECNT, EGT, Lns, My, NICNT1, Rd, TH]. We should probably understand that Jesus did not enter the room in the normal way [EGT, NICNT1]. Jesus' body was now of such a nature that he could pass through closed doors and show the disciples his wounds [Bar]. The 'doors' may be the main entrance of the house plus the door to the room where they were gathered [BECNT, Lns, NICNT1], or the gate plus the door of the room where they were [NTC]. It could also refer to the two doors that formed the gate [NTC]. The repetition of this fact by John (see also verse 26) indicates that he was emphasizing it. Jesus entered in spite of the doors being locked to the astonishment of the disciples [Kn].

QUESTION—To which group of disciples does the phrase 'the disciples' refer?

It could refer to just the eleven apostles, but see Luke 24:33 ('...the Eleven and those with them, assembled together') that indicates that more than the eleven were there [BECNT, ICC, Lns, NICNT1, TRT]. If Jesus appeared among them after the two from Emmaus arrived, these two would be included. Probably others as well were there in addition to the original apostles [ICC]. The exact number is uncertain but we should probably understand 10 disciples—the 12 apostles minus Judas and Thomas [Car].

QUESTION—What is indicated by the phrase 'the Jews'?

It refers to the Jewish leaders [AB, BECNT, Car, Kn, NTC, TH, TRT; CEV, NCV, NET, NLT, TEV].

20:20 And when-he-had-said this he-showed them (his) hands and (his) side. The disciples therefore[a] rejoiced[b] when-they-saw the Lord.

LEXICON—a. οὖν (LN 89.50): 'therefore' [Gdt, LN, Lns, NTC, WBC], 'then' [HTC NICNT2; KJV, NET, NRSV], 'consequently' [LN, My], 'so, accordingly, then, so then' [LN], not explicit [CEV, NASB, NCV, NIV, NJB, NLT, Ph, TEV]. The words 'The disciples therefore rejoiced' is translated 'At the sight of the Lord the disciples rejoiced' [AB]. This conjunction indicates result, often implying the conclusion of a process of reasoning [LN]. Here it reveals the fact that the sight of Jesus' hands and side was effective. It was *because of this* that they rejoiced [NICNT1].

b. aorist act. indic. of χαίρω (LN 25.125) (BAGD 1. p. 873): 'to rejoice' [AB, BAGD, Gdt, LN, NICNT2, NTC; NASB, NET, NRSV], 'to be glad' [BAGD, HTC, LN; KJV], 'to be/become filled with joy' [WBC; NJB,

NLT, TEV], 'to be overjoyed' [NIV, Ph, REB], 'to become happy' [CEV], 'to be thrilled' [NCV]. This verb means to enjoy a state of happiness and well-being [LN]. The aorist tense may indicate the sudden joy that came over them on realizing that it was Jesus [BECNT, NICNT1].

QUESTION—Why did Jesus show the disciples his hands and side?

He wanted to convince them that he was the same Jesus they had known even though now he was transformed however much from what they had known [CH, Lns, My, NICNT1, NICNT2, Rd, WBC]. He wanted to calm their fears [WBC]. Jesus' hands and side point to the wounds that the nails and spear had made in them [AB, Bar, BECNT, Car, EGT, Gdt, Kn, Lns, My, NICNT1, NTC, Rd, TRT]. 'Hands' probably means forearms/wrists since the weight of a person's body would tear the hands rather than suspend the person on the cross [Car, Kn]. The Greek word χείρ 'hand' can include the wrist and forearm [Car, TRT].

QUESTION—What relationship is indicated by the participial clause 'when they saw the Lord' (literally, 'having seen the Lord')?

It indicates the cause of the disciples joy [AB, Lns, NTC, TH; probably NICNT2; NJB, REB, TEV]: 'At the sight of the Lord the disciples rejoiced' [AB]. (All other translations seem to take this clause to be temporal indicating 'when they saw the Lord'.)

QUESTION—What prophecies does this verse fulfill?

It fulfills John 16:22 '…I will see you again and you will rejoice, and no one will take away your joy' [Car, EGT, ICC, NICNT1, NICNT2, TRT, WBC]. It also fulfills John 14:18 'I will not leave you as orphans; I will come to you' [Car, WBC].

QUESTION—What word is emphasized in this verse?

The pronoun τοῦτο 'this' occurs before the verb 'said' in Greek increasing its prominence [TRT].

20:21 So Jesus said to-them again, "Peace (be) with-you. As[a] the Father has-sent[b] me, so-I[c] send[d] you."

TEXT—Some manuscripts omit the name ὁ Ἰησοῦς 'Jesus'. GNT encloses 'Jesus' in brackets including it with a C decision indicating difficulty in making the decision.

LEXICON—a. καθώς (LN 64.14) (BAGD 1. p. 391): 'as' [AB, Gdt, HTC, WBC; KJV, NASB, NCV, NIV, NJB, NLT, NRSV, REB, TEV], 'just as' [BAGD, LN, NICNT2, NTC; CEV, NET, Ph], 'in comparison to' [LN]. This conjunction indicates similarity in events and states, with the possible implication of something being in accordance with something else [LN]. When καθώς is followed by καί (as here) it indicates 'as…so' or 'as…so also' [BAGD].

b. perf. act. indic. of ἀποστέλλω (LN 15.66) (BAGD 1.c. p. 99): 'to send' [BAGD, LN; all translations]. This verb means to cause someone to depart for a particular purpose [LN].

c. κἀγώ (BAGD 3.a. p. 386): 'so I' [AB, NICNT2, NTC; NJB, NLT, NRSV, Ph, REB, TEV], 'even so I' [Gdt, HTC; KJV], 'I also' [BAGD, WBC; NASB, NET], 'I too' [BAGD, Lns], 'I now' [NCV], 'I' [CEV, NIV]. The combined form κἀγώ is made by joining καί 'and' with ἐγώ 'I' [BAGD].
d. pres. act. indic. of πέμπω (LN 15.66) (BAGD 1. p. 641): 'to send' [BAGD, LN; all translations]. This verb means to cause someone to depart for a particular purpose [LN].

QUESTION—Why does Jesus repeat the phrase, 'Peace be to you'?
He repeats it because 'Peace' was foundational to their work as apostles [Gdt]. Jesus' sudden appearance to them had alarmed them. Even though their fear was somewhat diminished and they were now rejoicing, the greeting of 'Peace' could stand repeating [NTC]. The phrase is repeated to emphasize it [My, NICNT1]. It was the peace that was the result of Jesus' death and resurrection (see 14:27) [NICNT1].

QUESTION—Is there a difference in the meaning of the two Greek verbs (ἀποστέλλω and πέμπω) for 'to send' here?
1. There is no significant difference. They are rather being used synonymously here [AB, BECNT, Bar, Car, HTC, ICC, IVP, Kn, Lns, NICNT1, NICNT2, NTC, Rd, TH]. Note that the word ἀποστέλλω, used here for the way that God sent Jesus, is also used in John 17:18 about Jesus sending the disciples—'As you sent (ἀποστέλλω), me into the world, I have sent (ἀποστέλλω) them into the world' [AB, NICNT2]. Jesus uses the formula ὁ πέμψας με 'who sent me', when speaking of his Father, over twenty times (see for example 5:30) [HTC]. And the same verb (πέμπω) is used when referring to the sending of the Holy Spirit (see 14:26; 15:26; 16:7) [Bar, HTC].
2. When referring to himself he uses the more official term of an ambassador, but when referring to the disciples he uses the term of simply being sent [Gdt].

QUESTION—Where are the disciples being sent?
Some languages may require a destination to be made specific. If so, the phrase 'into the world' would be appropriate [HTC, Rd, TH, TRT]. In verse 17:18 both Jesus and the disciples are sent 'into the world' [NICNT1].

QUESTION—Was this sending limited to the twelve (eleven) disciples?
1. The sending was not confined to the original twelve apostles [AB, BECNT, IVP, Kn, Lns, NTC], it included all believers present [Lns], as well as later generations of believers (see 13:20) [BECNT].
2. It was given to the eleven apostles alone [ICC, NTC]. Although there were others in the room, Jesus had chiefly the eleven disciples in mind when he said this (see John 17:18, 20) [NTC].

20:22 And when-he-had-said this he-breathed-on[a] (them) and said to-them, "Receive[b] (the) Holy Spirit.[c]

LEXICON—a. aorist act. indic. of ἐμφυσάω (LN **23.185**) (BAGD p. 258): 'to breathe on' [BAGD, **LN**; all translations except NTC, WBC], 'to breathe into' [WBC], 'to blow' [NTC]. This verb means to breathe on something. The process of breathing on someone may have very important symbolic implications. In some instances this can be related to a blessing, as in John 20:22, but in some languages the act of breathing on a person almost inevitably suggests some harmful influence, often connected with the use of black magic. It may therefore be important to select some less specific term so as to avoid a symbolic meaning which would considerably distort the significance of this one passage in which ἐμφυσάω occurs in the NT [LN]. Jesus did this in order to hand on the Spirit to the disciples [BAGD]. In some languages this verb should be rendered as 'blew on' since breathe simply refers to the normal inhaling and exhaling of breath. But this was a significant action of Jesus and may require a more active verb such as 'to blow on' [TH].

b. aorist act. impera. of λαμβάνω (LN 57.125): 'to receive' [LN; CEV, all translations], 'to accept' [LN]. This verb means to receive or accept an object or benefit for which the initiative rests with the giver, but the focus of attention in the transfer is on the receiver [LN]. Since a literal understanding of this verb requires a 'taking in one's hand', it may be necessary to translate something like 'accept the Holy Spirit in your lives', 'welcome the Holy Spirit in your hearts', or 'make room for the Holy Spirit within you' [TH].

c. πνεῦμα (BAGD 5.a. p. 676): 'Spirit' [BAGD; all translations except KJV, Ph], 'spirit' [Ph], 'Ghost' [KJV]. The phrase πνεῦμα ἅγιον (without the definite article) is translated 'the Holy Spirit' [BAGD; all translations except Gdt, NICNT2, WBC; Ph], '(the) Holy Spirit' [Gdt, WBC], 'a holy Spirit' [AB], 'Holy Spirit' [NICNT2], 'holy spirit' [Ph]. This noun denotes 'the spirit' as that which differentiates God from everything that is not God, as the divine power that produces all divine existence, as the divine element in which all divine life is carried on, as the bearer of every application of the divine will. Here the phrase πνεῦμα ἅγιον without the article indicates 'the Holy Spirit' [BAGD].

QUESTION—Where else in Scripture does the word ἐμφυσάω 'to breathe on' occur?

This verb also occurs in the LXX of Genesis 2:7 where God breathes his Spirit into Adam making him into a 'living being' [BECNT, ICC, NICNT1]. It also occurs in Ezekiel 37:9 where it produces life from the dead ('Then he said to me, "Prophesy to the breath; prophesy, son of man, and say to it, 'This is what the Sovereign LORD says: Come from the four winds, O breath, and breathe into these slain, that they may live'"') [ICC, NICNT1].

QUESTION—What does the lack of an article before 'Holy Spirit' imply?

The lack of an article before the word πνεῦμα 'spirit/Spirit' makes no difference here. The reference is to the Holy Spirit [BECNT, BAGD, Bar, Car, CH, EGT, ICC, IVP, Kn, Lns, My, NICNT1, Rd, TH, TRT; all translations except AB, NICNT2; Ph]. The article is also missing in other places in the Bible where the reference is definitely to the Holy Spirit (see

Acts 2:4) [AB, TH]. The Spirit was promised to be given after Jesus was glorified (7:39; 16:7). It is this gift that is in focus here [Bar]. The article is also missing in 1:33; 7:39; Acts 1:2, 5, as well as many other places, but in each case it is God's Spirit that is being referred to [Lns]. The lack of an article shows that this bestowal of the Holy Spirit was not yet that bestowal spoken of in chapters 14–16 that would occur at Pentecost [Gdt].

QUESTION—What word is emphasized in this verse?

The pronoun τοῦτο 'this' occurs before the verb 'said' in Greek increasing its prominence (literally, 'and *this* having said')[TRT].

20:23 Whoever's sins you-forgive[a] they-have-been-forgiven for-them. Whoever's (sins) you-hold-(against them),[b] they-have-been-held-(against them)."

TEXT—Instead of the perfect tense ἀφέωνται 'have been forgiven', some manuscripts read the present tense ἀφίονται 'are forgiven', others read another form of the present tense ἀφίενται 'are forgiven', and still others read the future tense ἀφεθήσεται 'shall be forgiven'. GNT reads the perfect tense 'have been forgiven' with a B rating, indicating that the text is almost certain.

LEXICON—a. aorist act. subj. of ἀφίημι (LN 40.8) (BAGD 2. p. 126): 'to forgive' [BAGD, LN; all translations except Gdt; KJV], 'to remit' [BAGD, Gdt; KJV], 'to pardon' [BAGD, LN], 'to cancel' [BAGD], 'to dismiss' [Lns]. This verb means to remove the guilt resulting from wrongdoing. It is extremely important to note that the focus in the meanings of ἀφίημι is on the guilt of the wrongdoer and not on the wrongdoing itself. The event of wrongdoing is not undone, but the guilt resulting from such an event is pardoned. To forgive, therefore, means essentially to remove the guilt resulting from wrongdoing. Some languages make a clear distinction between guilt and sin, and terms for forgiveness are therefore related to guilt and not to the wrongdoing. Therefore, 'to forgive sins' is literally 'to forgive guilt'. Though terms for 'forgiveness' are often literally 'to wipe out', 'to blot out', or 'to do away with', it is obviously not possible to blot out or to wipe out an event, but it is possible to remove or obliterate the guilt [LN]. This verb refers to the remission of the guilt or debt of sin. It is used in the OT and NT predominantly in the religious sense of divine forgiveness [BAGD]. The concept of forgiveness is expressed in different ways. For example, 'to erase one's sins', 'to wipe out one's sins', 'to throw a person's sins away', 'to forget about a person's sins', or even 'to give a person's sins back to him' [TH]. When you forgive someone's sins, you release them from being punished for the sins (even though they deserve it). Or when you forgive someone you remove their guilt [TRT].

b. pres. act. subj. of κρατέω (LN **13.34**) (BAGD 2.e.ε. p. 448): 'to hold' [AB, LN, Lns], 'to hold unforgiven' [Ph], 'to hold back' [WBC], 'to hold (someone's sin) against them' [**LN**], 'to retain' [Gdt, HTC, NICNT2,

NTC; KJV, NASB, NET, NJB, NRSV], 'to not forgive' [CEV, NCV, NIV, NLT, TEV], 'to pronounce unforgiven' [REB], 'to keep, to cause to continue' [LN]. This verb means to cause a state to continue, on the basis of some authority or power [LN]. The verb 'to hold' has the meaning of 'to not forgive' [TH]. This verb clearly means here the opposite of 'to forgive' [EGT, Rd]. The present tense indicates a continued state of refusing to forgive [AB].

QUESTION—What other Scriptures parallel this verse?

In Matthew 16:19 and 18:18 Jesus says, 'I will give you the keys of the kingdom of heaven. Whatever you bind on earth will be bound in heaven, and whatever you loose on earth will be loosed in heaven' (16:19), and '...whatever you bind on earth will be bound in heaven, and whatever you loose on earth will be loosed in heaven' (18:18) [Bar, BECNT, Car, CH, HTC, ICC, Lns, NTC, Rd, WBC].

QUESTION—Who is the actor implied in the passive phrases 'they have been forgiven', 'they have not been forgiven'?

God is the one who has forgiven them or not forgiven them [AB, Car, Kn, My, NICNT2, Rd, TH, TRT].

QUESTION—What is implied by this endowment on the disciples to be able to forgive sins?

The authority to forgive sins is closely connected with the bestowal of the Holy Spirit enabling the disciples to do this [Bar, CH, EGT, Gdt, ICC, Lns, My, NICNT1, NICNT2, NTC, Rd]. This authority is exercised only as the Spirit directs [NICNT1]. In so doing, Jesus is revealing himself as present in the disciples forgiving sins on earth [Rd]. Jesus has given the disciples the authority to act on his behalf in the world [NICNT2].

DISCOURSE UNIT—20:24–31 [NTC; NET, NIV, Ph]. The topic is the response of Thomas [NET], Jesus appears to Thomas [NIV, Ph].

DISCOURSE UNIT—20:24–29 [AB, BECNT, Car, HTC, ICC, IVP, Lns, NICNT1, Rd, WBC; NCV, NLT, NRSV, TEV]. The topic is Jesus appears to Thomas.

20:24 But Thomas one of the Twelve, called the-Twin,[a] was not with them when Jesus came. **20:25** So the other disciples told him, "We-have-seen the Lord." But he said to-them, "Unless I-see the mark[b] of-the nails in his hands and put[c] my finger into the mark of-the nails and put my hand into his side, I-will- never[d] -believe."

LEXICON—a. Δίδυμος (LN 93.95) (BAGD p. 192): 'the Twin' [HTC, NTC; CEV, NJB, NRSV, Ph, REB, TEV], '(nicknamed) the Twin' [NLT], '(this name means) Twin' [AB, similarly WBC], 'Didymus' [Gdt, LN; KJV, NASB, NCV, NET, NIV], 'Didymos' [NICNT2]. This noun denotes the Greek name of the apostle Thomas (93.155) and means 'Twin' [BAGD, LN].

b. τύπος (LN **8.56**) (BAGD 1.f. p. 823): 'mark' [AB, NTC, WBC; NCV, NIV, NRSV, Ph, REB], 'scar' [**LN**; CEV, TEV], 'print' [AB, HTC, NICNT2; KJV], 'imprint' [NASB], 'hole' [NJB], 'wound' [LN; NET, NLT], 'place, position, region' [BAGD]. This noun denotes a visible impression or trace made as the result of a blow or pressure [LN]. It denotes the place where something is found, or at least should or could be found. Here it indicates the place where the nails had been [BAGD].

c. aorist act. subj. of βάλλω (LN 85.34) (BAGD 2.b. p. 131): 'to put' [AB, BAGD, LN; all translations except HTC; CEV], 'to place' [BAGD, HTC], 'to touch' [CEV]. This verb means to put or place some object or mass in a location, with the possible implication of force in some contexts [LN].

d. οὐ μή (LN **69.5**): 'never' [AB, NICNT2, TRT, WBC; NET, Ph, REB], 'definitely not' [NTC, TRT], 'in no wise' [Lns], 'certainly not' [BECNT, LN], 'by no means' [LN], 'not' [Gdt, HTC; CEV, KJV, NASB, NCV, NIV, NLT, NRSV, TEV]. This negative particle is also translated as a verb phrase: 'I refuse (to believe)' [NJB]. The negative particle combination is a marker of emphatic negation [HTC, LN, NICNT2, NICNT1]. Οὐ μή with the subjunctive or future indicative is the strongest form of negation—'in no way', 'not at all' [Lns]. It is very emphatic [AB, IVP].

QUESTION—Who were the 'Twelve'?

Here the 'Twelve' were the original twelve apostles minus Judas and Thomas. So technically it refers to only ten apostles [TH].

QUESTION—What is indicated by the imperfect tense of 'told' (literally 'were telling') in the phrase 'the other disciples told him'?

It indicates repeated action [AB, BECNT, Lns, NICNT1, NTC, TH; NCV, Ph, REB]: 'The other disciples kept on telling him' [Ph]. It indicates that they kept trying to convince Thomas [Lns]. It may indicate that they tried to tell him [AB, BECNT].

QUESTION—What did Thomas refuse to believe?

He refused to believe that Jesus rose from the dead [NTC, TH], or that the disciples saw him or that he was really alive [TH, TRT]. Thomas thinks their claim is absurd [Rd].

QUESTION—Had Thomas predicted Jesus' death?

John 11:16 informs us, 'Then Thomas (called Didymus) said to the rest of the disciples, "Let us also go, that we may die with him"'. We may well imagine him saying to the other disciples, 'I told you so' [Gdt, ICC].

20:26 And eight days later his disciples were inside again, and Thomas (was) with them. The doors being-locked Jesus came and stood among (them) and said, "Peace (be) with-you."

QUESTION—What is indicated by the phrase 'eight days later'?

The Jews counted the beginning and the end of a time period, hence eight days equals a week [Bar, HTC, IVP, WBC]—counting both Sundays [Bar].

It indicates the Sunday following Jesus' first resurrection appearances [AB, BECNT, Bar, Car, IVP, Lns, NICNT1, NICNT2, TH, WBC].

QUESTION—What is indicated by the adverb ἔσω 'inside'?

It indicates that the disciples were inside a house [AB, HTC, Lns, My, TH, TRT], or inside a room [TRT]. It was probably the same place that Jesus first appeared to them [EGT, HTC, ICC, Lns, My, NTC, TRT].

QUESTION—What is indicated by the repetition of the phrase τῶν υρῶν κεκλεισμένων 'the doors being locked'?

By repeating the fact that the doors were locked John means to emphasize the miraculous aspect of Jesus' appearance among the disciples [TH].

20:27 Then he-said to-Thomas, "Put[a] your finger here and see[b] my hands and put your hand into my side, and do- not -be[c] unbelieving,[d] but believe."[e]

LEXICON—a. pres. act. impera. of φέρω (LN **85.42**): 'to put' [HTC, **LN**; CEV, NCV, NET, NIV, NJB, NLT, NRSV, Ph, TEV], 'to bring' [NICNT2, NTC, WBC], 'to reach' [Gdt; KJV, NASB, REB], 'to reach out' [AB], 'to place' [LN]. This verb means to put or place an object by moving it to a particular point [LN].

b. aorist act. impera. of ὁράω (LN 24.1): 'to see' [Gdt, HTC, LN, NICNT2, NTC, WBC; NASB, NIV, NRSV], 'to look (at)' [CEV, NCV, NLT, REB, TEV], 'to examine' [AB, TRT; NET], 'to behold' [KJV]. The words ἴδε τὰς χεῖράς μου 'see my hands' is translated 'look, here are (my hands)' [NJB, Ph].

c. pres. (deponent = active) middle or passive impera. of γίνομαι (LN) (BAGD A.III.3.b. p. 517): 'to be' [LN]. This verb means to possess certain characteristics, with the implication of their having been acquired [LN]. The present imperative indicates that an action that has begun should be stopped [AB, BAGD (A.III.3.b. p. 517), NICNT1, NICNT2, NTC, TH, TRT, WBC; CEV, NCV, NET, NJB, NIV, NLT, REB, TEV]. (See following two items for version evidence).

d. ἄπιστος (LN 31.98) (BAGD 2. p. 85): 'unbelieving' [BAGD, LN], 'faithless' [BAGD], 'lacking in trust' [LN]. The phrase μὴ γίνου ἄπιστος 'do not be unbelieving' [NASB] is also translated 'do not be unbelieving anymore' [NJB, similarly REB], 'stop being unbelieving' [WBC], 'no longer be unbelieving' [NTC], 'become not unbelieving' [Gdt], 'be not faithless' [HTC; KJV], 'be no longer faithless' [NICNT2; similarly NLT], 'do not persist/continue in your unbelief' [AB; NET], 'stop being an unbeliever' [NCV], 'do not doubt' [NRSV], 'you must not doubt' [Ph], 'stop (your) doubting' [IVP, TRT; CEV, NIV, TEV]. This adjective is derived from ἀπιστέω 'to not believe (in)' (31.97) and pertains to not believing, with the implication of refusing to believe [LN].

e. πιστός (LN 31.86) (BAGD 2. p. 665): 'trusting' [BAGD, LN], 'cherishing faith, 'trust' [BAGD]. The adjective 'trusting' (implied 'to be…trusting') is translated 'believe(!)' [WBC; NCV, NET, NIV, NJB, NLT, NRSV, Ph, REB, TEV], 'have faith!' [CEV], '(be)…believing'

[Gdt, HTC, NTC; KJV, NASB], '(be) faithful' [NICNT2], '(become) a believer' [AB]. This adjective is derived from πιστεύω 'to trust' (31.85) and pertains to trusting [LN]. Here it refers to believing in the resurrection of Jesus [BAGD].

QUESTION—What was remarkable about Jesus' words to Thomas?
Jesus' words to Thomas parallel almost exactly Thomas's requirements:
'Unless I-see the mark of-the nails in his hands' – 'See my hands'.
'Put my finger into the mark of-the nails' – 'Put your finger here'.
'Put my hand into his side' – 'Put your hand into my side'.
'I will never believe' – 'Stop being unbelieving, but believe' [NTC].

QUESTION—What specific place does the adverb ὧδε 'here' refer to?
It may be necessary in some languages to expand this adverb to include the exact location such as 'put your finger here on the scars on my hands' or 'put your finger on my hand' [TH].

QUESTION—What is indicated by ἀλλά 'but (believe)'?
It is a strong adversative meaning 'but, on the contrary' [NICNT1].

QUESTION—What is the implied object of the command 'believe!'?
Jesus was encouraging Thomas to believe *that he was truly alive* [TRT].

20:28 Thomas answered him, "My Lord[a] and my God."

LEXICON—a. κύριος (LN 12.9) (BAGD 2.c.β. p. 459; 2.c.γ. p. 460): 'Lord' [BAGD, LN; all translations], 'Ruler, One who commands' [LN], 'lord, master' [BAGD]. This noun is a title for God and for Christ and denotes one who exercises supernatural authority over mankind. The most common equivalent of 'Lord' is a term meaning 'chief' or 'leader', but frequently this cannot be employed as a title for 'God'. One may, however, combine such an expression with a term for 'God' and employ a phrase meaning 'God our leader' or 'God our chief'. In some instances, however, a term for 'Lord' is related to a verb meaning 'to command' or 'to order', and therefore 'Lord' can be rendered as 'the one who commands us' and combined with 'God' may form a phrase such as 'God, the one who commands us' [LN]. The use of the term κύριος raises Jesus above the human level [BAGD 2.c.γ. p. 460].

QUESTION—What is implied in the reply of Thomas 'My Lord and my God'?
Thomas's reply means, '*You are* my Lord and my God' [AB, EGT, Lns, TH, TRT, WBC; CEV].

QUESTION—How are the nouns related in the genitive construction Ὁ κύριός μου καὶ θεός μου (literally, 'the Lord of me and God of me'), 'my Lord and my God'?
If the words Lord and God cannot be possessed ('my Lord…'), it may be necessary to translate something like, 'You are the one who rules over me and you are the God whom I worship' [TH].

QUESTION—What does Thomas' statement indicate?
It indicates that he recognizes that Jesus is God in human form [Bar, BECNT, Car, CH, Gdt, HTC, ICC, IVP, Kn, Lns, My, NICNT1, NICNT2,

NTC, TH, TRT, WBC]. In the OT the pair 'Lord' and 'God' are used together when referring to Yahweh (see Psalm 29:3; 35:23–24; Jeremiah 38:17; Zechariah 13:9) [BECNT, BAGD (3.c. p. 357), NICNT1, TRT]. See also Revelation 4:11 [TRT]. This statement of Thomas's corresponds to John 1:1, '...the Word was God'. Thomas now sees Jesus as one who has risen from the dead. Mere men do not do this kind of thing [NICNT1].

QUESTION—What words are emphasized in Thomas's reply, 'My Lord and my God'?

The repeated pronoun μου 'my' emphasizes the personal quality of Thomas's faith [BECNT, EGT, Gdt, Lns, My].

20:29 Jesus said to-him, "Have-you-believed/you-have-believed because you-have-seen me? Happy[a] (are) they-who have- not -seen and-yet[b] have-believed."

LEXICON—a. μακάριος (LN 25.119) (BAGD 1.b. p. 486): 'happy' [AB, BAGD, LN, WBC; Ph, REB], 'truly happy' [NCV], '(how) happy…!' [TEV], 'blessed' [BAGD, Gdt, HTC, NICNT2, NTC; CEV, KJV, NASB, NET, NIV, NJB, NLT, NRSV], 'fortunate' [BAGD]. This adjective indicates the quality of being happy, with the implication of enjoying favorable circumstances [LN]. This means 'blessed, fortunate, happy' usually in the sense of 'privileged recipient of divine favor' [BAGD].

b. καί [LN 89.124a]: 'and yet' [AB, HTC, WBC; KJV, NASB, NET, NIV, NJB, NRSV, Ph], 'and' [NICNT2], 'but' [LN]. The words 'Happy are they who have not seen and yet have believed' are translated 'How happy are those who believe without seeing me' [TEV, similarly Gdt; NCV, NLT, REB], 'blessed are they who, though not seeing, are yet believing' [NTC].

QUESTION—It is difficult to determine if the first sentence of Jesus' reply is a question or a statement. If it is a question it expects the answer 'Yes' [TH]. Which is correct?

1. It should be taken as a question [ICC, My; CEV, NASB, NET, NRSV, Ph, TEV]: 'Is it because you have seen me that you believe?' [Ph]. To take this interrogatively highlights Jesus' reproof of Thomas which is indicated by the emphatic forward positioning of the words '*because you have seen me* (have you believed)?' [My].

2. It should rather be taken as a statement [AB, Bar, Car, Gdt, HTC, Lns, NICNT1, NICNT2, NTC, Rd, WBC; KJV, NCV, NIV, NJB, NLT, REB]. The perfect tense 'you have believed' indicates that Thomas's unbelief has now been changed to belief [Rd]. Since this is the more difficult reading we have hesitatingly adopted it [AB].

QUESTION—Are Jesus' words a reprimand to Thomas or something else?

1. Jesus' response should be taken as a reprimand to Thomas [BECNT, CH, Gdt, My, NICNT1, Rd]. The eye-witness evidence of his fellow disciples should have been sufficient grounds for Thomas to believe that Jesus had really risen from the dead [My]. Jesus is showing Thomas that his faith is

limited to seeing and also is signaling a transition to believing in the testimony of the apostles [BECNT]. If Jesus' words are a reprimand to Thomas they are a very gentle one [NICNT1].
2. His response is not a reprimand of Thomas [Bar, Car, EGT, ICC, Lns]. Thomas's confession simply acts as a trigger to Jesus to pronounce a blessing on those who believe without seeing [Car]. Jesus accepts Thomas's confession but reminds him that there exists a higher faith than one based on sight [EGT]. The only reprimand to Thomas is in the words of verse 27, 'stop being unbelieving, but believe' [ICC]. The faith of all the other disciples was based on sight as well, even that of John himself (see verse 8) [Lns].

DISCOURSE UNIT—20:30–31 [AB, BECNT, ICC, IVP, Kn, Rd; NRSV]. The topic is the author's purpose [AB, Car, ICC, IVP, NICNT1; CEV, NASB, NCV, NLT, NRSV, TEV], conclusion of the Gospel [BECNT, HTC, Lns, Kn, WBC], epilogue [Rd].

20:30 **Now**[a] **Jesus also did many other signs**[b] **in-the-presence-of his disciples, that are- not -written in this book.**

TEXT—Some manuscripts omit αὐτοῦ 'his (disciples)'. GNT includes 'his' with a C decision, indicating difficulty in deciding whether or not to include it in the text.

LEXICON—a. μέν οὖν (BAGD 3. p. 593, 1.a.α. p. 502): 'now' [HTC, NICNT2, WBC; NET, NRSV], '(now) to be sure' [BAGD, NTC], 'of course' [AB], 'truly' [KJV], 'therefore' [Gdt; NASB], '(there were) indeed' [LN; REB], not explicit [all other translations]. Μέν is an affirmative particle. It introduces a concessive clause, followed by another clause with an adversative particle: 'to be sure...but', 'on the one hand...on the other hand', though in many cases the translation will not fit this scheme. Rather, the contrast is to be emphasized in the second clause often with 'but'. When μέν is used with οὖν and δέ (beginning of verse 31), as here (μέν οὖν...δέ), it means '(now) indeed...but' [BAGD (p. 502)]. This may be a case where some traces of classical usage can be seen in which οὖν is emphatic and means 'certainly, really, to be sure' [BAGD (p. 593)]. Οὖν has the sense of 'therefore' as follows: 'Those who have not seen the risen Christ and yet have believed are blessed; *therefore* this book has been composed, to the end that you may believe'. The preceding μέν is coupled with the δέ that introduces verse 31 and together they have the sense of 'on the one hand'...'on the other' [Car]. (See also the second question below for further examples).

b. σημεῖον (LN 33.477) (BAGD 2.a. p. 748): 'sign' [AB, BAGD, HTC, LN, NICNT2, NTC, WBC; KJV, NASB, NJB, NRSV, Ph, REB], 'miracle' [BAGD, Gdt; CEV, NCV, TEV], 'miraculous sign' [NET, NIV, NLT]. This noun denotes an event which is regarded as having some special meaning. Σημεῖον as an event with special meaning [LN, Lns, NTC] was inevitably an unusual or even miraculous type of occurrence, and in a number of contexts it may be rendered as 'miracle'. Certainly that is the referent of the term in John 2:23, ('many believed in him as they saw the signs he did'). For the Gospel of John, however, a σημεῖον is not simply a miraculous event but something that points to a reality with even greater significance. A strictly literal translation of σημεῖον as 'sign' might mean nothing more than a road sign or a sign on a building, and therefore in some languages σημεῖον in a context such as John 2:23 may be rendered as 'a miracle with great meaning' [LN]. It is a sign that consists of a 'wonder' or 'miracle', an event that is contrary to the usual course of nature and is performed by God himself, by Christ, or by men of God [BAGD]. Here 'sign' indicates a miracle by which Jesus has proven that he is the Messiah [My]. This word occurs at 2:11, 18; 3:2; 4:48, 54; 6:2, 14, 26, 30; 7:31; 9:16; 10:41, 47; 12:18, 37; 20:30.

QUESTION—What may be significant about these two final verses of this chapter?

Many scholars think that these two verses form the original conclusion of this Gospel [AB, EGT, ICC, Kn, Lns, My]. Verses 29 and 30 form the provisional conclusion of this Gospel [Rd].

QUESTION—There are three conjunctions clustered at the beginning of this verse, μέν, οὖν, and καί 'on one hand, therefore, also' respectively. The following show how the translations that made them explicit rendered them.

'*Now* Jesus, *to be sure…also* performed many other signs' [NTC].
'*Now* Jesus performed many other signs/miraculous signs' [NET, NRSV, similarly HTC, NICNT2, WBC].
'*And* many other signs *truly* did Jesus' [KJV].
'Jesus *therefore* did many miracles, other than these' [Gdt].
'*Therefore* many other signs Jesus *also* performed' [NASB].
'*Of course*, Jesus *also* performed many other signs' [AB].

20:31 But^a these are-written so-that you-might-believe that Jesus is the Christ^b the Son of God, and so-that believing you-may-have life^c in^d his name.^e

TEXT—Instead of the aorist tense πιστεύσητε 'you might believe/come to believe', some manuscripts read the present tense πιστεύητε 'you might be believing/continue to believe'. GNT follows NA in reading the aorist tense πιστεύ[σ]ητε 'you might believe/come to believe' with a C decision, but with the bracketed [σ] implying the present tense as an alternative and indicating difficulty in deciding between the two tenses. It seems that the translations and commentaries that support the position of the GNT are BECNT, Car, CH, Lns, NICNT2. Alternatively Bar, Gdt, ICC, NICNT1, and NTC support the present tense.

LEXICON—a. δέ (LN 89.124): 'but' [LN; all translations except NCV, REB], 'on the other hand' [LN], 'however' [Lns], not explicit [NCV, REB]. This conjunction indicates contrast [LN]. It corresponds to the particle μέν 'on the one hand' of the previous verse [ICC].

b. Χριστός (LN 53.82) (BAGD 1. p. 887): 'Christ' [BAGD, Gdt, HTC, LN, NICNT2, NTC, WBC; KJV, NASB, NCV, NET, NIV, NJB, Ph, REB], 'Messiah' [AB, BAGD, LN; CEV, NLT, NRSV, TEV], 'Anointed One' [BAGD]. This noun literally means 'one who has been anointed' and is a title for Jesus as the Messiah [LN]. In a number of languages Χριστός (or Μεσσίας) as a reference to the Messiah occurs in a transliterated form based either on Χριστός in Greek or on Messiah in Hebrew. However, in some languages an attempt is made to represent the significance of the terms Χριστός and Μεσσίας by translating 'God's appointed one' or 'God's specially chosen one' or 'the expected one' in the sense of one to whom everyone was looking for help and deliverance [LN].
c. ζωή (BAGD 2.b.a. p. 340): 'life' [BAGD; all translations except CEV], 'true life' [CEV]. The life referred to here is the supernatural life belonging to God and Christ, which the believers will receive in the future, but which they also enjoy here in this world [BAGD].
d. ἐν (LN 89.76): 'in' [AB, Gdt, HTC, NICNT2, NTC, WBC; CEV, NASB, NET, NIV], 'through' [LN; KJV, NCV, NJB, TEV], 'by the power of' [NLT], 'by' [LN; REB], 'by means of' [LN]. This preposition indicates the means by which one event makes another event possible [LN]. It means 'in union, in vital connection with, his name' [Lns].
e. ὄνομα (LN 33.126) (BAGD I.4.c.γ. p. 573): 'name' [BAGD, LN; all translations except CEV, Ph, TEV]. The phrase 'in his name' is translated 'as his disciples' [Ph]. The clause 'so that believing you might have life in his name' is translated 'If you have faith in him you will have true life' [CEV], 'that in that faith you may have life as his disciples' [Ph], 'that through your faith in him you may have life' [TEV]. This noun denotes the proper name of a person or object [LN]. 'In the name of God' or 'Jesus' means, in the great majority of cases, 'with mention of the name', or 'while calling on the name'. It can be translated 'through' or 'by the name' in which the effect brought about by the name is caused by the utterance of the name [BAGD].

QUESTION—To what does the word ταῦτα 'these (are written)' refer?

It refers to the things written down in the whole Book of John [EGT, My, TH, TRT]. It refers specifically to the signs recorded in John 1-12 (see 12:37) [BECNT]. It may refer to the signs/miracles of verse 30 [TH].

QUESTION—Who is the implied actor of γέγραπται 'are written'?

The implied actor is the author of the Gospel [NICNT1, TH, TRT]: 'I have written these' [TH].

QUESTION—What relationship is indicated by the present participle 'believing (you may have life)'?

The present participle indicates the means to have life [AB, HTC, WBC; CEV, NCV, NET, NIV, NLT, NRSV, Ph, REB, TEV]: 'by believing, you may come to have life through his name' [NCV].

QUESTION—The object of 'believing' is left implicit. What should be understood as the object?

The object of believing is that Jesus is the Christ the Son of God [AB; NJB, Ph, REB, TRT]: 'through this faith you may have life' [AB]. The object is Jesus [CEV, NLT, TEV]: 'by believing in him' [NLT].

QUESTION—Does the prounoun 'you (might believe)' refer primarily to believers or unbelievers?

1. It refers primarily to believers [AB, Bar, CH, Gdt, HTC, IVP, Kn, Lns, Rd, WBC]. Although the primary object of the Gospel is to strengthen the faith of believers [IVP, Rd, WBC], there is also an evangelistic intention as well with unbelievers in view [CH, IVP, WBC].
2. It refers primarily to unbelievers [Car, NICNT1]. John is out to win converts more than to encourage believers [NICNT1].
3. It probably includes both believers and unbelievers [TRT].

QUESTION—Should the phrase 'in his name' be construed with the verb 'believing' (that is, '*believing in his name*') or with the phrase 'you may have life' (that is, 'you may *have life in his name*')?

1. The phrase 'in his name' should be construed with the words 'you may have life' [AB, Bar, Gdt, HTC, IVP, My, NICNT1; probably KJV, NASB, NCV, NET, NIV, NJB, NRSV, REB]: 'you may have life through his name' [NCV]. The thrust of the words are: 'that you may have life on account of him, by his agency, in virtue of your believing relationship with him' [Bar]. John means that abundant life is the gift of Christ [NICNT1]. The life is in his name because it is in fellowship with Christ. Living in his name is living his own life [IVP].
2. It is better to take the phrase 'in his name' as joined with 'believing' [ICC, TH; CEV, NLT, TEV]: 'through your faith in him you may have life; [TEV], 'If you have faith in him, you will have true life' [CEV], 'that believing in his name, ye may have life' [ICC].

QUESTION—To what specific kind of life does the term ζωή refer?

It refers to: eternal life [NICNT2, NTC, TRT], eternal-divine life [HTC], abundant life [NICNT1], the life of the Father and the Son [IVP].

QUESTION—To what does a person's name refer?

1. It refers to the person himself [Bar, Gdt, HTC, NICNT1, TH, TRT; CEV, TEV]: 'through your faith in him you may have life' [TEV]. Abundant life is his gift [NICNT1].
2. It refers to the mention of his name [BAGD].

DISCOURSE UNIT—21:1–25 [Car, CH, Kn, NICNT1, NICNT2, WBC; NLT]. The topic is Jesus' last resurrection appearance [CH], epilogue [Car, Kn, NICNT1], Jesus' third appearance and Peter's commission [NICNT2], the mission of the church [WBC], epilogue: Jesus appears to seven disciples [NLT].

DISCOURSE UNIT—21:1–23 [Ph]. The topic is the risen Jesus and Peter.

DISCOURSE UNIT—21:1–14 [AB, Bar, Car, HTC, Kn, NICNT1, WBC; CEV, NCV, NET, NIV, NRSV, TEV]. The topic is Jesus' appearance by the seaside [Bar, Car, HTC, Kn, WBC; CEV, NCV, NET, NRSV, TEV], the fish sign [Kn], the miraculous draught of fish [NICNT1; NIV].

DISCOURSE UNIT—21:1–11 [NASB]. The topic is Jesus appears at the sea of Galilee.

21:1 After these-things^a Jesus revealed^b himself again to-the disciples by Lake^c Tiberias.^d He revealed himself in this way.

LEXICON—a. οὗτος (LN 92.29): 'this, this one' [LN]. The phrase μετὰ ταῦτα 'after these things' [NICNT2; NTC, KJV, NASB, NRSV] is also translated 'after this' [Gdt, HTC, WBC; NET, TEV], 'afterward' [NIV], 'later' [CEV, NCV, NLT], 'later on' [AB; NJB], 'some time later' [REB]. This demonstrative pronoun refers to an entity regarded as a part of the discourse setting, with a pejorative meaning in certain contexts [LN]. The phrase is a general reference to a later time and does not imply strict sequence. It barely means more than 'another time' [ICC]. If a language requires a more definite reference to time one could translate something like 'a few days later' [TH].

  b. aorist act. indic. of φανερόω (LN **24.19**) (BAGD 2.a. p. 853): 'to make visible' [**LN**], 'to make appear' [**LN**], 'to cause to be seen' [LN]. The words 'Jesus revealed himself' [AB, BAGD, HTC, NICNT2, WBC; NET, NJB] are also translated 'Jesus appeared (literally "... made himself visible ...")' [**LN**], 'Jesus appeared' [CEV, NIV, NLT, TEV], 'Jesus showed himself' [BAGD; KJV, NCV, NRSV, Ph, REB], 'Jesus manifested himself' [Gdt, NTC; NASB]. This verb means to cause to become visible [LN], or 'to show' or 'to reveal oneself' or 'to make (oneself) known' [BAGD]. In a number of languages the meaning of 'appeared to' must be expressed as two closely related events, so that in John 21:1 it may be necessary to translate 'Jesus came and was seen once more by his disciples' or 'Jesus came and once more his disciples saw him' [**LN**].

  c. θάλασσα (LN **1.70**) (BAGD 2. p. 350): 'lake' [BAGD, LN, NICNT2; CEV, NCV, TEV], 'sea' [AB, Gdt, HTC, LN, NTC, WBC; KJV, NASB, NET, NIV, NJB, NLT, NRSV, REB]. This noun denotes a particular body of water, normally rather large [LN]. The use of θάλασσα to refer to a lake such as the Lake of Galilee (Matthew 4:18; Mark 1:16) or the Lake of Tiberias (John 21:1) reflects Semitic usage, in which all bodies of water from oceans to pools could be referred to by a single term. Normal Greek usage would employ the word λίμνη 'lake, pool' (1.72). Many languages make a clear distinction between different types of bodies of water. The three principal bases for differentiation are (1) fresh, brackish, or salty, (2) relative size, that is, large versus small bodies of water, and (3) existence of an outlet. On the basis of this third type of distinction, a term to designate the Sea of Galilee would need to be different from that used in speaking of the Dead Sea, since the Sea of Galilee has an outlet while the

Dead Sea does not. Considerable care must be exercised in the choice of terms for such bodies of water, since failure to select the right terms may result in serious distortion of geography and therefore considerable misunderstanding of the geographical setting of biblical events [**LN**].

d. Τιβεριάς (LN **93.597**) (BAGD p. 815): 'Tiberias' [BAGD, **LN**; all translations except NCV, NLT], 'Galilee' [NCV, NLT]. This noun denotes a city on the west shore of the Lake of Galilee [LN]. Tiberias is a city on the west shore of the Lake Gennesaret, founded by Herod Antipas as the capital of his domain and named in honor of Emperor Tiberius [BAGD]. In verse 6:1 'Lake/Sea of Galilee' was also referred to as 'Lake/Sea of Tiberias' [AB, Bar, Car, CH, EGT, Gdt, HTC, ICC, NICNT1, NICNT2, TH, TRT].

21:2 **Simon Peter and Thomas called Didymus[a] and Nathanael of Cana in Galilee and the (sons) of Zebedee[b] and two others of his disciples were together.** **21:3** **Simon Peter said to-them, "I-am-going fishing."[c] They-said to-him, "We also will-come with you." So they-went-out and got into the boat,[d] but that night they-caught[e] nothing.**

LEXICON—a. Δίδυμος (LN 93.95) (BAGD p. 192): 'Didymus' [BAGD, Gdt, LN; KJV, NASB, NCV, NET, NIV], 'Didymos' [NICNT2], '(the) Twin' [BAGD, HTC, NTC; CEV, NJB, NLT, NRSV, Ph, REB, TEV]. The phrase 'called Didymus' is translated 'this/whose name means "Twin"' [AB; WBC]. This noun means 'twin' and is the Greek name of the apostle Thomas [BAGD, LN].

b. Ζεβεδαῖος (LN 93.137) (BAGD p. 337): 'Zebedee' [BAGD, LN; all translations except CEV]. The phrase 'the (sons) of Zebedee' is translated 'the brothers James and John' [CEV]. This noun denotes the father of the apostles James and John [BAGD, LN]. The names of the sons, James and John, are made explicit in Matthew 4:21 [BECNT].

c. pres. act. infin. of ἁλιεύω (LN **44.7**) (BAGD p. 37): 'to fish' [BAGD, **LN**; all translations]. This verb means to catch fish, whether by means of a line or by a net [LN]. If a particular language requires the manner of fishing to be specified, it should be fishing with nets [TH, TRT].

d. πλοῖον (LN 6.41) (BAGD 2. p. 673): 'boat' [BAGD, LN; all translations except KJV], 'ship' [BAGD, LN; KJV]. This noun denotes any kind of boat, from small fishing boats as on Lake Galilee to large seagoing vessels [LN]. Here it refers to a small fishing vessel used on Lake Gennesaret [BAGD]. This boat must have been large enough to hold seven men with their nets [TH, TRT].

e. aorist act. indic. of πιάζω (LN 18.3) (BAGD 2.b. p. 657): 'to catch' [BAGD, LN; all translations except Gdt], 'to take' [Gdt], 'to take hold of, to seize, to grasp (firmly)' [BAGD, LN]. This verb means to take hold of firmly and with a considerable measure of force [LN].

QUESTION—What was the intention of the other disciples?
They meant that they would go with him to help him fish [Lns, TH, TRT], the preposition σύν 'with' implies this [Lns].
QUESTION—What word is emphasized in this verse?
The pronoun ἡμεῖς 'we' is emphasized [TH].

21:4 But when-it-was already^a early-morning,^b Jesus stood on the shore. But^c the disciples did- not -realize that it-was Jesus.

LEXICON—a. ἤδη (LN 67.20): 'already' [NJB; NET, NJB], 'now' [KJV, NASB], 'as soon as' [NICNT2], not explicit [AB, HTC, WBC; CEV, NCV, NIV, NLT, NRSV, REB, TEV]. This adverb indicates a point of time preceding another point of time and implying completion [LN]. In some important Western texts this word is missing [AB].

b. πρωΐα (LN 67.187) (BAGD p. 725): 'early morning' [BAGD, LN]. The clause 'when it was already early morning' is translated 'when it was already very early morning' [NET], 'early in the morning' [NIV], 'early the next morning' [CEV, NCV], 'when the morning was already/now come' [Gdt; KJV], 'as soon as morning had come' [NICNT2], 'morning came' [REB], 'just as day was breaking' [HTC], 'when the day was already/now breaking' [NTC; NASB], 'now when day had broken' [WBC], 'just after daybreak' [AB; NRSV], 'just as dawn began to break' [Ph], 'as the sun was rising' [TEV], 'when it was already light' [NJB], 'at dawn' [NLT]. This noun denotes the early part of the daylight period [LN], or first light [NICNT1].

c. μέντοι (LN 89.130) (BAGD 2. p. 503): 'but' [BAGD, LN, NTC, WBC; CEV, KJV, NCV, NET, NIV, NLT, NRSV, REB, TEV], 'however' [Gdt, WBC], 'yet' [HTC, NICNT2; NASB], 'though' [BAGD; NJB], 'nevertheless, except' [LN], 'to be sure, indeed' [BAGD]. This conjunction indicates contrast, implying the validity of something irrespective of other considerations [LN].

21:5 Then Jesus said to-them, "Children,^a you-do- not^b -have any fish^c -do- you?" They answered him, "No."

LEXICON—a. παιδίον (LN **9.46**) (BAGD 3.c. p. 604): 'child' [BAGD, Gdt, HTC, **LN**; KJV, NASB, NET, NRSV], 'friend' [CEV, NCV, NIV, NJB, REB], 'lad' [AB, EGT, Lns, NICNT2, NTC], 'boy' [WBC], 'young man' [TEV], 'fellow' [NLT]. This noun denotes 'child, offspring', a person of any age for whom there is a special relationship of endearment and association—'my child, my dear friend, my dear man, my dear one, my dear lad'. In a number of languages παιδία in John 21:5 is better rendered as 'my good friends' or 'my dear friends' or 'my dear comrades'. In this context, not age, but the connotation of affection and endearment is in focus. [LN]. It is a form of familiar address on the part of a respected person, who feels himself on terms of fatherly intimacy with those whom he addresses [BAGD]. It is a term of affection that could be used to address one's spiritual children [IVP]. Jesus uses the term as referring to 'lads' or 'boys' [AB, Car, ICC, NTC] or 'guys' [Car]. It is a polite form of address that someone in authority would use to address a subordinate [Gdt, TRT].

b. μή (LN **69.15**) (BAGD C.1. p. 517, (also under μήτι p. 520)): 'not' [LN, WBC; TEV, NIV, NJB], not explicit [Gdt, HTC, NICNT2; CEV, KJV, NCV, NLT, REB]. This interrogative particle indicates that a negative response is expected to a question [BAGD, LN]. It means 'you probably have no fish, have you?' [BAGD (p. 520)].

c. προσφάγιον (LN **5.17**) (BAGD p. 719): 'fish' [BAGD, HTC, LN, WBC; NASB, NCV, NET, NIV, NLT, NRSV], 'meat' [KJV], 'catch' [NICNT2]. The question 'you do not have any fish, do you?' is translated 'have you caught anything' [CEV, similarly NJB, REB, TEV], 'you haven't caught anything to eat, have you?' [AB, similarly Gdt, NTC]. This noun denotes the flesh of fish as food [LN, NTC]. In literature outside the NT, προσφάγιον normally refers to some type of relish eaten with bread, but in John 21:5 (the only occurrence in the NT) the reference is to the flesh of fish [LN]. It denotes something eaten with bread [BAGD, EGT, Gdt, Lns, NICNT2], and so here it refers to fish [Lns, Gdt]. Here it probably refers in general to a 'bite to eat' [BECNT, Car]. It literally means 'side dish' usually referring to fish as an accompaniment to bread [AB, Rd].

QUESTION—Does Jesus' question expect a negative reply?

1. The particle μή when used in a queston expects a negative reply [AB, BAGD, Car, CH, Gdt, LN, Lns, ICC, HTC, IVP, Kn, My, NTC, Rd, NICNT1, NICNT2, TH, TRT, WBC; NASB, NET, NRSV]: 'Boys, you have not had any catch, have you?' [ICC]. The question expects a negative reply or expresses doubt or both [Car, WBC]. Jesus asks this question in order to focus the disciples' attention on the fact that their return to their former life has been a total failure. He is implying that without him they could do nothing [NTC].

2. In some contexts the particle μή in a queston expects a negative reply but here it expresses doubt and hesitation [Bar].

QUESTION—What may be indicated by the reply, 'No' of the disciples?

In some languages the proper negative response to Jesus' question might be 'Yes (we don't have any)' [TRT].

21:6 He said to-them, "Throw the net on the right side of-the boat, and you-will-find (some fish)." So they-threw (it), and they-were- no-longer[a] -able to-haul- it -in,[b] because-of[c] the large-number[d] of fish.

LEXICON—a. οὐκέτι (LN 67.130): 'no longer' [LN, NICNT2, NTC], 'not' [all translations except NICNT2, NTC]. This adverb indicates extension of time up to a point but not beyond [LN]. It contrasts the action of the disciples when the net was empty and they could draw it [EGT, My].

b. aorist act. infin. of ἕλκω (LN **15.212**) (BAGD 1.a. p. 251): 'to haul (in)' [AB, BAGD, HTC, NTC, WBC; NASB, NIV, NJB, NLT, NRSV], 'to haul (on board)' [REB], 'to pull (in/back into)' [**LN**; NCV, NET, TEV], 'to draw (in)' [BAGD, Gdt, LN, NICNT2; KJV], 'to drag...(up into)' [BAGD, LN; CEV]. This verb means to pull or drag something, requiring force because of the inertia of the object being dragged [LN]. The place to which they try to draw the net is probably into the boat [EGT, NICNT1; REB].

c. ἀπό (LN 89.25) (BAGD V.1. p. 87): 'because of' [BAGD, Gdt, LN, NICNT2, NTC, WBC; NASB, NET, NIV, NJB], 'for' [HTC; KJV]. The statement 'they were no longer able to pull it in, because of the large number of fish' is translated 'the net was so full of fish that they could not drag it up into the boat' [CEV], 'the number of fish was so great that they were not able to haul it in' [AB; similarly NCV, NLT, NRSV, REB, TEV]. This preposition in the genitive case indicates cause or reason, with focus on the source [LN]. Or it indicates cause, means, or outcome [BAGD].

d. πλῆθος (LN 59.9) (BAGD 2.a. p. 668): 'large number (of)' [BAGD, LN; NET, NIV], 'great number (of)' [NICNT2, NTC; NASB], 'multitude (of)' [BAGD, Gdt, LN; KJV], 'number (of)' [WBC], 'quantity (of)' [HTC; NJB]. This noun denotes a large number of countable objects or events, with the probable implication of some type of grouping [LN]. (See previous item for other renderings.)

QUESTION—What kind of net did the disciples use?

It was probably circular with small weights around the edge [TH]. It was probably a dragnet having floats around the top edge and weights on the bottom edge. This formed a semicircle as it was dragged along entrapping the fish [TRT]. It was probably dragged by the boat through the water [BECNT]. It was obviously a rather large net [HTC, Kn].

QUESTION—What is indicated by the imperfect tense of the verb, 'they were no longer able'?

It indicates that they kept on trying to draw the net in unsuccessfully [NTC]. Or it pictures the disciples using all their force [Lns].

21:7 So that disciple whom Jesus loved said to-Peter, "It-is the Lord." Then when- Simon Peter -heard that it-was the Lord he put-on[a] (his) outer-garment,[b] for he-was naked,[c] and threw[d] himself into the sea.

LEXICON—a. aorist mid. indic. of διαζώννυμι (LN 49.14) (BAGD p. 182): 'to put on' [BAGD, Gdt, HTC, LN; CEV, NASB, NLT, NRSV], 'to wrap around oneself' [NCV, NIV, TEV], 'to tie around/round oneself' [WBC; NJB], 'to fasten about' [REB], 'to belt about' [NTC], 'to tuck in' [AB; NET], 'to secure' [NICNT2], 'to gird' [LN; KJV], 'to fasten one's belt, to wear a narrow band of cloth around the waist, to tie around the waist' [LN]. This verb means to tuck up or hold a garment firmly in place by wrapping a belt, girdle, or piece of cloth around it [LN]. In the middle voice it means 'to put on an outer garment' (literally 'tie around oneself') [BAGD].

b. ἐπενδύτης (LN **6.172**) (BAGD p. 285): 'outer garment' [AB, BAGD, LN, NICNT2, WBC; NASB, NET, NIV, NJB, TEV], 'coat' [BAGD, LN; NCV, REB], 'fisher's coat' [KJV], 'fisherman's jacket' [NTC], 'garment' [AB], 'his/some clothes' [HTC; NRSV], 'the clothes he had taken off while he was working' [CEV], 'tunic' [NLT], 'cloak, robe' [LN]. This noun denotes any type of outer garment [LN].

c. γυμνός (LN 49.22) (BAGD 2. p. 167): 'naked' [BAGD, LN; KJV, NRSV], 'without an outer garment' [BAGD], 'stripped, bare' [BAGD]. The phrase 'for he was naked' [Gdt, NICNT2; KJV, NRSV] is also translated '(Peter had taken his clothes off)' [NCV, similarly TEV], '(for he had nothing on)' [NJB], 'for he was practically naked' [WBC], '(for he was otherwise naked)' [AB], '(for he had nothing on underneath it)' [NET], '(for he had taken it off)' [NIV], '(for he was/had stripped)' [NTC; REB], '(for he was/had stripped for work)' [HTC; NASB, NLT]. This adjective pertains to wearing no clothing or being scantily clothed [Car, Kn, LN, Lns, TH, TRT]. A person without an outer garment would not appear in public [BAGD].

d. aorist act. indic. of βάλλω (LN 15.215) (BAGD 1.b. p. 131): 'to throw' [BAGD, LN]. The words 'he...threw/cast/flung himself into/in the sea/lake' [Gdt, NICNT2, NTC, WBC; KJV, NASB] are also translated 'he jumped into the water/sea' [AB; CEV, NCV, NIV, NJB, NLT, NRSV, TEV], 'he...plunged into the water/sea' [NET, REB], 'he...sprang into the sea' [HTC].

QUESTION—To whom does the pronoun 'it' refer in the words, 'It is the Lord'?

In some languages it may be necessary to specify the antecedent of the pronoun 'it' by translating something like, 'The person on the shore is the Lord' or 'The one who spoke to us is the Lord' [TH], or 'That man on the shore is our Lord' [TRT].

QUESTION—What made the beloved disciple recognize who the person on the shore was?

When he saw the miracle of the huge catch of fish he deduced that it must be the Lord [IVP, Lns, NICNT1, Rd, WBC].

QUESTION—Was Peter completely naked or only stripped for work?

1. He was merely stripped to his undergarment for work [AB, Bar, BECNT, CH, EGT, Gdt, HTC, ICC, Kn, Lns, NICNT1, NICNT2, NTC, Rd, TH, WBC; NASB, NET, NLT]. Peter was naked in the sense that he had nothing on underneath his outer garment or fisherman's smock. So he tucks or secures this into his belt to allow him to swim more freely and jumps into the water [AB, Bar, HTC, NICNT2, TH]. He was naked in the sense that he wore no clothing over his undergarment [CH, EGT, Gdt, HTC, ICC, Kn, Lns, My, NTC, WBC]. Peter was naked except for the *subligaculum* 'apron/loincloth' that was required for decency [EGT, Gdt].

2. He was completely naked [IVP; possibly KJV, NCV, NJB, NRSV, TEV]. If he added his outer garment over his under garment and then jumped into the water, he would possibly be drowned or at least would be slowed

on his way to shore. He probably had been working naked and now he puts on his loincloth to swim to shore [IVP].
3. He was either naked or was stripped to his undergarment for work [Car]. Since γυμνός can either mean 'naked' or 'lightly clad', Peter was either completely bare under his outer garment or was working in only his loincloth or undergarment [Car].

QUESTION—Why did Peter jump into the water?
He intended to swim to the Lord or to shore [Gdt, NICNT1]. He wanted to be the first to greet Jesus [CH]. He was eager to prove his devotion to Jesus [Kn].

21:8 **The other disciples came in-the boat,ᵃ draggingᵇ the net of fish, for they-were not far from the land only about two-hundred cubits.ᶜ**

LEXICON—a. πλοιάριον (LN 6.42) (BAGD p. 673): 'boat' [BAGD, LN; all translations except KJV, NASB], 'little boat' [NASB], 'small boat' [LN], 'little ship' [KJV]. This noun is a diminutive form of πλοῖον 'boat, ship' (see 6.41 in verse 21:6), but in some contexts it is possible that the diminutive aspect of πλοιάριον is not relevant [LN]. It is probably no longer thought of as diminutive [BAGD]. This refers back as a synonym for the same boat referred to in verses 3 and 6 [Bar, NICNT1, NTC]. The two words πλοῖον and πλοιάριον are used interchangeably (see 6:17, 19, 22, and 23) [Lns, NICNT2].
  b. pres. act. participle of σύρω (LN **15.212**) (BAGD p. 794): 'to drag' [BAGD, LN; KJV, NASB, NCV, NET, NRSV], 'to drag in' [BAGD; CEV], 'to pull' [BAGD, **LN**; NLT, TEV], 'to tow' [NIV, NJB, REB], 'to draw' [BAGD, LN], 'to drag away' [BAGD]. This verb means to pull or drag, requiring force because of the inertia of the object being dragged [LN].
  c. πῆχυς (LN 81.25) (BAGD p. 657): 'cubit' [BAGD, LN], 'cubit, eighteen inches, half meter' [LN], 'forearm, ell' [BAGD]. The phrase 'about two hundred cubits' [NICNT2] is also translated 'about the distance of two hundred cubits' [Gdt], 'as it were two hundred cubits' [KJV], 'about a/one hundred yards' [all other translations]. This noun traditionally denotes the distance from the elbow to the end of the fingers, about eighteen inches or one-half meter [LN]. It measures precisely .462 of a meter [BAGD].

QUESTION—How did the disciples come to shore with the net?
If a language requires the means by which they propelled the boat to be explicit, it would have been by rowing [TRT, TH].

QUESTION—What is indicated by the conjunction γάρ 'for' in the clause '*for they were not far from the land*'?
It indicates how the disciples were able to come to the land [Gdt]. It explains why they did not just leave the boat there [My]. It explains why Peter jumped in the water to swim ashore since it was so close by [HTC].

QUESTION—How are the nouns related in the genitive phrase 'net of fish'?
The genitive indicates that the net contained the fish [Lns, My; CEV]: 'net full of fish'[CEV].

21:9 So when they-got-out on land they-saw (a) charcoal-fire[a] laid[b] with fish lying-on[c] (it) and bread.

LEXICON—a. ἀνθρακιά (LN 2.6) (BAGD p. 67): 'charcoal fire' [BAGD, LN; all translations except Gdt; KJV, NCV, NIV], 'fire of (hot/burning) coals' [Gdt; KJV, NCV, NIV]. The occurrence of ἀνθρακιά 'charcoal fire' in John 18:18 fits the context well, since a charcoal fire provides a maximum of heat with a minimum of smoke. The making and use of charcoal is widespread throughout the world, and there is generally no difficulty in obtaining a satisfactory term for 'charcoal'. However, where such a term does not exist, it is possible to speak of 'a wood fire' or simply 'a fire' [LN].

 b. pres. mid. or pass. (deponent = active) of κεῖμαι (LN 85.3) (BAGD 1.b. p. 426): 'to lie' [BAGD, LN], 'to be' [LN], 'to recline' [LN]. The words 'a charcoal fire laid with fish lying on it' is translated 'a charcoal fire already laid and fish placed on it' [NASB], 'a charcoal fire laid, and fish laid on' [NICNT2], 'a charcoal fire/a fire of burning coals there with fish (laid/lying) on it' [HTC, WBC; NIV, NRSV, REB, TEV], 'a fire of coals there, and (a) fish laid thereon' [Gdt; KJV], 'a charcoal fire with fish (cooking) on it' [CEV, NJB], 'a charcoal fire ready with fish placed on it' [NET], 'a charcoal fire all made and a fish lying on it' [NTC], 'a fire of hot coals. There were fish on the fire' [NCV], 'fish cooking over a charcoal fire' [NLT], 'a charcoal fire, with a fish laid on it' [AB]. This verb means to be in a place, frequently in the sense of 'being contained in' or 'resting on' [LN]. It can serve as a passive of τίθημι 'to be placed' [BAGD].

 c. pres. mid. or pass. (deponent = active) of ἐπίκειμαι (LN **85.4**) (BAGD 1. p. 294): 'to lie on' [BAGD, **LN**], 'to be on' [LN]. The words 'with fish lying on it' are translated 'and fish lying on the coals' [**LN**]. This verb means to be in a place on something [LN]. See previous item for version evidence.

QUESTION—What is indicated by the present tense of the Greek verb βλέπουσιν, 'they see'?

 It indicates that the disciples were surprised to see a charcoal fire already made with fish on it [Lns].

QUESTION—Who had made the fire on the shore?

 Jesus had made the fire with the fish on it [BECNT, Car, Gdt, ICC, IVP, Kn, Lns, NICNT2, NTC, Rd, WBC].

QUESTION—Does the singular Greek word ὀψάριον 'fish' indicate that there was only one fish or does it refer to fish in general?

 1. It indicates that there was only one fish on the fire [AB, BECNT, Gdt, Lns, NTC; NET]: 'they saw there a charcoal fire, with a fish laid on it' [AB, similarly Gdt, NTC; NET]. The plural of the word 'fish' in verse 10 supports the singular meaning of the word here [Gdt]. In verse 13 Jesus takes the singular fish and gives it to the disciples to eat—note the definite

article 'the' in verse 13. Compared with verse 6:11 it seems that this also is a miracle of much from little [Lns, NTC].
2. It indicates fish in the general sense of more than one [My, NICNT2; probably all other translations]. The words 'fish' and 'bread' are both without an article and are probably meant to be understood generically as an unspecified amount of food [NICNT2].

QUESTION—Does the Greek singular noun ἄρτος 'bread' indicate a single piece of bread, or bread in general?
1. It indicates a single loaf [Lns, NTC]. The singular ἄρτον 'bread' is certainly intentional (see the same singular when referring to the bread in verse 13). If several loaves were meant, the plural ἄρτοι would have been used. But also a single loaf would not have satisfied seven men [Lns]. It seems that this also is a miracle of much from little [Lns, NTC].
2. It rather indicates bread in the collective sense [AB, ICC, My, NICNT2]. So important a miracle as this would not have been only obliquely hinted at. There may have been one fish since Jesus does ask for more, but the singlular word 'bread' is probably meant as a collective word [AB].

21:10 Jesus said to-them, "Bring some-of[a] the fish that you-have- just - caught." **21:11** So Simon Peter went-aboard[b] and hauled the net onto land full of-large fish 153 (of them). And-although[c] there-were so-many the net was- not -torn.[d]

LEXICON—a. ἀπό (LN 63.20) (BAGD I. 6. p. 86): 'some of' [BAGD; all translations except Gdt; KJV], 'of' [Gdt; KJV], 'part of, 'one of, one among' [LN], 'from, away from' [BAGD]. This preposition in the genitive case indicates a part of a whole, whether consisting of countables or of mass [LN].
b. aorist act. indic. of ἀναβαίνω (LN 15.99): 'to go aboard/on board' [AB, HTC, LN, NTC, WBC; NET, NJB, NLT, NRSV, REB, TEV], 'to climb aboard' [NIV], 'to embark' [LN], 'to go up' [NICNT2; KJV, NASB]. The verb 'went aboard' is translated 'got back into the boat' [CEV], 'went into the boat' [NCV], 'went up on the boat' [Gdt]. This verb means to move up onto an object, with specialization of meaning in reference to boats [LN].
c. καί (LN 91.12): 'and/but although' [Gdt, HTC, NTC, WBC; NASB, NET], 'and/even though' [NRSV], 'and/but even though/with' [NICNT2; NCV, NIV], 'and yet' [NLT, REB], 'and for (all there were so many)' [KJV], 'even though...still' [TEV], 'yet/and in spite of' [AB; NJB], 'yet' [LN], 'but still' [CEV], 'then, indeed, how it is then' [LN]. This conjunction indicates emphasis, involving surprise and unexpectedness [LN].
d. aorist pass. indic. of σχίζω (LN 19.27) (BAGD 1. b. p. 797): 'to be torn' [AB, BAGD, HTC, LN, NICNT2, NTC, WBC; NASB, NET, NIV, NRSV, REB], 'to be broken' [Gdt; KJV, NJB], 'to be split' [BAGD, LN], 'to be divided' [BAGD]. This verb is also rendered actively: 'to rip'

[CEV], 'to tear' [NCV, NLT, TEV]. It means to split or to tear an object into at least two parts [LN].

QUESTION—Did Peter go aboard the boat or only up to it?
1. He went aboard the boat [AB, Bar, BECNT, Car, CH, EGT, Gdt, HTC, ICC, Rd, NICNT1, NTC, TH, TRT; CEV, NCV, NET, NJB, NLT, NRSV, REB, TEV]: 'Peter went up on the boat and drew the net to land' [Gdt]. Apparently the net was attached to the stern of the boat so that Peter had to actually board the boat first in order to get to the net [AB, Rd]. Peter went aboard the boat and unfastened the net from the boat and handed it to the others who were waiting at the edge of the water [Lns].
2. This could mean that Peter went aboard the boat or that he went up to the boat to bring the full net onto the land. It is more likely that he did the latter [NICNT2].

DISCOURSE UNIT—21:12–14 [NASB]. The topic is Jesus provides.

21:12 Jesus said to-them, "Come (and) have-breakfast."[a] Now none of-the disciples dared[b] ask[c] him, "Who are you?" They-knew it-was the Lord.

LEXICON—a. aorist act. impera. of ἀριστάω (LN **23.24**, 23.20) (BAGD 1. p. 106): 'to have (some) breakfast' [BAGD, HTC, **LN** (23.24), NICNT2, NTC, WBC; NASB, NET, NIV, NJB, NLT, NRSV, REB], 'to breakfast' [EGT, Gdt, Lns], 'to break one's fast' [ICC], 'to eat one's breakfast' [AB], 'to take breakfast' [Bar], 'to eat' [CEV, NCV, TEV], 'to dine' [KJV], 'to eat a meal, to have a meal' [LN (23.20)]. This verb means to eat the earlier meal of the day [LN (23.24)]. Or it is an idiom that literally means 'to break bread' and indicates to eat a meal, without reference to any particular time of the day or to the type of food involved [LN (23.20)]. If this latter meaning is chosen one would translate 'Come have something to eat' or '…have a meal' [**LN** (23.24)]. The Jews normally had two meals a day with ἄριστον 'breakfast' being the first although it could indicate an early lunch as well [BECNT, NICNT1]. Verse 4 ('it was…early morning') expects the meaning 'breakfast' even though the more common meaning in NT usage was a later meal [Car]. In classical Greek it meant 'to eat breakfast' [AB, TH].

b. imperf. act. indic. of τολμάω (LN 25.161) (BAGD 1.a. p. 821): 'to dare' [BAGD, LN; all translations except NTC; NASB, NJB], 'to venture' [NTC; NASB], 'to be bold enough' [NJB], 'to have the courage, to be brave enough' [BAGD]. This verb means to be so bold as to challenge or defy possible danger or opposition [LN].

c. aorist act. infin. of ἐξετάζω (LN **33.182**) (BAGD 2. p. 275): 'to ask' [BAGD, **LN**; all translations except AB, NICNT2, WBC, NASB], 'to inquire (of)' [AB, LN, NICNT2, WBC], 'to question' [BAGD; NASB], 'to examine' [BAGD]. This verb means to inquire intently, with the implication of careful examination [LN].

QUESTION—What is the meaning of the question, 'Who are you?'?

Since the disciples knew that it was the Lord, the meaning of this question must have been 'Is it *really* you?' It was Jesus whom they had known and yet it was not quite that same Jesus. Something was different [WBC].

QUESTION—What relationship is indicated by the participle εἰδότες, 'knowing (it was the Lord)'?

It indicates a causal relationship [AB, Lns, NICNT1, NTC, TH, TRT, WBC; NCV, NET, NRSV, TEV]: 'None of the disciples dared ask him, "Who are you?" because they knew it was the Lord' [TEV]. It might rather have a concessive relationship 'although they knew' [NICNT1, WBC].

21:13 **Jesus came and took the bread and gave (it) to-them, and likewise the fish.** **21:14** **This (was) now**[a] **(the) third (time) (that) Jesus was-revealed**[b] **to-the disciples after-he-was-raised**[c] **from (the) dead.**

LEXICON—a. ἤδη (LN) (BAGD): 'now' [AB, BAGD, Gdt, HTC, LN, NICNT2, NTC, WBC; KJV, NASB, NCV, NET, NIV, NRSV], 'then' [TEV], 'already' [BAGD, LN, Lns], 'by this time' [BAGD], not explicit [CEV, NJB, NLT, REB]. This adverb indicates a point of time preceding another point of time and implying completion [LN].

b. aorist pass. indic. of φανερόω (LN 24.19) (BAGD 2.b.β. p. 853): 'to be revealed' [HTC, NICNT2, WBC; NET], 'to be manifested' [NTC; NASB], 'to be made to appear, to be made visible, to be caused to be seen' [LN], 'to be made known, to show oneself, to appear' [BAGD]. This passive verb is also translated actively: 'to appear' [BAGD; CEV, NIV, NLT, NRSV, REB, TEV], 'to show oneself' [BAGD; KJV, NCV], 'to reveal oneself' [AB, BAGD; NJB], 'to manifest oneself' [Gdt]. This verb means to cause something/someone to become visible [LN]. The stress in the passive is on Jesus' revelation of himself [Car].

c. aorist. pass. participle of ἐγείρω (LN 23.94) (BAGD 2.c. p. 215): 'to be raised' [BAGD, HTC, NICNT2, WBC; CEV, NASB, NCV, NET, NIV, NLT, NRSV, TEV], 'to be raised to life, to be made to live again' [LN]. This verb is also translated actively: 'to rise' [BAGD, Gdt, NTC; KJV, NJB]. It is also translated as a noun: 'his resurrection (from the dead)' [AB; REB]. Εγείρω means to cause someone to live again after having once died [LN].

QUESTION—To what place did Jesus 'come'?

It is probably best to take the verb 'to come' as a pair with the verb 'to take' and translate something like, 'Jesus came/went/walked over and took the bread' [ICC, TH, TRT]. Jesus now steps forward from his position at a distance in order to distribute the breakfast [Gdt, My]. The verb 'to come' is superfluous and possibly merely stylistic [Bar].

QUESTION—What bread and fish did Jesus take?

The bread and fish are both singular both with the definite article 'the' referring back to the bread and fish the disciples saw on the fire when they came ashore [Lns, NICNT2, NTC]. The fish are not the ones caught by the disciples [NICNT2]. He took *the bread* referred to in verse 9 ('they-saw a charcoal fire there with fish lying on it and bread') [My, NTC, TRT]. The fish were those referred to in verses 9 and 10 [ICC, My].

QUESTION—How was this the third time that Jesus revealed himself?

In chapter 20 he had revealed himself to the ten disciples (20:19-23) and then later to the disciples plus Thomas (20:26–29) [AB, BECNT, Car, CH, Gdt, Lns, NICNT1, NTC, TH, TRT]. Jesus' appearance to Mary is not being counted [AB, Bar, BECNT, Gdt, IVP, Lns, Rd], nor are his appearances to the women, to Peter, and to the two disciples on the road to Emmaus [Lns]. Mary is not included here since this is only referring to the number of times Jesus appeared to *the disciples* [Bar, Car, Gdt, NICNT1, NTC]. We should not ignore the possibility that the author is thinking of the two appearances to the disciples as a group in a locked room as a single appearance and is including the appearance first to Mary as the second appearance [NICNT2].

QUESTION—Who is the actor of the passive verb, 'he was raised from the dead'?

It may be necessary to translate this something like, 'after God raised him from death' [TH, TRT].

DISCOURSE UNIT—21:15–25 [Bar; NCV, NIV]. The topic is Jesus and Peter and the beloved disciple [Bar], Jesus talks to Peter [NCV], Jesus reinstates Peter [NIV].

DISCOURSE UNIT—21:15–24 [Car]. The topic is Jesus and Peter and John.

DISCOURSE UNIT—21:15–23 [AB, Kn, WBC]. The topic is Jesus speaks to Peter [AB, WBC], the call [Kn].

DISCOURSE UNIT—21:15–19 [HTC, NICNT1; NET, NRSV, TEV]. The topic is Jesus and Peter [HTC; NRSV, TEV], Peter restored [NICNT1; NET].

DISCOURSE UNIT—21:15–17 [NASB]. The topic is the love motivation.

21:15 So when they-had-eaten-breakfast Jesus said to-Simon Peter, "Simon, (son) of-John, do-you-love[a] me more-than these?" He-said to-him, "Yes,[b] Lord, you-know that I-love/have-affection-for[c] you." He-said to-him, "Feed[d] my lambs."[e]

TEXT—Instead of the word Ἰωάννου 'of John', some manuscripts read Ἰωνᾶ 'Jona', and one manuscript omits this word. GNT reads 'of John' with a B rating, indicating that the text is almost certain.

LEXICON—a. pres. act. indic. of ἀγαπάω (LN 25.43, BAGD 1.a.β. p. 4): 'to love' [BAGD, LN; all translations except NIV], 'to truly love' [NIV], 'to regard with affection' [LN], 'to cherish' [BAGD]. This verb means to have love for someone or something, based on sincere appreciation and high regard [LN]. It means to love or have affection for a person [BAGD]. This is the love of intelligence and purpose, a whole-hearted devotion to someone [NTC]. It is a volitional, responsible kind of love [CH]. It is a love of intelligence, reason, and comprehension as well as purpose [Lns].

b. ναί (LN 69.1) (BAGD 1.a. p. 533): 'yes' [BAGD, LN; all translations except NTC], 'indeed' [LN, NTC], 'yes it is true that, yes it is so, sure' [LN]. This particle indicates an affirmative response to questions or statements or an emphatic affirmation of a statement [LN]. Peter is not agreeing to Jesus' full question that he loves Jesus more than the others. But he agrees in that he feels he has a similar emotion toward him that is like, but not the same as Jesus was asking [NTC].
c. pres. act. indic. of φιλέω (LN 25.33) (BAGD 1.a. p. 859): 'to love' [BAGD; all translations except NTC; Ph], 'to have affection for' [BAGD, LN, NTC], 'to be one's friend' [Ph], 'to like' [BAGD]. This verb is also translated as a pro-verb for 'to love': '(you know) I do' [CEV]. This verb means to have love or affection for someone or something based on association [LN]. It is the kind of love that results from liking or being fond of someone [CH]. It is the love of personal heart emotion [My].
d. pres. act. indic. of βόσκω (LN **23.10**, **44.1**) (BAGD 1. p. 145): 'to feed' [BAGD, **LN** (23.10); all translations except NICNT2, WBC; NASB, TEV], 'to tend' [BAGD, NICNT2; NASB], 'to take care of' [**LN** (44.1), WBC; TEV], 'to cause to eat' [LN (23.10)], 'to herd, to look after' [LN (44.1)]. This verb means to cause animals to eat, particularly pasturing animals. It is possible to interpret βόσκω in John 21:15 as meaning 'to tend' or 'to take care of', especially since it occurs in a figurative context referring to people. Such an interpretation may be classified as a figurative meaning. However, it seems more likely that in John 21:15 it should be understood as an instance of figurative usage, and as such it may also be interpreted as 'to take care of' [LN (23.10)]. It literally means to herd animals so as to provide them with adequate pasture and to take care of what other needs may be involved [LN (44.1)].
e. ἀρνίον (LN **11.29**, 4.25) (BAGD p. 108): 'lamb' [BAGD, LN (11.29, 4.25); all translations], 'a person who is like a lamb' [**LN** (11.29)], 'sheep' [BAGD, LN (4.25)], 'ram' [LN (4.25)]. This noun is used as a figurative extension of the meaning of ἀρνίον 'lamb', (4.25) and indicates a follower of Christ, with the implication of helplessness and dependence. Here the words 'Feed my lambs' could be translated, 'take care of my people, who are like lambs' [**LN** (11.29)]. Literally ἀρνίον indicates a sheep of any age [LN (4.25)]. Here it refers to the Christian community [BAGD].

QUESTION—Jesus' question, 'Do you love me more than these?' can mean either 'more than these other disciples love me', or 'or more than you love these other disciples', or 'more than you love the fishing gear and occupation'? Which is the probable meaning?

1. The words 'more than these' means 'more than these disciples love me' [Bar, BECNT, Car, CH, Gdt, HTC, IVP, Lns, My, NICNT1, NICNT2, NTC, Rd, TH, TRT, WBC; CEV, NET, NJB, Ph, TEV]: 'do you love me more than the others do?' [Gdt]. Jesus reminds Peter of his boast, 'Even if all fall away on account of you, I never will' (Matthew 26:33) [Gdt, Lns].

Jesus is referring Peter to his boast to lay down his life for him (John 13:37) [HTC].
2. 'More than these' means 'more than this boat, net, and the occupation of fishing' [EGT, ICC, Kn]. If Jesus had meant to compare Peter's love for him with the disciples' love for him, he would almost necessarily have had to use the second personal pronoun 'you' when asking—*you* more than *these*? The contrast intended is rather between Peter's love for *Jesus* and his love for *his old way of life*. Jesus' question means 'Do you love *me* more than *this boat, nets and your old occupation*' [EGT].

QUESTION—Though some persons have tried to assign certain significant differences of meaning between ἀγαπάω and φιλέω, it does not seem possible to insist upon a contrast of meaning in any and all contexts. For example, the usage in John 21:15–17 seems to reflect simply a rhetorical alternation designed to avoid undue repetition. There is, however, one significant clue to possible meaningful differences in at least some contexts, namely, the fact that people are never commanded to love each other with φιλέω or φιλία, but only with ἀγαπάω and ἀγάπη. Though the meanings of these terms overlap considerably in many contexts, there are probably some significant differences in certain contexts; that is to say, φιλέω and φιλία are likely to focus on love or affection based upon interpersonal association, while ἀγαπάω and ἀγάπη focus on love and affection based on deep appreciation and high regard. On the basis of this type of distinction, one can understand some of the reasons for the use of ἀγαπάω and ἀγάπη in commands to Christians to love one another. It would, however, be quite wrong to assume that φιλέω and φιλία refer only to human love, while ἀγαπάω and ἀγάπη refer to divine love. Both sets of terms are used for the total range of loving relations between people, between people and God, and between God and Jesus Christ [LN]. Which meaning is intended in this context?

1. In verses 15–17, there is an intended difference between ἀγαπάω and φιλέω [CH, Gdt, Lns, IVP, My, NTC; NIV, Ph]: 'Yes Lord, he replied, you know that I am your friend' [Ph], 'Indeed, Lord, thou dost know/knowest that I have affection for thee' [Lns, NTC]. Although there is no simple difference between the two words, yet the fact that Jesus switches to Peter's word in the final question to him suggests that there is a subtle distinction reflected in NIV's renderings ἀγαπάω 'truly love', versus φιλέω 'love'. The verb ἀγαπάω means an act of the will in which a person chooses to love someone whom they would not naturally love. The verb φιλέω means to be fond of someone or to like them [IVP]. Peter substitutes the word φιλέω for Jesus' term ἀγαπάω. The former means to cherish or love in the sense of personal attachment while the latter means to love in the spiritual sense, a reverential kind of love. He no longer dares to ascribe to himself this higher kind of love. His reply softens a full agreement with Jesus' question by qualifying the effect that a simple 'Yes' would have communicated [Gdt]. Any appeal to Aramaic not having two similar verbs is not valid since every language is capable of

expressing differences of thought whether by verbs or other parts of speech. Jesus' word ἀγαπάω outranks φιλέω that indicates the love of personal affection or liking and lacks the intelligence and high purpose of ἀγαπάω [Lns]. Peter is humbled by the memory of his fall and so will not use the higher word for love to describe his attitude toward Jesus but substitutes rather the word for the love of subjective affection [NTC].

2. There is no intended difference in verses 15–17 between ἀγαπάω and φιλέω [AB, BAGD (1.a. p. 859), Bar, BECNT, Car, EGT, HTC, ICC, Kn, LN, NICNT1, NICNT2, Rd, TH, WBC; all translations except NTC; NIV, Ph]. The following factors argue for the interchangeability of these two words: 1) John seems to use the two terms interchangeably in his Gospel; 2) Hebrew and Aramaic do not have different verbs for expressing love; 3) Peter responds to each question with a 'Yes' reply even though he uses the term φιλέω in his response showing no awareness that there is any difference between the meaning of the terms [AB]. Peter's affirmative reply to Jesus' question indicates that he was simply using a synonym for Jesus' term for love [Bar]. Both words are used in the NT to refer to God's love for man, the Father's love for the Son, Jesus' love for men, men's love for other men, men's love for Jesus, men's love for God and Jesus' love for the Father. Peter's positive response to Jesus' question shows that he considers his word just a synonym to Jesus' term [ICC]. NOTE—Although BECNT sides with this interpretation he still states that in verse 17 Jesus finally adopts Peter's word for 'love'. This seems to be counter to his position that the words mean the same thing.

QUESTION—To whom do the words, 'lambs' and 'sheep', in verses 15–17 refer?

They refer not to the animals but to Christian believers won to Jesus by the missionary efforts of the disciples [AB, LN, My, TH, TRT]. It includes the whole flock of believers and apostles [Gdt]. It may be wise to translate this metaphor as a simile such as, 'Take care of my followers, just as though they were lambs' [TH].

QUESTION—If the word βόσκω 'to feed' is being used metaphorically here, what does it mean?

It means 'to take care of' [LN, TH, TRT], 'to lead', 'to guide', 'to rule' Jesus' followers [TH]. It means to lead believers in the way of life [CH]. It refers to nourishing the flock in a spiritual sense, to have for them the kind of sympathy that springs from love [Gdt]. It refers to guiding and guarding them in their new spiritual way of life [ICC]. It refers to Jesus' command, '...teaching them to obey everything I have commanded you' (Matthew 28:20) [Lns].

QUESTION—What word is emphasized in this verse?

The pronoun σύ 'you' in the words 'you know' is emphatic [AB, NICNT1]. Peter's own recent actions did not reveal love so he cannot use them to support his claim, but he can appeal to *Jesus'* full knowledge of the situation

[NICNT1]. It is significant that the word σύ 'you' is made explicit and is repeated in all three verses 15–17 indicating emphasis on this pronoun [AB].

21:16 He-said to-him again (a) second-time, "Simon, (son) of-John, do-you-love[a] me?" He-said to-him, "Yes Lord, you know that I-love[b] you." He-said to-him, "Shepherd[c] my sheep."[d]

TEXT—Instead of Ἰωάννου 'of John', some manuscripts read Ἰωνᾶ 'Jona'. GNT reads 'of John' with a B rating, indicating that the text is almost certain.

LEXICON—a. pres. act. indic. of ἀγαπάω (LN 25.43): 'to love' [LN; all translations except NIV], 'to truly love' [NIV], 'to regard with affection' [LN]. This verb means to have love for someone or something, based on sincere appreciation and high regard [LN].
- b. pres. act. indic. of φιλέω (LN 25.33): 'to love' [LN; all translations except NTC; Ph], 'to have affection for' [LN, Lns, NTC], 'to be one's friend' [Ph]. This verb means to have love or affection for someone or something based on association [LN].
- c. pres. act. impera. of ποιμαίνω (LN **44.3**) (BAGD 2.a.α. p. 683): 'to shepherd' [**LN**, NICNT2, NTC; NASB, NET], 'to take care of' [**LN**; CEV, NCV, NIV, NLT, TEV], 'to care for' [Ph], 'to tend' [AB, BAGD, LN, HTC; NRSV, REB], 'to look after' [WBC; NJB], 'to lead' [Gdt], 'to feed' [KJV], 'to pasture' [LN], 'to herd, to (lead to) pasture' [BAGD]. This verb means to herd and tend flocks of sheep or goats [BAGD, LN]. It figuratively refers to activity that protects, rules, governs, fosters in the sense 'lead', 'guide', or 'rule' the direction of a congregation 'to tend God's flock' [BAGD]. It indicates a complete figure of leadership over God's people [IVP]. It carries the implication of protection and careful leading of those who belong to Christ [HTC]. 'Shepherding' connotes pastoral care [NICNT2].
- d. πρόβατον (LN 4.22, **11.30**) (BAGD 2. p. 703): 'sheep' [BAGD, LN (4.22)], 'a person who is like a sheep' [**LN** (11.30)]. This word is also translated figuratively '(take care of) my people, who are like sheep' [**LN** (11.30)]. This noun is a figurative extension of the meaning of πρόβατον 'sheep' (4.22), indicating a follower of Christ, with the implication of someone needing care and guidance [LN (11.30)]. The word 'sheep' also stands as a symbol of church members while the bishop is the shepherd [BAGD].

QUESTION—Does the verb ποιμαίνω 'to shepherd' differ in meaning from the verb 'to feed' in verse 15?
1. The verb 'to shepherd' here has a significant difference from the verb 'to feed' of verse 15 [AB, CH, Gdt, HTC, IVP, Kn, Lns, My, Rd, NICNT1]. 'Shepherding' is more general than 'feeding' and indicates the governing of the whole church [Gdt], or literally all the duties of a shepherd [Kn]. The meaning of exercising the role of shepherd is broader than simply feeding the flock [AB, Lns, My, NICNT1]. Taken strictly the differences

between 'lambs' and 'sheep' and 'feed' and 'shepherd' define the shepherd's total care for the whole flock [IVP, Rd].
2. The verbs 'to feed' of verse 15 and 'to shepherd' of verse 16 are used synonymously [Bar, Car, EGT, ICC, TH, WBC]. Finding a difference between these two verbs is a modern interpretation that was unknown to antiquity. The use of these verbs in the LXX does not reflect a difference in meaning since both are used to translate the same Hebrew root [ICC].

QUESTION—What word is emphasized in this verse?

Again the pronoun σύ 'you' in the phrase '*you* know' is emphatic [AB, NICNT1].

21:17 He-said to-him the third (time), "Simon (son) of-John, do-you-love[a] me?" Peter was-hurt[b] because he-said to-him the third (time), "Do-you-love[c] me?" And he-said to-him, "Lord, you know[d] everything. You know[e] that I-love[f] you." Jesus said to-him, "Feed[g] my sheep.

TEXT—Instead of Ἰωάννου 'of John', some manuscripts read Ἰωνᾶ 'Jona'. GNT reads Ἰωάννου 'of John' with a B rating, indicating that the text is almost certain.

LEXICON—a. pres. act. indic. of φιλέω (LN 25.33): 'to love' [LN; all translations except NTC, Ph], 'to have affection for' [LN, Lns, NTC], 'to be one's friend' [Ph]. This verb means to have love or affection for someone or something based on association [LN]. Now Jesus adopts Peter's word for love [IVP, NICNT1, NTC] coming down to Peter's level [NTC].

b. aorist pass. indic. of λυπέω (LN 25.275) (BAGD 2.a. p. 481): 'to be hurt' [AB; CEV, NCV, NCV, NIV, NJB, NLT, REB], 'to be deeply hurt' [Ph], 'to be grieved' [BAGD, Gdt, HTC, NICNT2, NTC; KJV, NASB], 'to be pained' [BAGD, WBC], 'to be distressed' [NET], 'to be made sad, to be saddened' [LN], 'to become sad, sorrowful' [BAGD]. This verb is also translated actively: 'to feel hurt' [NRSV], 'to become sad' [TEV]. This verb is derived from λύπη '(a) state of sadness' (25.273) and means to cause someone to be sad, sorrowful, or distressed [LN]. Here it means 'to become distressed' [BAGD]. The word refers to grief and does not mean to be annoyed [Is, NICNT1].

c. pres. act. indic. of φιλέω (LN 25.33): 'to love' [LN; all translations except NTC, Ph], 'to have affection for' [LN, Lns, NTC], 'to be one's friend' [Ph]. This verb means to have love or affection for someone or something based on association [LN].

d. perf. act. indic. of οἶδα (LN 28.1): 'to know' [LN; all translations], 'to know about, to have knowledge of, to be acquainted with' [LN]. This verb means to possess information about [LN].

e. pres. act. indic. of γινώσκω (LN 28.1) (BAGD 6.c. p. 161): 'to know' [LN; all translations except AB and NTC], 'to realize' [NTC], 'to know well' [AB], 'to know about, to have knowledge of, to be acquainted with' [LN]. This verb means to possess information about [LN].

f. pres. act. indic. of φιλέω (LN 25.33): 'to love' [LN; all translations except NTC, Ph], 'to have affection for' [LN, Lns, NTC], 'to be one's friend' [Ph]. This verb means to have love or affection for someone or something based on association [LN].

g. pres. active impera. of βόσκω (LN 23.10) (BAGD 1. p. 145): 'to feed' [AB, BAGD, Gdt, LN, NTC; CEV, KJV, NCV, NET, NIV, NJB, NLT, NRSV, Ph, REB], 'to tend' [BAGD, NICNT2; NASB], 'to take care of' [WBC; TEV], 'to cause to eat' [LN]. This verb means to cause animals to eat, particularly pasturing animals [LN].

QUESTION—Why does Jesus repeat his question three times to Peter?

Probably because Peter had denied him three times [Car, TRT]. It was probably meant to restore Peter to his position of leadership. He had denied Jesus three times and now he has the chance to affirm his love for him three times [NICNT1].

QUESTION—Why was Peter 'hurt' by Jesus question the third time?

1. Peter was hurt because he was asked the same question three times [AB, Bar, Car, EGT, ICC, NICNT1, NICNT2, Rd, WBC]. Since Peter had disowned Jesus three times, Jesus now requires him to confess his love three times [Car]. The use of the words 'second time' in verse 16 coupled with the words 'third time' here support the interpretation that it was the same question all three times with no change in meaning intended [EGT, NICNT1].

2. Peter was hurt because this time Jesus changes to Peter's word φιλέω [Gdt, Lns, My, NTC]. The phrase 'the third time' does not place emphasis on the word 'time' as though it was the number of repetitions that grieved Peter, but it emphasizes the fact that this time Jesus changes and uses Peter's own word in which Jesus questions even Peter's lower admission of love [Lns]. Jesus seems to doubt even the humble affection that Peter is claiming [Gdt, NTC]. This hurts Peter's feelings since he is sure that he really has this humbler form of affection for Jesus [Lns, NTC].

QUESTION—Peter uses two different words for know in this verse, σὺ οἶδας 'you know (everything)' and σὺ γινώσκεις 'you know (that I love you)'. Do the two words indicate a difference in knowing?

1. The two Greek words for 'to know' have the same meaning [NICNT1, TH]; all translations except AB, NTC. The majority of scholars believe that the two Greek words are used synonymously here [TH].

2. Peter intended a difference in using two words [ICC, IVP, Lns, NTC]: 'all things thou *knowest*, thou *dost realize* that I have affection for thee' [NTC, similarly Lns]. Peter relies on the omniscience of Jesus, 'you *know* everything' and then adds his deduction 'you *realize* that I do have affecton for you', meaning that Jesus had full penetrating insight into Peter's soul [Lns]. There is a difference in meaning of the words 'to know'. Peter's second use of 'know' (γινώσκω) may indicate, 'you must be able to see' [IVP].

QUESTION—What words are emphasized in this verse?
The twice repeated explicit pronoun σύ 'you' in this verse '*you* know everything…*you* know that I love you' is emphatic [AB, HTC, TH]. The word 'everything' is placed before the phrase 'you know' increasing its prominence [TRT]. In this verse there is a definite article before the phrase 'third time' that was missing before the words 'a second time' in the previous verse. Here it adds emphasis to this phrase [AB]. The pronoun μου 'my' in the phrase 'my sheep' is repeated in all three replies of Jesus emphasizing his ownership of the sheep [Gdt].

DISCOURSE UNIT—21:18–25 [NASB]. The topic is our times are in his hand.

21:18 "Truly[a] truly I-say to-you, when you-were young you-used-to-dress[b] yourself and walk where you-wanted. But when you-are-old,[c] you-will-stretch-out[d] your hands, and another will-dress[e] you and take[f] (you) where you-do- not -want (to go)."

LEXICON—a. ἀμήν (LN 72.6): 'truly' [LN], 'indeed, it is true that' [LN]. The clause 'Truly truly I say to you' [HTC; NASB] is also translated 'Verily, verily, I say unto you' [Gdt; KJV], 'Very truly, I tell you' [NRSV], 'Amen, amen, I tell you/say to you' [NICNT2, WBC], 'I tell you for certain' [CEV], 'I tell you truly' [Ph], 'I tell/am telling you the truth' [NCV, NIV, NLT, TEV], 'I tell you the solemn truth' [NET], 'In all/very truth I tell you' [NJB, REB], 'I most solemnly assure you' [NTC], 'Truly, I assure you' [AB]. This particle indicates strong affirmation of what is declared [LN]. Note how you translated this phrase in these previous references in John 1:51; 3:3, 5, 11; 5:19, 24–25; 6:26, 32, 47, 53; 8:34, 51, 58; 10:1, 7; 12:24; 13:16, 20–21, 38; 14:12; 16:20, 23 [TRT].
  b. imperf. act. indic. of ζωννύω (LN **49.8**) (BAGD p. 341): 'to dress' [**LN**; CEV, NIV, Ph], 'to gird' [BAGD, Gdt, HTC, NICNT2, NTC; KJV, NASB], 'to tie one's own belt' [NCV], 'to put on one's own belt' [WBC; NJB], 'to fasten one's own belt' [AB; NRSV, similarly REB], 'to tie (one's own clothes) around (oneself)' [NET]. The words 'you used to dress youself' are translated 'you were able to do as you liked; you dressed yourself' [NLT], 'you used to get ready' [TEV]. This verb means to dress oneself, including the fastening of one's belt as the final act in dressing [LN]. This verb refers to putting a belt around one's loose fitting clothes in preparation to go out of one's house or travel somewhere. The imperfect tense indicates customary action in the past [TH]. This idiom indicates the control a person has over his own life [TRT].
  c. aorist act. subj. of γηράσκω (LN **67.105**) (BAGD p. 158): 'to be old' [HTC, NICNT2; CEV, KJV, NCV, NET, NIV, NLT, REB, TEV], 'to become old' [Gdt, **LN**, NTC], 'to be an old man' [Ph], 'to grow old' [AB, BAGD, LN, WBC; NASB, NJB, NRSV]. This verb means to become old in age (referring to living beings) [LN].

d. fut. act. indic. of ἐκτείνω (LN 16.19) (BAGD 1. p. 245): 'to stretch out' [BAGD, LN; all translations except Gdt; CEV, KJV, NCV], 'to stretch forth' [Gdt; KJV], 'to hold out' [CEV], 'to put out' [NCV], 'to extend, to reach out' [LN]. This verb means to cause an object to extend in space (for example, by becoming straight, unfolded, or uncoiled) [LN]. When it refers to stretching out one's hand it refers to being crucified [BAGD].
   e. fut. act. indic. of ζωννύω (BAGD p. 341): 'to dress' [NIV, NLT, Ph], 'to gird' [Gdt, HTC, NICNT2, NTC; KJV, NASB], 'to tie someone' [NCV], 'to tie someone up' [NET, TEV], 'to bind someone fast' [REB], 'to put/wrap/fasten a belt around someone' [AB; CEV, NJB, NRSV], 'to put someone's belt on them' [WBC]. This verb here implies that someone will bind Peter in chains as a prisoner and so take control of his life [TRT]. This verb probably refers to the tying of a prisoner's arms to the crossbeam as part of the crucifixion routine [IVP].
   f. fut. act. indic. of φέρω (LN 15.166) (BAGD 4.b.β. p. 855): 'to take' [AB, LN, WBC; NCV, NJB, NLT, NRSV, Ph, TEV], 'to bring' [BAGD, LN, NICNT2, NTC; NASB, NET], 'to carry' [LN, HTC; KJV, REB], 'to lead' [Gdt; CEV, NIV], 'to fetch' [BAGD]. This verb means to cause to move to a place, with a possible implication of assistance or firm control [LN].

QUESTION—Does the phrase 'you will stretch out your hands' refer to crucifixion or to something else?
   1. It is probably a euphemism for crucifixion [BAGD, BECNT, Car, CH, IVP, Kn, WBC]. The words 'stretch out one's hands' in the ancient world was taken to refer to death by crucifixion [BECNT]. The stretching out referred to the tying of the prisoners hands to the horizontal crossbar of a cross [BECNT, IVP]. Verse 19 shows that this action pointed to Peter's death and he took Jesus' words as a prediction of his martyrdom (see 2 Peter 1:14) [Car, CH, Kn]. Verse 19 states that Peter's death would glorify God in the same way that the death of Jesus glorified God [Car, WBC].
   2. It refers to something else [EGT, Gdt, HTC, ICC, Lns, My, NICNT1, NICNT2, NTC, Rd]. It merely refers to the action of passivity to forceful handling [Gdt]. It refers in general to Peter's upcoming death as a martyr [Gdt, Lns, NICNT1, Rd]. It probably was a gesture of helplessness preceding his arrest and execution. It may have been a reference to martyrdom but not necessarily by crucifixion (see next verse) [NICNT2]. It may refer to Peter's stretching out his hands to allow others to tie them together [HTC]. To say that the words 'another will dress you and take you where you do not want to go' refer to the crucifixion of Peter would place the crucifixion before he is led to the cross [Lns, My]. It could point either to Peter's being tied up or to having his hands fastened to a cross [NTC].

JOHN 21:19   485

21:19 He-said this to-indicate[a] by-what-kind-of[b] death he-was-to-glorify[c] God. And after-saying this he-said to-him, "Follow me."

LEXICON—a. pres. act. participle of ὠημαίδω (LN 33.153) (BAGD 2. p. 747): 'to indicate' [AB; NIV, NJB, NRSV, REB, TEV], 'to indicate clearly' [LN; NET], 'to indicate (beforehand)' [BAGD], 'to signify' [Gdt, NICNT2, NTC, WBC; KJV, NASB], 'to show' [HTC; Ph, NCV], 'to tell (how)' [CEV], 'to let (someone) know' [NLT], 'to make evident' [LN], 'to foretell' [BAGD]. This verb means to cause something to be both specific and clear [LN].

  b. ποῖος (LN 58.30) (BAGD 1.a.γ. p. 684): 'what kind of' [BAGD, LN, NTC; NASB, NET, NLT], 'the kind of' [WBC; NIV, NJB, NRSV, Ph], 'the sort of' [AB], 'what sort of' [BAGD, LN], 'the manner of' [REB], 'the way in which' [TEV], 'how' [CEV, NCV], '(by) what (death)' [Gdt, HTC, NICNT2; KJV]. This interrogative adjective (dative case) refers to class or kind [LN].

  c. fut. act. indic. of δοξάζω (LN 87.8) (BAGD 2. p. 204): 'to glorify' [AB, BAGD, Gdt, HTC, NICNT2, NTC, WBC; KJV, NASB, NET, NIV, NLT, NRSV, REB], 'to give/bring glory to' [NCV, NJB, TEV], 'to honor' [LN; Ph], 'to bring honor to' [CEV], 'to respect' [LN], 'to clothe in splendor' [BAGD]. This verb means to attribute high status to someone by honoring them [LN]. It refers to the glory that comes in the next life especially in reference to martyrdom [BAGD]. For the Christian, glorifiying God is dying in obedience and faith [Bar].

QUESTION—Should the first sentence of this verse be put into parentheses?
  The following place this sentence in parentheses [AB, HTC, NTC, Ph; NCV, NET, NRSV, TEV]. This is an explanatory comment by the author of this Gospel [TH].

QUESTION—There are three third person pronouns in this verse. To whom do they refer?
  The first pronoun refers to Jesus, the second refers to Peter, and the third refers again to Jesus [TEV]: 'In saying this Jesus was indicating the way in which Peter would die and bring glory to God. Then Jesus said to him, "Follow me"' [TEV]. It is important to make sure that one's translation makes it plain that the second 'he' refers to Peter and not to Jesus [AB, TH, TRT; CEV, NCV, NET, NIV, NJB, Ph, REB, TEV]: '…in which way Peter would die and bring glory to God' [TEV].

QUESTION—What may this prophecy of Jesus have referred to?
  Church history records that Peter was crucified about 30 years later by Emperor Nero. He was crucified upside down because he felt unworthy to be crucified in the same position in which Jesus was crucified [TRT].

QUESTION—What is the sense of the verb, 'Follow me!' and what is the significance of the present tense of the imperative verb?
  'Follow me' is not meant literally as 'to follow behind someone' but figuratively in the sense of 'be my disciple' or the like [Bar, CH, Lns, My, NICNT1, NICNT2, NTC, TH, TRT], even on the path to martyrdom [Bar,

My]. Since Jesus is no longer on earth as a physical man, he is not asking Peter to follow him as a disciple would follow his master [Lns]. Jesus is asking Peter to follow him in the sense of joining him on a path in which He himself, as the great Shepherd of the sheep, gave up his life [Rd]. The word 'follow' may refer to nothing more than an invitation to take a walk with Jesus [BECNT, Gdt]. Since the next verse appears to show Jesus walking along with Peter and the Beloved Disciple, the literal sense cannot be ruled out. But it may refer to discipleship and death [AB, Car, EGT, ICC, WBC]. The present tense indicates 'to continue to follow' or 'to never stop following' [TRT], or 'to keep on following' [CH, NICNT1].

DISCOURSE UNIT—21:20–24 [NRSV, TEV]. The topic is Jesus and the beloved disciple.

DISCOURSE UNIT—21:20–23 [AB, NICNT1; NET]. The topic is Peter and the beloved disciple [AB; NET], the role of the beloved disciple [NICNT1].

21:20 Peter turned[a] (and) saw the disciple whom Jesus loved following (them), the-one-who also had-leaned-back[b] on- his -chest[c] during supper[d] and had-said, "Lord, who is it-that-is going-to-betray you?"

LEXICON—a. aorist pass. participle of ἐπιστρέφομαι (LN 16.13) (BAGD 2.a.α. p. 301): 'to turn' [BAGD, HTC, NICNT2, NTC; CEV, NCV, NIV, NJB, NRSV], 'to turn (a)round' [AB, BAGD, LN, Ph, WBC; NASB, NET, NLT, TEV], 'to turn about' [Gdt; KJV], 'to look round' [REB], 'to turn toward' [LN]. This verb means to turn around to or toward [LN].
  b. aorist act. indic. of ἀναπίπτω (LN 17.23) (BAGD 2. P. 59): 'to lean back' [AB, BAGD, NTC, WBC; NASB, NET, NIV], 'to lean' [BAGD, Gdt, NICNT2; KJV, NCV], 'to recline' [LN; NRSV], 'to lie' [HTC], 'to eat, to sit down to eat, to be at table, to dine' [LN]. The words 'who also had reclined on his bosom' are translated 'who had sat next to Jesus' [CEV], 'who had leaned/leaned back against Jesus' [NCV, NET, NIV], 'who had leant back close to his chest' [NJB], 'who had leaned over to Jesus' [NLT], 'who had leaned close to Jesus' [TEV], 'who had reclined next to Jesus' [NRSV], 'who at supper had leaned back close to him' [REB], 'who had his head on Jesus' shoulder' [Ph]. This verb means to be in a reclining position as one eats (with the focus either on the position or the act of eating) [LN].
  c. στῆθος (LN 8.36) (BAGD p. 767): 'chest' [AB, BAGD, LN; NET, NCV, NJB], 'breast' [BAGD, Gdt, HTC, NICNT2, NTC, WBC; KJV], 'bosom' [NASB], 'shoulder' [Ph], not explicit [CEV, NLT, NRSV, REB, TEV]. This noun indicates the trunk of the body from the neck to the abdomen [LN]. Note that the phrase 'on his bosom' is translated in various ways in item b. above.
  d. δεῖπνον (LN 23.25) (BAGD 1. p. 173): 'supper' [BAGD, LN; all translations except CEV, NET, TEV], 'meal' [CEV, NET, TEV], main

meal' [BAGD, LN], 'dinner' [BAGD]. This noun indicates the principal meal of the day, usually in the evening [BAGD, LN].

QUESTION—In what sense is the verb 'following' used here?

Here the verb is used in its literal sense of 'to come behind someone' or the like [NICNT1, NICNT2, TH].

QUESTION—To what incident do the words, '…the one who also had leaned back on his chest during supper', refer?

They refer to the occasion of the last supper recorded in 13:25 [AB, BECNT, IVP, Rd, NICNT1, NICNT2, TH, TRT].

21:21 So-when Peter saw him he-said to Jesus, "But[a] Lord, what-about[b] this-man?"

LEXICON—a. δέ (BAGD p. 171): 'but' [AB, BAGD; Ph], 'and' [BAGD, Gdt, Lns, WBC; KJV, NASB], not explicit [all other translations].

b. τίς (LN 92.14) (BAGD 1.b.δ. p. 819): 'what about?' [BAGD; all translations except Gdt; KJV], 'what?' [BAGD, Gdt, LN; KJV], 'what of?' [Lns], 'who?' [BAGD, LN], 'which one?' [BAGD]. This interrogative pronoun refers to someone or something [LN].

QUESTION—What is implied by Peter's question οὗτος δὲ τί, literally, 'this-one but/and what'?

Peter's question inquires about the destiny of the beloved disciple [BECNT, ICC]. If Peter understood that Jesus was predicting Peter's death, then he is asking the same question about the beloved disciple, 'How will his life end?' or 'Will he meet a similar fate?' [NICNT2, similarly NTC]. Many translations rendered it something like, 'what about this man?' It could also be translated, 'what will happen to him?' or 'what is he going to undergo?' or 'how are people going to treat him?' [TH]. Other translations render it or suggest, 'what shall befall him?' [Gdt], 'how will he die?' [TRT], 'what is to become of him?' [AB].

21:22 Jesus said to-him, "If I-want[a] him to-remain[b] until I-come,[c] what (is that) to you? You follow me."

LEXICON—a. pres. act. subj. of θέλω (LN 25.1) (BAGD 1. p. 355): 'to want' [LN, NICNT1; CEV, NASB, NCV, NET, NIV, NJB, NLT, TEV], 'to will' [Gdt, NTC, WBC; KJV], 'to like' [AB], 'to desire, to wish' [LN]. The words 'If I want' are also translated: 'If it is my will/wish' [HTC; NRSV, Ph], 'If it should be my will' [REB]. This verb means to desire to have or experience something [LN].

b. pres. act. infin. of μένω (LN 13.89) (BAGD 1.c.α. p. 504): 'to remain' [AB, BAGD, HTC, NICNT2, NTC, WBC; NASB, NIV], 'to live' [CEV, NCV, NET, TEV], 'to remain alive' [BAGD; NLT], 'to stay' [Ph, REB], 'to stay behind' [NJB], 'to tarry' [Gdt; KJV], 'to continue to live' [BAGD], 'to continue, to continue to exist, to still be in existence' [LN], 'to last, to persist' [BAGD]. This verb means to continue to exist [LN]. The meaning here is 'to stay/remain alive' [AB, BAGD, Bar, Car, HTC, NICNT2, TH], or 'to remain alive on earth' [Car],

c. pres. mid. (deponent = active) or pass. of ἔρχομαι (LN 15.81) (BAGD I.2.c. p. 311): 'to come' [AB, BAGD, Gdt, HTC, LN, NICNT2, NTC, WBC; KJV, NASB, NJB, NRSV, Ph, REB, TEV], 'to return' [TRT; CEV, NIV, NLT], 'to come back' [TRT; NCV, NET]. This verb means to move toward or up to the reference point of the viewpoint character or event [LN]. This 'coming' refers to Jesus' Second coming [Bar, CH, HTC, ICC, Kn, Lns, NICNT2], to the coming promised in 14:3 [ICC, NICNT2], or 1 John 2:28 [Kn].

QUESTION—Is the question, 'What is that to you?', real or rhetorical?

The question is rhetorical [BECNT, Car, CH, EGT, Gdt, ICC, IVP, Kn, Lns, My, NICNT1, NICNT2, NTC, Rd, TRT; NCV]. It is a mild reprimand [EGT, Gdt, NTC]. Jesus is saying in effect that this is not Peter's business [BECNT, Car, CH, ICC, Kn, My, NICNT1, NICNT2, WBC]. Jesus is telling Peter not to meddle in what he has in mind for the other disciple [Rd]. He is stressing to Peter that curiosity about John's future must be put in the background to his obedience to the command to follow him [NTC]. Jesus is gently indicating to Peter that he leave John's future in Jesus' hands [Lns]. Some render this question as a statement: 'That is not your business' [NCV, similarly IVP], 'that's not your concern' or 'that shouldn't matter to you' [TRT]. Others render it: 'what concern is that of yours?' [NET], 'what does it matter to you?' [NJB], 'is that your business?' [Ph], 'how does that/it concern you?' [AB, BAGD III.5.c. p. 710], 'what is that to do with you?' [WBC], 'why are you worried about that?' or 'why are you concerned about that?'[TH].

QUESTION—What words are emphasized in this verse?

The pronoun σύ 'you' in the words 'You follow me' are emphasized [AB, BECNT, Bar, Car, Gdt, ICC, Lns, My, NICNT1, NICNT2, WBC; NLT]: 'as for you, follow me' [NLT]. It contrasts Peter with the beloved disciple [AB, Gdt, NICNT2], or with the other disciples [My]. In the Greek the pronoun αὐτόν 'him' precedes the verb 'I want' (literally, if him I want) emphasizing it [Lns, TRT]: 'In case I will that he on his part remain until I come, what is that to thee? Do thou on thy part keep following me!' [Lns].

21:23 So the word went-out among the brothers that that disciple would-not -die. But[a] Jesus did- not -tell him that he-would- not -die but,[b] "If I-want him to-remain until I-come, what (is that) to you?"

TEXT—Instead of ἕως ἔρχομαι, [τί πρὸς σέ]; 'until I come, [what (is that) to you?]', one manuscript reads ἕως ἔρχομαι πρὸς σέ; 'until I come to you?', while others read ἕως ἔρχομαι 'until I come?'. GNT reads 'until I come, [what (is that) to you?]' with a C rating indicating difficulty in making the decision. It follows NA in placing the words 'what (is that) to you?' in brackets. AB also includes these words in brackets while Gdt and NJB omit them completely.

LEXICON—a. δέ (LN 89.124): 'but' [Gdt, LN, NICNT2, WBC; CEV, NCV, NET, NIV, NJB, NLT, TEV], 'yet' [HTC, NTC; KJV, NASB, NRSV],

'but in fact' [REB], 'as a matter of fact' [AB], 'yet, of course' [Ph], 'on the other hand' [LN]. This conjunction marks contrast [LN]. The position of this conjunction in the Greek indicates emphasis as we have translated it [AB].
  b. ἀλλά (LN 89.125): 'but' [Gdt, HTC, LN, NICNT2, NTC, WBC; KJV, NJB, NRSV], 'but only' [NASB], 'but rather' [NET], 'but simply' [Ph], 'on the contrary' [LN, Lns], 'instead' [LN]. This word is also translated: 'he only said' [NCV, NIV, NLT, REB], 'he simply said' [CEV], 'all he said was' [AB], 'rather he said' [TRT], 'he said' [TEV]. This conjunction is a marker of more emphatic contrast (as compared to δέ, 89.124) [LN]. It is a strong adversative [NICNT1]. John is making a sharp contrast between what Jesus did not say and what he did say [NICNT1].

QUESTION—What is the purpose of this verse?
This verse is included to explain that Jesus' statement to Peter about John was not a prophecy but a hypothetical statement [TH].

QUESTION—Who are 'the brothers'?
They refer to the Christian community in general who were brothers to each other [AB, ICC, My, NICNT1, NICNT2, NTC]. It refers to fellow believers or Christians, not to blood brothers [TRT].

QUESTION—To whom do the pronouns 'him', 'he', and 'him' refer?
The first 'him' refers to Peter, while the following 'he' and 'him' refer back to 'that disciple' [NICNT2, NTC, TRT; NJB]: 'Yet Jesus did not say to Peter, "He will not die," but, "If I want him to stay behind till I come"'[NJB].

21:24 This is the disciple who is-testifying[a] about these-things, and who has-written these-things, and we-know that his testimony is true.[b]

LEXICON—a. pres. act. participle of μαρτυρέω (LN 33.262) (BAGD 1.a. p. 492): 'to testify' [Gdt, LN, NTC, NICNT2; KJV, NASB, NET, NIV, NLT, NRSV], 'to tell' [CEV, NCV], 'to vouch for' [NJB, REB], 'to give one's testimony to' [Ph], 'to speak of' [TEV], 'to bear witness (to/about)' [BAGD, HTC, WBC], 'to be a witness (for)' [AB, BAGD]. This verb means to provide information about a person or an event concerning which the speaker has direct knowledge [LN].
  b. ἀληθής (LN 72.1) (BAGD 2. p. 36): 'true' [BAGD, LN; all translations except CEV, NLT, Ph], 'accurate' [NLT], 'reliable' [Ph], 'in accordance with truth, dependable' [BAGD]. This adjective is also translated as a noun: '(he is telling the) truth' [CEV]. This adjective pertains to something being in accordance with historical fact [LN].

QUESTION—To whom does the phrase, 'the disciple' refer?
It probably refers to the beloved disciple [AB, Bar, BECNT, Car, EGT, Gdt, HTC, ICC, IVP, NICNT1, NICNT2, Rd, TH, WBC], identified in verse 20 [TH]. Specifically it refers to John (BECNT, Car, CH, Lns, My, NTC), the son of Zebedee [BECNT, Car, CH].

QUESTION—To what does the phrase, 'these things' refer?

It probably refers to the complete Gospel of John chapters 1–21 [Bar, Car, EGT, Gdt, HTC, ICC, Lns, NICNT1, NTC, Rd]. It refers to the contents of this chapter—verses 1–23 [My].

QUESTION—To whom does the pronoun 'we' refer?

1. 'We' probably refers to the elders of the church at Ephesus [ICC, Lns, NTC]. It probably refers to the the elders of the church at Ephesus or to the elders of the churches in Ephesus and surroundings [NTC].
2. 'We' probably is the editorial 'we' referring just to the author himself [BECNT, Car].
3. Other views [AB, Bar, Gdt, HTC, My, NICNT1, TH]. 'We' refers to a group of people that includes the writer of verse 24 but does not include the disciple whom Jesus loved (verse 20) [TH]. It refers to the group that formed around the beloved disciple [AB, CH, IVP, Rd] to which he bequeathed his Gospel [Rd]. It refers to an apostolic Church able to verify and affirm the testimony of the beloved disciple [Bar, HTC]. It probably refers in general to people who were respected among the believers and who were familiar with the facts of the case [NICNT1]. It refers both to the Apostles and to believers who knew John and were part of his group at Ephesus [Gdt].

DISCOURSE UNIT—21:25 [Car; TEV]. The topic is the greatness of Jesus [Car], conclusion [TEV].

21:25 Now there-are also many other-things that Jesus did (that) if every-one-of-them[a] was-written, I-suppose[b] not-even[c] the world[d] itself would-contain[e] the books that-would-be-written.

TEXT—A few major Greek manuscripts include the word 'Amen' at the end of this verse. Only KJV joins them.

TEXT—Following this verse one manuscript and one version include John 7:53–8:11.

LEXICON—a. καθ' ἕν (BAGD 5.e. p. 232): 'every one (of them)' [HTC; NCV, NET, NIV, NRSV], '(they)...every one' [KJV], 'one after the other' [BAGD], '(they) all' [CEV, NLT], '(they)...one by one' [WBC; NTC], '(they...all)...one by one' [TEV], '(they)...in detail' [AB, Gdt; NASB], '(it)...in detail' [NJB], '(it...all)...in detail' [REB], 'every one' [NICNT2], 'each one' [Ph].

b. pres. mid. or pass. (deponent = active) of οἶμαι (LN **31.29**) (BAGD p. 562): 'to suppose' [BAGD, LN; all translations except AB, Gdt, WBC], 'to think' [BAGD, Gdt, LN, WBC], 'to imagine' [**LN**], 'to presume, to assume, to believe' [LN], 'to expect' [BAGD]. The combination 'suppose not even' is translated: '(I) doubt' [AB]. This verb means to regard something as presumably true, but without particular certainty [LN].

c. οὐδέ (LN 69.8) (BAGD 3. p. 591): 'not even' [BAGD, LN; KJV, NASB, NIV], 'not' [all translations except KJV, NASB, NIV]. This is a combination of the negative particle οὐ 'not' (69.3), and the postpositional particle δέ 'even' [LN].

d. κόσμος (LN 1.39) (BAGD 2. P. 446): 'world' [BAGD, LN; all translations], 'universe' [BAGD], 'earth' [LN]. Apparently the following translated the phrase αὐτὸν…τὸν κόσμον 'the world itself' as 'the whole world' [AB; CEV, NCV, NET, NIV, NLT, Ph, TEV]. This noun indicates the surface of the earth as the dwelling place of mankind, in contrast with the heavens above and the world below [LN]. The word κόσμος indicates the universe here [AB, TH]. Here the universe, as the greatest space conceivable, is not able to contain something [BAGD].

e. aorist. act. infin. of χωρέω (LN **80.4**) (BAGD 3.a. p. 889): 'to contain' [BAGD, Gdt, HTC, **LN**, NTC; KJV, NASB, NLT, NRSV], 'to hold' [BAGD, NICNT2; NJB, REB, TEV], 'to have room for' [BAGD, LN, WBC; CEV, NET, NIV], 'to be room for' [AB; Ph], 'to be big enough for' [NCV], 'to be space for' [LN]. The words 'not even the world itself would contain the books' is translated 'there would not be room in the whole world for all the books' [Ph]. This verb means to be a quantity of space [LN].

QUESTION—Should the negative 'not even', be construed with the verb 'to suppose', or with the verb 'to contain'?

1. It should be construed with the verb 'to suppose' [AB, Bar, Gdt, TRT, WBC; CEV, NJB]: 'I don't suppose there would be room enough in the whole world for all the books' [CEV]. The infinitive χωρέω 'to contain' would normally be negated by μή 'not', not by a form of οὐ (as here) [AB, Bar].
2. It should be construed with the verb 'to contain' [LN, HTC, NICNT1, NICNT2, NTC, TH; KJV, NASB, NCV, NET, NIV, NLT, NRSV, Ph, REB, TEV]: 'I imagine that the whole world could not hold the books that would be written' [LN]. The negative οὐδέ is remarkable being used with the infinitive of χωρέω. Perhaps it is more emphatic than μηδέ would have been [NICNT1].
3. In either case the same meaning is arrived at. But since what is actually negated is the contents of the supposition, it is better to translate this as though the verb 'to contain' were negated, 'in the whole world there would not be enough room for the books' [TH].

QUESTION—Is this claim a hyperbole or a statement of truth?

Here it is a hyperbolic expression, that is, a rhetorical overstatement BAGD, BECNT, Bar, Gdt, HTC, IVP, Lns, NICNT1, WBC]. In this case this seeming hyperbole is quite literally true [Car, IVP, NTC].

www.ingramcontent.com/pod-product-compliance
Lightning Source LLC
Chambersburg PA
CBHW071135300426
44113CB00009B/983